The

Elements

of

Typographic

Style

ALSO BY ROBERT BRINGHURST

POETRY

The Shipwright's Log · 1972
Cadastre · 1973
Bergschrund · 1975
Tzuhalem's Mountain · 1982
The Beauty of the Weapons: Selected Poems 1972–82 · 1982
Tending the Fire · 1985
The Blue Roofs of Japan · 1986
Pieces of Map, Pieces of Music · 1986
Conversations with a Toad · 1987
The Calling: Selected Poems 1970–1995 · 1995
Elements (with drawings by Ulf Nilsen) · 1995
The Book of Silences · 2001
Ursa Major: A Polyphonic Masque for Speakers and Dancers · 2003
The Old in Their Knowing · 2004

PROSE

Visions: Contemporary Art in Canada
(with Geoffrey James, Russell Keziere & Doris Shadbolt) · 1983
Ocean/Paper/Stone · 1984
The Raven Steals the Light (with Bill Reid) · 1984
Shovels, Shoes and the Slow Rotation of Letters · 1986
The Black Canoe (with photographs by Ulli Steltzer) · 1991
Boats Is Saintlier than Captains:
Thirteen Ways of Looking at Morality, Language and Design · 1997
A Short History of the Printed Word (with Warren Chappell) · 1999
A Story as Sharp as a Knife:
The Classical Haida Mythtellers and Their World · 1999
Carving the Elements: A Companion to the Fragments of Parmenides
(with Peter Koch et al) · 2004
Prosodies of Meaning: Literary Form in Native North America · 2004
The Solid Form of Language: An Essay on Writing and Meaning · 2004

TRANSLATION

Ghandl of the Qayahl Llaanas, *Nine Visits to the Mythworld* · 2000
Skaay of the Qquuna Qiighawaay, *Being in Being:*
The Collected Works of a Master Haida Mythteller · 2001
Parmenides, *The Fragments* · 2003

¶ THE ELEMENTS *of* TYPOGRAPHIC STYLE

version 3.1

Robert Bringhurst

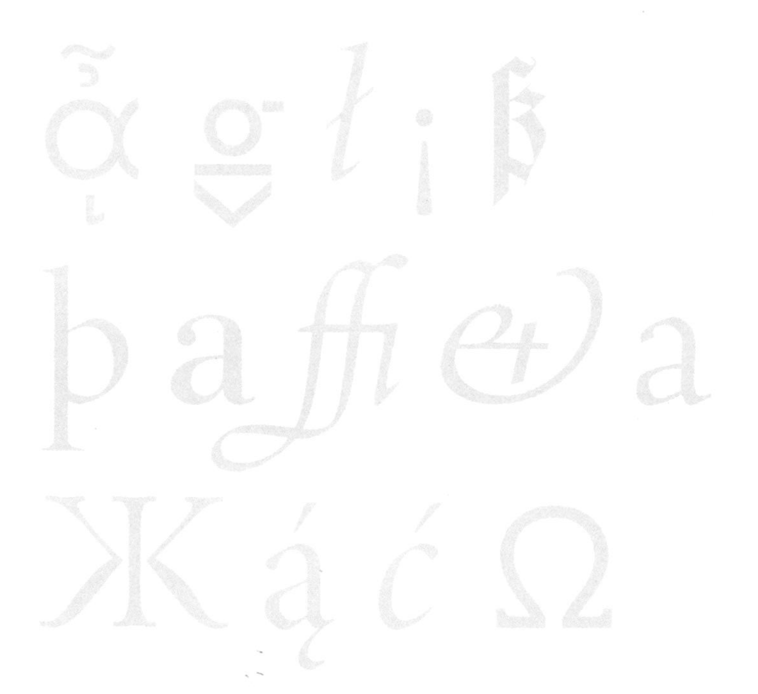

HARTLEY & MARKS, *Publishers*

Version 3.1 ¶ 5 4 3 2 1

HARTLEY & MARKS, PUBLISHERS

- PO Box 147
  Point Roberts, WA 98281
  USA
- 3661 West Broadway
  Vancouver, BC V6R 2B8
  Canada

This version of the third edition incorporates emendations to pages 91, 119, 182, 246, 288, 295, 303, 306, 311, 317, 318, 361–364, 373 and 381.

Designed & assembled in Canada;
printed & bound in China.

∞

Library of Congress Cataloguing in Publication Data:

Bringhurst, Robert.
The elements of typographic style / Robert Bringhurst. – 3rd ed.
p. cm.
Includes bibliographical references and index.
ISBN 0-88179-205-5 –
ISBN 0-88179-206-3 (pbk.)
1. Graphic design (Typography)
2. Type and type-founding.
3. Book design.
I. Title.
Z246.B74 2004
686.2'24 – dc22
2004053913

National Library of Canada Cataloguing in Publication Data:

Bringhurst, Robert, 1946–
The elements of typographic style / Robert Bringhurst. – 3rd ed., expanded and rev.
Includes bibliographical references and index.
ISBN 0-88179-205-5 (bound) –
ISBN 0-88179-206-3 (pbk.)
1. Layout (Printing)
2. Type and type-founding.
3. Book design.
4. Printing – Specimens.
I. Title.
Z246.B74 2004 686.2'24
C2004-902010-2

for my colleagues & friends

in the worlds of letters:

writers & editors,

type designers, typographers,

printers & publishers,

shepherding words and books

on their lethal and innocent ways

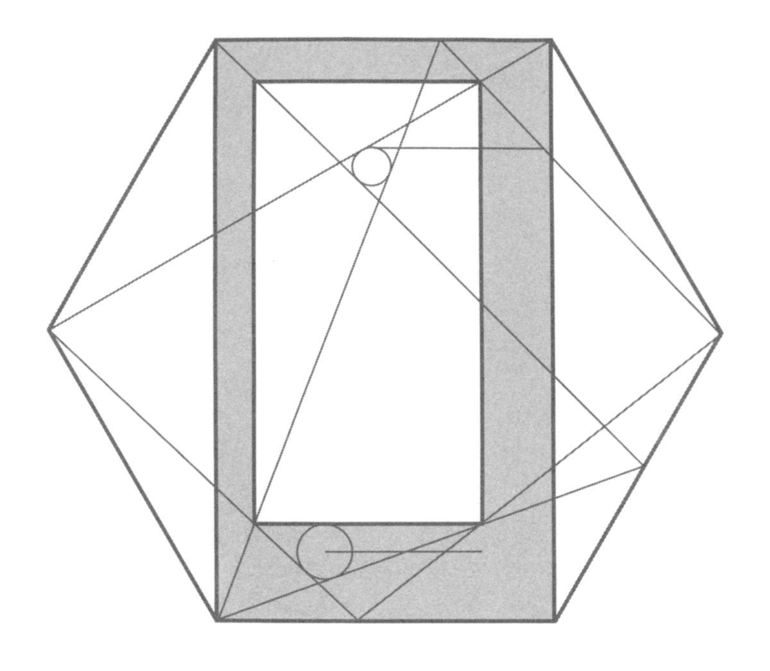

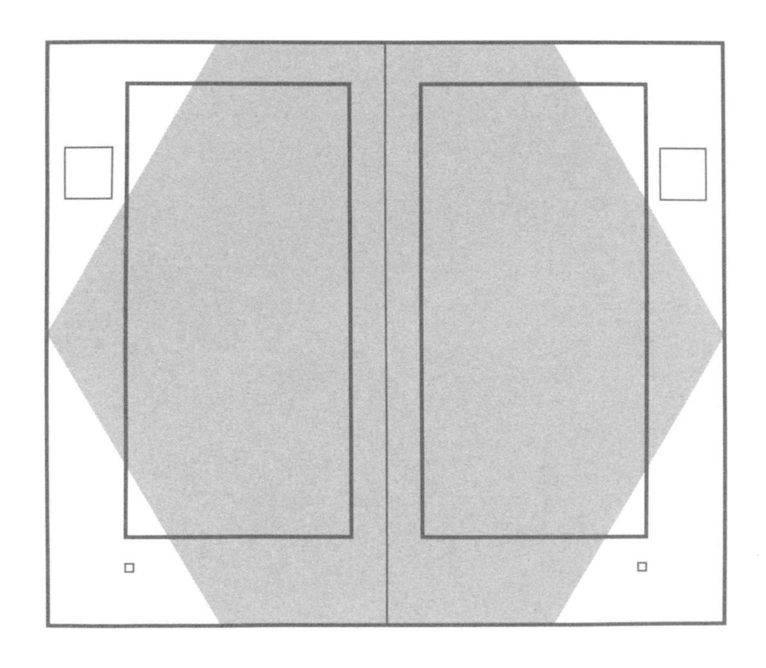

CONTENTS

— Everything written symbols can say has already passed by. They are like tracks left by animals. That is why the masters of meditation refuse to accept that writings are final. The aim is to reach true being by means of those tracks, those letters, those signs – but reality itself is not a sign, and it leaves no tracks. It doesn't come to us by way of letters or words. We can go toward it, by following those words and letters back to what they came from. But so long as we are preoccupied with symbols, theories and opinions, we will fail to reach the principle.

— But when we give up symbols and opinions, aren't we left in the utter nothingness of being?

— Yes.

KIMURA KYŪHO, *Kenjutsu Fushigi Hen*
[*On the Mysteries of Swordsmanship*],
1768

A true revelation, it seems to me, will only emerge from stubborn concentration on a solitary problem. I am not in league with inventors or adventurers, nor with travelers to exotic destinations. The surest – also the quickest – way to awake the sense of wonder in ourselves is to look intently, undeterred, at a single object. Suddenly, miraculously, it will reveal itself as something we have never seen before.

CESARE PAVESE, *Dialoghi con Leucò*,
1947

FOREWORD

There are many books about typography, and some of them are models of the art they teach. But when I set myself to compile a simple list of working principles, one of the benchmarks I first thought of was William Strunk and E.B. White's small masterpiece, *The Elements of Style.* Brevity, however, is the essence of Strunk & White's manual of literary technique. This book is longer than theirs, and for that there is a cause.

Typography makes at least two kinds of sense, if it makes any sense at all. It makes visual sense and historical sense. The visual side of typography is always on display, and materials for the study of its visual form are many and widespread. The history of letterforms and their usage is visible too, to those with access to manuscripts, inscriptions and old books, but from others it is largely hidden. This book has therefore grown into something more than a short manual of typographic etiquette. It is the fruit of a lot of long walks in the wilderness of letters: in part a pocket field guide to the living wonders that are found there, and in part a meditation on the ecological principles, survival techniques and ethics that apply. The principles of typography as I understand them are not a set of dead conventions but the tribal customs of the magic forest, where ancient voices speak from all directions and new ones move to unremembered forms.

One question, nevertheless, has been often in my mind. When all right-thinking human beings are struggling to remember that other men and women are free to be different, and free to become more different still, how can one honestly write a rulebook? What reason and authority exist for these commandments, suggestions and instructions? Surely typographers, like others, ought to be at liberty to follow or to blaze the trails they choose.

Typography thrives as a shared concern – and there are no paths at all where there are no shared desires and directions. A typographer determined to forge new routes must move, like other solitary travelers, through uninhabited country and against the grain of the land, crossing common thoroughfares in the silence before dawn. The subject of this book is not typographic solitude, but the old, well-traveled roads at the core of the tradition: paths that each of us is free to follow or not, and to enter and leave when we choose – if only we know the paths are there and have a sense of where they lead. That freedom is denied us if the tradition is concealed or left for dead. Originality is everywhere, but much originality is blocked if the way back to earlier discoveries is cut or overgrown.

If you use this book as a guide, by all means leave the road when you wish. That is precisely the use of a road: to reach individually chosen points of departure. By all means break the rules, and break them beautifully, deliberately and well. That is one of the ends for which they exist.

Letterforms change constantly yet differ very little, because they are alive. The principles of typographic clarity have also scarcely altered since the second half of the fifteenth century, when the first books were printed in roman type. Indeed, most of the principles of legibility and design explored in this book were known and used by Egyptian scribes writing hieratic script with reed pens on papyrus in 1000 BC. Samples of their work sit now in museums in Cairo, London and New York, still lively, subtle and perfectly legible thirty centuries after they were made.

Writing systems vary, but a good page is not hard to learn to recognize, whether it comes from Táng Dynasty China, the Egyptian New Kingdom or Renaissance Italy. The principles that unite these distant schools of design are based on the structure and scale of the human body – the eye, the hand and the forearm in particular – and on the invisible but no less real, no less demanding and no less sensuous anatomy of the human mind. I don't like to call these principles universals, because they are largely unique to our species. Dogs and ants, for example, read and write by more chemical means. But the underlying principles of typography are, at any rate, stable enough to weather any number of human fashions and fads.

It is true that typographers' tools are presently changing with considerable force and speed, but this is not a manual in the use of any particular typesetting system or medium. I suppose that most readers of this book will set most of their type in digital form, using computers, but I have no preconceptions about which brands of computers, or which versions of which proprietary software, they may use. The essential elements of style have more to do with the goals typographers set for themselves than with the mutable eccentricities of their tools. Typography itself, in other words, is far more device-independent than PostScript, which is the computer language used to render these particular letters, and the design of these pages, into typographic code. If I have succeeded in my task, this book should be as useful to artists and antiquarians setting foundry metal by hand and pulling proofs on a flat-bed press, as to those who check their work on a screen or laser printer, then ship it to high-resolution digital output devices by optical disk or long-distance telephone line.

Typography is the craft of endowing human language with a durable visual form, and thus with an independent existence. Its heartwood is calligraphy – the dance, on a tiny stage, of the living, speaking hand – and its roots reach into living soil, though its branches may be hung each year with new machines. So long as the root lives, typography remains a source of true delight, true knowledge, true surprise.

As a craft, typography shares a long common boundary and many common concerns with writing and editing on the one side and with graphic design on the other; yet typography itself belongs to neither. This book in its turn is neither a manual of editorial style nor a textbook on design, though it overlaps with both of these concerns. The perspective throughout is first and foremost typographic – and I hope the book will be useful for that very reason to those whose work or interests may be centered in adjacent fields.

This book owes much to the conversation and example, over the years, of several friends and master craftsmen – Kay Amert, Stan Bevington, Crispin Elsted, Glenn Goluska, Peter Koch, Vic Marks, George Payerle and others – and to the practice of two artists and exemplars: the late Adrian Wilson, and Hermann Zapf. Artists and scholars around the world have shared their knowledge freely. James Mosley, his staff and his successors at the St Bride Printing Library, London, have been particularly helpful. I am grateful to them all.

I have many others to thank as well for their contributions to the second and now the third edition of the book. Their names appear in the afterword, page 365.

R.B.

aperture: the opening in letters such as a, c, e, s

RENAISSANCE (15th & 16th centuries): modulated stroke; humanist [oblique] axis; crisp, pen-formed terminals; large *aperture*; italic equal to and independent of roman.

These charts show first and foremost the axis of the stroke, which is the axis of the pen that makes the letter. It is often very different from the axis of the lettershape itself. A pen that points northwest can make an upright letter or a letter that slopes to the northeast.

BAROQUE (17th century): modulated stroke; variable axis; modeled serifs and terminals; moderate aperture; italic subsidiary to roman and closely linked with it. A secondary vertical axis often develops in Baroque letters – but the *primary* axis of the penstroke is normally oblique.

NEOCLASSICAL (18th century): modulated stroke; rationalist [vertical] axis; refined, *adnate* serifs; *lachrymal* terminals; moderate aperture; italic fully subjugated to roman.

adnate: flowing into the stem; *lachrymal*: tear-drop shaped

ROMANTIC (18th & 19th centuries): hypermodulated stroke; intensified rationalist axis; abrupt, thin serifs; round terminals; small aperture; fully subjugated italic. In Neoclassical and Romantic letters alike, the *primary* axis is usually vertical and the *secondary* axis oblique.

REALIST (19th & early 20th centuries): unmodulated stroke; implied vertical axis; small aperture; serifs absent or abrupt and of equal weight with main strokes; italic absent or replaced by sloped roman.

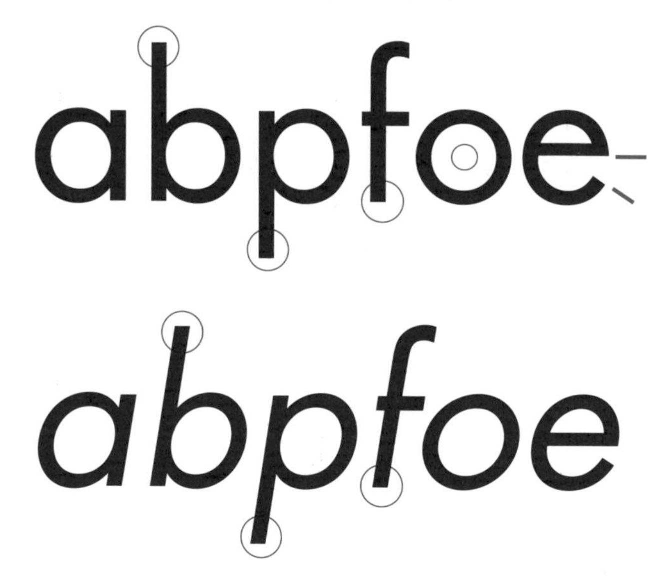

GEOMETRIC MODERNIST (20th century): unmodulated stroke; bowls often circular (no axis); moderate aperture; serifs absent or of equal weight with main strokes; italic absent or replaced by sloped roman. The modeling, however, is often much more subtle than it first appears.

LYRICAL MODERNIST (20th century): rediscovery of Renaissance form: modulated stroke; humanist axis; pen-formed serifs and terminals; large aperture; italic partially liberated from roman.

POSTMODERNIST (late 20th & early 21st century): frequent parody of Neoclassical, Romantic or Baroque form: rationalist or variable axis; sharply modeled serifs and terminals; moderate aperture. (There are many kinds of Postmodernist letter. This is one example.)

rigo Habraam numerã
ı a moſaica lege(ſeptim
r)ſed naturalı fuit ratio
idit enim Habraam de
m quoq; gentium patr
.s oés gentes hoc uıdelic
m eſt:cuius ille iuſtıtiæ
us eſt:qui poſt multas
imum omnium diuin
naſcerétur tradidit:ue
gnum:uel ut hoc quaſ
ſuos imitari conaret:au
um nobis modo eſt.Po

Roman type cut in 1469 by Nicolas Jenson, a French typographer working in Venice. The original is approximately 16 pt. The type is shown here as Jenson printed it, but at twice actual size. This is the ancestor of the type (Bruce Rogers's Centaur) shown at the top of page 12.

THE GRAND DESIGN

1.1 FIRST PRINCIPLES

1

1.1.1 *Typography exists to honor content.*

Like oratory, music, dance, calligraphy – like anything that lends its grace to language – typography is an art that can be deliberately misused. It is a craft by which the meanings of a text (or its absence of meaning) can be clarified, honored and shared, or knowingly disguised.

In a world rife with unsolicited messages, typography must often draw attention to itself before it will be read. Yet in order to be read, it must relinquish the attention it has drawn. Typography with anything to say therefore aspires to a kind of statuesque transparency. Its other traditional goal is durability: not immunity to change, but a clear superiority to fashion. Typography at its best is a visual form of language linking timelessness and time.

One of the principles of durable typography is always legibility; another is something more than legibility: some earned or unearned interest that gives its living energy to the page. It takes various forms and goes by various names, including serenity, liveliness, laughter, grace and joy.

These principles apply, in different ways, to the typography of business cards, instruction sheets and postage stamps, as well as to editions of religious scriptures, literary classics and other books that aspire to join their ranks. Within limits, the same principles apply even to stock market reports, airline schedules, milk cartons, classified ads. But laughter, grace and joy, like legibility itself, all feed on meaning, which the writer, the words and the subject, not the typographer, must generally provide.

In 1770, a bill was introduced in the English Parliament with the following provisions:

... all women of whatever age, rank, profession, or degree, whether virgins, maids, or widows, that shall ... impose upon, seduce, and betray into matrimony, any of His Majesty's subjects, by the scents, paints, cosmetic washes, artificial teeth, false hair, Spanish wool, iron stays, hoops, high heeled shoes [or] *bolstered hips shall incur*

the penalty of the law in force against witchcraft … and … the marriage, upon conviction, shall stand null and void.

The function of typography, as I understand it, is neither to further the power of witches nor to bolster the defences of those, like this unfortunate parliamentarian, who live in terror of being tempted and deceived. The satisfactions of the craft come from elucidating, and perhaps even ennobling, the text, not from deluding the unwary reader by applying scents, paints and iron stays to empty prose. But humble texts, such as classified ads or the telephone directory, may profit as much as anything else from a good typographical bath and a change of clothes. And many a book, like many a warrior or dancer or priest of either sex, may look well with some paint on its face, or indeed with a bone in its nose.

First Principles

1.1.2 *Letters have a life and dignity of their own.*

Letterforms that honor and elucidate what humans see and say deserve to be honored in their turn. Well-chosen words deserve well-chosen letters; these in their turn deserve to be set with affection, intelligence, knowledge and skill. Typography is a link, and it ought, as a matter of honor, courtesy and pure delight, to be as strong as the others in the chain.

Writing begins with the making of footprints, the leaving of signs. Like speaking, it is a perfectly natural act which humans have carried to complex extremes. The typographer's task has always been to add a somewhat unnatural edge, a protective shell of artificial order, to the power of the writing hand. The tools have altered over the centuries, and the exact degree of unnaturalness desired has varied from place to place and time to time, but the character of the essential transformation between manuscript and type has scarcely changed.

The original purpose of type was simply copying. The job of the typographer was to imitate the scribal hand in a form that permitted exact and fast replication. Dozens, then hundreds, then thousands of copies were printed in less time than a scribe would need to finish one. This excuse for setting texts in type has disappeared. In the age of photolithography, digital scanning and offset printing, it is as easy to print directly from handwritten copy as from text that is typographically composed. Yet the typographer's task is little changed. It is still to give the illusion of superhuman speed and stamina – and of superhuman patience and precision – to the writing hand.

Typography is just that: idealized writing. Writers themselves now rarely have the calligraphic skill of earlier scribes, but they evoke countless versions of ideal script by their varying voices and literary styles. To these blind and often invisible visions, the typographer must respond in visible terms.

The Grand Design

In a badly designed book, the letters mill and stand like starving horses in a field. In a book designed by rote, they sit like stale bread and mutton on the page. In a well-made book, where designer, compositor and printer have all done their jobs, no matter how many thousands of lines and pages they must occupy, the letters are alive. They dance in their seats. Sometimes they rise and dance in the margins and aisles.

Simple as it may sound, the task of creative non-interference with letters is a rewarding and difficult calling. In ideal conditions, it is all that typographers are really asked to do – and it is enough.

1.1.3 *There is a style beyond style.*

Literary style, says Walter Benjamin, "is the power to move freely in the length and breadth of linguistic thinking without slipping into banality." Typographic style, in this large and intelligent sense of the word, does not mean any particular style – my style or your style, or Neoclassical or Baroque style – but the power to move freely through the whole domain of typography, and to function at every step in a way that is graceful and vital instead of banal. It means typography that can walk familiar ground without sliding into platitudes, typography that responds to new conditions with innovative solutions, and typography that does not vex the reader with its own originality in a self-conscious search for praise.

From part 2 of Benjamin's essay on Karl Kraus, in *Illuminationen* (Frankfurt, 1955). There is an English translation in Walter Benjamin, *Reflections,* ed. Peter Demetz (New York, 1978).

Typography is to literature as musical performance is to composition: an essential act of interpretation, full of endless opportunities for insight or obtuseness. Much typography is far removed from literature, for language has many uses, including packaging and propaganda. Like music, it can be used to manipulate behavior and emotions. But this is not where typographers, musicians or other human beings show us their finest side. Typography at its best is a slow performing art, worthy of the same informed appreciation that we sometimes give to musical performances, and capable of giving similar nourishment and pleasure in return.

The same alphabets and page designs can be used for a biography of Mohandas Gandhi and for a manual on the use and deployment of biological weapons. Writing can be used both for love letters and for hate mail, and love letters themselves can be used for manipulation and extortion as well as to bring delight to body and soul. Evidently there is nothing inherently noble and trustworthy in the written or printed word. Yet generations of men and women have turned to writing and printing to house and share their deepest hopes, perceptions, dreams and fears. It is to them, not to the extortionist – nor to the opportunist or the profiteer – that the typographer must answer.

1.2 TACTICS

1.2.1 *Read the text before designing it.*

The typographer's one essential task is to interpret and communicate the text. Its tone, its tempo, its logical structure, its physical size, all determine the possibilities of its typographic form. The typographer is to the text as the theatrical director to the script, or the musician to the score.

1.2.2 *Discover the outer logic of the typography in the inner logic of the text.*

A novel often purports to be a seamless river of words from beginning to end, or a series of unnamed scenes. Research papers, textbooks, cookbooks and other works of nonfiction rarely look so smooth. They are often layered with chapter heads, section heads, subheads, block quotations, footnotes, endnotes, lists and illustrative examples. Such features may be obscure in the manuscript, even if they are clear in the author's mind. For the sake of the reader, each requires its own typographic identity and form. Every layer and level of the text must be consistent, distinct, yet (usually) harmonious in form.

The first task of the typographer is therefore to read and understand the text; the second task is to analyze and map it. Only then can typographic interpretation begin.

If the text has many layers or sections, it may need not only heads and subheads but running heads as well, reappearing on every page or two-page spread, to remind readers which intellectual neighborhood they happen to be visiting.

Novels seldom need such signposts, but they often require typographic markers of other kinds. Peter Matthiessen's novel *Far Tortuga* (New York, 1975; designed by Kenneth Miyamoto) uses two sizes of type, three different margins, free-floating block paragraphs and other typographic devices to separate thought, speech and action. Ken Kesey's novel *Sometimes a Great Notion* (New York, 1964) seems to flow like conventional prose, yet it shifts repeatedly in mid-sentence between roman and italic to distinguish what characters say to each other from what they say in silence to themselves.

In poetry and drama, a larger typographic palette is sometimes required. Some of Douglass Parker's translations from classical Greek and Dennis Tedlock's translations from Zuni use roman, italic, bold, small caps and full caps in various sizes to emulate the dynamic markings of music. Robert Massin's typographic performances of Eugène Ionesco's plays use intersecting lines of type, stretched and melted letters, inkblots, pictograms, and a separate typeface for each person in the play. In the works of other artists such as Guillaume Apollinaire and Guy Davenport, boundaries between author and designer sometimes vanish. Writing merges with typography, and the text becomes its own illustration.

See for example Aristophanes, *Four Comedies* (Ann Arbor, Michigan, 1969); Dennis Tedlock, *Finding the Center* (New York, 1972); Eugène Ionesco, *La Cantatrice chauve* (Paris, 1964), and *Délire à deux* (Paris, 1966). There are samples of Massin's work in *Typographia* n.s. 11 (1965).

The typographer must analyze and reveal the inner order of the text, as a musician must reveal the inner order of the music he performs. But the reader, like the listener, should in retrospect be able to close her eyes and see what lies inside the words she has been reading. The typographic performance must reveal, not replace, the inner composition. Typographers, like other artists and craftsmen – musicians, composers and authors as well – must as a rule do their work and disappear.

1.2.3 *Make the visible relationship between the text and other elements (photographs, captions, tables, diagrams, notes) a reflection of their real relationship.*

If the text is tied to other elements, where do they belong? If there are notes, do they go at the side of the page, the foot of the page, the end of the chapter, the end of the book? If there are photographs or other illustrations, should they be embedded in the text or should they form a special section of their own? And if the photographs have captions or credits or labels, should these sit close beside the photographs or should they be separately housed?

If there is more than one text – as in countless publications issued in Canada, Switzerland, Belgium and other multilingual countries – how will the separate but equal texts be arrayed? Will they run side by side to emphasize their equality (and perhaps to share in a single set of illustrations), or will they be printed back-to-back, to emphasize their distinctness?

Tactics

No matter what their relation to the text, photos or maps must sometimes be grouped apart from it because they require a separate paper or different inks. If this is the case, what typographic cross-references will be required?

These and similar questions, which confront the working typographer on a daily basis, must be answered case by case. The typographic page is a map of the mind; it is frequently also a map of the social order from which it comes. And for better or for worse, minds and social orders change.

1.2.4 *Choose a typeface or a group of faces that will honor and elucidate the character of the text.*

This is the beginning, middle and end of the practice of typography: choose and use the type with sensitivity and intelligence. Aspects of this principle are explored throughout this book and considered in detail in chapters 6, 7 and 11.

a A a

a a a

a *a* a

a *a* A

a a a

a *a*

a *a*

Letterforms have tone, timbre, character, just as words and sentences do. The moment a text and a typeface are chosen, two streams of thought, two rhythmical systems, two sets of habits, or if you like, two personalities, intersect. They need not live together contentedly forever, but they must not as a rule collide.

The root metaphor of typesetting is that the alphabet (or in Chinese, the entire lexicon) is a system of interchangeable parts. The word *form* can be surgically revised, instead of rewritten, to become the word *farm* or *firm* or *fort* or *fork* or *from*, or with a little more trouble, to become the word *pineapple*. The old compositor's typecase is a partitioned wooden tray holding hundreds of such interchangeable bits of information. These subsemantic particles, these bits – called *sorts* by letterpress printers – are letters cast on standardized bodies of metal, waiting to be assembled into meaningful combinations, then dispersed and reassembled in a different form. The compositor's typecase is one of the primary ancestors of the computer – and it is no surprise that while typesetting was one of the last crafts to be mechanized, it was one of the first to be computerized.

But the bits of information handled by typographers differ in one essential respect from the computer programmer's bits. Whether the type is set in hard metal by hand, or in softer metal by machine, or in digital form with a computer, every comma, every parenthesis, every *e*, and in context, even every empty space, has style as well as bald symbolic value. Letters are microscopic works of art as well as useful symbols. They mean what they are as well as what they say.

Typography is the art and craft of handling these doubly meaningful bits of information. A good typographer handles them in intelligent, coherent, sensitive ways. When the type is poorly chosen, what the words say linguistically and what the letters imply visually are disharmonious, dishonest, out of tune.

1.2.5 *Shape the page and frame the textblock so that it honors and reveals every element, every relationship between elements, and every logical nuance of the text.*

Selecting the shape of the page and placing the type upon it is much like framing and hanging a painting. A cubist painting in an eighteenth-century gilded frame, or a seventeenth-century still-life in a slim chrome box, will look no sillier than a nineteenth-century text from England set in types that come from seventeenth-century France, asymmetrically positioned on a German Modernist page.

If the text is long or the space is short, or if the elements are many, multiple columns may be required. If illustrations and text march side by side, does one take precedence over the other? And does the order or degree of prominence change? Does the text suggest perpetual symmetry, perpetual asymmetry, or something in between?

Again, does the text suggest the continuous unruffled flow of justified prose, or the continued flirtation with order and chaos evoked by flush-left ragged-right composition? (The running heads and sidenotes on the recto (righthand) pages of this book are set flush left, ragged right. On the verso (lefthand) pages, they are ragged left. Leftward-reading alphabets, like Arabic and Hebrew, are perfectly at home in ragged-left text, but with rightward-reading alphabets like Latin, Greek or Thai, ragged-left setting emphasizes the end, not the beginning, of the line. This makes it a poor choice for extended composition.)

Shaping the page goes hand in hand with choosing the type, and both are permanent typographical preoccupations. The subject of page shapes and proportions is addressed in greater detail in chapter 8.

Tactics

1.2.6 *Give full typographic attention even to incidental details.*

Some of what a typographer must set, like some of what any musician must play, is simply passage work. Even an edition of Plato or Shakespeare will contain a certain amount of routine text: page numbers, scene numbers, textual notes, the copyright claim, the publisher's name and address, and the hyperbole on the jacket, not to mention the passage work or background writing that is implicit in the text itself. But just as a good musician can make a heart-wrenching ballad from a few banal words and a trivial tune, so the typographer can make poignant and lovely typography from bibliographical paraphernalia and textual chaff. The ability to do so rests on respect for the text as a whole, and on respect for the letters themselves.

Perhaps the principle should read: Give full typographic attention *especially* to incidental details.

1.3 SUMMARY

There are always exceptions, always excuses for stunts and surprises. But perhaps we can agree that, as a rule, typography should perform these services for the reader:

- *invite the reader into the text;*
- *reveal the tenor and meaning of the text;*
- *clarify the structure and the order of the text;*
- *link the text with other existing elements;*
- *induce a state of energetic repose, which is the ideal condition for reading.*

While serving the reader in this way, typography, like a musical performance or a theatrical production, should serve two other ends. It should honor the text for its own sake – always assuming that the text is worth a typographer's trouble – and it should honor and contribute to its own tradition: that of typography itself.

2

RHYTHM & PROPORTION

2.1 HORIZONTAL MOTION

An ancient metaphor: thought is a thread, and the raconteur is a spinner of yarns – but the true storyteller, the poet, is a weaver. The scribes made this old and audible abstraction into a new and visible fact. After long practice, their work took on such an even, flexible texture that they called the written page a *textus,* which means cloth.

The typesetting device, whether it happens to be a computer or a composing stick, functions like a loom. And the typographer, like the scribe, normally aims to weave the text as evenly as possible. Good letterforms are designed to give a lively, even texture, but careless spacing of letters, lines and words can tear this fabric apart.

Another ancient metaphor: the density of texture in a written or typeset page is called its *color.* This has nothing to do with red or green ink; it refers only to the darkness or blackness of the letterforms in mass. Once the demands of legibility and logical order are satisfied, *evenness of color* is the typographer's normal aim. And color depends on four things: the design of the type, the spacing between the letters, the spacing between the words, and the spacing between the lines. None is independent of the others.

2.1.1 *Define the word space to suit the size and natural letterfit of the font.*

Type is normally measured in picas and points (explained in detail on pages 328–329), but horizontal spacing is measured in *ems,* and the em is a sliding measure. One em is a distance equal to the type size. In 6 point type, an em is 6 points; in 12 pt type it is 12 points, and in 60 pt type it is 60 points. Thus a one-em space is *proportionately* the same in any size.

12 pt em | 18 pt em | 24 pt em | 36 pt em

Typesetting machines generally divide the em into units. Ems of 18, 36 or 54 units, for example, are commonly found in the older machines. In newer devices, the em is generally a thousand units. Typographers are more likely to divide the em into simple fractions: half an em, a third of an em, and so on, knowing that the unit value of these fractions will vary from one machine to the next. Half an em is called an *en.*

Horizontal Motion

If text is set ragged right, the *word space* (the space between words) can be fixed and unchanging. If the text is *justified* (set flush left and right, like the text in this book), that space must usually be elastic. In either case, the size of the ideal word space varies from one circumstance to another, depending on factors such as letterfit, type color, and size. A loosely fitted or bold face will need a larger interval between the words. At larger sizes, when letterfit is tightened, the spacing of words can be tightened as well. For a normal text face in a normal text size, a typical value for the word space is a quarter of an em, which can be written M/4. (A quarter of an em is typically about the same as, or slightly more than, the set-width of the letter t.)

M/3	M/4	M/5

Language has some effect on the word space as well. In highly inflected languages, such as Latin, most word boundaries are marked by grammatical tags, and a smaller space is therefore sufficient. In English and other uninflected languages, good word spacing makes the difference between a line that has to be deciphered and a line that can be efficiently read.

If the text is justified, a reasonable *minimum* word space is a fifth of an em (M/5), and M/4 is a good average to aim for. A reasonable maximum in justified text is M/2. If it can be held to M/3, so much the better. But for loosely fitted faces, or text set in a small size, M/3 is often a better average to aim for, and a better minimum is M/4. In a line of widely letterspaced capitals, a word space of M/2 or more may be required.

For example: the word space native to the font used here is 227 units wide, or 227 thousandths of an em. The typesetting software is instructed to allow, in the main text, a minimum word space of 85%. That is 193 units: just under a fifth of an em. The maximum word space is set to 150%, which is 340 units: just over a third of an em.

2.1.2 *Choose a comfortable measure.*

Anything from 45 to 75 characters is widely regarded as a satisfactory length of line for a single-column page set in a serifed text face in a text size. The 66-character line (counting both letters and spaces) is widely regarded as ideal. For multiple-column work, a better average is 40 to 50 characters.

If the type is well set and printed, lines of 85 or 90 characters will pose no problem in discontinuous texts, such as bibliographies, or, with generous leading, in footnotes. But even with generous leading, a line that averages more than 75 or 80 characters is likely to be too long for continuous reading.

A reasonable working minimum for justified text in English is the 40-character line. Shorter lines may compose perfectly well with sufficient luck and patience, but in the long run, justified lines averaging less than 38 or 40 characters will lead to white acne or pig bristles: a rash of erratic and splotchy word spaces or an epidemic of hyphenation. When the line is short, the text should be set ragged right. In large doses, even ragged-right composition may look anorexic if the line falls below 30 characters, but in small and isolated patches – ragged marginal notes, for example – the minimum line (if the language is English) can be as little as 12 or 15 characters.

When the counters of the letterforms themselves, not just the spaces between words, are elastic, justification can be carried to greater extremes. See pp 190–192.

These line lengths are in every case averages, and they include empty spaces and punctuation as well as letters. The simplest way of computing them is with a copyfitting table like the one on page 29. Measure the length of the basic lowercase alphabet – abcdefghijklmnopqrstuvwxyz – in any face and size you are considering, and the table will tell you the average number of characters to expect on a given line. In most text faces, the 10 pt roman alphabet will run between 120 and 140 points in length, but a 10 pt italic alphabet might be 100 points long or even less, while a 10 pt bold might run to 160. The 12 pt alphabet is, of course, about 1.2 times the length of the 10 pt alphabet – but not exactly so unless it is generated from the same master design and the letterfit is unchanged.

On a conventional book page, the measure, or length of line, is usually around 30 times the size of the type, but lines as little as 20 or as much as 40 times the type size fall within the expectable range. If, for example, the type size is 10 pt, the measure might be around 30 × 10 = 300 pt, which is 300/12 = 25 picas. A typical lowercase alphabet length for a 10 pt text font is 128 pt, and the copyfitting table tells us that such a font set to a 25-pica measure will yield roughly 65 characters per line.

2.1.3 *Set ragged if ragged setting suits the text and the page.*

In justified text, there is always a trade-off between evenness of spacing and frequency of hyphenation. The best available compromise will depend on the nature of the text as well as on the specifics of the design. Good compositors like to avoid consecutive hyphenated line-ends, but frequent hyphens are better than sloppy spacing, and ragged setting is better yet.

Narrow measures – which make good justification extremely difficult – are commonly used when the text is set in multiple columns. Setting ragged right under these conditions will lighten the page and decrease its stiffness, as well as preventing an outbreak of hyphenation.

Horizontal Motion

Many unserifed faces look best when set ragged no matter what the length of the measure. And monospaced fonts, which are common on typewriters, always look better set ragged, in standard typewriter style. A typewriter (or a computer-driven printer of similar quality) that justifies its lines in imitation of typesetting is a presumptuous, uneducated machine, mimicking the outward form instead of the inner truth of typography.

❧ When setting ragged text with a computer, take a moment to refine your software's understanding of what constitutes an honest rag. Software is often predisposed to invoke a minimum as well as a maximum line. If permitted to do so, it will hyphenate words and adjust the word spaces regardless of whether it is ragging or justifying the text. Ragged setting with these parameters tends to produce an orderly ripple down the righthand side, making the text look like a neatly pinched piecrust. If that is what you want, fine; but it may not be. Unless the measure is excruciatingly narrow, you may prefer the greater variations of a hard rag. This means fixed word spaces, no minimum line, no letterspacing, and no hyphenation beyond what is inherent in the text. In a hard rag, hyphenated linebreaks may occur in words like *self-consciousness,* which are hyphenated anyway, but they cannot occur without manual intervention in words like *hyphenation* or *pseudosophisticated,* which aren't.

2.1.4 *Use a single word space between sentences.*

In the nineteenth century, which was a dark and inflationary age in typography and type design, many compositors were encouraged to stuff extra space between sentences. Generations of twentieth-century typists were then taught to do the same, by hitting the spacebar twice after every period. Your typing as well as your typesetting will benefit from unlearning this quaint Victorian habit. As a general rule, no more than a single space is required

AVERAGE CHARACTER COUNT PER LINE

	10	12	14	16	18	20	22	24	26	28	30	32	34	36	38	40
80	40	48	56	64	72	80	88	96	104	112	120	128	136	144	152	160
85	38	45	53	60	68	76	83	91	98	106	113	121	129	136	144	151
90	36	43	50	57	64	72	79	86	93	100	107	115	122	129	136	143
95	34	41	48	55	62	69	75	82	89	96	103	110	117	123	130	137
100	33	40	46	53	59	66	73	79	86	92	99	106	112	119	125	132
105	32	38	44	51	57	63	70	76	82	89	95	101	108	114	120	127
110	30	37	43	49	55	61	67	73	79	85	92	98	104	110	116	122
115	29	35	41	47	53	59	64	70	76	82	88	94	100	105	111	117
120	28	34	39	45	50	56	62	67	73	78	84	90	95	101	106	112
125	27	32	38	43	48	54	59	65	70	75	81	86	91	97	102	108
130	26	31	36	41	47	52	57	62	67	73	78	83	88	93	98	104
135	25	30	35	40	45	50	55	60	65	70	75	80	85	90	95	100
140	24	29	34	39	44	48	53	58	63	68	73	77	82	87	92	97
145	23	28	33	37	42	47	51	56	61	66	70	75	80	84	89	94
150	23	28	32	37	41	46	51	55	60	64	69	74	78	83	87	92
155	22	27	31	36	40	45	49	54	58	63	67	72	76	81	85	90
160	22	26	30	35	39	43	48	52	56	61	65	69	74	78	82	87
165	21	25	30	34	38	42	46	51	55	59	63	68	72	76	80	84
170	21	25	29	33	37	41	45	49	53	57	62	66	70	74	78	82
175	20	24	28	32	36	40	44	48	52	56	60	64	68	72	76	80
180	20	23	27	31	35	39	43	47	51	55	59	62	66	70	74	78
185	19	23	27	30	34	38	42	46	49	53	57	61	65	68	72	76
190	19	22	26	30	33	37	41	44	48	52	56	59	63	67	70	74
195	18	22	25	29	32	36	40	43	47	50	54	58	61	65	68	72
200	18	21	25	28	32	35	39	42	46	49	53	56	60	63	67	70
210	17	20	23	27	30	33	37	40	43	47	50	53	57	60	63	67
220	16	19	22	25	29	32	35	38	41	45	48	51	54	57	60	64
230	15	18	21	24	27	30	33	36	40	43	46	49	52	55	58	61
240	15	17	20	23	26	29	32	35	38	41	44	46	49	52	55	58
250	14	17	20	22	25	28	31	34	36	39	42	45	48	50	53	56
260	14	16	19	22	24	27	30	32	35	38	41	43	46	49	51	54
270	13	16	18	21	23	26	29	31	34	36	39	42	44	47	49	52
280	13	15	18	20	23	25	28	30	33	35	38	40	43	45	48	50
290	12	15	17	20	22	24	27	29	32	34	37	39	41	44	46	49
300	12	14	17	19	21	24	26	28	31	33	35	38	40	42	45	47
320	11	13	16	18	20	22	25	27	29	31	34	36	38	40	43	45
340	10	13	15	17	19	21	23	25	27	29	32	34	36	38	40	42
360	10	12	14	16	18	20	22	24	26	28	30	32	34	36	38	40

Read down, in the left column: lowercase alphabet length in points. *Read across,* in the top row: line length in picas.

after a period, a colon or any other mark of punctuation. Larger spaces (e.g., en spaces) are *themselves* punctuation.

The rule is sometimes altered, however, when setting classical Latin and Greek, romanized Sanskrit, phonetics or other kinds of texts in which sentences begin with lowercase letters. In the absence of a capital, a full *en space* (M/2) between sentences may be welcome.

Horizontal Motion

2.1.5 *Add little or no space within strings of initials.*

Names such as W. B. Yeats and J. C. L. Prillwitz need hair spaces, thin spaces or no spaces at all after the intermediary periods. A normal word space follows the *last* period in the string.

2.1.6 *Letterspace all strings of capitals and small caps, and all long strings of digits.*

Acronyms such as CIA and PLO are frequent in some texts. So are abbreviations such as CE and BCE or AD and BC. The normal value for letterspacing these sequences of small or full caps is 5% to 10% of the type size. If your software sees the em as 1000 PostScript units, that means 50 to 100 units of letterspacing.

With digital fonts, it is a simple matter to assign extra width to all small capitals, so that letterspacing occurs automatically. The width values of full caps are normally based on the assumption that they will be used in conjunction with the lower case, but letterspacing can still be automated through the use of kerning tables (see pages 33–34).

In titles and headings, extra letterspacing is often desirable. Justified lines of letterspaced capitals are generally set by inserting a normal word space (M/5 to M/4) between letters. This corresponds to letterspacing of 20% to 25% of the type size. But the extra space between letters will also require more space between lines. A Renaissance typographer setting a multi-line head in letterspaced text-size capitals would normally set blanks between the lines: the hand compositor's equivalent of the keyboard operator's extra hard return, or double spacing.

There is no generalized optimum value for letterspacing capitals in titles or display lines. The effective letterspacing of caps in good classical inscriptions and later manuscripts ranges from 5% to 100% of the nominal type size. The quantity of space is far less important than its balance. Sequences like LA or AVA may need no extra space at all, while sequences like NN and HIH beg to be pried open.

W A V A D O P A T T I M M I L T L

WAVADOPATTIMMILTL

Letterspaced caps, above; kerned but unletterspaced, below.

Many typographers like to letterspace all strings of numbers as well. Spacing is essential for rapid reading of long, fundamentally meaningless strings, such as serial numbers, and it is helpful even for shorter strings such as phone numbers and dates. Numbers set in pairs need not be letterspaced; strings of three or more may need a little air. This is the rationale behind the old European habit of setting phone numbers in the form 00 00 00 instead of 000-0000.

2.1.7 *Don't letterspace the lower case without a reason.*

A man who would letterspace lower case would steal sheep, Frederic Goudy liked to say. If this wisdom needs updating, it is chiefly to add that a woman who would letterspace lower case would steal sheep as well.

Nevertheless, like every rule, this one extends only as far as its rationale. The reason for not letterspacing lower case is that it hampers legibility. But there are some lowercase alphabets to which this principle doesn't apply.

Headings set in exaggeratedly letterspaced, condensed, unserifed capitals are now a hallmark, if not a cliché, of postmodern typography. In this context, secondary display can be set perfectly well in more modestly letterspaced, condensed, unserifed lower case. Moderate letterspacing can make a face such as lowercase Univers bold condensed more legible rather than less. Inessential ligatures are, of course, omitted from letterspaced text.

wharves and wharfingers

Lowercase Univers bold condensed, letterspaced 10%.

It would be possible, in fact, to make a detailed chart of lowercase letterforms, plotting their inherent resistance to letterspacing.

Near the top of the list (most unsuitable for letterspacing) would be Renaissance italics, such as Arrighi, whose structure strongly implies an actual linkage between one letter and the next. A little farther along would be Renaissance romans. Still farther along, we would find faces like Syntax, which echo the forms of Renaissance roman but lack the serifs. Around the middle of the list, we would find other unserifed faces, such as Helvetica, in which nothing more than wishful thinking bonds the letters to each other. Bold condensed sanserifs would appear at the bottom of the list. Letterspacing will always sabotage a Renaissance roman or italic. But when we come to the other extreme, the faces with no calligraphic flow, letterspacing of lowercase letters can sometimes be of genuine benefit.

Because it isolates the individual elements, letterspacing has a role to play where words have ceased to matter and letters are what count. Where letters function one by one (as in acronyms, web-site and e-mail addresses) letterspacing is likely to help, no matter whether the letters are caps, small caps or lower case.

daß
d a ß

Outside the domain of roman and italic type, the letterspacing of text has other traditional functions. Blackletter faces have, as a rule, no companion italic or bold, and no small caps. The simplest methods of emphasis available are underlining and letterspacing. The former was the usual method of the scribes, but letterspacing is easier for letterpress printers. In digitial typography, however, underlining is just as easy as letterspacing and sometimes does less damage to the page.

ЖКИ
жки

In Cyrillic, the difference between lower case and small caps is more subtle than in the Latin or Greek alphabets, but small caps are nonetheless important to skilled Cyrillic typographers. In former days, when Cyrillic cursive type was scarce and small caps almost nonexistent, Cyrillic was routinely set like fraktur, with letterspaced upright (roman) lower case where the small caps and the cursive (italic) would have been. Improved Cyrillic types have made that practice obsolete.

2.1.8 *Kern consistently and modestly or not at all.*

Inconsistencies in letterfit are inescapable, given the forms of the Latin alphabet, and small irregularities are after all essential to the legibility of roman type. *Kerning* – altering the space between selected pairs of letters – can increase consistency of spacing in a word like Washington or Toronto, where the combinations Wa and To are kerned. But names like Wisconsin, Tübingen, Tbilisi and Los Alamos, as well as common words like The and This, remain more or less immune to alteration.

Hand compositors rarely kern text sizes, because their kerning pairs must be manually fitted, one at a time. Computerized typesetting makes extensive kerning easy, but judgment is still required, and the computer does not make good judgment any easier to come by. Too little kerning is preferable to too much, and inconsistent kerning is worse than none.

In digital type, as in foundry type, each letter has a standard width of its own. But computerized typesetting systems can modify these widths in many ways. Digital fonts are generally kerned through the use of *kerning tables,* which can specify a reduction or increase in spacing for every possible pair of letters, numbers or symbols. By this means, space can be automatically added to combinations like HH and removed from combinations like Ty. Prefabricated kerning tables are now routine components of well-made digital fonts, but they still sometimes require extensive editing to suit individual styles and requirements. If you use an automatic kerning program, test it thoroughly before trusting its decisions, and take the time to repair its inevitable shortcomings.

There is more about kerning tables on pp 203–207.

Kerning tables generally subtract space from combinations such as Av, Aw, Ay, 'A, 'A, L', and all combinations in which the first element is T, V, W or Y and the second element is anything other than b, h, k or l. Not all such combinations occur in English, but a good kerning table will accommodate names such as Tchaikovsky, Tmolos, Tsimshian, Vázquez, Chateau d'Yquem and Ysaÿe.

The table also normally adds space to sequences like f', f), f], f?, f!, (*f,* [*f,* (J and [J. In some italics, space must also be added to *gg* and *gy.* If your text includes them, other sequences – *gf, gj, qf, qj,* for instance – may need attention as well.

Especially at larger sizes, it is common to kern combinations involving commas and periods, such as r, / r. / v, / v. / w, / w. / y, / y. But use care in kerning combinations such as F. / P. / T. / V. Capitals need their space, and some combinations are easy to misread. P.F. Didot may be misread as R E Didot if too enthusiastically kerned.

Töp

Töpf

(*f*")

w, f'

Numbers are often omitted from kerning tables, but numbers often need more kerning than letters do. Most fonts, both metal and digital, are equipped with *tabular figures* – figures that all have identical set-width, so columns of typeset figures will align. If you are forced to use such a font, heavy kerning will be required. A good text font will give you *proportional figures* instead. A digital font in the OpenType format may offer you four choices: proportional and tabular lining (titling) figures, and proportional and tabular old-style (text) figures. No matter how the figures are cut, when used in text, they are likely to need some kerning, to each other and to the en dash.

Horizontal Motion

1740–1900 1740–1900

Unkerned Sabon numerals, left, and well-kerned numerals, right

Whatever kerning you do, make sure it does not result in collisions with diacritics. Wolf can be kerned more than Wölfflin in many faces, and Tennyson more than Tête-à-tête. Also beware the composite effect of sequential kerns. The apostrophes in L'Hôtel and D'Artagnan can be brought up fairly close, but in L'Anse aux Meadows, two close kerns in a row will produce a collision.

’s

a’a

“¿

ck

ij

A kerning table written expressly for one language will need subtle alteration before it can do justice to another. In English, for example, it is normal to kern the combinations ’d ’m ’r ’s ’t, which appear in common contractions. In French, ’a ’â ’e ’é ’è ’ê ’o ’ô are kerned instead, because these appear in elisions. In Native American texts, apostrophes can appear in many other contexts. For Spanish, one kerns the combinations ‘¿ and “¿. For German, a careful typographer will take space out of the combinations ‚T „T ‚V „V ‚W „W and may add some space to ‚J and „J.

The letter *c* is not a full-fledged member of the German alphabet, and in former times it was always restricted, in German, to the ligatures *ch* and *ck*. English-speaking readers often find these combinations kerned too close for comfort in German-made fonts – or they find the right sidebearing of the *c* too close-cut to begin with. In fonts from the Netherlands, unusually tight kerning is common in the sequence *ij* instead.

Binomial kerning tables are powerful and useful typographic tools, but they eliminate neither the need nor the pleasure of making final adjustments by hand. Names like T.V.R. Murti and T.R.V. Murti, for example, pose microscopic typographic problems that no binomial kerning table can solve. Fonts with polynomial kerning tables – able to kern a given pair of letters in different ways according to context – have existed for a decade and may someday be the norm. For now, they are a rarity.

2.1.9 *Don't alter the widths or shapes of letters without cause.*

Type design is an art practiced by few and mastered by fewer – but font-editing software makes it possible for anyone to alter in a moment the widths and shapes of letters to which an artist may have devoted decades of study, years of inspiration and a rare concentration of skill. The power to destroy such a type designer's work should be used with caution. And arbitrarily condensing or expanding letterforms is the poorest of all methods for fitting uneditable copy into unalterable space.

In many fonts, the exclamation mark, question mark, semicolon and colon need a wider left sidebearing than manufacturers have given them, but the width of any character should be altered for one purpose only: to improve the set of the type.

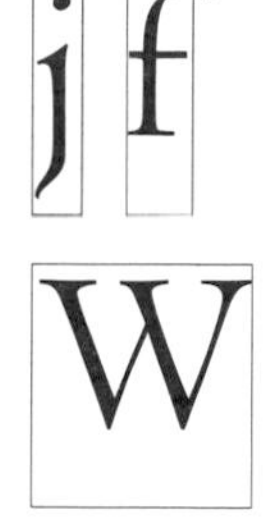

Typographic letters are made legible not only by their forms and by the color of the ink that prints them but also by the sculpted empty space between and around them. When type is cast and set by hand, that space is physically defined by blocks of metal. When the type is reduced to a *face,* photographically or digitally stored, the letter still has a room of its own, defined by its stated body height and width, but it is a virtual room. In the world of digital type, it is very easy for a designer or compositor with no regard for letters to squish them into cattle trains and ship them to the slaughter.

letterfit   letterfit

When letters are maltreated in this way, their reserve of legibility is sapped. They can do little in their turn except shortchange and brutalize the reader.

2.1.10 *Don't stretch the space until it breaks.*

Lists, such as contents pages and recipes, are opportunities to build architectural structures in which the space between the elements both separates and binds. The two favorite ways of destroying such an opportunity are setting great chasms of space that the eye cannot leap without help from the hand, and setting unenlightening rows of dots (*dot leaders,* they are called) that force the eye to walk the width of the page like a prisoner being escorted back to its cell.

The following examples show two among many ways of handling a list. Splitting titles and numbers apart, setting one flush left and the other flush right, with or without dot leaders, would only muffle the information:

	Introduction	7
Chapter **1**	The Sex of Centaurs	11
Chapter **2**	Poliphilo's Dream	43

Horizontal Motion

Prologue · *page 5*
Points of Possible Agreement · *page 9*
Irreconcilable Differences · *page 11*
Conclusion · *page 163*
Index · *page 164*

2.2 VERTICAL MOTION

2.2.1 *Choose a basic leading that suits the typeface, text and measure.*

Time is divisible into any number of increments. So is space. But for working purposes, time in music is divided into a few proportional intervals: halves, quarters, eighths, sixteenths and so on. And time in most music is measured. Add a quarter note to a bar whose time is already accounted for and, somewhere nearby, the equivalent of that quarter note must come out. Phrasing and rhythm can move in and out of phase – as they do in the singing of Billie Holiday and the trumpet solos of Miles Davis – but the force of blues phrasing and syncopation vanishes if the beat is actually lost.

Space in typography is like time in music. It is infinitely divisible, but a few proportional intervals can be much more useful than a limitless choice of arbitrary quantities.

The metering of horizontal space is accomplished almost unconsciously in typography. You choose and prepare a font, and you choose a measure (the width of the column). When you set the type, the measure fills with the varied rhythm of repeating letter shapes, which are music to the eye.

Vertical space is metered in a different way. You must choose not only the overall measure – the depth of the column or page – but also a basic rhythmical unit. This unit is the leading, which is the distance from one baseline to the next.

Eleven-point type *set solid* is described as 11/11. The theoretical face of the type is 11 points high (from the top of *d* to the bottom of *p*, if the type is full on the body), and the distance from the baseline of line one to the baseline of line two is also 11 points. Add two points of lead (interlinear space), and the type is set 11/13. The type size has not changed, but the distance from baseline to baseline has increased to 13 points, and the type has more room to breathe.

The text of the book you are reading, to take an example, is set 10/12 × 21. This means that the type size is 10 pt, the added lead is 2 pt, giving a total leading of 12 pt, and the line length is 21 picas.

A short burst of advertising copy or a title might be set with negative leading (18/15, for example), so long as the ascenders and descenders don't collide:

this is an example
of negative leading

Continuous text is very rarely set with negative leading, and only a few text faces read well when set solid. Most text requires positive leading. Settings such as 9/11, 10/12, 11/13 and 12/15 are routine. Longer measures need more lead than short ones. Dark faces need more lead than light ones. Large-bodied faces need more lead than smaller-bodied ones. Faces like Bauer Bodoni, with substantial color and a rigid vertical axis, need much more lead than faces like Bembo, whose color is light and whose axis is based on the writing hand. And unserifed faces often need more lead (or a shorter line) than their serifed counterparts.

Extra leading is also generally welcome where the text is thickened by superscripts, subscripts, mathematical expressions, or the frequent use of full capitals. A text in German would ideally have a little more lead than the same text in Latin or French, purely because of the increased frequency of capitals.

Bauer Bodoni and Bembo, both set 40/42.

2.2.2 *Add and delete vertical space in measured intervals.*

For the same reason that the tempo must not change arbitrarily in music, leading must not change arbitrarily in type.

Pages and columns are set most often to uniform depth, but ragged depths are better in some situations. A collection of short texts, such as catalogue entries, set in multiple-column pages, is likely to look better and read more easily if the text is not sawed into columns of uniform depth. A collection of short poems is bound to generate pages of varying depth as well – and so much the better.

Vertical Motion

Continuous prose offers no such excuse for variation. It is therefore usually set in pages of uniform depth, designed in symmetrical pairs. The lines and blocks of text on facing pages in this format should align, and the lines on the front and back of the leaf (the recto and verso pages) should align as well. Typographers check their reproduction proofs by holding them up to the light in pairs, to see that the text and crop marks match from page to page. Press proofs are checked in the same way, by holding them up to the light to see that textblocks *back each other up* when the sheet is printed on both sides.

Headings, subheads, block quotations, footnotes, illustrations, captions and other intrusions into the text create syncopations and variations against the base rhythm of regularly leaded lines. These variations can and should add life to the page, but the main text should also return after each variation precisely on beat and in phase. This means that the total amount of vertical space consumed by each departure from the main text should be an even multiple of the basic leading. If the main text runs 11/13, intrusions to the text should equal some multiple of 13 points: 26, 39, 52, 65, 78, 91, 104 and so on.

Subheads in this book are leaded in the simplest possible way, with a *white line* (that is, in keyboard terms, a hard return) before and after. They could just as well be leaded asymmetrically, with more space above than below, so long as the total additional lead is equivalent to an even number of text lines.

If you happen to be setting a text 11/13, subhead possibilities include the following:

- subheads in 11/13 small caps, with 13 pt above the head and 13 pt below;
- subheads in 11/13 bold u&lc (upper and lower case), with 8 pt above the head and 5 pt below, since 8 + 5 = 13;
- subheads in 11/13 caps with 26 pt above and 13 pt below;
- one-line subheads in 14/13 italic u&lc, with 16 pt above the head and 10 pt below. (The negative leading is merely to minimize coding in this case. If the heads are one line long, no cramping will occur.)

2.2.3 *Don't suffocate the page.*

Most books now printed in the Latin alphabet carry from 30 to 45 lines per page. The average length of line in most of those books is 60 to 66 characters. In English and the Romance languages, a word is typically assumed to average five letters plus a space. Ten or eleven such words fit on a line of 60 to 66 characters, and the page, if it is full, holds from 300 to 500 words.

Outside these conventional boundaries lie many interesting typographic problems. If the text deserves the honor, a handsome page can be made with very few words. A page with 17 lines of 36 characters each, as an example, will carry only 100 words. At the other extreme, a page with 45 lines of 70 characters each will carry 525 words. If you want more than 500 words to the page, it is time to consider multiple columns. A two-column book page will comfortably carry 750 words. If it must, it can carry a thousand.

However empty or full it may be, the page must breathe, and in a book – that is, in a long text fit for the reader to live in – the page must breathe in both directions. The longer the line, the more space necessary between lines. Two columns of short lines are therefore more compact than a single column of long lines.

2.3 BLOCKS & PARAGRAPHS

2.3.1 *Set opening paragraphs flush left.*

The function of a paragraph indent is to mark a pause, setting the paragraph apart from what precedes it. If a paragraph is preceded by a title or subhead, the indent is superfluous and can therefore be omitted, as it is here.

2.3.2 *In continuous text, mark all paragraphs after the first with an indent of at least one en.*

Typography like other arts, from cooking to choreography, involves a balance between the familiar and the unfamiliar, the dependably consistent and the unforeseen. Typographers generally take pleasure in the unpredictable length of the paragraph while accepting the simple and reassuring consistency of the paragraph indent. The prose paragraph and its verse counterpart, the stanza, are basic units of linguistic thought and literary style. The typographer must articulate them enough to make them clear, yet not so strongly that the form instead of the content steals the show. If the units of thought, or the boundaries between thoughts, look more important than the thoughts themselves, the typographer has failed.

❧ Ornaments can be placed in the paragraph indents, but few texts actually profit from ornamentation.

Blocks and Paragraphs

Paragraphs can also be marked, as this one is, by drop lines, but dropline paragraphs grow tiresome in long texts. They also increase the labor of revisions and corrections. ¶ Pilcrows, boxes and bullets can be used to mark the breaks in a stream of continuous text, sometimes with excellent results. This format is more economical of space than conventional indented paragraphs, but again, extra labor and expense may arise with emendations and corrections.

Outdented paragraphs and indented paragraphs are the two most obvious possibilities that remain. And outdented paragraphs bring with them other possibilities, such as the use of enlarged marginal letters.

All these variants, and others, have their uses, but the plainest, most unmistakable yet unobtrusive way of marking paragraphs is the simple indent: a white square.

How much indent is enough? The most common paragraph indent is one em. Another standard value is *one lead*. If your text is set 11/13, the indent would then be either 11 pt (one em) or 13 pt (one lead). One en (half an em) is the practical minimum.

Where the line is long and margins are ample, an indent of 1½ or 2 ems may look more luxurious than one em, but paragraph indents larger than three ems are generally counterproductive. Short last lines followed by new lines with large indents produce a tattered page.

Block paragraphs open flush left and are separated vertically from their neighbors by extra lead, usually a white line. Block paragraphs are common in business letters and memos, and because they suggest precision, crispness and speed, they can be useful in short documents of other kinds. In longer sequences, they may seem soulless and uninviting.

2.3.3 *Add extra lead before and after block quotations.*

Block quotations (like the one on pp 17–18 of this book) can be distinguished from the main text in many ways. For instance: by a change of face (usually from roman to italic), by a change in size (as from 11 pt down to 10 pt or 9 pt), or by indention.

Combinations of these methods are often used, but one device is enough. If your paragraph indent is modest, you may for consistency's sake want to use the same indent for quotations. And even if your block quotations are set in a size smaller than normal text, you may want to leave the leading unchanged. If the main text runs 10/12, the block quotations might run 10/12 italic or 9/12 roman. If you prefer greater density or are eager to save space, you might set them 9/11 or 9/10½.

However the block quotations are set, there must be a visible distinction between main text and quotation, and again between the quotation and subsequent text. This usually means a white line or half-line at the beginning and end of the block. But if the leading within the block quotation differs from the leading of the main text, these blanks before and after the quotation must be elastic. They afford the only opportunity for bringing the text back into phase.

Suppose your main text is 11/13 and a five-line block quotation set 10/12 intervenes. The depth of the quotation is $5 \times 12 = 60$. This must be bulked up to a multiple of 13 to bring the text back into phase. The nearest multiple of 13 is $5 \times 13 = 65$. The remaining space is $65 - 60 = 5$, and $5/2 = 2.5$, which is not enough. Adding 2.5 points before and after the quotation will not give adequate separation. The next multiple of 13 is $6 \times 13 = 78$, which is better: $78 - 60 = 18$, and $18/2 = 9$. Add 9 pt lead before and after the quotation, and the text will realign.

2.3.4 *Indent or center verse quotations.*

Verse is usually set flush left and ragged right, and verse quotations within prose should not be deprived of their chosen form. But to distinguish verse quotations from surrounding prose, they should be indented or centered on the longest line. Centering is preferable when the prose measure is substantially longer than the verse line. The following passage, for example, is centered on the first and longest line.

> *God guard me from those thoughts men think*
> *In the mind alone;*
> *He that sings a lasting song*
> *Thinks in a marrow bone.*

William Butler Yeats, "A Prayer for Old Age."

Suppose your main text is set on a 24-pica measure and you have decided to set verse quotations in italic at the text size. Suppose that the longest line in your quotation measures 269 points. The indent for this quotation might be computed as follows: 24 × 12 = 288 pt, which is the full prose measure, and 288 – 269 = 19 pt, which is the difference between the measure and the longest verse line. The theoretically perfect left indent for the verse quotation is 19/2 = 9.5 pt. But if another indent close to 9.5 pt is already in use, either for block quotations in prose, or as a paragraph indent, then the verse quotation might just as well be indented to match.

Suppose however that the longest line in the verse is 128 points. The measure, again, is 288 points, and 288 – 128 = 160. Half of 160 is 80 points. No other indent in the vicinity of 80 points is likely to be in use. The verse quotation would then be indented by precisely that amount.

2.4 ETIQUETTE OF HYPHENATION & PAGINATION

The rules listed below are traditional craft practice for the setting of justified text. Except for the last rule, they are all programmable, but the operation of these rules necessarily affects the spacing of words and thus the texture and color of the page. If decisions are left to the software, they should be checked by a trained eye – and no typesetting software should be permitted to compress, expand or letterspace the text automatically and arbitrarily as a means of fitting the copy. Copyfitting problems should be solved by creative design, not fobbed off on the reader and the text nor cast like pearls before machines.

For a brief discussion of software justification engines, which now do most of the work, see §9.4, page 190.

2.4.1 *At hyphenated line-ends, leave at least two characters behind and take at least three forward.*

Fi-nally is conventionally acceptable line-end hyphenation, but final-ly is not, because it takes too little of the word ahead to the next line.

2.4.2 *Avoid leaving the stub-end of a hyphenated word, or any word shorter than four letters, as the last line of a paragraph.*

2.4.3 *Avoid more than three consecutive hyphenated lines.*

2.4.4 *Hyphenate proper names only as a last resort unless they occur with the frequency of common nouns.*

2.4.5 *Hyphenate according to the conventions of the language.*

In English we hyphenate *cab-ri-o-let* but in French *ca-brio-let*. The old German rule which hyphenated *Glockenspiel* as *Glok-kenspiel* was changed by law in 1998, but when *össze* is broken in Hungarian, it still turns into *ösz-sze*. In Spanish the double consonants *ll* and *rr* are never divided. (The only permissible hyphenation in the phrase *arroz con pollo* is thus *arroz con po-llo*.) The conventions of each language are a part of its typographic heritage and should normally be followed, even when setting single foreign words or brief quotations.

Hart's Rules for Compositors (39th ed, 1983) includes a good, brief guide to hyphenation and punctuation rules for several European languages. Its fat successor, Ritter's *Oxford Guide to Style* (2002) is more thorough but much less handy. It is always worthwhile, however, to consult a style manual written in and for the language at issue – e.g., for French, the *Lexique des règles typographiques en usage à l'imprimerie nationale* (Paris, 1990).

2.4.6 *Link short numerical and mathematical expressions with hard spaces.*

All you may see on the keyboard is a space bar, but typographers use several invisible characters: the word space, fixed spaces of various sizes (em space, en space, thin space, figure space, etc) and a *hard space* or *no-break space*. The hard space will stretch, like a normal word space, when the line is justified, but it will not convert to a linebreak. Hard spaces are useful for preventing linebreaks within phrases such as *6.2 mm*, *3 in.*, *4 × 4*, or in phrases like *page 3* and *chapter 5*.

When it is necessary to break longer algebraic or numerical expressions, such as $a + b = c$, the break should come at the equal sign or another clear logical pause.

2.4.7 *Avoid beginning more than two consecutive lines with the same word.*

2.4.8 *Never begin a page with the last line of a multi-line paragraph.*

The typographic terminology is telling. Isolated lines created when paragraphs *begin* on the *last* line of a page are known as *orphans*. They have no past, but they do have a future, and they need not trouble the typographer. The stub-ends left when paragraphs *end* on the *first* line of a page are called *widows*. They have a past but not a future, and they look foreshortened and forlorn. It is the custom – in most, if not in all, the world's typographic cultures – to give them one additional line for company. This rule is applied in close conjunction with the next.

Etiquette of Hyphenation and Pagination

2.4.9 *Balance facing pages by moving single lines.*

Pages with more than two columns often look best with the columns set to varying depths. This is the vertical equivalent of ragged-right composition. Where there are only one or two main text columns per page, paired columns and facing pages (except at the end of a chapter or section) are usually set to a uniform depth.

Balance facing pages not by adding extra lead or puffing up the word space, but by exporting or importing single lines to and from the preceding or following spreads. The same technique is used to avoid widows, and to extend or shorten any chapters that would otherwise end with a meager few lines on the final page. But this balancing should be performed with a gentle hand. In the end, no spread of continuous text should have to run more than a single line short or a single line long.

2.4.10 *Avoid hyphenated breaks where the text is interrupted.*

Style books sometimes insist that both parts of a hyphenated word must occur on the same page: in other words, that the last line on a page must never end with a hyphen. But turning the page is not, in itself, an interruption of the reading process. It is far more important to avoid breaking words in those locations where the reader is likely to be distracted by other information. That is, whenever a map, a chart, a photograph, a pull-quote, a sidebar or other interruption intervenes.

2.4.11 *Abandon any and all rules of hyphenation and pagination that fail to serve the needs of the text.*

HARMONY & COUNTERPOINT

3

3.1 SIZE

3.1.1 *Don't compose without a scale.*

The simplest scale is a single note, and sticking with a single note draws more attention to other parameters, such as rhythm and inflection. The early Renaissance typographers set each book in a single font – that is, one face in one size – supplemented by hand-drawn or specially engraved large initial letters for the openings of chapters. Their pages show what sensuous evenness of texture and variety of rhythm can be attained with a single font of type: very much greater than on a typewriter, where letters have, more often than not, a single width and a single stroke-weight as well as a single size.

In the sixteenth century, a series of common sizes developed among European typographers, and the series survived with little change and few additions for 400 years. In the early days, the sizes had names rather than numbers, but measured in points, the traditional series is this:

A few examples of the many older names for type sizes:
6 pt: *nonpareil*
7 pt: *minion*
8 pt: *brevier* or *small text*
9 pt: *bourgeois* or *galliard*
10 pt: *long primer* or *garamond*
11 pt: *small pica* or *philosophy*
12 pt: *pica*
14 pt: *english* or *augustin*
18 pt: *great primer*

a a a a a a a a a a a a a a a a
6 7 8 9 10 11 12 14 16 18 21 24 36 48 60 72

This is the typographic equivalent of the diatonic scale. But modern equipment makes it possible to set, in addition to these sizes, all the sharps and flats and microtonal intervals between. Twenty-point, 22-point, 23-point, and 10½-point type are all available for the asking. The designer can now choose a new scale or tone-row for every piece of work.

These new resources are useful, but rarely all at once. Use the old familiar scale, or use new scales of your own devising, but limit yourself, at first, to a modest set of distinct and related intervals. Start with one size and work slowly from there. In time, the scales you choose, like the faces you choose, will become recognizable features of personal style.

3.2.1 *Use titling figures with full caps, and text figures in all other circumstances.*

Numerals, Capitals and Small Caps

So the date is 23 August 1832; it could be 3:00 AM in Apartment 6-B, 213-A Beacon Street; it is 27° C or 81° F; the price is $47,000 USD or £28,200; the postal codes are NL 1034 WR Amsterdam, SF 00170 Helsinki 17, Honolulu 96814, London WC1 2NN, New Delhi 110 003, Toronto M5S 2G5, and Dublin 2.

BUT IT IS 1832 AND 81° IN FULL CAPITALS.

١ ٢ ٣
٤ ٥ ٦ ٧
٨ ٩ ٠

The arabic numerals of Latin script are derived from the Indian numerals of Arabic script (above).

Arabic numerals – known in Arabic as Indian numerals, *arqām hindiyya,* because the Arabs obtained them from India – entered the scribal tradition of Europe in the thirteenth century. Before that (and for many purposes afterward) European scribes used roman numerals, written in capitals when they occurred in the midst of other capitals, and in lowercase in the midst of lowercase letters. Typographers have naturally inherited this custom of setting roman numerals so that they harmonize with the words:

Number xiii lowercase AND XIII UPPERCASE
AND THE NUMBER XIII IN SMALL CAPITALS
and the roman numeral xiii in italic

When arabic numerals joined the roman alphabet, they too were given both lowercase and uppercase forms. Typographers call the former *text figures, hanging figures, lowercase figures,* or *old-style figures* (OSF for short) and make a point of using them whenever the surrounding text is set in lowercase letters or small caps. The alternative forms are called *titling figures, ranging figures* or *lining figures,* because they range or align with one another and with the upper case.

Text 1234567890 figures
TITLING 1234567890 FIGURES
FIGURES 1234567890 WITH SMALL CAPS
Italic text 1234567890 figures

Text figures were the common form in European typography between 1540 and 1800. But in the mid-eighteenth century, when European shopkeepers and merchants were apt to write more numbers than letters, handwritten numerals developed proportions of their own. These quite literally middle-class figures entered the realm of typography in 1788, when a British punchcutter named Richard Austin cut a font of three-quarter-height lining figures for the founder John Bell.

Harmony and Counterpoint

Bell letters and 1234567890 figures
in roman *and 1234567890 in italic*

In the nineteenth century, which was not a great age for typography, founders stretched these figures up to cap height, and titling figures became the norm in commercial typography. Renaissance letterforms were revived in the early twentieth century, and text figures found their way back into books. But in news and advertising work, titling figures remained routine. In the 1960s, phototypesetting machines with their truncated fonts once again made text figures difficult to find. The better digital foundries now offer a wide selection of fonts with text figures and small caps. These are often sold separately and involve extra expense, but they are essential to good typography. It is better to have one good face with all its parts, including text figures and small caps, than fifty faces without.

It is true that text figures are rarely useful in classified ads, but they are useful for setting almost everything else, including good magazine and newspaper copy. They are basic parts of typographic speech, and they are a sign of civilization: a sign that dollars are not really twice as important as ideas, and numbers are not afraid to consort on an equal footing with words.

It is also true that a number of excellent text faces, both serifed and unserifed, were originally issued without text figures. Examples include Adrian Frutiger's Méridien, Eric Gill's Gill Sans, Paul Renner's Futura, Hans Eduard Meier's Syntax, Hermann Zapf's Comenius and Optima, and Gudrun Zapf-von Hesse's Carmina. In several of these cases, text figures were part of the original conception or even the finished design but were scuttled by the foundry. Many such missing components have belatedly been issued in digital form. With any text face that is missing text figures, it is reasonable to enquire whether commercial intimidation or, in effect, commercial censorship may not have played a role.

During most of the nineteenth and twentieth centuries, lining figures were widely known as 'modern' and text figures as 'old-style.' Modernism was preached as a sacred duty, and numbers, in a sense, were actually deified. Modernism is nothing if not complex, but its gospel was radical simplicity. Many efforts were made to reduce the Latin alphabet back to a single case. (The telegraph and teletype, with their unicameral alphabets, are also products of that time.) These efforts failed to make much headway where letters were concerned. With numbers, the campaign had considerable success. Typewriters soon came to have letters in both upper and lower case but numbers in upper case alone. And from typewriters have come computer keyboards.

Numerals, Capitals and Small Caps

Typographic civilization seems, nonetheless, determined to proceed. Text figures are again a normal part of type design – and have thus been retroactively supplied for faces that were earlier denied them. However common it may be, the use of titling figures in running text is illiterate: it spurns the truth of letters.

3.2.2 *For abbreviations and acronyms in the midst of normal text, use spaced small caps.*

This is a good rule for just about everything except two-letter geographical acronyms and acronyms that stand for personal names. Thus: 3:00 AM, 3:00 PM, the ninth century CE, 450 BC to AD 450, the OAS and NATO; World War II or WWII; but JFK and Fr J.A.S. O'Brien, OMI; HMS *Hypothesis* and USS *Ticonderoga*; Washington, DC, and Mexico, DF; J.S. Bach's Prelude and Fugue in B♭ minor, BWV 867.

Many typographers prefer to use small caps for postal abbreviations (San Francisco, CA 94119), and for geographical acronyms longer than two letters. Thus, the USA, or in Spanish, *los* EEUU, and Sydney, NSW. But the need for consistency intervenes when long and short abbreviations fall together. From the viewpoint of the typographer, small caps are preferable in faces with fine features and small x-height, full caps in faces with large x-height and robust form.

Genuine small caps are not simply shrunken versions of the full caps. They differ from large caps in stroke weight, letterfit, and internal proportions as well as in height. Any good set of small caps is designed as such from the ground up. Thickening, shrinking and squashing the full caps with digital modification routines will only produce a parody.

Sloped small capitals – *A B C D E F G* – have been designed and cut for relatively few faces in the history of type design. They can be faked with digital machinery, by sloping the roman small caps, but it is better to choose a face (such as this one, Robert Slimbach's Minion) which includes them, or to live without. Sloped (italic) text figures, on the other hand, are part of the basic requirement and are available for most good text fonts.

Harmony and Counterpoint

3.2.3 *Refer typographic disputes to the higher courts of speech and thinking.*

Type is idealized writing, and its normal function is to record idealized speech. Acronyms such as CD and TV or USA and UFO are set in caps because that is the way we pronounce them. Acronyms like UNESCO, ASCII and FORTRAN, which are pronounced not as letters but as words, are in the process of becoming precisely that. When a writer accepts them fully into her speech and urges readers to do likewise, it is time for the typographer to accept them into the common speech of typography by setting them in lower case: Unesco, Ascii (or ascii) and Fortran. Other acronymic words, such as *laser* and *radar,* have long since traveled the same road.

Logograms pose a more difficult question. An increasing number of persons and institutions, from e.e. cummings to WordPerfect, now come to the typographer in search of special treatment. In earlier days it was kings and deities whose agents demanded that their names be written in a larger size or set in a specially ornate typeface; now it is business firms and mass-market products demanding an extra helping of capitals, or a proprietary face, and poets pleading, by contrast, to be left entirely in the vernacular lower case. But type is visible speech, in which gods and men, saints and sinners, poets and business executives are treated fundamentally alike. Typographers, in keeping with the virtue of their trade, honor the stewardship of *texts* and implicitly oppose private ownership of *words.*

Logotypes and logograms push typography in the direction of hieroglyphics, which tend to be looked at rather than read. They also push it toward the realm of candy and drugs, which tend to provoke dependent responses, and away from the realm of food, which tends to promote autonomous being. Good typography is like bread: ready to be admired, appraised and dissected before it is consumed.

3.3.1 *Use the ligatures required by the font, and the characters required by the language, in which you are setting type.*

f + *f* + *i* → *ffi*

ل + ا ← لا

لا

The *lâm-alif* ligature above is from Nabih Jaroudi's Yakout Arabic. The *pi-tau*, *chi-rho* and *mu-alpha-iota* ligatures below are from Matthew Carter's Wilson Greek.

π + *τ* → *πτ*

χ + *ρ* → *χρ*

μ + *α* + *ι* → *μαι*

In most roman faces the letter f reaches into the space beyond it. In most italics, the *f* reaches into the space on both sides. Typographers call these overlaps *kerns.* Only a few kerns, like those in the arm of the *f* and the tail of the *j*, are implicit in a normal typefont, while others, like the overlap in the combination *To,* are optional refinements, independent of the letterforms.

Reaching into the space in front of it, the arm of the f will collide with certain letters – b, f, h, i, j, k, l – and with question marks, quotation marks or parentheses, if these are in its way.

Most of the early European fonts were designed primarily for setting Latin, in which the sequences fb, fh, fj, fk do not occur, but the sequences ff, fi, fl, ffi, ffl are frequent. The same set of ligatures was once sufficient for English, and these five ligatures are standard in traditional roman and italic fonts. As the craft of typography spread through Europe, new regional ligatures were added. An fj and æ were needed in Norway and Denmark for words such as *fjeld* and *fjord* and *nær.* In France an œ, and in Germany an ß (*eszett* or double-s) were required, along with accented and umlauted vowels. Double letters which are read as one – *ll* in Spanish, *ij* in Dutch, and *ch* in German, for example – were cast as single sorts for regional markets. An ffj was needed in Iceland. New individual letters were added, like the Polish ł, the Spanish ñ, and the Danish and Norwegian ø. Purely decorative ligatures were added to many fonts as well.

English continues to absorb and create new words – *fjord, gaffhook, halfback, hors d'œuvre* – that call for ligatures beyond the Latin list. As an international language, English must also accommodate names like *Youngfox, al-Hajji* and *Asdzą́ą́ Yołgai.* These sometimes make demands on the roman alphabet which earlier designers didn't foresee. In the digital world, some of these compound characters and ligatures can, in effect, take care of themselves. In text work, there is no burning need for a specially crafted fb or fh ligature when the digital forms can be cleanly superimposed, but in display work, such ligatures can be crucial. Recent type designers, alive to these polylingual demands on the alphabet, have often simplified the problem further by designing faces in which no sequence of letters involves a collision.

æœ as ch ct ﬀ ﬃ ﬄ ﬁ ﬂ fr
ÿ is ll q; ſt ſch ſh ſi ſl ſp ſſ ß ſſi ſſl ſt ſz us
Æ Œ æ œ *æ œ* ß *ß* ﬀ ﬁ ﬂ ﬃ ﬄ *ﬃ ﬄ*
ct ﬆ *ct ﬆ* ſh ſi ſl ſſ ﬅ *ſh ſi ſl ſſ ﬅ*

Top two lines: Ligatures from an italic font cut in the 1650s by Christoffel van Dijck. *Lower two lines*: Ligatures from Adobe Caslon, a digital face by Carol Twombly, after William Caslon, dating from about 1750. These are Baroque typefaces. As such, they include a set of ligatures with *f* and a second set formed with the *long* s (ſ, *ſ*). Long s and its ligatures were normal in European typography until late in the eighteenth century, though fonts designed to do without them were cut as early as the 1640s.

Separation of the letters *f* and *i* is sometimes crucial. In Turkish, *i* with a dot and *ı* without – or in capitals, *İ* and *I* – are two different letters. To set Turkish well, you need a face whose *f* is designed so it does not disguise the difference.

This does not do away with the question of the five Latin ligatures. Older typefaces – Bembo, Garamond, Caslon, Baskerville and other distinguished creations – are, thankfully, still with us, in metal and in digital revivals. Many new faces also perpetuate the spirit of these earlier designs. These faces are routinely supplied with the five basic ligatures because they require them. And for digital typographers, software is available that will automatically insert them.

ﬆ

Th

ﬀﬂ

Decorative ligatures such as *ﬆ* and *Th* are now deservedly rare. The ligature *ﬀﬂ* is rarer, but it has been cut for at least one typeface (Jonathan Hoefler's Requiem italic) and can be used in at least two words: German *Sauerſtoffflasche* (oxygen bottle) and *Sauerſtoffflaschenſpüler* (oxygen bottle washer).

Bembo, set with ligatures (above) and without (below)

If your software is inserting ligatures automatically, take a moment to verify two things: (1) that the software is inserting all the ligatures you want *and* none that you do not want; (2) that all these ligatures are staying where they're put.

ﬀj

Th

Good OpenType digital fonts usually include the five Latin ligatures (ﬀ, ﬃ, ﬄ, ﬁ, ﬂ), and many include the two Scandinavian ligatures (ﬀj, fj). There may also be a set of ornamentals and archaics (ct, sp, st, Th; fi, fk, fl, ffi, ffl, etc) – and sometimes there are more of these special-purpose ligatures (*quaints,* as typographers call them) in italic than in roman. Where such a feast of ligatures is present, they are usually divided into classes: *basic* and *discretionary.* If your software is conversant with OpenType fonts, it can be told to use the ligatures from either class or from both. But the classes are not always well defined. For now at least, fonts in the 'Adobe Originals' series all have the Th ligature misclassified as basic, not discretionary. Unless you edit the font to fix this error, you cannot get ﬁ, fj, ﬀ and ﬃ without getting Th also. If you *want* the Th ligature, this is fine. But Th has a different pedigree than ﬁ and its brethren. Stylistically, it belongs to a different register. These two registers can certainly be paired; they should not be arbitrarily blurred together.

Some software that inserts ligs automatically will also strip them out again as soon as the type is letterspaced. If you let such software justify a text by adding space between the letters, you may find ligatures present in one line and missing in the next. The solution for this is twofold: (1) good software and (2) intelligent justification. Ligatures should go where they are needed and then stay no matter what.

3.3.2 *If you wish to avoid ligatures altogether, restrict yourself to faces that don't require them.*

It is quite possible to avoid the use of ligatures completely and still set beautiful type. All that is required is a face with non-kerning roman and italic *f* – and some of the finest twentieth-century faces have been deliberately equipped with just this feature. Aldus, Melior, Mendoza, Palatino, Sabon, Trajanus and Trump Mediäval, for example, all set handsomely without ligatures. Full or partial ligatures do exist for these faces, and the ligatures may add a touch

ﬁ fi *ﬁ* *fi* ﬁ fi *ﬁ* *fi*

Ligatured and unligatured combinations in Sabon (left) and Trump Mediäval (right). In faces such as these, *f*-ligatures are optional – and in most such faces, only a partial set of ligatures exists.

of refinement – but when ligatures are omitted from these faces, no unsightly collisions occur.

The choice is wider still among sanserifs. Ligatures are important to the design of Eric Gill's Gill Sans, Ronald Arnholm's Legacy Sans, Martin Majoor's Scala Sans and Seria Sans but irrelevant to many unserifed faces. (Dummy ligatures, consisting of separate letters, are usually present on digital versions of those fonts, but using these dummies has no visible effect.)

Harmony and Counterpoint

3.4 TRIBAL ALLIANCES & FAMILIES

3.4.1 *To the marriage of type and text, both parties bring their cultural presumptions, dreams and family obligations. Accept them.*

Each text, each manuscript (and naturally, each language and each alphabet) has its own requirements and expectations. Some types are more adaptable than others in meeting these demands. But typefaces too have their individual habits and presumptions. Many of them, for instance, are rich with historical and regional connections – a subject pursued at greater length in chapter 7. For the moment, consider just the sociology of typefaces. What kinds of families and alliances do they form?

The union of uppercase and lowercase roman letters – in which the upper case has seniority but the lower case has the power – has held firm for twelve centuries. This constitutional monarchy of the alphabet is one of the most durable of European cultural institutions.

Aa

BbB

c*c*C

Dd

EeE*e*

Ff

Ornamental initials, small caps and arabic figures were early additions to the roman union. Italics were a separate tribe at first, refusing to associate with roman lower case, but forming an alliance of their own with roman (not italic) capitals and small caps. Sloped caps developed only in the sixteenth century. Roman, italic and small caps formed an enlarged tribal alliance at that time, and most text families continue to include them.

Bold and condensed faces became a fashion in the nineteenth century, partially displacing italics and small caps. Bold weights and titling figures have been added retroactively to many earlier faces (Bembo and Centaur for example), though they lack any historical justification. Older text faces, converted from metal to digital form, are usually available in two fundamentally different versions. The better digital foundries supply authentic reconstruc-

Tribal Alliances and Families

Primary:	roman lower case	1.1
Secondary:	Roman Upper Case	2.1
	ROMAN SMALL CAPS	2.2
	roman text figures: 123	2.3
	italic lower case	2.4
Tertiary:	*True Italic (Cursive) Upper Case & Swash*	3.1
	italic text figures: 123	3.2
	SLOPED SMALL CAPS	3.3
	Roman Titling Figures: 123	3.4
	bold lower case	3.5
Quaternary:	*False Italic (Sloped) Upper Case*	4.1
	Bold Upper Case	4.2
	BOLD SMALL CAPS	4.3
	bold text figures: 123	4.4
	bold italic lower case	4.5
Quintary:	*Italic Titling Figures: 123*	5.1
	Bold False Italic (Sloped) Upper Case	5.2
	bold italic text figures: 123	5.3
	Bold Titling Figures: 123	5.4
Sextary:	***Bold Italic Titling Figures: 123***	6.1

tions; others supply the fonts without small caps, text figures and other essential components, and usually burden them instead with an inauthentic bold.

Among recent text faces, two basic family structures are now common. The simplified model consists only of roman, italic and titling figures, in a range of weights – light, medium, bold and black, for example. The more elaborate family structure includes small caps and text figures, though these are sometimes present only in the lighter weights.

A family with all these elements forms a hierarchical series, based not on historical seniority but on general adaptability and frequency of use. And the series works the way it does not so much from force of custom as from the force of physiology. The monumentality of the capitals, the loudness of the bold face, the calligraphic flow and (most of the time) slope of italic, stand out effectively against a peaceful, largely perpendicular, roman ground. Reverse the order and the text not only looks peculiar, it causes the reader physical strain.

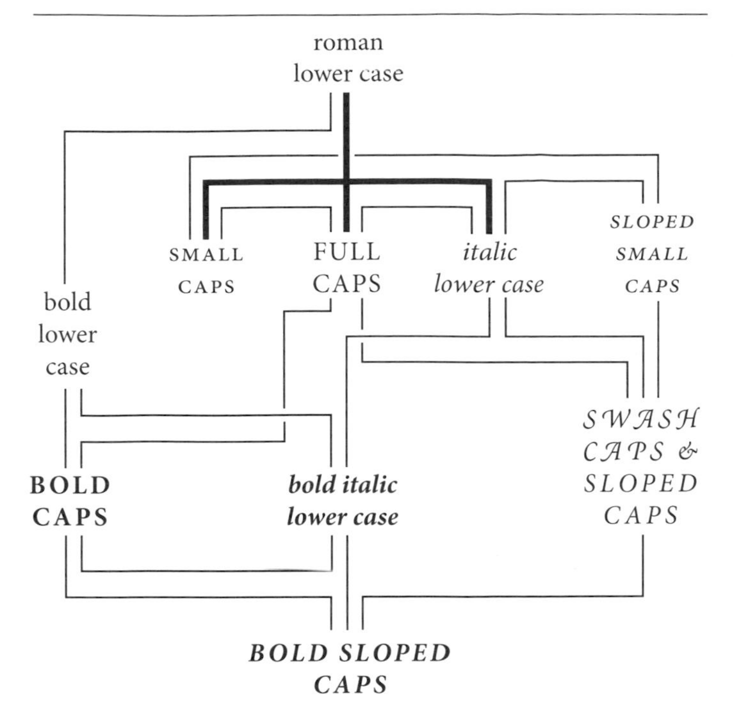

The chart at left is a grammatical road map of a conventional large family of type. (The heavy rules show the extent of the basic nuclear family.) The typographer can move directly along any of the lines – e.g., from roman lower case to bold lower case or to small or full caps. A sudden shift from roman lower case to bold caps or sloped caps short-circuits the conventions of typographic grammar.

Fonts in each of these categories are called into use, through a surprisingly complex grammar of editorial and typographic rules, by fonts in the category above. The typographer can intervene in this process at will, and alter it to any degree. But good type is good because it has natural strength and beauty. The best results come, as a rule, from finding the best type for the work and then guiding it with the gentlest possible hand.

The standard North American reference on the editorial tradition is the *Chicago Manual of Style,* now in its 15th edition (2003).

3.4.2 *Don't use a font you don't need.*

The marriage of type and text requires courtesy to the in-laws, but it does not mean that all of them ought to move in, nor even that all must come to visit.

Boldface roman type did not exist until the nineteenth century. Bold italic is even more recent. Generations of good typographers were quite content without such variations. Font manufacturers nevertheless now often sell these extra weights as part of a basic package, thereby encouraging typographers – beginners especially – to use bold roman and italic whether they need them or not.

Bold and semibold faces do have their value. They can be used, for instance, to flag items in a list, to set titles and subheads u&lc in small sizes, to mark the opening of the text on a complex page, or to thicken the texture of lines that will be printed in pale ink or as dropouts (negative images) in a colored field. Sparingly used, they can effectively emphasize numbers or words, such as the headwords, keywords and definition numbers in a dictionary. They can also be used (as they often are) to shout at readers, putting them on edge and driving them away; or to destroy the historical integrity of a typeface designed before boldface roman was born; or to create unintentional anachronisms, something like adding a steam engine or a fax machine to the stage set for *King Lear.*

3.4.3 *Use sloped romans sparingly and artificially sloped romans more sparingly still.*

It is true that most romans are upright and most italics slope to the right – but flow, not slope, is what really differentiates the two. Italics have a more cursive structure than romans, which is to say that italic is closer to longhand or continuous script. Italic serifs are usually *transitive*; they are direct entry and exit strokes, depicting the pen's arrival from the previous letter and its departure for the next. Roman serifs, by contrast, are generally *reflexive.* They show the pen doubling back onto itself, emphasizing the end of the stroke. Italic serifs therefore tend to slope at a natural writing angle, tracing the path from one letter to another. Roman serifs, especially at the baseline, tend to be level, tying the letters not to each other but to an invisible common line.

Some italics are more cursive than others; so are some romans. But any given italic is routinely more cursive than the roman with which it is paired.

e *e* l *l* m *m* u *u*

Baskerville roman and italic. Baskerville has less calligraphic flow than most earlier typefaces, but the italic serifs are, like their predecessors, *transitive and oblique,* showing the path of the pen from letter to letter. The roman serifs are *reflexive and level,* tying letters to a common line.

Early italic fonts had only modest slope and were designed to be used with upright roman capitals. There are some beautiful fifteenth-century manuscript italics with no slope whatsoever, and some excellent typographic versions, old and new, that slope as little as 2° or 3°. Yet others slope as much as 25°.

Harmony and Counterpoint

Italic and roman lived quite separate lives until the middle of the sixteenth century. Before that date, books were set in either roman *or* italic, but not in both. In the late Renaissance, typographers began to use the two for different features in the same book. Typically, roman was used for the main text and italic for the preface, headnotes, sidenotes and for verse or block quotations. The custom of combining italic and roman *in the same line,* using italic to emphasize individual words and mark specific classes of information, developed in the sixteenth century and flowered in the seventeenth. Baroque typographers liked the extra activity this mixing of fonts gave to the page, and the convention proved so useful to editors and authors that no subsequent change of typographic taste has ever driven it entirely away. Modulation between roman and italic is now a basic and routine typographic technique, much the same as modulation in music between major and minor keys. (The system of linked major and minor keys in music is, of course, another Baroque invention.)

Since the seventeenth century, many attempts have been made to curb the cursive, fluid nature of italic and to refashion it on the roman model. Many so-called italics designed in the last two hundred years are actually not italics at all, but sloped romans – otherwise known as *obliques.* And many are hybrids between the two.

As lowercase italic letterforms mutated toward sloped roman, their proportions changed as well. Most italics (though not all) are 5% to 10% narrower than their roman counterparts. But most sloped romans (unless designed by Eric Gill) are as wide or wider than their upright roman companions.

Renaissance italics were designed for continuous reading, and modern italics based on similar principles tend to have similar virtues. Baroque and Neoclassical italics were designed to serve as secondary faces only, and are best left in that role. Sloped romans, as a general rule, are even more devotedly subsidiary faces. They have been with us for ten centuries or more, but have rarely succeeded in rising above the status of calligraphic stunts or short-term perturbations of the upright roman.

In addition to families consisting of upright and sloped roman, there are now several families consisting of upright (or nearly upright) and sloped *italic.* Hermann Zapf's Zapf Chancery (ITC, 1979) is an example. The 'roman' is an italic with a slope of 4°; the 'italic' is also an italic, but with swash caps and a slope of 14°. Another example is Eaglefeather Informal (see p 271), in which the 'roman' is an italic with a slope of 0° and the 'italic' is in essence the same design with a slope of 10°.

1 adefmpru *adefmpru* [19 pt]
2 adefmpru ***adefmpru*** [18 pt]
3 adefmpru *adefmpru* [24 pt]
4 adefmpru *adefmpru* [18 pt]
5 adefmpru *adefmpru* [21 pt]

1 Adrian Frutiger's Méridien roman and *italic*; **2** Lucida Sans roman and *italic*, by Kris Holmes & Charles Bigelow; **3** Perpetua roman and its *italic* – actually a hybridized sloped roman – by Eric Gill; **4** Univers roman and its *oblique* (a pure sloped roman), by Adrian Frutiger; **5** Romulus roman and *oblique* (again a pure sloped roman), by Jan van Krimpen.

Typesetting software is capable of distorting letters in many different ways: condensing, expanding, outlining, shadowing, sloping, and so on. If the only difference between a roman and its companion font were slope, the roman font alone would be enough for the computer. Sloped versions could be generated at will. But italic is not sloped roman, and even a good sloped roman is more than simply roman with a slope.

Direct electronic sloping of letterforms changes the weight of vertical and sloped strokes, while the weight of the horizontal strokes remains the same. Strokes that run northwest-southeast in the parent form – like the right leg of the A or the upper right and lower left corners of the O – are rotated toward the vertical when the letter is given a slope. Rotation toward the vertical causes these strokes to thicken. But strokes running northeast-southwest, like the left leg of the A, and the other corners of the O, are rotated farther away from the vertical. Rotation away from the vertical thins them down. Stroke curvature is altered in this translation process as well. The natural inclinations of a calligrapher drawing a sloped roman differ from what is convenient for the machine. Even 'italic' capitals – which nowadays are rarely anything except sloped roman – require individual shaping and editing to reach a durable form.

Through the collaborative efforts of calligraphers, typographers and engineers, software for the design and editing of typographic letterforms continues to improve. As it does, it continues to mimic more and more closely those subtle and primitive tools that lie at the root of all typography: the stick, the brush, the chisel and the broadnib pen. Rules for transforming roman into good sloped roman forms, instead of into parodies, can surely be derived through close analysis of what the best scribes do. When parts of the procedure can be stated with mechanical precision, they can also be entrusted to machines. But rules for translating roman into *italic* cannot be stated clearly because no such rules exist. The two kinds of letterform have different genealogies, like apples and bananas. They form a common heritage and share an evolutionary source, yet neither one is a direct modification of the other.

A A *A* O O *O*

Adobe Caslon roman, the same roman sloped electronically, and the true 'italic' capitals as drawn. Caslon italics have an average slope of 20°.

a a *a* o o *o*

Palatino roman, the same roman sloped electronically, and the genuine italic, whose average slope is 9°.

A E M R S T Y

True italic capitals: the swash forms from Robert Slimbach's Minion italic. It is the structure, not the slope, of the letters that marks them as italic.

Once in a while, nevertheless, a typographer will pine for a sloped version of a font such as Haas Clarendon or André Gürtler's Egyptian 505, for which no italic, nor even a sloped roman, has been drawn. On such occasions, a sloped roman generated by computer may suffice as a temporary solution. But the slope should be modest (perhaps 10° maximum), because less slope yields less distortion.

3.5.1 *Change one parameter at a time.*

When your text is set in a 12 pt medium roman, it should not be necessary to set the heads or titles in 24 pt bold italic capitals. If boldface appeals to you, begin by trying the bold weight of the text face, u&lc, *in the text size.* As alternatives, try u&lc italic, or letterspaced small caps, or letterspaced full caps in the text weight and size. If you want a larger size, experiment first with a larger size of the text face, u&lc in the text weight. For a balanced page, the weight should *decrease* slightly, not increase, as the size increases.

Contrast

3.5.2 *Don't clutter the foreground.*

When boldface is used to emphasize words, it is usually best to leave the punctuation in the background, which is to say, in the basic text font. It is the words, not the punctuation, that merit emphasis in a sequence such as the following:

> … on the islands of **Lombok**, **Bali**, **Flores**,
> **Timor** and **Sulawesi**, the same textiles …

But if the same names are emphasized by setting them in italic rather than bold, there is no advantage in leaving the punctuation in roman. With italic text, italic punctuation normally gives better letterfit and thus looks less obtrusive:

> … on the islands of *Lombok, Bali, Flores,*
> *Timor* and *Sulawesi,* the same textiles …

If spaced small caps are used for emphasis – changing the stature and form of the letters instead of their weight or slope, and thereby minimizing the surface disturbance on the page – the question of punctuation does not arise. The punctuation used with small caps is (except for question and exclamation marks) usually the same as roman punctuation; it is only necessary to check it for accurate spacing:

> … on the islands of LOMBOK, BALI, FLORES,
> TIMOR and SULAWESI, the same textiles …

STRUCTURAL FORMS & DEVICES

4

4.1 OPENINGS

4.1.1 *Make the title page a symbol of the dignity and presence of the text.*

If the text has immense reserve and dignity, the title page should have these properties as well – and if the text is devoid of dignity, the title page should in honesty be the same.

Think of the blank page as alpine meadow, or as the purity of undifferentiated being. The typographer enters this space and must change it. The reader will enter it later, to see what the typographer has done. The underlying truth of the blank page must be infringed, but it must never altogether disappear – and whatever displaces it might well aim to be as lively and peaceful as it is. It is not enough, when building a title page, merely to unload some big, prefabricated letters into the center of the space, nor to dig a few holes in the silence with typographic heavy machinery and then move on. Big type, even huge type, can be beautiful and useful. But poise is usually far more important than size – and poise consists primarily of emptiness. Typographically, poise is made of white space. Many fine title pages consist of a modest line or two near the top, and a line or two near the bottom, with little or nothing more than taut, balanced white space in between.

4.1.2 *Don't permit the titles to oppress the text.*

In books, spaced capitals of the text size and weight are often perfectly adequate for titles. At the other extreme, there is a fine magazine design by Bradbury Thompson, in which the title, the single word BOOM, is set in gigantic bold condensed caps that fill the entire two-page spread. The text is set in a tall narrow column *inside the stem* of the big B. The title has swallowed the text – yet the text has been reborn, alive and talkative, like Jonah from the whale.

For examples of Thompson's work, see Bradbury Thompson, *The Art of Graphic Design* (1988).

Most unsuccessful attempts at titling fall between these two extremes, and their problem is often that the title throws its weight around, unbalancing and discoloring the page. If the title is set in a larger size than the text, it is often best to set it u&lc in a light titling font or a lightened version of the text font. Inline capitals (like the Castellar initials on pages 64 and 160) are another device that typographers have used since the fifteenth century to get large size without excessive weight.

There are other ways of creating large letters of light weight, but some of these are printerly instead of typographic. First of all, if the budget permits, the typographer can design the work to be printed in two or even in twenty different colors. An inexpensive alternative is the same one your monochrome desktop printer uses to render that colorful file: screening the type: breaking up the solid image with an electronic filter. (Note however that screened text always looks different on screen than on paper.)

10 20 30 40 50

60 70 80 90 100

Screened text. The numbers indicate the percentage of ink coverage permitted by the screen.

4.1.3 *Set titles and openings in a form that contributes to the overall design.*

Renaissance books, with their long titles and ample margins, generally left no extra space at the heads of chapters. In modern books, where the titles are shorter and the margins have been eaten by inflationary pressure, a third of a page sometimes lies vacant just to celebrate the fact that the chapter begins. But space alone is not enough to achieve the sense of richness and celebration, nor is absence of space necessarily a sign of typographic poverty.

Narrow row houses flush with the street are found not only in urban slums but in the loveliest of the old Italian hill towns and Mediterranean villages. A page full of letters presents the same possibilities. It can lapse into a typographic slum, or grow into a model of architectural grace, skilled engineering and simple economy. Broad suburban lawns and wide typographical front yards can also be uninspiringly empty or welcoming and graceful. They can display real treasure, including the treasure of empty space, or they can be filled with souvenirs of wishful thinking. Neoclassical birdbaths and effigies of liveried slaves, stable boys and faded pink flamingoes all have counterparts in the typographic world.

4.1.4 *Mark each beginning and resumption of the text.*

Structural Forms and Devices

The simplest way of beginning any block of prose is to start from the margin, flush left, as this paragraph does. On a peaceful page, where the text is announced by a head or subhead, this is enough. But if the text, or a new section of text, begins at the top of a page with no heading to mark it, a little fanfare will probably be required. The same is true if the opening page is busy. If there is a chapter title, an epigraph, a sidenote, and a photograph and caption, the opening of the text will need a banner, a ten-gallon hat or a bright red dress to draw the eye.

Fleurons (typographic ornaments) are often used to flag text openings, and are often printed in red, the typographer's habitual second color. The opening phrase, or entire first line, can also be set in small caps or in bold u&lc. Another excellent method of marking the start of the text, inherited from ancient scribal practice, is a large initial capital: a versal or lettrine. Versals can be treated in many ways. Indented or centered, they can stick up from the text. Flush left, they can be nested into the text (typographers call these drop caps, as opposed to elevated or stick-up caps). If there is room, they can hang in the left margin. They can be set in the same face as the text or in something outlandishly different. In scribal and typographic tradition alike, where the budget permits, versals too are generally red or another color in preference to black.

Elevated caps are easier to set well from a keyboard, but drop caps have closer links with the scribal and letterpress tradition. And the tooling and fitting of drop caps is something typographers do for fun, to test their skill and visual intuition. It is common practice to set the first word or phrase after the versal in caps, small caps or boldface, as a bridge between versal and normal text. Examples are shown on the following page.

In English, if the initial letter is A, I or O, a question can arise: is the initial letter itself a word? The answer to this question must come in the spacing of the text in relation to the versal. If the first word of the text is *Ahead,* for example, excessive space betwen the initial A and the rest of the word is bound to cause confusion.

Openings

O SCULETUR me osculo oris sui; quia meliora sunt ubera tua vino, ¶ fragantia unguentis optimis. Oleum effusum nomen tuum; ideo adolescentulae dilexerunt te.

T RAHE ME, post te curremus in odorem unguentorum tuorum. Introduxit me rex in cellaria sua; exsultabimus et laetabimur in te, memores uberum tuorum super vinum. Recti diligunt te.

« N IGRA SUM, sed formosa, filiae Ierusalem, sicut tabernacula Cedar, sicut pelles Salomonis. Nolite me considerare quod fusca sim, quia decoloravit me sol. Filii matris meae pugnaverunt contra me.... »

" A DIURO VOS, filiae Ierusalem, per capreas cervosque camporum, ne suscitetis, neque evigilare faciatis dilectam, quoadusque ipsa velit."

V OX DILECTI MEI; ecce iste venit, saliens in montibus, transiliens colles. ¶ Similis est dilectus meus capreae, hinnuloque cervorum. En ipse stat post parietem nostrum, respiciens per fenestras, prospiciens per cancellos. En dilectus meus loquitur mihi.

S URGE, propera, amica mea, columba mea, formosa mea, et veni. ¶ Iam enim hiems transiit; imber abiit, et recessit. ¶ Flores apparuerunt in terra nostra....

L AVI PEDES MEOS, quomodo inquinabo illos? ¶ Dilectus meus misit manum suam per foramen, et venter meus intremuit ad tactum eius. ¶ Surrexit ut aperirem dilecto meo; manus meae stillaverunt myrrham, et digiti mei pleni myrrha probatissima. Pessulum ostii mei....

Passages from the Song of Songs, set in Aldus 10/12 × 10 RR. Elevated cap: Castellar 54 pt. Drop caps: Aldus 42 pt, mortised line by line.

4.1.5 *If the text begins with a quotation, include the initial quotation mark.*

Quotation marks have a long scribal history as editorial signs added after the fact to other people's texts, but they did not come into routine typographic use until late in the sixteenth century. Then, because they interfered with established habits for positioning large initials, they were commonly omitted from the openings of texts. Some style books still prescribe this concession to convenience as a fixed procedural rule. But digital typography makes it simple to control the size and placement of the opening quotation mark, whether or not the text begins with a versal. For the reader's sake, it should be there.

4.2 HEADINGS & SUBHEADS

4.2.1 *Set headings in a form that contributes to the style of the whole.*

Headings can take many forms, but one of the first choices to make is whether they will be symmetrical or asymmetrical. Symmetrical heads, which are centered on the measure, are known to typographers as *crossheads.* Asymmetrical heads usually take the form of *left sideheads,* which is to say they are set flush left, or modestly indented or outdented from the left. *Right sideheads* work well in certain contexts, but more often as main heads than as subheads. A short, one-line head set flush right needs substantial size or weight to prevent the reader from missing it altogether.

These principles are reversed, of course, when setting leftward-reading alphabets such as Arabic and Hebrew.

One way to make heads prominent without making them large is to set them entirely in the margin, like the running heads (in typographic terms, they are *running shoulderheads*) used throughout this book.

4.2.2 *Use as many levels of headings as you need: no more and no fewer.*

As a rule it is best to choose a predominantly symmetrical or asymmetrical form for subheads. Mixing the two haphazardly leads to stylistic as well as logical confusion. But the number of levels available can be slightly increased, if necessary, by judicious combinations. If symmetrical heads are added to a basically asymmetrical series, or vice versa, it is usually better to put the visiting foreigners at the top or bottom of the hierarchical pile. Two six-level series of subheads are shown, by way of example, on the following pages.

In marking copy for typesetting, the various levels of subheads are generally given letters rather than names: A-heads, B-heads, C-heads, and so on. Using this terminology, the heads on the following pages run from A through F.

Main Section Title

Headings and Subheads

IF A MAN walk in the woods for love of them half of each day, he is in danger of being regarded as a loafer; but if he spends his whole day as a speculator, shearing off those woods and making earth bald before her time, he is esteemed an industrious and enterprising citizen.

MAIN CROSSHEAD

The ways by which you may get money almost without exception lead downward. To have done anything by which you earned money *merely* is to have been truly idle or worse.... If you would get money as a writer or lecurer, you must be popular, which is to go down perpendicularly....

Heavy Crosshead

In proportion as our inward life fails, we go more constantly and desperately to the post office. You may depend on it, that the poor fellow who walks away with the greatest number of letters ... has not heard from himself this long while.

MEDIUM CROSSHEAD

I do not know but it is too much to read one newspaper a week. I have tried it recently, and for so long it seems to me that I have not dwelt in my native region. The sun, the clouds, the snow, the trees say not so much to me....

Light Crosshead

You cannot serve two masters. It requires more than a day's devotion to know and to possess the wealth of a day.... Really to see the sun rise or go down every day, so to relate ourselves to a universal fact, would preserve us sane forever.

hypethral: from Greek ἐν ὑπαίθρῳ, 'in the open air'

RUN-IN SIDEHEAD Shall the mind be a public arena...? Or shall it be a quarter of heaven itself, an hypethral temple, consecrated to the service of the gods?

Main Section Title

❁ IF I AM TO BE a thoroughfare, I prefer that it be of the mountain brooks, the Parnassian streams, and not the town sewers.... I believe that the mind can be permanently profaned by attending to trivial things, so that all our thoughts shall be tinged with triviality.

Structural Forms and Devices

MAIN CROSSHEAD

Our very intellect shall be macadamized, as it were: its foundation broken into fragments for the wheels of travel to roll over; and if you would know what will make the most durable pavement, surpassing rolled stones, spruce blocks, and asphaltum, you have only to look into some of our minds....

The texts on this and the facing page are excerpts from HENRY DAVID THOREAU'S "Life Without Principle," *c.* 1854, first published in 1863. The type on the facing page is Adobe Caslon 10/12 × 21, and on this page, recut Monotype Centaur & *Arrighi* 11/12 × 21.

❦ ORNAMENTED CROSSHEAD ❦

Read not the Times. Read the Eternities.... Even the facts of science may dust the mind by their dryness, unless they are in a sense effaced each morning, or rather rendered fertile by the dews of fresh and living truth.

INDENTED SIDEHEAD

Knowledge does not come to us by details, but in flashes of light from heaven. Yes, every thought that passes through the mind helps to wear and tear it, and to deepen the ruts, which, as in the streets of Pompeii, evince how much it has been used.

Secondary Indented Sidehead

When we want culture more than potatoes, and illumination more than sugar-plums, then the great resources of a world are taxed and drawn out, and the result, or staple production, is not slaves, nor operatives, but ... saints, poets, philosophers....

Run-in Sidehead In short, as a snowdrift is formed where there is a lull in the wind, so, one would say, where there is a lull of truth, an *institution* springs up....

4.3 NOTES

4.3.1 *If the text includes notes, choose the optimum form.*

Notes

If notes are used for subordinate details, it is right that they be set in a smaller size than the main text. But the academic habit of relegating notes to the foot of the page or the end of the book is a mirror of Victorian social and domestic practice, in which the kitchen was kept out of sight and the servants were kept below stairs. If the notes are permitted to move around in the margins – as they were in Renaissance books – they can be present where needed and at the same time enrich the life of the page.

Footnotes are the very emblem of fussiness, but they have their uses. If they are short and infrequent, they can be made economical of space, easy to find when wanted and, when not wanted, easy to ignore. Long footnotes are inevitably a distraction: tedious to read and wearying to look at. Footnotes that extend to a second page (as some long footnotes are bound to do) are an abject failure of design.

Endnotes can be just as economical of space, less trouble to design and less expensive to set, and they can comfortably run to any length. They also leave the text page clean except for a peppering of superscripts. They do, however, require the serious reader to use two bookmarks and to read with both hands as well as both eyes, swapping back and forth between the popular and the persnickety parts of the text.

Sidenotes give more life and variety to the page and are the easiest of all to find and read. If carefully designed, they need not enlarge either the page or the cost of printing it.

Footnotes rarely need to be larger than 8 or 9 pt. Endnotes are typically set in small text sizes: 9 or 10 pt. Sidenotes can be set in anything up to the same size as the main text, depending on their frequency and importance, and on the overall format of the page.

4.3.2 *Check the weight and spacing of superscripts.*

If they are not too frequent, sidenotes can be set with no superscripts at all (as in this book), or with the same symbol (normally an asterisk) constantly reused, even when several notes appear on a single page. For endnotes, superscript numbers are standard. For footnotes, symbols can be used if the notes are few. (The traditional order is * † ‡ § ‖ ¶. But beyond the asterisk, dagger and double dagger, this order is not familiar to most readers, and never was.) Numbers are more transparent, and their order is much less easy to confuse.

Many fonts include sets of superscript numbers, but these are not always of satisfactory size and design. Text numerals set at a reduced size and elevated baseline are sometimes the best or only choice. Establishing the best size, weight and spacing for superscripts will, however, require some care. In many faces, smaller numbers in semibold look better than larger numbers of regular weight. And the smaller the superscripts are, the more likely they are to need increased character space.

Structural Forms and Devices

Superscripts frequently come at the ends of phrases or sentences. If they are high above the line, they can be kerned over a comma or period, but this may endanger readability, especially if the text is set in a modest size.

4.3.3 *Use superscripts in the text but full-size numbers in the notes themselves.*

In the main text, superscript numbers are used to indicate notes because superscript numbers minimize interruption. They are typographic asides: small because that is an expression of their relative importance, and raised for two reasons: to keep them out of the flow of the main text, and to make them easier to find. In the note itself, the number is not an aside but a target. Therefore the number in the note should be full size.[1]

a[1] b

1. Ba

To make them easy to find, the numbers of footnotes or endnotes can be hung to the left (like the marginal numbers on the following two pages and the footnote number below). Punctuation, apart from empty space, is not normally needed between the number and text of the note.

4.3.4 *Avoid ambiguity in the numbering and placement of endnotes.*

Readers should never be forced to hunt for the endnotes. As a rule, this means the endnotes should not appear in small clumps

1 This footnote is flagged by a superscript in the text, but the note itself is introduced by an outdented figure of the same size used for the text of the note. The main text on this page is set 10/12 × 21, and the note is 8/11.

at the end of each chapter. It is better to place them together at the end of the book. Wherever possible, they should also be numbered sequentially from the beginning to end of the book, and the notes themselves should be designed so the numbers are readily visible. If the notes are numbered anew for each section or chapter or essay, running heads will be needed along with the notes to point the way. If the running heads accompanying the notes say, for instance, "Notes to Pages 44–62," readers will know their way. But if the running heads say something like "Notes to Chapter 5," then chapter 5 must be identified as such by running heads of its own.

Notes

4.4 TABLES & LISTS

4.4.1 *Edit tables with the same attention given to text, and set them as text to be read.*

For graphic alternatives to typographic tables, see Edward R. Tufte, *The Visual Display of Quantitative Information* (2nd ed., 2001) and *Envisioning Information* (1990).

Tables are notoriously time-consuming to typeset, but the problems posed are often editorial as much as typographic. If the table is not planned in a readable form to begin with, the typographer can render it readable only by rewriting or redesigning it from scratch.

Tables, like text, go awry when approached on a purely technical basis. Good typographic answers are not elicited by asking questions such as "How can I cram this number of characters into that amount of space?"

If the table is approached as merely one more form of text, which must be made both good to read and good to look at, several principles will be clear:

1. All text should be horizontal, or in rare cases oblique. Setting column heads vertically as a space-saving measure is quite feasible if the text is in Japanese or Chinese, but not if it is written in the Latin alphabet.
2. Letterforms too small or too condensed for comfortable reading are not part of the solution.
3. There should be a minimum amount of furniture (rules, boxes, dots and other guiderails for traveling through typographic space) and a maximum amount of information.
4. Rules, tint blocks or other guides and dividers, where they are necessary at all, should run in the predominant reading direction: vertically in the case of lists, indices and some numerical tables, and horizontally otherwise.

5 A rule located at the edge of a table, separating the first or final column from the adjacent empty space, ordinarily serves no function.
6 A table, like any other text in multiple columns, must contain within itself an adequate amount of white space.

4.4.2 *Avoid overpunctuating lists.*

Structural Forms and Devices

A list is an inherently spatial and numerical arrangement. Speakers reciting lists often enumerate on their fingers, and lists set in type often call for equivalent typographic gestures. This means that the list should be clarified as much as possible through spatial positioning and pointing, usually done with bullets, dashes or numerals. (Examples occur on these two pages and throughout this book.) If the numbers are made visible either through position (e.g., by hanging them in the margin) or through prominence (e.g., by setting them in a contrasting face), additional punctuation – extra periods, parentheses or the like – should rarely be required.

Dot leaders (lines of dots leading the eye from one word or number to another) are rarely beneficial in tables.

4.4.3 *Set lists and columns of figures to align flush right or on the decimal.*

The numerals in many fonts are all of equal width, though there is sometimes an alternative, narrower form of the numeral one. This fitted one is generally used when setting figures in the midst of text, while the unfitted one (of standard numeral width) is often used when setting figures in columns. The font itself or the composition software will also include a figure space – a fixed blank space corresponding to the width of a standard, unkerned numeral. This makes it a simple matter to compose lists and columns of figures in rigorous mechanical alignment.

100
111
100
111

If you use proportionally fitted numerals (always the best choice for text), or kern the numeral permutations in a font with tabular figures, the individual figures will not align in columns or lists, but *columns* of figures can still be aligned. For much tabular matter (e.g., the first table overleaf) this is sufficient. If notes are required in a table with flush-right columns, the superscripts should be hung to the right (as in column 3, line 2 of the first example overleaf) so they will not disrupt the alignment.

8	98	998	9.75
9	99	999*	10
10	100	1000	10.25
11	101	1001	10.5

Above: aligning columns of nonaligning figures, with a hanging asterisk. *Below*: columns in mixed alignment.

Aster	2 : 3	24 × 36	0.667	$a = 2b$
Valerian	271 : 20	813 × 60	13.550	$6a = c$

4.4.4 *For text and numerals alike, choose harmonious and legible tabular alignments.*

Simple tables and lists of paired items, like the sample tables of contents on page 36, are often best aligned against each other, the left column flush right and the right column flush left. Financial statements and other numerical tables usually follow the opposite pattern: a column of words, on the left, aligns flush left, while the subsequent columns of numbers all align flush right or on the decimal. Any repeating character – a dimension sign or equal sign, for instance – is potentially of use in tabular alignment. But many columns with many different alignments can generate overall visual chaos. Occasionally it is better, in such cases, to set all columns or most columns either flush right or flush left, for the sake of general clarity.

4.5 FRONT & BACK MATTER

4.5.1 *Leave adequate space at the beginning and end of every publication.*

A brief research paper may look its best with no more space at beginning and end than is provided by the standard page margins. The same is rarely true of a book, whose text should generally be, and should seem to be, a living and breathing entity, not aged and shrink-wrapped meat. A chapbook or saddle-stitched booklet can begin directly with the title page. Otherwise, a half-title is customary, preceding the title page. It is equally customary to leave a blank leaf, or at least a blank page, at the end of a book. These blanks provide a place for inscriptions and notes and allow the text to relax in its binding.

4.5.2 *Give adequate space to the prelims.*

A text preceded by an interminable chain of forewords, prefaces, introductions and prologues is unlikely to be read. But a dedication that is stuffed, like a typographic afterthought, onto an already overfilled copyright page is no dedication at all. And a list of contents which is incomplete (or missing altogether), and which does not have the page to itself, is usually a sign of typographic desperation or of disregard for the reader.

Structural Forms and Devices

4.5.3 *Balance the front and back matter.*

Books are normally built up from gatherings or signatures – printed and folded sheets – with each signature forming a unit of 8, 12, 16, 24 or 32 pages. The 16-page signature is by far the most common. Typographers therefore work to make most of their books seem divinely ordained and conceived to be some multiple of 16 pages in length. Seasoned book typographers recite in their meditations not only the mantra of points and picas – 12, 24, 36, 48, 60, 72 … – but also the mantra of octavo signatures: 16, 32, 48, 64, 80, 96, 112, 128, 144, 160, 176, 192, 208, 224, 240, 256, 272, 288, 304, 320, 336, 352, 368, 384, 400…. These are the lengths of the books that we read.

In a work of continuous prose, the illusion of divine love for the number sixteen is obtained by straightforward copyfitting. If the length of the text is accurately measured, the page can be designed to yield a book of appropriate length. More complicated books are often surrounded by paraphernalia – not only the standard half-title, title page, copyright page, dedication page and some blanks, but also perhaps a detailed table of contents, a list of charts, illustrations and maps, a table of abbreviations, a page or two of acknowledgements, and a preface, counterbalanced by appendices, endnotes, bibliography, index and a colophon. Copyfitting the main text for a volume of this kind may be highly complex, and room may be taken up or conserved in the large aura of front and back matter. But for complex books and simple books alike, it is up to the typographer to balance the front matter, back matter and text. A wad of blank leaves at the end of a book is a sign of carelessness, not of kindliness toward readers who like to take notes.

ABCDEFGHIKL
MNOPQ RSTV
XYZabcdefghil
mnopqrsſtuvxyz
1234567890,. ’!?;:-⁹ ꝰ
Æ æ ct ff fi fl œ ſſ ſi ſt ſl ℞
& ã á à â ç ẽ é è ê ë ę ĩ í ì î ï ſſ

Iuris præcepta ſunt hæc, Honeſté viuere, alterum non lædere, ſuum cuiq; tribuere. Huius ſtudij duæ ſunt poſitiones, Publicum & priuatum. Publicum ius eſt, quod ad ſtatum rei Romanæ ſpectat. Priuatum, quod ad ſingulorum vtilitatem pertinet. Dicendum eſt igitur de iure priuato, quòd tripertitum eſt: collectum eſt enim ex naturalibus præceptis, aut gẽtium aut ciuilibus. Ius naturale eſt quòd

A 42 pt roman titling font (cut *c.* 1530, revised *c.* 1550) and a 16 pt italic text font (*c.* 1539). Both were cut by Claude Garamond, Paris. The italic is shown actual size and the roman reduced by about one fifth. Matrices for the roman font survive at the Plantin-Moretus Museum, Antwerp.

5

5.1 ANALPHABETIC STYLE

It falls to the typographer to deal with an increasing herd of flicks, squiggles, dashes, dots and ideographs that travel with the alphabet yet never quite belong. The most essential of these marks – period, comma, parentheses, and the like – are signs of logical pause and intonation, much like the rests and slurs in a musical score. Some, like the dollar and per cent signs, are stylized abbreviations. Others, like the asterisk and the dagger, are silent typographical cross-references. And a few that are normally unspoken have tried to sneak their way into the oral tradition. Speakers who say *quote unquote* or *who slash what* or *That's it, period!* are, of course, proving their debt to these enduring paraliterary signs.

Approached through the scribal and typographic tradition, the palette of analphabetic symbols is much more supple and expressive than it appears through the narrow grill of the typewriter keyboard. A typographer will not necessarily use more analphabetic symbols per page than a typist. In fact, many good typographers use fewer. But even the most laconic typographer learns to speak this sign language with an eloquence that conventional editing software, like the typewriter, seems to preclude.

5.1.1 *To invoke the inscriptional tradition, use the midpoint.*

The earliest alphabetic inscriptions have no analphabetic furniture at all, not even spaces between the words. As writing spread through Greece and Italy, spaces appeared between the words, and a further sign was added: the centered dot, for marking phrases or abbreviations. That dot, the *midpoint* or small bullet, remains one of the simplest, most effective forms of typographic punctuation – useful today in lists and letterheads and signage just as it was on engraved marble twenty centuries ago.

Suite 6 · 325 Central Park South

Roman calligraphers lettered their inscriptions with a flat brush held in the right hand. The flat brush – thick in one direction, thin in the other, like a broadnib pen – produces a *modulated stroke*. That is to say, the weight of the stroke varies predictably with direction. The letter O is an example. Because the brush is held in the scribe's right hand, the strokes are thickest in the northwest/southeast direction, at the natural inclination of the forearm and the hand. Using the same brush, Roman calligraphers also developed the subtle choreography of twists and turns at the stroke-ends that produces the imperial Roman serif. Roman capital letters have retained these forms for two thousand years.

愛さ

In Asian and European scripts alike, modulated strokes are usually serifed and unmodulated strokes are usually not. Transitive brush serifs are evident in the *mincho* typeface above, designed by Takaichi Hori. The same *kanji* and *kana* are shown below in an unserifed face designed by Yasubumi Miyake. *Mincho katsuji* or 'Ming Dynasty script' is, roughly, the Japanese counterpart of serifed roman – but its serif structure is more cursive, like that of italic.

O · I · M

When the centered dot or midpoint is made in the same way with the same tool, it becomes a small, curved wedge: a clockwise twist of the brush, with a short tail. Falling to the baseline, this tailed dot became our comma. The same inscriptional and calligraphic traditions have left us other useful marks, such as the double dot or colon (:), the virgule (/), the hyphen (-), and the long dash (– or —).

5.1.2 *Use analphabetic symbols and diacritics that are in tune with the basic font.*

A normal font of type now includes about two dozen mutant forms of the few ancient signs of punctuation (period, comma, colon, quotation marks, brackets, parentheses, dashes, and so on). It also includes about a dozen diacritics (acute and grave accents, the circumflex, tilde, ogonek, umlaut, and others), some legal and commercial logograms (@ # $ £ % ‰ etc) and a few arithmetical symbols. In the ISO Latin character sets (font tables defined by the International Organization for Standardization and now used as a standard by most digital foundries in Europe and North America), analphabetic symbols outnumber the basic Latin alphabet three to one.

On some fonts, these analphabetic characters are beautifully designed; on others they are not designed at all. Often they are simply borrowed from another font, which may have been drawn in a different weight and style.

Several analphabetic characters are notorious for poor design and should always be inspected when assessing a new font. These problem characters include *square brackets* [ ], which are often too dark; *parentheses* ( ), which are often too symmetrical and skinny; the asterisk *, the *pilcrow* ¶ and the *section sign* §, which are often stiff and bland; and the *octothorp* or numeral sign #, which is frequently too large for anything more interesting than chain-store propaganda. Fonts equipped with good versions of these characters must often lend them to those without. But not just any good version will do.

Analphabetic Symbols

a · * § & & ; ’ ! ?
1 2 3 4 8 † £ · z

Neoclassical analphabetics, after John Baskerville, above, and the neohumanist analphabetics of Hermann Zapf's Palatino, below. Analphabetics differ from one face to another, and from one historical period to another, just as much as the letterforms do – and they differ in essentially the same ways.

a · * § & & ; ’ ! ?
1 2 3 4 8 † £ · z

Baskerville, which is an eighteenth-century Neoclassical typeface, requires a Neoclassical asterisk: one with an even number of lobes, each in symmetrical teardrop form. But a twentieth-century neohumanist face like Palatino requires an asterisk with more calligraphic character – sharper, slightly asymmetrical lobes, more likely five than six in number, showing the trace of the broadnib pen. Well-made fonts are distinguished by similar differences in the question and exclamation marks, quotation marks and commas. Not even simple periods are freely interchangeable. Some are elliptical, diamond-shaped or square instead of round. Their weight and fitting varies as well. The *visible invisibility* of the marks of punctuation, which is essential to their function, depends on these details. So, therefore, does the visible invisibility of the typeface as a whole. In the republic of typography, the lowliest, most incidental mark is also a citizen.

5.1.3 *In heads and titles, use the best available ampersand.*

Earlier typographers made liberal use of ampersands, especially when setting italic – and relished their variety of form. The 16th-century French printer Christophe Plantin sometimes uses four quite different ampersands in the course of a single paragraph, even when setting something as unwhimsical as the eight-volume polylingual Bible on which he risked his fortune and to which he devoted more than six years of his life.

The ampersand is a symbol evolved from the Latin *et,* meaning *and.* It is one of the oldest alphabetic abbreviations, and it has assumed over the centuries a wonderful variety of forms. Contemporary offerings are for the most part uninspired, stolid pretzels: unmusical imitations of the treble clef. Often the italic font is equipped with an ampersand less repressed than its roman counterpart. Since the ampersand is more often used in display work than in ordinary text, the more creative versions are often the more useful. There is rarely any reason not to borrow the italic ampersand for use with roman text.

Shakespeare & Co.
Brown & Son
Smith & Daughter

Trump Mediäval italic (top) was designed by Georg Trump, Pontifex roman (second two lines) by Friedrich Poppl. In both, the italic ampersand is more stylish than the roman.

5.1.4 *Consider even the lowly hyphen.*

It is worth taking a close look at hyphens, which were once more subtle and various than they tend to be today. The hyphen was originally a simple pen stroke, often the thinnest stroke the broadnib pen could make, at an angle of 20° to 45° above horizontal. To distinguish the hyphen from the comma (which could also be written as a simple, canted stroke), the hyphen was often doubled, like an equal sign heading uphill.

Many Renaissance typographers preferred the canted hyphen with italic and the level hyphen with roman. Others mixed the two at random – one of several techniques once used to give a touch of scribal variety to the typeset page. But after the death of the master printer Robert Estienne in 1559 and of Claude Garamond in 1561, the level hyphen was the norm.

Most hyphens currently offered are short, blunt, thick, and perfectly level, like refugees from a font of Helvetica. This has sometimes been the choice of the designer, sometimes not. The double hyphen designed by Hermann Zapf in 1953 for his typeface Aldus, as an example, was omitted when the face was commercially issued in 1954. Foundry Centaur, designed by Bruce Rogers, had a hyphen inclined at 48°, but Monotype replaced it with a level bar when the face was adapted for machine composition in 1929. And the original Linotype issue of W.A. Dwiggins's Electra had a subtly tapered hyphen inclined at 7° from the horizontal; later copies of the face have substituted a bland, anonymous form.

If you are tempted to redesign an existing font, using a digital font editor, the hyphen is a good character to start on. It is a comparatively simple character, and you may be able to restore instead of subvert the designer's original intentions.

A few alternatives to the blunt and level hyphen are also still in circulation, and these are worth stealing on occasion for use with another face. The hyphen in Monotype Poliphilus is canted (as in the original design) at 42°. The hyphen in Monotype Blado (the companion italic to Poliphilus) is canted at 35° and tapered as well. The hyphens in most of Frederic Goudy's text faces are canted at angles ranging from 15° to 50°. Some digital versions preserve this feature; others are more homogenized. Canted and tapered hyphens are also to be found in many of the faces of Oldřich Menhart. (In the original version of Menhart's Figural, for example, the roman hyphen is tapered one way and the italic hyphen the other.) Frederic Warde's Arrighi, José Mendoza's Photina italic, and Warren Chappell's Trajanus all have hyphens that are level but asymmetrically serifed, which gives them a slight angular movement. The hyphen in Bram de Does's Trinité, a model of subtlety, is essentially level and unserifed but has a slight calligraphic lift at one end.

g-h

g-h

Poliphilus & *Blado,* above; Kennerley below.

g-h

g-h

fine-tuned / eagle-eye

Frederic Warde's Arrighi, left, and Warren Chappell's Trajanus, right

Hyphens also once varied considerably in width, but most now are standardized to a quarter of an em. Sometimes a shorter hyphen is better. Some of Gerard Unger's and Martin Majoor's economical Dutch hyphens (in faces such as Swift, Flora and Scala) measure no more than a fifth of an em.

Line-end hyphens are often best hung in the right margin, like the line-end hyphens on this and the facing page. This was easy to do for the scribes, who made it a common practice, but it is tedious to emulate in metal. Digital typography makes it potentially easy once again – though not all typesetting software is equally eager to oblige.

5.2 DASHES, SLASHES & DOTS

Dashes, Slashes and Dots

5.2.1 *Use spaced en dashes – rather than close-set em dashes or spaced hyphens – to set off phrases.*

Standard computer keyboards and typewriters include only one dash: the hyphen. Any normal font of text type, either roman or italic, includes at least three. These are the hyphen and two sizes of long dash: the en dash – which is one en (half an em, M/2) in width – and the em dash—which is one em (two ens) wide. Many fonts also include a subtraction sign, which may or may not be the same length and weight as the en dash, and some include a figure dash (equal to the width of a standard numeral). The *three-quarter em* dash, and the *three-to-em* dash, which is one third of an em (M/3) in length, are often missing but perfectly easy to make.

In typescript, a double hyphen (--) is often used for a long dash. Double hyphens in a typeset document are a sure sign that the type was set by a typist, not a typographer. A typographer will use an em dash, three-quarter em, or en dash, depending on context or personal style. The em dash is the nineteenth-century standard, still prescribed in many editorial style books, but the em dash is too long for use with the best text faces. Like the oversized space between sentences, it belongs to the padded and corseted aesthetic of Victorian typography.

Used as a phrase marker – thus – the en dash is set with a normal word space either side.

5.2.2 *Use close-set en dashes or three-to-em dashes between digits to indicate a range.*

Thus: 3–6 November; 4:30–5:00 PM; 25–30 mm. Set close in this way (and with careful attention to kerning and spacing), the dash stands for the word *to.* The hyphen is too short to serve this function, and in some faces the en dash (which is traditionally prescribed) appears too long. A *three-to-em* (M/3) dash is often the best choice. There is no need to edit the font in order to make such a creature. Typesetting software will happily condense the en or em dash by any desired amount.

When compound terms are linked with a dash in the midst of running prose, subtle clues of size and spacing can be crucial, and confusion can easily arise. A sentence such as *The office will be closed 25 December – 3 January* is a linguistic and typographic trap. When it stands all alone in a schedule or list, the phrase *25 December – 3 January* will be clear, but in running prose it is better both editorially and typographically to omit the dash and insert an honest preposition: *25 December to 3 January.*

5.2.3 *Use the em dash to introduce speakers in narrative dialogue.*

The em dash, followed by a thin space (M/5) or word space, is the normal European method of marking dialogue, and it is much less fussy than quotation marks:

— So this is a French novel? she said.
— No, he said, it's Manitoban.

Unicode (see p 181) defines a special character [U+2015] as the quotation dash. Fonts containing such a character are rare. The em dash is the typographic norm.

5.2.4 *In lists and bibliographies, use a three-em rule when required as a sign of repetition.*

Set without spaces, a line of true em dashes forms a continuous midline rule. A three-em rule (three consecutive em dashes) is the old standard bibliographical sign for the repetition of a name. For example:

Boas, Franz. *Primitive Art.* Oslo: Aschehoug, 1927. Reissued Cambridge, Mass.: Harvard University Press, 1928; New York: Dover, 1955.
———. *Tsimshian Mythology.* BAE Ann. Rep. 31. Washington, DC: Bureau of American Ethnology, 1916.

In recent years, many professional scholars have abandoned this style of bibliography, but the three-em rule still has many nonacademic uses.

5.2.5 *Use the virgule with words and dates, the solidus with split-level fractions.*

The slash, like the dash, is more various in real life than it is on the typewriter keyboard. A normal font of type includes a vertical bar and two slashes of differing inclinations. The steeper slash is the virgule (/), an alternative form of the comma. It is useful in dates (6/6/99 = 6.VI.99 = 6 June 99) and in text where a comma or parenthesis might otherwise have been used.

Wednesday / August 3 / 1977
Tibetan Guest House / Thamel / Kathmandu
Victoria University, Toronto / Ontario
he/she hit him/her

Dashes, Slashes and Dots

The other slash mark on the font is a solidus or fraction bar, used to construct fractions such as ³⁄₃₂. The solidus generally slopes at close to 45° and kerns on both sides. The virgule, not the solidus, is used to construct *level* fractions, such as 2π/3. (Notice, for instance, the difference in slope and kerning between the two slash marks in the type specification 8/9½.)

5.2.6 *Use a dimension sign* (×) *instead of the letter* x *when dimensions are given.*

4 × 4

A picture is 26 × 42 cm; studs are 2 × 4 and shelving is 2 × 10 inches; North American letter paper is 8½ × 11.

5.2.7 *Use ellipses that fit the font.*

i ... j

k....

l...,l

l, ... l

m...?

n...!

Most digital fonts now include, among other things, a prefabricated *ellipsis* (a row of three baseline dots). Many typographers nevertheless prefer to make their own. Some prefer to set the three dots flush ... with a normal word space before and after. Others prefer . . . to add *thin* spaces between the dots. Thick spaces (M/3) are prescribed by the *Chicago Manual of Style,* but these are another Victorian eccentricity. In most contexts, the Chicago ellipsis is much too wide.

Flush-set ellipses work well with some fonts and faces but not with all. At small text sizes – in 8 pt footnotes, for example – it is generally better to add space (as much as M/5) between the dots. Extra space may also look best in the midst of light, open letterforms, such as Baskerville, and less space in the company of a dark font, such as Trajanus, or when setting in bold face. (The ellipsis generally used in this book is part of the font and sets as a single character.)

In English (but usually not in French), when the ellipsis occurs at the end of a sentence, a fourth dot, the period, is added and the space at the beginning of the ellipsis disappears. . . . When the ellipsis combines with a comma, exclamation mark or question mark, the same typographic principle applies. Otherwise, a word space is required fore and aft.

5.2.8 *Treat the punctuation as notation, not expression, most of the time.*

Analphabetic Symbols

Now and again the typographer finds on his desk a manuscript in which the exclamation marks and question marks stand six or nine together. Certain words may be written in bold capitals and others may be underlined five times. If the page has been written by hand, the dashes may get longer, and the screamers (exclamations) may get taller as they go. With sufficient equipment and time, the typographer can actually come close to reproducing what he sees; he can even increase its dramatic intensity in any of several ways. Theatrical typography is a genre that flourished throughout most of the twentieth century, yet whose limits are still largely unexplored.

Most writing and typography nevertheless remain contentedly abstract, like a theater script or a musical score. The script of *Macbeth* does not need to be bloodstained and spattered with tears; it needs to be legible. And the score of Beethoven's *Hammerklavier Sonata* does not need bolder notes to mark fortissimos nor fractured notes to mark the broken chords. The score is abstract code and not raw gesture. The typeset script or musical score is also a performance in its way – but only of the text. The score is silent so the pianist can play. The script can whisper while the actors roar.

William Faulkner, like most American novelists of his generation, typed his final drafts. Noel Polk, a literary scholar and a specialist on Faulkner, has prepared new editions of these novels in recent years. He found that Faulkner usually typed three hyphens for a long dash and four or five dots for an ellipsis, but that once in a while he hammered away at the key, typing hyphens or dots a dozen or more in a row. Polk decided not to try to replicate Faulkner's keyboard jigs exactly, but he did not want to edit them entirely away. He evolved the rule of converting two, three or four hyphens to an em dash, and five or more hyphens to a two-em dash. Anything up to six dots, he replaced with a standard ellipsis, and he called for seven dots wherever Faulkner had typed seven dots or more.

See Joseph Blotner & Noel Polk, "Note on the Texts," in William Faulkner, *Novels 1930–1945* (New York: Library of America, 1985), p 1021, and *Novels 1936–1940* (1990), p 1108. Photoreproductions of Faulkner's holographs and typescripts have also been published in 25 volumes as *The Faulkner Manuscripts* (New York: Garland, 1986–87).

These are typographic decisions that other editors or typographers might have made in other ways. But the principle underlying them is sound. That principle is: punctuation is cold notation; it is not frustrated speech; it is typographic code.

Faulkner, we can presume, did not resort to bouts of extravagant punctuation because he was unable to express himself in words. He may, however, have been looking for some of the keys that the typewriter just doesn't have. The typographer's task is to know the vocabulary and grammar of typography, and to put them to meaningful use on Faulkner's behalf.

5.3 PARENTHESES

5.3.1 *Use the best available brackets and parentheses, and set them with adequate space.*

Typographic parentheses are traditionally pure line, like the virgule (/), the en dash (–) and the em dash (—). They are curved rules – usually portions of perfect circles, with no variation in weight – and in many older fonts they were loosely fitted, or set with plenty of space between them and the text they enclose. Parentheses in the form of swelled rules – thick in the middle and pointed at the ends – first appeared in the early Baroque, faded from view again in the Neoclassic age, and became the fashion, along with lining figures, in the nineteenth century. Many of the best twentieth-century text faces (Bruce Rogers's Centaur and the Monotype Corporation's Bembo, for example) were historical revivals that reasserted the older form.

(abc) (abc)

Monotype Centaur and Monotype Baskerville, above. Georg Trump's Trump Mediäval Antiqua and Karl-Erik Forsberg's Berling, below.

(abc) (abc)

The parentheses of some recent faces, such as Georg Trump's Trump Mediäval Antiqua and Hermann Zapf's Comenius, are modulated, asymmetrical strokes, based on the natural forms of the broadnib pen. In other recent designs (Zapf's Melior and Zapf International, and Karl-Erik Forsberg's Berling, for example), the parentheses are symmetrically thick in the middle and thin at the ends, like the nineteenth-century standard, but they are stretched into the form of a partial superellipse, which gives them greater tension and poise.

Parentheses in the form of nineteenth-century swelled rules are found by default on many digital fonts and have frequently been added, by mistake or by design, to alphabets with which they don't belong – historical revivals of the printing types of Garamond and Baskerville for example.

If you are forced to work with a font whose parentheses fall below standard, borrow a better pair from elsewhere. And whatever parentheses you use, check that they are not too tightly fitted (as in recent fonts they very often are).

In older German typeface classifi cations, *Antiqua* means roman and *mediäval* actually means Renaissance – because Italian Renaissance architects and scribes revived and updated romanesque and Carolingian forms from the medieval period. *Trump Mediäval Antiqua*, or Trump Medieval roman, despite its name, stems from late Renaissance forms.

5.3.2 *Use upright (i.e., "roman") rather than sloped parentheses, brackets and braces, even if the context is italic.*

Parentheses and brackets are not letters, and it makes little sense to speak of them as roman or italic. There are vertical parentheses and sloped ones, and the parentheses on italic fonts are almost always sloped, but vertical parentheses are generally to be preferred. That means they must come from the roman font, and may need extra spacing when used with italic letterforms.

This rule has been broken more often than followed since the end of the 16th century. It was followed more often than broken by the best of the early typographers who set books in italic: Aldus Manutius, Gershom Soncino, Johann Froben, Simon de Colines, Robert Estienne, Ludovico degli Arrighi and Henri Estienne II.

(efg) (*efg*)

The sloped square brackets usually found on italic fonts are, if anything, even less useful than sloped parentheses. If, perish the thought, there were a book or film entitled *The View from My [sic] Bed,* sloped brackets might be useful as a way of indicating that the brackets and their contents are actually part of the title. Otherwise, vertical brackets should be used, no matter whether the text is roman or italic: "The View from My [*sic*] Bed" and "*the view from my* [*sic*] *bed.*"

5.4.1 *Minimize the use of quotation marks, especially with Renaissance faces.*

Quotation Marks and Other Intrusions

Typographers got by quite well for centuries without quotation marks. In the earliest printed books, quotation was marked merely by naming the speaker – as it still is in most editions of the Vulgate and King James Bibles. In the High Renaissance, quotation was generally marked by a change of font: from roman to italic or the other way around. Quotation marks were first cut in the middle of the sixteenth century, and by the seventeenth, some printers liked to use them profusely. In books from the Baroque and Romantic periods, quotation marks are sometimes repeated at the beginning of every line of a long quotation. When these distractions were finally omitted, the space they had occupied was frequently retained. This is the origin of the indented block quotation. Renaissance block quotations were set in a contrasting face at full size and full measure.

“and”
„und“
« et »
»und«

Three forms of quotation mark are still in common use. Inverted and raised commas – “quote” and ‘quote’ – are generally favored in Britain and North America. But baseline and inverted commas – „quote“ – are more widely used in Germany, and many typographers prefer them to take the shape of sloped primes („–“) instead of tailed commas („–“). *Guillemets,* otherwise known as *duck-foot quotation marks, chevrons,* or *angle quotes* – « quote » and ‹ quote › – are the normal form in France and Italy, and are widely used in the rest of Europe. French and Italian typographers set their guillemets with the points out, « thus », while German-speaking typographers usually set them »the opposite way«. In either case, thin spaces are customary between the guillemets and the text they enclose.

An informative history of punctuation is M.B. Parkes, *Pause and Effect* (1993).

Quotation marks are sufficiently ingrained in modern editorial sign language that it is difficult, in many kinds of texts, to do entirely without them. But many nonprofessional writers overuse quotation marks. Good editors and typographers will reduce their appearance to a minimum, retaining only those that contribute real information.

When quotation marks (including guillemets) are used, the question remains, how many should there be? The usual British practice is to use single quotes first, and doubles within singles: *‘So does “analphabetic” mean what I think it means?’ she said suspiciously.* When this convention is followed, most quotation marks will be singles and therefore less obtrusive.

Common American practice is the reverse: *"So," she said, "does 'analphabetic' mean...?"* This convention, using singles within doubles instead of doubles within singles, ensures that quotation flags will stand out. But some faces – Matthew Carter's Galliard, for example – have prominent quotation marks, while others have forms that are more discreet. Consider the face as well as the text when deciding which convention to follow in marking quotations.

5.4.2 *Position quotation marks consistently in relation to the rest of the punctuation.*

Punctuation is normally placed inside a closing single or double guillemet if it belongs to the quotation, and outside otherwise. With other quotation marks, usage is less consistent. Most North American editors like their commas and periods inside the raised commas, "like this," but their colons and semicolons outside. Many British editors prefer to put all punctuation outside, with the milk and the cat. The kerning capabilities of digital typesetters, especially in the hands of advertising typographers, have evolved an intermediate third style, in which closing quotation marks are kerned over the top of commas and periods. Typographically, this is a good idea with some faces in large sizes, but a bad idea with many faces at text sizes, where a kerned quotation mark or apostrophe may look much like a question or exclamation mark.

"in."

"out".

"kern, 'kerning,' kerned."

When quotation marks are not kerned, it makes no *typographic* difference whether they follow commas and periods or precede them. The difference is one of editorial rather than visual discretion. But typographers, like editors, should be consistent, whichever route they choose.

5.4.3 *Omit the apostrophe from numerical plurals.*

Houses are built with 2 × 4s; children and parents live through the terrible twos; Europeans killed as many Europeans in the 1930s as they did Native Americans and Africans in the 1800s.

5.4.4 *Eliminate other unnecessary punctuation.*

Omit the period after metric units and other self-evident abbreviations. Set 5.2 m and 520 cm but 36 in. or 36″, and in bibliographical references, p 36f, or pp 396–424.

North American editors and typesetters tend to put periods after all abbreviations or (more rarely) after none. The former practice produces a text full of birdshot and wormholes; the latter can cause confusion. As a form of compromise, the Oxford house style, which is widely followed in Britain, has much to commend it. This rule is: use a period only when the word stops prematurely. The period is omitted if the abbreviation begins with the first letter of the word and ends with the last. Thus: Mrs Bodoni, Mr John Adams Jr and Ms Lucy Chong-Adams, Dr McBain, St Thomas Aquinas, Msgr Kuruwezi and Fr O'Malley; but Prof. Czesław Miłosz and Capt. James Cook.

Periods are equally unnecessary in acronyms and other abbreviations written with small or large capitals. Thus: 3:00 AM and 450 BC; Washington, DC, and Mexico, DF; Vancouver, BC, and Darwin, NT.

In the interests of typographic hygiene, unnecessary hyphens should likewise be omitted. Thus: avant garde, bleeding heart, halfhearted, postmodern, prewar, silkscreen and typeface, in preference to the hyphenated alternatives. (It is good editorial practice, however, to hyphenate compound adjectives unless they can be fused into single words or will stand out as proper nouns. Thus, one finds twentieth-century typefaces in limited-edition books but publishes a limited edition at the end of the twentieth century and rides the New York Subway in New York. And one finds lowercase letters in the lower case.)

Apostrophes are needed for some plurals, but not for others, and inconsistency is better than a profusion of unnecessary marks. Thus: do's and don'ts; the ayes have it but the I's don't; the ewes are coming but the you's are staying home.

5.4.5 *Add punctuation, or preserve it, where it is necessary to meaning.*

The phrase *twenty one night stands* is ambiguous when written, but if the speaker knows what he means, it will be perfectly clear when spoken. Typography answers to vocal inflection in distinguishing *twenty one-night stands* from *twenty-one nightstands.*

In the careful language of science and poetry, hyphens can be more important still. Consider the following list of names: Douglas-fir, balsam fir, Oregon ash, mountain-ash, redcedar, yellowcedar, Atlas cedar, white pine, yellow pine, blue spruce. All these names are correct as they stand. They would be less so if an eager but ignorant editor, or a typographer obsessed with graphic hygiene, tried to standardize the hyphens. The terms are written differently because some are made from nouns that are only borrowed, others from nouns that are generic. The balsam fir is what it claims to be: a fir; the Douglas-fir is not; it is a separate genus waiting for a proper English name. The Oregon ash, likewise, is an ash, but the mountain-ash is not, and the Atlas cedar is a cedar, but redcedar and yellowcedar (or yellow-cedar) are not. The differences, though subtle, are perfectly audible in the speech of knowledgeable speakers (who say **bal**sam ***fir*** and **Doug**las-**fir** and **moun**tain-**ash** and **Or**egon ***ash***). A good typographer will make the same distinctions subtly visible as well. In the present state of typographic art and editorial convention, this is done not by spattering the page with boldface syllables but by the judicious and subtle placement of hyphens.

5.5 DIACRITICS

5.5.1 *Use the accents and alternate sorts that proper names and imported words and phrases require.*

Simplicity is good, but so is plurality. Typography's principal function (not its only function) is communication, and the greatest threat to communication is not difference but sameness. Communication ceases when one being is no different from another: when there is nothing strange to wonder at and no new information to exchange. For that reason among others, typography and typographers must honor the variety and complexity of human language, thought and identity, instead of homogenizing or hiding it.

Typography was once a fluently multilingual and multicultural calling. The great typographers of the fifteenth and sixteenth centuries worked willingly with North Italian whiteletter, Italian or German blackletter, French script, Ashkenazi and Sephardic Hebrew, orthotic and cursive and chancery Greek. The best typographers of the twentieth century have followed their lead. But typographic ethnocentricity and racism also have thrived in

a a *a*
א א
α α

the last hundred years, and much of that narrow-mindedness is institutionalized in the workings of machines. Unregenerate, uneducated fonts and keyboards, defiantly incapable of setting anything beyond the most rudimentary Anglo-American alphabet, are getting scarcer but are still not difficult to find.

Diacritics

Recent digital technology has made it possible for any typographer to create special characters on demand – a luxury most have been without since the seventeenth century. Prepackaged fonts of impeccable design, with character sets sufficient to set any word or name in any European and many Asian languages, and the software to compose and kern these characters, are also now available even to the smallest home and desktop operations. Yet there are large-circulation newspapers in North America still unwilling to spell correctly even the names of major cities, composers and statesmen, or the annual list of winners of the Nobel Prize, for fear of letters like ñ and é.

Neither typographers nor their tools should labor under the sad misapprehension that no one will enjoy or even mention crêpes flambées or aïoli, no one will have a name like Antonín Dvořák, Søren Kierkegaard, Stéphane Mallarmé or Chloë Jones, and no one will live in Óbidos or Århus, in Kroměříž or Øster Vrå, Průhonice, Nagykőrös, Dalasýsla, Kırkağaç or Köln.

5.5.2 *Remap the font driver and keyboard to suit your own requirements.*

The conventional computer keyboard includes a number of characters – @ # ^ + = { } | \ ~ < > – rarely required by most typesetters, while frequently needed characters, such as the en dash, em dash, acute accent, midpoint and ellipsis, are nowhere to be seen. Unless your keyboard fits your needs as is, remap it. It should give you ready access to whatever accented and analphabetic characters you regularly use.

Unless your composition software places ligatures automatically, you may find it easiest to insert them through a substitution routine after the text is fully set. Some typographers, however, (and I am one of them) prefer to rearrange their fonts or keyboards so that all the basic ligatures are accessible directly from the keyboard, as they are on a Monotype machine. Open and close quotes can also be inserted through substitution routines, but most typing and typesetting software will insert them automatically. (This means, of course, that in words or names such as

Dutch *'s-Hertogenbosch* or Navajo *'Áshį́į́h 'Asdzáán,* the software will always make the wrong choice, which the typographer must then correct by hand – or through yet another search-and-replace routine.)

Compositors who seldom use accented characters often prefer to set them through mnemonic codes, using a function key that momentarily redefines the keyboard. Software that operates in this way may produce ó from the combination o + /, ř from r + v, Ů from U + o, and so on. But if you use accented characters with any frequency, you may find it worth your while to map them directly to the keyboard. One way to do this is to install the standard prefabricated keyboards for each language you may need. This, however, requires swapping from one to another as different languages or even different names come up in multilingual text, and it requires you to memorize a lot of different layouts. Another solution is to create a custom keyboard (or even several keyboards) that will meet your own particular requirements.

Analphabetic Symbols

A typical customized keyboard for a Latin font is shown overleaf. The purpose of this particular layout is general multilingual text work. This could mean something as complex as polylingual manuals and packaging for technical products sold on the global market, or something as simple as addressing an envelope to Poland, or spelling the names correctly in the program for a symphony performance in Chicago or Detroit.

The keyboard shown accommodates more than twenty European languages, including Albanian, Basque, Breton, Catalan, Danish, Dutch, English, Faroese, Finnish, Flemish, French, Frisian, German, Hungarian, Icelandic, Italian, Norwegian, Polish, Portuguese, Romansch, Spanish, Swedish and Welsh. It will also accommodate many African and Native American languages and most of the Pacific languages written in Latin script (including Bahasa Indonesia, Bikol, Cebuano, Fijian, Hawaiian, Hiligaynon, Ilocano, Malay, Tagalog and Tahitian).

Tagalog is the primary language of the Philippines. Bikol, Cebuano, Hiligaynon and Ilocano are other Philippine languages with several million speakers each.

Expanded to its maximum dimensions, a standard keyboard will give direct access to 47 × 6 = 282 glyphs. This is enough to handle all current European versions of the Latin alphabet.

The individual characters are identified and discussed in appendices A & B, pages 288–320.

Sample Layout for an Expanded Keyboard

Cntrl	¡	Ŵ	Ŷ	£	ź	Ź	ż	Ż	í	Í	ú	×	
SHIFT	!	ŵ	ŷ	$	%	°	&	*	(	)	Ú	+	
Plain	1	2	3	4	5	6	7	8	9	0	-	=	
Alt	â	ê	î	ô	û	Â	Ê	Î	Ô	Û	–	—	
Cntrl	Ø	É	È	Å	Þ	Ý	Ù	Ì	Ò		Ś	ś	
SHIFT	**Q**	**W**	**E**	**R**	**T**	**Y**	**U**	**I**	**O**	**P**	Ő	Ű	
Plain	**q**	**w**	**e**	**r**	**t**	**y**	**u**	**i**	**o**	**p**	[	]	
Alt	ø	é	è	å	þ	ý	ù	ì	ò	¶	ő	ű	
Cntrl	À	§	Đ	Ä	Ë	Ï	Ö	Ü	Ł	Ÿ	Ć		
SHIFT	**A**	**S**	**D**	**F**	**G**	**H**	**J**	**K**	**L**	**:**	”/“		
Plain	**a**	**s**	**d**	**f**	**g**	**h**	**j**	**k**	**l**	**;**	’/‘		
Alt	à	ß	ð	ä	ë	ï	ö	ü	ł	ÿ	ć		
Cntrl	Ã	Õ	Ç	Ą	Ę	Ñ	Ó	«	»	¿		Ń	Æ
SHIFT	**Z**	**X**	**C**	**V**	**B**	**N**	**M**	µ	…	**?**		Á	Œ
Plain	**z**	**x**	**c**	**v**	**b**	**n**	**m**	,	.	/		á	œ
Alt	ã	õ	ç	ą	ę	ñ	ó	ª	·	º		ń	æ

Ambiguous characters are as follows. **Row 1**: *Shift-6* is the degree sign. *Alt-hyphen* is an en dash, and *Alt-equal* is an em dash. **Row 4**: *Alt-comma* is the ordinal A. *Alt-period* is a midpoint. The *slash* key is a virgule, not a fraction bar or solidus. *Alt-slash* is the ordinal o.

The two extra keys shown to the right in the bottom row are placed in different positions by different keyboard manufacturers. On an ordinary keyboard, one of these keys carries the backslash and pipe; the other carries the swung dash and floating grave. Here, the *backslash* key is reassigned to carry upper- and lowercase a-acute and n-acute. The *swung dash* key is reassigned to the four typographic diphthongs or ligatured vowels. The single and double quotation mark keys follow the "smart quotes" convention. All other keys are coded one to one; they give a single complete glyph for each stroke.

There are 188 characters in the keyboard layout shown. By employing the *Shift-Cntrl* and *Shift-Alt* combinations, another 94 characters can be added: enough to accommodate all variations on the Latin alphabet used in Eastern and Western Europe.

("Alt" and "Control" are keyboard codes of the PC persuasion. On the Macintosh keyboard, the counterparts are the "Option" and "Command" keys.)

CHOOSING & COMBINING TYPE

6

6.1 TECHNICAL CONSIDERATIONS

6.1.1 *Consider the medium for which the typeface was originally designed.*

Typographic purists like to see every typeface used with the technology for which it was designed. Taken literally, this means that virtually all faces designed before 1950 must be set in metal and printed letterpress, and the majority must be set by hand. Most typographers apply this principle in a more relaxed and complex way, and settle for preserving something rather than everything of a type's original character.

On the technical side, several things can be done to increase the chance that a letterpress typeface will survive translation to digital composition and offset printing.

6.1.2 *When using digital adaptations of letterpress faces, choose fonts that are faithful to the spirit as well as the letter of the old designs.*

Letterpress printing places the letterform *into* the paper, while offset printing lays it on the surface. Many subtle differences result from these two approaches to printing. The letterpress adds a little bulk and definition to the letter, especially in the thin strokes, and increases the prominence of the ends of thin serifs. Metal typefaces are designed to take advantage of these features of letterpress printing.

On the offset press – and in the photographic procedures by which camera-ready art and offset printing plates are prepared – thin strokes tend to get thinner and the ends of delicate serifs are eaten away. In a face like Bembo, for instance, offset printing tends to make features like the feet of i and l, and the heads and feet of H and I, slightly convex, while letterpress printing tends to make them slightly concave.

Ili

Faces designed for photographic manipulation and offset printing are therefore weighted and finished differently from letterpress designs. And adapting a letterpress face for digital composition is a far from simple task.

Digital fonts poorly translated from metal originals are sometimes too dark or light or blunt throughout, or uneven in stroke weight, or faithless in their proportions. They sometimes lack text figures or other essential components of the original design. But digital translations can also be *too faithful* to the original. They sometimes neglect the subtle adjustments that the shift from three-dimensional letterpress to two-dimensional offset printing requires.

6.1.3 *Choose faces that will survive, and if possible prosper, under the final printing conditions.*

a a

a a

Bembo and Centaur, Spectrum and Palatino, are subtle and beautiful alphabets, but if you are setting 8 pt text with a laser printer on plain paper at 300 dpi, the refined forms of these faces will be rubbed into the coarse digital mud of the imaging process. If the final output will be 14 pt text set directly to plate at 2800 dpi, then printed by good offset lithography on the best coated paper, every nuance may be crystal clear, but the result will still lack the character and texture of the letterpress medium for which these faces were designed.

lr

Some of the most innocent looking faces are actually the most difficult to render by digital means. Optima, for example – an unserifed and apparently uncomplicated face – is (in its authentic form) entirely constructed of subtle tapers and curves that can be adequately rendered only at the highest resolutions.

a a

a a

Faces with blunt and substantial serifs, open counters, gentle modeling and minimal pretensions to aristocratic grace stand the best chance of surviving the indignities of low resolution. Amasis, Caecilia, Lucida Sans, Stone and Utopia, for example, while they prosper at high resolutions, are faces that will also survive under cruder conditions lethal to Centaur, Spectrum, Linotype Didot or almost any version of Bodoni.

6.1.4 *Choose faces that suit the paper you intend to print on, or paper that suits the faces you wish to use.*

Most Renaissance and Baroque types were made to be pressed into robust, lively papers by fairly robust means. They wilt when placed on the glossy, hard-surfaced sheets that came into vogue toward the end of the eighteenth century. Most Neoclassical and Romantic types, on the other hand, were designed to require smooth papers. Rough, three-dimensional papers break their fragile lines. Geometric Modernist types such as Futura, and overhauled Realist types such as Helvetica, can be printed on rough and smooth papers alike, because they are fundamentally *monochrome*. (That is to say, the stroke is nearly uniform in width.) But the aura of machine precision that emanates from a type like Futura is reinforced by a smooth paper and contradicted (*or* counterbalanced) by a paper that feels homespun.

The types associated with these historical categories are epitomized on pp 12–15 and explored in more detail in chapter 7.

6.2 PRACTICAL TYPOGRAPHY

6.2.1 *Choose faces that suit the task as well as the subject.*

You are designing, let us say, a book about bicycle racing. You have found in the specimen books a typeface called Bicycle, which has spokes in the O, an A in the shape of a racing seat, a T that resembles a set of racing handlebars, and tiny cleated shoes perched on the long, one-sided serifs of ascenders and descenders, like pumping feet on the pedals. Surely this is the perfect face for your book?

Actually, typefaces and racing bikes are very much alike. Both are ideas as well as machines, and neither should be burdened with excess drag or baggage. Pictures of pumping feet will not make the type go faster, any more than smoke trails, pictures of rocket ships or imitation lightning bolts tied to the frame will improve the speed of the bike.

The best type for a book about bicycle racing will be, first of all, an inherently good type. Second, it will be a good type for books, which means a good type for comfortable long-distance reading. Third, it will be a type sympathetic to the theme. It will probably be lean, strong and swift; perhaps it will also be Italian. But it is unlikely to be carrying excess ornament or freight, and unlikely to be indulging in a masquerade.

6.2.2 *Choose faces that can furnish whatever special effects you require.*

If your text includes an abundance of numerals, you may want a face whose numerals are especially well designed. Palatino, Pontifex, Trump Mediäval and Zapf International, for example, all recommend themselves. If you prefer three-quarter-height lining numerals, your options include Bell, Trajanus and Weiss.

If you need small caps, faces that lack them (such as Frutiger and Méridien) are out of the running. If you need a range of weights, Spectrum is disqualified but Frutiger may work. If you need matching phonetics, your options include Stone Serif and Sans, Lucida Sans, and Times Roman. For the sake of a matching Cyrillic, you might choose Charter, Minion, Lazurski, Officina, Quadraat, Warnock, or, among the unserifed faces, Syntax, Myriad or Futura. For the sake of a matching Greek, you might choose Georgia or Palatino, or for the sake of a matching Cherokee, Plantagenet. To obtain a perfectly mated sanserif, you might choose Haarlemmer, Legacy, Lucida, Le Monde, Officina, Quadraat, Scala, Seria or Stone. These matters are explored in more detail in chapter 11, which addresses individual typefaces.

Special effects can also be obtained through more unorthodox combinations, which are the subject of §6.5.

6.2.3 *Use what there is to the best advantage.*

If there is nothing for dinner but beans, one may hunt for an onion, some pepper, salt, cilantro and sour cream to enliven the dish, but it is generally no help to pretend that the beans are really prawns or chanterelles.

When the only font available is Cheltenham or Times Roman, the typographer must make the most of its virtues, limited though they may be. An italic, small caps and text figures will help immensely if they can be added, but there is nothing to be gained by pretending that Times Roman is Bembo or Cheltenham is Aldus in disguise.

As a rule, a face of modest merits should be handled with great discretion, formality and care. It should be set in modest sizes (better yet, in one size only) with the caps well spaced, the lines well leaded, and the lower case well fitted and modestly kerned. The line length should be optimal and the page impeccably proportioned. In short, the typography should be richly and superbly *ordinary*, so that attention is drawn to the quality of the composition, not to the individual letterforms. Only a face that warrants close scrutiny should be set in a form that invites it.

Using what there is to best advantage almost always means using less than what is available. Baskerville, Helvetica, Palatino and Times Roman, for example – which are four of the most widely available typefaces – are four faces with nothing to offer

Baskerville roman
and its italic

Helvetica roman
and its oblique

Palatino roman
and its italic

Times New Roman
and its italic

Baskerville is an English Neoclassical face designed in Birmingham in the 1750s by John Baskerville. It has a rationalist axis, thoroughgoing symmetry and delicate finish.

Helvetica is a twentieth-century Swiss revision of a late nineteenth-century German Realist face. The first weights were drawn in 1956 by Max Miedinger, based on the Berthold Foundry's old Odd-job Sanserif, or Akzidenz Grotesk, as it is called in German. The heavy, unmodulated line and tiny aperture evoke an image of uncultivated strength, force and persistence. The very light weights issued in recent years have done much to reduce Helvetica's coarseness but little to increase its readability.

Palatino is a lyrical modernist face with a neohumanist architecture, which is to say that it is *written,* not drawn, and that it is based on Renaissance forms. It was created in 1948 by Hermann Zapf.

Times Roman – properly Times *New* Roman – is an historical pastiche drawn by Victor Lardent for Stanley Morison in London in 1931. It has a humanist axis but Mannerist proportions, Baroque weight, and a sharp, Neoclassical finish.

one another except public disagreement. None makes a good companion face for any of the others, because each of them is rooted in a different concept of what constitutes a letterform. If the available palette is limited to these faces, the first thing to do is choose *one* for the task at hand and ignore the other three.

Historical Consider-ations

6.3 HISTORICAL CONSIDERATIONS

Typography, like other arts, preys on its own past. It can do so with the callousness of a grave robber, or with the piety of unquestioning ancestor worship. It can also do so in thoughtful, enlightened and deeply creative ways.

Roman type has been with us for more than five centuries. Its root components – the roman upper and lower case, basic analphabetic symbols, and the arabic numerals – have been with us for much longer yet. There are typographers who resolutely avoid using any typeface designed in an earlier era, but even they must learn something of how the older letterforms functioned, because the ancient forms are living in the new. Typographers who willingly use the old faces, and who wish to use them intelligently, need to know all they can learn about the heritage they enjoy.

6.3.1 *Choose a face whose historical echoes and associations are in harmony with the text.*

abc
abc

Any contemporary library will furnish examples of typographic anachronism. There are books on contemporary Italy and on seventeenth-century France set in typefaces such as Baskerville and Caslon, cut in eighteenth-century England. There are books about the Renaissance set in faces that belong to the Baroque, and books about the Baroque set in faces from the Renaissance. To a good typographer it is not enough merely to avoid these kinds of laughable contradictions. The typographer seeks to *shed light* on the text, to generate insight and energy, by setting every text in a face and form in which it actually belongs.

It is not that good typographers object to mixing centuries and cultures. Many take delight in doing so – especially when they have no other choice. A text from ancient Athens, for example, cannot be set in an ancient Athenian version of roman type. A face designed in North America in the 1990s may well be used instead. Texts from seventeenth-century France or eighteenth-century England also might be set perfectly well in faces of recent design. But a face that truly suits an historical text is likely to have some fairly clear historical content of its own. There is no typeface *equally suited* to texts from Greek antiquity, the French Baroque and the English Neoclassical period – though faces equally *unsuited* to each of them abound.

The historical affiliations of individual typefaces are discussed in chapters 7 and 11.

6.3.2 *Allow the face to speak in its natural idiom.*

Books that leap historical boundaries and mix historical subjects can pose complex and exciting typographic problems. But often, if a text calls for a Renaissance type, it calls for Renaissance typography as well. This usually means Renaissance page proportions and margins, and an absence of bold face. It may also mean large Renaissance versals, Renaissance style in the handling of quotations, and the segregation of roman and italic. If the text calls for a Neoclassical type, it likewise often calls for Neoclassical page design. When you undertake to use an historical typeface, take the trouble to learn the typographic idiom for which it was intended. (Works of reference that may be useful in solving particular problems are listed in the bibliography, page 357.)

6.4 CULTURAL & PERSONAL CONSIDERATIONS

6.4.1 *Choose faces whose individual spirit and character is in keeping with the text.*

Accidental associations are rarely a good basis for choosing a typeface. Books of poems by the twentieth-century Jewish American poet Marvin Bell, for example, have sometimes been set in Bell type – which is eighteenth-century, English and Presbyterian – solely because of the name. Such puns are a private amusement for typographers; they also sometimes work. But a typographic page so well designed that it attains a life of its own will be based on real affinities, not on an inside joke.

abc
abc

Letterforms have character, spirit and personality. Typographers learn to discern these features through years of working first-hand with the forms, and through studying and comparing the work of other designers, present and past. On close inspection, typefaces reveal many hints of their designers' times and temperaments, and even their nationalities and religious faiths. Faces chosen on these grounds are likely to give more interesting results than faces chosen through mere convenience of availability or coincidence of name.

a a
a a
a G
a

If, for example, you are setting a text by a woman, you might prefer a face, or several faces, designed by a woman. Such faces were rare or nonexistent in earlier centuries, but there are now a number to choose from. They include Gudrun Zapf-von Hesse's admirable Alcuin, Carmina, Diotima and Nofret families; Elizabeth Friedländer's Elizabeth; Kris Holmes's Sierra and Lucida; Kris Holmes's and Janice Prescott Fishman's Shannon; Carol Twombly's handsome text face Chaparral and her titling faces Charlemagne, Lithos, Nueva and Trajan; Zuzana Ličko's Journal and Mrs Eaves, and Ilse Schüle's Rhapsodie. For some purposes, one might also go back to the work of Elizabeth Colwell, whose Colwell Handletter, issued by ATF in 1916, was the first American typeface designed by a woman.

But perhaps a text by a French author, or a text dealing with France, might best be set in a French typeface, without regard to the gender of author or designer. The choices include Garamond, Jannon, Mendoza, Méridien, Vendôme and many others, but even this abbreviated list covers considerable range. Garamond – of which there are many recent revivals – was designed in sixteenth-century Paris. It owes much to Italian forms and belongs to the world of Renaissance Catholicism. Jannon is equally elegant but nonconformist. It belongs to the Reformation rather than the Renaissance, and its designer, Jean Jannon, was a French Protestant who suffered all his life from religious persecution. Vendôme, designed by François Ganeau, is a witty twentieth-century face much indebted to Jannon. Mendoza, designed in Paris in 1990, goes back to the tough humanist roots from which Garamond sprang. Méridien, from the 1950s, is more in touch with the secular spirit of twentieth-century Swiss industrial design, yet it includes a regal, even imperious, upper case and a very crisp and graceful italic. These five different faces invite additional differences in page design, paper and binding as well as different texts, just as different musical instruments invite different phrasings, different tempi, different musical modes or keys.

Even nations such as Greece and Thailand, which have alphabets of their own, share in a multinational tradition of type

Garamond roman
and its italic

Jannon roman
and its italic

Mendoza roman
and its italic

Méridien roman
and its italic

Vendôme roman
and its oblique

Stempel Garamond is the Stempel Foundry's replica of a text roman and italic designed by Claude Garamond (*c.* 1490–1561). (Compare the reproductions of some of Garamond's actual type on page 74.)

Monotype 'Garamond' 156 is a revival of a type designed by Jean Jannon (1580–1658), the greatest typecutter of the French Baroque. Jannon's type was once misidentified as Garamond's and is still routinely sold under his name.

Mendoza was designed about 1990 by José Mendoza y Almeida. Adrian Frutiger's Méridien and François Ganeau's Vendôme are products of the 1950s. Ganeau – who worked as a painter, sculptor and set designer more than as a typographer – based Vendôme on Jannon's letters, but moved them playfully in the direction of French Neoclassicism.

design. Nevertheless, some typefaces seem more redolent of national character than others. Frederic Goudy, for example, is widely regarded as the most ebulliently American of all American type designers. The sensitive typographer would not choose one of Goudy's faces to set, let us say, the text of the Canadian or Mexican constitution.

Cultural and Personal Considerations

This subject is a lifelong study, and for serious typographers it is a lifelong source of discovery and delight. Here it is pursued at greater length in chapter 11. Appendix D (page 333) is a cross-indexed list of type designers.

6.5 THE MULTICULTURAL PAGE

Consistency is one of the forms of beauty. Contrast is another. A fine page, even a fine book, can be set from beginning to end in one type in one size. It can also teem with variety, like an equatorial forest or a modern city.

6.5.1 *Start with a single typographic family.*

a A *a*
a A *a*
a A *a*
a A *a*

Most pages, and most entire documents, can be set perfectly well with only one family of type. But perhaps the page confronting you requires a chapter title, two or three levels of subheads, an epigraph, a text in two languages, block quotations within the text, a couple of mathematical equations, a bar graph, several explanatory sidenotes, and captions for photographs and a map. An extended type family, such as Legacy, Lucida, Quadraat, Seria or Stone, may provide sufficient resources even for this task. Another possibility is Gerard Unger's comprehensive series known as Demos, Praxis and Flora – which is a family with no surname to unite it. Each of these series includes both roman and italic in a range of weights, matching serifed and unserifed forms, and other variations. If you restrict yourself to faces within the family, you can have variety and homogeneity at the same time: many shapes and sizes but a single typographic culture. Such an approach is well suited to some texts, poorly suited to others.

You can also, of course, mix faces at random, by drawing them out of a hat.

Between these two extremes is the wide arena of thoughtful mixing and matching, in which the typographic intelligence often does its most creative work and play.

6.5.2 *Respect the integrity of roman, italic and small caps.*

It has been the normal practice of type designers since the middle of the sixteenth century to offer text faces in the form of a matched triad, consisting of roman, italic and small caps. Because some of these marriages are more successful than others, it is wise to examine the roman and the italic both separately and together when choosing a text face.

Choosing and Combining Type

There are several celebrated instances in which an italic designed by one artist has been happily and permanently married to another designer's roman. These matches always involve some redrawing (and the face that is most heavily redrawn is almost always the italic, which is the subsidiary and 'feminine' font in post-Renaissance typography). There are also instances in which a roman and its italic have been designed by the same artist many years apart. But casual liaisons, in which the roman of one family is paired momentarily with the italic of another, have little hope of success. Mixing small caps from one face with full caps from another is even less likely to succeed.

If you use type strictly in the Renaissance manner, treating the roman and italic as separate but equal, not mixing them on the line, you may find that greater latitude is possible. Jan van Krimpen's Lutetia italic mixes well with his later Romanée roman, for example, if the two are not too intimately combined. One is visibly more mature than the other, but they are close in color and structure, and they are patently the work of the same designer.

6.5.3 *Consider bold faces on their own merits.*

The original boldface printing types are the blackletters used by Gutenberg in the 1440s. For the next two centuries, blackletter fonts were widely used not only in Germany but in France, Spain, the Netherlands and England. (That is why blackletter fonts are occasionally sold in the USA as 'Olde English.')

Boldface romans, however, are a nineteenth-century invention. Bold italic is even more recent, and it is hard to find a successful version designed before 1950. Bold romans and italics have been added retroactively to many earlier faces, but they are often simply parodies of the original designs.

Before using a bold weight, especially a bold italic, ask yourself whether you really need it at all. If the answer is yes, you may want to avoid type families such as Bembo, Garamond or Baskerville, to which bold weights have been retroactively added but do not in fact belong. You might, instead, choose a twentieth-century family such as Apollo, Nofret or Scala, in which a range of weights is part of the original design.

If your text face lacks a bold weight, you may also find an appropriate bold close by. Hermann Zapf's Aldus, for example, is a twentieth-century family on the Renaissance model, limited to roman, italic and small caps. But Aldus is a close cousin of the same designer's Palatino family, which does include a bold, and Palatino bold sits comfortably enough with Aldus text.

a aardvark; **b** *balloon;* **3** thruppence

Aldus 16 pt roman and italic with Palatino 15 pt bold

Equally interesting results can often be obtained by reaching much farther afield. The normal function of boldface type is, after all, to contrast with the roman text. If the bold is used in small amounts, and bold and roman are not too intimately combined, a difference in structure as well as weight may be an asset. Under these conditions, a typographer is free to choose both roman and bold on their own merits, seeking basic compatibility rather than close genetic connection.

c chinstrap; **d** *daffodil*; **6** saxophone

Sabon 16 pt roman and italic with Zapf International 15 pt demibold

A text might be set in Sabon, for example, with Zapf International as a titling face and Zapf International demi or heavy for subheads and flags. Structurally, these are very different faces, with very different pedigrees. But Sabon has the calm and steady flow required for setting text, while Zapf International's vitality makes it a good face for titling – and this vitality persists even in the boldest weights. The bold weights of fonts that are closer in structure Sabon often look splayed and deformed.

Fifteenth-century typographers – Nicolas Jenson for example – rarely mixed fonts except when mixing languages. They loved an even page. Bold roman is therefore an appendage they did happily without. If, nevertheless, you were using one of the fine text faces based on Jenson's single roman font and wanted to embellish it with bold, you might consider using Jenson's kind of bold. The only dark faces he cut were blackletters.

Elève elephant; **fool** filibuster; **lvi** phytogenic

Bruce Rogers's Centaur (here 16 pt) with Karlgeorg Hoefer's San Marco (12 pt). Centaur is based on the roman that Nicolas Jenson cut at Venice in 1469. San Marco is based on the rotundas he cut there in the 1470s.

6.5.4 *Choose titling and display faces that reinforce the structure of the text face.*

Titling faces, display faces and scripts can be chosen on much the same principles as bold faces. Incestuous similarity is rarely a necessity, but empathy and compatibility usually are. A geometrically constructed, high-contrast face such as Bauer Bodoni, beautiful though it may be, has marginal promise as a titling face for a text set in Garamond or Bembo, whose contrast is low and whose structure is fundamentally calligraphic. (Bodoni mixes far more happily with Baskerville – of which it is not a contradiction but rather an exaggeration.)

6.5.5 *Pair serifed and unserifed faces on the basis of their inner structure.*

When the basic text is set in a serifed face, a related sanserif is frequently useful for other elements, such as tables, captions or notes. In complicated texts, such as dictionary entries, it may also be necessary to mix unserifed and serifed fonts on the same line. If you've chosen a family that includes a matched sanserif, your problems may be solved. But many successful marriages between serifed and unserifed faces from different families are waiting to be made.

Frutiger Méridien Univers

The version of Frutiger used here is the recent revision known as Frutiger Next.

Suppose your main text is set in Méridien – a serifed roman and italic designed by Adrian Frutiger. It would be reasonable to look first of all among Frutiger's other creations for a related sanserif. Frutiger is a prolific designer of types, both serifed and unserifed, so there are several from which to choose. Univers is his most widely used sanserif. But another of his unserifed faces – the one to which he gave his own name – is structurally much closer to Méridien and works handsomely as a companion.

Hans Eduard Meier's Syntax is a sanserif much different in structure from either Frutiger or Univers. It is based on serifed Renaissance forms like those of Garamond. It works well with such faces as Stempel or Adobe Garamond, or with Sabon, another descendant of Garamond, designed by Meier's contemporary and countryman, Jan Tschichold.

If your choice falls on a more geometric sanserif, such as Futura, a Renaissance roman will hardly suffice as a serifed companion. Many romans based on the work of Bodoni, however, breathe much the same spirit as Futura. They aspire not to calligraphic motion but to geometric purity.

Gabocse escobaG
Gabocse escobaG
Gabocse escobaG

Syntax and Minion, above; Futura and Berthold Bodoni, center; Helvetica and Haas Clarendon, below.

6.6 MIXING ALPHABETS

6.6.1 *Choose non-Latin faces as carefully as Latin ones.*

a א
a א
a א

Mixing Latin letters with Hebrew or Arabic is, in principle, scarcely different from mixing roman with blackletter or serif with sans. Different though they look, and even though they read in different directions, all these alphabets spring from the same source, and all are written with similar tools. Many structural similarities underlie the obvious differences. A book involving more than one alphabet therefore poses some of the same questions posed by a bilingual or polylingual book set entirely in Latin letters. The typographer must decide in each case – after studying the text – whether to emphasize or minimize the differences. In general, the more closely different alphabets are mixed, the more important it becomes that they should be close in color and in size, no matter how superficially different in form.

The Latin, Greek and Cyrillic alphabets are as closely related in structure as roman, italic and small caps. (And in most Cyrillic faces, the lower case is close in color and shape to Latin small caps.) Random marriages of Latin and Greek, or Latin and Cyrillic, look just as ungainly and haphazard as random combinations of roman, italic and small caps – but excellent sets of related faces have developed, and a few homogeneous polyglot families have been designed.

Plato and Aristotle both quote
the line of Parmenides that says
πρώτιστον μὲν *Ἔρωτα* θεῶν μητίσατο
πάντων: "The first of all the gods to
arise in the mind of their mother was
PHYSICAL LOVE."
Греки боготворили природу и
завещали миру свою религию,
то есть *философию и искусство,*
says a character named Shatov in
Dostoevsky's novel *Demons*: "The
Greeks deified nature and bequeathed
to the world their religion, which is
philosophy and art."

Robert Slimbach's Minion roman, italic and small caps, with upright and cursive forms of Minion Cyrillic and Minion Greek.

The text on this page is set in ITC Mendoza 10/13 with 12 pt GFS Neo Hellenic. On the facing page, the roman and italic are Figural 10/13; the Greek is 10.5 pt GFS Porson. The caps in both Greek fonts have been resized. (The original edition of Cornford's book, printed in 1912, was set in the curious combination of Century Expanded and Porson Greek.)

ΦΥΣΙΣ AS THE SOUL / THE SOUL AS ΓΝΩΣΙΣ. The second proposition of Thales declares that the All is alive, or has Soul in it (τὸ πᾶν ἔμψυχον). This statement accounts for the mobility of φύσις. Its motion, and its power of generating things other than itself, are due to its life (ψυχή), an inward, spontaneous principle of activity. (Cf. Plato, *Laws* 892c: φύσιν βούλονται λέγειν γένεσιν τὴν περὶ τὰ πρῶτα· εἰ δὲ φανήσεται ψυχὴ πρῶτον, οὐ πῦρ οὐδὲ ἀήρ, ψυχὴ Δ' ἐν πρώτοις γεγενημένη, σχεδὸν ὀρθότατα λέγοιτ' ἂν εἶναι διαφερόντως φύσει.)...

It is a general rule that the Greek philosophers describe φύσις as standing in the same relation to the universe as soul does to body. Anaximenes, the third Milesian, says: οἷον ἡ ψυχὴ ἡ ἡμετέρα ἀὴρ οὖσα συγκρατεῖ ἡμᾶς, καὶ ὅλον τὸν κόσμον πνεῦμα καὶ ἀὴρ περιέχει. "As our soul is air and holds us together, so a breath or air embraces the whole cosmos."[1]...

The second function of Soul – knowing – was not at first distinguished from motion. Aristotle says, φαμὲν γὰρ τὴν ψυχὴν λυπεῖσθαι χαίρειν, θαρρεῖν φοβεῖσθαι, ἔτι δὲ ὀργίζεσθαί τε καὶ αἰσθάνεσθαι καὶ διανοεῖσθαι· ταῦτα δὲ πάντα κινήσεις εἶναι δοκοῦσιν. ὅθεν οἰηθείη τις ἂν αὐτὴν κινεῖσθαι. "The soul is said to feel pain and joy, confidence and fear, and again to be angry, to perceive, and to think; and all these states are held to be movements, which might lead one to suppose that soul itself is moved."[2] Sense-perception (αἴσθησις), not distinguished from thought, was taken as the type of all cognition, and this is a form of action at a distance.[3]

1 Frag. 2. Compare Pythagoras' "boundless breath" outside the heavens, which is inhaled by the world (Arist., *Phys.* 213*b*22), and Heraclitus' "divine reason," which surrounds (περιέχει) us and which we draw in by means of respiration (Sext. Emp., *Adv. Math.* vii.127).

2 *De anima* 408*b*1.

3 *De anima* 410*a*25: Those who make soul consist of all the elements, and who hold that like perceives and knows like, "assume that perceiving is a sort of being acted upon or moved and that the same is true of thinking and knowing" (τὸ Δ' αἰσθάνεσθαι πάσχειν τι καὶ κινεῖσθαι τιθέασιν· ὁμοίως δὲ καὶ τὸ *νοεῖν* τε καὶ γιγνώσκειν).

All such action, moreover, was held to require a continuous vehicle or medium, uniting the soul which knows to the object which is known. Further, the soul and its object must not only be thus linked in physical contact, but they must be *alike* or *akin*....

It follows from this principle that, if the Soul is to know the world, the world must ultimately consist of the same substance as Soul. Φύσις and Soul must be homogeneous. Aristotle formulates the doctrine with great precision:

The texts on this and the facing page are adapted from F.M. CORNFORD'S *From Religion to Philosophy: A Study in the Origins of Western Speculation* (London, 1912). Some of the Greek quotations have been extended, and some have been moved from the footnotes into the main text. This makes Cornford's prose seem more pedantic and less lucid than it really is, but it poses a harder test for the type and at the same time permits a more compact typographic demonstration.

ὅσοι δ' ἐπὶ τὸ γινώσκειν καὶ τὸ αἰσθάνεσθαι τῶν ὄντων, οὗτοι δὲ λέγουσι τὴν ψυχὴν τὰς ἀρχάς, οἱ μὲν πλείους ποιοῦντες, ταύτας, οἱ δὲ μίαν, ταύτην, ὥσπερ Ἐμπεδοκλῆς μὲν ἐκ τῶν στοιχείων πάντων, εἶναι δὲ καὶ ἕκαστον ψυχὴν τούτων, λέγων οὕτως

γαίῃ μὲν γὰρ γαῖαν ὀπώπαμεν, ὕδατι δ' ὕδωρ,
αἰθέρι δ' αἰθέρα δῖαν, ἀτὰρ πυρὶ πῦρ αΐδηλον,
στοργῇ δὲ στοργήν, νεῖκος δέ τε νείκεϊ λυγρῷ.

τὸν αὐτὸν δὲ τρόπον καὶ Πλάτων ἐν τῷ Τιμαίῳ τὴν ψυχὴν ἐκ τῶν στοιχείων ποιεῖ· γιγνώσκεσθαι γὰρ τῷ ὁμοίῳ τὸ ὅμοιον, τὰ δὲ πράγματα ἐκ τῶν ἀρχῶν εἶναι.

«Those who laid stress on its knowledge and perception of all that exists, identified the soul with the ultimate principles, whether they recognized a plurality of these or only one. Thus, Empedocles compounded soul out of all the elements, while at the same time regarding each one of them as a soul. His words are,

«*With earth we see earth, with water water,*
«*with air bright air, ravaging fire by fire,*
«*love by love, and strife by gruesome strife.*

«In the same manner, Plato in the *Timaeus* constructs the soul out of the elements. Like, he there maintains, is known by like, and the things we know are composed of the ultimate principles....»[4]

4 *De anima* 404b8–18.

These lines are from §5 of Anna Akhmatova's В сороковом году.

Но я предупреждаю вас,

But I'm warning you,

Что я живу в последний раз.

this is my last existence.

Ни ласточкой, ни кленом,

Not as a swallow, not as a maple,

Ни тростником и ни звездой ...

not as a cat-tail and not as a star ...

The words of Anna Akhmatova in the letters of Vadim Lazurski. The type is Lazurski Cyrillic with its companion roman.

Greek letters, like Greek words, are used for many purposes in non-Greek-speaking countries. Physicists and fraternity members, astronomers and novelists have raided the old alphabet for symbols. Because of their frequent use in mathematics and technical writing, a grab-bag of Greek letters lurks somewhere in nearly every digital typesetting system. α, β, γ, θ, π, Ω (alpha, beta, gamma, theta, pi, cap omega) and their brethren are usually housed, with other mathematical symbols, in a ghetto called the pi font. But setting Greek *text* with such a font is not a thankful task. Pi fonts lack the breathing marks and accents used in the classical language, and even the two simple diacritics (acute and diaeresis) that survive in modern Greek; and some pi fonts include only ten Greek caps – Γ Δ Θ Λ Ξ Π Σ Φ Ψ Ω – because the others – Α Β Ε Η Ζ Ι Κ Μ Ν Ο Ρ Τ Υ Χ – have familiar roman forms, though not in every case the same phonetic value.

A text that includes even a single Greek quotation calls for a Greek text font rather than a pi font. A text font will include not only the full alphabet but matching punctuation and all the monotonic (modern) or polytonic (classical) diacritics. It will include two forms of lowercase sigma (ς, used at the ends of words, and σ, used everywhere else). If it is a polytonic font, it will include in addition three sets of long vowels with iota subscripts (ᾄ, ῇ, ῲ, etc). With luck, the font will include a sensible kerning table as well. This is a lot to ask from an industry in which there is, officially, no culture other than commerce and no purpose except monetary gain. It is a lot to ask, but not by itself enough. In Greek as in any other alphabet, *the face must suit the text.* It must also suit the context, which is likely to be roman and italic.

There may be 60,000 fonts of type for the Latin alphabet now on the market in digital form. These comprise some 7,000 families. Perhaps two per cent of them are truly useful for text work – but a hundred families of type is still a very generous number, and the available text faces cover a wide stylistic range. With a little scrounging, one can turn up several dozen digital fonts of Greek – but again, only a small percentage of these have any real potential for text work. It is therefore often best to choose a Greek font *first,* and then a roman and italic to go with it, even when only a few Greek words or a single Greek quotation is present in the text you are going to set.

Two Greek text fonts with eminent credentials – Victor Scholderer's New Hellenic, designed in 1927, and Richard Porson's Porson, designed in 1806 – are shown, in their digital incarnations, on pages 108–109. Porson's Greek was first commissioned by Cambridge University Press, but it became in the twentieth century the favorite Greek at Oxford, while Scholderer's New Hellenic became the favorite Cambridge Greek. New Hellenic in particular has an eminent Renaissance pedigree further discussed in §11.7.

ἄβγ

ἄβγ

6.6.2 *Match the continuity of the typography to the continuity of thought.*

A text composed in a single dialect may be full of leaps and holes, while a text that hops and skips through several languages and alphabets may in fact be tracing a path that is perfectly smooth. The continuity, or lack of continuity, that underlies the text should as a rule be revealed, not concealed, in the cloth the typographer weaves.

An author who quotes Greek or Hebrew or Russian or Arabic fluently and gracefully in speech should be permitted to do likewise on the page. Practically speaking, this means that when the alphabets are mixed, they should be very closely balanced both in *color* and in *contrast.*

abyohi ἄβγοθι *abyohi*

abyohi ἄβγοθι *abyohi*

Mixing Alphabets

abyohi ἄβγοθι *abyohi*

Victor Scholderer's New Hellenic paired with José Mendoza's Mendoza (above), with Peter Matthias Noordzij's Caecilia (center) and with Adobe Jenson (below). Mendoza is a face with very low contrast (the thicks and thins are nearly the same). New Hellenic and Caecilia have an unmodulated stroke – in other words, no contrast at all. New Hellenic and Adobe Jenson have stylistic compatibility of a different kind. Both stem from the work of Nicolas Jenson, who in 1469 cut the father of this roman and in 1471 the grandfather of this Greek.

Flow and *slope* are other factors to consider, especially when balancing Latin and Greek. Many Greek text faces (the Porson and Didot Greeks for example) are structurally comparable to italics. That is, they are cursive. Some of them are upright nonetheless (like the Didot), and some (like the Porson) slope. When roman, italic and Greek are combined on the page, the Greek may be upright like the roman, or it may harmonize with the italic in flow and slope. It may also stand aloof, with a gait and inclination of its own.

6.6.3 *Balance the type optically more than mathematically.*

Two other factors of importance when types sit side by side are their *torso* (x-height) and *extension.* When a long-limbed Greek is paired with a short-limbed Latin, the difference will stand out. Large disparities in x-height are far more obvious still. In metal, this is a harsh typographic constraint. In the digital medium, it is easy to match the torso of any Greek face to that of any Latin face exactly, through microscopic adjustments in size. But an optical, not mathematical, match is the goal. Classical Greek, beneath its cloud of diacritics, needs more room to breathe than roman type. And when setting Greek in footnotes, the minimum practical size is the size at which the accents are still legible.

abyohi ἄβγοθι *abyohi*

abyohi ἄβγοθι abyohi

abyohi ἄβγοϑι *abyohi*

Above: The Greek of Richard Porson paired with W. A. Dwiggins's Electra. *Center*: Didot Greek paired with Adobe Caslon. *Below*: The Bodoni Greek of Takis Katsoulides paired with the Esprit roman and italic of Jovica Veljović. Electra italic and Porson Greek both have a slope of 10°, while the Caslon italic slopes at 20°. Porson, with its rationalist axis, also has a structural kinship to Electra. The Didot Greek, though Neoclassical in form, is closer in color to Caslon. Katsoulides's more playful Bodoni Greek is closer both in structure and in spirit to Esprit.

The type on page 109 looked fine when it was first roughed out in bald Greek letters identical in x-height to the roman. When the bald sorts were replaced with accented letters, the Greek was still mathematically correct but optically too large. Balance was restored by shrinking the Greek from 11 to 10.5 pt. The x-height of the type is (as usual in a Neoclassical text face) only about two fifths of the body size. The difference in x-height between 10.5 and 11 pt type is accordingly two fifths of half a point. That is roughly 70 µm, which is less than 0.003 inch. Not much, but enough to unbalance or balance the page.

6.7 NEW ORTHOGRAPHIES

No writing system is fixed. Even our ways of writing classical Latin and Greek continue to change, along with our ways of writing and spelling such rapidly mutating languages as English. But many languages old to speech are new to writing, and many have not yet decided their literate form.

In North America, for example, Navajo, Hopi, Tlingit, Cree, Ojibwa, Inuktitut and Cherokee, among others, have evolved quite stable writing systems, in which a substantial printed literature has accrued. But many Native American languages are still being written in different ways by every scholar and student who happens by. Some, like Tsimshian, Fox and Kwakwala, already possess a considerable written literature, but in cumbersome scripts that even scholars have ceased to use.

Typographers must generally confront these problems piecemeal. Alphabets are often created by fiat, but it is usually in tiny increments that real typographic style evolves.

New Orthographies

đ ğ
Ђ љ
ڤ ڗ

6.7.1 *Add no unnecessary characters.*

Colonial expansion has carried the Arabic alphabet across the north of Africa and much of southern Asia, Cyrillic script across the north of Asia, and the Latin alphabet around the world. For better or for worse, most of those learning to read and write in newly literate languages are exposed to writing in a colonial language first. For readers and typographers alike, the basic Latin, Cyrillic or Arabic alphabet is therefore often the easiest place to start, and the fewer additional symbols required the better. The dream of a common language, imposed upon many minority cultures, has proven for most to be a nightmare. But in a world where there are hundreds of ancestral and classical languages and literatures instead of one or two, prayers for renewed diversification often entail the dream of a common script.

> Wa′giên sq!ê′ñgua lā′na hîn sā′wan, "K!wa la t!āla′ñ ł gia′ḷītc!în."

> Wagyaan sqqinggwa llaana hin saawan, "Kkwa lla ttaalang hl gyadliittsin."

A sentence in the Haida language, in the earliest standard orthography (first used in 1900) and a more recent, simplified version. In the former, glottalized consonants are marked by exclamations and long vowels by macrons. In the latter, both are notated by doubling. (Translation: *Then the one in the bow said, 'Let us take it aboard.'*)

6.7.2 *Add only characters that are visually distinct.*

The texture of the typographic page depends not only on how the type is designed, set and printed, but also on the frequency of different letters. Latin looks smoother than English (and much smoother than German) because it uses fewer ascending and descending letters, no accented characters, and (in the hands of most editors) very few caps. Polynesian languages – Maori and Hawaiian, for example – which are long on vowels and short on consonants, compose into a texture even creamier than Latin, and require an even smaller alphabet.

Most languages need more, not fewer, consonants than the basic Latin alphabet provides. There may be (as in Haida and Tlingit) four forms of *k*, or (as in the Khoisan languages of southwest Africa) 36 different clicks – and if each is lexically significant, each needs a distinctive typographic form.

Vowels are fairly easy to elaborate when need be; except for the y, they have no extenders. Navajo, for example, involves twelve forms of *a* – a, aa, ą, ąą, á, áá, áa, aá, ą́, ą́ą́, ą́ą, ąą́ – all easily distinguished. Typographically, it would be no problem to add another dozen forms.

In the Navajo alphabet (*saad bee 'ál'íní*), long vowels are written double and nasal vowels are written with an ogonek. High tone is marked with an acute. Long high vowels carry two acutes, one on each vowel. Long falling vowels carry an acute on the first vowel only, long rising vowels carry an acute on the second vowel only. Glottalized (ejective) consonants are followed by apostrophes.

Consonants are not quite so easy to ramify, just because so many have extenders. Typographically deficient forms therefore often crop up. Lakhota, for example – the language of the Sioux – requires two forms of *h*. The missionary Stephen Riggs, who published the first Lakhota dictionary and grammar in 1852, chose to mark the second form with an overdot: *ḣ*. This character is easily mistaken for *li*. More recent Lakhota orthographies (including the Txakini system, developed by Violet Catches, a native speaker) replace Riggs's dotted *h* with *x*. This is easier to type. More importantly, it is harder to misread.

In the Tlingit language, spoken and written in southern Alaska, northern British Columbia and the Yukon, underscores are used to mark uvular consonants, which is fine for k̲ and x̲, but maybe not so fine for g̲. A form like ġ or ğ or ḡ, though less consistent, is more compact and, once again, harder to misread.

The desire for consistency was not the only factor that led earlier linguists to write g̲ instead of ğ. The Tlingit alphabet was developed, like many early twentieth-century writing systems, using only the keyboard of a North American typewriter. Recent Tlingit publications are typeset with computers using modified fonts of Palatino or Stone, but the iron metaphor of the typewriter has not yet loosed its hold.

Elsewhere in the world, the mechanical typewriter and letterpress are still economically viable tools – and this need not prevent new alphabet design. The Pan Nigerian face shown overleaf was cut and cast commercially for hand composition in 1983. Mechanical typewriters using a monospaced version of the font entered production in 1985. Digital versions now also exist.

àbɓcdɗeəẹ́fghiîịjkƙl
AƁCDƊEƎẸ́FGHIÎỊJKƘL
MNÒỌPRSṢTÛỤ̄VWYZ
mnòọprsṣtûụ̄vwyz

New Orthographies

Pan-Nigerian alphabet designed in 1983 by Hermann Zapf, in collaboration with Victor Manfredi. This normalizes the missionary orthographies that had been used for Hausa, Igbo, Yoruba, Edo, Fulfulde and several other Nigerian languages.

6.7.3 *Avoid capricious redefinition of familiar characters.*

Mayan languages have been written in roman script since the 1550s, but more than one orthography remains in use. Perhaps the oldest, based on the manuscript tradition of the *Popol Vuh,* uses the numerals 3 and 4 and the digraphs 4h and 4, [*including* the comma] to write glottalized consonants. The Quiché words for sun and moon, for example, can be written *k'ih* and *ic',* or *kkih* and *icc,* or *3ih* and *i4,* and the word for blood can be written *quit'z* or *quittz* or *qui4,.* In the final case – but not in any of the others – the comma is part of the word and not a mark of punctuation.

Though it is not as picturesque as Mayan hieroglyphs, this alphanumeric script appeals to some scholars and amateurs, perhaps because of its very strangeness. Typographically, it begs for clarification, either through the creation of unambiguous new symbols or through reversion to plain old roman letters (which is now a common practice).

6.7.4 *Don't mix faces haphazardly when specialized sorts are required.*

ʔaƛ'aqə́m is Upper Chehalis, meaning *you will emerge;* ɪntɚ-næʃənḷ fənɛɾɪks (*international phonetics*) is English.

If a text involves setting occasional words such as ʔaƛ'aqə́m or ɪntɚ-næʃənḷ fənɛɾɪks, it is best to plan for them from the beginning. Two standard phonetic alphabets are in use: the international (IPA) and the American. But the extra characters involved have been cut for only a few faces. (Lucida Sans, Stone and Times Roman are examples. Stone phonetic – which is used here – exists in both serifed and unserifed forms.) The typographer therefore has two choices: to set the entire text in a face for which matching phonetic characters are available, so that phonetic transcriptions can enter the text transparently and at will; or to set the main text in a suitably contrasting face, and switch to the phonetic font (along with its matching text font, if required) each time a phonetic transcription occurs.

If contrasting faces are used for phonetic transcriptions and main text, each entire phonetic word or passage, not just the individual phonetic characters, should be set in the chosen phonetic face. Patchwork typography, in which the letters of a single word come from different faces and fonts, is a sign of typographic failure. Forms such as 'θatθɛ̨łi' and 'ˀeθ̂ə́n heldéłi' (formerly employed in writing the Native Canadian language Chipewyan) or 'Θraētona' and 'Usaδan' (still used in writing the ancient language Avestan) are typographically problematic because they mix two alphabets *within a single word*. Such mixtures are almost sure to fail unless all the fonts involved have been designed as a single family. (Here they succeed, because a unified Latin and Greek are used.)

6.8 BUILDING A TYPE LIBRARY

6.8.1 *Choose your library of faces slowly and well.*

Some of the best typographers who ever lived had no more than one roman font at a time, one blackletter and one Greek. Others had as many as five or six romans, two or three italics, three blackletters, three or four Greeks. Today, the typographer can buy fonts by the thousand on compact discs, and use the telephone to download thousands more: more fonts than any human could use, yet never a complete selection.

With type as with philosophy, music and food, it is better to have a little of the best than to be swamped with the derivative, the careless, the routine.

The stock fonts supplied with software packages and desktop printers are sometimes generous in number, but they are the wrong fonts for many tasks and people, and most of them are missing essential parts (small caps, text figures, ligatures, diacritics and important analphabetics).

Begin by buying one good face or family, or a few related faces, with all the components intact. And instead of skipping from face to face, attempting to try everything, stay with your first choices long enough to learn their virtues and limitations before you move on.

AISC

HYLO

MWG

RUIX

PTEK

Carol Twombly's Lithos (1988) and Adrian Frutiger's Herculanum (1990) and Rusticana (1991) are typefaces based on early Mediterranean inscriptions. In this example, Lithos is printed solid, Herculanum with a medium screen, Rusticana with a light screen.

7

Printing from movable type was first invented not in Germany in the 1450s, as Europeans often claim, but in China in the 1040s. In preference to Gutenberg, we should honor a scholarly engineer by the name of Bí Shēng (畢昇). The earliest surviving works printed in Asia from movable type seem to date from the thirteenth century, but there is a clear account of the typesetting process, and Bí Shēng's role in its development, by the eleventh-century essayist Shěn Kuò (沈括).

Shěn Kuò's account is contained in his *Mèngxī Bǐtán* (夢溪筆談), "Dream Creek Essays." For more information in English, see Denis Twitchett, *Printing and Publishing in Medieval China* (1983) and Thomas F. Carter, *The Invention of Printing in China and Its Spread Westward*, 2nd ed. (1955).

The new technology reached Korea before the middle of the thirteenth century and Europe by the middle of the fifteenth. There it intersected the already long and fertile history of the roman letter. And there typesetting flourished as it had failed to do in China, because of the far smaller number of glyphs European scripts required. Even at the end of the nineteenth century, most printing in China was done by the same method used in the eighth century to make the first printed books: entire pages of text were carved by hand into wooden printing plates. Corrections were made by drilling out the error, installing a wooden plug, and cutting the new characters. Text, in other words, was treated just like woodcut illustrations. To this day, a page of type is known in Chinese as *huóbǎn* (活板), "a living plank."

7.1 THE EARLY SCRIBAL FORMS

The earliest surviving European letterforms are Greek capitals scratched into stone. The strokes are bony and thin, almost ethereal – the opposite of the heavy substance they are carved in. The letters are made primarily from straight lines, and when curved forms appear, they have a very large *aperture*. This means that forms like S and C and M, which can be relatively open or relatively closed, are about as open as they can get. These early Greek letters were drawn freehand, not constructed with compasses and rule, and they have no serifs – neither the informal entry and exit strokes left by a relaxed and fluent writer, nor the symmetrical finishing strokes typically added to letters by a formal scribe.

In time, the strokes of these letters grew thicker, the aperture lessened, and serifs appeared. The new forms, used for inscriptions throughout the Greek empire, served as models for formal lettering in imperial Rome. And those Roman inscriptional letters – written with a flat brush, held at an angle like a broadnib pen, then carved into the stone with mallet and chisel – have served in their turn as models for calligraphers and type designers for the past two thousand years. They have a modest aperture, a *modulated* stroke (a stroke whose thickness varies with direction), and they have lively but full and formal serifs.

The Early Scribal Forms

ABCSPQR

Trajan, designed by Carol Twombly in 1988, is based on the inscription at the base of Trajan's Column, Rome, carved in AD 113.

Between the Roman inscriptions and Gutenberg's time, there were many further changes in European letterforms. Narrow rustic capitals, wide uncials and other forms evolved. Writing spread to the farthest corners of Europe, and many regional scripts and alphabets arose. Monastic scribes – who were designers, copyists and archivists as well – kept many of the older letterforms alive. They used them for titles, subheads and initials, choosing newer and more compact scripts for running text. Out of this rich multiplicity of letters, a basic dichotomy evolved: *majuscules* and *minuscules*: large formal letters and smaller, more casual ones: the upper and lower case, as we call them now.

CAROLUS MAGNUS
Caroline or Carolingian means of the time
of the Emperor Charlemagne: «Big Charles».

Carol Twombly's Charlemagne (above), Gudrun Zapf-von Hesse's Alcuin (center) and Gottfried Pott's Carolina (below) are typefaces based on Carolingian majuscules and minuscules from ninth- and tenth-century European manuscripts.

Many of the old scribal conventions survive in typesetting today. Titles are still set in large, formal letters; large initials mark the beginnings of chapters or sections; small capitals mark an opening phrase. The well-made page is now what it was then: a window into history, language and the mind: a map of what is being said and a portrait of the voice that is silently speaking.

In the later Middle Ages and the early Renaissance, a well-trained European scribe might know eight or ten distinct styles of script. Each was defined as precisely as a typeface, stored like a font in the human memory, and each had certain uses. Sacred scriptures, legal documents, romance literature, business and personal letters all required different scripts, and particular forms evoked specific languages and regions.

Historical Interlude

When the technology of movable type arrived, Europe was rich with Gothic, Byzantine, Romanesque and humanistic hands, and with a wealth of older letters. They are all still with us in some way, but the humanistic hand, based on the Carolingian minuscule, has become the central form: the roman lower case, evolving into a thousand variations, sports and hybrids, like the willow or the rose.

7.2 THE TYPOGRAPHIC LATIN LETTER

Several systems are in use for classifying typefaces. Some of them use fabricated terms such as 'garalde' and 'didone.' Others rely on familiar but vague labels such as 'old style,' 'modern' and 'transitional.' All these systems work to a certain extent, but all leave much to be desired. They are neither good science nor good history.

Rigorously scientific descriptions and classifications of typefaces are certainly possible, and important research has been under way in this field for several years. Like the scientific study of plants and animals, the infant science of typology involves precise measurement, close analysis, and the careful use of technically descriptive terms.

But letterforms are not only objects of science. They also belong to the realm of art, and they participate in its history. They have changed over time just as music, painting and architecture have changed, and the same historical terms – Renaissance, Baroque, Neoclassical, Romantic, and so on – are useful in each of these fields.

The art history of Latin letterforms is treated in greater detail in an incomplete series of essays in *Serif* magazine, issues 1–5 (1994–97).

This approach to the classification of letterforms has another important advantage. Typography never occurs in isolation. Good typography demands not only a knowledge of type itself, but an understanding of the relationship between letterforms and the other things that humans make and do. Typographic history is just that: the study of the relationships between type designs and the rest of human activity – politics, philosophy, the arts, and the history of ideas. It is a lifelong pursuit, but one that is informative and rewarding from the beginning.

7.2.1 *The Renaissance Roman Letter*

Renaissance roman letters developed among the scholars and scribes of northern Italy in the fourteenth and fifteenth centuries. Their translation from script to type began in Italy in 1465 and continued for more than a century. Like Renaissance painting and music, Renaissance letterforms are full of sensuous

abcefgnopj

abcefgnopj

abcefgnopj

abcefgnopj

Four twentieth-century reconstructions of Renaissance roman typefaces. Centaur (top) was designed by the American typographer Bruce Rogers, Boston, *c.* 1914, after Nicolas Jenson, Venice, 1469. Bembo (second) was cut by Monotype, London, in 1929, based on the design of Francesco Griffo, Venice, 1499. Adobe Garamond (third) was designed by Robert Slimbach, San Francisco, 1988, after Claude Garamond, Paris, *c.* 1540. DTL Van den Keere (bottom) is Frank Blokland's reconstruction of a font cut for Christophe Plantin by Hendrik van den Keere, Antwerp, in 1575.

and unhurried light and space. They have served as typographic benchmarks for five hundred years.

The earliest surviving roman punches or matrices may well be Garamond's, cut in Paris in the 1530s. For earlier type, we have no evidence beyond the printed books themselves. The basic structure and form of these early typefaces is clear beyond dispute, but in their subtlest details, all the existing replicas of fifteenth-century Italian type are hypothetical reconstructions.

Historical Interlude

Like Roman inscriptional capitals, Renaissance roman lowercase letters have a modulated stroke (the width varies with direction) and a *humanist* axis. This means that the letters have the form produced by a broadnib pen held in the right hand in a comfortable and relaxed writing position. The thick strokes run NW/SE, the axis of the writer's hand and forearm. The serifs are crisp, the stroke is light, and the contrast between thick strokes and thin strokes is generally modest.

In summary, the characteristics of the early Renaissance roman letter are these:

- *stems vertical*
- *bowls nearly circular*
- *modulated stroke*
- *consistent humanist axis*
- *modest contrast*
- *modest x-height*
- *crisp, oblique head serifs (on letters such as* b *and* r*)*
- *abrupt, flat or slightly splayed bilateral foot serifs (on letters such as* r, l *and* p*)*
- *abrupt, pen-formed terminals on* a, c, f *and* r
- *rising crossbar in* e, *perpendicular to the stroke axis*
- *the roman font is solitary (there is no italic or bold)*

In later Renaissance forms (from 1500 on), the letterforms grow softer, smoother and more self-contained in subtle ways:

- *head serifs become more wedge-shaped*
- *foot serifs become adnate (flowing smoothly into the stem) instead of abrupt*
- *terminals of* c, f *and* r *become less abrupt and more lachrymal (teardrop-shaped)*
- *crossbar of* e *becomes horizontal*

7.2.2 *The Renaissance Italic Letter*

Rome is located in the midst of Italy. Why is roman type a category separate from italic? It seems a question to which typographers might possess the answer. But the question and the answer both have as much to do with politics and religion as with calligraphy and typography.

Roman type consists of two quite different basic parts. The upper case, which does indeed come from Rome, is based on Roman imperial inscriptions. The lower case was developed in northern Europe, chiefly in France and Germany, in the late Middle Ages, and given its final polish in Venice in the early Renaissance. Nevertheless, it too is Roman in the larger sense. While the roman upper case is a legacy of the Roman Empire, the lower case is a legacy of the Holy Roman Empire, the pagan empire's Christianized successor. It acquired its fundamental form at the hands of Christian scribes, many of them employed during the late eighth century as administrators and teachers by the Holy Roman Emperor Charlemagne.

Italic letterforms, on the other hand, are an Italian Renaissance creation. Some early italics come from Rome, others from elsewhere in Italy, and when they were first converted to type, italics were still full of local flavor and freshness. But the earliest italic fonts, cut between 1500 and 1540, consist of lower case only. They were used with upright roman caps but not in conjunction with the roman lower case.

abcefgnopxyz

abcefgnopxyz

Two revivals of Renaissance italic type. Monotype Arrighi (above) is derived from one of a series of italics designed by Frederic Warde, London and Paris, 1925–29, after Ludovico degli Arrighi, Rome, 1524. Monotype Bembo italic (below) was cut in London in 1929, based on the work of both Arrighi and Giovanantonio Tagliente, Venice, 1524.

The characteristics of the Renaissance italic letter can be summarized as follows:

- *stems vertical or of fairly even slope, not exceeding 10°*
- *bowls generally elliptical*
- *light, modulated stroke*
- *consistent humanist axis*
- *low contrast*
- *modest x-height*
- *cursive forms with crisp, oblique entry and exit serifs*
- *descenders serifed bilaterally or not at all*
- *terminals abrupt or lachrymal*
- *italic lower case paired with small, upright roman capitals, and with occasional swash capitals; italic otherwise fully independent of roman*

Early Renaissance italics are known as *Aldine* italics, in honor of the scholar and publisher Aldus Manutius, who commissioned the first italic type from Francesco Griffo in 1499. Strange to say, in 2004, not a single authentic reconstruction of an Aldine italic appears to be on the market, in either metal or digital form. Monotype Bembo roman and Monotype Poliphilus are both based on Griffo's work, but their companion italics are not; they come from a different age. The digital italic nearest to an Aldine in design is Giovanni Mardersteig's Dante italic, but even this has sloped instead of upright capitals.

See page 210 for reproductions of two Aldine italics.

ae

eQubdaffglopsspz

abefop*abefop*

Two recent typefaces in the Mannerist tradition. Poetica (above) is a chancery italic based on sixteenth-century models. It was designed by Robert Slimbach and issued by Adobe in 1992. Galliard (below), designed by Matthew Carter, was issued by Linotype in 1978. It is based on letterforms cut in the sixteenth century by Robert Granjon.

7.2.3 *The Mannerist Letter*

Mannerist art is Renaissance art to which subtle exaggerations – of length, angularity or tension, for example – have been added. Mannerist typographers, working chiefly in Italy and France early in the sixteenth century, began the practice of using roman and italic in the same book, and even on the same page – though rarely on the same line. It was also during the Mannerist period that sloped roman capitals were first added to the italic lower case.

There are many fine sixteenth-century examples of Mannerist typefaces, including roman titling fonts with long, delicate extenders, chancery italics with even longer and often ornamented extenders, and text faces with short extenders but increased tension in the forms. Digital interpretations of a number of these faces have recently been made. Two significant examples – one ornate and one restrained – are shown overleaf.

abefop *abefop*

abefop *abefop*

abefop *abefop*

abefop *abefop*

Four revivals of Baroque typefaces. Monotype 'Garamond' (top) is based on fonts cut in France by Jean Jannon, about 1621. DTL Elzevir (second) is based on fonts cut by Christoffel van Dijck at Amsterdam in the 1660s. Linotype Janson Text (third) is based on fonts cut by Miklós Kis, Amsterdam, about 1685. Adobe Caslon (bottom), by Carol Twombly, is based on faces cut by William Caslon, London, in the 1730s.

7.2.4 *The Baroque Letter*

Baroque typography, like Baroque painting and music, is rich with activity and takes delight in the restless and dramatic play of contradictory forms. One of the most obvious features of any Baroque typeface is the large *variation in axis* from one letter to the next. Baroque italics are *ambidextrous*: both right- and lefthanded. And it was during the Baroque that typographers first made a habit of mixing roman and italic *on the same line.*

Historical Interlude

In general, Baroque letterforms appear more modeled and less *written* than Renaissance forms. They give less evidence of the direct trace of the pen. Yet they take many different forms, and they thrived in Europe throughout the seventeenth century, endured through much of the eighteenth, and enjoyed an enthusiastic revival during the nineteenth.

Baroque letterforms generally differ from Renaissance letters in the following ways:

- *stroke axis of the roman and italic lower case varies widely within a single alphabet*
- *slope of italic averages 15° to 20° and often varies considerably within a single alphabet*
- *contrast increased*
- *x-height increased*
- *aperture generally reduced*
- *further softening of terminals from abrupt to lachrymal*
- *roman head serifs become sharp wedges*
- *head serifs of italic ascenders become level and sharp*

7.2.5 *The Rococo Letter*

The historical periods listed here – Renaissance, Baroque and so on – belong to all the arts, and they are naturally not limited, in typography, to roman and italic letters. Blackletter and script types passed through the same phases as well. But the Rococo period, with its love of florid ornament, belongs almost entirely to blackletters and scripts.

Roman and italic type was certainly used by Rococo typographers, who often surrounded their texts with typographic ornaments, engraved medallions, and so on. They produced a good deal of Rococo *typography*, but not much Rococo roman and italic *type*. Several romans and italics that might indeed be classified abcefgnopy

CEFOTZ

abcefgnopy

DTL Fleischmann. Note the ornate forms of *g*, *y* and several of the capitals, and the exaggerated contrast in italic *o*. This exaggerated contrast is typical of the Romantic types cut by Firmin Didot and Giambattista Bodoni after Fleischman's death in 1768. But Romantic types have an obsessively vertical axis. The primary axis of Fleischman's type is oblique. Structurally, these letters belong to the Baroque. But their tendency to ornamentation and exaggeration sets them apart from earlier Baroque types. That is a reason for calling them Rococo.

Though he was born and trained in Germany, Fleischman moved to the Netherlands before his 30th birthday and remained there the rest of his life. *Fleischmann* is the German spelling of his name; the Dutch form *Fleischman* is the one he chose to use in all his published specimens. The digital versions of Fleischman's type, published in the Netherlands, were created by the German type designer Erhard Kaiser, who christened them *Fleischmann.*

as Rococo were, however, cut in Amsterdam in 1738–39 by the German-born punchcutter Johann Michael Fleischman. Digital versions of these fonts have recently been released by the Dutch Type Library in 's-Hertogenbosch.

7.2.6 *The Neoclassical Letter*

Generally speaking, Neoclassical art is more static and restrained than either Renaissance or Baroque art, and far more interested in rigorous consistency. Neoclassical letterforms follow this pattern. In Neoclassical letters, an echo of the broadnib pen can still be seen, but it is rotated away from the natural writing angle to a strictly vertical or *rationalist* axis. The letters are moderate in contrast and aperture, but their axis is dictated by an idea, not by the truth of human anatomy. They are products of the Rationalist era: frequently beautiful, calm forms, but forms oblivious to the more complex beauty of organic fact. If Baroque letterforms are ambidextrous, Neoclassical letters are, in their quiet way, *neitherhanded.*

abefop*abefop*
abefop*abefop*
abefop*abefop*

Three twentieth-century revivals of Neoclassical letterforms. *Above*: Monotype Fournier, which is based on types cut by Pierre Simon Fournier, Paris, about 1740. *Center*: Monotype Baskerville, which is based on the designs of John Baskerville, Birmingham, about 1754. *Below*: Monotype Bell, based on the types cut in London in 1788 by Richard Austin for the typefounder and publisher John Bell.

The first Neoclassical typeface, known as the *romain du roi* or King's Roman, was designed in France in the 1690s, not by a typographer but by a government committee consisting of two priests, an accountant and an engineer. Other Neoclassical faces were designed and cut in France, England, Italy and Spain during the eighteenth and nineteenth centuries, and some of them have remained in continuous use throughout all subsequent changes of style and fashion.

The American printer and statesman Benjamin Franklin deeply admired the Neoclassical type of his English contemporary John Baskerville, and it is partly due to Franklin's support that Baskerville's type became more important in the United States and France than it ever was in Baskerville's native land. But the connection between Baskerville and America rests on more than Benjamin Franklin's personal taste. Baskerville's letters correspond very closely to the federal style in American architecture. They are as purely and unperturbably Neoclassical as the Capitol Building, the White House, and many another federal and state edifice. (The Houses of Parliament in London and in Ottawa, which are Neogothic instead of Neoclassical, call for typography of a different kind.)

In brief, Neoclassical letterforms differ from Baroque letters as follows:

- *predominantly vertical axis in both roman and italic*
- *slope of italic generally uniform, averaging 14° to 16°*
- *serifs generally adnate, but thinner, flatter, more level*

7.2.7 *The Romantic Letter*

Neoclassicism and Romanticism are not sequential movements in European history. They marched through the eighteenth century and much of the nineteenth side by side: vigorously opposed in some respects and closely united in others. Both Neoclassical and Romantic letterforms adhere to a rationalist axis, and both look more drawn than written, but it is possible to make some precise distinctions between the two. The most obvious difference is one of contrast. In Romantic letters we will normally find the following:

- *abrupt modulation of the stroke*
- *vertical axis intensified through exaggerated contrast*
- *hardening of terminals from lachrymal to round*
- *serifs thinner and more abrupt*
- *aperture reduced*

This remarkable shift in type design – like *all* structural shifts in type design – is the record of an underlying change in handwriting. Romantic letters are forms from which the broadnib pen has vanished. In its place is the pointed and flexible quill. The broadnib pen produces a smoothly modulated stroke whose thickness varies with direction, but the pointed quill performs quite differently. The stroke of a flexible quill shifts suddenly from thin to thick to thin again, in response to changes in pressure. Used with restraint, it produces a Neoclassical flourish. Used with greater force, it produces a more dramatic and Romantic one. Dramatic contrast, which is essential to much Romantic music and painting, is essential to Romantic type design as well.

Romantic letters can be extraordinarily beautiful, but they lack the flowing and steady rhythm of Renaissance forms. It is that rhythm which invites the reader to enter the text and read. The statuesque forms of Romantic letters invite the reader to stand outside and *look* at the letters instead.

abefop *abefop*

abefop *abefop*

abefop *abefop*

abefop *abefop*

Four revivals of Romantic letterforms. Monotype Bulmer (top) is based on a series of fonts William Martin cut in London in the early 1790s. Linotype Didot (second), drawn by Adrian Frutiger, is based on fonts Firmin Didot cut in Paris between 1799 and 1811. Bauer Bodoni (third) is based on fonts cut by Giambattista Bodoni at Parma between 1803 and 1812. Berthold Walbaum (bottom) is based on types cut by Justus Erich Walbaum, Weimar, about 1805.

7.2.8 *The Realist Letter*

The nineteenth and twentieth centuries have entertained a bewildering variety of artistic movements and schools – Realism, Naturalism, Impressionism, Expressionism, Art Nouveau, Art Deco, Constructivism, Cubism, Abstract Expressionism, Pop Art, Op Art, and many more. Virtually all of these movements have raised waves in the typographic world as well, though not all are important enough to merit a place in this brief survey. One of these movements – one which has not by any means yet expired – is typographic Realism.

The Realist painters of the nineteenth century – Gustave Courbet, François Millet and many others – turned their backs on the subjects and poses approved by the academy. They set out instead to paint ordinary people doing their ordinary tasks. Realist type designers – Alexander Phemister, Robert Besley

abcefgnop
abcefgnop

Akzidenz Grotesk (above) is a Realist typeface issued by the Berthold Foundry, Berlin, in 1898. It is the immediate ancestor of Morris Benton's Franklin Gothic (1903) and of Helvetica, issued by the Haas Foundry in 1952. Haas Clarendon (below), designed in 1951 by Hermann Eidenbenz, is a revival of an earlier Realist face, the first Clarendon, cut by Benjamin Fox for Robert Besley, London, 1845.

and others, who have not achieved the posthumous fame of the painters – worked in a similar spirit. They made blunt and simple letters, based on the script of people denied the opportunity to learn to read and write with fluency and poise. Realist letters very often have the same basic shape as Neoclassical and Romantic letters, but most of them have heavy, slab serifs or no serifs at all. The stroke is often uniform in weight, and the aperture (often a gauge of grace or good fortune in typefaces) is tiny. Small caps, text figures and other signs of sophistication and elegance are almost always missing.

7.2.9 *Geometric Modernism: The Distillation of Function*

Early modernism took many intriguing typographic forms. One of the most obvious is geometric. The sparest, most rigorous architecture of the early twentieth century has its counterpart in the equally geometric typefaces designed at the same time, often by the same people. These typefaces, like their Realist predecessors, make no distinction between main stroke and serif. Their serifs are equal in weight with the main strokes or are missing altogether. But most Geometric Modernist faces seek purity more than populism. Some show the study of archaic inscriptions, and some include text figures and other subtleties, but their shapes owe more to pure mathematical forms – the circle and the line – than to scribal letters.

abcefgnop
abcefgnop

Two Geometric Modernist typefaces. Futura (above) was designed in Germany in 1924–26 by Paul Renner. Memphis (below) was designed in 1929 by Rudolf Wolf, art director at the Stempel Foundry. The original design for Futura included text figures and many highly geometric, alternative characters which have never been issued in metal, though The Foundry (London) issued them in digital form in 1994.

abefop*abefop*
abefop*abefop*
abefop*abefop*
abefop*abefop*

Four neohumanist or Lyrical Modernist typefaces. Spectrum (top) was designed by Jan van Krimpen in the Netherlands during the 1940s and issued by both Enschedé and Monotype in 1952. Palatino (second) was designed by Hermann Zapf, Frankfurt, 1948. Dante (third) was designed by Giovanni Mardersteig, Verona, 1952. Pontifex (bottom) was designed by Friedrich Poppl, Wiesbaden, 1974. All but the last were originally cut by hand in steel, just like Renaissance faces.

7.2.10 *Lyrical Modernism: The Rediscovery of Humanist Form*

Another major phase of modernism in type design is closely allied with abstract expressionist painting. Painters in the twentieth century rediscovered the physical and sensory pleasures of painting as an act, and the pleasures of making organic instead of mechanical forms. Designers of type during those years were equally busy rediscovering the pleasures of *writing* letterforms rather than drawing them. In rediscovering calligraphy, they rediscovered the broadnib pen, the humanist axis and humanist scale of Renaissance letters. Typographic modernism is fundamentally the reassertion of Renaissance form. There is no hard line between modernist design and Renaissance revival.

7.2.11 *The Expressionist Letter*

In yet another of its aspects, typographic modernism is rough and concrete more than lyrical and abstract. Rudolf Koch, Vojtěch Preissig and Oldřich Menhart are three designers who explored this path in the early part of the twentieth century. They are in some respect the typographic counterparts of expressionist painters such as Vincent van Gogh and Oskar Kokoschka. More recent painters and type designers, such as Zuzana Ličko, have proven that the genre is still richly productive.

Expressionist designers use many different tools. Koch and Preissig often cut their own letters in metal or wood. Menhart worked with a pen and rough paper. Ličko has exploited the

abcefghijop

abefop*abefop*

Two Expressionist types – one Modernist and one Postmodern. Preissig (above) was designed in New York in 1924 by the Czech artist Vojtěch Preissig. It was cut and cast in Prague in 1925. Zuzana Ličko's Journal (below) was designed in Berkeley in 1990 and issued in digital form by Emigre.

harsh economies of digital plotting routines, slicing from control point to control point not with a knife, file or chisel but with digitized straight lines.

7.2.12 *Elegiac Postmodernism*

Historical Interlude

Modernism in type design has its roots in the study of history, the facts of human anatomy, and in the pleasures of calligraphy. Like the Renaissance itself, modernism is more than a phase or fad that simply runs its course and expires. It remains very much alive in the arts generally and in type design in particular, though it no longer seems the final word. In the last decades of the twentieth century, critics of architecture, literature and music – along with others who study human affairs – all perceived movements away from modernism. Lacking any proper name of their own, these movements have come to be called by the single term postmodernism. And postmodernism is as evident in the world of type design as it is in other fields.

Postmodern letterforms, like Postmodern buildings, frequently recycle and revise Neoclassical, Romantic and other premodern forms. At their best, they do so with an engaging lightness of touch and a fine sense of humor. Postmodern art is for the most part highly self-conscious, but devoutly unserious. Postmodern designers – who frequently are or have been Modernist designers as well – have proven that it is possible to infuse Neoclassical and Romantic form, and the rationalist axis, with genuine calligraphic energy.

abefop *abefop*

abefop *abefop*

Two Postmodern faces. Esprit (above) was designed by Jovica Veljović, Beograd, 1985. Nofret (below) was designed by Gudrun Zapf-von Hesse, Darmstadt, 1990. Both types sing, where many Postmodern faces merely screech. But the song is elegiac more than lyrical.

abefop*abefop*

abefop*abefop*

Two Geometric Postmodern faces: Triplex Sans (above) and Officina Serif (below). Triplex italic was designed by John Downer in 1985. Its companion romans – one with serifs, one without – were designed by Zuzana Ličko in 1989–90, and the full *ménage à trois* was issued in 1990 by Emigre. Officina (ITC, 1990) was designed by Erik Spiekermann. It has been issued in both serifed and unserifed versions.

7.2.13 *Geometric Postmodernism*

Some Postmodern faces are highly geometric. Like their predecessors the Geometric Modernist faces, they are usually slab-serifed or unserifed, but often they exist in both varieties at once or are hybrids of the two. They are rarely, it seems, based on the pure and simple line and circle, but almost always on more mannered, often asymmetric forms. And like other Postmodern types, they are rich with nostalgia for something premodern. Many of these faces are indebted to older industrial letterforms, including typewriter faces and the ubiquitous factory folk-art of North American highway signs. They recycle and revise not Romantic and Neoclassical but Realist ideas. To this industrial unpretentiousness, however, they often add not only Postmodern humor but also the fruits of typographic sophistication: text figures, small caps, large aperture, and subtle modeling and balancing of forms.

Postmodern art, like Neoclassical art, is above all an art of the surface: an art of reflections rather than visions. It has thrived in the depthless world of high-speed offset printing and digital design, where modernism starves. But the world of the scribes, in which the craft of type design is rooted, was a depthless world too. It was the world of the Gothic painters, in which everything is present in one plane. In that respect at least, postmodernism and modernism alike confront the basic task with which typography began. That is the task of answering in two (or little more than two) dimensions to a world that has many.

7.3 MECHANICAL TYPESETTING

7.3.1 *The Linotype Machine*

The Linotype machine, invented in the 1880s by Ottmar Mergenthaler and much modified over the years, is a kind of cross between a casting machine, a typewriter, a vending machine and a backhoe. It consists of a series of slides, belts, wheels, lifts, vises, plungers and screws, controlled from a large mechanical keyboard. Its complex mechanism composes a line of matrices, justifies the line by sliding tapered wedges into the spaces between the words, then casts the entire line as a single metal slug for letterpress printing.

For a detailed account of the growth of mechanized typesetting, see Richard E. Huss, *The Development of Printers' Mechanical Typesetting Methods 1822–1925* (1973).

Typeface design for the Linotype was restricted by three basic factors. First, kerning is impossible without special compound matrices. (The basic italic *f* in a Linotype font therefore always has a stunted head and tail.) Second, the em is divided into only 18 units, which discourages subtlety of proportion. Third, the italic and roman matrices are usually paired. In most faces, each italic letter must therefore have the same width as its counterpart in roman.

A number of typefaces designed for the Linotype were artistically successful in spite of these constraints. Hermann Zapf's Aldus and Optima, Rudolph Růžička's Fairfield, Sem Hartz's Juliana, and W.A. Dwiggins's Electra, Caledonia and Falcon were all designed for the Linotype machine. Linotype Janson, adapted by Zapf in 1952 from the seventeenth-century originals of Miklós Kis, is another eminent success. Many Linotype faces have nevertheless been modified in the course of digitization, to make use of the kerning capabilities of digital machines and restore the independent proportioning of roman and italic.

7.3.2 *The Monotype Machine*

In 1887, in competition with Mergenthaler, Tolbert Lanston created a machine that stamped individual letters in cold metal and assembled them into lines. This device was soon abandoned for another – built in 1900 by Lanston's colleague John Bancroft – that cast individual letters from molten metal rather than cold-stamping them. It was soon sold worldwide as the Monotype machine. It is two machines in fact, a terminal and an output device, and in this respect resembles most computer-driven typesetting machines. But the Monotype terminal carries a large mechanical keyboard, including seven full alphabets as well as analphabetics. The keyboard punches holes in a paper tape, like a narrow player-piano roll, by driving pins with compressed air. The output device is the caster, which reads the paper tape by blowing more compressed air through the punched holes, then casts and assembles the letters.

The Monotype em, like the Linotype em, is divided into only 18 units, but italic and roman are independent in width, kerning is possible, and because the type remains in the form of separate letters, typeset lines can be further adjusted by hand. Characters larger than 24 pt are cast individually and left for hand assembly. In fact, the Monotype machine is a portable typefoundry as much as it is a composing machine – and it is increasingly used as such, even though its unit system imposes restrictions on letterform design, and it is incapable of casting in hard metal.

7.3.3 *Two-Dimensional Printing*

From the middle of the fifteenth century to the middle of the twentieth, most roman letters were printed by a technique rooted in sculpture. In this process, each letter is carved at actual size on the end of a steel punch. The punch is then struck into a matrix of softer metal, the matrix is fitted into a mold, and three-dimensional metal type is cast from an alloy of lead, tin and antimony. The cast letters are locked in a frame and placed in a printing press, where they are inked. Their image is then imprinted *into* the paper, producing a tactile and visual image. The color and sheen of the ink join with the smooth texture of crushed paper, recessed into the whiter and rougher fibers surrounding the letters and lines. A book produced by this means is a folding inscription, a flexible sculpture in low relief. The black light of the text *shines out from within* a well-printed letterpress page.

Renaissance typographers reveled in the physical depth and texture they could achieve by this method of printing. Neoclassical and Romantic printers, like Baskerville, often took a different view. Baskerville printed his sheets by letterpress – since he had no other method – but then had them ironed like laundry to remove the sculptural tinge.

With the development of lithography, at the end of the eighteenth century, printing moved another step back toward the two-dimensional world of the medieval scribes. Since the middle of the twentieth century, most commercial printing has been by two-dimensional means. The normal method is offset photolithography, in which a photographic or digital image is etched into a plate, inked, *offset* to a smooth intermediary blanket, then laid flat on the surface of the page.

In the early days of commercial offset printing, type was still set with Linotype or Monotype machines. Proofs were pulled in a letterpress, then cut, pasted and photographed. Type designers saw their work altered by this process. Most letters designed to be printed in three dimensions look weaker when printed in two. But other letters prospered: geometric letters, which evoked the world of the draftsman rather than the goldsmith, and flowing letters recalling the heritage of the scribe.

7.3.4 *Phototype Machines*

Light flashes through the image of a letter carried on glass or photographic film; the size of the letter is altered with a lens; its target location is fixed by a mirror, and it is exposed like any other photographic image onto photosensitive paper or film. Machines that operate on this principle are the natural children of the camera and the offset press. They were designed and patented in the 1890s and in regular use for setting titles and headlines by 1925, though it was not until the 1960s that they came to dominate the trade.

Just as the sophistication and subtlety of handset type seemed at first to be swept aside when composing machines appeared, so the sophistication slowly achieved with Linotype and Monotype machines seemed to be swept aside by this new technological wave. The photosetters were fast, but they knew nothing of subtle changes in proportion from size to size. Their fonts lacked ligatures, text figures and small caps. American-made fonts lacked even the simplest accented characters. The choice of faces was poor. And with the sudden, widespread use of these complex but simplistic machines came the final collapse of the old craft system of apprenticeships and guilds.

Phototypesetting machines and their users had only begun to answer these complaints when digital equipment arrived to replace them. Some excellent faces were designed for phototype machines – from Adrian Frutiger's Apollo (1962) to Bram de Does's Trinité (1982) – but in retrospect, the era of phototype seems only a brief interregnum between hot metal and digital composition. The important innovation of the period was not, after all, the conversion of fonts from metal to film, but the introduction of microcomputers to edit, compose and correct the text and to drive the last generations of photosetting machines.

7.3.5 *Historical Recutting and Twentieth-Century Design*

New typefaces have been designed in vast numbers in the past hundred years, and many old ones have been resuscitated. From 1960 to 1980, most new types and revivals were designed for photosetting, and since 1980, almost all have been planned for digital composition. But most of the older faces now sold in digital form have already passed through another stylistic filter. They were recut in the early twentieth century, either as foundry type or as matrices for the Monotype or Linotype machines. Typography was radically reformed between 1920 and 1950, through the commercial reinvention of typographic history. It is worth looking back at this process to see something of what went on, because its legacy affects us still.

Two separate companies – one based in England, one in America – rose up around the Monotype machine and followed two quite separate development programs. The English company, advised during its heyday by a scholar named Stanley Morison, cut a series of facsimiles based on the work of Francesco Griffo, Giovanantonio Tagliente, Ludovico degli Arrighi and other early designers. It was Morison who conceived the idea of turning independent Renaissance faces into families by mating one designer's roman with another's formerly self-sufficient italic. The fruits of this enterprise included Poliphilus and Blado (one of Griffo's romans mated with an altered version of one of Arrighi's italics), Bembo (a later version of the same roman, paired with an altered version of one of Tagliente's italics), and the brilliantly successful shotgun marriage of Centaur roman (designed by Bruce Rogers) with the Arrighi italic (designed by Frederic Warde). This program was supplemented by commissioning new faces from artists such as Eric Gill, Alfred Fairbank, Jan van Krimpen and Berthold Wolpe.

a *a*

a *a*

a *a*

Lanston Monotype, as the American company was called, made some historical recuttings of its own and issued many new and historically based faces designed by its own advisor, Frederic Goudy. A third campaign to recreate typographic history in marketable form was mounted by Linotype, under the direction of the English master printer George William Jones.

Several of the larger typefoundries – including ATF (American Type Founders) in the United States, Deberny & Peignot in France, Enschedé in the Netherlands, Stempel in Germany and Grafotechna in Czechoslovakia – continued ambitious programs of their own, lasting in some cases into the 1980s. Revivals of faces by Claude Garamond, Miklós Kis and other early designers came from these foundries during the twentieth century, along with important new faces by such designers as Hermann Zapf, Jan van Krimpen, Adrian Frutiger, Oldřich Menhart and Hans Eduard Meier. Zapf's Palatino, which became the most widely used (and most widely pirated) face of the twentieth century, was cut by hand in steel and cast as a foundry type in the ancient way, in 1949–50, while phototype machines and a few cumbersome early computers were humming no great distance away.

Historical Interlude

The earlier history of type design is the history of forms made by individual artists and artisans who began their careers as apprentices and ended them as independent masters and small businessmen. The scale of the industry enlarged in the seventeenth and eighteenth centuries, and questions of fashion increasingly superseded questions of artistry. By the end of the nineteenth century, commercial considerations had changed the methods as well as the taste of the trade. Punches and matrices were increasingly cut by machine from large pattern letters, and calligraphic models were all but unknown.

The twentieth-century rediscovery of the history and principles of typographic form was not associated with any particular technology. It occurred among scholars and artists who brought their discoveries to fruition wherever they found employment: in typefoundries, typesetting-machine companies, art schools and their own small, independent studios.

Despite commercial pressures, the best of the old metal foundries, like the best of the new digital ones, were more than merely market-driven factories. They were cultural institutions, on a par with fine publishing houses and the ateliers of printmakers, potters, weavers and instrument makers. What made them so was the stature of the type designers, living and dead, whose work they produced – for type designers are, at their best, the Stradivarii of literature: not merely makers of salable products, but artists who design and make the instruments that other artists use.

7.3.6 *Digital Typography*

Mechanical Typesetting

It is much too soon to summarize the history of digital typography, but the evolution of computerized bitmapping, hinting and scaling techniques has proceeded very quickly since the development of the microchip at the beginning of the 1970s. At the same time, the old technologies, freed from commercial duties, have by no means died. Foundry type, the Monotype, the Linotype and letterpress remain important artistic instruments, alongside brush and chisel, pencil, graver and pen.

Typographic style is founded not on any one technology of typesetting or printing, but on the primitive yet subtle craft of writing. Letters derive their form from the motions of the human hand, restrained and amplified by a tool. That tool may be as complex as a digitizing tablet or a specially programmed keyboard, or as simple as a sharpened stick. Meaning resides, in either case, in the firmness and grace of the gesture itself, not in the tool with which it is made.

7.4 THE PLURALITY OF TYPOGRAPHIC HISTORY

の

굉

無

Every alphabet is a culture. Every culture has its own version of history and its own accumulation of tradition – and this chapter has dwelt on the recent history of one alphabet only. The Arabic, Armenian, Burmese, Cherokee, Cree, Cyrillic, Devanagari, Georgian, Greek, Gujarati, Hebrew, Japanese, Korean, Malayalam, Tamil and Telugu alphabets and syllabaries – to name only a few – have other histories of their own, in some cases every bit as intricate and long as – or longer than – the history of Latin letterforms. So, of course, has the logographic script of Chinese. These histories have touched at certain points; at other points, they diverge. Here at the beginning of the twenty-first century, an unusual degree of convergence can be seen. But the challenge and excitement of multilingual typography still lies largely in the fact that different typographic histories momentarily share the page. Typographers working with multiple alphabets are multiply blessed: with a chance to learn the cultural history as well as the typographic technicalities of every script concerned.

The histories of Greek and Cyrillic types are taken up more briefly in chapter 11, and the legacies of individual typefoundries are summarized briefly in appendix E, page 346.

SHAPING THE PAGE

8

A book is a flexible mirror of the mind and the body. Its overall size and proportions, the color and texture of the paper, the sound it makes as the pages turn, and the smell of the paper, adhesive and ink, all blend with the size and form and placement of the type to reveal a little about the world in which it was made. If the book appears to be only a paper machine, produced at their own convenience by other machines, only machines will want to read it.

8.1 ORGANIC, MECHANICAL & MUSICAL PROPORTION

A page, like a building or a room, can be of any size and proportion, but some are distinctly more pleasing than others, and some have quite specific connotations. A brochure that unfolds and refolds in the hand is intrinsically different from a formal letter that lies motionless and flat, or a handwritten note that folds into quarters and comes in an envelope of a different shape and size. All of these are different again from a book, in which the pages flow sequentially in pairs.

Much typography is based, for the sake of convenience, on standard industrial paper sizes, from 35 × 45 inch press sheets to 3½ × 2 inch conventional business cards. Some formats, such as the booklets that accompany compact discs, are condemned to especially rigid restrictions of size. But many typographic projects begin with the opportunity and necessity of selecting the dimensions of the page.

There is rarely a free choice. A page size of 12 × 19 inches, for example, is likely to be both inconvenient and expensive because it is just in excess of 11 × 17, which is a standard industrial unit. And a brochure that is 5 × 9 inches, no matter how handsome, might be unacceptable because it is too wide to fit into a standard business envelope (4×9½). But when the realm of practicality has been established, and it is known that the page must fall within certain limits, how is one to choose? By taking whatever is easiest, or biggest, or whatever is the most convenient standard size? By trusting to blind instinct?

Instinct, in matters such as these, is largely memory in disguise. It works quite well when it is trained, and poorly otherwise.

But in a craft like typography, no matter how perfectly honed one's instincts are, it is useful to be able to calculate answers exactly. History, natural science, geometry and mathematics are all relevant to typography in this regard – and can all be counted on for aid.

Organic, Mechanical and Musical Proportion

Scribes and typographers, like architects, have been shaping visual spaces for thousands of years. Certain proportions keep recurring in their work because they please the eye and the mind, just as certain sizes keep recurring because they are comfortable to the hand. Many of these proportions are inherent in simple geometric figures – equilateral triangle, square, regular pentagon, hexagon and octagon. And these proportions not only seem to please human beings in many different centuries and countries, they are also prominent in nature far beyond the human realm. They occur in the structures of molecules, mineral crystals, soap bubbles, flowers, as well as books and temples, manuscripts and mosques.

Two very useful works on natural form and structure are D'Arcy Thompson, *On Growth and Form* (rev. ed., 1942) and Peter S. Stevens, *Patterns in Nature* (1974). An equally important book on structures made by humans is Dorothy Washburn & Donald Crowe, *Symmetries of Culture: Theory and Practice of Plane Pattern Analysis* (1988).

The tables on pages 148–149 list a number of page proportions derivable from simple geometric figures. These proportions occur repeatedly in nature, and pages that embody them recur in manuscripts and books from Renaissance Europe, Táng and Sòng dynasty China, early Egypt, precolumbian Mexico and ancient Rome. It seems that the beauty of these proportions is more than a matter of regional taste or immediate fashion. They are therefore useful for two purposes. Working and playing with them is a way of developing good typographic instincts, and they serve as useful references in analyzing old designs and calculating new ones.

For comparison, several other proportions are included in the tables. There are several simple numerical ratios, several standard industrial sizes, and several proportions involving four irrational numbers important in the analysis of natural structures and processes. These numbers are $\pi = 3.14159\ldots$, which is the circumference of a circle whose diameter is one; $\sqrt{2} = 1.41421\ldots$, which is the diagonal of a unit square; $e = 2.71828\ldots$, which is the base of the natural logarithms; and $\varphi = 1.61803\ldots$, a number discussed in greater detail on page 155. Certain of these proportions reappear in the structure of the human body; others appear in musical scales. Indeed, one of the simplest of all systems of page proportions is based on the familiar intervals of the diatonic scale. Pages that embody these basic musical proportions have been in common use in Europe for more than a thousand years.

Sizing and spacing type, like composing and performing music or applying paint to canvas, is largely concerned with intervals and differences. As the texture builds, precise relationships and very small discrepancies are easily perceived. Establishing the overall dimensions of the page is more a matter of limits and sums. In this realm, it is usually sufficient, and often it is better, if structural harmony is not so much enforced as implied. That is one of the reasons typographers tend to fall in love with books. The pages flex and turn; their proportions ebb and flow against the underlying form. But the harmony of that underlying form is no less important, and no less easy to perceive, than the harmony of the letterforms themselves.

Shaping the Page

The page is a piece of paper. It is also a visible and tangible proportion, silently sounding the thoroughbass of the book. On it lies the textblock, which must answer to the page. The two together – page and textblock – produce an antiphonal geometry. That geometry alone can bond the reader to the book. Or conversely, it can put the reader to sleep, or put the reader's nerves on edge, or drive the reader away.

The textblock is known in Chinese as *yèxīn* (頁心), a useful phrase. *Yè* means *page*; *xīn* means *heart* and *mind.*

Arithmetic and mathematics also drive away some readers, and this is a chapter peppered with both. Readers may well ask whether all this is necessary, merely in order to choose where some letters should sit on a piece of paper and where the paper itself should be trimmed. The answer, naturally, is no. It is not in the least necessary to understand the mathematics in order to perform the actions that the math describes. People walk and ride bicycles without mathematical analyses of these complex operations. The chambered nautilus and the snail construct perfect logarithmic spirals without any need of logarithmic tables, sliderules or the theory of infinite series. The typographer likewise can construct beautiful pages without knowing the meaning of symbols like π or φ, and indeed without ever learning to add and subtract, if he has a well-educated eye and knows which buttons to push on the calculator and keyboard.

The mathematics are not here to impose drudgery upon anyone. On the contrary, they are here entirely for pleasure. They are here for the pleasure of those who like to examine what they are doing, or what they might do or have already done, perhaps in the hope of doing it still better. Those who prefer to act directly at all times, and to leave the analysis to others, may be content in this chapter to study the pictures and skim the text.

Chromatic Scale of Page Proportions

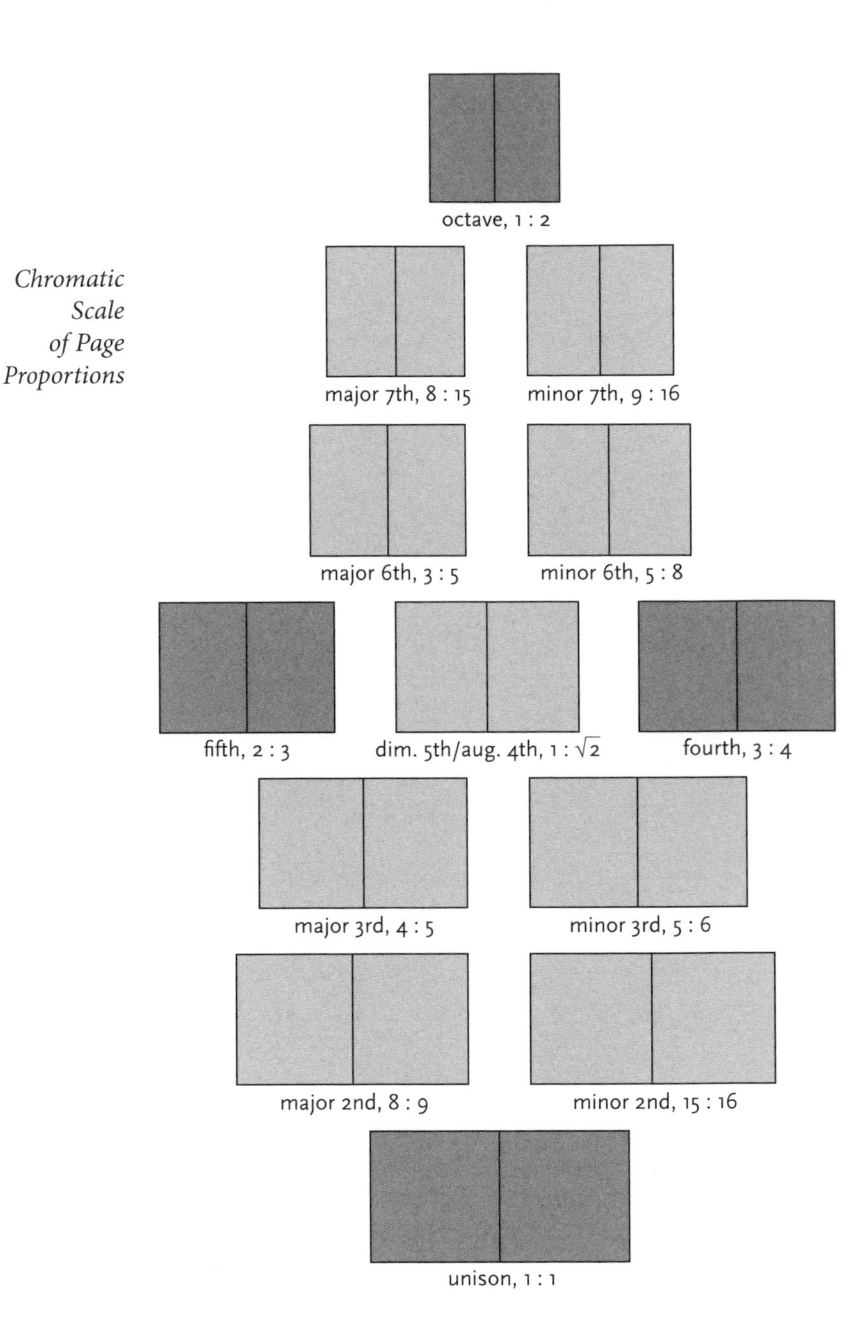

Page proportions corresponding to the chromatic scale, from unison (at the bottom) to octave (at the top). The musical correlations are shown in detail on the facing page.

interval	ratio	proportion	notes	page
octave	1 : 2	1 : 2	C – C′	*double square*
major 7th	8 : 15	1 : 1.875	C – B	*narrow books*
minor 7th	9 : 16	1 : 1.778	C – B♭	
major 6th	3 : 5	1 : 1.667	C – A	
minor 6th	5 : 8	1 : 1.6	C – A♭	~ 1 : φ
fifth	2 : 3	1 : 1.5	C – G	
dim. 5th / *aug. 4th*	$1 : \sqrt{2}$	1 : 1.414	C – G♭ / C – F♯	*self-replicating page*
fourth	3 : 4	1 : 1.333	C – F	
major 3rd	4 : 5	1 : 1.25	C – E	~ φ : 2
minor 3rd	5 : 6	1 : 1.2	C – E♭	*wide books*
major 2nd	8 : 9	1 : 1.125	C – D	
minor 2nd	15 : 16	1 : 1.067	C – D♭	
unison	1 : 1	1 : 1	C – C	*square page*

The value for the diminished 5th/augmented 4th is calculated here according to the system of equal temperament. All other intervals are calculated according to the system of just intonation.

Page shapes derived from the chromatic scale. Two-page spreads that embody these proportions are shown on the facing page.

The perfect intervals (fifth and fourth) coincide exactly with the favorite page shapes of the European Middle Ages, which are still in use today: the page proportions 2 : 3 and 3 : 4. Renaissance typographers made extensive use of narrower pages, corresponding to the larger impure intervals (major and minor sixth, major and minor seventh).

Each page shape has a counterpart with which it alternates. If a sheet whose proportions are 5 : 8 is folded in half, it produces a sheet whose proportions are 4 : 5. If this is folded once again, it produces another sheet whose proportions are 5 : 8. In the same way, the proportion 1 : 2 alternates with the proportion 1 : 1. The proportion $1 : \sqrt{2}$, corresponding to the diminished fifth and augmented fourth of equal temperament, is the only one that alternates with itself.

In musical terms, these alternating proportions form harmonic inversions. (The harmonic inversion of a fifth, for example, is a fourth, and the harmonic inversion of a minor sixth is a major third.) The total of each such pair of intervals is always one octave.

		Page & Textblock Proportions		Sample sizes in inches		
octave	**A**	Double Square	1 : 2	4.5 × 9	5 × 10	5.5 × 11
	B	Tall Octagon	1 : 1.924	4.7 × 9	5.2 × 10	5.7 × 11
major 7th		8 : 15	1 : 1.875	4.8 × 9		
	C	Tall Hexagon	1 : 1.866			5.9 × 11
	D	Octagon	1 : 1.848	4.9 × 9	5.4 × 10	6 × 11
		5 : 9	1 : 1.8	5 × 9		
minor 7th		9 : 16	1 : 1.778		5.1 × 9	
	E	HEXAGON = $1 : \sqrt{3}$	1 : 1.732	4.9 × 8.5	5.2 × 9	6.4 × 11
	F	Tall Pentagon	1 : 1.701	5 × 8.5	5.3 × 9	6.5 × 11
major 6th		3 : 5	1 : 1.667	5.1 × 8.5		
		Legal Sheet	1 : 1.647			8.5 × 14
	G	GOLDEN SECTION	1 : 1.618	5.3 × 8.5	5.6 × 9	6.8 × 11
minor 6th		5 : 8	1 : 1.6	5 × 8		
	H	PENTAGON	1 : 1.539	5.5 × 8.5	5.9 × 9	7.2 × 11
➤ *fifth*		2 : 3	1 : 1.5		6 × 9	7.3 × 11
	Z	ISO = $1 : \sqrt{2}$	1 : 1.414	6.4 × 9	7.1 × 10	7.8 × 11
		5 : 7	1 : 1.4			
	J	Short Pentagon	1 : 1.376	6.5 × 9	7.3 × 10	8 × 11
➤ *fourth*		3 : 4	1 : 1.333	6.8 × 9	7.5 × 10	9 × 12
	K	Tall Half Octagon	1 : 1.307	6.9 × 9	7.7 × 10	8.4 × 11
		Letter Sheet	1 : 1.294			8.5 × 11
major 3rd		4 : 5	1 : 1.25	7.2 × 9	8 × 10	8.8 × 11
	L	Half Octagon	1 : 1.207		8.3 × 10	9.1 × 11
minor 3rd		5 : 6	1 : 1.2	7.5 × 9		
	M	Truncated Pentagon	1 : 1.176		8.5 × 10	9.4 × 11
		6 : 7	1 : 1.167	7.7 × 9		
		e : π	1 : 1.156			
	N	Turned Hexagon	1 : 1.155	7.8 × 9	8.7 × 10	9.5 × 11
major 2nd		8 : 9	1 : 1.125	8 × 9	8.9 × 10	9.8 × 11
	O	Tall Cross Octagon	1 : 1.082	8.3 × 9	9.2 × 10	10.2 × 11
minor 2nd		15 : 16	1 : 1.067	8.4 × 9	9.4 × 10	10.3 × 11
	P	Turned Pentagon	1 : 1.051	8.6 × 9	9.5 × 10	10.5 × 11
unison	**Q**	SQUARE	1 : 1	9 × 9	10 × 10	11 × 11
	R	Broad Pentagon	1 : 0.951	8.9 × 8.5	10 × 9.5	11 × 10.5
	S	Broad Cross Octagon	1 : 0.924	9.2 × 8.5	10 × 9.2	11 × 10.1
major 2nd		9 : 8	1 : 0.889	9.6 × 8.5		11 × 9.8
	T	Broad Hexagon	1 : 0.866	9.8 × 8.5	10 × 8.7	11 × 9.5
	U	Full Cross Octagon	1 : 0.829	10.3 × 8.5	10 × 8.3	11 × 9.1
major 3rd		5 : 4	1 : 0.8	10.6 × 8.5		11 × 8.8
		Landscape Letter	1 : 0.773	11 × 8.5	10 × 7.7	

	Column Proportions		Sample sizes in picas			
a	Quadruple Square	1 : 4	10 × 40	11 × 44	12 × 48	*double octave*
	$1 : \sqrt{15}$	1 : 3.873	10 × 39			
	4 : 15	1 : 3.75		12 × 45		*major 14th*
	5 : 18	1 : 3.6	10 × 36	12 × 43		
	9 : 32	1 : 3.556	11 × 39			*minor 14th*
	$1 : \sqrt{12}$	1 : 3.464	11 × 38		15 × 52	
b	Octagon Wing	1 : 3.414		12 × 41		
	3 : 10	1 : 3.333		12 × 40	15 × 50	*major 13th*
	$1 : 2\varphi$	1 : 3.236				
	5 : 16	1 : 3.2			15 × 48	*minor 13th*
	$1 : \sqrt{10}$	1 : 3.162	12 × 38			
	$1 : \pi$	1 : 3.142		14 × 44		
c	Double Pentagon	1 : 3.078	12 × 37	14 × 43	16 × 49	
d	Triple Square	1 : 3	12 × 36	14 × 42	16 × 48	*twelfth*
e	Wide Octagon Wing	1 : 2.993				
z	$1 : 2\sqrt{2} = 1 : \sqrt{8}$	1 : 2.828				
f	Pentagon Wing	1 : 2.753		16 × 44		
	$1 : e$	1 : 2.718	14 × 38		18 × 49	
	3 : 8	1 : 2.667		15 × 40	18 × 48	*eleventh*
	$1 : \sqrt{7}$	1 : 2.646				
g	Extended Section	1 : 2.618				
h	Tall Octagon Column	1 : 2.613			18 × 47	
i	Mid Octagon Column	1 : 2.514				
	2 : 5	1 : 2.5	16 × 40	18 × 45	20 × 50	*major 10th*
j	Short Octagon Column	1 : 2.414				
	5 : 12	1 : 2.4			20 × 48	*minor 10th*
k	Hexagon Wing	1 : 2.309	16 × 37	20 × 46		
m	Double Truncated Pentagon	1 : 2.252				
	4 : 9	1 : 2.25		20 × 45		*major 9th*
	$1 : \sqrt{5}$	1 : 2.236	17 × 38		21 × 47	
	5 : 11	1 : 2.2		20 × 44	24 × 53	
	15 : 32	1 : 2.133			24 × 52	*minor 9th*
A	Double Square	1 : 2	18 × 36	21 × 42	24 × 48	*octave*

[The intervals listed in the right hand column on this page are *compound intervals* of the chromatic scale. Octave + minor 2nd = minor 9th; octave + major 3rd = major 10th; octave + fifth = twelfth, etc.]

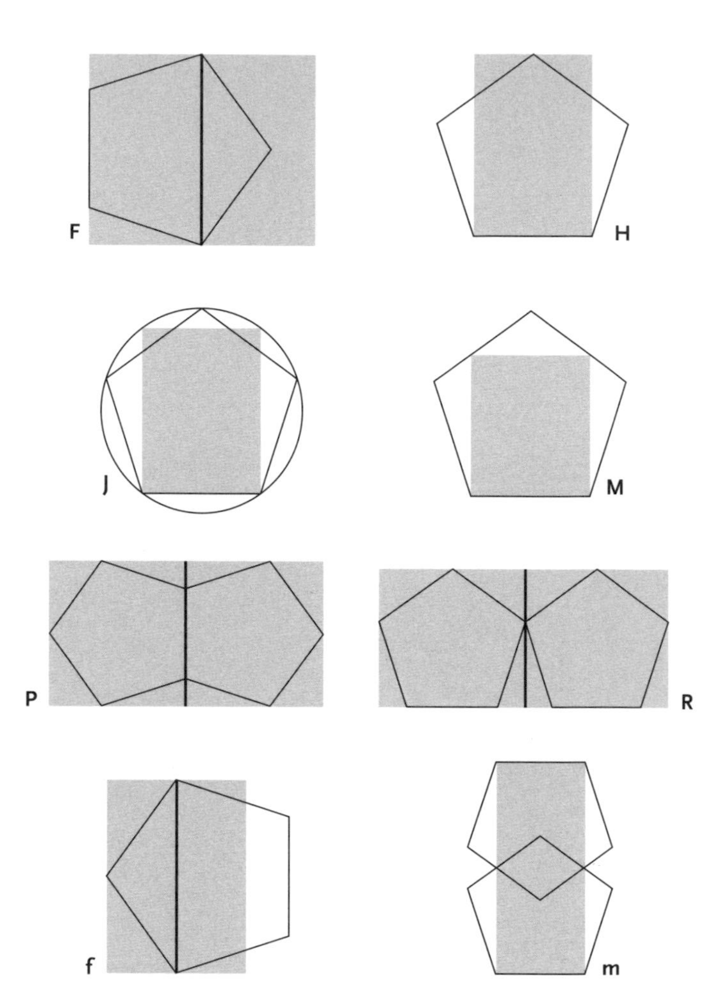

F, P, R and f are shown here as two-page spreads. H, J, M and m are shown as single pages.

Pages derived from the pentagon: **F** the Tall Pentagon page, 1 : 1.701; **H** Pentagon page, 1 : 1.539; **J** Short Pentagon page, 1 : 1.376; **M** the Truncated Pentagon page, 1 : 1.176; **P** Turned Pentagon page, 1 : 1.051; **R** the Broad Pentagon page, 1 : 0.951; **f** Pentagon Wing, 1 : 2.753; **m** the Double Truncated Pentagon, 1 : 2.252. The pentagon page differs by 2% from the North American standard small trade book size, which is half the size of a letter sheet: 5½ × 8½ inches. A more eminent page proportion, the *golden section,* is also present in the pentagon (see page 156). In nature, pentagonal symmetry is rare in inanimate forms. Packed soap bubbles seem to strive for it but never quite succeed, and there are no mineral crystals with true pentagonal structures. But pentagonal geometry is basic to many living things, from roses and forget-me-nots to sea urchins and starfish.

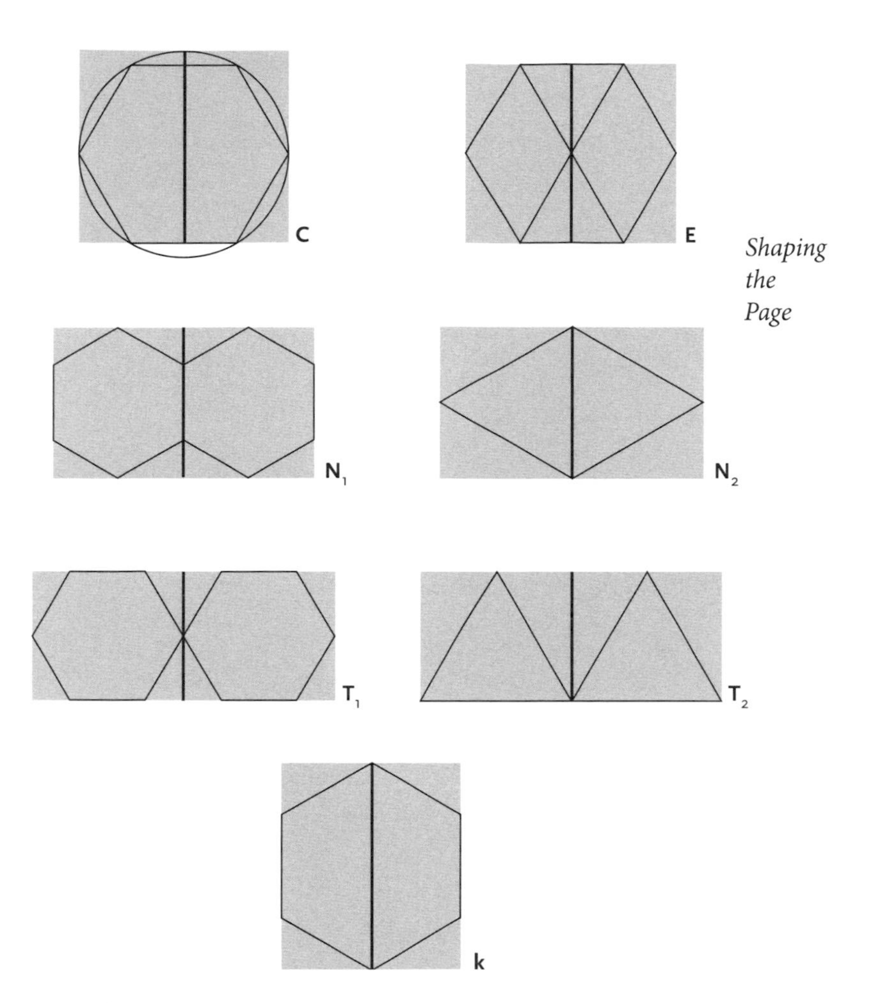

Pages derived from the hexagon: **C** the Tall Hexagon page, 1 : 1.866; **E** Hexagon page, $1 : \sqrt{3} = 1 : 1.732$; **N** Turned Hexagon page, 1 : 1.155; **T** Broad Hexagon page, 1 : 0.866; **k** Hexagon Wing, 1 : 2.309. The hexagon consists of six equilateral triangles, and each of these page shapes can be derived directly from the triangle instead. The hexagon merely clarifies their existence as mirror images, like the pages of a book. Hexagonal structures are present in both the organic and the inorganic world – in lilies and wasps' nests, for example, and in snowflakes, silica crystals and sunbaked mudflats. The proportions of the broad hexagon page are within one tenth of one per cent of the natural ratio π/e, while the turned hexagon page (which is the broad hexagon rotated 90°) approximates the ratio e/π. (The hexagon page used in this book is analyzed on page 6.)

All formats on this page are shown as two-page spreads.

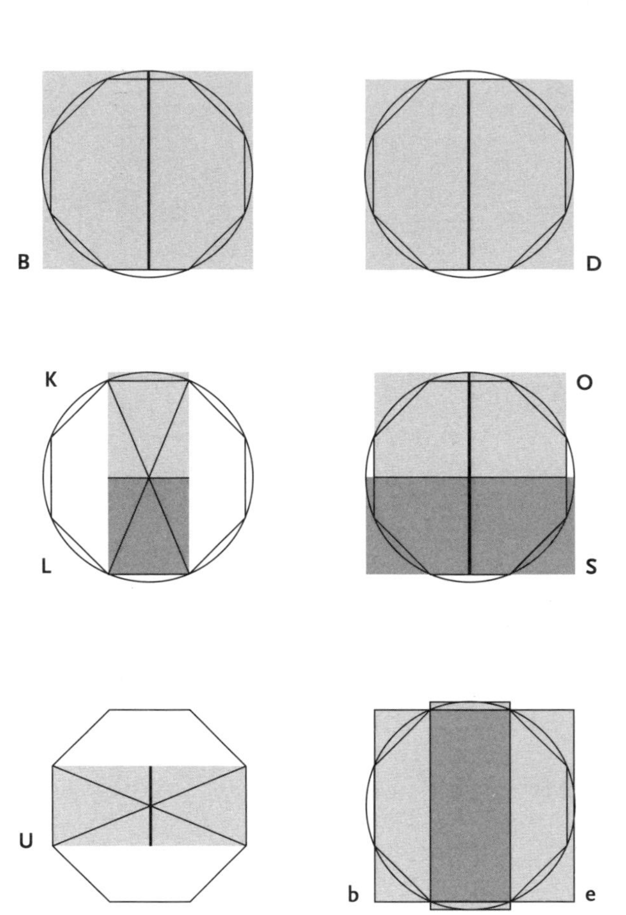

B, D, O, S and U are shown as two-page spreads.

Pages derived from the octagon: **B** the Tall Octagon page, 1 : 1.924; **D** Octagon page, 1 : 1.848; **K** Tall Half Octagon page, 1 : 1.307; **L** Half Octagon page, 1 : 1.207; **O** Tall Cross Octagon, 1 : 1.082; **S** Broad Cross Octagon page, 1 : 0.924; **U** the Full Cross Octagon page, 1 : 0.829; **b** Octagon Wing, 1 : 3.414; **e** Wide Octagon Wing, 1 : 2.993; **h**, **i**, **j** Tall, Middle and Short Octagon Columns, 1 : 2.613, 1 : 2.514 and 1 : 2.414. The tall half octagon page (**K**), used in Roman times, differs by a margin of 1% from the standard North American letter size. Are proportions derived from the hexagon and pentagon livelier and more pleasing than those derived from the octagon? Forms based on the hexagon and pentagon are, at any rate, far more frequent than octagonal forms in the structure of flowering plants and elsewhere in the living world.

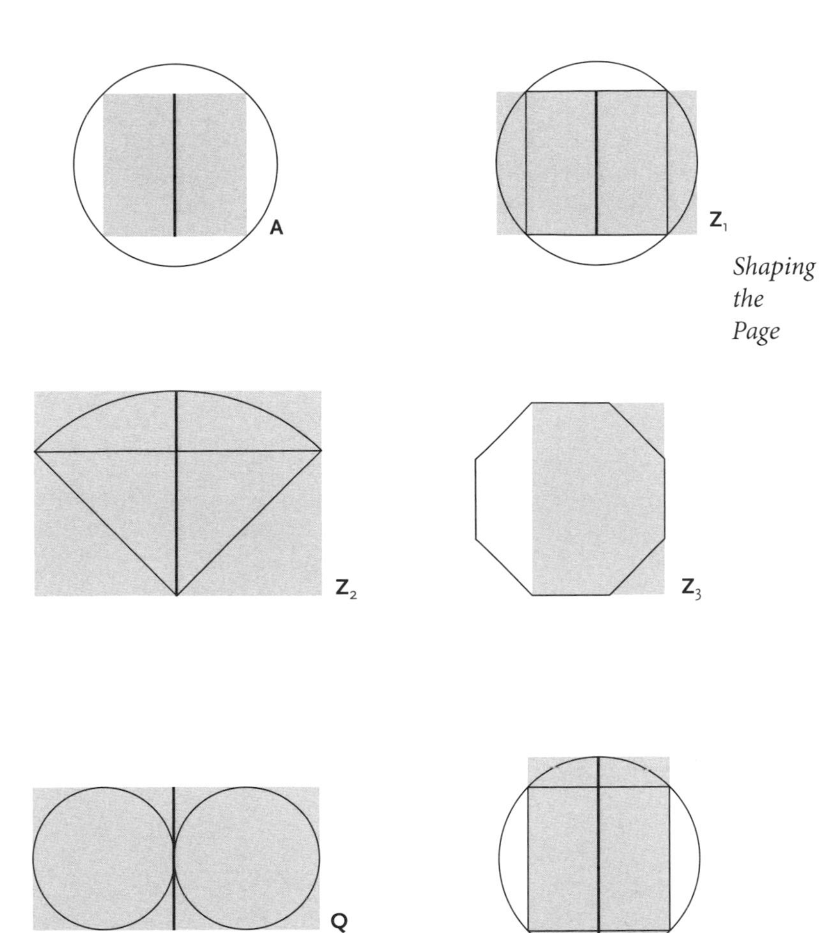

Shaping the Page

Pages derived from the circle and square: **A** Double Square page, 1 : 2; **Z** the Broad Square page, which is the ISO standard, $1 : \sqrt{2} = 1 : 1.414$; **Q** the Perfect Square; **z** Double ISO, $1 : 2\sqrt{2} = 1 : 2.828$. The proportion $1 : \sqrt{2}$ is that of side to diagonal in a square. A rectangle of these proportions (and no others) can be halved or doubled indefinitely to produce new rectangles of the same proportion. The proportion was chosen for that reason as the basis for ISO (International Organization for Standardization) paper sizes. The A4 sheet, for example, is standard European letter size, 210 × 297 mm = 8¼″ × 11⅝″. An 8½″ × 12″ book page also embodies this proportion.

Except for Z_3, all formats on this page are shown as two-page spreads.

The ISO or broad square page is latent not only in the square but in the octagon.

ISO sheet sizes:		
	A0 = 841 × 1189 mm	A3 = 297 × 420 mm
	A1 = 594 × 841 mm	A4 = 210 × 297 mm
	A2 = 420 × 594 mm	A5 = 148 × 210 mm

When a sheet whose proportions are $1 : \sqrt{2}$ is folded in half, the result is a sheet half as large but with *the same proportions.* Standard paper sizes based on this principle have been in use in Germany since the early 1920s. The basis of the system is the A0 sheet, which has an area of 1 m². Yet precisely because it is *reciprocal with nothing but itself,* the ISO page is, in isolation, the least musical of all the major page shapes. It needs a textblock of another shape for contrast.

8.2 THE GOLDEN SECTION

The golden section is a symmetrical relation built from asymmetrical parts. Two numbers, shapes or elements embody the golden section when the smaller is to the larger as the larger is to the sum. That is, $a : b = b : (a + b)$. In the language of algebra, this ratio is $1 : \varphi = 1 : (1 + \sqrt{5})/2$, and in the language of trigonometry, it is $1 : (2 \sin 54°)$. Its approximate value in decimal terms is $1 : 1.61803$.

The second term of this ratio, φ (the Greek letter *phi*), is a number with several unusual properties. If you *add* one to φ, you get its square ($\varphi \times \varphi$). If you *subtract* one from φ, you get its reciprocal ($1/\varphi$). And if you multiply φ endlessly by itself, you get an infinite series embodying a single proportion. That proportion is $1 : \varphi$. If we rewrite these facts in the typographic form mathematicians like to use, they look like this:

$$\varphi + 1 = \varphi^2$$

$$\varphi - 1 = 1/\varphi$$

$$\varphi^{-1} : 1 = 1 : \varphi = \varphi : \varphi^2 = \varphi^2 : \varphi^3 = \varphi^3 : \varphi^4 = \varphi^4 : \varphi^5 \ldots$$

If we look for a numerical approximation to this ratio, $1 : \varphi$, we will find it in something called the Fibonacci series, named for the thirteenth-century mathematician Leonardo Fibonacci. Though he died two centuries before Gutenberg, Fibonacci is important in the history of European typography as well as mathematics. He was born in Pisa but studied in North Africa. On his return, he introduced Arabic mathematics to North Italian scholars and also arabic numerals to the North Italian scribes.

As a mathematician, Fibonacci took an interest in many problems, including the problem of unchecked propagation. What happens, he asked, if everything breeds and nothing dies? The answer is a logarithmic spiral of increase. Expressed as a series of integers, such a spiral takes the following form:

0 · 1 · 1 · 2 · 3 · 5 · 8 · 13 · 21 · 34 · 55 · 89 · 144 · 233 · 377 · 610 ·
987 · 1,597 · 2,584 · 4,181 · 6,765 · 10,946 · 17,711 · 28,657 …

Here each term after the first two is *the sum of the two preceding*. And the farther we proceed along this series, the closer

The Golden Section

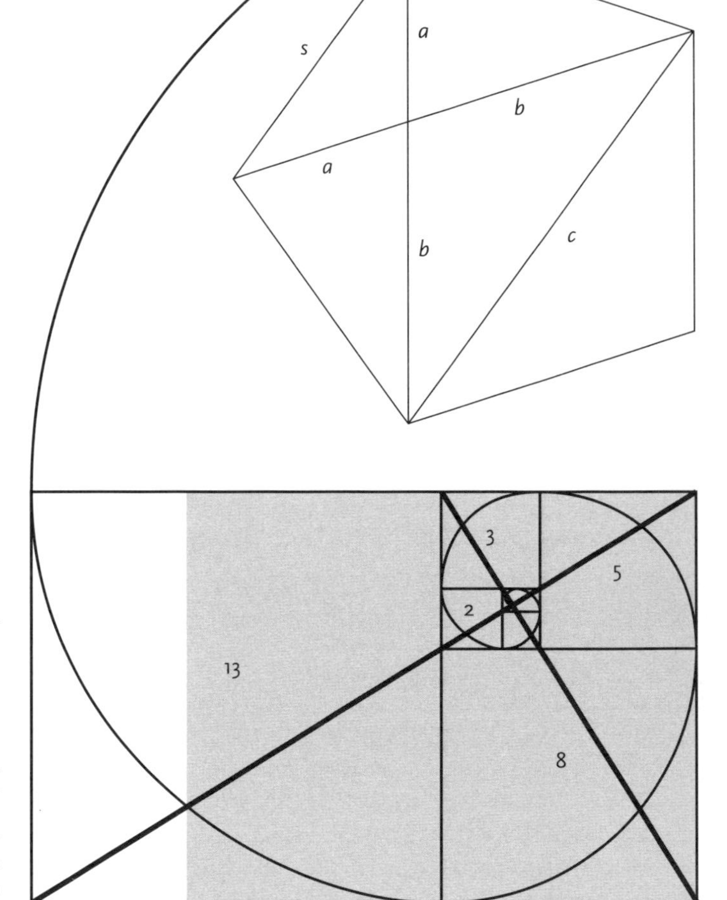

The screened area represents a two-page spread in which each page embodies the golden section. The root of the spiral, which is the navel of the page, lies at the intersection of the diagonals. This is a Renaissance structure: precisely measured and formed, yet open-ended, unconfined. Like Thoreau's vision of the mind (page 66), it is *hypethral*. (Compare the equally elegant but closed, medieval structure on page 173 and the resolutely linear structure on page 154.)

G Golden Section, $1 : \varphi = 1 : 1.618...$. In the pentagon, the side *s* and the chord *c* embody the golden section. The smaller is to the larger as the larger is to the whole, or $s : c = c : (s + c)$. When two chords intersect, they divide each other in the same proportion: $a : b = b : c$, where $c = a + b$. Moreover, $b = s$. Thus, $a : s = s : c = c : (s + c) = 1 : \varphi$.

An evolving sequence of figures that embody the golden section also defines the path of a logarithmic spiral. And if the lengths of the sides of the figures are rounded off to the nearest whole numbers, the result is a Fibonacci series of integers.

we come to an accurate approximation of the number φ. Thus 5 : 8 = 1 : 1.6; 8 : 13 = 1 : 1.625; 13 : 21 = 1 : 1.615; 21 : 34 = 1 : 1.619, and so on.

In the world of pure mathematics, this spiral of increase, the Fibonacci series, proceeds without end. In the world of mortal living things, of course, the spiral soon breaks off. It is repeatedly interrupted by death and other practical considerations – but it is visible nevertheless in the short term. Abbreviated versions of the Fibonacci series, and the proportion 1 : φ, can be seen in the structure of pineapples, pinecones, sunflowers, sea urchins, snails, the chambered nautilus, and in the proportions of the human body as well.

If we convert the ratio 1 : φ or 1 : 1.61803 to percentages, the smaller part is roughly **38.2%** and the larger **61.8%** of the whole. But we will find the *exact* proportions of the golden section in several simple geometric figures. These include the pentagon, where they are relatively obvious, and the square, where they are somewhat more deeply concealed. Sunflowers, snails and humans who use the golden section *choose* it; they do not invent it.

The golden section, 1 : φ, differs by roughly one per cent from the interval of the minor sixth in the chromatic scale. The proportion 5 : 8, which is the arithmetic value of the minor sixth in music, is often used in typography as a rough approximation to the golden section.

The golden section was much admired by classical Greek geometers and architects, and by Renaissance mathematicians, architects and scribes, who often used it in their work. It has also been much admired by artists and craftsmen, including typographers, in the modern age. Paperback books in the Penguin Classics series have been manufactured for more than half a century to the standard size of 111 × 180 mm, which embodies the golden section. The Modulor system of the Swiss architect Le Corbusier is based on the golden section as well.

If type sizes are chosen according to the golden section, the result is again a Fibonacci series:

(a) 5 · 8 · 13 · 21 · 34 · 55 · 89 …

These sizes alone are adequate for many typographic tasks. But to create a more versatile scale of sizes, a second or third interlocking series can be added. The possibilities include:

(b) 6 · 10 · 16 · 26 · 42 · 68 · 110 …
(c) 4 · 7 · 11 · 18 · 29 · 47 · 76 …

All three of these series – **a**, **b** and **c** – obey the Fibonacci rule (each term is the sum of the two terms preceding). Series **b** is also related to series **a** by simple doubling. The combination of **a** and **b** is therefore a two-stranded Fibonacci series with incremental symmetry, forming a very versatile scale of type sizes:

(**d**) 6 · 8 · 10 · 13 · 16 · 21 · 26 · 34 · 42 · 55 · 68 …

The Golden Section

The double-stranded Fibonacci series used by Le Corbusier (with other units of measurement) in his architectural work is similarly useful in typography:

(**e**) 4 6½ 10½ 17 27½ 44½ 72
5 8 13 21 34 55 89 …

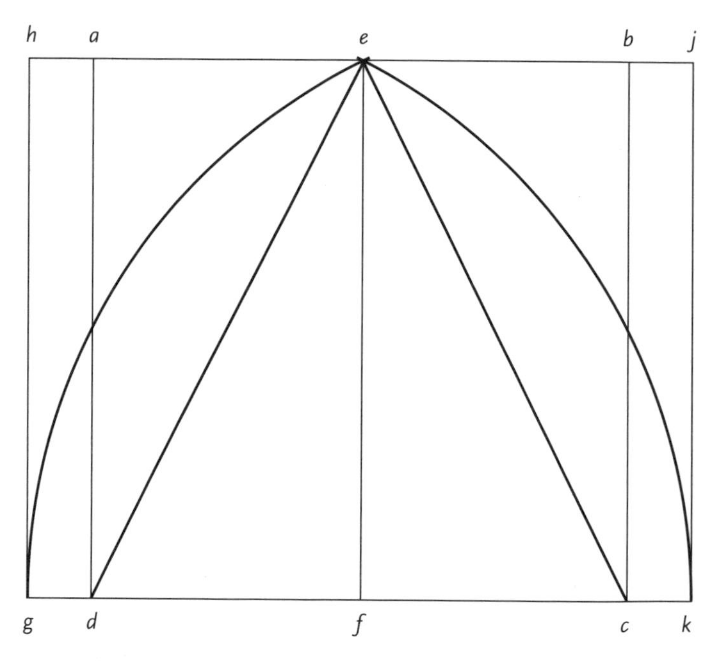

Finding the golden section in the square. Begin with the square *abcd*. Bisect the square (with the line *ef*) and draw diagonals (*ec* and *ed*) in each half. An isosceles triangle, *cde*, consisting of two right triangles, is formed. Extend the base of the square (draw the line *gk*) and project each of the diagonals (the hypotenuse of each of the right triangles) onto the extended base. Now $ce = cg$, and $de = dk$. Draw the new rectangle, *efgh*. This and its mirror image, *ejkf*, each have the proportions of the golden section. That is to say, $eh : gh = gh : (gh + eh) = ej : jk = jk : (jk + ej) = 1 : \varphi$. (Contrast this with figure Z_2 on page 153.)

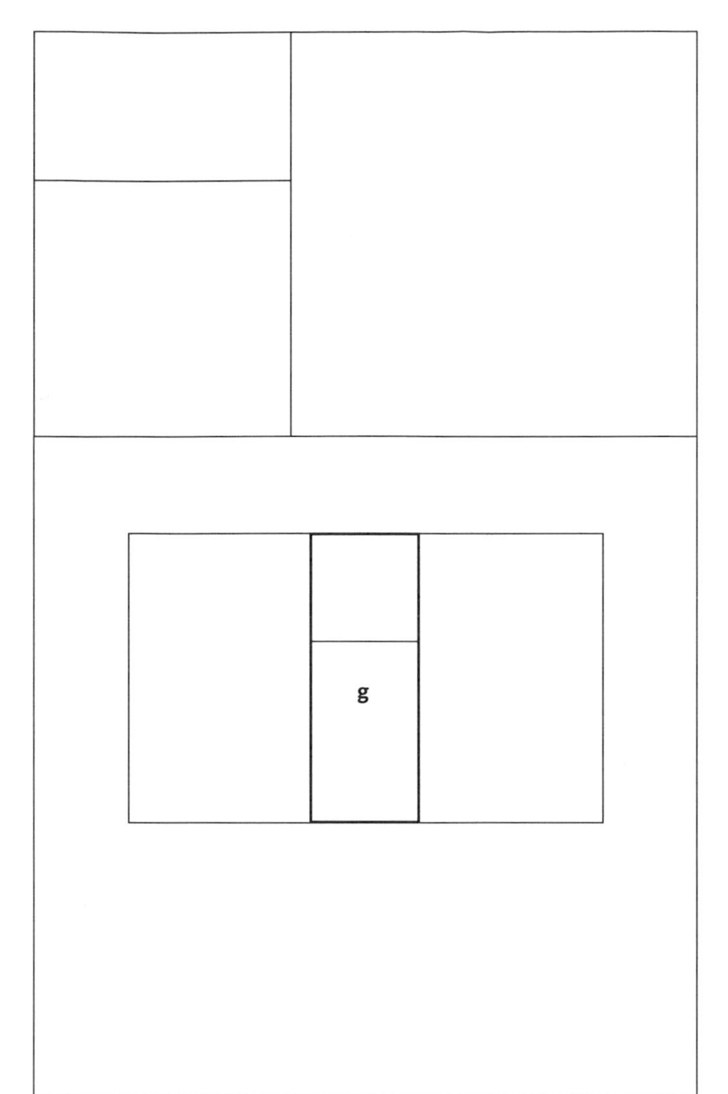

The relationship between the square and the golden section is perpetual. Each time a square is subtracted from a golden section, a new golden section remains. If two overlapping squares are formed within a golden-section rectangle, two smaller rectangles of golden-section proportions are created, along with a narrow column whose proportions are $1 : (\varphi + 1) = 1 : 2.618$. This is **g**, the Extended Section, from the table on page 149. If a square is subtracted from this, the golden section is restored.

The Golden Section

THIS PARAGRAPH, for example, is indented according to the golden section. The indent is to the remainder of the line as that remainder is to the full text measure. Here the measure is 21 picas, and the indent is 38.2% of that, which is to say 8 picas.

The amount of *sinkage* (the extra white space allowed at the top of the page) is 7 lines (here equal to 7 picas). Add the extra pica of white space created by the indent itself, and you have an imaginary 8-pica square of empty space in the upper left corner of the textblock.

The size of the elevated cap is related in turn to the size of the indent and the sinkage. Eight picas is 96 pt, and 61.8% of that is 59.3 pt. But the relationship between 59 or 60 pt type and an 8-pica indent would be difficult to perceive, because a 60 pt letter is not visibly 60 pt high. The initial used has an actual 60 pt cap height instead. Depending on the face, such a letter could be anywhere from 72 to 100 pt nominal size; here it is 84 pt Castellar.

8.3 PROPORTIONS OF THE EMPTY PAGE

8.3.1 *Choose inherently satisfying page proportions in preference to stock sizes or arbitrary shapes.*

The proportions of a page are like an interval in music. In a given context, some are consonant, others dissonant. Some are familiar; some are also inescapable, because of their presence in the structures of the natural as well as the man-made world. Some proportions also seem particularly linked to living things. It is true that wastage is often increased when an 8½ × 11 inch page is trimmed to 7¾ × 11 or 6¾ × 11, or when a 6 × 9 book page is narrowed to 5⅝ × 9. But an organic page looks and feels different from a mechanical page, and the shape of the page itself will provoke certain responses and expectations in the reader, independently of whatever text it contains.

the text m…
quoting and reading…

8.4.2 *Shape the textblock so that it bal… the shape of the overall page.*

The proportions that are useful for the shapes of pages are equally useful in shaping the textblock. This is not to say that the proportions of the textblock and the page should be the same. They often were the same in medieval books. In the Renaissance, many typographers preferred a more polyphonic page, in which the proportions of page and textblock differ. But it is pointless for them to differ unless, like intervals in music, they differ to a clear and purposeful degree.

For all the beauty of pure geometry, a perfectly square block of type on a perfectly square page with even margins all around is a form unlikely to encourage reading. Reading, like walking, involves navigation – and the square block of type on a square block of paper is short of basic landmarks and clues. To give the reader a sense of direction, and the page a sense of liveliness and poise, it is necessary to break this inexorable sameness and find a new balance of another kind. Some space must be narrow so that other space may be wide, and some space emptied so that other space may be filled.

In the simple format shown overleaf, a page whose proportions are 1 : 1.62 (the golden section) carries a textblock whose proportions are 1 : 1.8 [5 : 9]. This difference constitutes a primary visual chord which generates both energy and harmony in the with t...

column, two co...

Proportions of the Empty Page

cept of the page survives t... books). There are early books that are ... others that are close to square, and many shap...

In medieval Europe, most books, though certainly ... settled down to proportions ranging from 1 : 1.5 to 1 : 1.25. Paper – once the mills were built in Europe – was commonly made in sheets whose proportions were 2 : 3 [1 : 1.5] or 3 : 4 [1 : 1.33]. These proportions, which correspond to the acoustically perfect musical intervals of fifth and fourth, also reproduce one another with each fold. If a sheet is 40 × 60 cm [2 : 3] to start with, it folds to 30 × 40 [3 : 4], which folds to 20 × 30, and so on. The 25 × 38 inch [roughly 2 : 3] and 20 × 26 inch [roughly 3 : 4] press sheets used in North America today are survivors of this medieval tradition.

The page proportion $1 : \sqrt{2}$, which is now the European standard, was also known to the medieval scribes. And the tall half octagon page, 1 : 1.3 (the shape enshrined now in North American letter paper) has a similar pedigree. The British Museum has a Roman wax-tablet book of precisely this proportion, dated to about AD 300.

Renaissance typographers continued to produce books in the proportions 1 : 1.5. They also developed an enthusiasm for narrower proportions. The proportions 1 : 1.87 (tall hexagon), 1 : 1.7 (tall pentagon), 1 : 1.67 [3 : 5], and of course 1 : 1.62, the golden section, were used by typographers in Venice before the end of the fifteenth century. The narrower page was preferred especially for works in the arts and sciences. Wider pages, better able to carry a double column, were preferred for legal and ecclesiastical texts. (Even now, a Bible, a volume of court reports or a manual on mortgages or wills is likely to be on a wider page than a book of poems or a novel.)

Renaissance page proportions (generally in the range of 1 : 1.4 to 1 : 2) survived through the Baroque, but Neoclassical books are often wider, returning to the heavier Roman proportion of 1 : 1.3.

8.5 MARGINS & SATELLITES

8.5.1 *Bring the margins into the design.*

Shaping the Page

In typography, margins must do three things. They must *lock the textblock to the page* and *lock the facing pages to each other* through the force of their proportions. Second, they must *frame the textblock* in a manner that suits its design. Third, they must *protect the textblock*, leaving it easy for the reader to see and convenient to handle. (That is, they must leave room for the reader's thumbs.) The third of these is easy, and the second is not difficult. The first is like choosing type: it is an endless opportunity for typographic play and a serious test of skill.

Perhaps fifty per cent of the character and integrity of a printed page lies in its letterforms. Much of the other fifty per cent resides in its margins.

8.5.2 *Bring the design into the margins.*

The boundaries of the textblock are rarely absolute. They are nibbled and punctured by paragraph indents, blank lines between sections, gutters between columns, and the sinkage of chapter openings. They are overrun by hanging numbers, outdented paragraphs or heads, marginal bullets, folios (page numbers) and often running heads, marginal notes and other typographic satellites. These features – whether recurrent, like folios, or unpredictable, like marginal notes and numbers – should be designed to give vitality to the page and further bind the page and the textblock.

8.5.3 *Mark the reader's way.*

Folios are useful in most documents longer than two pages. They can be anywhere on the page that is graphically pleasing and easy to find, but in practice this reduces to few possibilities: (**1**) at the head of the page, aligned with the outside edge of the textblock (a common place for folios accompanied by running heads); (**2**) at the foot of the page, aligned with or slightly indented from the outside edge of the text; (**3**) in the upper quarter of the outside margin, beyond the outside edge of the text; (**4**) at the foot of the page, horizontally centered beneath the textblock.

The fourth of these choices offers Neoclassical poise but is not the best for quick navigation. Folios near the upper or lower outside corner are the easiest to find by flipping pages in a small book. In large books and magazines, the bottom outside corner is generally more convenient for joint assaults by eye and thumb. Folios placed on the inner margin are rarely worth considering. They are invisible when needed and all too visible otherwise.

It is usual to set folios in the text size and to position them near the textblock. Unless they are very black, brightly colored or large, the folios usually drown when they get very far away from the text. Strengthened enough to survive on their own, they are likely to prove a distraction.

8.5.4 *Don't restate the obvious.*

In Bibles and other large works, running heads have been standard equipment for two thousand years. Photocopying machines, which can easily separate a chapter or a page from the rest of a book or journal, have also given running heads (and running feet, or footers) new importance.

Except as insurance against photocopying pirates, running heads are nevertheless pointless in many books and documents with a strong authorial voice or a unified subject. They remain essential in most anthologies and works of reference, large or small.

Like folios, running heads pose an interesting typographic problem. They are useless if the reader has to hunt for them, so they must somehow be distinguished from the text, yet they have no independent value and must not become a distraction. It has been a common typographic practice since 1501 to set them in spaced small caps of the text size, or if the budget permits, to print them in the text face in a second color.

8.6 PAGE GRIDS & MODULAR SCALES

8.6.1 *Use a modular scale if you need one to subdivide the page.*

Grids are often used in magazine design and in other situations where unpredictable graphic elements must be combined in a rapid and orderly way.

Modular scales serve much the same purpose as grids, but they are more flexible. A modular scale, like a musical scale, is a prearranged set of harmonious proportions. In essence, it is a measuring stick whose units are *indivisible* (or are treated as

Standard grid for three-column magazine

such) and are *not of uniform size*. The traditional sequence of type sizes shown on page 45, for example, is a modular scale. The single- and double-stranded Fibonacci series discussed on pp 157–158 are modular scales as well. These scales can, in fact, be put directly to use in page design by altering the units from points to picas. More examples of modular scales are shown on the following page.

It is perfectly feasible to create a new modular scale for any project requiring one, and the scale can be founded on any convenient single or multiple proportion – a given page size, for example, or the dimensions of a set of illustrations, or something implicit in the subject matter. A work on astronomy might use a modular scale based on star charts or Bode's law of interplanetary distances. A book on Greek art might be laid out using intervals from one or more of the Greek musical scales or, of course, the golden section. A work of modernist literature might be designed using something more deliberately arcane – perhaps a scale based on the proportions of the author's hand. Generally speaking, a scale based on two ratios ($1:\varphi$ and $1:2$, for example) will give more flexible and interesting results than a scale founded on just one.

The Half Pica Modular scale illustrated overleaf is actually a miniaturized version of the architectural scale of Le Corbusier, which is based in turn on the proportions of the human body.

See Le Corbusier, *The Modulor* (2nd ed., 1954).

Examples

The formula for designing a perfect page is the same as the formula for writing one: start at the upper left hand corner and work your way across and down; then turn the page and try again. The examples on the following pages show only a few of the many kinds of typographic structures that might evolve along the way.

In fact, the weaving of the text and the tailoring of the page are thoroughly interdependent. We can discuss them one by one, and we can separate each in turn into a series of simple, unintimidating questions. But the answers to these questions must all, in the end, fold back into a single answer. The page, the pamphlet or the book must be seen as a whole if it is to look like one. If it appears to be only a series of individual solutions to separate typographic problems, who will believe that its message coheres?

In analyzing the examples on the following pages, these symbols are used:

Proportions: P = page proportion: h/w
T = textblock proportion: d/m

Page size: w = width of page (trim-size)
h = height of page (trim-size)

Textblock: m = measure (width of primary textblock)
d = depth (height) of primary textblock (excluding running heads, folios, etc)
λ = line height (type size plus added lead)
n = secondary measure (width of secondary column)
c = column width, where there are even multiple columns

Margins: s = spine margin (back margin)
t = top margin (head margin)
e = fore-edge (front margin)
f = foot margin
g = internal gutter (on a multiple-column page)

Page and textblock proportions (P and T in the examples) are given here as single values (1.414, for example). To find the same values in the table on page 148, look up the corresponding *ratio* (1 : 1.414, for example).

P = variable; T = 1.75. Margins: $t = h/12$; $f = 3t/2$; $g = t/2$ or $t/3$. Text columns from Isaiah Scroll A, from Qumran Cave 1, on the Dead Sea. The column depth is 29 lines and the measure is 28 picas, giving a line length of roughly 40 characters. Elsewhere in the scroll, column widths range from 21.5 to 39 picas. Paragraphs begin on a new line but – in keeping with the crisp, square Hebrew characters – are not indented. (Palestine, perhaps first century BC.) Original size: 26 × 725 cm.

P = 1.5 [2 : 3]; T = 1.7 [tall pentagon]. Margins: $s = t = w/9$; $e = 2s$. The text is a fantasy novel, Francesco Colonna's *Hypnerotomachia Poliphili,* set in a roman font cut by Francesco Griffo. (Aldus Manutius, Venice, 1499.) Original size: 20.5 × 31 cm.

Examples

P = 1.62 [golden section]; T = 1.87 [tall hexagon]. Margins: $s = w/9$; $t = s$; $e = 2s$. Secondary column: $g = w/75$; $n = s$. The text is in Claude Garamond's 14 pt roman; the sidenotes are 12 pt italic. The gutter between main text and sidenotes is tiny: 6 or 7 pt against a main text measure of 33.5 picas. But the differences in size and face prevent any confusion. The text is a history of the Hundred Years' War. (Jean Froissart, *Histoire et chronique,* Jean de Tournes, Paris, 1559.) Original size: roughly 21 × 34 cm.

This grid is analyzed on the facing page.

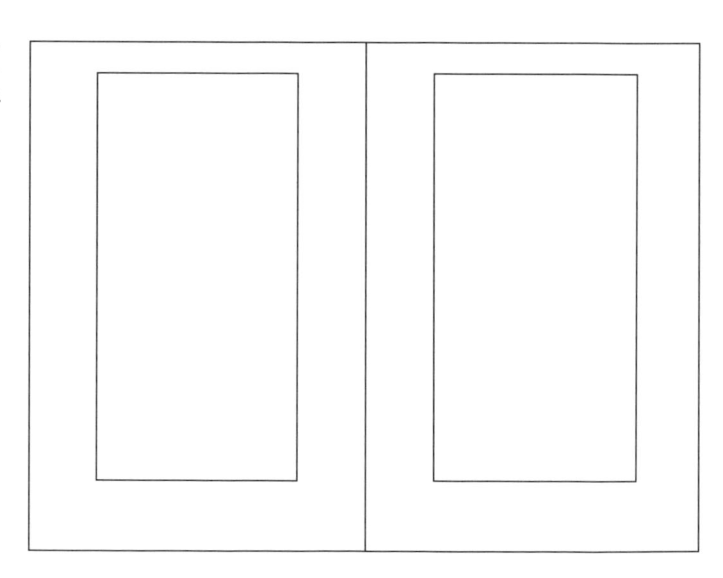

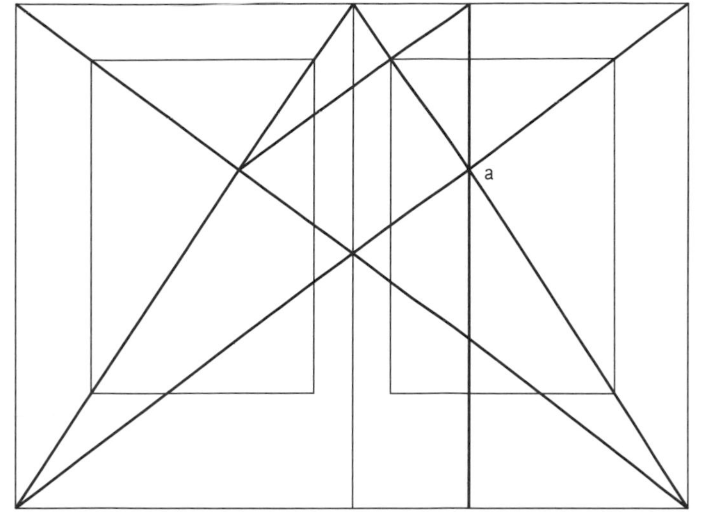

P = T = 1.5 [2 : 3]. Margins: $s = w/9$; $t = h/9$; $e = 2s$; $f = 2t$. The margins are thus in the proportion $s : t : e : f = 2 : 3 : 4 : 6$. A sound, elegant and basic medieval structure, which will work for any proportion of page and textblock, so long as the two remain in unison. Spine and head margins may be ninths, tenths, twelfths or any other desired proportion of the page size. Twelfths, of course, give a fuller and more efficient page, with less white space. But if the page proportion is 2 : 3 and the spine and head margins are ninths, as shown here, the consonance of textblock and page is considerably deepened, because $d = w$, which is to say, the depth of the textblock matches the width of the page. Thus $m : w = d : h = w : h = m : d = s : t = e : f = 2 : 3$. Point a, where the half and full diagonals intersect, is one third of the way down and across the textblock and the page. Jan Tschichold, 1955, after Villard de Honnecourt, France, c. 1280. See Tschichold's *The Form of the Book* (1991).

Scribes employing this format often designed their pages so that the line height was an even factor of the spine margin. If $\lambda = s/3$, the depth of the textblock will be 27 lines. If $\lambda = s/4$, the depth of the textblock will be 36 lines.

FACING PAGE: P = 1.5 [2 : 3]; T = 2 [double square]. Margins: $s = e = w/5$; $t = s/2$. The text is a book of poems, set throughout in a chancery italic with roman capitals. The designer and publisher of this book was a master calligrapher, certainly aware of the tradition that the inner margins should be smaller than the outer. He followed that tradition himself with books of prose, but in this book of poems he chose to center the textblock on the page. The text throughout is set in one size. Titles are set in the capitals of the text font, letterspaced about 30%. There are no running heads or other diversions. (Giangiorgio Trissino, *Canzone,* Ludovico degli Arrighi, Rome, *c.* 1523.) Original size: 12.5 × 18.75 cm.

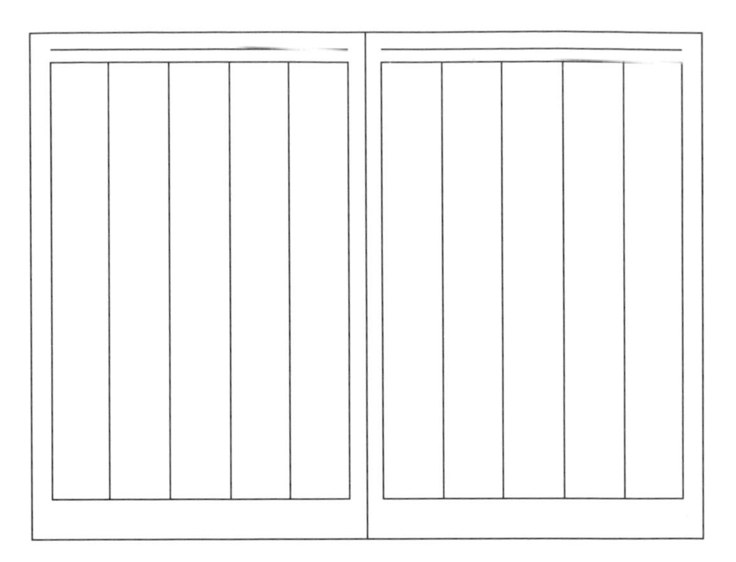

P = 1.5 [2 : 3]; T = 1.54 [pentagon textblock]. Margins: $s = w/20$; $t = s = h/30$; $e = w/15 = 4s/3$; $f = 2t$. This is the format used for the index to the fifth edition of the *Times Atlas of the World* (London, 1975). The page is a standard medieval shape. The text is set in 5.5 pt Univers leaded 0.1 pt on a 12-pica measure, in five subdivided columns per page. Columns are separated by thin vertical rules. Keywords and folios, at the top of the page, are in 16 pt Univers semibold. (Because of their prominence, these running heads are included here in calculating the size and shape of the textblock.) The text is 204 lines deep, yielding an average of 1000 names per page for 217 pages. This index is a masterpiece of its kind: a potent typographic symbol, an efficient work of reference, and a comfortable text to browse. Original size: 30 × 45 cm.

This grid is analyzed on the facing page.

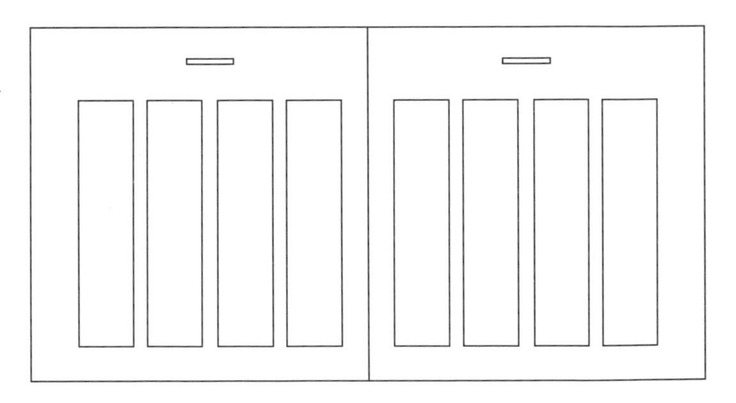

P = 1.414 [$\sqrt{2}$]; T = 1.62 [φ, the golden section]. Margins: $s = t = w/9$ and $e = f = 2s$. This is a simple format for placing a golden-section textblock on an ISO page, locking the two together with margins in the proportions 1 : 2. Two possible locations for folios are shown: in the upper outside margin and (as an alternative) underneath the lower outside corner of the textblock. There is also ample room for sidenotes in the fore-edge if required. If the spine and top margins on these pages are increased to $w/8$, while the textblock and page are held at their original proportion, the relationship of the margins becomes $e = f = \varphi s$, another golden section.

FACING PAGE: P = 1.1; T = 0.91; $c = w/6$. Margins: $s = w/14$; $e = 2s$; $t = 3s$; $f = 3s/2$; $g = m/20$. The proportions of the textblock are the *reciprocal of the proportions of the page*: 0.91 = 1/1.1, which is to say that the textblock is the same shape as the page, rotated 90°. But if the gutters are removed from the textblock and the four columns closed up solid, the textblock collapses to the same shape *in the same orientation* as the page. In other words, the textblock has been expanded from the same shape to the reciprocal shape of the page *entirely by the addition of white space*. The text is the Greek Bible, lettered in uncials, about 13 characters per line. There are no spaces between the words, but there is some punctuation, and the text has a slight rag, with line breaks carefully chosen. This subtle piece of craftsmanship was produced in Egypt in the fourth century. It is the Codex Sinaiticus, Add. Ms. 43725, at the British Library, London. Original size: 34.5 × 38 cm.

P = 1.414 [$\sqrt{2}$]; T = 2 [double square]. Margins: $s = w/12$; $f = 2t = h/9$; $e = w/3$. The wide fore-edge of this manuscript book had a purpose: it was deliberately left free for sidenotes to be added by the owner. The text is a sequence of short poems by the Roman poet Horace, written in Caroline minuscule. (Ms. Plut. 34.1, Laurentian Library, Florence; tenth century.)

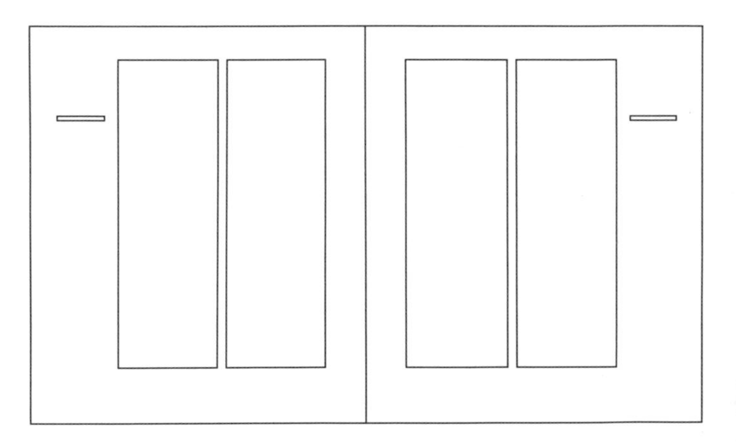

P = 1.176 [truncated pentagon page]; T = 1.46. Margins: $s = h/11$; $t = 5s/6$; $e = 5s/2$; $f = 3s/2$. Columns: $c = 3w/10$; $g = s/4$. The text (set in Friedrich Poppl's Pontifex, 11/13 × 17 RR) is a series of essays on twentieth-century art, published in Canada in 1983, with many full-page illustrations. Original size: 24 × 28 cm.

8.8.1 *Improvise, calculate, and improvise some more.*

Numerical values – used by all typographers in their daily work – give an impression of exactness. Careful measurement and accurate calculation are indeed important in typography, but they are not its final purpose, and moments arise in every project when exactness bumps its head against approximation. On the mechanical side, paper expands and contracts, and printing presses, folding machines and trimming knives – not to speak of typesetting hardware and software – all have their margins of error. The typographer can rarely profit from these variations and cannot entirely prevent them. On the planning side, however, imprecision can often be put to better use.

Some typographers prefer to design by arithmetic from the outset, in a space composed of little invisible bricks called points and picas. Others prefer to work in the free two-dimensional space of a sketchpad, converting their layouts afterward to typographic measure. Most work involves a combination of these methods, with occasional collisions between the two. But the margins of inexactness that crop up in the rounding of units, in conflicts between optical and arithmetic spacing and centering, in combining proportions, and in translating from one form of measurement to another should be welcomed as opportunities, not as inconsistencies to be ignored, glossed over or begrudged. The equal temperament of the typesetting machine and the just intonation of the sketchpad should be used to test and refine one another until the final answer sings.

8.8.2 *Adjust the type and the spaces within the textblock using typographic increments, but rely on free proportions to adjust the empty space.*

Proportions are more flexible than picas, and it is usually convenient and appealing to work in even units. A margin of 5.32 picas, for example, begs to be altered to 5 or 5¼ or 5½. But picas per se are less important than proportions, and the system of typographic sizes and units serves the interrelations of letterforms better than it serves the interrelations of empty space. As a general rule, it is better to make incremental jumps in the textblock first and to readjust the margins thereafter – paying more attention in the latter case to absolute proportion than to convenient units of measurement. When space is measured purely in points, the temptation to rearrange it into even picas is miraculously lessened.

Improvisations and Adjustments

8.8.3 *Keep the page design supple enough to provide a livable home for the text.*

Architects build perfectly proportioned kitchens, living rooms and bedrooms in which their clients will make, among other things, a mess. Typographers likewise build perfectly proportioned pages, then distort them on demand. The text takes precedence over the purity of the design, and the typographic texture of the text takes precedence over the absolute proportions of the individual page.

If, for instance, three lines remain at the end of a chapter, looking forlorn on a page of their own, the design must flex to accommodate them. The obvious choices are: (1) running two of the previous spreads a line long (that is, adding one line to the depth of two pairs of facing pages), which will leave the final page one line short; (2) running half a dozen of the previous spreads a line short, thereby bumping a dozen lines along to the final page; or (3) reproportioning some non-textual element – perhaps an illustration or the sinkage, if any, at the head of the chapter.

Spacious chapter heads stand out in a book, as they are meant to. Reproportioning the sinkage is therefore a poor option unless all chapter heads can be reproportioned to match. And running six spreads short is, on the face of it, clearly a greater evil than running two spreads long.

If there are only a few pages to the document, the whole thing can, and probably should, be redesigned to fit the text. But in a book of many pages, widow lines, orphaned subheads, and the runt ends of chapters or sections are certain to require reproportioning some spreads. A rigid design that demands an invariant page depth is therefore inappropriate for a work of any length. Altering the leading on short pages to preserve a standard depth (vertical justification, it is sometimes called) is not a solution. Neither is stuffing extra space between the paragraphs. These antics destroy the fabric of the text and thus strike at the heart of the book.

9

The state of the art has more by far to do with the knowledge and skill of its practitioners than with the subtleties of their tools, but tools can constrain that skill or set it free. The limitations of the tools are therefore also of some interest. They are of special interest now, because they are subject to rapid change.

9.1 THE HUNDRED-THOUSAND CHARACTER ALPHABET

It is often said that the Latin alphabet consists of 26 letters, the Greek of 24 and the Arabic of 28. If you confine yourself to one case only, a narrow historical window and the dialect in power, this assertion can hold true. If you include both caps and lower case, accented letters and a global set of consonants and vowels – á à â å ã ä ą ă ā æ ǽ ç ć č ċ ð đ é ł ñ ň ņ ő š ś ş þ ű ů ū ŵ ý ž ź ż and all the rest – the Latin alphabet is not 26 letters long after all; it is closer to 600 and able to increase at any time. The alphabet that classicists now use for classical Greek, with its long parade of vowels and diacritics – ά ὰ ᾶ ἀ ἄ ἂ ἆ ἁ ἅ ἃ ἇ ᾷ ᾇ, and so on – is modest by comparison: fewer than 300 glyphs altogether.

To the 600-character globalized Latin alphabet, mathematicians, grammarians, chemists and even typographers are prone to make additions: arabic numerals, punctuation, technical symbols, letters borrowed from Hebrew, Greek and Cyrillic, and, where the letterforms require or invite them, a few typographic ligatures and alternates as well. There is no hope at this stage of counting the number of sorts or glyphs precisely, but the total is clearly over a thousand.

At the end of the eighteenth century, an English-speaking hand compositor's standard lower case had 54 compartments, holding roman or italic *a* to *z*, arabic numerals, basic ligatures, spaces and punctuation. The upper case had another 98, containing caps and analphabetics. That total, 98 + 54 = 152, is the English-speaking hand compositor's minimum basic allotment. When more sorts are required, as they very often are, supplementary cases are used. Two pair give 304 compartments; three pair give 456; four pair give 608. This has been the ordinary typographic ballpark for some time. How Gutenberg's cases were arranged we do not know, but we know how big they were. He used not 26

Printing enthusiasts sometimes speak of *the lay of the case* as if it were universal law – but the lay of the case is as localized as the lay of the land. Hand compositors often set not from paired but from single cases. These have been reduced to as few as 89 compartments but sometimes contain 400 or more.

but 290 different sorts, in one face and one size, in an unaccented script, to set his 42-line Bible. The Monotype machine, built five centuries later, with 255 (later 272) positions in a standard matrix case, had fallen only a little ways behind.

Many computer keyboards have over 100 keys, but only 47 are tied to characters. (This odd number is made even by the spacebar.) Each character key has, at minimum, a plain and a shift position, reaching 94 characters in all: ordinarily the 94 basic ASCII characters. But the keys can be remapped and can easily be coded to reach four characters each instead of two. (An example of such a keyboard is shown on page 92.) When more than 47 × 4 = 188 characters are needed at one time, more than one keyboard map is in order as well. Function keys are normally used to jump from one map to another: Latin to Greek to Cyrillic to Hebrew for example.

Early computers and e-mail links were, by comparison, living in typographic poverty. The alphabet they used was the basic character set defined by the American Standard Code for Information Interchange, or ASCII. Each character was limited to seven bits of binary information, so the maximum number of characters was $2^7 = 128$. Thirty-three of those were normally subtracted for control codes, and one was the code for an empty space. This leaves 94: not even enough to hold the standard working character set of Spanish, French or German. The fact that such a character set was long considered adequate tells us something about the cultural narrowness of American civilization, or American technocracy, in the midst of the twentieth century.

The extended ASCII character set, which has been in general use since 1980, is made from eight-bit characters. This gives $2^8 = 256$ slots altogether. As a rule, glyphs are assigned to some 230 of these. Editing and composition software often limits the working selection to 216 or less. The upper register of this set – altogether invisible on a normal computer keyboard – is usually filled out with characters selected from the Latin 1 Character Set established by ISO (the International Organization for Standardization, Geneva). These characters – *ä ç é ñ* and so on – are identified and discussed in appendix B, page 301.

The allotment of 216 or 230 characters is meagre but adequate for basic communication in all the 'official' languages of Western Europe and North America. This ignores the needs of mathematicians, linguists and other specialists, and of millions of normal human beings who use the Latin alphabet for Czech, Hausa, Hungarian, Latvian, Navajo, Polish, Romanian, Turkish, Vietnamese, Welsh, Yoruba, and so on. The extended ASCII character set is the alphabet not of the real world nor of the UN General Assembly but of NATO: a technological memento of the them-and-us mentality that thrived in the Cold War.

Good, affordable software that would handle thousands of characters efficiently was for sale (and in fact was widely used) in the early 1980s. Standardization within the industry shrank this palette down, then enormously increased it. Some typographic tools have not caught up. Typographically sectarian and culturally stunted software is widespread.

Earlier typographers were free to cut another punch at any time and cast another character. The freedom to do likewise exists with the computer. But finding room for all these letters in a shared standard alphabet involves, in the digital world, a shift from eight-bit to sixteen-bit characters. When we make this change, the alphabet increases to $2^{16} = 65{,}536$ characters. The first version of a standard set of characters this size – known as Unicode – was roughed out at the end of the 1980s and published in the early 1990s. By the year 2000, the rudiments of Unicode were embedded in the operating systems of home computers, and major digital founders had adopted it as the new encoding standard.

The State of the Art

It is, like any standard, less than perfect, but it forms a working protocol both for a global Latin alphabet and for the technological coexistence of Arabic, Bengali, Chinese, Cyrillic, Devanagari, Greek, Hebrew, Korean, Latin, Thai, Tibetan and hundreds of other scripts. It was soon clear, however, that 65,000 characters wasn't enough. To extend the set, $2^{10} = 2{,}048$ of the original allotment were assigned to function in pairs. This permits an additional $1024^2 = 1{,}048{,}576$ characters. In its latest published form (version 4.0.0, issued in 2003), Unicode defines 96,382 characters, sets 137,468 aside for private use, and still has roughly 878,000 free for future allocation.

See *The Unicode Standard*, Version 4.0.0 (2003), on line at *www.unicode.org.*

Few of us may need (and few may want to memorize) 100,000 characters. Typographers working in Chinese have often mastered 20,000; those who work in Korean learn 3,000 or more; most literate humans learn a thousand characters or fewer. Yet authors, editors, typographers and ordinary citizens who just want to be able to spell Dvořák, Miłosz, Mą'ii or al-Fārābī, or to quote a line of Sophocles or Pushkin, or the Vedas or the Sutras or the Psalms, or to write $\varphi \neq \pi$, are beneficiaries of a system this inclusive. So is everyone who want to read their e-mail in an alphabet other than Latin or a language other than English.

ä ő
あ ɤ
ث 字 ∇̇
ή̣ y
צ ṝ ٣
ŭ̈
й
тц
ở
℘
⇆
ƛ

There may also never be a font of 100,000 well-made characters designed by one designer. But good fonts with well over ten thousand characters, keyed to the Unicode system, are now readily available. Computer operating systems now support them. More importantly, fonts for particular symbol sets and alphabets can be linked and tuned to one another by adjusting weight, letterfit and scale. This kind of typographic diplomacy is a task of some importance – and when character sets are joined in this way, sharing typographic space whether or not they are all on one font, Unicode can serve as a coordinating mechanism.

Unicode is relatively new, but many of the resources it catalogues are ancient. Composition software, communication links and keyboards are just starting to catch up.

9.2 THE SUBSTANCE OF THE FONT

Within the tiny confraternity of metal typefounders and letterpress printers there is a subtribe that can argue day and night about recipes for type metal. In such a company, the question of whether to add or subtract five per cent of tin or antimony, or one per cent of copper, can lead to a long and heated exchange. In the community of digital founders and programmers, there is a corresponding subtribe capable of arguing till death about the merits of one digital format versus another.

Type metal is typically 60% to 80% lead, 15% to 30% antimony and 5% to 10% tin. Some founders also like to add a trace of copper.

Between 1980 and 2000, several digital font formats were introduced. Each one's sponsors claimed their product was superior to its predecessors, and sometimes they had grounds to make such claims. In every case, however, it has turned out that what genuinely matters is not the format used so much as the level of hands-on workmanship, good sense and attention to detail. In metal and digital founding alike, the standard is set by the human who does the work, not by the recipe or by the brand name of the tools.

Bitmapped fonts came into use in the 1970s. Fonts of this sort are defined by simple addition and subtraction: *this pixel on, that pixel off, these pixels on, those pixels off.* In 1982, with the introduction of PostScript, bitmapped printer fonts rapidly gave way to fonts defined as scalable outlines. A decade later came the TrueType format, which differs from PostScript in two essential respects. First, PostScript and TrueType take a quite different approach to hinting (that is, they have different ways of addressing the problems caused by inadequate resolution). Second, their descriptive mathematics are different. Both interpret letterforms in terms of Bézier splines (that is to say, they rely on algebraic techniques developed by Paul de Casteljau and Pierre Bézier in France in the 1960s and 1970s) – but PostScript splines are cubic, while TrueType's are quadratic.

In mechanics, a spline is a flexible strip that will bend under tension. Boatbuilders and furniture makers use them for laying out curves. In mathematics, a spline is a curve that behaves as if it had fiber: sturdy enough to hold itself up yet limber enough to straighten and bend, stretch and retract.

Think of a curve as a tensile line, bent by means of a lever attached to each end. Such a curve can be mathematically defined in terms of four points. Two of these are the *endpoints* of the curve. The other two, at the far ends of the levers, are known as the curve's *control points*. If the two imaginary levers can be controlled independently, then cubic equations [as for example, $f(t) = (1 - t)^3\text{E}_1 + 3t(1 - t)^2\text{C}_1 + 3t^2(1 - t)\text{C}_2 + t^3\text{E}_2$] will be required to describe the curve, and it is called a cubic spline.

The levers themselves *are not part of the curve*, and the control points are usually off the curve. In the simplest case, however, these imaginary levers have a length of zero. Then the control points and the endpoints coincide, and the curve is a straight line.

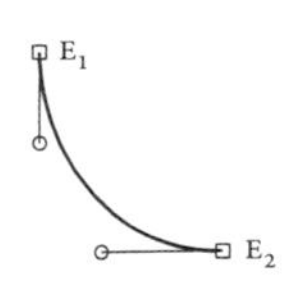

One way to simplify a cubic spline is to tie the levers together so that both control points coincide (or so that one control point has a fixed relation to the other). If that is done, the mathematical description can be simplified from cubic to quadratic [along the lines, $f(t) = (1 - t)^2\text{E}_1 + 2t(1 - t)\text{C} + t^2\text{E}_2$].

A simple cubic spline, above, and the same curve (more or less) reconceived as two quadratic splines, below.

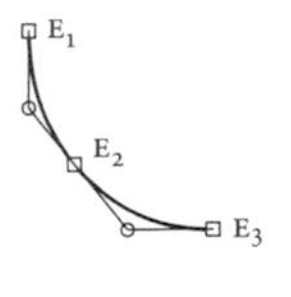

There are some other complications. A cubic spline, for instance, can have additional anchors or points of inflection; a quadratic spline cannot. In brief, cubic splines can be simple or complex; quadratic splines can only be comparatively simple. So translating a cubic spline to quadratic form can mean converting one spline into several (and the translation even then may be imperfect). A TrueType letterform will therefore often have more splines than the equivalent form in PostScript, but these are usually defined by fewer points, and mathematically speaking, the points are usually simpler to describe.

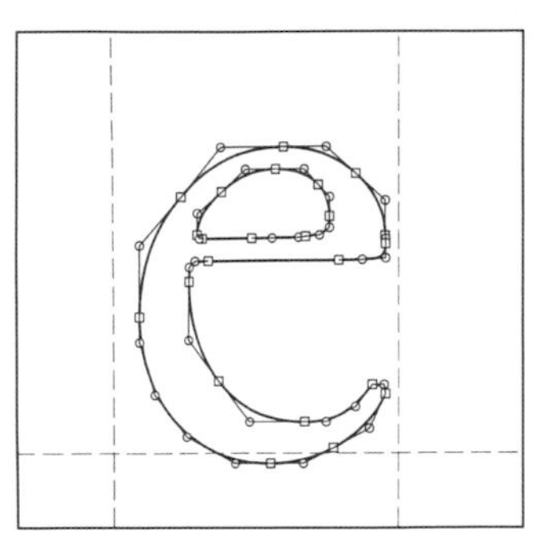

All quadratic splines can be perfectly expressed as cubic splines, but *not vice versa*. In quadratic equations, the highest power is *two* (e.g., x squared: x^2); in cubic equations, it is three (e.g., x cubed: x^3).

The *e* on the left, encoded in PostScript, is described by way of 18 cubic splines defined by 60 points. The *e* on the right, encoded in TrueType, is described by way of 23 quadratic splines defined by 52 points. Endpoints are represented by squares, control points by circles.

Several font formats based on PostScript have developed over the years. The one that has prospered is the early version known as Type One. PostScript fonts are accordingly referred to as PS, T-1 or PS-1. (For most purposes, these are synonymous.) Tens of thousands of fonts are now available in this format. Many are available now in TrueType (TT) format too (often directly converted from PostScript). In both, the level of technical quality ranges – like the design – from pathetic to superb.

The Substance of the Font

A promising amplification of PS-1, developed at the beginning of the 1990s, is known as Multiple Master (MM). Fonts in the MM format are continuously adjustable along any of several axes, determined by the designer. These axes can include, for example, width, weight, optimal size, extender length, terminal shape or serif formation. To date, however, relatively few such fonts have actually been made.

aaaaaaaaaa

Adobe Jenson MM is scalable both for weight and for optimal size. Here one letter of uniform weight is scaled from 6 to 72 pt optimal size. The forms are then resized to the same x-height so their shapes and effective weights can be compared. If each letter is set at the size intended, optical balance is achieved.

In Adobe's terminology, the size axis is called *optical*, not optimal size. What is at issue, however, is physical scale, which is visceral as much as optical.

The initial TrueType format led to two important variations. These are Graphic Extension (GX) fonts, first released in 1994, and TrueType Open (TTO), dating from 1995. These formats are significant for their ability to accommodate large character sets together with automatic contextual substitution of variants and ligatures. Both these capabilities are essential for many Asian scripts (Arabic, Devanagari, Tibetan and Malayalam for example). They are also vital to many historical forms (and possibly some future forms) of Greek and Latin script.

Makers of editorial and composition software did not respond to these advances as eagerly as hoped. Partly for this reason, an agreement was reached in the late 1990s between the originators of PostScript (Adobe Systems) and the inheritors of TrueType (Microsoft) on yet another font format known as OpenType (OT or OTF). Outwardly, an OpenType font resembles a GX or TTO font. It can include a colossal character set with multiple encodings. (It can hold, for example, thousands of Chinese or

Korean characters, and a complete pan-European set of Lati
Greek and Cyrillic with regional variants.) Several styles of figures and several sets of small caps can reside on the same font with the u&lc. The font can also include a set (or many sets) of rules for automatic substitution of alternates and ligatures and automatic repositioning of glyphs in certain contexts. And the letterforms within an OT font can be described in *either* cubic or quadratic terms. The kernel of the font, in other words, can be either PS or TT.

The St… of the Ar…

The composition software has to work with such a font to bring its features into play. When run with parochial software, an OT font's OT features disappear. It behaves like a normal T-1 or TT font with 216 or fewer accessible characters.

Several thousand OT fonts have now been issued – and again, the quality ranges from dismal to superb. Some OT fonts in fact take no advantage of the format's capabilities; they are functionally identical to plain vanilla PS or TT fonts. Others are rich and subtle. Without opening the package and checking out the contents, there is no real way to tell.

Typography and typefounding will not save the world. But peaceful coexistence and exchange among all the world's writing systems could be a gesture in that direction. Even this modest goal is a good ways off and may never be reached. But it is now a perceptible goal, which is something in itself.

9.3 THE MULTIDIMENSIONAL FONT

9.3.1 *Glyphs and Characters*

Typographers are frequently surprised to learn that small caps, text figures, swashes and other things they need and use are nowhere to be found in the lengthening Unicode catalogue. But Unicode lists *textual* not *typographic* symbols. Its aim is to embrace all linguistically meaningful signs, not all their typographically desirable forms and permutations. Because of inconsistencies in its original design, and because it has absorbed inconsistent ISO standards, even the recently purified version of Unicode includes some lingering compound characters. In theory, however, authors, editors and denizens of Unicode think and transmit elemental signs (f + f + i, for instance, rather than *ffi*), and typographers transform these underlying abstract entities into their endlessly varying outward manifestations.

This mode of thinking about text transmission and typography has proven very fruitful, especially in relation to non-Latin scripts. And it has prompted type designers and founders to distinguish with some care between a character set and a *glyph palette.* The plain and swash forms of *z* in Arrighi or Poetica, for example, are different glyphs (or different *sorts,* a hand compositor would say) that correspond to a single character. In fact this distinction between characters and glyphs has been familiar to scribes for millennia. It was also familiar to Gutenberg.

In the early days of letterpress, punchcutters frequently cut multiple versions of common letters and other characters (such as the hyphen), so that their subtle, often subliminal, variations would invigorate the page. A hand compositor reaching into the typecase for an *e* might then come up with any of several similar but not identical forms. Few readers may have consciously noticed the difference, yet each of these slyly variant letters contributed its mote of vitality to the page. After five hundred years on the library shelf, that vitality remains. It comes in part from the artistry of the cutters, and in part from the use of a system that lets the glyphs outnumber the characters.

For the origins of Sophia, see Stanley Morison, *Politics and Script* (1972): 98–103, and the review of Sophia and Mantinia in *Print* 48.2 (New York, 1994): 121–22.

Matthew Carter's Sophia, to take a more recent example, is a digital face consisting only of capitals, yet it includes multiple glyphs for many characters. There are four forms of T, three forms each of E, F and R, two forms of A, C, G, H, I, K and many other letters. Some of the variant forms are independent; others are components used in custom-building ligatures. Sophia's stake in the character set is small, because it has no lower case, but its glyph palette is relatively large (and Carter has been urged to make it larger).

Apart from special cases like Sophia and Zapfino, most fonts of Latin type are limited at present to only one glyph for most characters, and a few contextual glyphs like *ff* and *ffi.* At the level of the *family* there are several glyphs per character: a, *a,* ᴀ, **a**, ***a*** and sometimes many more. But in English the rules for choosing among these glyphs are editorial as much as typographic. In the Arabic alphabet, by contrast, multiple glyphs are essential in every font, and the choice of glyph is governed mostly by scriptorial or typographic rules. There are no capitals, small caps or italics in Arabic script, but ligatures are frequent, and even a font of simplified Arabic type contains about a hundred basic glyphs for the 28 Arabic letters, because most letters have four different forms: initial, medial, final and free-standing.

THE INTELLECT OF MAN
IS FORCED TO CHOOSE +
PERFECTION OF THE LIFE
OR OF THE WORK +
— AND IF IT TAKE THE
SECOND MUST REFUSE +
A HEAVENLY MANSION,
RAGING IN THE DARK +
WILLIAM · BUTLER · YEATS

Matthew Carter's Sophia (Carter & Cone, 1993) is a face with alternate glyphs for many characters. Many of these alternates form ligatures.

This explains the necessity for 'private use' characters in Unicode. Typographic ligatures, text figures, small caps, swashes and other alternate glyphs are placed in that domain. The composition software must then be taught to find them.

Lexical ligatures (æ, œ, ß, etc) are those whose usage is defined by lexicographers and grammarians. These are in Unicode. *Typographic* ligatures (ff, fi, ct, etc) are those whose usage is primarily a matter of typographic style. The distinction is by no means absolute.

9.3.2 *Manual, Random and Programmed Variation*

The text is a string of characters; the font is a palette of glyphs – along with all the information (width tables, kerning tables and so on) needed for stringing the glyphs to match the characters. If we think about typography in these terms, it is clear that every font could offer the typographer a different range of choices: a different palette of glyphs, in other words, mapped perhaps in many different ways, to the same set of standard characters.

Zuzana Ličko's type family Mrs Eaves (Emigre, 1996) is an example. There are five basic members of the family: roman, italic, bold roman, and two sizes of small caps. The roman, italic and bold are each equipped with a supplementary battery of 71 ligatures. Some of these are subtle, some distinctly cheeky. A supporting piece of software, engineered by Just van Rossum, lets the compositor decide which ligatures to use, then implants them automatically wherever the equivalent string of characters appears. This is how most systems for handling optional ligatures ought to work – and how, perhaps, one day, they will.

How many ligatures is a lot? There are only 10 or 12 nowadays (æ, œ, Æ, Œ, ß, fi, fl, ff, ffi, ffl; sometimes fj and ffj) in a normal Latin text font, but there are 36 in the font for Gutenberg's 42-line Bible (*c.* 1455), 45 in Robert Granjon's second civilité (*c.* 1570), 55 in Robert Slimbach's Poetica (1992), 70 in Francesco Griffo's first italic (1499), and about 350 in each font of Claude Garamond's Royal Greeks (*c.* 1541).

ae æ cky ee ffy ffr gg ggy gi
ip it ky oe œ sp ſs ſs Th tt tty ty
ae æ cky ct ee fb ff ffy ffr ft ggy gi gy ip
it ky oe œ OO sp ſs st py tt tty ty tw

Some of the ligatures in Zuzana Ličko's typeface Mrs Eaves. There are 30 ligatures for the caps, 40 for the lower case, and one hybrid (Th). Each of these exists in three forms: roman, italic and bold. The face (though not its complement of ligatures) is based on John Baskerville's roman and italic. It is named for Sarah Ruston Eaves (Mrs Richard Eaves), who for sixteen years was Baskerville's resident housekeeper and lover, and for another eleven years (after the death of her first husband) was his lawful wedded wife.

If every font can have a slightly different set of glyphs, pointless to expect the composition software by itself to cho effectively among them. Three other possibilities suggest them selves: (1) the choice of glyphs can be left to the typographer, who picks them and inserts them each by hand; (2) where there are variant forms of single letters, the choice can be left to chance; (3) the rules for choosing glyphs can be tailored to the typeface and embedded in the font itself.

The
of the

The first of these options has been the normal practice with foundry type for centuries. Poetica, Sophia and Zapf Renaissance, in their ordinary PostScript incarnations, belong to the same tradition. By including extra glyphs for certain characters, these faces offer digital typographers the same degree of freedom (and require in return the same investment of skill and attention) that hand compositors have enjoyed since the days of Gutenberg, Ratdolt and Jenson.

The second option – letting the designer's chosen variants assert themselves at random – is an old and distinguished method too. Francesco Griffo, Claude Garamond and Simon de Colines are three of many early masters who cut multiple forms of letters. Some alternates (with forms like v and n) were used selectively at the beginnings and ends of words, in contexts where their extra width was useful to the line. Others, which differed among themselves scarcely enough to reach the threshold of visibility, could serve – and did serve – to enliven the text at random.

David Pye discusses the importance of *the threshold of visibility* in his perceptive book *The Nature and Art of Workmanship* (1968).

Another kind of random variation involves the interaction of the craftsman's skill and the texture of materials. The letterforms of Griffo and Colines were cut with immense care. But the letters they cut were struck by hand in brass, then cast and dressed and set by hand, inked by hand with handmade ink and printed by hand in a handmade wooden press on handmade paper. Every step along the way introduced small variations planned by no one. In the world of the finely honed machine, those human-scale textures are erased. A sterile sameness supervenes.

The computer is, on the face of it, an ideal device for reviving the old luxury of *random variations at the threshold of perception* (quite a different thing from chaos). But conventional typesetting software and hardware focuses instead on the unsustainable ideal of absolute control – and has been hamstrung in the past by the idea of a single glyph per character. There have been several recent attempts to introduce a layer of random variation, but all have had to work against the grain of technological development.

…n early example was Erik van Blokland and Just van Ros…s typeface Beowolf. In its first experimental version (1990), …is face relied on the output device to create truly random perturbations from a single set of letterforms. Though it would not work on all systems, and the evolving hardware and software quickly passed it by, it remains an important landmark in the effort to teach computers what typography really entails.

…ie Open… version of …mann Zapf's Zapfino, the sequence $p + p$ can automatically convert to $p_1 + p_2$, but there are several other options. Four of these are shown below.

dapper
dapper
dapper
dapper

eeeeeeeee eeeeeeeee eeeeeeeee

Beowolf (FontShop, 1990) is at root a statuesque text roman drawn by Erik van Blokland. The letterforms are sent to the output device through a subroutine, devised by Just van Rossum, that provokes distortions of each letter within predetermined limits in unpredetermined ways. Three degrees of randomization are available. Within the specified limits, every letter is a surprise.

Those are two options: manual and random substitution. There is still the third: building glyph-selection rules into the font itself. This gives *predictable* variation. It is now the reigning method for achieving typographic variation, because this is the method adopted by the sponsors of GX, TTO and OT fonts.

For now, therefore, the goal of pleasing randomness – constrained but unplanned variation – goes begging in computerized typography. Is it worth pursuing? Communication requires control, just as life requires control, but it also requires a context beyond its control. Unpremeditated grace is as crucial to the liveliness of the page as it is to the liveliness of the garden.

9.4 METHODS OF JUSTIFICATION

9.4.1 *Use the best available justification engine.*

Most of the type set in the past five hundred years is justified type, and most of it has been justified line by line, by the simple expedient of altering the space between the words. There are, however, better ways. Scribes justify text as they write, by introducing abbreviations and subtly altering the widths of letters. Gutenberg replicated the feat by cutting and casting a host of abbreviations and ligatures along with multiple versions of certain letters, differing modestly in width. In the early 1990s, Peter Karow and Hermann Zapf devised a means of doing much the same in the

Nations are not truly great solely because the individuals
composing them are numerous, free, and active; [nor corporations because of their market share and profits;] but
they are great when these numbers, this freedom, and this
activity [or this market share and profit] are employed in
the service of an ideal higher than that of an ordinary
[hu]man, taken by himself. – MATTHEW ARNOLD [& EVE
SMITH]

FL/RR,
invarian
spacing, le
spacing anc
glyph shape.

Nations are not truly great solely because the individuals
composing them are numerous, free, and active; [nor corporations because of their market share and profits;] but
they are great when these numbers, this freedom, and this
activity [or this market share and profit] are employed in the
service of an ideal higher than that of an ordinary [hu]man,
taken by himself. – MATTHEW ARNOLD [& EVE SMITH]

Justified by
wordspacing
only.

Nations are not truly great solely because the individuals
composing them are numerous, free, and active; [nor corporations because of their market share and profits;] but they
are great when these numbers, this freedom, and this activity
[or this market share and profit] are employed in the service
of an ideal higher than that of an ordinary [hu]man, taken
by himself. – MATTHEW ARNOLD [& EVE SMITH]

Justified by
letterspacing
only.

Nations are not truly great solely because the individuals
composing them are numerous, free, and active; [nor corporations because of their market share and profits;] but they are
great when these numbers, this freedom, and this activity [or
this market share and profit] are employed in the service of
an ideal higher than that of an ordinary [hu]man, taken by
himself. – MATTHEW ARNOLD [& EVE SMITH]

Justified by glyph
reshaping only.

Nations are not truly great solely because the individuals
composing them are numerous, free, and active; [nor corporations because of their market share and profits;] but they are
great when these numbers, this freedom, and this activity [or
this market share and profit] are employed in the service of
an ideal higher than that of an ordinary [hu]man, taken by
himself. – MATTHEW ARNOLD [& EVE SMITH]

Justified by a
combination of
wordspacing, let-
terspacing and
glyph reshaping.

digital medium – and without relying on scribal abbreviations. When the method they had devised was first offered for sale, it was rejected. Now it is being absorbed. The justification engine used in setting this book is in essence the one imagined by Zapf and engineered by Karow more than a decade ago: an electronic version of what Gutenberg envisioned in the 1440s, as he analyzed the work of master scribes.

Methods of Justification

Unlike a Monotype or Linotype machine, the computer is perfectly capable of calculating the pros and cons of linebreaks over a whole paragraph. It can break a line in one place, then go back and break it again, and again, and again, if subsequent lines give it reason to do so. Hand compositors have been known to do the same – but rejustification by hand is a tedious business. The computer, once it learns the trick, can do it in an flash.

Another thing computer software can do – because Karow taught it how – is justify text by making subtle alterations in the widths of letters.

Good justification is calculated paragraph by paragraph instead of line by line. And the best computer justification now relies on microscopic adjustments to the space *between and within the letters* as well as the space between the words. In this book, for example, the justification engine has been permitted to vary the intercharacter spacing by ±3% and to adjust the width of individual glyphs by ±2%. The bulk of the work is still done by adjusting the spaces between words, but there are more letters than spaces in these lines. Tiny adjustments to spaces within and between the letters therefore go a long way toward creating a page of even color and texture.

In English, where on average there are five times more letters than spaces on a page, the allowable elasticity in intra- and intercharacter spacing should usually be held to around one fifth of the elasticity permitted in the spaces between words.

9.5 PIXELS, PROOFS & PRINTING

9.5.1 *If the text will be read on the screen, design it for that medium.*

Like a forest or a garden or a field, an honest page of letters can absorb – and will repay – as much attention as it is given. Much type now, however, is composed not for the page but for the screen of a computer. That screen can be alive with flowing color, but the best computer monitors have dismal resolution (about 140 dpi: less than a quarter the current norm for laser printers and less than 6% of the norm for professional digital typesetting). When the text is crudely rendered, the eye goes looking for distraction, which the screen is all too able to provide.

The screen mimics the sky, not the earth. It bombards the eye with light instead of waiting to repay the gift of vision. It is not simultaneously restful and lively, like a field full of flowers, or the face of a thinking human being, or a well-made typographic page. And we read the screen the way we read the sky: in quick sweeps, guessing at the weather from the changing shapes of clouds, or like astronomers, in magnified small bits, examining details. We look to it for clues and revelations more than wisdom. This makes it an attractive place for the open storage of pulverized information – names, dates, library call numbers, for instance – but not so good a place for thoughtful text.

The screen, in other words, is a reading environment even more fugitive than the newspaper. Intricate, long sentences full of unfamiliar words stand little chance. At text size, subtle and delicate letterforms stand little chance as well. Superscripts and subscripts, footnotes, endnotes, sidenotes disappear. In the harsh light and coarse resolution of the screen, such literate accessories are difficult to see; what is worse, they dispel the essential illusion of speed. So the links and jumps of hypertext replace them. All the subtexts then can be the same size, and readers are at liberty to skip from text to text like children switching channels on TV. When reading takes this form, both sentences and letterforms retreat to blunt simplicity. Forms bred on newsprint and signage are most likely to survive. Good text faces for the screen are therefore as a rule faces with low contrast, a large torso, open counters, sturdy terminals, and slab serifs or no serifs at all.

If it has anything significant to say, a text that scrolls across the screen still needs the typographer's attention, just like any printed text. It may be that the reader, not the typographer, will actually choose the typeface. The typographer may still have some control over other factors of typographic rhythm – type size, measure, leading. Most importantly, the typographer shapes the virtual page, determining the form and frequency of heads, the orientation and placement of illustrations, the disposition of lists and paragraphs. The typographer gives outward and visible form to the text's intrinsic, invisible order. This determines, in large part, who will read the text and how.

9.5.2 *Check the type at every stage.*

Pixels, Proofs and Printing

Digital letterforms can be printed directly on paper with laser printers; they can be typeset onto photosensitive paper, negative film or positive film, from which lithographic printing plates, letterpress blocks or serigraphic stencils are then made; or they can be etched directly onto printing plates that run on an offset press. Each of these electrostatic and photographic transformations provides an opportunity for overexposing or underexposing the type.

Check for accurate color and sharpness in the letterforms at every stage, and check for consistency throughout. Inconsistent exposure is often encountered when the work is set a section at a time, or when corrected pages are rerun. But even when all the work is run at once on one machine, inconsistencies can occur. If, for instance, two shelf lots of film or photosensitive paper are inadvertently mixed, the same machine settings will give two different results.

Mechanical errors are also not unknown in the superficially sanitized, high-tech world of computerized type. Many a finely tooled page has been spoiled in the end by a loose roller or unlubricated ratchet. Check the output against a grid to make sure the leading is consistent, multiple columns align as they should, and the textblock is not trapezoidal unless it is meant to be.

9.5.3 *Follow the work to the printer.*

All typographic decisions – the choice of the type, the choice of size and leading, the calculation of margins and the shaping of the page – involve assumptions about the printing. It is well to find out in advance whether these assumptions stand any chance of being fulfilled. Good printers have much else to teach their clients, and the best typographer can always find something to learn. But the path from the editor's desk to the pressroom floor remains a journey often fraught with danger and surprise. The reason is that it is frequently a journey between economic realms. On the one side, a singular thing, a manuscript, moves slowly through the hands of individual human beings – author, editor, typographer – who make judgements and decisions one by one, and who are free (for a time at least) to change their minds. On the other side, an immensely expensive commodity (blank paper) passes at great speed and irreversibly through an immensely expensive (and therefore obsessively hungry) machine.

Digital methods have helped to bring editing, typography and type design back, in some respects, to the close relationship they enjoyed in the golden age of letterpress. But everything the writer, type designer, editor and typographer do is still contingent on the skills and methods of the printer – and while typography, for many, has returned to cottage scale, printing has enlarged to the dimensions of heavy industry. The freedom afforded by cheap and standardized typesetting hardware and software also comes at a price. That price is the danger of weary sameness and thinness in all the work the typographer does. The use of standard industrial papers, inks, presses and binding machinery can easily erase whatever remains of the typographer's personal touch. Yet printing is what typography is usually thought to be for.

If only by default, it falls to the typographer more than to anyone else to bridge this gap between a world focused on the perfect final proof and the world of its industrial replication. No one else works as close to that frontier as the typographer, and no one has a greater need to understand what happens on both sides.

The margins of books cannot be calculated correctly until the binding method is chosen, and they cannot be right in the end unless the chosen method is followed. The type cannot be chosen without coming to some decision about the kind of paper it will be printed on, and cannot look right in the end if that decision is later betrayed. A change of one eighth inch in the folding pattern or trim size will ruin a precisely measured page.

Yet another way to undercut the type is to print it with the wrong ink. Color control is important whether or not color is used, for there are many hues of black, some veering toward red, some veering toward blue. Redder blacks are acceptable on ivory paper. If the paper is closer to gray or white, the black of the ink should move closer to blue. But it will be process black by default – and the density of the type will be at the mercy of the press foreman's final color adjustments – if the text and process-color illustrations are printed in one go.

Ink gloss is rarely a problem on uncoated paper. On coated stock, the sheen of the ink is frequently out of control. For the sake of legibility in artificial light, inks that are used for printing text on a coated sheet should have *less* reflectivity than the paper, rather than more.

6 MAINTAINING THE SYSTEM

9.6.1 *Consult the ancestors.*

aining
System

Typography is an ancient craft and an old profession as well as a constant technological frontier. It is also in some sense a trust. The lexicon of the tribe and the letters of the alphabet – which are the chromosomes and genes of literate culture – are in the typographer's care. Maintaining the system means more than merely buying the newest fonts from digital foundries and the latest updates for typesetting software.

The rate of change in typesetting methods has been steep – perhaps it has approximated the Fibonacci series – for more than a century. Yet, like poetry and painting, storytelling and weaving, typography itself *has not improved.* There is no greater proof that typography is more art than engineering. Like all the arts, it is basically immune to progress, though it is not immune to change. Typography at its best is sometimes as good, and at its worst is just as bad, as it ever was. The speed of certain processes has certainly increased; some old, hard tricks have come to seem easy, and some new ones have been learned. But the quality of typography and printing, their faithfulness to themselves, and the inherent grace and poise of the finished page, is not greater now than it was in 1465. In several respects, digital typography still lags far behind the methods and resources of Renaissance compositors and medieval scribes.

Maintaining the system means openness to the surprises and gifts of the future; it also means keeping the future in touch with the past. This is done by looking with equal eagerness at the old work and the new. Reproductions, of course, are fine as far as they go, but you will never know what a fifteenth-century manuscript or printed book is like until you touch one, smell one, hold one in your hands.

9.6.2 *Look after the low- as well as the high-technology end.*

A digital typographer is now likely to use two rather flimsy but capable pieces of hardware: a computer, with keyboard and screen, and some kind of proofing device, usually a laser printer. The rest of the system – another computer which imposes the work for the press, and a high-resolution digital plate-maker or other output device – may be miles away.

In the typographer's computer there are likely to be a number of interdependent pieces of software. These will probably include a text editor, composition software, a library of digital fonts, a font manager, and a font editor. There may also be a photo editor and some electronic drawing tools. And the composition software will nowadays include a host of tools for manipulating type, erasing the ancient boundary between text and illustration. All these tools are new, but the craft is old.

The State of the Art

Outside the hardware, but no less essential to the system, more primitive tools are still required: a pica stick, a sketch pad, a drawing board and instruments, and a library of reference works and examples of fine typography for discussion and inspiration. It is the latter, low-technology end of most typesetting systems that is usually in the most urgent need of upgrading.

One good typeface is better and more useful than an infinity of poor ones. Here as always, good means several things. It means that the letterforms themselves are clearly envisioned, lucidly rendered and, beyond all that, convincing. It means they make mute, irrefutable sense to both body and mind. It means that the fabric in which these letterforms are held is well made too. If the type is metal, it means that the metal is well cast – hard, sharp, free of bubbles or sags – and evenly dressed. If the type is digital, it means that the glyphs are correctly aligned and consistently sized, with accurate widths and sensitive kerning instructions. A font of type *can be* (and may or may not be in fact) an electronic artefact of immense sophistication: not only a masterpiece of design but an intangible piece of craftsmanship enriched by many skilled and often uncredited eyes and minds.

Some observers are dismayed and some excited by the complexity of the equipment most typographers now use. Some are excited and others unnerved by the evident power of that equipment and the ease of its operation. Yet inside that complexity, typography persists as what it is: the making of meaningful, durable, abstract, visible signs. When the system crashes, the craft, its purposes, its values and all its possibilities remain.

GROOMING THE FONT

10

Writing begins with the making of meaningful marks. That is to say, leaving the traces of meaningful gestures. Typography begins with arranging meaningful marks that are already made. In that respect, the practice of typography is like playing the piano – an instrument quite different from the human voice. On the piano, the notes are already fixed, although their order, duration and amplitude are not. The notes are fixed but they can be endlessly rearranged, into meaningful music or meaningless noise.

Pianos, however, need to be tuned. The same is true of fonts. To put this in more literary terms, fonts need to be *edited* just as carefully as texts do – and may need to be re-edited, like texts, when their circumstances change. The editing of fonts, like the editing of texts, begins before their birth and never ends.

You may prefer to entrust the editing of your fonts, like the tuning of your piano, to a professional. If you are the editor of a magazine or the manager of a publishing house, that is probably the best way to proceed. But devoted typographers, like lutenists and guitarists, often feel that they themselves must tune the instruments they play.

10.1 LEGAL CONSIDERATIONS

10.1.1 *Check the license before tuning a digital font.*

Digital fonts are usually licensed to the user, not sold outright, and the license terms vary. Some manufacturers claim to believe that improving a font produced by them is an infringement of their rights. No one believes that tuning a piano or pumping up the tires of a car infringes on the rights of the manufacturer – and this is true no matter whether the car or the piano has been rented, leased or purchased. Printing type was treated the same way from Bí Shēng's time until the 1980s. Generally speaking, metal type and phototype are treated that way still. In the digital realm, where the font is wholly intangible, those older notions of ownership are under pressure to change.

The Linotype Library's standard font license says that "You may modify the Font-Software to satisfy your design requirements." FontShop's standard license has a similar provision: "You do have the right to modify and alter Font Software for your customary personal and business use, but not for resale or further distribution." Adobe's and Agfa Monotype's licenses contain no such provision. Monotype's says instead that "You may not alter Font Software for the purpose of adding any functionality.... You agree not to adapt, modify, alter, translate, convert, or otherwise change the Font Software...."

Grooming the Font

If your license forbids improving the font itself, the only legal way to tune it is through a software override. For example, you can use an external kerning editor to override the kerning table built into the font. This is the least elegant way to do it, but a multitude of errors in fitting and kerning can be masked, if need be, by this means.

10.2 ETHICAL & AESTHETIC CONSIDERATIONS

10.2.1 *If it ain't broke....*

Any part of the font can be tuned – lettershapes, character set, character encoding, fitting and sidebearings, kerning table, hinting, and, in an OpenType font, the rules governing character substitution. What doesn't need tuning or fixing shouldn't be touched. If you want to revise the font just for the sake of revising it, you might do better to design your own instead. And if you hack up someone else's font for practice, like a biology student cutting up a frog, you might cremate or bury the results.

10.2.2 *If the font is out of tune, fix it once and for all.*

One way to refine the typography of a text is to work your way through it line by line, putting space in here, removing it there, and repositioning errant characters one by one. But if these refinements are made to the font itself, you will never need to make them again. They are done for good.

10.2.3 *Respect the text first of all, the letterforms second, the type designer third, the foundry fourth.*

The needs of the text should take precedence over the layout of the font, the integrity of the letterforms over the ego of the designer, the artistic sensibility of the designer over the foundry's desire for profit, and the founder's craft over a good deal else.

10.2.4 *Keep on fixing.*

Check every text you set to see where improvements can be made. Then return to the font and make them. Little by little, you and the instrument – the font, that is – will fuse, and the type you set will start to sing. Remember, though, this process never ends. There is no such thing as the perfect font.

10.3 HONING THE CHARACTER SET

10.3.1 *If there are defective glyphs, mend them.*

If the basic lettershapes of your font are poorly drawn, it is probably better to abandon it rather than edit it. But many fonts combine superb basic letterforms with alien or sloppy supplementary characters. Where this is the case, you can usually rest assured that the basic letterforms are the work of a real designer, whose craftsmanship merits respect, and that the supplementary characters were added by an inattentive foundry employee. The latter's errors should be remedied at once.

You may find for example that analphabetic characters such as @ + ± × = · – — © are too big or too small, too light or too dark, too high or too low, or are otherwise out of tune with the basic alphabet. You may also find that diacritics in glyphs such as å ç é ñ ô ü are poorly drawn, poorly postioned, or out of scale with the letterforms.

1 + 2 = 3 < 9 > 6±1 · 2 × 4

a + *b* = *c* · a@b · © 2007

1 + 2 = 3 < 9 > 6±1 · 2 × 4

a + *b* = *c* · a@b · © 2007

José Mendoza y Almeida's Photina is an excellent piece of design, but in every weight and style of Monotype digital Photina, as issued by the foundry, arithmetical signs and other analphabetics are out of scale and out of position, and the copyright symbol and *at* sign are alien to the font. The raw versions are shown in grey, corrected versions in black.

é ù ô ã → é ù ô ã

Frederic Goudy's Kennerley is a homely but quite pleasant type, useful for many purposes, but in Lanston's digital version, the letterforms are burdened with some preposterous diacritics. *Above left*: four accented sorts as issued by the foundry. *Above right*: corrected versions. All fonts are candidates for similar improvement. *Below left*: four accented sorts from Robert Slimbach's carefully honed Minion, as originally issued by Adobe in 1989. *Below right*: the same glyphs, revised by Slimbach ten years later, while preparing the OpenType version of the face.

á è ï û → á è ï û

10.3.2 *If text figures, ligatures or other glyphs you need on a regular basis don't reside on the base font, move them.*

For readable text, you almost always need text figures, but most digital fonts are sold with titling figures instead. Most digital fonts also include the ligatures fi and fl but not ff, ffi, ffl, fj or ffj. You may find at least some of the missing glyphs on a supplementary font (an 'expert font'), but that is not enough. Put all the basic glyphs together on the base font.

If, like a good Renaissance typographer, you use only upright parentheses and brackets (see §5.3.2), copy the upright forms from the roman to the italic font. Only then can they be kerned and spaced correctly without fuss.

[*f*]

10.3.3 *If glyphs you need are missing altogether, make them.*

Standard ISO digital text fonts (PostScript or TrueType) have 256 slots and carry a basic set of Western European characters. Eastern European characters such as ą ć đ ė ğ ħ ī ň ő ŗ ş ť ů are usually missing. So are the Welsh sorts ŵ and ŷ, and a host of characters needed for African, Asian and Native American languages.

The components required to make these characters may be present on the font, and assembling the pieces is not hard, but you need a place to put whatever characters you make. If you need only a few and do not care about system compatibility, you can place them in wasted slots – e.g., the ^ < > \ | ~ ` positions, which are accessible directly from the keyboard, or slots such as ¢ ÷ ^{1} ^{2} ^{3} ™ ¤ ‰ ¦, which can be reached through insertion utilities or by typing character codes or by customizing the keyboard.

If you need to add many such characters, you will need to make a supplementary font or, better yet, an enlarged font (TrueType or OpenType). If these are for your own use only, the extra characters can be placed wherever you wish. If the fonts are to be shared, every new glyph should be labeled with its PostScript name and Unicode number.

10.3.4 *Check and correct the sidebearings.*

The spacing of letters is part of the essence of their design. A well-made font should need little adjustment, except for refining the kerning. Remember, however, that kerning tables exist for the sake of problematical sequences such as *f**, *gy*, *"A*, *To*, *Va* and *74*. If you find that simple pairs such as *oo* or *oe* require kerning, this is a sign that the letters are poorly fitted. It is better to correct the sidebearings than to write a bloated kerning table.

The spacing of many analphabetics, however, has as much to do with editorial style as with typographic design. Unless your fonts are custom made, neither the type designer nor the founder can know what you need or prefer. I habitually increase the left sidebearing of semicolon, colon, question and exclamation marks, and the inner bearings of guillemets and parentheses, in search of a kind of Channel Island compromise: neither the tight fitting preferred by most anglophone editors nor the wide-open spacing customary in France. If I worked in French all the time, I might increase these sidebearings further.

abc: def; ghx? klm! «non»

abc: def; ghx? klm! « hmm »

abç : déf ; ghx ? klm ! « oui »

Three options for the spacing of basic analphabetics in Monotype digital Centaur: foundry issue (top); French spacing (bottom); and something in between. Making such adjustments one by one by the insertion of fixed spaces can be tedious. It is easier by far, if you know what you want and you want it consistently, to incorporate your preferences into the font.

10.3.5 *Refine the kerning table.*

Digital type can be printed in three dimensions, using zinc or polymer plates, and metal type can be printed flat, from photos or scans of the letterpress proofs. Usually, however, metal type is printed in three dimensions and digital type is printed in two. Two-dimensional type can be printed more cleanly and sharply than three-dimensional type, but the gain in sharpness rarely equals what is lost in depth and texture. A digital page is therefore apt to look aenemic next to a page printed directly from handset metal.

This imbalance can be addressed by going deeper into two dimensions. Digital type is capable of refinements of spacing and kerning beyond those attainable in metal, and the primary means of achieving this refinement is the kerning table.

Always check the sidebearings of figures and letters *before* you edit the kerning table. Sidebearings can be checked quickly for errors by disabling kerning and setting characters, at ample size, in pairs: 11223344 ... qqwweerrttyy.... If the spacing within the pairs appears to vary, or if it appears consistently cramped or loose, the sidebearings probably need to be changed.

The function of a kerning table is to achieve what perfect sidebearings cannot. A thorough check of the kerning table therefore involves checking all feasible permutations of characters: 1213141516 ... qwqeqrqtqyquqiqoqpq ... (a(s(d(f(g(h(j(k(l ...)a)s)d)f)g ... –1–2–3–4–5 ... TqTwTeTrTtTyTuTiToTp ... and so on. This will take several hours for a standard ISO font. For a full pan-European font, it will take several days.

Class-based kerning (now a standard capability of font editing software) can be used to speed the process. In class-based kerning, similar letters, such as *a á â ä à å ã ă ā ą*, are treated as one and kerned alike. This is an excellent way to begin when you are kerning a large font, but not a way to finish. The combinations Ta and Tä, Ti and Tï, il and íl, i) and ï), are likely to require different treatment.

Kerning sequences such as Tp, Tt and f(may seem to you absurd, but they can and do occur in legitimate text. (Tpig is the name of a town in the mountains of Dagestan, near the southern tip of the Russian Federation; Ttanuu is an important historical site on the British Columbia coast; sequences such as $y = f(x)$ occur routinely in mathematics.) If you know what texts you wish to set with a given font, and know that combinations such as

“Ask Jeff” or ‘Ask Jeff’. Take the chef d’œuvre! Two of [of] (of) ‘of’ “of” of? of! of*. *Two of [of] (of) ‘of’ “of” of? of! of*.* Ydes, Yffignac and Ygrande are in France: so are Ypres, Les Woëvres, the Fôret de Wœvres, the Voire and Vauvise. Yves is in heaven; D’Amboise is in jail. Lyford’s in Texas & L’Anse-aux-Griffons in Québec; the Łyna in Poland. Yriarte, Yciar and Ysaÿe are at Yale. Kyoto and Ryotsu are both in Japan, Kwikpak on the Yukon delta, Kvæven in Norway, Kyulu in Kenya, not in Rwanda…. Walton’s in West Virginia, but «Wren» is in Oregon. Tlálpan is near Xochimilco in México, The Zygos & Xylophagou are in Cyprus, Zwettl in Austria, Fænø in Denmark, the Vøringsfossen and Værøy in Norway. Tchula is in Mississippi, the Tittabawassee in Michigan. Twodot is here in Montana, Ywamun in Burma. Yggdrasil and Ymir, Yngvi and Vóden, Vídrið and Skeggjöld and Týr are all in the Eddas. Tørberget and Vråg, of course, are in Norway, Ktipas and Tmolos in Greece, but Vázquez is in Argentina, Vreden in Germany, Von-Vincke-Straße in Münster, Vdovino in Russia, Ytterbium in the periodic table. Are Toussaint L’Ouverture, Wölfflin, Wolfe, Miłosz and Wū Wǔ all in the library? 1510–1620, 11:00 pm, and the 1980s are over.

The font on this page is straight off the shelf: a magnificently complex piece of digital engineering capable of setting bad type in five different scripts and over a hundred different languages.

On the facing page is a well-groomed version of the same font: the same big set of plain vanilla letterforms, tuned to set type well.

Some but not all of the lapses in the original kerning table are circled.

Part of a text file designed to test for missing or dislocated glyphs and for lapses in the kerning table. Raw font at left; groomed font at right.

There are many versions of Times New Roman. The version tested here is Times New Roman PS MT, version 2.76, the default text font in recent versions of the Microsoft Windows operating system. This is a

"Ask Jeff" or 'Ask Jeff'. Take the chef d'œuvre! Two of [of] (of) 'of' "of" of? of! of*. *Two of [of] (of) 'of' "of" of? of! of**. Ydes, Yffignac and Ygrande are in France: so are Ypres, Les Woëvres, the Fôret de Wœvres, the Voire and Vauvise. Yves is in heaven; D'Amboise is in jail. Lyford's in Texas & L'Anse-aux-Griffons in Québec; the Łyna in Poland. Yriarte, Yciar and Ysaÿe are at Yale. Kyoto and Ryotsu are both in Japan, Kwikpak on the Yukon delta, Kvæven in Norway, Kyulu in Kenya, not in Rwanda.... Walton's in West Virginia, but «Wren» is in Oregon. Tlálpan is near Xochimilco in México. The Zygos & Xylophagou are in Cyprus, Zwettl in Austria, Fænø in Denmark, the Vøringsfossen and Værøy in Norway. Tchula is in Mississippi, the Tittabawassee in Michigan. Twodot is here in Montana, Ywamun in Burma. Yggdrasil and Ymir, Yngvi and Vóden, Vídrið and Skeggjöld and Týr are all in the Eddas. Tørberget and Våg, of course, are in Norway, Ktipas and Tmolos in Greece, but Vázquez is in Argentina, Vreden in Germany, Von-Vincke-Straße in Münster, Vdovino in Russia, Ytterbium in the periodic table. Are Toussaint L'Ouverture, Wölfflin, Wolfe, Miłosz and Wū Wǔ all in the library? 1510–1620, 11:00 PM, and the 1980s are over.

TrueType-flavored OpenType font, including pan-European Latin, Greek, Vietnamese, Cyrillic, Hebrew and Arabic glyphs. It lacks the text figures, ligatures and small caps typical of full-featured OpenType fonts, and its OT features are actually limited to the Arabic character set. The kerning is good as far as it goes, but it does not go nearly far enough.

these will never occur, you can certainly omit them from the table. But if you are preparing a font for general use, even in a single language, remember that it should accommodate the occasional foreign phrase and the names of real and fictional people, places and things. These can involve some unusual combinations. (A few additional examples: McTavish, FitzWilliam, O'Quinn, *dogfish,* jack o'-lantern, Hallowe'en.)

It is also wise to check the font by running a test file – a specially written text designed to hunt out missing or malformed characters and kerning pairs that are either too tight or too loose. On pages 204–205 is a short example of such a test file, showing the difference between an ungroomed font and a groomed one.

It is nothing unusual for a well-groomed ISO font (which might contain around two hundred working characters) to have a kerning table listing a thousand pairs. Kerning instructions for large OpenType fonts are usually stored in a different form, but if converted to tabular form, the kerning data for a pan-European Latin font may easily reach 30,000 pairs. For a well-groomed Latin-Greek-Cyrillic font, decompiling the kerning instructions can generate a table of 150,000 pairs. Remember, though, that the number isn't what counts. What matters is the intelligence and style of the kerning. Remember too that there is no such thing as a font whose kerning cannot be improved.

10.3.6 *Check the kerning of the word space.*

The word space – that invisible blank box – is the most common character in almost every text. It is normally kerned against sloping and undercut glyphs: quotation marks, apostrophe, the letters A, T, V, W, Y, and often to the numerals 1, 3, 5. It is *not,* however, normally kerned more than a hair either to or away from a preceding lowercase *f* in either roman or italic.

A cautionary example. Most of the Monotype digital revivals I have tested over the years have serious flaws in the kerning tables. One problem in particular recurs in Monotype Baskerville, Centaur & Arrighi, Dante, Fournier, Gill Sans, Poliphilus & Blado, Van Dijck and other masterworks in the Monotype collection. These are well-tried faces of superb design – yet in defiance of tradition, the maker's kerning tables call for a large space (as much as M/4) to be added whenever the *f* is followed by a word space. The result is a large white blotch after every word ending in *f* unless a mark of punctuation intervenes.

Is it east of the sun

and west of the moon — or

is it west of the moon

and east of the sun?

Monotype digital Van Dijck, before and after editing the kerning table. As issued, the kerning table adds 127 units (thousandths of an em) in the roman, and 228 in the italic, between the letter *f* and the word space. The corrected table adds 6 units in the roman, none in the italic. Other, less drastic refinements have also been made to the kerning table used in the second two lines.

This error – documented in methodical tests of Monotype fonts in 1991 – was still present in fonts purchased from Agfa Monotype in the summer of 2004.

Professional typographers may argue about whether the added space should be zero, or ten, or even 25 thousandths of an em. But there is no professional dispute about whether it should be on the order of an eighth or a quarter of an em. An extra space that large is a prefabricated typographic error – one that would bring snorts of disbelief and instantaneous correction from Stanley Morison, Bruce Rogers, Jan van Krimpen, Eric Gill and others on whose expertise and genius the Monotype heritage is built. But it is an easy error to fix for anyone equipped with the requisite tool: a digital font editor.

10.4 HINTING

10.4.1 *If the font looks poor at low resolutions, check the hinting.*

Digital hints are important chiefly for the sake of how the type will look on screen. Broadly speaking, hints are of two kinds: generic hints that apply to the font as a whole and specific hints applicable only to individual characters. Many fonts are sold unhinted, and few fonts indeed are sold with hints that cannot be improved.

Manual hinting is tedious in the extreme, but any good font editor of recent vintage will include routines for automated hinting. These routines are usually enough to make a poorly hinted text font more legible on screen. (In the long run, the solution is high-resolution screens, making the hinting of fonts irrelevant except at tiny sizes.)

Grooming the Font

The presumption of common law is that inherited designs, like inherited texts, belong in the public domain. New designs (or in the USA, the software in which they are enshrined) are protected for a certain term by copyright; the *names* of the designs are also normally protected by trademark legislation. The names are often better protected, in fact, because infringements on the rights conferred by a trademark are often much easier to prove than infringements of copyright. Nevertheless there are times when a typographer must tinker with the names manufacturers give to their digital fonts.

Text fonts are generally sold in families, which may include a smorgasbord of weights and variations. Most editing and typesetting software takes a narrower, more stereotypical view. It recognizes only the nuclear family of roman, italic, bold and bold italic. Keyboard shortcuts make it easy to switch from one to another of these, and the switch codes employed are generic. Instead of saying "Switch to such and such a font at such and such a size," they say, for instance, "Switch to this font's italic counterpart, whatever that may be." This convention makes the instructions transferable. You can change the face and size of a whole paragraph or file and the roman, italic and bold should all convert correctly. The slightest inconsistency in font names can prevent this trick from working – and not all manufacturers name their fonts according to the same conventions. For the fonts to be linked, their family names must be identical and the font names must abide by rules known to the operating system and software in use.

If, for example, you install Martin Majoor's Scala or Scala Sans (issued by FontShop) on a PC, you will find that the italic and the roman are unlinked. These are superbly designed fonts, handsomely kerned and fully equipped with the requisite text figures and small caps – almost everything a digital font should be – but the PC versions must be placed in a font editor and renamed in order to make them work as expected.

PROWLING THE SPECIMEN BOOKS

11

Type is idealized writing – yet there is no end of typefaces, as there is no end to visions of the ideal. The faces discussed in this chapter cover a wide historical range – Renaissance, Baroque, Neoclassical, Romantic, Modern and Postmodern. They also constitute a wide stylistic variety – formal, informal, fluid, crisp, delicate and robust. The emphasis, however, is on types I like to read and to reread. Each face shown seems to me of both historical and practical importance, and each seems to me one of the finest of its kind. Each also has its limitations. I've included some very well-known types, such as Baskerville and Palatino; some others, such as Romulus Sans, Heraklit, and Manuscript Cyrillic, that are undeservedly forgotten; and several that are new enough they have not yet had time to establish themselves. Some, like Photina and Vendôme, have long been known in Europe but are rarely seen in North America; others, such as Deepdene, have had just as unbalanced a reception the other way round.

Most readers of this book will have access to digital catalogues, maintained on font vendors' websites. Now that type is principally a digital commodity, printed type specimens are quickly disappearing. Yet they remain an invaluable resource. because the Web, like the subway, is not a destination. Printing is still what type is for. By giving printed samples here, and pointing out some landmarks as well as hidden features, I hope to make it easier to navigate at will among the disembodied spectres.

Almost all faces listed in this chapter now exist in digital form, though a few are still missing essential components – text figures, for example – in their digital incarnations. Many such shortcomings have been remedied in recent years because typographers have made their wishes known. Yet some digital foundries continue making faces in abbreviated, deformed or pirated form. The presence of a typeface in this list is by no means an endorsement of every or any marketed version. (I have noted some of the instances, but not all, in which a font I wanted to include seemed first to require drastic editing.)

Buyers of type should be aware that they are always buying a copy of someone's original design. Licensed copies are preferable to unlicensed copies for two important reasons. First, if the designer is still alive, the license implies that the fonts are being

Candido, leggiadretto, & caro guanto;
Che copria netto auorio, & fresche rose;
Chi vidi al mondo mai si dolci spoglie?
Cosi haues s'io del bel velo altretanto.
O inconstantia de l'humane cose.
Pur questo è furto; & vië, ch'io me ne spoglie.

Four Italic Benchmarks

stro, & domino Iesu Christo. Gratias ago deo meo semper pro uobis de gratia dei, quæ data est uobis per Christū Iesum, quod in omnibus ditati estis per ipsum, in omni sermone, & omni co- gnitione (quibus rebus testimonium Iesu Christi confirmatū fuit in uobis) adeo, ut nō destituamini in ullo dono, expectātes reue

Nuda latus Marti, ac fulg
Thermodoontiaca munita

Le génie étonnant qui lui donna naissance.
Toi qui sus concevoir tant de plans à la fois,
A l'immortalité pourquoi perdre tes droits?

Many thousands of types, including thousands of copies of earlier foundry types, are currently for sale. This page shows four of the thousands of excellent types that are *not* for sale. None of these fonts now exists in original form – and to the best of my knowledge, no reasonably faithful metal, photographic or digital copies of these fonts have yet been made. From top to bottom, they are:

1 The Petrarca Italic: a 12 pt Aldine italic designed and cut by Francesco Griffo in 1503 for Gershom Soncino, who printed with it at Fano, on the Adriatic coast, east of Florence. (Note the two forms of *d* throughout.)

2 The Froben Italic: a 12 pt Aldine italic cut for Johann Froben by the unidentified Master of Basel (possibly Peter Schoeffer the Younger). Froben started using this type in 1519.

3 The Colines St Augustin Italic [enlarged]: a 13 pt italic designed and cut by Simon de Colines, Paris. Colines had cut several romans by the time he finished this type, in 1528, but it may have been his first italic.

4 Firmin Didot Italic N° 1: a 12 pt Neoclassical italic cut by the 19-year-old Firmin Didot in his father's shop in Paris, 1783.

For more about Colines, see Kay Amert, "Origins of the French Old Style: The Types of Simon de Colines" (1992), and Fred Schreiber, *Simon de Colines* (Provo, Utah, 1995).

sold with the designer's permission and that royalties from the sale are being paid. Second, the license gives some hope – though rarely, alas, a guarantee – that the fonts are not being sold in truncated or mutilated form.

11.1 NOMENCLATURE & SYNONYMY

Prowling the Specimen Books

Only one guiding principle is stated in this chapter:

11.1.1 *Call the type by its honest name if you can.*

The oldest types usually come to us without distinctive names and with only meager clues to who designed them. Setting this record straight, establishing the chronology, and giving credit where credit is due is the basic work of typographic history. People who admire the old types like to talk about them too. For that purpose they need names. These are bestowed for pure convenience, but out of pure affection.

Newer types, and copies of the old ones, need names too. As objects of commerce, they are almost always named by those who sell them, with or without the designer's cooperation. Early in his career, Hermann Zapf designed a type that he called Medici. After some consultation between founder and designer, that name was scrapped. When the first fonts were advertised for sale, they were known as Palatino.

The name *Palatino* alludes to the 16th-century Italian calligrapher Giovanni Battista Palatino, but the type is not based on any alphabet Palatino himself designed. The ultimate source of the name is the Mons Palatinus – the Palatine hill in Rome, site of a major temple of Apollo and of several imperial palaces.

That, however, is not the end of the story. A decade after its release as both a foundry type and Linotype machine face, Palatino became the object of commercial envy among the manufacturers of fonts for phototype machines. Zapf's design – or rather, his two quite different designs, one for the Linotype, one for the foundry – were then copied right and left, and the copies were sold under names like Pontiac, Patina, Paladium and Malibu. A more recently plagiarized version is sold as Book Antiqua. Max Miedinger's Helvetica – though not so distinguished a face nor so original a design in the first instance – has also been an object of widespread commercial envy. It is copied to this day under names such as Vega, Swiss and Geneva. Zapf's Optima is plagiarized as Oracle; Friedrich Poppl's Pontifex is plagiarized as Power, and so on.

The problem is not new. Nicolas Jenson's roman and Greek types were copied by other printers in the 1470s. So were Griffo's types, and Caslon's and Baskerville's and Bodoni's in their days. So are they now; though now, with these artists safely dead and their work in the public domain, we are free both to make the copies honest and to give them honest names.

Part of the problem is that, in most jurisdictions, type designs themselves are not effectively protected as intellectual property. Courts have not learned to distinguish between typographic artistry and typographic plagiarism. Names, however, can easily be registered as trademarks. Competitors who plagiarize designs can then be forced to give their copies different names. In the literary world, the law works the other way around. It is the substance and the text, not the title, of a story, poem or book that is protected by copyright legislation.

Other complications sometimes spring from this anomaly in the law. The first sizes and weights of Paul Renner's Futura were issued by the Bauer Foundry, Frankfurt, in 1927. The type was a commercial as well as artistic success, and other founders soon copied the design. Sol Hess at Lanston Monotype redrew the face and called it Twentieth Century; ATF sold its own imitation as Spartan. But the Futura that the Bauer Foundry had issued was a timid incarnation of Renner's original design. Renner drew many alternate characters; Bauer issued, for each letter, only the single most conventional of Renner's several forms. In 1993, when David Quay and Freda Sack at The Foundry, London, made a digital translation of Renner's original design, the conventions of the trade prevented them from calling it Futura. Their version – artistically the earliest known version of Futura, though commercially one of the latest to be produced – was sold instead under the trade name Architype Renner. Though it was not Renner's choice, this is a serviceable name to the serious typographer, because it plays no invidious tricks and it plainly acknowledges the originating designer.

cordia uale

Type categories such as *roman* and *italic* are not fixed. This is the enlarged trace of a 16 pt serifed type cut in central Italy in 1466–67, probably by Konrad Sweynheym. It is the second type used by Sweynheym and his partner Arnold Pannartz, who printed books with it at Rome from 1467 to 1473. Like Gudrun Zapf-von Hesse's Alcuin type, designed five centuries later, it is really neither roman nor italic. It is rooted in the Carolingian scriptorial tradition, which precedes any such division.

The balance of this chapter is a litany of names, with the briefest of histories attached. Part of every font's history is that it was born in a certain medium. At the beginning of each entry, that medium is shown by a simple code:

H = originally a metal type for hand composition
M = originally for machine composition in metal
P = originally designed for photosetting
D = originally designed in digital form

11.2 SERIFED TEXT FACES

abcëfghijõp 123 AQ *abcéfghijôp*

Albertina P This graceful, understated text family – embracing Latin, Greek and Cyrillic – was designed in 1965 by the Dutch calligrapher Chris Brand. The Latin portion of the family was issued by Monotype, not in metal but as one of the corporation's first proprietary faces for photocomposition. Technology then moved on, and Albertina was left behind. The Latin component was issued anew in digital form by DTL (the Dutch Type Library) in 1996, complete with its requisite text figures and both roman and italic small caps. The Cyrillic and Greek followed at last in 2004. The forms are quiet and alert, the width economical, and the axis is that of the humanist hand. The crisp italic, with its subtly elliptical dots, slopes at a modest 5°. There is a full range of weights. (See also pp 275, 280.)

AQ 123 ábçdèfghijklmñöpqrstûvwxyz

abcëfghijõp AQ 123 ABCËFGHIJÕP

Alcuin D A strong and graceful Carolingian face designed in 1991 by Gudrun Zapf-von Hesse and first issued by URW. As a genuine Carolingian, Alcuin is rooted in handwritten scripts that predate by 600 years the separation of roman and italic. It is neither of these itself, though it contains the seeds of both. As such, it does not have and does not need a sloped companion face. There is instead an extensive range of weights with text figures and small caps. This is everything required for setting excellent text. The face should not be used where editorial inflexibility demands the use of roman and italic. (See also pp 120, 212.)

Digital translations of Palatino (on the left) and Aldus (on the right). These are two related faces designed in 1948–53 by Hermann Zapf. To illustrate the difference in proportion, selected characters of both are shown here at 72 pt. The basic alphabets (Palatino above, Aldus below) are also shown at 18 pt.

(Note that neither of these cuts was ever intended to be seen at the 72 pt size. Display sizes of foundry Palatino are more delicate than this, and Aldus is a text face for which no display sizes were designed. But the enlargements facilitate comparison.)

aa bb cc

éé ff gg

ññ ôô tt

CC HH

abcdefghijklmnopqrstuvwxyz

abcdefghijklmnopqrstuvwxyz

1 2 3 4 5 6 7 8 9 0 · A B C D É F G

1 2 3 4 5 6 7 8 9 0 · A B C D É F G

A B C D E F G H I J K L M N O

A B C D E F G H I J K L M N O

abcdefghijklmnopqrstuvwxyz

abcdefghijklmnopqrstuvwxyz

abcëfghijõp 123 AQ *abcéfghijôp*

Aldus M Roman and italic, designed in 1953 by Hermann Zapf as a text-size Linotype companion for his new foundry face, Palatino. Aldus is narrower than Palatino and has a lower midline (smaller x-height). It is a crisply sculptured and compact text face, rooted in Renaissance scribal tradition. Small caps and text figures are essential to the spirit of the face, but it needs no ligatures. Digital Aldus preserves the Linotype equality of set-width in roman and italic. Palatino, Michelangelo and Sistina are the allied titling faces, and Palatino bold can be used when a bold companion is required. (See also pp 64, 104, 214.)

a

abcëfghijõp 123 AQ *abcéfghijôp*

Amethyst D Canadian printer and punchcutter Jim Rimmer designed the caps for this face in Vancouver in 1994 and initially called the face Maxwellian. He rechristened it Amethyst in 1999, when he drew the lower case. In 2002, after the first printing trials, Rimmer revised the book weight, darkening it by roughly 2%. It became a working typeface at that point. The fonts come rough from the foundry and must be edited in order to set text. It is worth the effort. Rimmer's affection for Frederic Goudy is visible in Amethyst and in some of his other faces – Albertan, for example. It is also visible in Kaatskill, a transgenerational collaboration for which Goudy drew the roman and Rimmer the italic.

a

abcëfghijõp 123 AQ *abcéfghijôp*

Apollo P Adrian Frutiger's Apollo was commissioned for the Monophoto machine in 1960 and produced in 1962. Frutiger used the opportunity to rethink his first text face, Méridien, drawn eight years earlier. Apollo lacks the sharpness of Méridien, but its smaller eye, blunter serifs and reduced modulation can make it a better choice for text, and it comes with the f-ligatures, text figures and small caps that Méridien lacks. (See also page 238.)

n

abcëfghijõp 123 AQ *abcéfghijôp*

Arrus D This is an elegant and graceful text face designed by calligrapher Richard Lipton for Bitstream in 1991. It is distinguished by the symmetrically notched roman foot serifs and asymmetri-

n

cally notched head serifs. There is a full range of weights, with text figures and small caps. The same designer's Cataneo, an equally graceful chancery italic (Bitstream, 1994), makes an excellent companion face for Arrus.

abcëfghijõp 123 AQ *abcéfghijôp*

g

Baskerville H John Baskerville designed this roman and italic in the 1750s. The initial versions were cut by John Handy under Baskerville's watchful eye. The result is the epitome of Neoclassicism and eighteenth-century rationalism in type – a face far more popular in Republican France and the American colonies than in eighteenth-century England, where it was made.

Many of the digital faces sold under Baskerville's name are passably faithful to his designs, but small caps and text figures, often omitted, are essential to the spirit of the original, and to an even flow of text. The digital version shown here is Monotype Baskerville. At least two Cyrillic versions also exist: one produced by Monotype and one produced by ParaType under license from ITC. (See also pp 13, 56, 77, 84, 97, 129, 280.)

abcëfghijõp 123 AQ *abcéfghijôp*

a

Bell H The original Bell type was cut in London in 1788 by Richard Austin for a publisher named John Bell. It was warmly greeted there and in the USA and was widely used at Boston and Philadelphia in the 1790s. It remains useful for period design work, as an alternative to Baskerville. Monotype cut a facsimile in 1931, and this version has been digitized. Bell has more variation in axis than Baskerville, but it too is an English Neoclassical face. The serifs are very sharp, but the overall spirit is nevertheless closer to brick than to granite, evoking Lincoln's Inn more than St Paul's, and Harvard Yard more than Pennsylvania Avenue. Bell numerals are three-quarter height, neither hanging nor fully ranging. (See also pp 47, 129.)

abcëfghijõp 123 AQ *abcéfghijôpy*

a

Bembo H Bembo was produced by Monotype in 1929, based on a roman cut at Venice by Francesco Griffo in 1495. The fifteenth-century original had no italic, and Monotype tested two possibilities as a companion face. One was Fairbank italic; the other was the softer Bembo italic shown here. This italic is in essence a revision of Blado (the italic cut for Poliphilus), with sidelong reference to a font designed in Venice in the 1520s by Giovanni Tagliente. Bembo roman and italic are quieter and farther from their sources than Centaur and Arrighi. They are nevertheless serene and versatile faces of genuine Renaissance structure, and they have in some measure survived the transition to digital composition and offset printing. Text figures and small caps are essential. The bold fonts are irrelevant to the spirit of the face. (See also pp 51, 122, 124, 242.)

Bembo is named for the Venetian writer Pietro Bembo (1470–1547) because the roman on which it is based was first used in Bembo's little book *De Aetna*, published by Aldus in 1496.

abcëfghijõpy! AQ *abcéfghijôpy*

Berling H Designed by the Swedish typographer and calligrapher Karl-Erik Forsberg. This face was issued in 1951 by the foundry from which it takes its name, the Berlingska Stilgjuteriet in Lund, Sweden. It is a neohumanist design, with vigorous modulation of the stroke. Ascenders and descenders are even more frequent in Swedish than in English, and Berling's descenders are unusually short. The ascenders are of normal height but designed to require no ligatures. The face has a Scandinavian sharpness and clarity, with sharply beaked f, j, y and ! in the roman. The titling figures are well formed, but the text figures (omitted from every digital cut I have seen) are decidedly better. (See also page 84.)

f!

abcëfghijõp 123 AQ *abcéfghijôp*

Bodoni H Giambattista Bodoni of Parma, one of the most prolific of all type designers, is also the nearest typographic counterpart to Byron and Liszt. That is to say, he is typography's arch-romantic. His hundreds of faces, designed between about 1765 and his death in 1813, embrace considerable variety, and more than 25,000 of his punches are in the Bodoni Museum in Parma. The revivals issued in his name reflect only a tiny part of this legacy, and many are simply parodies of his ideas. The typical features of Bodoni revivals are abrupt hairline serifs, ball terminals, vertical axis, small aperture, high contrast and exaggerated modulation. The ITC Bodonis, digitized in 1994–95 under the direction of Sumner Stone, are the closest of all the revivals to Bodoni's mature style. (There are three versions, based on 6, 12 and 72 pt originals.) Other favorites are the Bodoni cut by Louis Hoell for the Bauer Foundry, Frankfurt, in 1924, and the Berthold Foundry version,

a

g

produced in 1930. Both have been issued in digital form. Small caps and text figures are essential to all of these designs. The version shown is the Bauer. (See also pp 13, 131.)

abcëfghijõp 123 AQ *abcéfghijôp*

o

Bulmer H William Martin of Birmingham was the brother of Robert Martin, Baskerville's chief assistant. He may have learned to cut punches from Baskerville's punchcutter John Handy and may have got his first lessons in type design from Baskerville himself. He moved to London in 1786 and in the early 1790s started cutting types full of Baskervillean shapes yet considerably harsher than Baskerville's. The serifs were abrupt and the contrast much increased. This was the inception of English Romantic typography. Martin's types were sponsored and promoted by the printer William Bulmer, whose name overshadowed that of the designer. They were copied in 1928 by Morris Benton for ATF, and then by Monotype and Intertype. Several digital versions now exist. The most comprehensive of these is the one released by Monotype in 1994. (See also page 131.)

abcëfghijõp 123 AQ *abcéfghijôp*

p

Caecilia D This face, first issued by Linotype in 1991, was designed in the Netherlands by Peter Matthias Noordzij, whose wife is named Cécile. An earlier bearer of the name, Caecilia Metella, was the fourth wife of the Roman general Lucius Cornelius Sulla (*c.* 138–78 BC), whose army plundered Athens in 86 BC. On his return from that campaign, he led the winning side in the Roman civil war of 82 and was installed as Roman Dictator. In 81 BC, his wife Caecilia was stricken with an unidentified disease – caught, some Romans claimed, from Sulla himself. As Caecilia lay dying, her husband divorced her and had her carried out of the house to avoid contamination. A later Caecilia, also a native of Rome, is revered in the Christian tradition as the patron saint of music. The type that shares the name of these three women is a graceful, sturdy face, useful for text of many kinds. It is a neohumanist slab-serif, perhaps the first of its kind, with a slab-serifed true italic to match. The italic is built to Renaissance parameters, sloping at a modest 5°. There is a range of weights, with small caps and text figures. Licensed versions are sold as PMN Caecilia. There is no face called Sulla. (See also page 112.)

abcëfghijõp 123 AQ *abcéfghijôp*

Californian H The ancestor of this face is Frederic Goudy's University of California Old Style, cut as a proprietary typeface in 1938. Lanston Monotype issued it publicly in 1956 under the name Californian. The digital version shown is FB Californian, made in 1990 by David Berlow for the Font Bureau, Boston. It is useful to compare this with ITC Berkeley, a more pasteurized interpretation of the same original, produced in 1983 by Tony Stan for photocomposition. While Berkeley retains many virtues of the original type, it has lost much of its character. It also lacks the text figures and small caps required by the design. These are present in Berlow's version. (See overleaf.)

The diacritics have been repositioned in these fonts of FB Californian.

abcëfghijõp 123 AQ *abcéfghijôp*

Carmina D Gudrun Zapf-von Hesse designed this face, released by Bitstream in 1987. While it builds upon her earlier text faces, Diotima and Nofret, Carmina is more versatile and lyrical (hence the name: *carmina* are songs or lyrical poems). There is a good range of weights. Like many early digital fonts, however, it was issued in a Procrustean character set making no provision for text figures. Such figures were a part of the original design but still have never been released.

a

abcëfghijõp 123 AQ *abcéfghijôp*

Cartier P Canadian typographer Carl Dair began working on this face in the Netherlands in 1957. At his death in 1967, the display version of the roman was effectively complete, but the italic was still an overwrought and over-narrow draft. No text weight or small caps had been drawn. The type was hurriedly issued for filmsetting nevertheless, in time for the Canadian centenary in 1967. Cartier roman then became, despite its weaknesses, the *de facto* Canadian national typeface, often used for stamps and other celebratory projects. It was in principle a roman with enough French Gothic flavor to assert a crucial difference between Ottawa and Washington. The letterforms are rooted in Dair's study of fifteenth-century Parisian and Florentine printing, especially the work of Ulrich Gering and Antonio Miscomini.

o

In the 1970s, British typographer Robert Norton confused things slightly by producing a tamed and sanitized version of

FB Californian (on the left) and ITC Berkeley (on the right) are both derived from Frederic Goudy's University of California Old Style. To facilitate comparison, these two cuts are shown here at slightly different sizes: 74 pt (FB Californian) and 77 pt (ITC Berkeley). In the lower half of the page, both fonts are shown at 18 pt (Californian above, Berkeley below).

aa bb cc

éé ff gg

ññ ôô tt

AA HH

abcdefghijklmnopqrstuvwxyz

abcdefghijklmnopqrstuvwxyz

1234567890 · ABCDÉ

1234567890 · ABCDÉ

ABCDEFGHIJKLMNO

ABCDEFGHIJKLMNO

abcdefghijklmnopqrstuvwxyz

abcdefghijklmnopqrstuvwxyz

Cartier and giving it the name of an English colonial partisan: Raleigh. (Raleigh, however, is almost never seen as a book face because Norton gave it no italic.) In the 1990s another Canadian, Rod McDonald, undertook to rescue the design. He gave Dair's roman and italic the editing required to make them useful at text size, supplied the missing small caps, semibold and bold weight, and gave the type its first meticulous fitting. The result, called Cartier Book, began to circulate in 1998 and was issued by Agfa Monotype in 2000. Greek and Cyrillic companion faces are now underway. So is a suite of fleurons (maple leaf, spruce limbs, etc) for which Dair made some preliminary drawings.

g

abcëfghijõp 123 AQ *abcéfghijôp* — *Adobe Caslon, shown at 20 pt*

abcëfghijõp 123 ſo *ſo abcéfghijôp* — *Great Primer Founder's Caslon, at 24 pt*

abcëfghijõp 123 ſo *ſo abcéfghijôp* — *Pica Founder's Caslon, at 21 pt*

abcëfghijõp 123 ſo *ſo abcéfghijôp* — *Brevier Founder's Caslon, at 21 pt*

Caslon H William Caslon designed and cut a large number of romans, italics and non-Latin faces between 1720 and his death in 1766. His work is the typographic epitome of the English Baroque and is remarkably well preserved. He published thorough specimens, and a large collection of his punches is now in the St Bride Printing Library, London. There is not much doubt that Caslon was the first great English typecutter, and in the English-speaking world his type has long possessed the semilegendary, unexciting status of the pipe and slippers, good used car and favorite chair. Typographic opportunists have therefore freely helped themselves to Caslon's reassuring name, and many of the faces sold as Caslons now are merely parodies. Adobe Caslon, drawn by Carol Twombly in 1989, is a respectful, sensitive and well-made digital descendant of the originals, equipped not only with text figures and small caps, but with optional swash caps, ornaments and other antiquarian accessories. It is now made as an OpenType font with a pan-European Latin character set but without Greek and Cyrillic. (No one, alas, has yet made a digital version of Caslon's handsome polytonic Greeks.)

a *p*

For those in search of more historical veracity, Justin Howes has produced digital versions directly from printed specimens of several sizes of the original Caslon types. These preserve, in their perfectly static way, a taste of the dynamic, rugged texture of printing in Caslon's time. They are issued as Founder's Caslon, by H.W. Caslon & Co. (See also pp 12, 51, 66, 113, 126.)

a

abcëfghijõp 123 AQ *abcéfghijôp*

Centaur & Arrighi H Centaur roman was designed by Bruce Rogers in 1912–14, based on the roman type cut at Venice by Nicolas Jenson in 1469. In 1928, the face was mildly sanitized in the course of transposition to the Monotype machine. Frederic Warde drew the Arrighi italic in 1925, based on a chancery font designed by the calligrapher Ludovico degli Arrighi in the 1520s. In 1929, after several revisions, Rogers chose Warde's face as the companion italic for Centaur, provoking more revisions still. The fonts are used both separately and together.

Printed letterpress, Centaur and Arrighi are unrivalled in their power to re-evoke the typographic spirit of the Venetian Renaissance. In the two-dimensional world of digital composition and offset printing, this power is easily lost. The problem is aggravated by weaknesses in the digitization of Arrighi, destroying the balance achieved when the faces were married in metal.

Morris Benton's Cloister Old Style (ATF, 1913–25), George Jones's Venezia (Shanks, 1916; Linotype 1928), Ernst Detterer's Eusebius (Ludlow, 1924), Ronald Arnholm's Legacy (ITC, 1992) and Robert Slimbach's Adobe Jenson (Adobe, 1996) are other significant attempts to do some justice to the same original. (See also pp 12, 16, 67, 79, 84, 105, 122, 124, 186, 202.)

William Morris's Golden Type, cut in 1890, was the first modern attempt to recreate Jenson's roman. A more successful version was the Doves Roman, drawn by Emery Walker and cut by Edward Prince in 1900. But Walker's type has vanished just like Jenson's own. After using it for sixteen years, Thomas Cobden-Sanderson threw it surreptitiously into the Thames from Hammersmith Bridge.

abcëfghijõp 123 AQ *abcèfghijôp*

Chaparral D The evergreen oaks of the California foothills are known in Spanish as *chaparros.* The lean and sunny landscape in where they thrive is known as *chaparral.* Carol Twombly completed this extraordinarily clean and seemingly imperturbable typeface in 1997 and retired soon thereafter as staff designer at Adobe. Most good text types owe their power in part to the rhythmic modulation of the line. Here there is some modulation, but very little, and the power comes from the path of the stroke: the subtle out-of-roundness of the bowls and microscopic taper of the stems. There is a range of weights, and the character set is pan-European Latin.

AQ ábcdèfghijklmñöpqrstûvwxyz

Clarendon H Clarendon is the name of a whole genus of Victorian typefaces, spawned by a font that Benjamin Fox cut for Robert Besley at the Fann Street Foundry, London, in 1845. These faces reflect the hearty, stolid, bland, unstoppable aspects of the British Empire. They lack cultivation, but they also lack menace and guile. They squint and stand their ground, but they do not glare. In other words, they consist of thick strokes melding into thick slab serifs, fat ball terminals, vertical axis, large eye, low contrast and tiny aperture. The original had no italic, as the face had nothing of the fluent hand or sculpted nib left in its pedigree. (Stephenson Blake did however issue a sloped roman version of Besley's original Clarendon – known to them as Consort – in foundry metal in 1953.)

Hermann Eidenbenz drew a version of Clarendon for the Haas Foundry in Münchenstein, Switzerland, in 1951, and in 1962 the foundry finally added the light weight that transformed the series, paring it down from premodern ponderousness to postmodern insubstantiality. In this guise, as a kind of nostalgic steel frame from which all the Victorian murk has been removed, the face has many genuine uses. Monotype Clarendon lacks the presence of Haas Clarendon, which is the version shown.

A related face – a kind of muted Clarendon – is Morris Fuller Benton's Century Schoolbook, issued by ATF in 1924 and in machine form by Monotype in 1928. This too is now available in a light weight and in digital form. (See also pp 106, 132.)

abcëfghijõp 123 AQ *abcéfghijôp*

Comenius P The seventeenth-century Czech theologian Jan Ámos Komenský, or Comenius, is remembered for his efforts to establish universal public education throughout Europe and for his insistence that there is no incongruity between sacred and secular learning. The typeface aptly named for him is distinguished by its lucid blend of humanist and rationalist forms. It was designed by Hermann Zapf and first released by Berthold in 1980. The axis in the roman varies, and the bowls are asymmetrical. The result is a face alive with static energy. The italic is consistent in its axis and full of vibrant motion. There are two bold weights, both graceful and dramatic in their contrast. The requisite text figures were designed but have never been issued.

Diotima roman (on the left) and the normal weight of Nofret roman (on the right): two related faces designed some thirty years apart by Gudrun Zapf-von Hesse. Diotima was designed as a foundry face for letterpress printing. Nofret was designed initially for the medium of phototype. They are shown here for comparison at 70 pt and 18 pt, both in digital form.

aa bb cc

éé ff gg

ññ ôô tt

AA HH

abcdefghijklmnopqrstuvwxyz

abcdefghijklmnopqrstuvwxyz

1 2 3 4 5 6 7 8 9 0

1 2 3 4 5 6 7 8 9 0

A B C D E F G H I J K L M N O P Q

A B C D E F G H I J K L M N O P Q

abcdefghijklmnopqrstuvwxyz

abcdefghijklmnopqrstuvwxyz

abcëfghijõp 123 AQ *abcéfghijôp*

Dante H Roman and italic, designed by Giovanni Mardersteig and cut by hand in steel in 1954 by Charles Malin. Monotype adapted the face for machine setting in 1957 and in the early 1990s produced a digitized version. In its foundry form, Dante is one of the great achievements of twentieth-century typography: a finely tooled and stately neohumanist roman coupled with a very lively and lucid italic.

g

Mardersteig was the greatest modern scholar of Francesco Griffo's work, and his Dante – though not in fact a copy of any of Griffo's types – has more of Griffo's spirit than any other face now commercially available. Used with a reduced size of the upright roman capitals, Dante italic is also the nearest modern counterpart to a true Aldine italic. The Monotype digital version is, however, somewhat coarser than its metal antecedents. Small caps and text figures are, of course, quintessential to the design. (See also page 133.)

abcëfghijõp 123 AQ *abcéfghijôp*

Deepdene M This may be the gentlest and most lyrical of Frederic Goudy's many book faces. The aperture is larger than usual with Goudy, the x-height is modest, the axis is serenely neohumanist, and the drawing is graceful and even. Goudy drew the roman in 1927, naming it after his house in Marlborough, New York. (The house was named in turn for Deepdene Road on Long Island.) The italic – which slopes at only 3° – was completed the following year, when the face was issued by Lanston Monotype. Light as it is, the italic also has the strength to function as an independent text face. Small caps and text figures (included in the Lanston digital version) are requirements of the design. The swash characters available on supplementary fonts are less an asset than a temptation.

g

The alignment and character fit of Lanston digital Deepdene have been edited to produce the font used here.

abcëfghijõp 123 AQ *abcéfghijôp*

Diotima H Designed by Gudrun Zapf-von Hesse and cut by the Stempel Foundry, Frankfurt, in 1953, Diotima is now issued by Linotype-Hell in digital form. The roman is wide and the italic markedly narrow. There are small caps but no bold weights. The face is named for the earliest woman philosopher on record:

g

Diotima of Mantinea, whose metaphysic of love is recited in Plato's *Symposium* by her former student, Socrates. Diotima is part of an extended family of faces by the same designer that has accrued over more than thirty years. Its relatives include the Nofret series, Ariadne (a font of swash initials) and the handsome inline titling face, Smaragd. (See also page 224.)

abcëfghijõp 123 AQ *abcéfghijôp*

a

Documenta D Frank Blokland started work on this sturdy, open text face in 1986. It was issued by his firm, DTL, in 1993. Small caps and text figures are supplied for the full range of weights. An equally unpretentious and well-made sanserif companion face was released in 1997.

abcëfghijõp 123 AQ *abcéfghijôp*

g

Electra M Several early twentieth-century book faces are creative variations on Neoclassical and Romantic form. This makes them seem, in retrospect, significant precursors of postmodern design. Three were created in the USA for the Linotype machine and became immediate staples of American publishing. One is Rudolph Růžička's Fairfield, issued in 1940. The others are W.A. Dwiggins's Electra, issued in 1935, and his Caledonia, issued in 1938. In their original Linotype form, Electra was the liveliest of the three, though in digital form this may no longer be the case. Electra was first issued with a sloped roman in lieu of an italic, but in 1940 Dwiggins himself replaced this sloped roman with the simple, crisp italic now normally used. Small caps and text figures are inherent in the design. (See also page 113.)

abcëfghijõp 123 AQ *abcéfghijôp*

a

Esprit P Designed by Jovica Veljović in Beograd and issued through ITC, New York, in 1985. A sharply serifed roman and italic of variable axis, large x-height and small aperture. The strokes and bowls of the lower case are full of oblique lines and asymmetric curves which add further energy to the basically rowdy Neobaroque structure. A related but somewhat simpler face is the same designer's earlier Veljović. Small caps and text figures are implicit in the design– but the italic text figures, drawn long ago, have yet to be released. (See also pp 113, 135.)

AHQ 123 *ábçdèfghijklmñöpqrstûvwxyz*

Fairbank M In 1928, when English calligrapher Alfred Fairbank designed this face and offered it to Monotype, the corporation considered it as a possible companion for their new Bembo roman. It is narrow and has a slope of only 4°, yet it is full of tensile strength, and in the estimation of Monotype's typographical advisor, Stanley Morison, even after it was tamed by Monotype draftsmen, it overpowered the dignified and soft-spoken roman to which it was betrothed. A new and milder italic – the present Bembo italic – was cut to replace it. Fairbank's italic has since remained a typographic loner, routinely misdescribed (against its designer's explicit wish) as 'Bembo Condensed Italic.'

In fact, a typographic loner is what it needs to be. The humanist italics from which it descends – those of Griffo, the Master of Basel, and Arrighi – were employed on their own for setting extended texts, not as helpmeets to existing roman faces. Fairbank has the same rich potential.

When Robin Nicholas and Carl Cossgrove at Monotype finally digitized the face, in 2003, they returned to Fairbank's drawings, restoring the original upright capitals and the long extenders of the lower case. They also added several needless but legitimate swash characters and a wholly illegitimate set of lining figures that has no basis whatsoever in chancery tradition or in Fairbank's personal aesthetic. To make a working digital version of this highly useful type, Fairbank's own text figures must be moved from the swash font to the base font.

abcëfghijõp 123 AQ *abcéfghijôp*

Fairfield M A text face designed by Rudolph Růžička for the Linotype machine and issued in 1939. Fairfield has a rationalist axis, like the Electra of Růžička's friend and colleague W. A. Dwiggins, and it remained, like Electra, a standard text face in American publishing for roughly forty years. Alex Kazcun digitized Fairfield in 1991, replacing the narrow Linotype italic *f* and *j* with kerning characters and narrowing the set of the italic. He also increased the contrast of the face (thereby delicately tilting it from a pre- to a postmodern design), added additional weights to the range, and included Růžička's alternate italic, oddly rechristened the 'caption font.'

d p g

a

a

o

y

abcëfghijõp 123 AQ *abcéfghijôp*

Figural H The real Figural was designed in Czechoslovakia by Oldřich Menhart in 1940 and finally cut and cast by the Grafotechna Foundry, Prague, in 1949. A digital version was created by Michael Gills and issued by Letraset in 1992. Except to a few fortunate letterpress printers, this muffled digital version is the only form in which the type is currently available.

Menhart was the master of Expressionism in type design, and Figural is among his finest creations: a rugged but graceful roman and italic, deliberately preserving the expressive irregularity of pen-written forms. The same designer's Manuscript is similar in character but rougher, and his Monument is a congenial titling face for use with either Manuscript or Figural. Though digital Figural lacks the marvellous abrasiveness of the original, it is still a good text face for use at modest size. But like all of Menhart's work, Figural deserves a more authentic digital revival. (See also page 109.)

abcëfghijõp 123 AQ *abcéfghijôp*
CFGIT·*CFGIJOQT*

Fleischmann H This is a digital family based on roman and italic fonts cut by Johann Michael Fleischman [*sic*] in Amsterdam in 1738–39. Fleischman was a prolific, and skilled punchcutter and founder whose work, like Bodoni's, covers considerable range. In the late 1730s, he and his competitor Jacques-François Rosart both cut text types that are truly Rococo. The architecture of these fonts is fundamentally Baroque, but exaggerated contrast is found in the roman and italic *o* and *g*, and in all the round uppercase letters. The serifs on the caps are ostentatious and abrupt. Erhard Kaiser's digital interpretation, issued by DTL in 1995, is a little tamer than the metal. It includes text figures, small caps and a range of ornamental ligatures. (See also page 128.)

abcëfghijõp 123 AQ *abcéfghijôp*

Fournier H The typefaces of Pierre-Simon Fournier come from the same historical period – and much the same rationalist spirit – as Baskerville's designs and the Bell type of Richard Austin. Yet these faces are by no means all alike. The types of Fournier are as

French as Bell and Baskerville are English, and Fournier's type is Fournier's, speaking subtly of the man himself.

Fournier is also famous for his use of ornaments. Like Mozart, he moves between pure, and surprisingly powerful, Neoclassicism and airy Rococo. His letters have more variation of axis than Baskerville's, his romans are a little narrower, and his italics are sharper. Late in his life, he cut some of the first condensed roman faces. And like Mozart, he delights in sliding backward from the Neoclassical forms he pioneered to the older forms of the Baroque, which he admired and inherited.

In one important respect, however, Fournier turned his back on the Baroque. He cut his romans and italics as coequal, independent fonts which differ quite deliberately in x-height. In 1925, Monotype cut two separate series based on his work. These were issued in metal as Monotype Fournier and Monotype Barbou. Only the former has been digitized, but both series preserve Fournier's disparate proportioning of roman and italic. Modern editorial convention is still stuck in the Baroque and often demands that roman and italic be mixed on a single line. But Fournier should be used, I think, in Fournier's fashion, or else it should be recut. (See also page 129.)

x*x*o*o*
b*b*p*p*

abcëfghijõp 123 AQ *abcéfghijôp*

Galliard P Galliard was once the name of a type size – 9 pt – as well as a dance and its musical form. The family of type now known by this name was designed by Matthew Carter, issued initially by Mergenthaler in 1978, and later licensed by ITC. It is a crisp, formal but energetic roman and italic, based on the designs of the sixteenth-century French typecutter Robert Granjon. Enough of Granjon's work survives, both in steel and in print, to prove that he was one of the finest punchcutters who ever lived. Galliard is Carter's homage to the man as well as to his work. It is also the preeminent example of a Mannerist revival typeface.

Text figures and small caps are implicit in the design. For period typography, additional sets of Mannerist ligatures and swash capitals are available as well. The best of the several digital versions appears, not surprisingly, to be Carter's own, released in 1992 by Carter & Cone. The obvious titling face is Carter's Mantinia (page 284) – another act of homage to an artist of extraordinary intellect, precision and exemplary technical skill. (See also page 125.)

f

a

Garamond (1) H Claude Garamond (or Garamont), who died in 1561, was one of several great typecutters at work in Paris during the early sixteenth century. His teacher, Antoine Augereau, and his gifted contemporaries are remembered now only by scholars, while Garamond suffers posthumous fame. Many of his punches and matrices survive in museum collections, and his style is not hard to learn to recognize. This has not prevented people from crediting him with type he could not possibly have designed and would not, perhaps, have admired.

Garamond's romans are stately High Renaissance forms with humanist axis, moderate contrast and long extenders. He cut several beautiful italics as well, with some of the first sloped capitals, but he took no apparent interest in the radical new idea of actually *pairing* italics with romans. Revivals of his roman faces are often mated instead with italics based on the work of a younger artist, Robert Granjon. Three Garamond and Garamond/Granjon revivals worthy of serious consideration are:

The large sorts above are from William Ross Mills's "1520 Garamond," a titling face closer than any other digital version to Garamond's actual designs. It is issued by Tiro Typeworks, Vancouver.

1 Stempel Garamond, issued by the Stempel Foundry in 1924 and later digitized by Linotype;
2 Granjon, drawn by George William Jones and issued by Linotype in 1928 – now also in the Linotype digital library – and
3 Adobe Garamond, drawn by Robert Slimbach, issued in digital form by Adobe in 1989, and re-released in 2000 in the form of pan-European Latin OpenType.

Jan Tschichold's Sabon, listed separately on page 231, is also closely based on Garamond's originals. Small caps and text figures exist and are essential to all of these designs.

18 pt Stempel Garamond abcëfghijõp 123 AQ *abcéfghijôp*

18 pt Linotype Granjon abcëfghijõp 123 AQ *abcéfghijôp*

18 pt Adobe Garamond abcëfghijõp 123 AQ *abcéfghijôp*

a

Stempel Garamond is the only one of these in which the italic as well as the roman is based on a genuine Garamond. (The model used, Garamond's *gros romain* italic, is reproduced on page 74.) The rhythm and proportions of the Stempel face are, however, much changed from the original, and the *f*'s are deformed.

An entirely separate strain of designs, based on the work of Jean Jannon, is also sold under the name Garamond. These are discussed in the following entry. (See also pp 101, 122, 232.)

Garamond (2) **H** Jean Jannon, born in 1580, was the earliest of the great typographic artists of the European Baroque. He was also a French Protestant, printing illegally in a Catholic regime, and the type he cut and cast during the early seventeenth century was seized in 1641 by agents of the French crown. (Jannon may later have been reimbursed.) After two centuries in storage, it was revived and misidentified as the work of Claude Garamond. The surviving punches are still at the Imprimerie Nationale, Paris.

Jannon's type is elegant and disorderly: of widely varying axis and slope, sharply serifed and asymmetrical. The best revivals of these lovely, distinctly non-Garamondian letters are:

1 ATF 'Garamond,' drawn by M.F. Benton and issued in 1918–20;
2 Lanston's 'Garamont,' which was drawn by Frederic Goudy and issued in 1921;
3 Monotype 'Garamond,' issued in 1922; and
4 Simoncini 'Garamond,' drawn by Francesco Simoncini and issued in metal by the Simoncini Foundry, Bologna, in 1958.

Monotype has been particularly thorough in Jannon's case, issuing two different cuts of italic, both in metal and in digital form. Monotype 156, in which the slope of the caps varies rambunctiously, is closer to Jannon's originals. Monotype 176 was the corporate revision: an attempt to bring the unrepentant French typecutter, or at least his italic upper case, back into line. But irregularity lies at the heart of the Baroque, and at the heart of Jannon's letters, just as it may lie at the heart of his refusal to conform to the state religion of his day. I prefer Monotype 156 italic (called 'alternate' in digital form) for that reason.

abcëfghijõp 123 AQ *abcéfghijôp*

18 pt Monotype 'Garamond'

abcëfghijõp 123 AQ *abcéfghijôp*

18 pt Simoncini 'Garamond'

As issued, Simoncini Garamond lacks text figures and small caps. They have been added to the version shown here.

Yet another version of Jannon's type is sold as 'Garamond 3.' This is the ATF 'Garamond' of 1918 as adapted in 1936 for the Linotype machine, now re-revised for digital composition. It is perfectly serviceable as a text face, but it lacks both the slightly disheveled grace of Monotype 'Garamond' and the more carefully combed and erect grace of the Simoncini version.

ITC 'Garamond,' designed in the 1970s by Tony Stan, also has nothing to do with Garamond's type. It is a radically distorted form of Jannon's: distant from the spirit of the Baroque and of the Renaissance alike. (See also pp 101, 126, 232.)

Stempel Garamond roman (on the left) is indeed based on the work of Claude Garamond (though its *f*, in both roman and italic, is distorted in a misguided attempt to escape the need for ligatures). Monotype 'Garamond' (on the right) is based on the work of Jean Jannon. These two excellent types come from different centuries and spirits as well as different hands. Surely they also therefore merit different names. They are shown here side by side, the Stempel at 70 pt and the Monotype at 78 pt, and one above the other, both at 18 pt.

aa dd éé

ff ôô *õõ*

rr *kk xx*

AA HH

abcdefghijklmnopqrstuvwxyz

abcdefghijklmnopqrstuvwxyz

1 2 3 4 5 6 7 8 9 0 · A B C D É F G

1 2 3 4 5 6 7 8 9 0 · A B C D É F G

A B C D E F G H I J K L M T

A B C D E F G H I J K L M N T

abcdefghijklmnopqrstuvwxyz

abcdefghijklmnopqrstuvwxyz

abcëfghijõp 123 AQ *abcéfghijôp*

Haarlemmer M Jan van Krimpen drew this face for Monotype in 1938 to fulfill a private commission. It was issued at last in 1996, in digital form, by DTL. The roman is based on Romulus. The italic however was a new design in 1938. In the 1940s, Van Krimpen revised Haarlemmer into Spectrum. While digitizing the face, Frank Blokland created an unserifed companion, based largely on Van Krimpen's Romulus Sans. This was issued in 1998 as Haarlemmer Sans. (See also page 248.)

a

abcëfghijõp 123 AQ *abcéfghijôp*

Hollander D Few things are more useful in the typographic world than plain, sturdy, unpretentious and good-natured fonts of type. Hollander is one of several families of such type designed by Gerard Unger in 1983, but not issued until 1986. The same designer's Swift (1985) and Oranda (1992) are similar. Hollander has greater bulk than Swift but also sharper serifs. It therefore suffers more from harsh commercial treatment (low resolution, low-grade presswork, low-grade paper).

a

Jannon See *Garamond* (2), page 231.

Janson See *Kis*, page 235.

abcëfghijõp 123 AQ *abcéfghijôp*

Jenson H Many types of many kinds claim to be inspired by the roman cut at Venice in 1469 by Nicolas Jenson. Some of these derivatives are masterpieces; others are anything but. Bruce Rogers's Centaur is deservedly the best known recreation of Jenson's roman, but Monotype's digital Centaur is a two-dimensional ghost of Rogers's three-dimensional homage to the original Jenson type. Adobe Jenson, drawn by Robert Slimbach and issued in 1995, retraces Rogers's steps and also Frederic Warde's. The italic is based on the same model as Warde's Arrighi italic – a separate design later revised to serve as Centaur's italic. When only the digital fonts are compared, it is clear – to me at least – that Adobe Jenson has better balance between roman and italic and is generally more tolerant of the fundamental flimsiness of two-dimensional printing, though it is otherwise when the two are printed letterpress

a

a

(using polymer plates for Adobe Jenson). Other families of type with which these should be compared are M.F. Benton's Cloister and Ronald Arnholm's Legacy. (Adobe Jenson and Cloister are closer than Adobe Jenson and Centaur in some interesting respects.) The family has been issued both in Multiple Master and OpenType form. The OT versions include small caps, text figures, swash italic, a few fleurons, and a pan-European Latin character set. (See also pp 16, 112, 186.)

abcëfghijõp 123 AQ *abcéfghijôp*

p

Joanna H Designed by the English artist Eric Gill and cut by the Caslon Foundry, London, in 1930. The Monotype version was produced in 1937. This is a face of spartan simplicity, with flat serifs and very little contrast but considerable variation in stroke axis. The italic has a slope of only 3° and is full of roman forms, but it is sufficiently narrower than the roman to minimize confusion. Text figures are essential to Gill's design. Gill Sans is an obvious and very satisfying companion face.

abcëfghijõp 123 AQ *abcéfghijôp*

f

Journal D A rough and eminently readable face designed by Zuzana Ličko, issued in 1990 by Emigre. Text figures and small caps are part of the design. There is a wide version known as Journal Ultra as well as a range of weights. (See also page 134.)

abcëfghijõp 123 AQ *abcèfghijôp*

p

Kennerley H This was Frederic Goudy's first successful typeface, designed in 1911. (Goudy was 46 at the time, but his career as a type designer was just beginning.) By his own account, the designer wanted a new type with some of the flavor of Caslon – and Kennerley has Caslon's homey unpretentiousness, though it has returned to Renaissance forms for its underlying architecture and many of its structural details. The italic was drawn seven years after the roman, but Goudy had found his style; the two mate well. The text figures and small caps required by the design are included in Lanston's digital version.

(The spelling 'Kennerly' appears in some type catalogues, but the face was commissioned by and named for the publisher Mitchell Kennerley, 1878–1950.) (See also page 201.)

abcëfghijõpz 123 AQ *abcéfghijlôp*

Kinesis D Designed by Mark Jamra and issued by Adobe in 1997. Kinesis breaks several conventions of type design quite handsomely. The descenders have prominent, canted bilateral serifs. The ascenders, however, have no serifs at all: only an asymmetrically flared termination of the stroke, which is lightly cupped in the roman and beveled in the italic. Dots of i and j are tapered; so are the cross strokes of f and t, and all the unilateral serifs (except in the roman lowercase z). All the bilateral serifs, however, are blunt and nearly uniform in stroke-width. The italic includes some sloped roman forms (*i*, *l*) along with the cursive, triangular bowls of Mannerist calligraphy. The OpenType version of the family, issued in 2002, includes text figures and small caps in a wide range of weights but no East European characters.

abcëfghijõp 123 AQ *abcéfghijnôp*

Kis H The Hungarian Miklós Kis is a major figure in Dutch typography, as well as that of his own country. He spent most of the 1680s in Amsterdam, where he learned the craft and cut some wonderfully toothy and compact Baroque type. For many years Kis's work was incorrectly ascribed to the Dutch punchcutter Anton Janson and taken to be the epitome of Dutch Baroque design. Commerce has no conscience, and to this day, Kis's type is sold, even by people who know better, under Janson's name.

Some of Kis's original punches and matrices found their way to the Stempel Foundry in Frankfurt, and Stempel Foundry Janson is in consequence Kis's actual type, with German sorts (ä, ß, ü, etc) rather clumsily added by other hands. Linotype Janson was cut in 1954, based on the Kis originals, under the supervision of Hermann Zapf. Monotype Janson and Monotype Erhardt are also adapted – less successfully, I think – from Kis's designs. Linotype Janson Text (1985) seems to me the most successful digital version. It was prepared under the supervision of Adrian Frutiger, based on Kis's originals and on Zapf's excellent Linotype machine version. (See also page 126.)

abcëfghijõp 123 AQ *abcéfghijôp*

Legacy D Ronald Arnholm's Legacy (ITC, 1992) is, I think, the blandest of the many twentieth-century attempts to give new, two-dimensional life to the old three-dimensional type of the master typographer Nicolas Jenson. Blandness, however, is not always a disadvantage in a printing type, and Legacy is of interest on other grounds. It marries a redrawing of Jenson's roman with a redrawing of one of Garamond's italics, rather than one of Arrighi's, and it is the only revival of Jenson's roman that exists in both serifed and unserifed forms.

The model underlying the roman is reproduced on page 16 and the model underlying the italic on page 74. Legacy has a substantially larger eye than either, and in this respect it violates both Jenson's and Garamond's sense of proportion. It is nevertheless a family with many merits and uses. (See also page 258.)

abcefghijop 123 AO *abcefghijop*
abcefghijop 123 AO *abcefghijop*
bpbpbpbpbpbpbpbpbpbp

Lexicon D Designed by Bram de Does in 1992 and issued in digital form by Enschedé. Lexicon was commissioned, as the name suggests, for a new Dutch dictionary. It was therefore designed to be as compact as a Bible type but to function in a range of sizes and to allow many shades and degrees of emphasis. There are six weights (A–F), with both roman and italic small caps in every weight, and in each weight there are two forms of roman and italic lower case: N° 1 with short extenders; N° 2 with extenders of normal length. Lexicon 2A (the light weight with normal extenders) makes an excellent text face for a variety of uses, and Lexicon 1B (the second weight with short extenders) a good companion face for notes and other compact matter.

abcefghijop 123 AQ *abcefghijop*

Manuscript H This was designed in Czechoslovakia by Oldřich Menhart during World War II and issued by Grafotechna, Prague, in 1951. Manuscript is even rougher than the same designer's Figural, but its rough forms are painstakingly chosen and juxtaposed. The roman and italic are perfectly balanced with each other and within themselves. The numerals are large, but their alignment satisfyingly uneven. There is a matching Cyrillic. (The version shown is a trial digitization by Alex White.)

abcëfghijõp 123 AQ *abcéfghijôp*

Mendoza D Designed by José Mendoza y Almeida, Paris, and released by ITC in 1991. This is a forceful and resilient neohumanist text face with low contrast and a spartan finish, closer in some ways to the tough and lovely text romans and italics of sixteenth-century Paris than anything else now to be found in digital form. Mendoza prospers under careful handling but is robust enough to survive printing conditions lethal to other text faces. Small caps and text figures are implicit in the design, but the ligatures are best recut or forgotten. There is also an extensive range of weights. (See also pp 101, 108, 112.)

a

abcëfghijõp 123 AQ *abcéfghijôp*

Méridien H/P This was Adrian Frutiger's first text face, designed in 1954 for Deberny & Peignot, Paris. The roman was cut and cast for hand composition, but the italic, despite its impeccable balance and flow, was forced to wait. It was then released (with a new incarnation of the roman) only in the form of phototype. The roman caps, which have unusual authority and poise, make an excellent titling face in themselves. The same designer's Frutiger makes a useful sanserif companion. But in the absence of small caps and text figures, the related Apollo is often more useful for text. (See also pp 58, 101, 105, 238.)

g

abcëfghijõp 123 AQ *abcéfghijôp*

Minion D The first version of this family, designed near San Francisco by Robert Slimbach, was issued by Adobe in 1989. Multiple Master and OpenType versions have been issued more recently. Minion is a fully developed neohumanist text family which is, in the typographic sense, especially economical to set. That is to say that it gives, size for size, a few more characters per line than most text faces without appearing squished or compressed. Small caps and text figures are essential to the design, and these are available across the range, in several weights of both roman and italic. The OpenType form of the face, called Minion Pro, includes a set of typographic ornaments, swash italics, and upright and cursive Greek and Cyrillic. Slimbach's chancery italic, Poetica, is a useful companion face. (Minion Pro is the face in which this book is set. See also pp 106, 107, 201, 280.)

a

Digital versions of Adrian Frutiger's Méridien (on the left) and Apollo (on the right). The former – initially a foundry face, though matricies were only engraved for the roman – was finished in 1954. Apollo, designed for filmsetting, was completed in 1962. Selected letters are shown here at 72 pt (Méridien) and 80 pt (Apollo). The basic alphabets (Méridien above, Apollo below) are both shown at 18 pt.

aa bb cc

éé ff *ff*

gg pp tt

CC HH

abcdefghijklmnopqrstuvwxyz

abcdefghijklmnopqrstuvwxyz

1 2 3 4 5 6 7 8 9 0 · A B C D É

1 2 3 4 5 6 7 8 9 0 · A B C D É

A B C D E F G H I J K L M N O

A B C D E F G H I J K L M N O

abcdefghijklmnopqrstuvwxyz

abcdefghijklmnopqrstuvwxyz

abcëfghijõp 123 AQ *abcéfghijôp*

Nofret P Nofret, which means 'beautiful one,' was a popular woman's name in early Egypt. In 1984 an exhibition prepared by the Cairo Museum opened in Munich under the title *Nofret: Die Schöne: Die Frau in Alten Ägypten,* and in that year, Gudrun Zapf-von Hesse's typeface Nofret was released by the Berthold Foundry. It is in many respects a rethinking of the same designer's Diotima, drawn three decades earlier. It is more compact than Diotima in the roman, but of similar width in the italic. There is a wide range of weights, and even the heaviest of these retains its poise. This is not in the typographic sense an egyptian; it is an answer to the question, *What might happen to a typographic egyptian if it acquired feminine grace?* Small caps and text figures are implicit in the design. (See also pp 135, 224.)

e

abcëfghijõp 123 AQ *abcéfghijôp*

Officina D Designed by Eric Spiekermann and colleagues, and issued in 1990 through ITC. This is a narrow and plain yet robust text face, inspired by the typewriter and useful for setting much matter that might, in an earlier age, have stayed in typescript form. It is sturdy enough to withstand rough treatment (low-grade laser printing, for example) yet sufficiently well-built to prosper under better printing conditions. There is a sanserif counterpart. Cyrillic versions of both Officina Serif and Officina Sans were designed in 1994 by Tagir Safaev and issued in digital form by ParaGraph (now ParaType). (See also page 136.)

e

abcëfghijõp 123 AQ *abcéfghijôp*

18 pt digital Palatino Linotype

abcëfghijõp 123 AQ *abcéfghijôp*

18 pt Linotype digital Aldus

Palatino H/M This roman and italic were designed in 1948 by Hermann Zapf. The foundry version was cut in steel by August Rosenberger at the Stempel Foundry, Frankfurt. Zapf then adapted it for the Linotype machine. In photo and digital form, it has become the most widely used of all neohumanist faces, among typographic professionals and amateurs alike. As the most universally admired of Zapf's designs, it is also the most heavily pirated.

In its authentic incarnations, Palatino is a superbly balanced, powerful and graceful contribution to typography – but its close relative, Aldus, which was designed expressly for text setting, is often a better choice for that purpose, in company with Palatino as a display face. There is a bold weight, designed in 1950. A bold italic was added, evidently to combat existing forgeries, nearly thirty years later. The extended Palatino family includes two sets of display capitals (Michelangelo and Sistina), a text Greek (Heraklit) and Greek capitals (Phidias). Small caps and text figures are essential to the face.

Because it was first designed as a display face for handsetting in metal, then adapted for use in text sizes on the Linotype machine, there are two fundamentally different yet authentic versions of Palatino italic. There is a wide version, originally matching the roman letter-for-letter in set-width, as required by the Linotype machine, and a narrower, more elegant version intended for hand composition. The current digital versions are based on the foundry design. The OpenType digital fonts (known officially as 'Palatino Linotype' rather than Linotype Palatino) include a new Greek and Cyrillic along with a full pan-European character set and, in some incarnations, also *chữ quốc-ngữ*, the Latin character set employed for Vietnamese. (See also pp 15, 59, 77, 97, 104, 133, 211, 214, 254, 278, 281.)

abcëfghijõp 123 AQ *abcéfghijôp*

Photina P A text face with predominantly rationalist axis, small aperture and narrow set-width but unmistakable calligraphic energy. It was designed by José Mendoza y Almeida and first issued by Monotype in 1972 for photocomposition. There is a range of weights, and the bold versions are gracefully designed. Photina's proportions are deliberately close to those of Univers, which makes an excellent sanserif companion. This is one of the first and one of the finest postmodern text faces. Small caps and text figures are implicit in the design. (See also page 200.)

abcëfghijõp 123 AQ *abcèfghijôp*

[illegible]

Plantagenet D William Ross Mills designed the initial version of Plantagenet in the mid 1990s. It was issued by his firm, Tiro Typeworks, in 1996. In 2004, he produced a thorough revision, released as Plantagenet Novus. The new version includes pan-European Latin and Greek character sets with additional sorts for Native American languages that are written in Latin letters, a matching set of Cherokee syllabics, and a range of ornaments and swashes. Why should a face with Neoclassical structure and a character set that links classical Greece and Native America bear the nickname of the Anglo-Norman family that gave England all her kings from Henry II in 1154 to Richard III in 1485? I do not know. But *Plantagenet* is an old French name for the broom plant (in modern French, *la plante genêt*). It is said that Geoffrey of Anjou, founder of the family and an avid hunter, wore a sprig of it in his hat and had it planted as cover for birds. Broom was brought, along with the Latin alphabet, from Europe to North America, where both have since run wild.

AQ 123 AQ ábcdèfghijklmñöpqrstûvwxyz

eaqbābefeghghijklnōb Q U A styml

Poetica D A chancery italic designed by Robert Slimbach and issued by Adobe in 1992. The basic family consists of four variations on one italic, with varying amounts of swash. There are also five fonts of swash capitals, two of alternate lowercase letters, two fonts of lowercase initials, two of lowercase terminals, two sets of small caps (ornamented and plain), a font of fractions and standard ligatures, another of ornamental ligatures, one font of analphabetic ornaments, and one font entirely of ampersands. The basic face is a plain neohumanist italic, well suited for extended text. The supplementary fonts permit any desired degree of typographic play or ostentation. (See also page 125.)

abcëfghijõp 123 AQ *abcéfghijôp*

Poliphilus & Blado H Poliphilus, meaning 'Multiple Love,' is the name of the lead character in Francesco Colonna's fantasy novel *Hypnerotomachia Poliphili,* "The Dream-Fight of Poliphilus," which Aldus Manutius printed in 1499 in a newly revised roman type by Francesco Griffo. In 1923, Monotype tried to replicate this font for use on their machine. The result was Monotype Poliphilus. It was an early experiment in the resuscitation of Renaissance designs, and the Monotype draftsmen copied the actual letterpress impression, including much of the ink squash, instead of par-

Bembo (on the left) and Poliphilus (on the right): two attempts at reproducing a fifteenth-century Venetian type in twentieth-century terms. Both of these types are based on the same original lower case, but on two different sets of original capitals. They are shown here at 74 pt and at 18 pt.

(Poliphilus, of course, was never meant to be seen in public enlarged to this degree. It was created as a text face only. The largest size cut in metal matrix form is 16 pt.)

aa bb cc

éé ff gg

ññ ôô tt

AA CC

abcdefghijklmnopqrstuvwxyz

abcdefghijklmnopqrstuvwxyz

1 2 3 4 5 6 7 8 9 0 · A B C D É F G

1 2 3 4 5 6 7 8 9 0 · A B C D É F G

A B C D E F G H I J K L M N O

A B C D E F G H I J K L M N O

abcdefghijklmnopqrstuvwxyz

abcdefghijklmnopqrstuvwxyz

ing back the printed forms to restore what the punchcutter had carved. The result is a rough, somewhat rumpled yet charming face, like a Renaissance aristocrat, unshaven and in stockinged feet, caught between the bedroom and the bath. In the squeaky clean world of offset printing, this roughness has finally come into its own.

a

Six years after producing Poliphilus, Monotype repeated its experiment with a very different result. Monotype Bembo (1929) is based on an earlier state of the same original: the same lower case with an earlier set of capitals. The differences between lowercase Monotype Bembo and Poliphilus, great as they are, are entirely differences of interpretation, not of design.

Blado, the italic companion to Poliphilus, is not based upon any of Griffo's own superb italics (one of which is shown on page 210) but on a font designed in a very different intellectual milieu, by Ludovico degli Arrighi about 1526. (Arrighi died soon after finishing that type – probably his sixth italic – and it was acquired by the master printer Antonio Blado of Rome. No type called Arrighi existed when the 1923 revival was made. Monotype chose nevertheless to name their revival of the face for the printer who used it, not the calligrapher who designed it.)

y

abcëfghijõp 123 AQ *abcéfghijôp*

Pontifex P Designed by Friedrich Poppl in Wiesbaden and issued in 1976 by Berthold in Berlin. Pontifex is one of several eminent twentieth-century faces built on Mannerist lines. Other examples include Adrian Frutiger's Méridien, Georg Trump's Trump Mediäval, and Matthew Carter's Galliard. These are four quite different faces, designed by four quite different artists for three different typographic media, but they share several structural presumptions. All have a humanist axis in the roman but an unusually large x-height, a tendency toward sharpness, angularity and tension in the conformation of individual letters, and a considerable slope – 12° to 14° – in the italic. These are features inherited from French Mannerist typecutters such as Jacques de Sanlecque, Guillaume Le Bé and Robert Granjon. Galliard is in fact a revival of Granjon's letters, while Pontifex, Trump and Méridien are independent modern creations sympathetic in spirit to the earlier Mannerist work. Together, these faces demonstrate the considerable range and depth of what one could call the neomannerist aspect of the Modernist tradition. (See also pp 78, 133.)

a

y

abcëfghijõp 123 AQ *abcéfghijôp*

Quadraat D Fred Smeijers's Quadraat, issued by FontShop in 1993, is a study in contrasts: a tensile and large-eyed yet smoothly flowing roman married to an angular, broken but robust italic. The creative ingenuity involved here extends to the matching Cyrillic and the companion sanserif as well. The fonts as issued are expertly kerned and sold with the requisite parts – small caps and text figures – intact. Some fine types were made during the late twentieth century, and this is one. It is not pretty; its beauty is deeper and stranger than that. (See also pp 260, 281.)

g

abcëfghijõp 123 AQ *abcéfghijôp*

Requiem D Requiem is pretty where Quadraat is not, but its beauty runs deeper than prettiness too. In its way, this is the equal of the great neohumanist book types of the early twentieth century: Bembo, Centaur and Dante. It is however the fruit of a later age, more self-conscious and self-involved. Its models are also therefore later: scripts of the High Renaissance, which were likewise acutely self-aware. And Requiem, unlike Bembo, Centaur and Dante, was born in the digital medium, where two dimensions have to do the work of three. It was created by Jonathan Hoefler in New York City, who drew the caps in the early 1990s and completed the family in 1999. It grew out of a commission from a magazine suspiciously entitled *Travel and Leisure,* but like any good type, it savors of self-discipline no less than self-indulgence. The italic, like Robert Slimbach's Poetica, is indebted to the work of Ludovico degli Arrighi and includes a set of artful, playful ligatures to prove it. The roman caps, with which the project started, are grounded in Arrighi's work as well. The roman lower case owes more to another sixteenth-century calligrapher, Ferdinando Ruano. (See also pp 51, 285.)

p

22 pt Rialto (for titling)

abcëfghijõp 123 AQ *abcéfighijôp*

21 pt [sic] Rialto Piccolo (for text)

abcëfghijõp 123 AQ *abcéfighijôp*

Rialto D Requiem is pretty; Rialto is prettier still, but again, its beauty is deeper than that. Named for the best-loved bridge in Venice, it is the product of joint effort by Venetian calligrapher Giovanni de Faccio and Austrian typographer Lui Karner. The result is a face of extraordinary calligraphic loveliness which is nevertheless strong enough (properly used) for the texts of substantial books. Proper use begins with remembering that there are two sets of fonts. Rialto itself is actually a titling face, happiest at 18 pt and above. Rialto Piccolo is the better choice at 16 pt and below – which is to say, the choice for all text sizes. Besides the roman and italic there are small caps and semibold, a full set of ligatures and good italic alternates. The italic slopes at 2°, and the roman and italic share a single set of caps. It was issued in 1999 by *df* Type in Texing, near Vienna. (See also page 285.)

abcefghijop 123 AO *abcefghijop*

Romanée H Designed by Jan van Krimpen and cut in steel by Paul Helmuth Rädisch at the Enschedé Foundry in Haarlem, Netherlands. The roman owes much to the spirit of Garamond. Van Krimpen designed it in 1928 as a companion for an italic cut in the middle of the seventeenth century by another of Garamond's admirers, Christoffel van Dijck. But Van Krimpen remained dissatisfied with the relationship between the two faces, cut in the same land three hundred years apart. In 1948 he designed an italic of his own – his last type – to mate with Romanée roman. The new italic is distinguished by its prominent descenders, serifed on both sides, and it has much less slope than the italic of Van Dijck. Like the italics of the early sixteenth century – and unlike the italics of both Garamond and Van Dijck – it mates a cursive lower case with upright capitals.

"United they fall, apart they stand as fine designs," said Van Krimpen's younger colleague, Sem Hartz. And it is true that Romanée italic stands very well on its own. Perhaps these faces are best used in the Renaissance manner – not the manner of Van Dijck but the manner of Garamond, his predecessors and colleagues – with the italic set in separate passages rather than laced into the midst of roman text. Digital Romanée, though it has now existed for years, is still awaiting commercial release.

abcëfghijõp 123 AQ *abcéfghijôp*

Romulus H It has been said with some justice that Jan van Krimpen designed three roman types: Lutetia (1925), Romanée (1928), and a third to which at various times in the 1930s and 1940s he gave the names Romulus, Haarlemmer, Sheldon and

Spectrum. The italic sequence is different: Lutetia (1925), Cancelleresca Bastarda (1934), Haarlemmer (1938), Spectrum (*c.* 1942) and Romanée (1949). For Romulus, Van Krimpen initially designed no italic. Instead, on Stanley Morison's advice, he drew a second version of the roman that slopes at 11°. He soon atoned for this however by designing the most elaborate and technically challenging italic of his career, the Cancelleresca Bastarda, and incorporating it into the Romulus family.

a

Regarded solely as a roman and sloped roman, Romulus looks like a well-made but impoverished type. In reality, it is part of a large family issued in part between 1931 and 1936: the forerunner of other large families such as Legacy, Scala and Quadraat. As of 2004, DTL has digitized only the serifed roman and oblique. These will be of greater use when they are joined by the rest of the family: Cancelleresca Bastarda, Romulus Sans, Romulus Greek, and Romulus Open Capitals. (See also pp 58, 248.)

abcëfghijõp 123 AQ *abcéfghijôp*

Sabon H/M Designed by Jan Tschichold. The foundry version was issued by Stempel in 1964, followed by Monotype and Linotype machine versions in 1967. The series consists of a roman, italic, small caps and semibold, based broadly on the work of Claude Garamond and his pupil Jacques Sabon, who was once employed, after Garamond's death, to repair and complete a set of his teacher's punches. The structure of the letterforms is faithful to French Renaissance models, but Tschichold's face has a larger eye than any but the tiniest sizes cut by Garamond. The type was intended as a general-purpose book face, and it serves this purpose extremely well, though it is bland in comparison with Garamond's originals. (See also pp 34, 52, 104.)

p

abcëfghijõp 123 AQ *abcéfghijôpy*

Scala D A crisp, neohumanist text face with sharp serifs and low contrast, designed by Martin Majoor in the 1980s for the Vredenburg concert hall in Utrecht. (This may explain why it is named after an opera house in Milan.) It was publicly issued by FontShop International, Berlin, in 1991. This face has many of the merits of Eric Gill's Joanna – not to mention several merits distinctively its own – without Joanna's eccentricities. Small caps and text figures are implicit in the design – and the basic licensed

a

fonts of FF Scala come pre-equipped with text figures and a full set of ligatures, as if they were really meant for setting type instead of merely typing. There is also an unserifed branch of the family. (See also pp 260, 262–63.)

abcëfghijõp 123 AQ *abcéfghijôp*

Seria D Like Scala, this is the work of Martin Majoor, issued by FontShop in 2000. The designer has written that after completing Scala he wanted to produce a more "literary" face. Whether Seria is really more literary than Scala, I cannot say. Its small eye and long extenders do make it a less utilitarian face, but I have used it myself – and its matching sanserif – with great satisfaction for both literary and nonliterary texts. The italic slopes at only one degree. Italic and roman alike have upright caps, but not the same upright caps. Those of the italic are slightly but recognizably cursive. (See also page 261.)

a

ábçdèfghijklmñöpqrstûvwxyz 123

AQAQAQAEDEEGGMMM

Silentium D Designed by Jovica Veljović and issued in OpenType form by Adobe in 2000. This is a Carolingian face, like Gudrun Zapf-von Hesse's Alcuin. There is necessarily no italic, but there are four sets of caps (one written, three drawn, including one inline and one reversed set, useful for versals), many scribal alternates and ligatures, and an impressive set of ornaments.

g

abcëfghijõp 1234689 AQ *abcéfghijôp*

Spectrum H/M This is a refinement of Haarlemmer, designed by Jan van Krimpen in the early 1940s, then delayed by the Second World War and issued by both Enschedé and Monotype in 1952. It was Van Krimpen's last general text face and is now the one most widely used. The roman and italic are reserved, elegant and well matched. The axis is humanist, the aperture large, and the serifs simultaneously sharp and flat (a feature neither unwelcome nor contradictory in typography). Small caps and the distinctive Spectrum text figures, with their very short extenders, are essential to the design. A semibold was added by Sem Hartz and cut by Monotype in 1972. (See also pp 133, 248.)

a

Digital versions of three types by Jan van Krimpen: Romulus (left), Haarlemmer (middle) and Spectrum (right). Selected characters of Romulus are shown here at 78 pt, Haarlemmer at 72 pt, Spectrum at 82 pt. The basic lowercase alphabets of all three are shown at 18 pt.

The italics and the numerals of these three faces are quite distinct, but in the roman, the differences are such as one might expect to find among different sizes of a single hand-cut type.

á á á b b b

b b b c c c

f f f g g g i i i

C C C I I I

abcdefghijklmnopqrstuvwxyz

abcdefghijklmnopqrstuvwxyz

abcdefghijklmnopqrstuvwxyz

1234567890

1234567890 / 1234567890

abcdefghijklmnopqrstuvwxyz

abcdefghijklmnopqrstuvwxyz

abcdefghijklmnopqrstuvwxyz

abcëfghijõp 123 AQ *abcéfghijôp*

Swift D This large-eyed face was designed by Gerard Unger and first issued in 1987 by Rudolf Hell in Kiel. It is avowedly a newspaper type, but it has many additional uses. Though the eye is large and the set is narrow, the letters are crisp and open, with chisel-tipped, wedge-shaped terminals and serifs. The axis is humanist and the aperture large. The italic is taut and fluent, with a slope of 6°. The torso of these letterforms is large enough that Swift can function well without text figures and small caps, but these have now been issued by Elsner & Flake. Unger's sanserif family Praxis and his erect sanserif italic Flora make useful companion faces for Swift.

a

abcëfghijõp 123 AQ *abcéfghijôp*

Trajanus H/M Warren Chappell's Trajanus was issued in 1939 as a foundry face by Stempel and in machine form by Linotype. The angular, black forms echo the early humanist scripts of the Renaissance and some of the earliest roman printing types, used in Italy and Germany until they were superseded by the early Venetian whiteletter and then by the Aldine roman and italic. But Trajanus is a remarkably graceful face, and the roman is matched by an equally crisp and fluent italic. The figures, like those of Bell, are three-quarter height lining forms.

a

There is a companion bold face designed by Chappell and a Trajanus Cyrillic designed by Hermann Zapf. Chappell's own sanserif, Lydian, is another related design, slightly darker than Trajanus but of similar angularity. After long delay, Linotype issued a digital version in 1997. The Cyrillic, however, exists only as Linotype metal matrices.

Trinité P A text family designed in 1978–81 by Bram de Does for the Enschedé Foundry in Haarlem. The commission began with a challenge: to create in the elastic and ephemeral world of phototype something as resonant and reserved as the handcut metal types of Jan van Krimpen. The impressive result was issued in film form in 1982 by Bobst/Autologic in Lausanne but never effectively distributed. Trinité was issued again in digital form by the Enschedé Font Foundry in 1991.

The sample of Trinité is overleaf.

There are three weights of wide roman, two weights of narrow roman, two weights of small caps and two weights of italic.

Q ábbbçdddêfffggg O
(hhhijijijkkklllmñòppp)
A qqqrstüvwxyyyž IJ
+ 1234567890 =

Q ábbbbçddddêffffggg O
{hhhhijijijkkkklllmñòpppp}
A qqqqrstüvwxyyyž IJ
+ 1234567890 =

Q ábbbçdddêfffggg O
(hhhijijijkkklllmñòppp)
A qqqrstüvwxyyyž IJ
+ 1234567890 =

Trinité roman wide (above), italic (center) and roman narrow (below). All three ranges of each roman face are shown together, and all four ranges of the italic. In each range, only the extending letters vary.

All weights and widths of roman and italic come in three ranges: with short, normal and long extenders. The capitals remain the same in height; so does the torso of the lower case, but the extenders range to different depths and altitudes. Both weights of italic are also issued in chancery form (with curved extenders). The ordinary roman (Trinité 2, with the normal extenders, in either the wide or the narrow width) makes a fine text face for conventional use. The wide version is 9% wider than the narrow and keeps the same internal rhythm. (In wide and narrow versions alike, for example, the set-widths of the roman letters *i*, *n* and *m* are in exactly the proportion 1:2:3.) The roman letters slope at 1°, the italics at 3°.

There are no separate characters for ligatures in Trinité. They construct themselves from parts. The *f* + *i* and *f* + *j*, for instance, combine to form the ligatures *fi* and *fj*. (This is the reason for the dancing dots on *i* and *j* in different versions of the face. In Trinité 1 and 2, the dots meld with the arch of the *f*. In Trinité 3, the tallest version, the dots tuck under the arm of *f* instead.) In its present form, with pi fonts, expert sets and other variants, the full family consists of 81 separate digital fonts. Half a dozen of these would be ample for many normal texts. The technical complexities of the series ought not to obscure the simple beauty of the face, which is rooted in the heritage of Van Krimpen and of Italian Renaissance forms. Even the arithmetical signs in Trinité have a slight scribal asymmetry. This is sufficient to enliven the forms for text use yet not enough to render them dysfunctionally ornate. Small caps and text figures are essential components of the family.

p

abcëfghijõp 123 AQ *abcéfghijôp*

Trump Mediäval H/M This is a very robust text face, designed by Georg Trump. It was first issued in 1954 by the Weber Foundry, Stuttgart, as a foundry type, and in machine form by Linotype. It is a strong, angular roman and italic with humanist axis but Mannerist torque and proportions. The aperture is moderate; the serifs are substantial and abrupt. The numerals, both in text form and in titling form, are notably well designed. The digital version retains the Linotype nonkerning *f*. There is a range of weights but only a partial set of ligatures. A number of Trump's excellent script faces – Codex, Delphin, Jaguar, Palomba and Time Script, for example – and his slab-serifed titling face called City, are potentially useful companions. (See also pp 52, 84.)

a

abcëfghijõp 123 AQ *abcéfghijôp*

a

Van den Keere H This is a family of digital romans, modeled on a 21 pt font that Hendrik van den Keere of Ghent cut in 1575 for Christophe Plantin of Antwerp. There are several weights, all with the requisite small caps and other components. But in his long, illustrious career as a punchcutter, Van den Keere did not cut a single italic. The italic paired here with his roman is based on the work of his older friend and colleague François Guyot. The digital versions of these types were produced by Frank Blokland in 's-Hertogenbosch and issued by DTL in 1995–97. (See also page 122.)

abcëfghijõp 123 AQ *abcéfghijôp*

g

Van Dijck H The type family now called Van Dijck – first issued by Monotype in 1935 – is based on an italic cut in Amsterdam about 1660 by Christoffel van Dijck and a roman which is probably also his. (Original matrices for the italic still survive; the roman is known only from printed specimens.) These are calm and graceful Dutch Baroque faces, modest in x-height, narrow in the italic and relatively spacious in the roman. A comparison of Van Dijck's work with that of Miklós Kis illuminates the range of Dutch Baroque tradition, but there is plenty of range in Van Dijck's work on its own. His blackletter types are very ornate, while his romans and italics breathe a deep and deliberate serenity, not unlike the works of his great contemporaries, the painters Pieter de Hooch and Jan Vermeer. The digital version of Monotype Van Dijck has unfortunately lost much of the power and resiliency of the Monotype metal version. (See also pp 51, 207.)

abcëfghijõp 123 AQ *abcéfghijôp*

a

Veljović P Designed by Jovica Veljović and issued in 1984 by ITC. Veljović is a lively postmodern face, with much inherent movement wrapped around its rationalist axis, and much prickly energy emerging in the long, sharp, abrupt wedge serifs. There is a wide range of weights. Fonts with text figures are produced by Elsner & Flake. Small caps, though part of the original design, have evidently never been released. Veljović makes an excellent companion for the same designer's Gamma or Esprit and can be mated with his fine script face Ex Ponto. (See also page 15.)

abcëfghijõp 123 AQ *abcéfghijôp*

abcëfghijõp 123 AQ *abcéfghijôp*

16 pt Berthold Walbaum

20 pt Monotype Walbaum

Walbaum H Justus Erich Walbaum, who was a contemporary of Beethoven, ranks with Giambattista Bodoni and Firmin Didot as one of the great European Romantic designers of type. He was the latest of the three, but he may well have been the most original. Walbaum cut his fonts at Goslar and Weimar early in the nineteenth century. His matrices were bought by the Berthold Foundry a century later, and Berthold Walbaum, in its metal form, is Walbaum's actual type. Berthold digital Walbaum is a close and careful translation. Monotype Walbaum, different though it is, is also quite authentic. The Berthold version is based on Walbaum's larger fonts, and the Monotype version on his small text sizes.

Each of the major Romantic designers had his own effect on design in the twentieth century. Firmin Didot's ghost is palpable in Adrian Frutiger's Frutiger, Bodoni's ghost in Paul Renner's Futura, and Walbaum's spirit is alive in some of the later work of Hermann Zapf. Yet each of these instances involves a real creative leap, not imitation. (See also page 131.)

g

The letterfit of Berthold digital Walbaum has been edited extensively to produce the fonts used here.

abcëfghijõp 123 AQ *abcéfghijôp*

the qua sp fghj xyz

Zapf Renaissance D Designed by Hermann Zapf in 1984–85 and issued in 1986 by Scangraphic. This family returns, after forty years, to many of the principles that animated one of Zapf's first typefaces, Palatino. But Zapf Renaissance is designed for the high-technology, two-dimensional world of digital imaging instead of the slower, more multidimensional world of the artist printer's handpress. The result is a less printerly and sculptural, more scribal and painterly typeface – and one which at the same time is more tolerant of digital typography's capricious, even licentious, freedom with size. The family includes a roman, italic, small caps, semibold and swash italic with a rich assortment of pilcrows and fleurons.

Palatino Linotype Greek – actually much closer in time to Zapf Renaissance than it is to the original Palatino – makes a fine Greek companion to this roman. (See also page 254.)

a

Linotype digital Palatino (on the left) and Zapf Renaissance (on the right). Both are shown here at 72 pt and 18 pt.

These types have much in common, but Palatino was first designed as a foundry face, with weight and proportion changing from size to size and the expectation that it would be printed in three dimensions. Zapf Renaissance was designed as a freely scalable digital face, in which one pattern serves for every size, and with the expectation that it would be printed in two dimensions only.

aa bb cc

éé ff gg

ññ ôô tt

AA HH

abcdefghijklmnopqrstuvwxyz

abcdefghijklmnopqrstuvwxyz

1 2 3 4 5 6 7 8 9 0 · A B C D É F G

1 2 3 4 5 6 7 8 9 0 · A B C D É F G

A B C D E F G H I J K L M N O

A B C D E F G H I J K L M N O

abcdefghijklmnopqrstuvwxyz

abcdefghijklmnopqrstuvwxyz

14 pt unserifed Etruscan cut by William Caslon for Oxford University Press, about 1745. Unserifed scripts are as old as writing itself, but this is one of the earliest unserifed types.

11.3 UNSERIFED TEXT FACES

Unserifed letters have a history at least as long, and quite as distinguished, as serifed letters. Unserifed capitals appear in the earliest Greek inscriptions. They reappear at Rome in the third and second centuries BC, and in Florence in the early Renaissance. Perhaps it is no more than an accident of history that the unserifed letters of fifteenth-century Florentine architects and sculptors were not translated into metal type in the 1470s.

Many rotundas and Greek types cut in the 1460s and 1470s include sanserif forms, but none is consistently unserifed. (A recent example on similar lines is Karlgeorg Hoefer's San Marco, shown on page 252.)

At Athens and again at Rome, the modulated stroke and bilateral serif were the scribal trademarks and symbols of empire. Unserifed letters, with no modulation or, at most, a subtle taper in the stroke, were emblems of the Republic. This link between unserifed letterforms and populist or democratic movements recurs time and again, in Renaissance Italy and in the eighteenth and nineteenth centuries in northern Europe.

Unserifed types were first cut in the eighteenth century, but they were cut at first for alphabets other than Latin. A sanserif Latin printing type was cut for Valentin Haüy, Paris, in 1786 – but Haüy's type was meant to be invisible. It was designed to be embossed, without ink, for the blind to read with their fingers. The first unserifed Latin type for the sighted – cut by William Caslon IV, London, about 1812 – was based on signwriters' letters and consisted of capitals only. Bicameral (upper- and lowercase) unserifed roman fonts were apparently first cut in Leipzig in the 1820s.

The importance of the Haüy italic was first pointed out by James Mosley. For more on the history of unserifed letters, see his essay "The Nymph and the Grot," *Typographica* n.s. 12 (1965), and Nicolete Gray, *A History of Lettering* (1986).

Most, though not all, of the unserifed types of the nineteenth century were dark, coarse and tightly closed. These characteristics are still obvious in faces like Helvetica and Franklin Gothic, despite the weight-reductions and other refinements worked on them over the years. These faces are cultural souvenirs of some of the bleakest days of the Industrial Revolution.

During the twentieth century, sanserifs have evolved toward

much greater subtlety, and in this evolution there seem to be three major factors. One is the study of archaic Greek inscriptions, with their light, limber stroke and large aperture. Another is the pursuit of pure geometry: typographic meditation first on the circle and the line, then on more complex geometric figures. The third is the study of Renaissance calligraphy and humanistic form – vitally important in the recent history of serifed and unserifed letters alike. But in retrospect it seems that both type designers and founders were for many years strangely reluctant to believe that one could simply write a humanist letter and *leave the serifs off.* When this is done, everything happens and nothing happens: if the stroke has width, the stroke-end too has shape and form; it takes the serif's place.

Unserifed Text Faces

abcëfghijõp 123 AQ *abcéfghijôp*

fi

Caspari D Designed by Gerard Daniëls and issued by the Dutch Type Library in 1993. This is a subtly crafted and simple text face with the essential humanist attributes, including large aperture, a genuine italic with a modest slope of 6°, text figures, small caps and impressive economy of form. It was one of the first unserifed faces issued in a form truly suitable for text work, with all working parts in place. Daniëls added a Cyrillic version in 2003. One thing still missing is a book weight. (See also pp 264–65.)

AQ *ábçdèfghijklmñöpqrstûvwxyz*

fi

Flora P/D Designed by Gerard Unger, released by Rudolf Hell in 1985 and licensed through ITC in 1989. Flora is a true sanserif italic – and it was, I believe, the first unserifed italic to approximate chancery form. It can be used very happily alone but is designed to function also as a companion to Unger's Praxis (unserifed roman) and Demos (serifed roman and italic). Because its slope is only 2.5°, Flora functions best with Praxis when it is used for setting separate blocks of text.

Unger has spoken persuasively about the importance of horizontals in his type designs. He associates the strong horizontal thrust of Hollander and Swift with the flat Dutch landscape in the midst of which he lives. But in most of his italics – Swift, Hollander and Flora included – it is verticals that seem to matter most. (See also page 264.)

See Gerard Unger, "Dutch Landscape with Letters," in issue 14 of the Dutch journal *Gravisie* (Utrecht, 1989): 29–52.

abcëfghijõp 123 AQ *abcéfghijôp*

18 pt Original Frutiger

abcëfghijõp 123 AQ *abcéfghijôp*

18 pt Frutiger Next

fi

Frutiger P/D Adrian Frutiger designed this face in 1975, initially for signage at the Paris-Roissy Airport. It was then issued by Mergenthaler for use on their photosetting machines and immediately prospered as a typeface. What it lacked in the way of humanist structure it made up for in its open, fresh geometry, wide aperture and balance. It also mated well with the same designer's Méridien and Apollo, though such a mixture was not apparently part of the original design plan, and the fonts did not match in weight or body size. In the conversion from signage to typeface, a sloped roman was added, rather than a genuine italic.

In 1999–2000, Frutiger redrew the face, adding a true italic, incorporating subtle curves into the stems of the roman characters, and altering the range to include a book weight. There are other small improvements – repositioning of the diacritics, for example – which make the newer version better for text work, though there are still, as in Méridien, no text figures or small caps. The revised version, issued by Linotype in 2001, is known as Frutiger Next. (See also pp 105, 264–65.)

abcëfghijõp 123 AQ *abcéfghijôp*

Futura H This was the first and remains the best of the geometric sanserif faces, designed by Paul Renner in 1924–26 and issued by the Bauer Foundry, Frankfurt, in 1927. Futura is a subtly crafted face, but many copies have been made, under various names, in metal, film and digital form. By no means all these cuts are equally well made – and not all weights that have been added to the family are Renner's own designs.

Geometric though it is, Futura is one of the most rhythmical sanserifs ever made. Its proportions are graceful and humane – close to those of Centaur in the vertical dimension. This helps to make it suitable – like all the unserifed faces examined here – for setting extended text. (Which is not, of course, to say that it is suitable for texts of every kind.) The new digital version issued by Neufville in Barcelona includes text figures and small caps, which were part of Renner's original design but never issued in metal. (See also pp 14, 106, 133, 212, 264.)

fi

abcëfghijõp 123 AQ *abcéfghijôp*

Gill Sans M Designed by Eric Gill and issued by Monotype in 1927. Gill Sans is a distinctly British but highly readable sanserif, composed of latently humanist and overtly geometric forms. The aperture varies (it is large in *c*, moderate in roman *s*, smaller in roman *e*). The italic, like Fournier's, cut two centuries before, was a revolutionary achievement in its time. Books have been set successfully in Gill Sans, though it requires a sure sense of color and measure. Text figures and small caps – very useful when the face is used for text work – were finally added by the Monotype design staff in 1997. (See also pp 264, 277.)

e

abcëfghijõp 123 AQ *abcéfghijôp*

Haarlemmer Sans D Frank Blokland at the Dutch Type Library created this face as a digital companion to Jan van Krimpen's Haarlemmer while digitizing the latter in the mid 1990s. Haarlemmer itself, cut by Monotype, began as a private commission. So did Haarlemmer Sans, six decades later. The face has been publicly available since 1998. Small caps and text figures are implicit in the design. (See also page 233 – and compare Van Krimpen's Romulus Sans, page 260.)

e

abcëfghijõp 123 AQ *abcéfghijôp*

Legacy Sans D Designed by Ronald Arnholm and issued via ITC in 1992. To the best of my knowledge, this is the only published attempt to make an unserifed version of Nicolas Jenson's roman. Arnholm drew the serifed version first, and in the process made some drastic changes to Jenson's proportions, yet resemblances remain. The italic is based not on Arrighi but on Garamond's *gros romain*. There is more modulation of the stroke in Legacy Sans than in most unserifed types. Text figures and small caps are part of the design. (See also pp 235, 264.)

abcëfghijõp 123 AQ *abcéfghijôp*

Lucida Sans D This admirable sans, designed by Kris Holmes and Charles Bigelow in 1985, is part of the largest type family in the world. The Lucida tribe now includes not just serifed and unserifed roman and italic but also Greek, Hebrew, Vietnamese, pan-Asian and pan-European Latin and Cyrillic, a full phonetic character set, a multitude of mathematical symbol sets, swash italic, blackletter, script, a slightly rumpled offshoot known as Lucida Casual, a higher-contrast series called Lucida Bright, a series designed for crude resolutions, called Lucida Fax, a set of fixed-pitch typewriter fonts, and another fixed-pitch font, called Lucida Console, designed for terminal emulation. Yet the basic text figures and small caps, which are essential for civilized text work, are still omitted by every digital foundry that has merchandised the face. (See also page 264.)

e

abcëfghijõp 123 AQ *abcéfghijôp* — *18 pt Original Optima*

abcëfghijõp 123 AQ *abcéfghijôp* — *18 pt Optima Nova*

BCDEFGHIJKLMNOPRSW — *18 pt Original Optima*

BCDEFGHIJKLMNOPRSW — *18 pt Optima Nova*

Optima H/M/D Designed by Hermann Zapf in 1952–55 and issued in 1958, both as a foundry face by Stempel and in the form of metal matrices for the Linotype machine. The taper of the stroke in these original metal versions derives from unserifed Greek inscriptions and the unserifed roman inscriptions of Renaissance Florence, but in other respects the architecture of Optima is Neoclassical. The original Optima 'italic' is pure sloped roman. There is a range of weights and a matching text Greek, designed by Zapf and issued by Linotype in 1971 (but the Greek, to the best of my knowledge, has never been digitized.)

a

a

fi

Optima Nova – digital a revision undertaken by Zapf and Akira Kobayashi – was completed in 2003. It involves many changes to the roman, including the sharpening of the terminals (especially visible in a, c, f, s, C, G) and a return to the original subtle taper of the mainstrokes. (This taper, present in the metal typeface, was abandoned in the first conversion to digital format because of the staircasing it caused at low resolutions.) Roman text figures were also a part of the original foundry design, cut in steel a trial size but not offered for sale. These are revived in Optima Nova, and italic text figures have been added. The diacritics have been repositioned, and the width of some roman letters (D and W for instance) has noticeably changed. The italic is a new design, drawn by Kobayashi under Zapf's supervision. Optima

Nova italic slopes at 15° (compared with 11° in the original) and includes cursive forms of a, e, f, g and l. (See also page 264.)

abcëfghijõp 123 AQ *abcéfghijôp*

Quadraat Sans D Fred Smeijers, a typographer based in Arnhem, Netherlands, is one of the few people trained as a type designer first and self-taught as a punchcutter second. FontShop International released the serifed version of his Quadraat in 1993 and the unserifed version in 1997. These are postmodern fonts, but they are strongly rooted in Dutch Baroque tradition. Quirkiness is a hallmark of the Baroque, and these are among the quirkier text faces I have ever used. They are also among the most rigorously designed. Quadraat Sans, like its serifed partner, is not pretty, nor does it need to be. It is intelligent instead. Text figures and small caps are standard equipment. (See also pp 244, 264.)

a

AQ abcdefghijklmnopqrstuvwxyz

Romulus Sans H Jan van Krimpen's major project in the 1930s was the large Romulus family: serifed and unserifed roman, chancery italic, sloped roman, open titling, and Greek. Many designers have now embarked on similar projects, but in 1930, no one had done so. The most interesting part of the project was Romulus Sans, meant to challenge the new and revolutionary sans of Eric Gill (released in 1927). Four weights of the unserifed roman had been cut in a single size (12 pt) when Van Krimpen's employer, the Enschedé Foundry, halted the project. Romulus Sans is the basis for Frank Blokland's Haarlemmer Sans (page 258).

abcëfghijõp 123 AQ *abcéfghijôpy*

Scala Sans D A fine neohumanist sanserif designed by Martin Majoor and issued by FontShop International, Berlin, in 1994. This is as fully humanized as any sanserif I know. It has a crisp and very legible italic and small caps. Text figures and the full array of standard ligatures are present on the basic font. In the italic, even the geometric letters at the tail of the Latin alphabet (*v, w, y*) are cursive in their sharp and bony way. The relationship between the serifed and unserifed forms of Scala is studied in detail on pp 262–63. (Scala Sans is the unserifed face used throughout this book. See also pp 246, 264.)

a

abcëfghijõp 123 AQ abcéfghijôp

Seria Sans D Like its serifed counterpart, Martin Majoor's Seria Sans explores the common ground between Italian Renaissance structure and the world of Dutch reserve. The extenders are long and graceful, and the stroke weight subtly varied in fact though optically uniform. Seria Sans goes a long way toward fulfilling the dream of a pure sanserif type that began with Edward Johnston, Eric Gill and Jan van Krimpen. The italic, like its serifed cousin, slopes at only one degree and so shares many of its capitals with the roman. The family was issued by FontShop, Berlin, in 2000. (See also page 246.)

a

abcëfghijõp 123 AQ *abcéfghijôpy*

17 pt Original Syntax

abcëfghijõp 123 AQ *abcéfghijôpy*

17 pt "Linotype Syntax"

Syntax H/D This was the last sanserif text face commercially cast in metal, and in my opinion the best. Hans Eduard Meier designed the original version in Switzerland in the late 1960s, and it was cut and cast at the Stempel Foundry, Frankfurt, in 1969. The roman is a true neohumanist sanserif. Renaissance shapes that we are used to seeing in company with serifs and a modulated stroke are simply rendered in unserifed and (almost) unmodulated form. The italic, however, is a hybrid: primarily sloped roman. Close scrutiny reveals that in Syntax the roman is sloped too. The italic slopes at 12° and the roman at something close to half a degree. Half a degree, however, is enough to add perceptible vitality and motion to the forms. The stroke width changes very subtly, and the stroke ends are trimmed at a variety of angles. There are several weights, but as usual in neohumanist faces, the weights above semibold are severely distorted.

a

For text use, the original Syntax was hampered by the absence of text figures and small caps. Meier redrew the entire family in the late 1990s, adding these components, making very small adjustments to the roman and greater alterations to the italic. The new italic letterforms are narrower than the old, and three of them – *f, j, y* – are more cursive than before. Meier also added serifed and semiserifed versions of the face. These revisions add substantially to the range and versatility of the type, but the core of Meier's achievement remains exactly where it was: in the naked structure of the roman. (See also page 264.)

For a Native American variant of Syntax, see Dell Hymes, "Victoria Howard's 'Gitskux and His Older Brother'," in Brian Swann, ed., *Smoothing the Ground: Essays on Native American Oral Literature* (Berkeley, 1983).

Martin Majoor's Scala and Scala Sans, shown here at 74 pt and 18 pt.

The serifed and unserifed forms of Scala are closely related and highly compatible, but there are many subtle differences as well. Taking the serifs away from an alphabet changes the relative widths of the characters, which changes the rhythm of the face. In Scala roman, for example, the unserifed caps are uniformly narrower than the serifed caps. The unserifed lower case is slightly narrower too, but most of the difference comes in the straight-legged letters h *through* n.

aa bb cc

éé ff gg

ññ ôô tt

AA HH

abcdefghijklmnopqrstuvwxyz

abcdefghijklmnopqrstuvwxyz

1 2 3 4 5 6 7 8 9 0 · A B C D É F G

1 2 3 4 5 6 7 8 9 0 · A B C D É F G

A B C D E F G H I J K L M N

A B C D E F G H I J K L M N

O P Q R S T U V W X Y Z

O P Q R S T U V W X Y Z

aa bb *cc*
éé ff gg
ññ ôô tt
AA HH

abcdefghijklmnopqrstuvwxyz
abcdefghijklmnopqrstuvwxyz
1 2 3 4 5 6 7 8 9 0
1 2 3 4 5 6 7 8 9 0
A B C D E F G H I J K L M N
A B C D E F G H I J K L M N
O P Q R S T U V W X Y Z
O P Q R S T U V W X Y Z

In Scala italic, many lowercase letters are actually wider in the sans than in the serifed form, though the alphabet is narrower overall. And Scala Serif has a clearly modulated stroke, while Scala Sans is optically (not actually) monochrome. Thinned and tapered strokes occur in the sans and serifed forms alike (in the brow of roman a, *the bar of roman* e, *and in the roman and italic* g, *for example) – but the unserifed stroke is never thinned as much as the stroke with serifs.*

Italicization Quotient of Thirteen Unserifed 'Italics'

Sample	Cursive characters	Score
abcdefghijklmnopqrstuvwxyz FUTURA: Cursive characters: none		0
abcdefghijklmnopqrstuvwxyz ORIGINAL FRUTIGER: Cursive characters: none		0
abcdefghijklmnopqrstuvwxyz ORIGINAL OPTIMA: Cursive characters: none		0
abcdefghijklmnopqrstuvwxyz ORIGINAL SYNTAX: Cursive characters: *bcdpq*		5
abcdefghijklmnopqrstuvwxyz GILL SANS: Cursive characters: *abcdfpq*		7
abcdefghijklmnopqrstuvwxyz OPTIMA NOVA: Cursive characters: *abdefglpqu*		10
abcdefghijklmnopqrstuvwxyz CASPARI: Cursive characters: *abcdeghmnpq*		11
abcdefghijklmnopqrstuvwxyz FLORA: Cursive characters: *abcdefghmnpqru*		14
abcdefghijklmnopqrstuvwxyz LUCIDA SANS: Cursive characters: *abcdefghmnpqru*		14
abcdefghijklmnopqrstuvwxyz SCALA SANS: Cursive characters: *abcdefhmnpqtuvwy*		16
abcdefghijklmnopqrstuvwxyz LEGACY SANS: Cursive characters: *abcdefghkmnpqrtuy*		17
abcdefghijklmnopqrstuvwxyz QUADRAAT SANS: Cursive characters: *abcdefghjmnpquvwy*		17
abcdefghijklmnopqrstuvwxyz TRIPLEX: Cursive characters: *abcdefghiklmnopqrtuvwxyz*		24

Flora and Lucida Sans are shown here at 17 pt, all other samples at 18 pt.

Triplex italic – the most broken alphabet here – appears to get the highest score. Conclusion: brokenness can coexist with cursiveness, though the two are not the same.

SOME ITALICS are not italic at all – that is, they are not cursive. Others are very italic indeed. This is one of the salient differences among sanserif types. We can measure this aspect of a typeface, in a crude way, by counting how many letters in the basic lower case have visibly cursive characteristics. This tells us nothing whatsoever about how *good* or *bad* the typeface is. It tells us, instead, something about the *kind* of goodness it may or may not possess.

The same analysis can be performed on serifed italics too. But it is normal, in a serifed italic of humanist form, for every letter in the lower case to be noticeably cursive. There are no purely sanserif italics for which this seems to be true. (John Downer's Triplex italic lower case is close to 100% cursive in this sense, despite its highly geometric form – but it is not 100% unserifed.)

The features that mark an unserifed letter as cursive are often very subtle. In a letter such as *b, h, m, p* or *r,* for example, it is usually only the shape of the bowl, or the angle and the height at which the curved strokes enter or leave the stem, that reveals its cursive form.

b*b* p*p* r*r* · b*b* p*p* r*r*

In Frutiger (on the left, above), the oblique forms of *b, p* and *r* are no more cursive than the upright. In Legacy Sans (on the right, above), the oblique forms are visibly italic. They differ from the corresponding roman forms in structure as well as in slope.

The g can be cursive or noncursive, no matter whether it has the binocular form that is usual in serifed roman faces or the monocular form that is typical both of chancery italics such as Trinité and of Realist sanserifs such as Helvetica.

g*g* g*g* *g* · g*g* g*g* *g*

1 2 3 4 5 6

In Syntax (1), the oblique g keeps its essentially uncursive roman form. In Legacy Sans (2), the italic g differs more from the roman: it develops at least a little bit of swing as well as a slope. The g from DTL Elzevir italic (3) – a Baroque serifed face, based on the work of Christoffel van Dijck – provides a comparison. The g of Frutiger (4) is monocular but not cursive, even when it slopes. In Gerard Daniëls's Caspari (5), the italic g is monocular and cursive, like the g in Méridien italic (6).

Blackletters

The first types cut in Europe, including all those used by Johann Gutenberg, were blackletters. Scripts and printing types of this kind were once used throughout Europe – in England, France, Hungary, Poland, Portugal, the Netherlands and Spain, as well as Germany – and some species thrived even in Italy. They are the typographic counterpart of the Gothic style in architecture, and like Gothic architecture, they are a prominent part of the European heritage, though they flourished longer and more vigorously in Germany than anywhere else.

de heeft hy ons gheuandet die vten
hoghen opgegaen is Inlichte here
denghenē die in duysterniſſe ſittē eñ
in die ſcheme des doots. om te leydē

A 14-point textura cut by Henric Pieterszoon Lettersnider, probably at Antwerp in 1492. (Matrices for this font – likely the oldest set of matrices in existence – are now in the Enschedé Museum in Haarlem.)

Blackletter scripts, like roman scripts, exist in endless variety. Blackletter types are somewhat simpler, and not all of them need concern us here. But it is worth noting the presence of four major families: *textura, fraktur, bastarda* and *rotunda*. (Another variety of blackletter often listed in type catalogues is Schwabacher. This is bastarda by its domestic German name.) None of these families is confined to a particular historical period. All four of them have survived, like roman and italic, through many historical variations. Their differences are many and complex, but they can usually be distinguished by reference to the lowercase *o* alone. Though it is written with only two penstrokes, the *o* in a textura looks essentially hexagonal. In a fraktur, it is normally flat on the left side, curved on the right. In a bastarda, it is normally pointed at top and bottom and belled on both sides. In a rotunda, it is essentially oval or round.

Typical lowercase forms in textura, fraktur, bastarda and rotunda

Blackletters can be used in many contexts for emphasis or contrast – even in a world devoted to roman and italic – and need not be confined to the mastheads of newspapers or the titles of religious tracts. Type designers have also not abandoned them. Some excellent blackletters have been drawn in the twentieth century – by German artists such as Rudolf Koch and by the American Frederic Goudy.

A O ábçdèfghijklmñöpqrstûvwxyz ß

Clairvaux D The blackletter of the White Monks. The Cistercian abbey of Clairvaux, about half way from Paris to Basel, was founded by St Bernard in 1115 and thrived throughout the twelfth century. The typeface of the same name, designed by Herbert Maring and issued by Linotype in 1990, has much of the simplicity espoused by the old Cistercian order. It is also closer than any other bastarda to the forms of the Caroline minuscule, and thus more legible than most to modern eyes.

A O ábçdèfghijklmñöpqrstûvwxyz ß

Duc de Berry D A light French bastarda, designed by Gottfried Pott, issued in digital form by Linotype in 1991. Jean de France, the Duke of Berry (1340–1416) would, I think, have found these letterforms familiar, but they are not based on the script in any of the lavish Books of Hours he once owned.

A O ábçdèfghijklmñöpqrſtûvwxyz ß

Fette Fraktur H This heavy, Romantic fraktur was designed by Johann Christian Bauer and issued by his foundry at Frankfurt about 1850. It provides strong evidence that the Victorian 'fat face' is inherently more congenial to blackletter than to roman.

A O ábçdèfghijklmñöpqrstûvwxyz ß

Goudy Text M Designed by Frederic Goudy and issued by Monotype in 1928. This is a narrow, smooth, lightly ornamented textura, relatively legible in the upper as well as the lower case. There is a second set of capitals, known as Lombardic caps. In machine form and digital form alike, the type is poorly fitted, but it is worth the work of salvage.

A O abcdefghijklmnopqrstuvwxyz

Goudy Thirty M This was one of Frederic Goudy's last typefaces, deliberately conceived as his memorial to himself. ('Thirty' is, of course, journalists' code for 'end of story.') It is a light and simple rotunda, designed in 1942, issued by Lanston Monotype in 1948 and now available from the Lanston Type Co. in digital form. There are two versions, differing in the forms of *a, s, w* and several of the capitals.

A O abcdefghijklmnopqrsſtuvwxyz

Rhapsodie H This is an energetic, legible Schwabacher (German bastarda) designed by Ilse Schüle and issued by Ludwig & Mayer, Frankfurt, in 1951. There is an alternate set of ornamental capitals. I have not found a digital version of the face.

A O ábcdèfghíjklmñőpqrstûvwxyz ß

San Marco D Designed by Karlgeorg Hoefer and issued in digital form by Linotype in 1991. This is the first digital blackletter inspired by the rotundas cut at Venice in the 1470s by Nicolas Jenson. San Marco too is a rotunda – the genus of blackletter most closely connected to Italy and structurally closest to roman forms. It is named for the round-vaulted cathedral of San Marco, at the ceremonial center of Jenson's city. (See also page 105.)

A abcdefghijklmnopqrſstuvwxyz

Trump Deutsch H Designed by Georg Trump and issued in metal by the Berthold Foundry in 1936. This is a dark, wide, concave, unornamented and energetic textura. Both upper and lower case are open and easily legible forms. To the best of my knowledge, it has never yet been digitized.

A O ábçdèfghíjklmñőpqrstûvwxyz ß

Wilhelm Klingspor Schrift H Rudolf Koch completed this narrow, ornamental textura in 1925, naming it in honor of the recently deceased co-owner of the Klingspor Bros. Foundry in Offenbach, where Koch was chief designer. Not all the alternate glyphs in the handsome metal versions have been digitized.

Uncial letters were widely used by European scribes from the fourth through the ninth century AD, both for Latin and for Greek, but they had vanished from common use in the time of Gutenberg. Uncials were not cut into type until the nineteenth century, and then only for scholarly or antiquarian purposes. In the twentieth century, however, many designers – Sjoerd de Roos, William Addison Dwiggins, Frederic Goudy, Oldřich Menhart, Karlgeorg Hoefer and Günter Gerhard Lange, among others – took an interest in uncial forms, and one artist and printer, Victor Hammer, devoted his typographic life to them.

It is often said that *uncial* (from Latin *uncia*) means 'inch.' The two words are indeed related, but a better translation of *uncial* is simply 'small measure' or 'small standard.'

Historically, uncials are unicameral – they have only one case, as all European alphabets did until the late Middle Ages – but not all recent uncials are likewise. Early uncials, like recent ones, are sometimes serifed, sometimes not, and may be modulated or monochrome. They are now used chiefly for display, but some are quiet enough for extended texts.

AQ 123 ábçðèfghíjklmñôp

qrstűvwxyz 123 ÐGJQ 456

American Uncial H This is the fourth type Victor Hammer designed, the second for which he cut the punches, and the first he produced after fleeing to the USA from Austria in 1939. All Hammer's types are uncials. Only two – this one and its predecessor Pindar – are bicameral. American Uncial was cast privately in Chicago in 1945, then commercially by Klingspor and marketed in Europe as Neue Hammer Unziale. Most digital types sold as 'American Uncial' are actually copies of a different face: a unicameral uncial called Samson, which Hammer designed in Italy in the 1920s. Digital versions of the real American Uncial are sold, like their metal forebears, under the name Neue Hammer Unziale.

ábçðèfghijklmñôp

qrstüvwxyz 123 æœþð

Omnia D Lightly serifed, round, cursive uncials with a large aperture and humanist axis, designed by Karlgeorg Hoefer. This is a unicameral face, issued by Linotype in 1991.

Script Types

In ordinary usage, script is what is not type; it is writing: the mode of visual language used in public by calligraphers and in private by other literate humans, including typographers themselves. When script hardens, breaks and starts to look like type, we often call it printing – yet printing is what printers do with type, even type that looks like script, which we are likely to call script type. An innocent observer might conclude that English is an undernourished language, whose speakers cannot generate a new word even when they need one.

At the root of this confusion is a portion of good sense. Type is writing edited or imitated, translated or paraphrased, honored or mocked – but writing itself is a fluid and linear version of more disconnected epigraphic signs. The difference between 'type' and 'script' reiterates the difference between *glyphic* and *graphic*, or carved and written, characters. That difference was established at least 1500 years before the printing press was born.

The craving to mate roman with italic appears to be an effort to have type and script, or glyphic and graphic, at once. This explains in part why it is difficult to classify a typeface like Poetica. Is it a script, or is it a solitary (romanless) italic?

On the early history of printed scripts, see Stanley Morison's essay "On Script Types," *The Fleuron* 4 (1921): 1–42.

Scripts have thrived as foundry type, phototype and digital type, and several fine designers – Imre Reiner, for example – have focused as exclusively on scripts as others have on romans. But scripts had an importance in the world of commercial letterpress that they lack in the world of two-dimensional printing. Handwritten originals are expensive to photoengrave for reproduction on the letterpress. Specially commissioned calligraphy is easy to include, by way of scanning or photography, in artwork destined for the offset press. The best script to supplement a typographic page is now therefore more likely to be custom made.

Dozens of excellent script types are available. They include Arthur Baker's Marigold and Visigoth, Roger Excoffon's Choc and Mistral, Karlgeorg Hoefer's Salto and Saltino, Günter Gerhard Lange's Derby and El Greco, Michael Neugebauer's Squire, Friedrich Peter's Magnificat and Vivaldi, Imre Reiner's Matura and Pepita, Robert Slimbach's Caflisch and Sanvito, and Georg Trump's Jaguar and Palomba. I have chosen to illustrate here only a handful of the scripts that particularly interest me. Two of these – Eaglefeather and Tekton – are architectural scripts and could have been included just as easily among the text types. I have put them here instead for what they reveal about the process of transition from writing to printing, script to type, and script type to roman and italic.

abcëfghijõp 123 ABDQ *abcéfghijôp*

Eaglefeather D This is a family of type created in 1994 by David Siegel and Carol Toriumi-Lawrence, based on some of the architectural lettering of Frank Lloyd Wright (1867–1959). Eaglefeather is issued in two forms, called formal and informal, but only the roman lower case actually differs. The two share one italic, one set of roman caps, small caps, figures and analphabetics. Eaglefeather Informal (the version shown) is actually two italics. The 'roman' is a crisp, unserifed italic with no slope. The 'italic' is the same set of letters with a slope of 10°. The series also includes small caps.

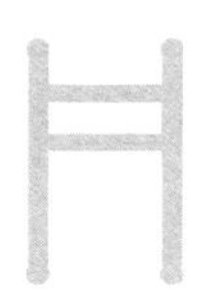

AQ 123 ábçdèfghijklmñöpqrstûvwxyz
AA EEE 4 ¢ čďį fpgh ik vz

Ex Ponto D This rough-edged, lyrical script was designed by Jovica Veljović and issued by Adobe in three weights in 1995. The design was completed in exile, and its name, Ex Ponto, alludes to the *Epistulae ex Ponto*, 'letters from the Black Sea,' written in exile before AD 13 by the Roman poet Ovid. The newer OpenType version of the face includes three sets of capitals and a wide assortment of variant letters and ligatures.

AO abcdefghijklmnopqrstuvwxyz

Legende H A wide, dark, disconnected script with a small eye but excellent legibility. It was designed by Ernst Schneidler and issued by the Bauer Foundry, Frankfurt, in 1937. This is one of the best modern exemplars of a class of Mannerist scripts inaugurated by Robert Granjon at Lyon in 1557. Typographers call them *civilités*.

The name *civilité* stems from the use of Granjon's script in an early French translation of one of Desiderius Erasmus's best-sellers, *De civilitate morum puerilium libellus*: 'A little book for children about civilized behavior.'

AQ 123 ábçdèfghijkmñöprstûvwxyz

Ondine H This is a dark but open, lucid, disconnected pen script designed by Adrian Frutiger and originally issued by Deberny & Peignot, Paris, in 1953. It was one of Frutiger's earliest designs and it remains his only script face. (An *ondine* is a sea-nymph, and Frutiger's Ondine is full of waves.)

AQ ábçdèfghijklmñöpqrstûvwxyz

Present H A light, broad, disconnected brush script designed by Friedrich Sallwey and issued by the Stempel Foundry, Frankfurt, in 1974. In digital form, the family has been enlarged to include both regular and condensed versions in three weights.

abcdëfghijõp 123 AQ *abcéfghijôp*

Tekton D Designed by David Siegel, based on the lettering of architect Frank Ching, and issued by Adobe in 1989. Multiple Master, GX and OpenType versions followed. The latter include text figures and small caps. In modest sizes, Tekton is functionally a sanserif. At larger sizes, its serifs are visible as tiny beads. The 'italic' is an oblique. The original script can be seen in Ching's book *Architectural Graphics* (New York, 1975; 2nd ed. 1985), which is printed from handwritten pages. (The third edition of the book, published in 1996, is set in semicondensed digital Tekton.)

AQ 123 ábçdèfõghijklmñöpqirstûvwxyz

AQ 123 ábçàdèfõghijklmñöpqirstûvwxyz

AQ 654 ábçàdèfõghijklmñöpqirstûvwxyz

AQ 456 ábçdèfoghijklmñöpqirstûvwxyz

Zapfino D This calligraphic tour de force designed by Hermann Zapf was issued by Linotype in 1998 as a set of four alphabets with a separate font of supplementary ligatures. In 2004 an enlarged, OpenType version appeared under the name Zapfino Extra. That incarnation of the family includes small caps, additional alternates and swashes, and a darker version of one of the alphabets, known as Zapfino Forte. It is an exemplary marriage of artistic and technical ability. Effective use of such a type requires considerable patience and skill. It therefore makes a useful training ground for typographers and calligraphers alike. (See also page 190.)

νηχόμενόν τε λέανδρον ὁμοῦ καὶ λύχνο

Δράσαντι δ᾽ αἰσχρά, δεινὰ τἀπιτίμια

πρὸς τὸν θεόν, καὶ θεὸς ἦν ὁ λόγος.

Three early Greek types. Above: The Complutensian Greek, a 16 pt orthotic font cut by Arnaldo Guillén de Brocar at Alcalá de Henares, near Madrid, in 1510. Center: The 10 pt cursive cut by Francesco Griffo, Venice, in 1502 [here shown at twice actual size]. Bottom: An 18 pt chancery Greek cut by Robert Granjon in the 1560s.

11.7 GREEKS

Greek type has a long and complex history peculiarly its own, yet closely entwined with the history of roman. The first full fonts of Greek were cut in Venice and Florence by Nicolas Jenson, Francesco Griffo and others who were simultaneously cutting the first roman and italic faces. Simon de Colines, Claude Garamond, Robert Granjon, Miklós Kis, Johann Fleischman and William Caslon cut good Greeks as well, and their type was widely used. Yet the first Greek book printed in Greece itself was the Mt Athos Psalter of 1759, and the first secular printing press in Greece was established only during the War of Independence, with help from Ambroise Firmin-Didot, in 1821.

Greek adaptations of popular roman faces – Baskerville, Caledonia, Helvetica, Times New Roman, Univers and others – have been issued by Linotype, Monotype and other firms, and are widely used in Greece. But there, as in much of Eastern Europe, the more lyrical forms of modernism have been slower to arrive. Even in the multinational world of classical studies, where Greek types that will harmonize with neohumanist romans are perennially needed, they are in very short supply.

Three important classes of Greek type have been with us since the fifteenth century. These are the *orthotic,* the *cursive,* and the *chancery script.* Orthotic Greek is analogous to roman in the Latin alphabet. It is, in other words, *not cursive.* The letters are relatively self-contained, usually upright, and may or may not have serifs. Cursive Greek type – which exists in both sloped and vertical forms – is analogous to italic. Chancery Greeks are merely elaborate forms of the cursive, but they attained in Greek a level

Orthotic is from the Greek word ὀρθός, meaning upright; *cursive* from the Latin *currere,* to run or to hurry; and *chancery* from the Latin *cancelli,* literally 'little crabs.' *Cancelli* came to be the Latin term for a lattice or grate, and then for the ornamental barrier that stood between officials and petitioners at court. It is in other words *the bar* to which lawyers are still called. Chancery scripts flourished where lawyers worked.

of typographic intricacy never yet approached by chancery italic type in the Latin alphabet.

The orthotic Greek types of the Renaissance resemble Renaissance romans yet differ from them too, in several interesting ways. The stroke is usually quite uniform in thickness, the stroke-ends are sharply rectangular, and the serifs, when present, are usually short, abrupt and unilateral. The geometric figures of triangle, circle and line are prominent in the underlying structure of these faces, though not to the exclusion of more complex curves. This is the oldest form of Greek type, first seen in the partial alphabets cut by Peter Schoeffer the Elder at Mainz and by Konrad Sweynheym at Subiaco, near Rome, in 1465. It is also the style of the first full-fledged and polytonic Greek type, cut by Nicolas Jenson at Venice in 1471.

Polytonic Greeks are fonts with a full complement of Alexandrian diacritics. See page 295 for details.

The finest early example of orthotic Greek, in the opinion of many historians, is the Complutensian Greek of Arnaldo Guillén de Brocar, cut in Spain in 1510. A few years after that, orthotic Greeks completely disappeared. They were not revived until the end of the nineteenth century. The most widely used modern version is the New Hellenic type designed by Victor Scholderer in London in 1927.

The first cursive Greek font was cut by an unidentified craftsman at Vicenza, west of Venice, in 1475. The second, cut at Venice by Francesco Griffo, did not appear for another twenty years – and it was not a simple cursive like the anonymous font from Vicenza but an elaborate chancery script. Griffo cut a simple Greek cursive in 1502, but chancery Greeks remained the fashion throughout Europe for the next two hundred years.

A simple Greek cursive can be turned to a chancery script by the addition of ligatures, and a chancery script converted to simple cursive by leaving the ligatures out. But the battery of ligatures involved often runs to several hundred, and sometimes to more than a thousand.

Chancery Greeks were cut by many artists from Garamond to Caslon, but Neoclassical and Romantic designers – including Baskerville, Bodoni, Alexander Wilson and Ambroise Firmin-Didot – all returned to simpler cursive forms. Firmin-Didot's Greek is still in frequent use, in France and Greece alike, but in the English-speaking world the cursive Greek most often seen is the one designed in 1806 by Richard Porson.

Neohumanist Greeks, such as Jan van Krimpen's Antigone, Hermann Zapf's Heraklit and Palatino Greek, and Robert Slimbach's Minion Greek, have opened a new chapter in the history of the Greek alphabet, bringing the humanist structure of Renaissance roman and italic into the Greek lower case. Ironically, these types have evolved just as the custodians of European culture were abandoning the study of the classics.

Greek, like Latin, evolved into bicameral form in the late Middle Ages. The upper case in the two alphabets shares the same heritage, and more than half the uppercase forms remain identical. (The same is true of Greek and Latin uncials.) But the Greek lower case has evolved along a different path. There is a quiet and formal Greek hand, not dissimilar in spirit to the roman lower case, but the usual Greek minuscule is cursive. As a consequence, most Greek faces are like Renaissance italics: upright, formal capitals married to a flowing, often sloping, lower case. No real supporting face has developed in the Greek typographic tradition: no face that augments and contrasts with the primary alphabet as italic does with roman.

Ἄᾳ

That of course is subject to change. Several twentieth-century designers have added bold and inclined variants to their Greeks, in imitation of Latin models, and a shift in usage may be underway. But several of the faces shown here are solitary designs. They are meant to be used alone or as supplementary faces themselves, for setting Greek intermixed with roman.

άβγδεζηϑικλμνξοπρσςτυφχψω

άβγδεζηϑικλμνξοπρσςτυφχψω

Albertina D Chris Brand designed this Greek in the 1960s, together with Albertina Latin and Cyrillic. Initially only the Latin face was produced. The Greek was issued only in 2004, by DTL. It exists in both upright and cursive form – but for now at least, only in a monotonic version. (See also pp 213, 280.)

αβγδεζηϑικλμνξοπρσςτυφχψω

Antigone H Designed by Jan van Krimpen and issued by Enschedé in 1927. This is a delicately sculpted neohumanist Greek, intended for the setting of lyric poetry. It was cut specifically to match the same designer's Lutetia roman and italic, but it composes well with his other Latin faces, including Romanée and Spectrum. There is no digital version of Antigone.

ἄβγδεζῆϑικλμνξοπϱσςτυφχψῳ

φ

Bodoni H Giambattista Bodoni designed and cut a large number of Greeks in the course of his career. Some are Neoclassical, others Romantic in structure; some are sloped cursives, and some are inscriptional faces consisting of capitals only. The so-called Bodoni Greek known to the typographic trade is not in truth Bodoni's, though it looks as though it should be one of his designs. It is an upright version of a font (the 18 pt Longus Greek) that Bodoni cut in sloped form in 1786.

I do not know which founder cut the first commercial adaptation of Bodoni's Greeks, but it was in use in Germany in the 1850s. Several German founders copied the initial trade version, and it served as the standard Greek type in German books for over a hundred years. The font shown here is a new digital interpretation, made in 1993 for the Greek Font Society, Athens, by Takis Katsoulides. It is Romantic in architecture but has been spared the exaggerated contrast found in many recent romans and italics that are advertised as Bodonis. As issued by GFS, the family includes both sloped and upright forms, a bold, and Greek small caps. (See also page 113.)

ἄβγδεζῆθικλμνξοπρσςτυφχψῳ

Α Β Γ Δ Ε Ζ Η Θ Κ Λ Μ Ξ

φ

Didot H More than one typographer has wondered why Didot Greeks look so little like the Didot romans. The reason is that the original versions were cut in different eras by father and son, and they embody the two punchcutters' different relationships to two distinct typographic traditions. The original Didot Greeks are the work of Ambroise Firmin-Didot, whose father, Firmin Didot, cut the best-known Didot romans and italics. The romans, cut in the thick of the French Revolution, have a strictly rationalist structure. They have left every vestige of Baroque variety behind.

Λ

Didot Greeks have a lefthandedness learned from the Mannerist and Baroque Greeks of Granjon, Jannon, Kis, Caslon and Fleischman. The capitals are openly schizophrenic, with adnate, Neoclassical serifs on the thin strokes and abrupt, Romantic serifs on the thick ones. The digital version shown here was made for the Greek Font Society, Athens, by Takis Katsoulides in 1993. (See also page 113.)

ΑΒΓΔΕΖΗΘΘΙΚΛΜΝΞΟΟΠΡΣϹΤΥΦΧΨΩ

Diogenes D An alphabet of pure archaic capitals, designed by Christopher Stinehour, Berkeley, in 1996. The face was commissioned by the printer Peter Rutledge Koch for use in an edition of the fragments of Parmenides. It is based on inscriptions of the fifth century BC from the old Greek city of Phokaia and its colony Elea, on the coast of Italy, where Parmenides was born. A slightly darker book weight (shown above) was added in 2003.

ἄβγδεζῆθικλμνξοπρσςτυφχψῳ

Gill Sans M This face was designed in the 1950s by Monotype draftsmen, not by Eric Gill himself, as a companion for the Gill Sans roman. Since the roman had also been modified from Gill's original drawings, Gill Sans Greek is twice removed from the artist for whom it is named. It is nevertheless a clean and usable design. The lower case, like its Latin counterpart, includes a few residual serifs. There are several weights, both upright and oblique, but no book weight has been commercially issued.

αβγδεζηϑικλμνξοπϱσςτυφχψω

Heraklit H/M This face was designed by Hermann Zapf and issued both by Stempel and by Linotype in 1954. It is a neohumanist text Greek, intended to be used with the same designer's Palatino and Aldus. There is a companion Greek titling face called Phidias: the Greek counterpart to Zapf's Michelangelo. Palatino Linotype Greek (page 278) is Heraklit's digital successor.

ἄβγδεζῆθικλμνξοπρσςτυφχψῳ

New Hellenic M Designed by Victor Scholderer and issued by Monotype in 1927. This is an orthotic Greek, reasserting the tradition of Nicolas Jenson, Antonio Miscomini and Arnaldo Guillén de Brocar, instead of the cursive and chancery Greek tradition of Francesco Griffo, Simon de Colines and Claude Garamond. It is open, erect, gracious and stable, with minimal modulation of the stroke and minimal serifs. There are well-made variant forms of several letters. A digital version of the face, shown here, was made in 1993 for the Greek Font Society by Takis Katsoulides. (This is sold as *Neo* rather than *New* Hellenic. See also pp 108, 112.)

The digital New Hellenic shown here has been modified as follows: side bearings of several analphabetics have been revised, a kerning table has been added, all the caps and five alternate glyphs (ϐ, ʒ, ϵ, ϲ, ω) have been resized.

ἄβγδεζῆθικλμνξοπϱσςτυφχψῳ

ἄβγδεζῆθικλμνξοπρσςτυφχψῳ

φ

Palatino D As part of the transformation of Palatino into the pan-European 'Palatino Linotype,' Hermann Zapf created an upright and italic Greek in two weights, based on his earlier Heraklit. The full range of monotonic and polytonic characters is included. The digitization, however, was done at Microsoft, not at Linotype. While the letterforms are lovely, kerning is nonexistent, and the diacritics are so pale they vanish at text sizes. When the diacritics are strengthened (as in the first of the two specimen lines above), this Greek mates handsomely not just with Palatino but with many Latin faces. (See also pp 239, 281.)

ἄβγδεζῆθικλμνξοπρσςτυφχψῳ

φ

Porson H Designed by the English classicist Richard Porson for Cambridge University and cut by Richard Austin beginning in 1806. The face was soon copied by several founders, and in 1912 an edited version was issued by Monotype. This has been the standard Greek face for the Oxford Classical Texts for over a century. It is a calm yet energetic face of Neoclassical design that composes well with many romans. During its long and fruitful career, the Porson lower case has been fitted with several different series of caps, none of which quite matches Porson's original design. The digital version of the face shown here and elsewhere in this book is the one produced in 1996 by George Matthiopoulos for the Greek Font Society, Athens – edited by reducing the size of the caps some 10%. (See also pp 109, 113.)

ἄβγδεζῆθικλμνξοπρσςτυφχψῳ

αἱ γὰ γγ εἶ θ πυ σθ τλ τῇ χω καὶ

φ

Wilson D Greek fonts this well-made have always been rare, though Greeks which aimed at this result were once common. At present, this is the only digital Greek of its kind. It was made by Matthew Carter in 1995, based on the Greek fonts of the eighteenth-century master punchcutter, physician and astronomer Alexander Wilson of Glasgow. The face is rich with alternate forms and ligatures, a few of which are shown here.

The Cyrillic alphabet was adapted from Greek in the ninth century, and the first Cyrillic type was cut in Kraków by Ludolf Borchtorp in 1490. An improved Cyrillic was cut in Prague in 1517 by the Belarusian Frantsysk Skaryna, but the first Cyrillic cursive was not cut until 1583. The subsequent history of Cyrillic is largely parallel to that of Latin type, with the important exception that there is no humanist or Renaissance phase, and the intimate linkage between upright and italic which is now taken for granted in Western European typography did not develop in the context of Cyrillic. Only in the eighteenth century were upright and cursive forms paired. Slavic type, like Slavic literature, passed more or less directly from the medieval to the late Baroque. For this and for other, more overtly political reasons, the neohumanist movement in type design also came late to Cyrillic letters.

Prowling the Specimen Books

With minor variations, Cyrillic is now used by close to half a billion people, writing in Russian, Ukrainian, Belarusian, Bulgarian, Macedonian and other Slavic languages. In Serbia and Montenegro it is used for Serbo-Croatian, and in Moldova for Romanian. It is also now the common alphabet for a host of unrelated languages, from Abkhaz to Uzbek, spoken and written across what once was the Soviet Union.

Several excellent type designers have worked in Russia and the neighboring republics in the past century. The list includes Vadim Lazurski from Odessa, Galina Bannikova from Sarapul, Anatoli Shchukin from Moscow, Pavel Kuzanyan and Solomon Telingater from Tbilisi. Few of their designs have been available in the West; many, in fact, have yet to be produced in type at all.

Linotype, Monotype, ParaType and other foundries have issued Cyrillic versions of Baskerville, Bodoni, Caslon, Charter, Frutiger, Futura, Gill Sans, Helvetica, Jannon, Kabel, Officina, Plantin, Syntax, Times, Univers and other Latin faces. Nearly all these have their uses, including setting multilingual texts, where matching Latin and Cyrillic fonts may be required. But not all of these derivative Cyrillics can claim to be distinguished designs, and not all are suited to running text.

Cyrillic text fonts are increasingly constructed with the same variations as the better Latin text types: roman, italic and small caps, with text as well as titling figures, often in several weights. Roman type is known in Russian as прямой шрифт (*pryamoi shrift*, 'upright type'). Italic is called курсив (*kursiv*) or

Text figures are available for all Cyrillic faces shown on the following pages.

курсивный шрифт (*kursivnyi shrift*). Unserifed Cyrillics, like Latin sanserifs, are often made with an oblique (наклонный шрифт = *naklonnyi shrift*, 'sloped type') in place of an italic.

абвгдежофщ АЖО *абвгдежофщ*

Д

Albertina D Like Albertina Greek, this was designed by Chris Brand in the 1960s but not produced until 2004. It mates perfectly with its Greek and Latin companions. (See also pp 213, 275.)

абвгдежофщ АЖО *абвгдежофщ*

Д

Baskerville M Baskerville himself did not design a Cyrillic, but Cyrillic adaptations of his roman and italic have been made by several foundries. The best of these is Monotype's, designed in 1930 by the young Harry Carter, who would soon grow into a great type historian. For some Russian texts of the eighteenth century and later, a face of Western origin and French Enlightenment spirit is highly appropriate. Baskerville Cyrillic is one obvious choice for this purpose – especially for bilingual publications, if Baskerville happens to suit the translation. (See also page 216.)

абвгдежофщ АЖО *абвгдежофщ*

Д

Lazurski H This is a neohumanist Cyrillic designed by the Russian book designer Vadim Lazurski. It was produced in 1962 in two forms, under two names. In Russia it was issued for machine setting as Garnitura Lazurskogo. The foundry version, edited by Giovanni Mardersteig and cut under his direction by Ruggiero Olivieri, is known as Pushkin. In that form, it has only been used at Mardersteig's press, the Officina Bodoni in Verona. Vladimir Yefimov adapted it for photosetting in 1984, adding a bold weight. Both the Cyrillic and its Latin companion were issued in digital form by ParaGraph, Moscow, in 1991. The requisite text figures were added in 1997. (See also page 110.)

абвгдежофщ АЖО *абвгдежофщ*

Д

Minion D A neohumanist Cyrillic designed by Robert Slimbach as a companion to his Minion Latin. It was first issued by Adobe in 1992, and re-issued in pan-European OpenType format in 2000. (See also pp 107, 237.)

абвгдежофщ АЖО *абвгдежофщ*

Palatino D Palatino Cyrillic, like Palatino Greek, was designed by Hermann Zapf in the 1990s as part of the transformation of Palatino into 'Palatino Linotype.' It is particularly useful for multilingual work. (See also pp 239, 278.)

абвгдежофщ АЖО *абвгдежофщ*

Quadraat D Most Cyrillic adaptations of Latin faces have an air of superficiality about them. Fred Smeijers's Quadraat Cyrillic is a wonderful exception to that rule. (See also page 244.)

абвгдежофщ АЖО *абвгдежофщ*

Warnock D Warnock, like Minion, is a pan-European family of type – Latin, Greek and Cyrillic – designed by Robert Slimbach and issued by Adobe in OpenType format in 2000. It is spikier than Minion, and more artificial (plainly *drawn* instead of *written*). It is also steeper (the italic slopes at 15° instead of 12°). The Cyrillic seems to me the most successful branch of the family.

11.9 INSCRIPTIONAL & CALLIGRAPHIC CAPITALS

Every text begins at least once. Most stop and start again repeatedly before they run their course. These beginnings – of sentences, paragraphs, chapters or sections – are the doors and windows of the text. European scribes began to mark the major ones with large, sometimes ornate capital letters – versals – even before the Latin alphabet developed a lower case.

In many early printed books, space is left for such initials to be painted in by hand. Printers also began to print them, in multiple colors, as early as 1459. Many fine alphabets of capitals have sprung from this tradition: fonts of type designed for setting titles or short texts, or to be used one letter at a time. Some of these alphabets – Carol Twombly's Lithos and Gudrun Zapf-von Hesse's Smaragd, for example – are *glyphic* or inscriptional; others are purely calligraphic.

Because they are meant for use with other fonts of text size, many fonts of inscriptional initials are inlines: the interior of the stroke has been carved away to lighten the face. Jan van Krimpen's Lutetia and Romulus Open Capitals, for example, were made by hollowing out the caps of these text faces. But Cristal, designed by Rémy Peignot, and Castellar, designed by John Peters, were created from the start as inline types and exist in no other form.

The capitals from any text font can, of course, be enlarged for use as versals, but the proportions often suffer as a result, and specially proportioned titling capitals exist for only a few text faces (Giovanni Mardersteig's Dante and John Hudson's Manticore are examples). From time to time, however, the capitals from a bicameral text or titling face develop a separate life of their own. This has occurred, for example, with Berthold Wolpe's Albertus, Carl Dair's Cartier, Herb Lubalin's Avant Garde, and with Georg Trump's Codex and Delphin. The faces listed below were all designed specifically as capitals for titling, not text.

Samples of many of these faces are shown on page 287.

A E G Q W

Ariadne H Calligraphic initials designed by Gudrun Zapf-von Hesse and issued by the Stempel Foundry, Frankfurt, in 1954. These initials combine especially well at text size with the same designer's Diotima and at larger sizes with Palatino and Aldus.

ABCDXYZ

Augustea H/M Sharply serifed, formal inscriptional capitals, designed by Aldo Novarese and Alessandro Butti, issued in metal by the Nebiolo Foundry, Torino, in 1951. There is an inline version, originally sold as Augustea Filettata, now digitized as Augustea Open. A lower case was also later added to the capitals. The result is known as Augustea Nova. (See also page 287.)

ABCDEFGHIJKLM
NOPQRSTUVWXYZ

Castellar M Inline capitals, asymmetrically inscribed, so that the hollowed strokes are light on the left, dark on the right. The face was designed by John Peters and issued by Monotype in 1957. (See also pp 64, 160, 287.)

ABCDEFGHIJKLM
NOPQRSTUVWXYZ

Charlemagne D These lighthearted Caroline capitals, based on the Carolingian titling scripts and versals of the ninth and tenth centuries, were designed by Carol Twombly and issued in digital form by Adobe in 1989. The newer OpenType version of the face includes a pan-European Latin character set. (See also pp 120, 287.)

ABCDEFGHIJKLM
AKMNRUVXYZ
NOPQRSTUVWXYZ

Herculanum D Designed by Adrian Frutiger and issued in digital form by Linotype in 1990. There are many variant letters. Herculanum was a Roman city near present-day Naples, buried, like Pompeii, by the eruption of Vesuvius in AD 79. The face that bears its name is based on written and painted Roman letters of the first and second centuries AD. These unofficial and informal Roman inscriptions have been a source of inspiration to Frutiger for half a century. The capitals of his Ondine (page 271), designed in the early 1950s, derive from them as well. (See also page 118.)

ABCDEFGHIJKLM
NOPQRSTUVWXYZ
ΓΔΘΛΞΠΣΥϒΦΨΩ
ĄČĚĘĢİĽŐŞŰŮŹ

Lithos D Unserifed capitals with a large aperture and cheerful form, based on early Greek inscriptional letters, designed by Carol Twombly and issued by Adobe in several weights. There are many subtle modulations in the stroke. The new OpenType version of the face includes pan-European Latin and Greek. An important precursor of this face is Robert Foster's now neglected Pericles, issued by ATF in 1934. (See also page 118.)

ABBAGGIIL&LLQQŒRRTTT
ABCDEFGHIJKLM
NOPQRSTUVWXYZ
YYYLA ÆCIVTT UPH&C

Inscriptional and Calligraphic Capitals

Mantinia D This is a complex face based on letterforms found in the work of the painter Andrea Mantegna (1431–1506). Andrea del Castagno, Fra Angelico and other fifteenth-century artists lavished as much care on their letterforms as on their human figures, but no Renaissance painter took the alphabet more seriously than Mantegna. The type that honors him was designed by Matthew Carter and issued by Carter & Cone in 1992.

ABCD**BCDE**

Michelangelo and *Sistina* H Two sets of serifed capitals designed by Hermann Zapf as complements to Palatino and Aldus. The original versions of both – the light, athletic Michelangelo and the darker, more ecclesiastical Sistina – were cut by August Rosenberger and issued by the Stempel Foundry in 1950–51. There is a third member of the series, Phidias, a Greek counterpart to Michelangelo. (See also page 287.)

ABCDPQR

Monument H Open inline capitals, designed by Oldřich Menhart and cast in 1950 by the Grafotechna Foundry, Prague. The imperial stillness typical of Roman inscriptional letters is transformed to a kind of stately folk dance under Menhart's hand.

ABCDEFGHIJKLMN
OPQRSTUVWXYZ

Neuland H Dark, rugged, unserifed roman capitals, designed and cut by Rudolf Koch and issued in metal by the Klingspor Foundry,

Offenbach, in 1923. Koch cut the original punches freehand, without pattern drawings. Each size in the foundry version therefore has many idiosyncracies of its own. These subtleties are lost in all the existing digital versions. (See also page 287.)

Requiem Titling D The Requiem family, designed by Jonathan Hoefler (1999), includes not only two display weights of roman and italic but also two weights of banner letters, augmented by floriated terminals, spacers and connectors. (See also page 244.)

ABCDEFGHIJKLM

ILYTLYTIYLTITLYIR

NOPQRSTUVWXYZ

Rialto Titling D This set of elegant, light calligraphic capitals is part of the Rialto family, designed by Giovanni De Faccio and Lui Karner, issued in 1999. (See also page 244.)

A B C D E F G H I J K L M
N O P Q R S T U V W X Y Z

Rusticana D This is one of a group of three faces designed by Adrian Frutiger based on the more populist, less imperial varieties of Roman inscriptions. The other members of the family are Herculanum and Pompeijana. Rusticana owes its form to Roman inscriptional lettering of the fourth and fifth centuries AD. (See also page 118.)

A B C D E F G H I J K L M
N O P Q R S T U V W X Y Z

Smaragd D A set of light but powerful inline capitals designed by Gudrun Zapf-von Hesse and issued by the Stempel Foundry in 1952. *Smaragd* means emerald: the substance on which the secrets of Hermes Trismegistos – the Greek incarnation of Thoth, the inventor of writing – were reputedly engraved.

A A B C D E F G H I J K L M M
N O P Q R S T U V W X X Y Z

Sophia D Designed by Matthew Carter and issued by Carter & Cone in 1993. This complex face with its many variant glyphs is based primarily on the alphabet found on an inscribed cross, made in Constantinople in the mid sixth century. The cross was a gift to the Bishop of Rome from the Byzantine Emperor Justin II and his wife (later also his regent) the Empress Sophia. (See also pp 186–87.)

A B C D E F G H I J K L M
N O P Q R S T U V W X Y Z

Trajan D Serifed capitals, based on the inscription at the base of Trajan's Column, Rome, carved at the beginning of the second century AD. The face was drawn by Carol Twombly and issued in digital form by Adobe. In its OpenType version, it includes the full pan-European Latin character set. (See also page 120.)

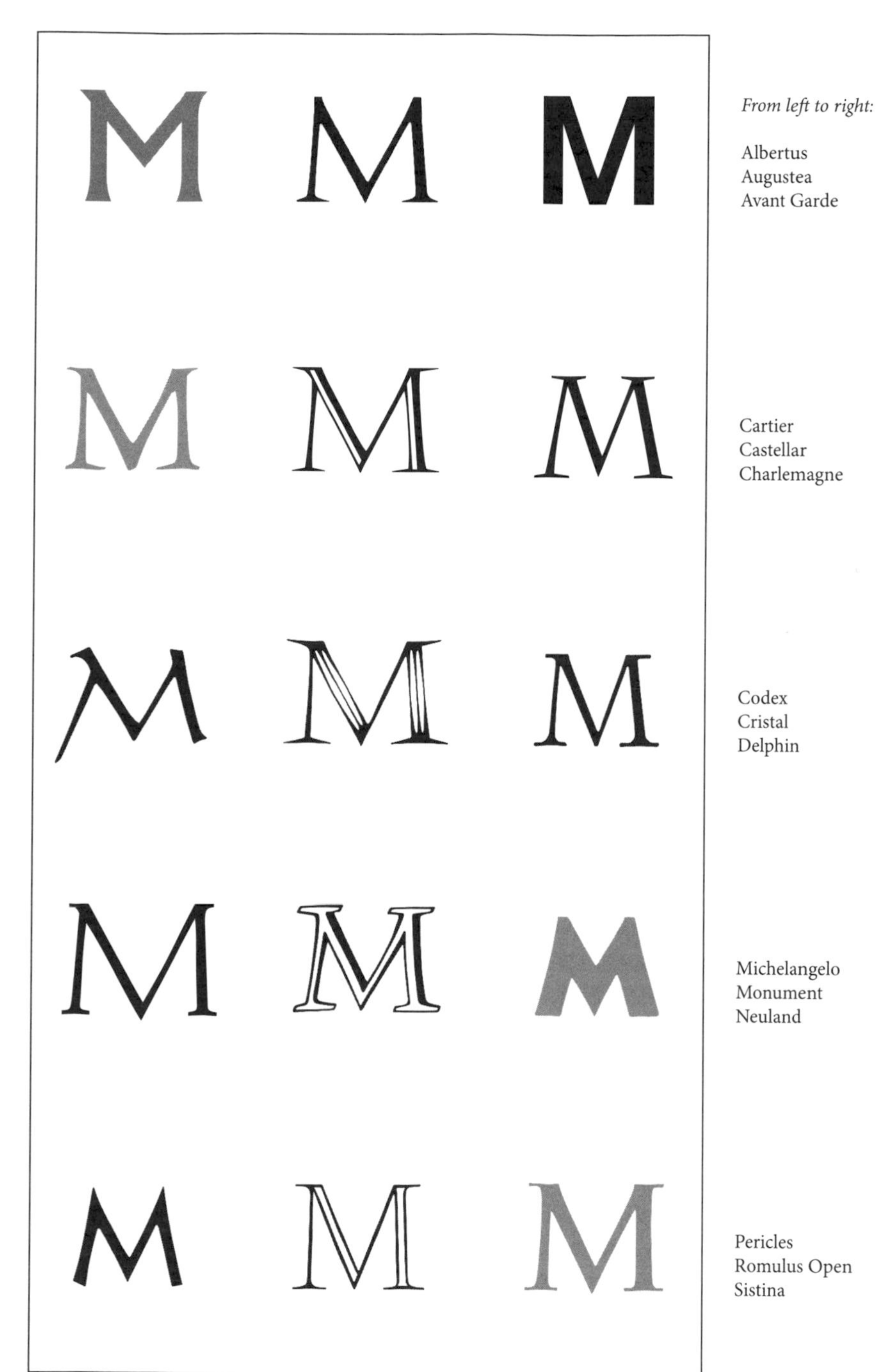

From left to right:

Albertus
Augustea
Avant Garde

Cartier
Castellar
Charlemagne

Codex
Cristal
Delphin

Michelangelo
Monument
Neuland

Pericles
Romulus Open
Sistina

APPENDIX A: THE WORKING ALPHABET

A census taken today will be inaccurate tomorrow, but in its travels through the world, the Latin alphabet has evolved to a working set of over 600 characters (counting caps and lower case), reinforced by about 500 more of its closest allies, Greek and Cyrillic. A few of the characters listed below are tied to a single language. Most are used by dozens or hundreds of languages. Three examples at most are given for each.

All *italicized* terms in this list are discussed in appendix B, page 301.

Additional Latin Letters		Examples of usage
æ Æ	*aesc*	Faroese; Icelandic
ɓ Ɓ	hooktop B	Fulfulde; Hausa; Kpelle
ð Ð	*eth; edh*	Faroese; Icelandic
đ Đ	*dyet*	Serbo-Croatian; Vietnamese
ɗ Ɗ	hooktop D	Fulfulde; Hausa
ɖ Ɖ	hooktail D	Ewe
ə Ǝ/Ə	*schwa*	Azeri; Kanuri; Lushootseed
ɛ Ɛ	African epsilon	Dinka; Ewe; Twi
ƒ Ƒ	hooktail F	Ewe
ɣ Ɣ	African gamma	Ewe; Kpelle
ħ Ħ	*barred H*	Maltese
ı	*dotless i*	Azeri; Turkish
ɨ Ɨ	barred i	Micmac; Mixtec; Sahaptin
ƙ Ƙ	hooktop K	Hausa
ĸ K‘	kra	Old Greenlandic
ł Ł	*barred L*	Heiltsuk; Navajo; Polish
ⱡ Ⱡ	double-barred L	Kutenai
ƛ	blam (barred lambda)	Lillooet; Nuxalk; Okanagan
ŋ Ŋ	*eng*	Ewe; Northern Saami; Wolof
ø Ø	*slashed O*	Danish; Faroese; Norwegian
ơ Ơ	*horned O*	Vietnamese
ɔ Ɔ	open O	Atsina; Ewe; Twi
œ Œ	*ethel*	French; archaic English
ſ	*long s*	Irish; archaic pan-European
ß	*eszett*	German; recent English
þ Þ	*thorn*	Anglo-Saxon; Icelandic
ŧ Ŧ	*barred T; tedh*	Northern Saami; Havasupai
ư Ư	*horned U*	Vietnamese

ʋ	Ʋ	curly v	Ewe
ƿ		*wynn*	early English
ƴ	Ƴ	hooktop y	Fulfulde
ȝ		*yogh*	Anglo-Saxon; early English
ʒ	Ʒ	*ezh*	Skolt

Inflected Latin Letters			Examples of usage
á	Á	a-*acute*	Czech; Icelandic; Spanish
à	À	a-*grave*	Dogrib; French; Italian
ȁ	Ȁ	a-*double grave*	Serbo-Croatian poetics
â	Â	a-*circumflex*	Cree; French; Welsh
ǎ	Ǎ	a-*caron* / a-wedge	romanized Mandarin
ä	Ä	a-*umlaut*	Estonian; Finnish; German
å	Å	a-*ring* / round a	Arikara; Cheyenne; Swedish
ā	Ā	a-*macron* / long a	Cornish; Latvian; Maori
ă	Ă	a-*breve* / short a	Latin; Romanian; Vietnamese
ȃ	Ȃ	a-*arch*	Serbo-Croatian poetics
ã	Ã	a-*tilde*	Portuguese; Vietnamese
ả	Ả	a-*hoi*	Vietnamese
ấ	Ấ	a-*circumflex-acute*	Vietnamese
ầ	Ầ	a-*circumflex-grave*	Vietnamese
ẫ	Ẫ	a-*circumflex-tilde*	Vietnamese
ẩ	Ẩ	a-*circumflex-hoi*	Vietnamese
ậ	Ậ	a-*circumflex-underdot*	Vietnamese
ắ	Ắ	a-*breve-acute*	Vietnamese
ằ	Ằ	a-*breve-grave*	Vietnamese
ẵ	Ẵ	a-*breve-tilde*	Vietnamese
ẳ	Ẳ	a-*breve-hoi*	Vietnamese
ặ	Ặ	a-*breve-underdot*	Vietnamese
ä́	Ä́	a-*umlaut-acute*	Tutchone
ä̀	Ä̀	a-*umlaut-grave*	Tutchone
ǟ	Ǟ	a-*umlaut-macron*	Tutchone
ạ	Ạ	a-*underdot* / a-*nang*	Twi; Vietnamese
a̱	A̱	a-*underscore*	Kwakwala; Tsimshian
á̱	Á̱	a-*acute-underscore*	Kwakwala
ą	Ą	a-*ogonek* / tailed a	Polish; Lithuanian; Navajo
ą́	Ą́	a-*acute-ogonek*	Navajo; Western Apache
ą̀	Ą̀	a-*grave-ogonek*	Dogrib; Gwichin; Sekani
ǽ	Ǽ	*aesc-acute*	Old Icelandic; linguistics
ǣ	Ǣ	*aesc-macron* / long aesc	Anglo-Saxon; Old Norse

ḃ	Ḃ	b-*overdot* / dotted b	Old Gaelic
ć	Ć	c-*acute*	Polish; Serbo-Croatian
ĉ	Ĉ	c-*circumflex*	Esperanto
č	Č	c-*caron* / c-wedge / cha	Czech; Latvian; Lithuanian
ċ	Ċ	c-*overdot* / dotted c	Maltese; Old Gaelic
c̓	C̓	*glottal* c	Kalispel; Kiowa; Nuxalk
č̓	Č̓	*glottal* cha	Comox; Kalispel; Lillooet
ç	Ç	c-*cedilla* / soft c	Albanian; French; Turkish
ḋ	Ḋ	d-*overdot* / dotted d	Old Gaelic
ď	Ď	d-*palatal hook* / d-háček	Czech; Slovak
d̄	D̄	d-*macron*	Old Basque
ḍ	Ḍ	d-*underdot*	Twi; romanized Arabic
d̦	D̦	d-*undercomma*	Livonian
é	É	e-*acute*	Czech; French; Hungarian
è	È	e-*grave*	Catalan; French; Italian
ȅ	Ȅ	e-*double grave*	Serbo-Croatian poetics
ê	Ê	e-*circumflex*	French; Portuguese; Welsh
ě	Ě	e-*caron* / e-wedge	Czech; romanized Mandarin
ė	Ė	e-*overdot* / dotted e	Lithuanian
ë	Ë	e-*diaeresis* / e-trema	Albanian; French
e̊	E̊	e-*ring*	Arikara; Cheyenne
ē	Ē	e-*macron* / long e	Cornish; Maori
ĕ	Ĕ	e-*breve* / short e	Latin
ȇ	Ȇ	e-*arch*	Serbo-Croatian poetics
ẽ	Ẽ	e-*tilde*	Vietnamese
ẻ	Ẻ	e-*hoi*	Vietnamese
ế	Ế	e-*circumflex-acute*	Vietnamese
ề	Ề	e-*circumflex-grave*	Vietnamese
ễ	Ễ	e-*circumflex-tilde*	romanized Mandarin
ê̌	Ê̌	e-*circumflex-caron*	romanized Mandarin
ê̄	Ê̄	e-*circumflex-macron*	Vietnamese
ể	Ể	e-*circumflex-hoi*	Vietnamese
ệ	Ệ	e-*circumflex-underdot*	Vietnamese
ẹ	Ẹ	e-*underdot* / e-*nang*	Twi; Vietnamese
ę	Ę	e-*ogonek* / tailed e	Polish; Lithuanian; Navajo
ę́	Ę́	e-*acute-ogonek*	Navajo; Western Apache
ę̀	Ę̀	e-*grave-ogonek*	Dogrib; Gwichin; Sekani
ə́		*schwa-acute*	Comox; Lushootseed; Sechelt

ɛ̈	Ɛ̈	African epsilon *umlaut*	Dinka
ɛ̃	Ɛ̃	African epsilon *tilde*	Kpelle; Twi
ḟ	Ḟ	f-*overdot* / dotted f	Old Gaelic
ǵ	Ǵ	g-*acute*	romanized Macedonian
ĝ	Ĝ	g-*circumflex*	Aleut; Esperanto
ǧ	Ǧ	g-*caron*	Heiltsuk; Kwakwala; Skolt
ġ	Ġ	g-*overdot* / dotted g	Iñupiaq; Kiksht; Maltese
ğ	Ğ	g-*breve*	Azeri; Tatar; Turkish
g̓	G̓	*glottal* g	American linguistics
g̲	G̲	g-*underscore*	Tlingit
ģ	Ģ	g-(*turned*) *undercomma*	Latvian; Livonian
ĥ	Ĥ	h-*circumflex*	Esperanto
ḣ	Ḣ	h-*overdot*	Old Lakhota
ḥ	Ḥ	h-*underdot*	romanized Arabic & Hebrew
í	Í	i-*acute*	Icelandic; Gaelic; Spanish
ì	Ì	i-*grave*	Dogrib; Italian; Sekani
ȉ	Ȉ	i-*double grave*	Serbo-Croatian poetics
î	Î	i-*circumflex*	French; Romanian; Welsh
ǐ	Ǐ	i-*caron* / i-wedge	romanized Mandarin
	İ	*dotted I*	Azeri; Tatar; Turkish
ï	Ï	i-*diaeresis*	French
i̊	I̊	i-*ring*	Arikara; Cheyenne
ī	Ī	i-*macron* / long i	Cornish; Latvian; Maori
ĭ	Ĭ	i-*breve* / short i	Latin; Vietnamese
ȋ	Ȋ	i-*arch*	Serbo-Croatian poetics
ĩ	Ĩ	i-*tilde*	Guaraní; Kikuyu; Vietnamese
ỉ	Ỉ	i-*hoi*	Vietnamese
ị	Ị	i-*underdot* / i-*nang*	Igbo; Vietnamese
į	Į	i-*ogonek* / tailed i	Chiricahua; Dogrib; Navajo
į́	Į́	i-*acute-ogonek*	Chiricahua; Mescalero; Navajo
į̀	Į̀	i-*grave-ogonek*	Dogrib; Gwichin; Sekani
ĵ	Ĵ	j-*circumflex*	Esperanto
ǰ	J̌	j-*caron* / j-wedge	American linguistics
ḱ	Ḱ	k-*acute*	romanized Macedonian
k̓	K̓	*glottal* k	Comox; Kiowa; Osage
ǩ	Ǩ	k-*caron*	Skolt

Inflected Latin Letters

ķ	Ķ	k-*undercomma*	Latvian; Livonian
k̲	K̲	k-*underscore*	Sahaptin; Tlingit
ĺ	Ĺ	l-*acute*	Slovak
ľ	Ľ/Ľ	l-*palatal hook*	Slovak
l̓	L̓	*glottal* l	Heiltsuk; Nisgha; Tsimshian
ḷ	Ḷ	l-*underdot* / syllabic l	romanized Sanskrit
ļ	Ļ	l-*cedilla* / soft l	Latvian
l̦	L̦	l-*undercomma*	Livonian; Romanian
ḻ	Ḻ	l-*underscore*	romanized Malayalam
ḹ	Ḹ	l-*underdot-macron*	romanized Sanskrit
ł̣	Ł̣	*barred l-underdot*	Iñupiaq
ƛ̓	Ƛ̓	*glottal* blam	Kalispel; Lillooet; Nuxalk
m̓	M̓	*glottal* m	Kwakwala; Nisgha; Tsimshian
ṁ	Ṁ	m-*overdot* / dotted m	Gaelic; romanized Sanskrit
ṃ	Ṃ	m-*underdot*	romanized Sanskrit
ń	Ń	n-*acute*	Chiricahua; Navajo; Polish
ǹ	Ǹ	n-*grave*	romanized Mandarin
n̓	N̓	*glottal* n	Kwakwala; Nisgha; Tsimshian
ṅ	Ṅ	n-*overdot* / dotted n	romanized Sanskrit
n̊	N̊	n-*ring*	Arikara
ň	Ň	n-*caron* / n-wedge	Czech; romanized Mandarin
ñ	Ñ	n-*tilde*	Basque; Catalan; Spanish
ņ	Ņ	n-*cedilla* / soft n	Latvian
n̦	N̦	n-*undercomma*	Latvian
ṇ	Ṇ	n-*underdot*	Twi; romanized Sanskrit
ṉ	Ṉ	n-*underscore*	romanized Malayalam
ó	Ó	o-*acute*	Gaelic; Navajo; Spanish
ő	Ő	o-*double-acute*	Hungarian
ò	Ò	o-*grave*	Catalan; Dogrib; Italian
ȍ	Ȍ	o-*double grave*	Serbo-Croatian poetics
ô	Ô	o-*circumflex*	French; Portuguese; Welsh
ǒ	Ǒ	o-*caron* / o-wedge	romanized Mandarin
ȯ	Ȯ	o-*overdot* / dotted o	Livonian
ö	Ö	o-*umlaut*	Hopi; German; Turkish
o̊	O̊	o-*ring*	Arikara; Cheyenne
ō	Ō	o-*macron* / long o	Cornish; Maori
ŏ	Ŏ	o-*breve* / short o	Latin; romanized Korean

ȏ	Ȏ	o-*arch*	Serbo-Croatian poetics
õ	Õ	o-*tilde*	Estonian; Portuguese
ỏ	Ỏ	o-*hoi*	Vietnamese
ȱ	Ȱ	o-*overdot-macron*	Livonian
ȫ	Ȫ	o-*umlaut-macron*	Livonian
ȭ	Ȭ	o-*tilde-macron*	Livonian
ố	Ố	o-*circumflex-acute*	Vietnamese
ồ	Ồ	o-*circumflex-grave*	Vietnamese
ỗ	Ỗ	o-*circumflex-tilde*	Vietnamese
ổ	Ổ	o-*circumflex-hoi*	Vietnamese
ộ	Ộ	o-*circumflex-underdot*	Vietnamese
ọ	Ọ	o-*underdot* / o-nang	Igbo; Vietnamese; Yoruba
ǫ	Ǫ	o-*ogonek* / tailed o	Navajo; Seneca; Old Icelandic
ǫ́	Ǫ́	o-*acute-ogonek*	Navajo; Slavey; Old Icelandic
ǫ̀	Ǫ̀	o-*grave-ogonek*	Dogrib; Gwichin; Sekani
ǿ	Ǿ	*slashed o-acute*	Old Icelandic; linguistics
ớ	Ớ	*horned o acute*	Vietnamese
ờ	Ờ	*horned o grave*	Vietnamese
ỡ	Ỡ	*horned o tilde*	Vietnamese
ở	Ở	*horned o hoi*	Vietnamese
ợ	Ợ	*horned o underdot*	Vietnamese
ɔ́	Ɔ́	open o *acute*	Dangme
ɔ̈	Ɔ̈	open o *umlaut*	Dinka
ɔ̃	Ɔ̃	open o *tilde*	Kpelle; Twi
ɔ̨	Ɔ̨	open o *ogonek*	Kiowa; American linguistics
p̓	P̓	*glottal* p	Kiowa; Kwakwala; Osage
ṗ	Ṗ	p-*overdot* / dotted p	Old Gaelic
q̓	Q̓	*glottal* q	Kwakwala; Nuxalk; Tsimshian
ŕ	Ŕ	r-*acute*	Sorbian; Old Basque
r̊	R̊	r-*ring*	Arikara
ř	Ř	r-*caron* / r-wedge	Alutiiq; Czech; Sorbian
ṛ	Ṛ	r-*underdot* / syllabic r	romanized Sanskrit
ŗ	Ŗ	r-*cedilla* / soft r	Latvian
r̦	R̦	r-*undercomma*	Livonian; Romanian
ṟ	Ṟ	r-*underscore*	romanized Malayalam
ṝ	Ṝ	r-*underdot-macron*	romanized Sanskrit

ś	Ś	s-*acute* / sharp s	Polish; romanized Sanskrit
s̓	S̓	*glottal* s	American linguistics
š	Š	s-*caron* / s-wedge	Czech; Omaha; Latvian
ṡ	Ṡ	s-*overdot* / dotted s	Old Gaelic
ẛ		dotted *long s*	Old Gaelic
š̓	Š̓	*glottal* s-*caron*	Lakhota; Omaha
ṣ	Ṣ	s-*underdot*	Yoruba; romanized Arabic
s̱	S̱	s-*underscore*	Tlingit
ş	Ş	s-*cedilla*	Turkish
ș	Ș	s-*undercomma*	Romanian

ṫ	Ṫ	t-*overdot* / dotted t	Old Gaelic
ť	Ť	t-*palatal hook* / t-háček	Czech; Slovak
t̓	T̓	*glottal* t	Kiowa; Tsimshian
t̄	T̄	t-*macron*	Lakhota; Old Basque
ṭ	Ṭ	t-*underdot*	romanized Arabic & Hebrew
ț	Ț	t-*undercomma*	Livonian; Romanian

ú	Ú	u-*acute*	Icelandic; Navajo; Spanish
ű	Ű	u-*double-acute*	Hungarian
ù	Ù	u-*grave*	Dogrib; Italian; Sekani
ȕ	Ȕ	u-*double grave*	Serbo-Croatian poetics
û	Û	u-*circumflex*	French; Welsh
ǔ	Ǔ	u-*caron* / u-wedge	romanized Mandarin
ü	Ü	u-*umlaut*	Estonian; German; Turkish
ů	Ů	u-*ring* / u-kroužek	Arikara; Cheyenne; Czech
ū	Ū	u-*macron* / long u	Cornish; Lithuanian; Maori
ŭ	Ŭ	u-*breve* / short u	Latin; romanized Korean
ȗ	Ȗ	u-*arch*	Serbo-Croatian poetics
ũ	Ũ	u-*tilde*	Kikuyu; Vietnamese
ủ	Ủ	u-*hoi*	Vietnamese
ǘ	Ǘ	u-*umlaut-acute*	romanized Mandarin
ǜ	Ǜ	u-*umlaut-grave*	romanized Mandarin
ǖ	Ǖ	u-*umlaut-macron*	romanized Mandarin
ǚ	Ǚ	u-*umlaut-caron*	romanized Mandarin
ụ	Ụ	u-*underdot* / u-nang	Igbo; Vietnamese
ų	Ų	u-*ogonek* / tailed u	Lithuanian; Mescalero; Polish
ų́	Ų́	u-*acute-ogonek*	Mescalero; Navajo
ų̀	Ų̀	u-*grave-ogonek*	Gwichin; Sekani; Tagish

ứ	Ứ	*horned u acute*	Vietnamese
ừ	Ừ	*horned u grave*	Vietnamese

ữ Ữ *horned u tilde* Vietnamese
ử Ử *horned u hoi* Vietnamese
ự Ự *horned u underdot* Vietnamese

ẃ Ẃ w-*acute* Welsh
ẁ Ẁ w-*grave* Welsh
w̓ W̓ *glottal* w Heiltsuk; Klamath; Tsimshian
ŵ Ŵ w-*circumflex* Chichewa; Welsh
ẅ Ẅ w-*diaeresis* Tsimshian
ẘ W̊ w-*ring* Arikara
w̆ W̆ w-*breve* Gã; Twi

x̂ X̂ x-*circumflex* Aleut
x̓ X̓ *glottal* x Chiwere; Tsimshian
x̣̓ X̣̓ *glottal* x *underdot* Tsimshian
x̌ X̌ x-*caron* / x-wedge Heiltsuk; Kwakwala
x̣ X̣ x-*underdot* Nuxalk; Okanagan
x̱ X̱ x-*underscore* Sahaptin; Tlingit
x̧ X̧ x-*cedilla* romanized Caucasian

ý Ý y-*acute* Faroese; Icelandic; Welsh
ỳ Ỳ y-*grave* Welsh
y̓ Y̓ *glottal* y Heiltsuk; Klamath; Tsimshian
ŷ Ŷ y-*circumflex* Welsh
ÿ Ÿ y-*diaeresis* / y-umlaut French; Dutch
ȳ Ȳ y-*macron* Cornish; Livonian
ÿ̓ Ÿ̓ *glottal* y-*umlaut* Tsimshian
ỹ Ỹ y-*tilde* Guaraní; Twi; Vietnamese
ỷ Ỷ y-*hoi* Vietnamese
ỵ Ỵ y-*underdot* / y-nang Vietnamese

ź Ź z-*acute* / sharp z Polish; Sorbian
z̓ Z̓ *glottal* z Lillooet
ž Ž z-*caron* / z-wedge / zhet Czech; Latvian; Lithuanian
ż Ż z-*overdot* / dotted z Maltese; Polish
ẓ Ẓ z-*underdot* romanized Arabic

ǯ Ǯ *ezh-caron* Klamath; Skolt

Basic and Inflected Greek Letters

Basic Greek

α	Α	alpha / 1
β	Β	beta / 2
γ	Γ	gamma / 3
δ	Δ	delta / 4
ε	Ε	epsilon / 5
ζ	Ζ	zeta / 7
η	Η	eta / 8
θ	Θ	theta / 9
ι	Ι	iota / 10
κ	Κ	kappa / 20
λ	Λ	lambda / 30
μ	Μ	mu / 40
ν	Ν	nu / 50
ξ	Ξ	xi / 60
ο	Ο	omicron / 70
π	Π	pi / 80
ρ	Ρ	rho / 100
σ	Σ	sigma / 200
τ	Τ	tau / 300
υ	Υ	upsilon / 400
φ	Φ	phi / 500
χ	Χ	khi / 600
ψ	Ψ	psi / 700
ω	Ω	omega / 800

Alternate Greek

ϐ	alternate beta
ϑ	alternate theta
ϰ	alternate kappa
ϖ	alternate pi
ς	terminal sigma
ϲ	lunate sigma
Ϲ	lunate cap sigma
ϕ	alternate phi
	(etc)

Monotonic Greek

ά		alpha tonos
έ		epsilon tonos
ή		eta tonos
ί		iota tonos
ϊ	Ϊ	iota dialytika
ΐ		iota dialytika tonos
ό		omicron tonos
ύ		upsilon tonos
ϋ	Ϋ	upsilon dialytika
ΰ		upsilon dialytika tonos
ώ		omega tonos

Polytonic Greek

ά		alpha oxeia
ὰ		alpha bareia
ᾶ		alpha perispomene
ἀ	Ἀ	*α* psili
ἄ	Ἄ	*α* psili oxeia
ἂ	Ἂ	*α* psili bareia
ἆ	Ἆ	*α* psili perispomene
ἁ	Ἁ	*α* daseia
ἅ	Ἅ	*α* daseia oxeia
ἃ	Ἃ	*α* daseia bareia
ἇ	Ἇ	*α* daseia perispomene
ᾳ	ᾼ	alpha iota
ᾴ		*ᾳ* oxeia
ᾲ		*ᾳ* bareia
ᾷ		*ᾳ* perispomene
ᾀ	ᾈ	*ᾳ* psili
ᾄ	ᾌ	*ᾳ* psili oxeia
ᾂ	ᾊ	*ᾳ* psili bareia
ᾆ	ᾎ	*ᾳ* psili perispomene
ᾁ	ᾉ	*ᾳ* daseia
ᾅ	ᾍ	*ᾳ* daseia oxeia
ᾃ	ᾋ	*ᾳ* daseia bareia
ᾇ	ᾏ	*ᾳ* daseia perispomene
έ		epsilon oxeia
ὲ		epsilon bareia
ἐ	Ἐ	*ε* psili
ἔ	Ἔ	*ε* psili oxeia
ἒ	Ἒ	*ε* psili bareia
ἑ	Ἑ	*ε* daseia
ἕ	Ἕ	*ε* daseia oxeia
ἓ	Ἓ	*ε* daseia bareia
ή		eta oxeia
ὴ		eta bareia
ῆ		eta perispomene
ἠ	Ἠ	*η* psili
ἤ	Ἤ	*η* psili oxeia
ἢ	Ἢ	*η* psili bareia
ἦ	Ἦ	*η* psili perispomene
ἡ	Ἡ	*η* daseia
ἥ	Ἥ	*η* daseia oxeia
ἣ	Ἣ	*η* daseia bareia
ἧ	Ἧ	*η* daseia perispomene
ῃ	ῌ	eta iota
ῄ		*ῃ* oxeia
ῂ		*ῃ* bareia
ῇ		*ῃ* perispomene
ᾐ	ᾘ	*ῃ* psili
ᾔ	ᾜ	*ῃ* psili oxeia
ᾒ	ᾚ	*ῃ* psili bareia

ᾖ ᾞ *ῃ* psili perispomene
ᾑ ᾙ *ῃ* daseia
ᾕ ᾝ *ῃ* daseia oxeia
ᾓ ᾛ *ῃ* daseia bareia
ᾗ ᾟ *ῃ* daseia perispomene

ί iota oxeia
ὶ iota bareia
ῖ iota perispomene
ἰ Ἰ *ι* psili
ἴ Ἴ *ι* psili oxeia
ἲ Ἲ *ι* psili bareia
ἶ Ἶ *ι* psili perispomene
ἱ Ἱ *ι* daseia
ἵ Ἵ *ι* daseia oxeia
ἳ Ἳ *ι* daseia bareia
ἷ Ἷ *ι* daseia perispomene
ϊ Ϊ iota dialytika
ΐ *ϊ* oxeia
ῒ *ϊ* bareia
ῗ *ϊ* perispomene

ό omicron oxeia
ὸ omicron bareia
ὀ Ὀ *ο* psili
ὄ Ὄ *ο* psili oxeia
ὂ Ὂ *ο* psili bareia
ὁ Ὁ *ο* daseia
ὅ Ὅ *ο* daseia oxeia
ὃ Ὃ *ο* daseia bareia

ῤ rho psili
ῥ rho daseia

ύ upsilon oxeia
ὺ upsilon bareia
ῦ upsilon perispomene
ὐ ᾿Υ *υ* psili
ὔ ῎Υ *υ* psili oxeia
ὒ ῍Υ *υ* psili bareia
ὖ ῏Υ *υ* psili perispomene
ὑ Ὑ *υ* daseia
ὕ Ὕ *υ* daseia oxeia
ὓ Ὓ *υ* daseia bareia
ὗ Ὗ *υ* daseia perispomene
ϋ Ϋ upsilon dialytika
ΰ *ϋ* oxeia
ῢ *ϋ* bareia
ῧ *ϋ* perispomene

ώ omega oxeia
ὼ omega bareia
ῶ omega perispomene
ὠ Ὠ *ω* psili
ὤ Ὤ *ω* psili oxeia
ὢ Ὢ *ω* psili bareia
ὦ Ὦ *ω* psili perispomene
ὡ Ὡ *ω* daseia
ὥ Ὥ *ω* daseia oxeia
ὣ Ὣ *ω* daseia bareia
ὧ Ὧ *ω* daseia perispomene

ῳ ῼ omega iota
ῴ *ῳ* oxeia
ῲ *ῳ* bareia
ῷ *ῳ* perispomene
ᾠ ᾨ *ῳ* psili
ᾤ ᾬ *ῳ* psili oxeia
ᾢ ᾪ *ῳ* psili bareia
ᾦ ᾮ *ῳ* psili perispomene
ᾡ ᾩ *ῳ* daseia
ᾥ ᾭ *ῳ* daseia oxeia
ᾣ ᾫ *ῳ* daseia bareia
ᾧ ᾯ *ῳ* daseia perispomene

Numeric Greek

ϝ digamma / old 6
ϛ stigma / new 6
ϙ qoppa / 90
ϡ sampi / 900
ϟ alternate qoppa
α′ right horn (for numerals 1–999)
͵α left horn (for 1000 and up)

Linguists' Greek

ᾱ Ᾱ long alpha
ᾰ Ᾰ short alpha
ῑ Ῑ long iota
ῐ Ῐ short iota
ῡ Ῡ long upsilon
ῠ Ῠ short upsilon
γ̇ γ-*overdot*
δ̂ δ-*circumflex*
θ̂ θ-*circumflex*
ƛ glam (*glottal* λ)

Basic and Inflected Cyrillic Letters

To people raised on the Latin alphabet, it can come as a surprise that the cursive form of Cyrillic т is *m*, the cursive form of д is *∂* or *g*, and the cursive form of ѣ is *ѣ*. Typical lowercase cursive forms are therefore shown for all Cyrillic letters in this list.

The invariant letter Ӏ, often romanized as *h* or *x̧*, is an independent letter of the alphabet in some Caucasian languages but more often used in digraphs and trigraphs, *e.g.*, Abaza ЧӀ and чӀ, ЧӀв and чӀв.

Russian Cyrillic

а	А	*а*	= a
б	Б	*б/δ*	= b
в	В	*в*	= v
г	Г	*г/ī*	= g
д	Д	*∂/g*	= d
е	Е	*е*	= e/ie
ж	Ж	*ж*	= ž
з	З	*з*	= z
и	И	*и*	= i
й	Й	*й*	= j/ĭ
к	К	*к*	= k
л	Л	*л*	= l
м	М	*м*	= m
н	Н	*н*	= n
о	О	*о*	= o
п	П	*n/ū*	= p
р	Р	*р*	= r
с	С	*с*	= s
т	Т	*m/m̄*	= t
у	У	*у*	= u
ф	Ф	*ф*	= f
х	Х	*х*	= x/kh
ц	Ц	*ц*	= c/ts
ч	Ч	*ч*	= č/ch
ш	Ш	*ш*	= š/sh
щ	Щ	*щ*	= shch
ъ	Ъ	*ъ*	= ‘hard’
ы	Ы	*ы*	= y
ь	Ь	*ь*	= ‘soft’
э	Э	*э*	= è
ю	Ю	*ю*	= yu/iu
я	Я	*я*	= ya/ia

Other Cyrillic

ӑ	Ӑ	*ӑ*	= ă	Chuvash
ӓ	Ӓ	*ӓ*	= ä	Mari, &c
ӕ	Ӕ	*ӕ*	= æ	Ossetian
а̏	А̏	*а̏*	= ȁ	Serbo-Croatian
ґ	Ґ	*ґ*	= g	Ukrainian
ѓ	Ѓ	*ѓ*	= ǵ/gj	Macedonian, &c
ғ	Ғ	*ғ*	= ğ/gh	Bashkir; Kazakh, &c
ҕ	Ҕ	*ҕ*	= ğ/gh	Abkhaz; Yakut, &c
ё	Ё	*ё*	= yo	Bashkir; Tajik, &c
ӗ	Ӗ	*ӗ*	= ĕ	Chuvash
ә	Ә	*ә*	= ə/ä	Bashkir; Tatar, &c
ӛ	Ӛ	*ӛ*	= ë	Khanty
ђ	Ђ	*ђ*	= đ/džy	Serbo-Croatian
ѕ	Ѕ	*ѕ*	= ż/dz	Macedonian
ћ	Ћ	*ћ*	= ć/chy	Serbo-Croatian
е̏	Е̏	*е̏*	= ȅ	Serbo-Croatian
ѐ	Ѐ	*ѐ*	= è	Macedonian
є	Є	*є*	= ye/ě	Ukrainian
ӂ	Ӂ	*ӂ*	= dž	Moldovan
ӝ	Ӝ	*ӝ*	= dž	Udmurt
җ	Җ	*җ*	= ż/ǰ	Kalmyk; Tatar, &c
ӟ	Ӟ	*ӟ*	= dź	Udmurt
ҙ	Ҙ	*ҙ*	= ð/ź	Bashkir
ӡ	Ӡ	*ӡ*	= ǰ/dz	Abkhaz
ѝ	Ѝ	*ѝ*	= ì	Macedonian
ӣ	Ӣ	*ӣ*	= ī	Tajik
ӥ	Ӥ	*ӥ*	= ï	Udmurt
и̏	И̏	*и̏*	= ȉ	Serbo-Croatian
i	İ	*i*	= î	Khakass
і	І	*і*	= i	Belarusian, &c
Ӏ	Ӏ	*Ӏ*	= h/x̧	Abaza; Ingush, &c
ї	Ї	*ї*	= ï/yi	Ukrainian
ј	Ј	*ј*	= j/y	Macedonian, &c
ќ	Ќ	*ќ*	= kj	Macedonian, &c
қ	Қ	*қ*	= k	Kazakh; Tajik, &c
ҟ	Ҟ	*ҟ*	= q’	Abhkaz
ҝ	Ҝ	*ҝ*	= g	Azeri
ӄ	Ӄ	*ӄ*	= q	Chukchi, &c
ҡ	Ҡ	*ҡ*	= q	Bashkir
љ	Љ	*љ*	= lj	Macedonian, &c

њ	Њ	*њ*	= nj	Macedonian, &c
ң	Ң	*ң*	= ņ/ng	Bashkir; Tuvan, &c
ӈ	Ӈ	*ӈ*	= nj/ñ	Khanty; Koryak, &c
ҥ	Ҥ	*ҥ*	= ngh	Altay; Yakut, &c
ӧ	Ӧ	*ӧ*	= ö	Altay; Shor, &c
о̏	О̏	*о̏*	= ȍ	Serbo-Croatian
ҩ	Ҩ	*ҩ*	= ò	Abhkaz
ҧ	Ҧ	*ҧ*	= p’	Abkhaz
р̏	Р̏	*р̏*	= ȑ	Serbo-Croatian
ҫ	Ҫ	*ҫ*	= ş	Bashkir; Chuvash
ҭ	Ҭ	*ҭ*	= ţ/t	Abkhaz
ҵ	Ҵ	*ҵ*	= ts’	Abkhaz
ў	Ў	*ў*	= ŭ/w	Belarusian; Uzbek
ӯ	Ӯ	*ӯ*	= ū	Tajik
ӱ	Ӱ	*ӱ*	= ü	Altay; Khanty, &c
ӳ	Ӳ	*ӳ*	= ű	Chuvash, &c
у̏	У̏	*у̏*	= ȕ	Serbo-Croatian
ү	Ү	*ү*	= ü/ū	Bashkir; Kazakh, &c
ұ	Ұ	*ұ*	= ʉ	Kazakh
ө	Ө	*ө*	= ō/ö	Tuvan; Yukaghir, &c
ӫ	Ӫ	*ӫ*	= ő	Khanty
ҳ	Ҳ	*ҳ*	= h/ħ	Tajik; Uzbek, &c
ҷ	Ҷ	*ҷ*	= č̦	Abkhaz; Tajik
ӌ	Ӌ	*ӌ*	= č/ǰ	Shor
ҹ	Ҹ	*ҹ*	= dž/c	Azeri
ӵ	Ӵ	*ӵ*	= ċ	Udmurt
ӹ	Ӹ	*ӹ*	= ÿ	Mari
ҽ	Ҽ	*ҽ*	= tç	Abkhaz
ҿ	Ҿ	*ҿ*	= tç’	Abkhaz
һ	Һ	*һ*	= h	Bashkir; Buryat, &c
џ	Џ	*џ*	= dž	Macedonian, &c
ԝ	Ԝ	*ԝ*	= w	Yukaghir

Old Cyrillic

ё	Ё	*ё*	yo	ѣ	Ѣ	*ѣ*	yat
є	Є	*є*	yest	ѥ	Ѥ	*ѥ*	ye
ѕ	Ѕ	*ѕ*	zelo	ξ	Ξ	*ξ*	ksi
і	І	*ї*	izhe	ѱ	Ѱ	*ѱ*	psi
ћ	Ћ	*ћ*	derv	ѳ	Ѳ	*ѳ*	fita
ѡ	Ѡ	*ѡ*	ot	ѵ	Ѵ	*ѵ*	izhitsa

International Phonetics

VOWELS

a ɐ ɑ ɒ æ ʌ
e ə ɘ ɛ ɜ ɞ
i ɨ ɪ ɤ
o ɵ ø œ ɶ ɔ
u ʉ ʊ ɯ y ʏ

CONSONANTS

b ɓ ʙ β
c ç ɕ
d ɗ ɖ ð
f ɸ
g ɠ ɢ ʛ ɣ
h ħ ɦ ʜ
j ʝ ɟ ʄ
k
l ɭ ʎ ʟ ɬ ɮ
m ɱ
n ɲ ŋ ɳ ɴ
p
q
r ɾ ɽ ɹ ɻ ɺ
ʀ ʁ
s ʂ ʃ
t ʈ θ
v ʋ
w ʍ ɥ ɰ
x χ ɧ
z ʑ ʐ ʒ
ʔ ʡ ʕ ʢ
ǃ ʘ ǀ ǂ ǁ
[ʩ ʪ ʫ ʬ ʭ]

INFLECTIONS

↑ ↓ ↗ ↘
˥ ˦ ˧ ˨ ˩
˩˥ ˥˩ ˦˥ ˩˨ ˧˦˧
ː ˑ ˈ ˌ .

This is only the skeleton of the IPA, which also admits the use of over fifty diacritics. For the names and functions of the symbols, see the *Handbook of the International Phonetic Association* (1999).

Visual Index of Analphabetic Characters

All the *italicized* terms are individually discussed in appendix B. The remaining terms are treated in three groups: (1) arithmetical signs; (2) currency signs; and (3) musical signs.

Single Stroke

- ˙ *overdot*
- · *midpoint*
- . *period*
- ̣ *underdot*
- • *bullet*
- ’ *apostrophe*
- ‘ *inverted comma; turned comma*
- , *comma*
- ̦ *undercomma*
- ´ *acute*
- ` *grave*
- ′ *prime*
- ' *dumb quote*
- ¯ *macron*
- - *hyphen*
- − *subtraction*
- _ *lowline*
- – en *dash*
- — em *dash*
- ‾ *vinculum*
- | *bar*
- ⁄ *solidus*
- / *virgule*
- \ *backslash*
- ¬ *negation*
- [ ] *square brackets*
- ⟨ ⟩ *angle brackets*
- √ *radical*
- ‹ › *guillemets*
- > greater than
- < less than
- ˇ *caron*
- ˆ *circumflex*
- ̑ *arch*
- ˘ *breve*
- ∧ *dumb caret*
- ˛ *ogonek*
- ¸ *cedilla*
- ̉ *hoi*
- ʔ *glottal stop*
- ˜ *tilde*
- ~ *swung dash*
- ( ) *parentheses*
- { } *braces*
- ˚ *ring*
- ° *degree*

Double Stroke

- ¨ *diaeresis/umlaut*
- : *colon*
- ; *semicolon*
- “ ” *quotation*
- „ “ *quotation*
- ¡ ! *exclamation*
- ¿ ? *question*
- ″ *double prime*
- ˝ *double acute*
- ̏ *double grave*
- " *dumb quote*
- = equal
- ¦ *pipe*
- ‖ *double bar*
- + addition
- × *dimension*
- « » *guillemets*
- ⟦ ⟧ *square brackets*
- ♮ natural
- ♭ flat

Multiple Stroke

- … *ellipsis*
- ÷ division
- ≠ *unequal*
- ± plus-or-minus
- # *octothorp*
- ♯ sharp
- ¤ *louse*

Pictograms

- * *asterisk*
- † *dagger*
- ‡ *double dagger*
- ☞ *fist*
- ❧ *hedera*

Modified Letters

- @ *at*
- © *copyright*
- ¢ cent
- € euro
- & & *ampersand*
- ƒ guilder
- £ sterling
- ℗ *phonomark*
- ¶ *pilcrow*
- ® *registered*
- § *section*
- $ dollar
- ™ *trademark*
- ¥ yen
- Ø *null*
- % *per cent*
- ‰ *per mille*

There is, of course, no limit to the number of typographic characters. Still less is there a limit to the number of variant glyphs by which these characters are realized. This appendix lists characters included on standard ISO (PS-1, TrueType or OpenType) and pan-European (TTO or OpenType) Latin text fonts. It also lists a few additional characters of long-standing typographic importance. Unicode numbers are given in square brackets at the end of each entry. Some characters (especially diacritics) have more than one address in Unicode. As a rule, only one of these addresses is given here. Two addresses are given for characters (such as *aesc*) that occur in both the upper and lower case.

acute An accent used on vowels – á é í ó ú ý ǽ – in Czech, French, Gaelic, Hungarian, Icelandic, Italian, Navajo, Spanish and other languages, and on consonants – ć ń ŕ ś ź – in Basque, Croatian, Polish and romanized Sanskrit. In romanized Chinese it is used with vowels and a nasal – á é í ń ó ú ǘ – to mark the rising tone. It is also used with Cyrillic consonants – ѓ and ќ – in Macedonian, and with all the vowels in Greek. Upper- and lowercase versions of the basic six acute vowels appear on standard ISO Latin text fonts. Pan-European fonts usually include both upper- and lowercase forms of the basic five acute consonants and the old Icelandic vowel *ǽ*. The acute schwa (ə́) and open o (ɔ́) and the Athapaskan high nasal vowels – ą́ ę́ į́ ǫ́ ų́ – are present only on specialized fonts. [U+0301]

á

aesc This ligature is a letter of the alphabet in Danish, Norwegian, Anglo-Saxon and Old Norse, corresponding in part to the Swedish *ä*. It is also sometimes used (unnecessarily) in Latin. In English, words of Greek origin were formerly spelled with æ corresponding to Greek αι (alpha iota). Thus *aesthetics* in older texts is *æsthetics*. Deliberate archaism and pedantically correct quotation still, therefore, require the ligature even in English. *Aesc* (*æsc* in the older spelling) is pronounced *ash*. [U+00C6, +00E6]

æ *æ* Æ

ampersand A scribal abbreviation for *and*, dating back to Roman times. It takes many forms – *&* *&* & & &c – all derived from the Latin word *et*. [U+0026]

&

⟨a⟩

angle brackets These useful characters are missing from most text fonts, but they are readily found on pi fonts and on some fonts of blackletter and Greek. They serve many functions in mathematical and scientific writing. In the editing of classical texts, angle brackets are used to mark editorial *additions* while *braces* mark the editor's *deletions*. See also *square brackets*. [U+2329, +232A]

’a

apostrophe Also called *raised comma* or *single close-quote*. A mark of elision in English, French, Italian and many other languages. It grew from that use in English to become also a sign of the possessive. (*It's* = *it is*, but *John's* = *Johnes* = belonging to John.) A superimposed apostrophe (not to be confused with the *acute*) is the standard symbol in linguistics for a glottalized consonant: m̓ p̓ q̓ w̓, etc. As a matter of convenience, these symbols are often converted to consonants *followed* by normal apostrophes: m’ p’ q’, etc. Apostrophized consonants of this sort are frequent in typography. The apostrophized *d* and *t* (ď and ť, whose capital forms are Ď and Ť) are letters of the alphabet in Czech; so are ľ and Ľ in Slovak, while ch’, k’, k̲’, l’, s’, t’, tl’, ts’, x’, x̲’ and their corresponding capitals (written with apostrophes, not carons) are letters of the alphabet in Tlingit. Used alone, the apostrophe often serves as a sign for the glottal stop. In Unicode, these functions are carefully distinguished. See also *dumb quotes, glottal stop, palatal hook* and *quotation marks*. [U+02BC, +0313, +0315, +2019]

ȃ

arch A diacritic used with vowels and one syllabic consonant – ȃ ȇ ȋ ȏ ȗ ȓ (and the corresponding Cyrillic letters, а̑ е̑ и̑ о̑ у̑ р̑) – to mark the long falling tone in Serbo-Croatian. Though not employed in ordinary writing, these forms are used in teaching, in linguistics, and in some editions of metrical poetry. Few text fonts include either the arch or the composite glyphs in which it is used. Not to be confused with the circumflex, which is pointed. Also known as a *dome* or *inverted breve*. It has also been called a *cap*, which leads to confusion. [U+0311]

± =
< + >
× ÷

arithmetical signs Only eight basic signs, + − ± × ÷ < = >, are included in most text fonts. When other mathematical symbols, such as ≠ ≈ ∇ ≡ √ ⩽ ⩾, are required, it is generally best to take all signs, including the basic ones, from the same technical font so that all forms match in color and size. [U+002B, +2212, +00B1, +00D7, 00F7, 003C, 003D, 003E, &c.]

asterisk This is usually a superscript, used primarily for marking referents and keywords. In European typography, it is widely used to mark a person's year of birth (as the dagger, substituting for a cross, is used to mark the year of death). In philology, it marks hypothetically reconstructed or fetal forms. The asterisk takes many forms (* * ✲ ★ * ⋆, for example). It appears in the earliest Sumerian pictographic writing and has been in continuous use as a graphic symbol for at least 5,000 years. [U+002A]

at A commercial symbol meaning *at* or *at the rate of.* Electronic mail has given it new life, and it is now therefore occasionally well designed. Still, it has no role in normal text. [U+0340]

backslash This is an unsolicited gift of the computer keyboard. Basic though it may be to elementary computer operations, it has no accepted function in typography. [U+005C]

\

bar The vertical bar is used in mathematics as a sign of absolute value, in prosodical studies to mark a caesura, and in propositional calculus (where it is called *Sheffer's stroke*) as a sign of noncon-junction. In bibliographical work, both single and double bars are used. Also called *caesura.* [U+007C]

|

barred H A letter of the Maltese alphabet (and of the IPA), corresponding to Arabic ح (*ḥ*). Its Maltese name is *h maqtugha,* "cut h." It is found on pan-European fonts. [U+0126, +0127]

ħ Ħ

barred L This is a basic letter of the alphabet in Chipewyan, Navajo, Polish, and many other languages. Henryk Mikołaj Górecki's Symphony N° 3, for example, is entitled *Symfonia Pieśni Żałosnych,* "Symphony of Sorrowful Songs." Also known by its Polish name, *ew.* The barred L is present on most Latin text fonts but often inaccessible to narrow-minded software. [U+0141, +0142]

ł Ł

barred T In Northern Saami, barred T represents a sound like *th* in English *thing* [IPA θ]). In Havasupai, it represents a dental *t.* It is normally included on pan-European Latin text fonts. Also known as *tedh,* by analogy with *edh* (ð). [U+0166, +0167]

ŧ Ŧ

braces Braces are rarely required in text work, but they can function perfectly well as an extra and outer (or inner) set of parentheses: { ([–]) }. In mathematics they are used to mark

{a}

phrases and sets. In editing classical papyri, braces are often used to mark editorial deletions. [U+007B, +007D]

brackets See *angle brackets* and *square brackets.*

ă

breve An accent used on vowels and consonants – ă ĕ ĭ ğ ŏ ŭ – in Malay, Romanian, Turkish, Vietnamese, and in some forms of romanized Korean. In English, it is used in informal phonetic transcriptions to mark lax (or so-called 'short') vowels. In writings on metrics and prosody, it is the sign of a quantitatively short vowel or syllable. It is also used on the Russian *i* (й, whose cursive form is *ŭ*) and on a second vowel, ў, in Belarusian and Uzbek. The breve is always rounded, and should not be confused with the angular caron. (*Breve* is two syllables, with the stress on the first, as in *brave, eh?*) Also called *short.* [U+0306]

•b

bullet A large version of the midpoint, used chiefly as a typographic flag. Bullets are commonly hung, like numbers, in the margin to mark items in a list, or centered on the measure to separate larger blocks of text. See also *midpoint.* [U+2022]

ǎ

caron An inverted circumflex. It is used on consonants and vowels – č ě ň ř š ž – in Croatian, Czech, Lithuanian, Northern Saami, Slovak, Slovene, Sorbian and other scripts. In romanized Thai, the caron indicates a rising tone. In romanized Chinese, it marks the retroflexive third tone (falling/rising tone) of standard Mandarin: ǎ ě ê̌ ǐ ň ǒ ǔ ǚ. It is also used in new scripts for sevferal Native American languages. For no good reason, most ISO fonts include a prefabricated upper- and lowercase š and ž, while other combinations must be built with the floating accent. Pan-European fonts contain a larger but still incomplete set of caroned letters, usually č ě ň ř š ž and Č Ď Ě Ň Ř Š Ť Ž. Also called a *wedge* or a *háček* (*hah-check*), which is its Czech name. In Czech, however, this character is actually a variant of the *palatal hook,* which can take the form of caron or apostrophe. [U+030C]

ç

cedilla A diacritic used with consonants, such as the ç in Catalan, French, Nahuatl and Portuguese, and ç and ş in Turkish. In Latvian and Romanian, the *undercomma* is preferred. Not to be confused with the *ogonek* or nasal hook, which curves the other way and is used with vowels. The name means *little z.* Turkish ş and Ş are missing from standard ISO text fonts. [U+0327]

circumflex A diacritic used on vowels – â ê î ô û ŵ ŷ – in Cree, French, Portuguese, Romanian, Vietnamese, Welsh and many other languages. In transliterated texts (e.g., from Arabic, Greek, Hebrew and Sanskrit), it is sometimes used as a substitute for the macron, to mark long vowels. In romanized Thai, a circumflex signifies a falling tone. Most Latin text fonts include all the circumflected vowels except Welsh ŵ and ŷ. [U+0302]

colon A grammatical marker inherited from the medieval European scribes. It is also used in mathematics to indicate ratios and in linguistics as a mark of prolongation. The name is from Greek. In classical rhetoric and prosody, a *colon* (plural, *cola*) is a long clause, and a *comma* is a short one. [U+003A]

comma A grammatical marker, descended from early scribal practice. In German, and often in East European languages, the comma is used as an open quote. Throughout Europe, it is also used as a decimal point, where most North Americans expect a period. In North American usage, the comma separates thousands, while a space is preferred in Europe. Thus 10,000,000 = 10 000 000, but a number such as 10,001 is typographically ambiguous. It could mean either ten and one one-thousandth or ten thousand and one. See also *quotation marks.* [U+002C]

copyright On poorly designed fonts, the copyright symbol sometimes appears as a superscript, but its rightful place in typography is on the baseline: ©. [U+00A9]

curl See *hoi.*

currency symbols Most ISO character sets of recent vintage include six genuine currency signs – $ £ € ƒ ¥ ¢ – and one imaginary sign, ¤. That so-called 'general currency sign,' the *louse,* has no typographic function. It merely holds a place on the font to which a real symbol for local currency (rupee, cruzeiro, peseta, etc) can be assigned. The cent sign (¢), now an American typographical heirloom, is equally irrelevant for most work. It remains in the character set chiefly out of nostalgia.

The dollar sign, a slashed S, is descended from an old symbol for the shilling. The same sign has come to be used for currencies with many other names: sol, peso, escudo, yuan, etc. The sign of the pound sterling, a crossed cursive L, actually stands for the Latin *libra* (also the source of the abbreviation *lb*, used for the pound avoirdupois). This £ sign is now used not only for British currency but for the pound, lira or livre of many African and Middle Eastern states. The sign for Dutch guilders is ƒ, for *florin*, which is the old name for the currency. This ƒ is often cut shorter and wider than the normal italic lowercase *f*. The sign for the shekel (Hebrew *sheqel*), the Israeli currency unit, is ₪. See also *louse*. [U+0024, +00A2, +00A3, +00A5, +0192, +20AC, &c.]

dagger A reference mark, used chiefly with footnotes. In European typography, it is also a sign of mortality, used to mark the year of death or the names of deceased persons, and in lexicography to mark obsolete forms. In editing classical texts, daggers are used to flag passages judged to be corrupt. Also called *obelisk, obelus* or *long cross*. [U+2020]

dashes Latin text fonts include, at minimum, an em dash, en dash and hyphen. A figure dash and three-quarter em dash are sometimes included as well, and a three-to-em dash more rarely. [U+2013, +2014, &c.]

degree Used in mathematics and in normal text to give temperatures, inclinations, latitudes, longitudes and compass bearings. Not to be confused with the *superior o* or *ordinal o* used in abbreviations such as Nº, nor with the *ring*, a diacritic. [U+00B0]

diaeresis / umlaut A diacritic used with vowels – ä ë ï ö ü ẅ ÿ – in many languages, including Albanian, Dinka, Estonian, Finnish, German, Swedish, Turkish, Welsh, and less frequently also in English, Greek, Spanish, Portuguese and French. Linguists distinguish between the *umlaut*, which marks a *change* in pronunciation of a single vowel (as in the German *schön*) and the *diaeresis*, which marks the *separation* of adjacent vowels (as in naïve and Noël). The typographic symbol is the same, but in reference to English and the Romance languages, the correct term is usually diaeresis, while umlaut is correct in reference to most other languages in which the symbol is used. Except for the Welsh ẅ and African ɛ̈ and ɔ̈, the umlauted or diaeretic vowels are present on most Latin text fonts. Also called *tréma*, its French name.

In Hungarian there are two forms of umlaut: the double dot, which is used for short vowels, and the *double acute* or *long umlaut*, used for long vowels (ű is the long form of ü).

The letter *ÿ* is a vowel sometimes used in archaic French and still required in the modern form of a few personal names and place names. It is also an alternate form of the *ij* ligature in Flemish. [U+0308]

diesis An alternate name for the *double dagger*.

dimension sign An unserifed x, usually square, also known as a multiplication sign. See *arithmetical signs*. [U+00D7]

×

dotless i and **dotted I** These are both letters of the alphabet in Turkish, where the lowercase form of I is ı and the uppercase form of i is İ. The dotless form signifies a back vowel (IPA ɯ), the dotted one a front vowel (IPA i, as in English *liter*. [U+0130, +0131]

ıIİi

dome See *arch*.

double acute A diacritic used on two Hungarian vowels: ő and ű. Also called *long umlaut*. The name 'Hungarian umlaut' (used in PostScript jargon) is unhelpful, since the short umlauted vowels ö and ü also appear in Hungarian. Not to be confused with the double prime nor with the close quote. [U+030B]

ő

double bar This is a standard symbol in bibliographical work and an old standard reference mark in European typography. It is missing from most text fonts but is easily made by kerning two single bars together. [U+2016]

‖

double dagger A reference mark for footnoting. Also called *diesis* or *double obelisk*. [U+2021]

‡

double grave A Serbo-Croatian diacritic used, like the arch, with five vowels and one syllabic consonant: ȁ ȅ ȉ ȍ ȕ ȑ (and in Cyrillic, а̏ е̏ и̏ о̏ у̏ р̏). This is a prosodic sign, to indicate the short falling tone. Though not employed in ordinary writing, the double grave is used in teaching, in linguistics, and in editions of metrical poetry. It is rarely found on text fonts. [U+030F]

ȍ

double prime An abbreviation for inches (1″ = 2.54 cm) and for seconds of arc (360″ = 1°). Not to be confused with quotation marks, the double acute, nor with dumb quotes. Prime and double prime are rarely found on text fonts. See also *prime*. [U+2033]

60″

a ^ b

dumb caret Also known, in vain, as the *ascii circumflex.* This is a stray, like the backslash and dumb quotes, ossified into the standard ASCII keyboard. The true circumflex (ˆ) is a different and genuine character. So is the *logical and* (∧, the sign of logical conjunction). Since it has no typographic function, the dumb caret also has no typographic form. In other words, this is not really a character at all. It is a wasted slot on the keyboard, waiting for something else to take up residence. [U+005E]

"a'i'a"

dumb quotes These are refugees from the typewriter keyboard. Typesetting software interprets quotation-mark keystrokes in context, converting the dumb quotes to smart quotes (never infallibly). Yet the dumb quotes are still there, taking space on the font. They have no typographic function. See also *double prime, quotation marks* and *prime.* [U+0022, +0027]

đ Đ

dyet A basic letter of the alphabet in Serbo-Croatian (where it has the sound of IPA d͡ʒ) and Vietnamese (where it is now IPA d and used to be ɗ). The uppercase form of the letter is, as a rule, graphically the same as the uppercase *eth,* but it is notionally different. It therefore has a different Unicode address. [U+0110, +0111]

…

ellipsis The sign of elision and of rhetorical pause: three dots. [U+2026]

ŋ Ŋ

eng A letter of the alphabet in Northern Saami and in many African languages. Lowercase eng is also used in linguistics and lexicography to represent the *ng* sound in the word *wing.* (Note the different sounds represented by the same letters in the words *wing, Wingate, singlet* and *singe*: ŋ, n-g, ŋg, ndʒ.) The eng is found on pan-European and pan-African fonts. [U+014A, +014B]

ß *ß*

eszett The *ss* ligature, *long s + short s* (ſ + s). It was once essential for setting English and is still essential for German. Not to be confused with the Greek beta, β. Also known as *sharp s.* Note that *not all instances* of *ss* in German turn to ß. [U+00DF]

ð Đ

eth A letter of the alphabet in Anglo-Saxon, Faroese, Icelandic, and in IPA. The uppercase eth is the same as the uppercase *dyet,* but the lowercase forms are not interchangeable, and the letters represent quite different sounds. (The name *eth,* also spelled *edh,* is pronounced like the *eth* in *whether.*) [U+00D0, +00F0]

ethel A ligature formerly used in English and still essential for setting French. English words and names derived from Greek were formerly spelled with the ethel (or *œthel*) corresponding to the Greek οι (omicron iota). Thus the old form of *ecumenical* is *œcumenical* (from οἶκος, Greek for 'house') and the Greek name Οἰδίπους (Oidípous), Latinized as Oedipus, was formerly written Œdipus. The ligature is required, therefore, for deliberate archaism and for academically correct quotation from older English sources, as well as for spelling French terms such as *hors d'œuvre*. In IPA, œ, ɶ and ɵ are three different letters. [U+0152, +0153]

œ Œ

ew See *barred* L.

exclamation In Spanish, the inverted exclamation mark is used at the beginning of the phrase and the upright mark at the end. In mathematics, the upright exclamation mark is the symbol for factorials ($4! = 4 \times 3 \times 2 \times 1$). It is also often used to represent the palatal clicks of the Khoisan languages of Africa. Thus, for example, the name !Kung. British printers often call the exclamation mark a *screamer*. [U+0021, +00A1]

¡a!

ezh This is an altered form of z, generally representing a sound like that of *z* in English *azure* or *j* in French *justice*, which is the sound of Czech ž or Polish ż. Ezh is a letter of the alphabet in Skolt, a language of the Saami family, spoken in northern Russia and Finland. The lowercase form is also part of the IPA and therefore present on any font of phonetic characters. Not to be confused with *yogh*. [U+01B7, +0292]

Ʒ

figures A text font normally includes at least one set of figures, which usually ought to be (and usually are not) text figures (OSF). Supporting fonts and OpenType fonts often include three further sets: titling (i.e., lining) figures, superiors and inferiors. The superiors are used for exponents, superscripts and the numerators of fractions, the inferiors for the denominators of fractions. For chemical formulae (H_2O etc) and mathematical subscripts, lowered inferior figures are needed. [U+0030—0039; +00B2, +00B3, +00B9, +2070, +2074—2079; +2080—2089]

1 2 3

4 5

fist The typographer's fist is neither a blunt instrument nor a closed purse. It is a silent, pointing hand. All too often, however, it is overdressed, with ruffles at the cuff. A Baroque invention, the

fist is missing from the standard ISO character set and must be found on a supplementary font. [U+261A—261F]

fractions Three fractions – ¼ ½ ¾ – appear on most ISO text fonts, and six more – ⅛ ⅓ ⅜ ⅝ ⅔ ⅞ – on some pan-European fonts. [U+00BC—00BE; +2153—215E]

glottal stop The glottal stop is a sound in search of a character: a basic sound in many languages now written in Latin letters, but one for which the Latin, Greek and Cyrillic alphabets have no traditional symbol. Linguists use the character ʔ or ˀ – a gelded question mark – to represent this sound, but the symbol most commonly used in setting texts is the apostrophe. In romanized Arabic the inverted comma or open quote (ʻ) is often used to represent the letter *ʻain* (ع), whose phonetic symbol is ʕ or ˤ, and the apostrophe (ʼ) is used to represent *hamza* (ء, أ, إ, etc), the Arabic glottal stop. Thus, the Koran in romanized Arabic is *al-Qurʼān*; Arab is *ʻarab*; the family is *al-ʻāʼila*. Also known by its Spanish name, *saltillo*, "little leap." See also *apostrophe, inverted comma* and *quotation marks*. [U+0294, +02BC, +02C0]

grave An accent used with vowels – à è ì ò ù ỳ – in French, Italian, Portuguese, Catalan, Vietnamese and many other languages. In romanized Chinese it is used with vowels – à è ì ò ù ǜ – to mark the falling tone. In Gaelic the grave is normally used instead of the macron to mark elongated vowels. The basic five grave vowels are present on most Latin text fonts. [U+0300]

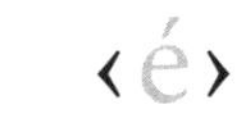

guillemets Single and double guillemets are widely used as quotation marks with the Latin, Cyrillic and Greek alphabets in Europe, Asia and Africa. Attempts to introduce them into North America have met with only slight success. In French and Italian, the guillemets almost always point out, «thus» and ‹thus›, but in German they more frequently point in, »so« and ›so‹. Single guillemets should not be confused with angle brackets nor with the arithmetical operators meaning greater-than and less-than.

Guillemet means Little Willy, in honor of the sixteenth-century French typecutter Guillaume [William] Le Bé, who may have invented them. Also called *chevrons, duck feet* and *angle quotes*. [U+00AB, +00BB, +2039, +203A]

háček See *caron* and *palatal hook*.

hedera An ivy leaf: a type of fleuron. (*Hedera* is the Latin name for ivy.) This is one of the oldest of all typographic ornaments, present in early Greek inscriptions. [U+2619, +2766, +2767]

hoi This is one of the five tonemarks used with vowels in the Vietnamese alphabet. It resembles a small dotless question mark and signifies the dipping-rising tone. The spelling in Vietnamese is, naturally, *hỏi* – and the name in Vietnamese does mean "question." In English it is also called a *curl.* [U+0309]

horned o A letter of the Vietnamese alphabet, representing a close mid-back unrounded vowel (IPA ɤ). [U+01A0, +01A1]

horned u Another basic Vietnamese letter, representing a close back unrounded vowel (IPA ɯ). [U+01AF, +01B0]

hyphen The shortest of the dashes. [U+002D]

inverted breve See *arch.*

inverted comma Also called a single open-quote, and used for that purpose in English, Spanish and many other languages. In Hawaiian, it represents the glottal stop (Hawai'i, Moloka'i). In transliterated Arabic and Hebrew, however, it represents the letter *'ain* (ع) or *ayin* (ע), a pharyngeal continuant (IPA ʕ), while its opposite, the apostrophe, represents the glottal stop. Thus: Sunni and Shī'a; King Ibn Sa'ūd. Only the well-curved form of the glyph (' instead of ') is useful in transliteration. See also *glottal stop, quotation marks, reversed apostrophe.* [U+2018]

kropka See *overdot.*

kroužek See *ring.*

letters At least three varieties of letters appear in an ordinary font of Latin type. There is normally a full basic alphabet of upper and lower case and a partial alphabet of superior letters. The superiors are used to abbreviate ordinal numbers: English 1st, 2nd, 3rd; French 1re, 2e (*première, deuxième*); Spanish 2a, 2o (*segunda, segundo*), etc. They are also used in a few verbal abbreviations, such as 4o = quarto; 8o = octavo; Mr = mister; No = number, but in English most such forms are now archaic. The basic ISO alphabet includes only two superior letters, the *ordinal a* and *ordinal o*, which are essential for setting text in Romance languages. (They are called ordinals because they are used for ordinal numbers: first, second, third....) A fuller set – conventionally limited to ᵃ ᵇ ᵈ ᵉ ⁱ ˡ ᵐ ⁿ ᵒ ʳ ˢ ᵗ – is often to be found on an 'expert' or OpenType font.

a B

x^{ab} A

Qu T

s ſ *ſ*

OpenType fonts routinely include small caps in addition to u&lc and superior letters. Full pan-European fonts also include a complete set of Cyrillic and Greek characters. Some fonts include swashes and quaints such as the *long s* (ſ) and its ligatures.

Note that the identity of the letters varies from language to language. The digraph *ch*, for example, is regarded as a single letter in Czech, Lithuanian and Spanish; *ll* is treated as a single letter in Spanish and Basque; *dd, ff, ng, ll, ph, rh, th* are all treated as single letters in Welsh; and in Serbo-Croatian the digraphs *dz, lj, nj* are regarded as single letters (corresponding to Cyrillic џ, љ and њ). [U+0041—005A; +0061—007A; +00C0—00D6; +00D8—00F6; +00F8—00FF, &c.]

fi *ffi* ß

ct *sp*

ligatures Basic ISO fonts are limited to two typographic ligatures, *fi* and *fl*. Rigid definitions of the glyph set, leaving no provision for additional ligatures (such as *ff, ffi, ffl, fj*) are a hazard to typography. Ligatures required by the design of the individual typeface should always reside on the basic font.

The *lexical* ligatures *æ, Æ, œ, Œ* and *ß* are bonafide Unicode characters, separately listed in this appendix. *Typographic* ligatures such as *fi* and *ſt* are glyphs, not characters; they are now consigned to the 'private use' section of Unicode.

logical not See *negation*.

ſ *ſ*

long s This taller form of *s* looks like *f* without its crossbar. (Note however that the roman form usually *does* have a spur on the left.) Long s was commonly used in English (uſed in Engliſh, *uſed in Engliſh*, USED IN ENGLISH) through the end of the eighteenth century. It was then the normal form of *s* in initial and medial positions. Short *s* was used at the ends of words and (usually) as the second *s* in a pair. Long s + short s forms the ligature ß, still used in German. Long s itself is still routinely used in blackletter though archaic in roman and italic. It often entails a substantial further set of ligatures – e.g., ſb ſh ſi ſk ſl ſſ ſſi ſſl. [U+017F]

long umlaut See *double acute*.

louse From *Filzlaus,* "pubic louse," a German name for the currency symbol placeholder (¤). Also known in English as a *sputnik.* Since the symbol is parasitic (it takes up space on the font but offers nothing in return), *louse* may be the better name. Having no true function, it has no authentic form. [U+00A4]

¤

lowline This is a standard ISO character, positioned as a baseline rule. Not to be confused with the *underscore.* [U+005F]

a_a

macron A diacritic used to mark long vowels – ā ē ī ō ū – in many languages: Fijian, Hausa, Latvian and Lithuanian, among others. It marks long vowels in romanized Arabic, Greek, Hebrew, Japanese, Sanskrit and other languages, and level tones in romanized Chinese. Some writers of Lakhota (Sioux) also use it to write de-aspirated consonants (c̄ k̄ p̄ t̄). [U+0304]

ā

midpoint An ancient European mark of punctuation, widely used in typography to flag items in a vertical list and to separate items in a horizontal line. A closely spaced midpoint is also often used to separate syllables or letters, especially in Catalan when one *l* adjoins another. (In Catalan as in Spanish, *ll* is treated as a single letter. When one *l* is adjacent to but separate from another, they are written *l·l.* Examples: the Catalan words *cel·les* [cells], *col·lecció* [collection] and *paral·lel.*) The same sign is used in mathematics for scalar multiplication and in symbolic logic for logical conjunction. Also called *interpoint.* [U+00B7]

(Upper- and lowercase *L* + *midpoint* [L· & l·] are needlessly treated by ISO, and therefore by Unicode, as single characters: U+013F & +0140.)

l·l

mu The Greek lowercase *m* represents the prefix *micro-* = 10^{-6}. Thus milligrams is written *mg* and micrograms *μg.* (A millionth of a meter or *micron,* formerly written *μ,* is now ordinarily written *μm.*) [U+03BC]

μ

musical signs Three elementary musical symbols – ♭ ♯ ♮, the flat, sharp and natural – are needed for setting normal texts that make reference to standard European musical pitches and keys (Beethoven's Sonata Op. 110 in A♭, Ennemond Gaultier's Suite for Lute in F♯m, the drop from C♯ to C♮, etc). These characters are, however, missing from most text fonts. (The octothorp is not an adequate substitute for the sharp.) [U+266D—266F]

♭ ♯ ♮

nang See *underdot.*

nasal hook See *ogonek.*

¬b

negation The negation sign used in the propositional calculus (symbolic logic) was formerly the swung dash (~). Since the swung dash is also used as a sign of similarity, this created confusion. The usual form of the negation sign now is the angled dash (¬). This is part of the standard ISO Latin character set and is included on most digital text fonts, even though it is useless without the other logical operators, such as ∪ ∩ ∧ ∨ ≡, which are almost never found on text fonts. Also called *logical not.* [U+00AC]

Ø

null Also known as a slashed or crossed zero. This glyph is used to distinguish zero from the letters *O* and *o*. But the null in its usual form is easily confused with *slashed o* (ø, *ø*), a letter of the alphabet in Danish and Norwegian, and even with the Greek letter phi (φ, ϕ). The crossed form of the null, ɵ, is also confusible with theta (θ). A null glyph is present on some text fonts and on many phonetic and technical fonts. (As an alternate form of zero, this glyph has no address of its own in Unicode.)

numeral sign See *octothorp.*

obelisk Also *obelus* (plural, *obeli*). Synonym for *dagger.*

#36

octothorp Otherwise known as the numeral sign. It has also been used as a symbol for the pound avoirdupois, but this usage is now archaic. In cartography, it is a traditional symbol for *village*: eight fields around a central square. That is the source of its name. *Octothorp* means eight fields. [U+0023]

ą

ogonek A diacritic used with vowels – ą ę į ǫ ų – in Lithuanian, Navajo, Polish and other languages. Also called a *nasal hook.* Not to be confused with the cedilla, which is used with consonants and curves the other way. *Ogonek* is a Polish diminutive, meaning 'little tail.' It is also the Polish name for the stem of an apple. Vowels with ogonek are known as *tailed vowels.* A *reversed ogonek* is used in the Bashkir consonant ҙ. [U+0328]

ordinal a, ordinal o See *letters.*

overdot A diacritic used with consonants – ċ ġ ṁ ṅ ż – in Maltese, Polish, old Gaelic and romanized Sanskrit, and with vowels – ė and İ – in Lithuanian and Turkish. In phonetics, it is widely employed as a sign of palatalization. Often known by its Polish name, *kropka.* See also *dotless i and dotted I.* [U+0307]

palatal hook A diacritic used in the Czech and Slovak alphabets to mark the so-called soft or palatal consonants. It usually looks like an apostrophe or single close quote but is differently fitted (cut closer on the left). In some fonts it also differs slightly from the apostrophe in shape and size. It combines with ascending lowercase consonants (ď, ľ, ť) and one capital (Ľ). The uppercase forms of ď and ť are Ď and Ť (and Ľ is an alternate form of Ľ). The caron form is used for both the caps and lower case of non-ascending letters (Č, č, Ř, ř). In Czech, both these forms of the diacritic are known as *háček,* "hook." Also sometimes called the *apostrophe accent.* See also *undercomma.* [U+030C]

paragraph See *pilcrow.*

parentheses These are used as phrase markers in grammar and in mathematics, and sometimes to isolate figures or letters in a numerical or alphabetical list. [U+0028, +0029]

per cent Parts per hundred. Not to be confused with the symbol c/o, 'in care of,' which is also sometimes cut as a single character. [U+0025]

per mille Parts per thousand (61‰ = 6.1%). Though it is very rarely needed in text typography, this sign has been given a place in the standard ISO Latin character set. [U+2030]

period The normal sign for the end of a sentence in all the languages of Europe. But it is also a letter of the alphabet in Tlingit, pronounced as a glottal stop, and in phonetics it is the sign of a syllable boundary. Also called *full point* or *full stop.* [U+002E]

phonomark The copyright symbol used for sound recordings. Also sometimes known, oddly, as the *publish* symbol. [U+2117]

pilcrow An old scribal mark used at the beginning of a paragraph or main text section. It is still used by typographers for that very purpose, and occasionally as a reference mark. Well-designed faces offer pilcrows with some character – ¶ ¶ ¶ ¶ ¶ ¶ ¶ – in preference to the overused, bland standard, ¶. [U+00B6]

pipe Despite its importance to computer programmers and its presence on the standard ASCII keyboard, the pipe has no function in typography. This is another key, and another slot in the font, that begs to be reassigned to something typographically useful. Also called a *broken bar* or *parted rule*. [U+00A6]

prime An abbreviation for feet ($1' = 12''$) and for minutes of arc ($60' = 1°$). Single and double primes should not be confused with apostrophes, dumb quotes or genuine quotation marks, though in some faces (frakturs especially) these glyphs may all have a similar shape and a pleasant slope. See also *apostrophe, double prime, dumb quotes* and *quotation marks*. [U+2032]

question In Spanish, the inverted question mark is used at the beginning of the phrase, in addition to the upright question mark at the end. [U+003F, +00BF]

quotation marks A standard ISO font includes four forms of guillemet and six forms of Anglo-Germanic quotation mark: ‘ ’ ‚ „ “ ”. One of these is also the apostrophe. Another is graphically identical to the comma but separately encloded. In English and Spanish, common usage is ‘thus’ and “thus”; in German, it is ‚thus‘ and „thus“. This parallels the difference in usage of guillemets. In the Romance languages, guillemets point outward; in German they normally point in: in French, “comme ça” *et* «comme ça»; in German, „auf diese Weise“ *und* »diese Weise«. See also *double prime, dumb quotes* and *prime*. [U+2018—201F]

radical sign The sign of the square root, normally used in conjunction with the *vinculum*: $\sqrt{10} = 3.16227766\ldots.$ [U+221A]

registered trademark This is properly a superscript, though the otherwise similar copyright symbol is not. [U+00AE]

reversed apostrophe(s) Mutant forms of the single and double open quote. They appear in several American advertising and text faces cut in the first years of the twentieth century and in some made at the end of that century as well. [U+201B, +201F]

ring Also called *kroužek*. A diacritic used in Arikara, Cheyenne, Czech, Danish, Norwegian, Swedish and other languages. The Scandanavian *round* A (å, Å = IPA ɔ) is present on ISO text fonts, but ů and Ů (*u* with *kroužek*), just as common in Czech, must be found on an East European or pan-European font, or built from component parts. In Arikara and Cheyenne, the ring marks devoiced letters. Uppercase or small cap round A or *A-ring* is the symbol for ångström units (10^4 Å = 1 μm). [U+030A]

schwa A rotated *e*, representing a short, bland vowel (in the jargon of phonetics, a mid central unrounded vowel). It occurs in many African and Native American alphabets. Two uppercase forms are current in Africa: Ǝ and Ə. Note that the first of these is horizontally *mirrored* instead of rotated. [U+018E, +01DD, +0259.]

ə

section A scribal form of double *s*, now used chiefly with reference to legal codes and statutes, when citing particular sections for reference. (The plural abbreviation, meaning sections, is written by doubling the symbol: §§.) [U+00A7]

§

semicolon A grammatical marker, hybrid between colon and comma, derived from European scribal practice. In Greek, however, the same symbol is used as a question mark. [U+003B]

slashed o This is a basic letter of the alphabet in Norwegian and Danish, generally corresponding to the Swedish *ö*. The lowercase form is also part of the IPA. Henrik Ibsen's last play, for example, was *Når vi døde vågner*, and one of his first was *Fru Inger til Østråt*. The letter is sometimes needed in English too, for setting names such as Jørgen Moe and Søren Kierkegaard. [U+00D8, +00F8]

solidus The fraction bar. Used with superior and inferior numbers to construct piece fractions. The *solidus* was a Roman imperial coin introduced by Constantine in AD 309. There were 72 *solidi* to the *libra,* the Roman pound, and 25 *denarii* to the *solidus.* The British based their own imperial coinage and its symbols – *£/s/d*, for pounds, shillings and pence – on the Roman model, and *solidus* became in due course not only a byword for shilling but also the name of the slash mark with which shillings and pence were written. (Given the design and fitting of the characters on most modern type fonts, the solidus is now best used for fractions alone. An italic virgule is usually the best character for setting

references to British imperial money.) See also *virgule*, which is a separate character. [U+2044]

sputnik See *louse*.

[a]

[[a]]

square brackets These essentials of text typography are used for interpolations into quoted matter and as a secondary and inner set of parentheses. In the editing of classical texts, square brackets normally mark editorial *restorations* while angle brackets mark editorial and conjectural insertions, and braces mark deletions. Double square brackets are used by textual scholars to mark deletions made not by the editor but by the original author or scribe. In editing manuscripts and papyri, square brackets also mark hiatuses caused by physical damage. [U+005B, +005D]

a ~ b

swung dash A rare character in text but important in logic and mathematics as the sign of similarity ($a \sim b$) and in lexicography as a sign of repetition. The same sign has been used in symbolic logic to indicate negation, but to avoid confusion, the angular negation sign or *logical not* (¬) is preferred. In the eyes of ISO and Unicode, the swung dash found on computer keyboards is an *ascii tilde* – a character of use to computer programmers but meaningless to typographers. Most fonts actually carry a swung dash, not a tilde, in this position. To Unicode, the true swung dash has a different address. Not to be confused with *tilde*, a smaller character used as a diacritic. [U+007E; +2053, +223C]

tedh Another name for ŧ/Ŧ, the *barred T*.

Þ þ

thorn A basic letter of the alphabet in Anglo-Saxon and Middle English, as well as in Icelandic: *Þótt þu langförull legðir....* Its sound is that of IPA θ: voiceless *th*, as in English *thorn*. Not to be confused with *wynn*. [U+00DE, +00FE]

ã

tilde A diacritic used on vowels – ã ẽ ɛ̃ ĩ õ ɔ̃ ũ ỹ – in many languages (Estonian, Kikuyu, Portuguese, Twi, Vietnamese...) and on at least one consonant (ñ) in many more. Ã, ã, Ñ, ñ, Õ, õ are found on standard ISO text fonts. Pan-European fonts include the old Greenlandic vowels Ĩ, ĩ, Ũ, ũ as well. [U+0303]

a™

trademark This is a superscript, found on most text fonts but useless except for commercial work. [U+2122]

turned undercomma This diacritic is a variant of the undercomma, used in the lowercase form of the Latvian soft g (ģ). The uppercase form of this letter is Ģ. (The *g* is the only palatalized Latvian letter that happens to have a descender.) See also *undercomma.* [U+0326, used in U+0123]

ģ

umlaut See *diaeresis.*

undercomma This is a variant form of the cedilla, popularized in the early twentieth century through the use of typewriters which lacked a real cedilla subscript. Through long habituation, it is now preferred to the cedilla by many writers and some typographers working in Latvian and Romanian. In these languages it is used to mark the soft (palatal) consonants: ļ ņ ŗ ș ț and their uppercase counterparts. It has become, in other words, a variant form of the *palatal hook.*

Because of its descender, Latvian lowercase palatal *g* (ģ) is marked with a raised and inverted form of this diacritic, the *turned undercomma.* [U+0326]

ņ

underdot A diacritic used with consonants – ḍ ḥ ḷ ḹ ṛ ṝ ṣ ṭ ẓ – in romanized Arabic, Hebrew and Sanskrit, and primarily with vowels in Igbo, Yoruba, Twi, and many other African alphabets. In Vietnamese, it is a tonemark signifying low glottalized vowels (ạ ặ ậ ệ ị ợ ự &c). Editors of inscriptions and papyri routinely use the underdot to mark all letters whose reading is uncertain. Its typographic nickname, *nang,* is a simplified form of its Vietnamese name, *nặng.* It is missing from most Latin text fonts. Like the period, it can take many shapes, but in African scripts, a squarish or elongated dot is often preferred. [U+0323]

ạ

underscore A diacritic required for many African and Native American languages, and useful for some purposes in English. It is also used as an alternative to the underdot in setting romanized Arabic and Hebrew. To clear descenders, a repositioned version of the character is required. See also *lowline.* [U+0332]

a̲

unequal A useful symbol missing from most ISO text fonts. It is essential in setting mathematics and, on occasion, important in general text. [U+2260]

$0 \neq 1$

vertical rule See *bar.*

A A

vinculum An overbar or overline, used in mathematics ($\sqrt{10}$) and in the sciences ($\overline{AB}$) to signify the unity of a group. The name is Latin for *bond* or *chain.* [U+203E]

a/c

virgule An oblique stroke, used by medieval scribes and many later writers as a form of comma. It is also used to build *level* fractions (e.g., π/3), to represent a linebreak when verse is set as prose, and in dates, addresses and elsewhere as a sign of separation. In writing the Khoisan languages of western Africa, it is sometimes used to represent dental or lateral clicks. Also called *slash* or *front slash* (to distinguish it from the *backslash*). It is poorly positioned on many fonts and consequently needs some subtle editing. Compare *solidus.* [U+002F]

wedge Another name for the *caron.*

ƿ

wynn This is an archaic English predecessor of the modern letter *w.* It appears only in specialized fonts designed for medievalists, and it is all too easy to confuse with *thorn,* but out of faithfulness to the manuscript tradition, it is occasionally used in printing Middle English texts. [U+01BF, +01F7]

yen See *currency symbols.*

ȝ

yogh This is an archaic Western European form of *y,* sometimes still used in Old and Middle English texts. The twelfth-century English poet Layamon, for example, wrote at a time when the English alphabet included aesc, eth, thorn and yogh, and the letter yogh appeared where we now put a *y* in Layamon's name: Laȝamon. The pronunciation varies with context between the sound of *y* in English *layer* and that of *g* in German *sagen.* Yogh is very rarely found on text fonts. The numeral 3 is not an adequate substitute. [U+021C, +021D]

NOTE: A number of reference works (including the first three editions of *The Unicode Standard,* both editions of Pullum & Ladusaw's *Phonetic Symbol Guide,* and the first two editions of *The Elements of Typographic Style*) fail to distinguish *yogh* from *ezh.* The two characters *can* be graphically identical and therefore can be realized by one in the same glyph, but they are different in origin and sound – and also different now in Unicode.

APPENDIX C: GLOSSARY OF TERMS

Names of individual characters and diacritics (circumflex, dyet, midpoint, virgule, etc) are not in this glossary. Look for them in appendix B. For summary definitions of historical categories (Renaissance, Baroque, etc), see chapter 7.

10/12 × 18 Ten on twelve by eighteen, which is to say, ten-point (10 pt) type set with 12 pt leading (2 pt extra lead, in addition to the body size of 10 pt, for a total of 12 pt from baseline to baseline) on a measure of 18 picas.

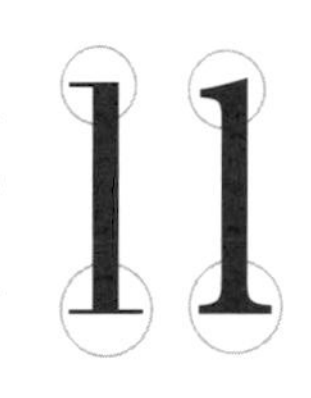

Abrupt and *Adnate* Serifs are either *abrupt* – meaning they break from the stem suddenly at an angle – or they are *adnate*, meaning that they flow smoothly into or out of the stem. In the older typographic literature, adnate serifs are generally described as bracketed.

Aldine Relating to the publishing house operated in Venice by Aldus Manutius between 1494 and 1515. Most of Aldus's type – which included roman, italic and Greek – was cut by Francesco Griffo of Bologna. Type that resembles Griffo's, like typography that resembles Aldus's, is called Aldine. Monotype Poliphilus and Bembo roman are Aldine revivals, though their companion italics are not. No Aldine italics or Aldine Greeks are in circulation at the present time.

Analphabetic A typographic symbol used with the alphabet but lacking a place in the alphabetical order. Diacritics such as the acute, umlaut, circumflex and caron are analphabetics. So are the asterisk, dagger, pilcrow, comma and parentheses.

Aperture The openings of letters such as C, c, S, s, a and e. Humanist faces such as Bembo and Centaur have large apertures, while Romantic faces such as Bodoni and Realist faces such as Helvetica have small apertures. Very large apertures occur in archaic Greek inscriptions and in typefaces such as Lithos, which are derived from them.

Axis In typography, the axis of a letter generally means the axis of the stroke, which in turn reveals the axis of the pen or other tool used to make the letter. If a letter has thick strokes and thin ones, find the thick strokes and extend them into lines. These lines reveal the axis (or *axes*; there may be several) of the letter. Not to be confused with *slope*.

Ball Terminal A circular form at the end of the arm, leg or brow in letters such as a, c, f, j, r and y. Ball terminals are found in many romans and italics of the Romantic period, some Realist faces, and in many recent faces built on Romantic lines. Examples: Bodoni, Scotch Roman and Haas Clarendon. See also *beak terminal* and *teardrop terminal*.

Baseline Whether written by hand or set into type, the Latin lowercase alphabet implies an invisible staff consisting of at least four lines: topline, midline, baseline and beardline. The topline is the line reached by ascenders in letters like b, d, h, k, l. The midline marks the top of letters like a, c, e, m, x, and the top of the torso of letters like b, d, h. The baseline is the line on which all these letters rest. The beardline is the line reached by descenders in letters like p and q. The cap line, marking the top of uppercase letters like H, does not necessarily coincide with the topline of the lower case.

Round letters like e and o normally dent the baseline. Pointed letters like v and w normally pierce it, while the foot serifs of letters like h and m usually rest precisely upon it.

Bastarda A class of *blackletter* types. See page 266.

Beak Terminal A sharp spur, found particularly on the f, and also often on a, c, j, r and y, in many twentieth-century romans and, to a lesser degree, italics. Examples: Apollo, Berling, Calisto, Méridien, Perpetua, Pontifex, Veljović.

Bicameral A bicameral alphabet is two alphabets joined. The modern Latin alphabet, which you are reading, is an example. It has an upper and a lower case, as closely linked and yet as easy to distinguish as the Senate and the House of Representatives. Unicameral alphabets (the Arabic, Hebrew and Devanagari alphabets, for example) have only one case. Tricameral alphabets have three – and a normal font of roman type is tricameral, if it includes an upper case, a lower case and small caps.

Bilateral Extending to both sides. Bilateral serifs, which are always *reflexive*, are typical of roman faces, while unilateral serifs are typical of romans, Carolingians and italics.

Bitmap A digital image in unintelligent form. A letterform can be described morphologically, as a series of reference points and trajectories that mimic its perimeter, or embryologically, as the series of penstrokes that produce the form. Such descriptions are partially independent of size and position. The same image can also be described quite accurately but superficially as the addresses of all the dots (or *bits*) in its digital representation. This sort of description, a bitmap, ties the image to one orientation and size.

Blackletter Blackletter is to typography what Gothic is to architecture: a general name for a wide variety of forms that stem predominantly from the north of Europe. Like Gothic buildings, blackletter types can be massive or light. They are often tall and pointed, but sometimes round instead. Compare *whiteletter*. The categories of blackletter include bastarda, fraktur, quadrata, rotunda and textura. See page 266.

Bleed As a verb, to bleed means to reach to the edge of the printed page. As a noun, it means printed matter with no margin. If an image is printed so that it reaches beyond the trim line, it will bleed when the page is trimmed. Photographs, rules, solids and background screens or patterns are often allowed to bleed. Type can rarely do so.

Blind In letterpress work, printing blind means printing without ink, producing a colorless impression.

Blind Folio A page which is counted in the numbering sequence but carries no visible number.

Block Quotation A quotation set off from the main text, forming a paragraph of its own, often indented or set in a different face or smaller size than the main text. A *run-in quotation*, on the other hand, is run in with the main text and usually enclosed in quotation marks.

Body (1) In reference to foundry type: the actual block of typemetal from which the sculpted mirror-image of the printed letter protrudes. (2) In reference to phototype or digital type: the rectangular face of the metal block that the letter would be mounted on *if it were* three-dimensional metal instead of a two-dimensional image or bitmap. Retained as a fiction for use in sizing and spacing the type.

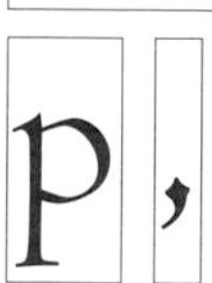

Body Size In graphic terms, the *height* of the *face* of the type, which in letterpress terms is the *depth* of the *body* of the type. Originally, this was the height of the face of the metal block on which each individual letter was cast. In digital type, it is the height of its imaginary equivalent, the rectangle defining the space owned by a given letter, and not the dimension of the letter itself. Body sizes are usually given in points – but European type sizes are often given in Didot points, which are 7% larger than the points used in Britain and North America.

Bowl The generally round or elliptical forms which are the basic bodyshape of letters such as C, G, O in the upper case, and b, c, e, o, p in the lower case. Also called *eye.*

Cap Height The distance from baseline to cap line of an alphabet, which is the approximate height of the uppercase letters. It is often less, but sometimes greater, than the height of the ascending lowercase letters. See also *baseline* and *x-height.*

Chancery A class of cursive letterforms, generally featuring extra ligatures and lengthened and curved extenders. Many, but not all, chancery letterforms are also *swash* forms.

Cicero A unit of measure equal to 12 Didot points. This is the continental European counterpart to the British and American *pica,* but the cicero is slightly larger than the pica. It is equivalent to 4.52 mm or 0.178 inch. See *point.*

Color The darkness of the type as set in mass, which is not the same as the *weight* of the face itself. The spacing of words and letters, the leading of lines, and the incidence of capitals, not to mention the properties of the ink and of the paper it is printed on, all affect the color of the type.

Contrast In the analysis of letterforms, this usually refers to the degree of contrast between the thick strokes and thin strokes of a given letter. In Romantic faces such as Bulmer and Bodoni, the contrast is high. In unmodulated faces such as Gill Sans and Futura, contrast is low or nonexistent.

Counter The white space enclosed by a letterform, whether wholly enclosed, as in *d* or *o,* or partially, as in *c* or *m.*

Crosshead A heading or subhead centered over the text. Compare *sidehead.*

Cursive Flowing. Often used as a synonym for *italic.*

Dingbat A typographic glyph or symbol subject to scorn because it has no apparent relation to the alphabet. Many dingbats are pictograms – tiny pictures of churches, airplanes, skiers, telephones, and the like, used in the tourist industry. Others are more abstract symbols – check marks, crosses, cartographic symbols, the emblems of the suits of playing cards, and so on. Compare *fleuron* and *hedera.*

Dot Leader A row of evenly spaced periods or midpoints, occasionally used to link flush-left text with flush-right numerals in a table of contents or similar context. (There are none in this book.)

DPI Dots per inch. The usual measure of output *resolution* in digital typography and in laser printing.

Drop Cap A large initial capital or *versal* mortised into the text. (See page 64 for examples.) Compare *elevated cap.*

Drop Folio A folio (page number) dropped to the foot of the page when the folios on other pages are carried near the top. Drop folios are often used on chapter openings.

Dropline Paragraph A paragraph marked by dropping directly down one line space from the end of the previous paragraph, without going back to the left margin. (See page 40 for an example.)

Glossary of Typographic Terms

Elevated Cap A large initial capital or versal rising up from the beginning of the text instead of nested down into it.

Em In linear measure, a distance equal to the type size, and in square measure, the square of the type size. Thus an em is 12 pt (or a 12 pt square) in 12 pt type, and 11 pt (or an 11 pt square) in 11 pt type. Also called *mutton*.

En Half an em. To avoid misunderstanding when instructions are given orally, typographers often speak of ems as *muttons* and ens as *nuts*.

Extenders Descenders and ascenders; i.e., any parts of the letterform that extend below the baseline, as in p and q, or above the midline, as in b, d and f.

Eye Synonym for *bowl* in the lower case. *Large eye* means large *x-height,* while *open eye* means large *aperture.*

FL Flush left, which means set with an even left margin. By implication, the right margin is ragged. To be more precise, one could write FL/RR, meaning flush left, ragged right.

FL&R Flush left and right, which is to say *justified.*

Fleuron A horticultural dingbat. That is to say, a typographic ornament ordinarily in the shape of a flower or leaf. Some fleurons are designed to be set in bulk and in combinations, to produce what amounts to typographic wallpaper.

Flush and Hung Set with the first line FL and subsequent lines indented, like the entries in this glossary.

Folio In bibliography, a page or leaf; but in typography, a folio is normally a typeset page *number*, not the page itself.

Font A set of sorts or glyphs. In the world of metal type, this means a given alphabet, with all its accessory characters, in a given size. In relation to phototype, it usually means the assortment of standard patterns forming the glyph palette, without regard to size, or the actual filmstrip or wheel on which these patterns are stored. In the world of digital type, the font is the glyph palette itself or the digital information encoding it. (The older British spelling, *fount*, has not only the same meaning but also the same pronunciation.)

Fore-edge The outside edge or margin of a book page; i.e., the edge or margin opposite the spine.

FR Flush right. With an even right margin. By implication, the left margin is ragged. The sidehead on this page is an example.

Glossary of Typographic Terms

Fraktur A class of *blackletter* types. See page 266.

Glyph An incarnation of a character. See *sort*.

Gutter The blank column between two columns of type or the margins at the spine between two facing textblocks.

Hanging Figures Text figures.

Hair Space Normally M/24 *or* the width of a slip of paper.

Hard Space A word space that will not translate into a line-break. Also called *no-break space*.

Hint The letterforms that make up a digital font are usually defined mathematically in terms of outlines or templates, which can be freely scaled, rotated and moved about. When pages are composed, these outlines are given specific locations and sizes. They must then be *rasterized*: converted into solid forms made up of dots at the resolution of the output device. If the size is very small or the resolution low, the raster or grid will be coarse, and the dots will fill the mathematical template very imperfectly. Hints are *the rules of compromise* applied in this process of rasterization. At large sizes and high resolutions, they are irrelevant. At smaller sizes and lower resolutions, where distortion is inevitable, they are crucial. *Hinted* fonts include hints as integral parts of the font definition. See also *bitmap*.

Humanist Humanist letterforms originated among the humanists of the Italian Renaissance and persist to the present day. They are of two primary kinds: roman and italic, both of which derive from Roman capitals and Carolingian minuscules. Humanist letterforms show the clear trace of a broadnib pen held by a right-handed scribe. They have a *modulated* stroke and a *humanist axis*.

Humanist Axis An oblique stroke axis reflecting the natural inclination of the writing hand. See pp 12–15.

Inline A letter in which the inner portions of the main strokes have been carved away, leaving the edges more or less intact. Inline faces lighten the color while preserving the shapes and proportions of the original face. *Outline* letters, on the other hand, are produced by drawing a line around the outsides of the letters and removing the entire original form. Outline letters, in consequence, are fatter than the originals and have less definition. Castellar, Smaragd and Romulus Open Kapitalen are examples of inline faces.

IPA International Phonetic Association and its alphabet. The organization was founded in 1886. The alphabet is a set of phonetic letters, diacritics and tonemarks, widely used but – like any scientific system – subject to constant refinement and modification. (See page 299.)

ISO International Organization for Standardization, headquartered in Geneva. An agency for international cooperation on industrial and scientific standards. Its membership consists of the national standards organizations of more than one hundred countries.

Italic A class of letterforms more cursive than roman but less cursive than script, developed from the Carolingian hand in fifteenth-century Italy. In most italics, the separate letters are implicitly connected by their *transitive* serifs.

Justify To adjust the length of the line so that it is flush left and right on the measure. Type in the Latin alphabet is commonly set either justified or FL/RR (flush left, ragged right).

Kern (1) Part of a letter that extends into the space of another. In many alphabets, the roman *f* has a kern to the right, the roman *j* a kern to the left, and the italic *f* one of each. (2) As a verb, to kern means to alter the fit of certain letter combinations – *To* or *VA*, for example – so that the limb of one projects over or under the body or limb of the other.

Lachrymal Terminal See *teardrop terminal.*

Lead [rhyming with *red*] Originally a strip of soft metal (typemetal or brass) used for vertical spacing between lines of type. Now meaning the vertical distance from the baseline of one line to the baseline of the next. Also called *leading.*

Lettrine Literally, 'a large letter.' Synonym for *versal.*

Ligature Two or more letters tied into a single character. The sequence ffi, for example, forms a ligature in most Latin text faces.

Lining Figures Figures of even height. Usually synonymous with *titling figures*, but some lining figures are smaller and lighter than the uppercase letters.

Logogram A specific typographic form tied to a certain word. Example: the nonstandard capitalizations in the names e.e. cummings, ПараГраф, TrueType and WordPerfect.

Lowercase Figures Synonym for *text figures* or old-style figures.

M/3 A third of an em: e.g., 4 pt in 12 pt type; 8 pt in 24 pt type.

Measure The standard length of the line; i.e., column width or width of the overall textblock, usually measured in picas.

Mid Space A space measuring M/4, a fourth of an em.

Modulation In relation to typography, modulation means a variation – usually cyclical and predictable – in the width of the stroke. In monochrome (unmodulated) letterforms such as Frutiger, the stroke is always fundamentally the same width. In a face such as Bembo or Centaur, the stroke is based on the trace of a broadnib pen, which makes thin cross strokes and thicker pull strokes. When letters are written with such an instrument, regular modulation automatically occurs.

Monotonic Modern Greek retains only one of the old tonic accent marks, the ὀξεῖα (*oxeia*) or acute. (Greek has often, in fact, been written and sometimes set this way, but the practice did not become official until 1982.) Fonts designed for setting Greek this way are known as monotonic. Their acute (renamed the *tonos*) is usually vertical. Compare *polytonic.*

Mutton An *em.* Also called mutton quad.

Negative Leading Leading – that is to say, line space – smaller than the body size. Type set 16/14, for example, is set with negative leading.

Neohumanist Recent letterforms that revive and reassert *humanist* principles are called neohumanist.

Nut An *en.*

Old-Style Figures (OSF) A common synonym for *text figures.*

Orthotic A class of Greek scripts and types that flourished in Western Europe between 1200 and 1520, revived in the early twentieth century. Orthotic Greeks are noncursive and usually bicameral. In other words, they are analogous to the roman form of Latin script. Both caps and lower case are usually upright. Serifs, when present, are usually short, abrupt and unilateral. The geometric figures of circle, line and triangle are usually prominent in their underlying structure. Victor Scholderer's New Hellenic is an example.

Pi Font A font of assorted mathematical or other symbols, designed to be used as an adjunct to one or more text fonts.

Pica A unit of measure equal to 12 *points.* Two different picas are in common use. (1) In traditional printers' measure, the pica is 4.22 mm or 0.166 inch: close to, but not exactly, one sixth of an inch. This is the customary British and American unit for measuring the length of the line and the depth of the textblock. (2) The PostScript pica is precisely one sixth of an inch: 0.166666…″. The difference between these units is roughly 0.03%. (Note: the continental European counterpart to the pica is the *cicero*, which is 7% larger.)

Piece Fraction A fraction (such as 5⁄64) that is not included in the font and must therefore be made on demand from separate components.

Point (1) In traditional British and American measure, a point is a twelfth of a *pica*, which makes it 0.3515 mm, or 0.01383 inch. In round numbers, there are 72 points per inch, or 28.5 points per centimeter. (2) In continental Europe a larger point, the Didot point, is used. The Didot point (one twelfth of a *cicero*) is 0.38 mm or 0.01483 inch. In round numbers, there are 26.5 Didot points per centimeter, or 67.5 per inch. (3) Nearly all digital typesetting devices, like the PostScript and TrueType languages they employ, make the point precisely 1⁄72 inch and the pica precisely one sixth of an inch.

Polytonic Classical Greek has been set since the fifteenth century with an array of tonic accents and other diacritics inherited from the Alexandrian scribes. These diacritics – *oxeia* (acute), *bareia* (grave), *perispomene* (circumflex), *psili* (smooth breathing), *daseia* (rough breathing), diaeresis and iota subscript – are used singly and in many combinations. Modern Greek retains only the acute (reinterpreted to a vertical mark called the *tonos*) and an occasional diaeresis. Greek fonts equipped with the full set of accents are accordingly known as polytonic Greeks, and modern Greek fonts as *monotonic*.

Quad An *em*. Also called *mutton quad*.

Quaint An antiquated sort or glyph, used to recreate the typographic flavor of a bygone age. The *ct*, *sp* and *st* ligatures, and the long s and its ligatures, are examples.

Ranging Figures Synonymous with *lining figures*.

Raster Digital grid. See *hint*.

Rationalist Axis Vertical axis, typical of Neoclassical and Romantic letterforms. See pp 12–13. Compare *humanist axis*.

Reflexive A type of *serif* that concludes the stroke of the pen by drawing back upon itself. Reflexive serifs are typical of roman faces, including the face in which these words are set. They always involve a sudden, small stoppage and reversal of the pen's direction, and more often than not they are *bilateral*. See also *transitive*.

Resolution In digital typography, resolution is the fineness of the grain of the typeset image. It is usually measured in dots per inch (dpi). Laser printers, for example, generally have a resolution between 300 and 1200 dpi, and platemakers or typesetting machines a resolution significantly greater than 1200 dpi. The resolution of the conventional television screen is only about 50 dpi, and the resolution of most computer screens is also very low: between 72 and 133 dpi. But other factors besides resolution affect the apparent roughness or fineness of the typeset image. These factors include the inherent design of the characters, the skill with which they are digitized, the *hinting* technology used to compensate for coarse *rasterization*, and the nature of the surface on which they are reproduced.

Rotunda A class of *blackletter* types. See page 266.

RR Ragged right, which is to say unjustified.

m

Sanserif From the earlier English forms *sans serif* and *sans surryphs*, without serifs: synonymous with *unserifed.*

m

T L

i *i*

Serif A stroke added to the beginning or end of one of the main strokes of a letter. In the roman alphabet, serifs are usually *reflexive* finishing strokes, forming unilateral or bilateral stops. (They are unilateral if they project only to one side of the main stroke, like the serifs at the head of T and the foot of L, and bilateral if they project to both sides, like the serifs at the foot of T and the head of L.) *Transitive* serifs – smooth entry or exit strokes – are usual in italic.

There are many descriptive terms for serifs, especially as they have developed in roman faces. They may be not only unilateral or bilateral, but also long or short, thick or thin, pointed or blunt, abrupt or adnate, horizontal or vertical or oblique, tapered, triangular, and so on. In texturas and some frakturs, they are usually *scutulate* (diamond-shaped), and in some architectural scripts, such as Eaglefeather and Tekton, the serifs are virtually round.

Sidehead A heading or subhead set flush left (more rarely, flush right) or slightly indented. Compare *crosshead.*

n

Slab Serif An abrupt or adnate serif of the same thickness as the main stroke. Slab serifs are a hallmark of the so-called egyptian and clarendon types: two groups of Realist faces produced in substantial numbers since the early nineteenth century. Memphis, Rockwell and Serifa are examples. A more recent example is PMN Caecilia.

Slope The angle of inclination of the stems and extenders of letters. Most (but not all!) italics slope to the right at something between 2° and 20°. Not to be confused with *axis*.

Solid Set without additional *lead*, or with the line space equivalent to the type size. Type set 11/11 or 12/12, for example, is set solid.

Sort A single piece of metal type; thus a letter or other character in one particular style and size. In the world of digital type, where letters have no physical existence until printed, the word *sort* has been largely displaced by the word *glyph*. A glyph is a version – a conceptual, not material, incarnation – of the abstract symbol called a character. Thus, *z* and *ʐ* are alternate glyphs (in the same face) for the same character.

Stem A main stroke that is more or less straight, not part of a bowl. The letter *o* has no stem; the letter *l* consists of stem and serifs alone.

Swash A letterform reveling in luxury. Some swash letters carry extra flourishes; others simply occupy an extra helping of space. Swash letters are usually cursive and swash typefaces therefore usually italic. True italic capitals (as distinct from sloped roman capitals) are usually swash. (*The Caps in this Sentence are Examples.*) Hermann Zapf's Zapf Renaissance italic and Robert Slimbach's Poetica are faces in which the swash can be extended to the lower case.

Teardrop Terminal A swelling, like a teardrop, at the end of the arm in letters such as a, c, f, g, j, r and y. This feature is typical of typefaces from the Late Renaissance, Baroque and Neoclassical periods, and is present in many recent faces built on Baroque or Neoclassical lines. Examples: Jannon, Van Dijck, Kis, Caslon, Fournier, Baskerville, Bell, Walbaum, Zapf International, Galliard. Also called *lachrymal terminal*. See also *ball terminal* and *beak terminal*.

Textblock The part of the page normally occupied by text.

Text Figures Figures – 123456 – designed to match the lowercase letters in size and color. Most text figures are ascending and descending forms. Also called *oldstyle figures*. Compare *lining figures, ranging figures* and *titling figures*.

Textura A class of *blackletter* types. See page 266.

Thick Space A space usually measuring M/3, a third of an em.

Thin Space In letterpress work, a space measuring M/5, a fifth of an em. In computer typesetting, sometimes understood as M/6 or M/8. Compare *hair space, mid space* and *thick space*.

Three-to-em One-third em. Also written M/3. See also *thick.*

Titling Figures Figures – 123456 – designed to match the uppercase letters in size and color. Compare *text figures.*

m

Transitive A type of serif which flows directly into or out of the main stroke without stopping to reverse direction, typical of many italics. Transitive serifs are usually unilateral: they extend only to one side of the stem. See also *reflexive.*

Type Size See *body size.*

U&lc Upper and lower case: the normal form for setting text in the Latin, Greek and Cyrillic alphabets, all of which are now *bicameral.*

Unicameral Having only one case – like the Arabic, Hebrew, Thai and Tibetan scripts, and many roman titling faces. Compare *bicameral.*

Unicode A scheme, begun in 1988, for standardized encoding of all the characters in all the world's scripts. See page 181.

Versal A large initial capital, either elevated or dropped. Also called *lettrine.*

Weight The darkness (blackness) of a typeface, independent of its size. See also *color.*

ao

Whiteletter The generally light roman letterforms favored by humanist scribes and typographers in Italy in the fifteenth and sixteenth centuries, as distinct from the generally darker *blackletter* script and type used for ecclesiastical and legal texts. Whiteletter is the typographic counterpart to Romanesque in architecture, as blackletter is the counterpart to Gothic.

White Line A line space.

Word Space The space between words. When type is set FL/RR, the word space may be of fixed size. When the type is *justified,* the word space is usually elastic.

x-height The distance between the baseline and the midline of an alphabet, which is normally the approximate height of the unextended lowercase letters – a, c, e, m, n, o, r, s, u, v, w, x, z – and of the torso of b, d, h, k, p, q, y. The relation of x-height to cap height is an important characteristic of any *bicameral* Latin typeface, and the relation of x-height to *extender* length is a crucial property of any Latin or Greek lower case. See also *baseline, cap height* and *eye.*

APPENDIX D: TYPE DESIGNERS

A biographical index of designers important to typographic history, and of all those doing important work in the present day, would be a book in itself. The following list is little more than a cross-reference to important designers whose work is mentioned elsewhere in this book.

LUDOVICO DEGLI ARRIGHI (*c.* 1480–1527) Italian calligrapher and designer of at least six chancery italic fonts. Frederic Warde's Vicenza and Arrighi (the italic companion to Centaur) are based on one of his faces. Monotype Blado (the italic companion to Poliphilus) is a rough approximation of another.

ANTOINE AUGEREAU (*c.* 1490–1534) Parisian punchcutter and printer. Author of several text romans and at least one Greek. Along with his contemporary Simon de Colines, Augereau defined the style of French typography later identified with the name of his most famous apprentice, Claude Garamond. This activity came to an end when he was hanged and his corpse was publicly burnt, on Christmas Eve of 1534, for printing a psalm without permission.

RICHARD AUSTIN (*c.* 1765–1830) English punchcutter producing Neoclassical and Romantic faces. He cut the original Bell type, the first Scotch Roman, and the original version of Porson Greek. W.A. Dwiggins's Caledonia is based primarily on Austin's work.

JOHN BASKERVILLE (1706–1775) English calligrapher, printer and businessman. Designer of a series of Neoclassical romans, italics and one Greek. Most of the faces sold in his name are based on his work and some resemble it closely. His punches are now at the University Library, Cambridge, and the St Bride Printing Library, London. A set of original matrices, formerly in Paris, is now in the Frutiger Foundry, Münchenstein, Switzerland.

LUCIAN BERNHARD (1885–1972) German immigrant to the USA. Painter, poet, industrial designer and typographer. Author of a large number of roman faces, distinguished by their long extenders. These were cut and cast primarily by ATF and Bauer.

CHARLES BIGELOW (1945–) American typographer and scholar. Codesigner, with Kris Holmes, of the Lucida family.

ARCHIBALD BINNEY (1762–1838) Scottish immigrant to the USA. He was trained as a punchcutter in Edinburgh. With James Ronaldson, another Scottish immigrant, he established the Binney & Ronaldson Foundry in Philadelphia, where he cut Baroque, Neoclassical and Romantic type.

FRANK BLOKLAND (1959–) Dutch type designer and founder of the Dutch Type Library in 's-Hertogenbosch. His faces include Berenice and Documenta. His historical revivals include DTL Van den Keere and its companion, Guyot italic.

GIAMBATTISTA BODONI (1740–1813) Italian punchcutter, printer and prolific designer of type, working at Rome and Parma. Bodoni is best known for his dark and razor-sharp Romantic romans, italics and sometimes wildly ornamental Greeks, but he also designed and cut a large number of Neoclassical fonts. Bauer Bodoni, Berthold Bodoni, and some of the other faces now sold in his name are based on his work. His punches are in the Museo Bodoniano, Parma.

LUDOLF BORCHTORP (*c.* 1470–*c.* 1510) Polish mathematician and engraver. Author of the first fonts of Cyrillic type, which he evidently cut in Kraków about 1490, for the printer Szwajpolt Fiol.

CHRIS BRAND (1921–1999) Dutch calligrapher, the designer of the Albertina family. Some of his finest work – including the Hebrew face Zippora, the Elsschot family and the Denise italic – has yet to be released.

DAN CARR (1951–) American punchcutter, poet, typographer and printer. Proprietor, with Julia Ferrari, of the Golgonooza Letter Foundry, Ashuelot, New Hampshire. Carr is one of the few active punchcutters now living. Designer and cutter of Regulus foundry roman and Parmenides foundry Greek; designer of the digital family Chêneau.

MATTHEW CARTER (1937–) English-born American type designer, punchcutter and scholar, based in Cambridge, Massachusetts. His text faces include Auriga, Charter, Galliard and Manutius; his titling faces include Mantinia and Sophia. His historical revivals include Wilson Greek.

WILLIAM CASLON (1692–1766) English engraver, punchcutter and typefounder; author of many Baroque romans, italics, Greeks and other non-Latin faces. ATF Caslon, Monotype Caslon, and Carol Twombly's Adobe Caslon are closely based on his work. A collection of his punches is now in the St Bride Printing Library, London.

WARREN CHAPPELL (1904–1991) American book artist, trained in Germany, where he studied with Rudolf Koch. His typefaces include Trajanus, Lydian and the still unmanufactured Eichenauer.

SIMON DE COLINES (*c.* 1480–1547) French master printer, typographer and punchcutter. Author of a dozen or more roman fonts, several italics, several blackletters and a fine cursive Greek. Colines as much as any single person appears to be responsible for creating the typographic style of the French golden age. Garamond and Augereau were part of the same circle. None of Colines's faces has evidently yet been translated to digital form.

CARL DAIR (1912–1967) Canadian book designer and typographer, working chiefly in Toronto. Designer of the Cartier family, which was left incomplete at Dair's death and later improved and completed by Rod McDonald.

GERARD DANIËLS (1966–) Dutch type designer and typographer, trained under Gerrit Noordzij in The Hague. Designer of Caspari.

ISMAR DAVID (1910–1996) German-born American book designer, architect, graphic artist and type designer. His faces include David Hebrew, released by Intertype in 1954, and a number of photolettering faces still awaiting digital revival.

GIOVANNI DEFACCIO (1966–) Italian calligrapher. With Lui Karner, he is codesigner of the Rialto family, produced by their digital foundry *df*Type.

FRANÇOIS-AMBROISE DIDOT (1730–1804) Parisian printer and publisher. Designer of several Neoclassical romans and italics, cut under his supervision by Pierre-Louis Vafflard. Father of Firmin Didot and founder of the Didot dynasty in printing and typography.

FIRMIN DIDOT (1764–1836) Parisian printer and punchcutter; son of F.-A. Didot and student of Pierre-Louis Vafflard; father of Ambroise Firmin-Didot. Author of several Neoclassical faces as well as the Romantic fonts for which he is posthumously known. Monotype Didot and Linotype's digital Didot (drawn by Adrian Frutiger) are based on his work.

BRAM DE DOES (1934–) Dutch typographer, formerly chief designer at Joh. Enschedé en Zonen, Haarlem. Designer of the Trinité and Lexicon families.

WILLIAM ADDISON DWIGGINS (1880–1956) American designer and typographer. Dwiggins designed typefaces exclusively for the Linotype machine. In the 1930s and 1940s, he also created the typographic house style at Alfred Knopf, New York. His serifed faces include Caledonia, Eldorado, Electra and Falcon. His only completed sanserif is Metro. His one uncial face is Winchester. Many of his type drawings are now in the Boston Public Library.

ALFRED FAIRBANK (1895–1982) English calligrapher and designer of Fairbank italic.

AMBROISE FIRMIN-DIDOT (1790–1876) French scholar, typecutter and printer. He was the son of Firmin Didot (whose full name he took as his own surname) and grandson of François-Ambroise Didot. Author of the first Didot Greek fonts.

JOHANN MICHAEL FLEISCHMAN (1701–1768) German-born punchcutter and founder working in the Netherlands. A prolific and skilled cutter of romans, italics and ornamental blackletters. Also the author of several Arabic and Greek fonts. His early romans and italics are Baroque, but in the 1730s he cut a series of text fonts idiosyncratic and self-conscious enough to be called Rococo. Most of his surviving material is now at the Enschedé Museum in Haarlem.

KARL-ERIK FORSBERG (1914–1995) Swedish calligrapher and typographer, designer of the Berling text roman. His titling faces include Carolus, Ericus and Lunda.

PIERRE SIMON FOURNIER (1712–1768) French printer and punchcutter. Author of many French Neoclassical fonts and typographic ornaments. Nearly all of his original material has been damaged or lost. Monotype Fournier and Barbou are based on his work, and W.A. Dwiggins's Electra owes much to the study of it.

HENRI FRIEDLAENDER (1904–1996) Israeli book and type designer, born in France of a Dutch father and English mother, and trained primarily in Germany. In 1950, after twenty years on the drawing table, a trial casting of his Hadassah Hebrew family was made by the Amsterdam Foundry. After further revision, working versions were issued beginning in 1958.

ADRIAN FRUTIGER (1928–) Swiss immigrant to France. A prolific and versatile designer of type and signage. He was involved in the early transition from metal type to phototype. His serifed faces include Apollo, Breughel, Glypha, Iridium and Méridien. His sanserifs include Avenir, Frutiger, and

Univers. His titling and script types include Herculanum, Ondine, Pompeijana and Rusticana.

CLAUDE GARAMOND (*c.* 1490–1561) French punchcutter, working chiefly in Paris. Author of many roman fonts, at least two italics, and a full set of chancery Greeks. His surviving punches and matrices are now at the Plantin-Moretus Museum in Antwerp and at the Imprimerie Nationale, Paris. Stempel Garamond roman *and* italic, Linotype Granjon roman, Günter Gerhard Lange's Berthold Garamond roman, Robert Slimbach's Adobe Garamond roman, and Ronald Arnholm's Legacy *italic* are all based on his designs. Monotype Garamond is not. (See also pp 230–32.)

The spelling *Garamont* is now customary in France. The English spelling *Garamond* is derived from the Latin *Garamondius*, often used by Garamont himself.

ERIC GILL (1882–1940) English engraver and stonecutter, working in England and Wales. His serifed faces include Joanna, Perpetua and Pilgrim. His one unserifed face is Gill Sans. Perpetua Greek is also his, but Gill Sans Greek is by other hands. Gill's type drawings are now in the St Bride Library, London. Some of the matrices and punches for his types are now at the University Library, Cambridge; others are in the Clark Library, Los Angeles – but none of these punches were cut by Gill himself.

FREDERIC GOUDY (1865–1947) American type designer and founder. His serifed faces include University of California Old Style (later adapted for machine composition as Californian), Deepdene, Italian Old Style, Kaatskill, Kennerley, Village Nº 1 and Village Nº 2. His blackletters include Franciscan, Goudy Text and Goudy Thirty. His titling faces include Forum, Goudy Old Style and Hadriano. Goudy Sans is his only unserifed face. His only uncial is Friar. Most of Goudy's original material was destroyed by fire in 1939. What survives is at the Rochester Institute of Technology.

ROBERT GRANJON (*c.* 1513–1590) French typecutter working at Paris, Lyon, Antwerp, Frankfurt and Rome. Author of many Renaissance and Mannerist romans, italics, scripts, several Greeks, a Cyrillic, some Hebrews, and the first successful fonts of Arabic type. Some of his punches and matrices survive at the Plantin-Moretus Museum, Antwerp and the Nordiska Museet, Stockholm. Matthew Carter's Galliard is based primarily on Granjon's Ascendonica roman and italic.

FRANCESCO GRIFFO (*c.* 1450–1518) Bolognese punchcutter, working in Venice, Bologna and elsewhere in Italy. Author of at least seven romans, three italics, four Greeks and a Hebrew. None of Griffo's actual punches or matrices are known to survive, and the house of Aldus Manutius in Venice, where he did most of his work, has vanished. (The site is now occupied by a bank.) Griffo's letterforms have nonetheless been patiently reconstructed from the printed books in which his type appears. Giovanni Mardersteig's Griffo type is an exacting replica of one of Griffo's fonts. Monotype Bembo roman is based more loosely on the same font. Monotype Poliphilus is a rough reproduction of the same lower case with different caps. Mardersteig's Dante roman and italic are also based on a close study of Griffo's work. The italics, overall, have received far less attention than the romans.

Giovanni Mardersteig's postscript to Pietro Bembo, *De Aetna* (Verona: Officina Bodoni, 1969) gives a good introduction to Griffo's roman types and their derivatives. More important still is the series of essays collected in Mardersteig's *Scritti* (1988).

ARNALDO GUILLÉN DE BROCAR (*c.* 1460–1524) Spanish master printer and typographer working at Alcalá de Henares, which is now a suburb of Madrid. Author of several romans and at least two Greek fonts. The most notable of these is the Complutensian Greek type, cut about 1510.

Complutensian means 'from Complutum,' which is the old Roman name for Alcalá.

FRANÇOIS GUYOT (*c.* 1510–1570) Punchcutter and typefounder, born at Paris. He moved to Antwerp in the 1530s and spent most of the rest of his life there, cutting type for the printer Christophe Plantin and others.

VICTOR HAMMER (1882–1967) Austrian-born printer working chiefly in Italy and the USA. All of Hammer's types are uncials. These include American Uncial, Andromache, Hammer Uncial, Pindar and Samson. His type drawings and punches are now at the University of Kentucky, Lexington.

JONATHAN HOEFLER (1970–) American type designer and digital founder. He established the Hoefler Type Foundry, New York, in 1989. Designer of Hoefler Text, Hoefler Titling, Gestalt, the Requiem family, and other faces.

KRIS HOLMES (1950–) American calligrapher. Designer of Isadora and Sierra; codesigner with Janice Fishman of Shannon, and with Charles Bigelow of the Lucida family.

JOHN HUDSON (1968–) English/Canadian type designer and expert in multilingual digital encoding. Designer of Aeneas and Manticore. Cofounder, with Ross Mills, of Tiro Typeworks in Vancouver.

MARK JAMRA (1956–) American typographer and graphic artist, trained in Switzerland. Designer of several artful postmodern faces, including Jamille, Latienne and Kinesis.

JEAN JANNON (1580–1658) French punchcutter and printer. His romans and italics, cut at Paris and Sedan, appear to be the first Baroque types ever made. Much of his material survives at the Imprimerie Nationale, Paris, where his type is known as the *caractères de l'université*. Monotype 'Garamond,' Linotype 'Garamond' 3, ATF 'Garamond,' Lanston 'Garamont' and Simoncini 'Garamond' are based on his work. (See pp 230–32.)

NICOLAS JENSON (*c*. 1420–1480) French punchcutter and printer, working in Venice. Author of at least one roman, one Greek and five rotundas. Jenson's punches and matrices have long vanished, but his type has often been copied from his printed books. Bruce Rogers's Centaur, Ronald Arnholm's Legacy roman and Robert Slimbach's Adobe Jenson roman are based on his. Karlgeorg Hoefer's San Marco is based in large part on Jenson's rotundas.

In addition to his 16 pt roman, Jenson cut at least the caps for a 12 pt font. In addition to his five rotundas (ranging from 12 to 21 pt), he also cut at least the lower case for a sixth and smaller font.

GEORGE WILLIAM JONES (1860–1942) English printer and type designer. Author of Linotype Estienne, Linotype Granjon, and the Venezia roman, which was later mated with an italic by Frederic Goudy. All Jones's faces are historical reconstructions. Linotype Granjon was the first commercial adaptation of a Garamond roman, mated with a Granjon italic.

LUI KARNER (1948–) Austrian typographer and letterpress printer. Codesigner, with Giovanni DeFaccio, of the Rialto family and partner in the digital foundry *df*Type.

MIKLÓS TÓTFALUSI KIS (1650–1702) Hungarian scholar, printer and typecutter. Kis was trained in Amsterdam and worked there and in Kolozsvár (now Cluj, Romania). Stempel Janson is struck and cast primarily from his surviving punches. Linotype Janson Text (both the metal and digital versions) and Monotype Erhardt are based on his work.

RUDOLF KOCH (1876–1934) German calligrapher and artist. His titling faces include Koch Antiqua and Neuland. His blackletters include Claudius, Jessen, Wallau and Wilhelm Klingspor Schrift. Kabel is his only sanserif. Much of his material, formerly in the Klingspor Archive, Offenbach, is now in the Haus für Industriekultur, Darmstadt.

HENK KRIJGER (1914–1979) Dutch typographer and visual artist, born and raised in Sumba, Indonesia. His Indonesian name is Senggih. Designer of several titling faces, the most important of which is Raffia.

JOOS LAMBRECHT (*c*. 1510–1556) Flemish punchcutter, typefounder and printer. Author of several fine romans, one italic and at least one textura. All of his original material has perished, but printed specimens survive.

VADIM VLADIMIROVICH LAZURSKI (1909–1994) Russian calligrapher and book designer. His Lazurski family includes both Cyrillic and Latin alphabets. The Cyrillic also exists in a proprietary foundry version known as Pushkin.

GUILLAUME LE BÉ *the elder* (1525–1598) French punchcutter working in Paris, Florence, Venice and Rome. Author of many Hebrew fonts, some fine romans and music types.

HENRIC PIETERSZOON LETTERSNIDER (*fl.* 1492–1511) Dutch punchcutter working at Gouda, Antwerp, Rotterdam and Delft. Author of a substantial number of blackletter types and fonts of large initials.

ZUZANA LIČKO (1961–) Slovakian immigrant to the USA. Cofounder of *Emigre* magazine and its offshoot, the Emigre digital foundry. Designer of Journal, Electrix, Modula and other faces. With John Downer, codesigner of Triplex.

RICHARD LIPTON (1953–) American graphic artist. Designer of Arrus. Codesigner, with Jacqueline Sakwa, of the script face Cataneo.

MARTIN MAJOOR (1960–) Dutch graphic artist trained at the Arnhem Academy. Designer of the Scala and Seria families.

GIOVANNI MARDERSTEIG (1892–1977) German immigrant to Italy. A master printer, scholar, typographer and type designer. Author of Dante, Fontana, Griffo and Zeno. His material is at the Officina Bodoni, Verona.

GABRIEL MARTÍNEZ MEAVE (1972–) Mexican type designer, working near Mexico City. His faces include Organica, Integra, Neocodex and Mexica.

ROD MCDONALD (1947–) Canadian graphic artist and type designer working in Toronto and, since 2002, in Halifax. His work includes the Laurentian family and Cartier Book, a family of type begun by Carl Dair.

HANS EDUARD MEIER (1922–) Swiss typographer. Designer of Barbedor, Syndor and the several versions of Syntax.

JOSÉ MENDOZA Y ALMEIDA (1926–) French graphic artist and type designer, working in Paris. His faces include Mendoza, Photina, Pascal, Fidelio (a chancery script), Sully Jonquières (an upright italic) and Convention.

OLDŘICH MENHART (1897–1962) Czech type designer and calligrapher. His serifed Latin faces include Figural, Menhart and Parliament. His Manuscript family includes both Latin and Cyrillic faces. His titling faces include Czech Uncial and Monument.

WILLIAM ROSS MILLS (1970–) Canadian type designer. Co-founder with John Hudson of Tiro Typeworks in Vancouver. Author of the Plantagenet Novus family (Latin, Greek and Cherokee) and two families of Canadian Syllabic type, Uqammaq and Pigiarniq, for setting Inuktitut. His historical revivals include the 1520 Garamond Roman.

ANTONIO DI BARTOLOMEO MISCOMINI (*c.* 1445–*c.* 1495) Italian punchcutter and printer, probably born in Bologna. He did most of his work in Venice, Modena and Florence, where he printed during the early 1490s and brought his roman and orthotic Greek types to final form.

GERRIT NOORDZIJ (1950–) Dutch typographer and teacher. From 1960 to 1990 he was responsible for training type designers at KABK (Koninklijke Academie van Beeldende Kunsten: The Royal Academy of Fine Arts) in The Hague, and thereby profoundly affected the course of modern type design in the Netherlands and elsewhere. Only one of his own designs is publicly available at present: the Ruse family, issued in digital form by the Enschedé Font Foundry.

Noordzij's 'Ruse' was originally 'Rus-E': version E of a face designed for a Russian bibliography. Specimens of five of his romans, four italics, two Greeks and one bastarda are included in Lommen & Verheul, *Haagse Letters* (1996).

PETER MATTHIAS NOORDZIJ (1961–) Dutch typographer and digital founder. Designer of PMN Caecilia and proprietor of the Enschedé Font Foundry.

FRIEDRICH PETER (1933–) Canadian calligrapher and visual artist, born in Dresden and trained in Berlin. Designer of the script faces Vivaldi and Magnificat.

ALEXANDER PHEMISTER (1829–1894) Scottish punchcutter. Author of the Old Style Antique issued by Miller & Richard, Edinburgh, beginning in 1858. In 1861 he moved to Boston where he worked for the Dickenson Foundry.

FRIEDRICH POPPL (1923–1982) German calligrapher. His serifed faces include Pontifex and Poppl Antiqua. His sanserif is Laudatio. His titling faces include Nero and Saladin. His script types include Poppl Exquisit and Residenz.

JEAN-FRANÇOIS PORCHEZ (1964–) French type designer; founder and proprietor of Porchez Typofonderie in Malakoff, near Paris. Designer of Angie, Apolline, Parisine, and the extensive Le Monde family, created for the Paris newspaper *Le Monde*.

RICHARD PORSON (1759–1808) English classical scholar. He designed the original Porson Greek, which was cut in steel by Richard Austin. Monotype Porson and the digital GFS Porson are based closely on his work.

EUDALD PRADELL (1721–1788) Catalan punchcutter and typefounder, working in Barcelona and Madrid. Some of the best eighteenth-century Spanish books are printed in his types.

VOJTĚCH PREISSIG (1873–1944) Czech artist, typographer and teacher, working in Czechoslovakia and in New York City. Preissig designed several text and titling faces, including the one that bears his name. His surviving drawings are in the Strahov Abbey, Prague.

ERHARD RATDOLT (1447–1528) German punchcutter and printer working at Augsburg and Venice. Author of at least ten blackletters, three romans and one Greek. In 1486 he issued the first known type specimen. (The one surviving copy is in the Munich State Library.)

IMRE REINER (1900–1987) Hungarian artist and designer working in Germany, the USA and Switzerland. He was a skilled wood engraver and book illustrator. Author of several Expressionist script faces.

PAUL RENNER (1878–1956) German typographer, type designer and teacher. Designer of Futura, Renner Antiqua, Renner Grotesk and the blackletter Ballade. His drawings for Futura are now in the Fundición Tipográfica Bauer, Barcelona.

JIM RIMMER (1934–) Canadian punchcutter and type designer. He has produced digital revivals of several of Frederic Goudy's faces and made new text faces – notably Amethyst and Albertan – in similar spirit. His titling faces include Credo, a revival of Robert Foster's Pericles.

BRUCE ROGERS (1870–1957) American typographer, working chiefly in Boston, London and Oxford. Designer of Montaigne and Centaur. The original drawings for Centaur are now in the Newberry Library, Chicago.

SJOERD HENDRIK DE ROOS (1877–1962) Dutch designer, typographer and printer. Author of the uncials Libra and Simplex, the Nobel sanserif, and De Roos roman and italic.

RUDOLPH RŮŽIČKA (1883–1978) Czech-born American typographer. Designer of Linotype Fairfield and Primer.

JACQUES DE SANLECQUE *the elder* (1558–1648) French punchcutter, student of Guillaume Le Bé the elder. Author of several fine romans and italics, music type, and a number of non-Latin faces, including Armenian, Samaritan and Syriac.

JACQUES DE SANLECQUE *the younger* (1613–1659) Son of the preceding. French punchcutter and founder revered for his technical finesse in cutting small sizes.

VICTOR SCHOLDERER (1880–1971) English classical scholar and librarian. Designer of the New Hellenic Greek.

FRANTSYSK HEORHII SKARYNA (*c.* 1488–*c.* 1540) Belarusian physician, translator and printer, educated at Kraków and Padova. Author of several fonts of Cyrillic type, with which he printed at Prague and Vilnius.

ROBERT SLIMBACH (1956–) American type designer, on staff at Adobe since 1987. His faces include Cronos, Adobe Garamond, Giovanni, Minion, Poetica, Slimbach, Utopia, Kepler and Warnock. His script faces include Sanvito and Caflisch. The Myriad family is a joint design by Slimbach and Carol Twombly.

FRED SMEIJERS (1961–) Dutch typographer and type designer. Author of the Quadraat family, Reynard, and the useful book *Counterpunch.*

ERIK SPIEKERMANN (1947–) German graphic artist and one of the founders of the FontShop digital foundry. Designer of the Meta and Officina families.

SUMNER STONE (1945–) American type designer and first director of the type department at Adobe Systems. Author of Silica, Cycles, Stone Print, and of the Stone typeface family, which includes serifed, unserifed and 'informal' series.

KONRAD SWEYNHEYM (*c.* 1415–1477) German monk and letterpress printer, working in central Italy. He is probably the author of the two romans and one Greek which he and his partner Arnold Pannartz used at Subiaco and Rome between 1464 and 1473.

GIOVANANTONIO TAGLIENTE (*fl.* 1500–1525) Italian calligrapher and designer of at least one chancery italic type. Monotype Bembo italic is derived from this font.

AMEET TAVERNIER (*c.* 1522–1570) Flemish typecutter and printer working primarily at Antwerp. Author of many romans, italics, blackletters and civilité script types.

GEORG TRUMP (1896–1985) German artist and type designer, initially a pupil of Ernst Schneidler. His serifed text faces include Mauritius, Schadow and Trump Mediäval. His blackletters include Trump Deutsch. His titling faces and scripts include Codex, Delphin, Jaguar and Time.

JAN TSCHICHOLD (1902–1974) German immigrant to Switzerland. Designer of the Sabon family and the Saskia script. Several of Tschichold's unproduced phototype designs were destroyed in the Second World War.

CAROL TWOMBLY (1959–) American type designer and visual artist. From 1988 to 1999 she was one of two type designers on staff at Adobe Systems. Her work includes the text family Chaparral and the titling faces Charlemagne, Lithos, Nueva, Trajan and Viva. Adobe Caslon is her digital revival of the work of William Caslon. With Robert Slimbach, she is the codesigner of the Myriad family.

GERARD UNGER (1942–) Dutch type designer and teacher. His serifed faces include Amerigo, Demos, Hollander, Oranda, Paradox and Swift. His unserifed faces include Argo, Flora and Praxis.

HENDRIK VAN DEN KEERE (*c.* 1540–1580) Belgian typecutter, working at Ghent and Antwerp. He cut many romans and blackletters, at least one script type (a civilité) and several fonts of music type. DTL Van den Keere roman is based on his work.

CHRISTOFFEL VAN DIJCK (1606–1669) Dutch punchcutter. Author of several Baroque romans, italics and blackletters. Monotype Van Dijck and DTL Elzevir are based on his work. Jan van Krimpen's Romanée and Gerard Unger's Hollander echo it in various ways. Most of Van Dijck's material has perished. The few surviving punches and matrices are at the Enschedé Museum, Haarlem.

JAN VAN KRIMPEN (1892–1958) Dutch typographer, for many years chief designer at Joh. Enschedé en Zonen, Haarlem. His type designs include Lutetia, Romanée, Romulus, Sheldon, Spectrum, Haarlemmer, Cancelleresca Bastarda (a chancery italic), Romulus Sans, Antigone Greek, Double Augustin Open Capitals, Lutetia Open Capitals and Romulus Open Capitals. Except for Haarlemmer and Sheldon, all these faces were first cut at Enschedé by Paul Helmuth Rädisch. Much of his work is still awaiting digital revival.

JOVICA VELJOVIĆ (1954–) Calligrapher and type designer born in Kosovo, trained in Belgrade, now working in Germany. His types include Gamma, Esprit, Ex Ponto, Silentium and Veljović.

JUSTUS ERICH WALBAUM (1768–1837) German typefounder and printer, author of several Neoclassical and Romantic faces. Both Berthold Walbaum and Monotype Walbaum are based on his surviving punches and matrices.

FREDERIC WARDE (1894–1939) American typographer, working chiefly in France, Italy and England. Designer of the

Vicenza and Arrighi italics. Some of Warde's drawings are in the Newberry Library, Chicago. Punches and matrices for the early (handcut) Arrighi are now at the Rochester Institute of Technology.

EMIL RUDOLF WEISS (1875–1942) German poet, painter, calligrapher and type designer. Author of a fraktur, a textura (Weiss Gotisch), a rotunda (Weiss Rundgotisch), Weiss Antiqua roman and italic, a suite of typographic ornaments, and three series of titling caps or initials. All these were cut by Louis Hoell and issued by the Bauer Foundry, Frankfurt.

ALEXANDER WILSON (1714–1786) Scottish punchcutter, typefounder and astronomer, working at Camlachie, near Glasgow. Author of the best romans, italics and Greeks produced in the Scottish Enlightenment.

BERTHOLD WOLPE (1905–1989) German calligrapher and typographer who spent his later life in England. Pegasus is his text face. His titling faces include Albertus and Hyperion.

HERMANN ZAPF (1918–) German master calligrapher, type designer, artist and teacher. His types include the roman and italic faces Aldus, Comenius, Euler, Hunt Roman, Marconi, Melior, Optima, Orion, Palatino, Zapf Book and Zapf Renaissance; the blackletters Gilgengart, Winchester and Stratford; the titling faces Kompakt, Michelangelo, Sistina and Zapf International; the Greeks Attika, Euler, Heraklit, Optima, Palatino Greek and Phidias; and the script faces Venture, Zapf Chancery, Zapf Civilité and Zapfino.

GUDRUN ZAPF-VON HESSE (1918–) German calligrapher and book artist. Her text and titling faces include Alcuin, Carmina, Diotima, Nofret, Ariadne and Smaragd.

A reliable encyclopedia of the world's typefoundries – metal, photographic and digital; present and past – would be a very useful document. It would also be a thick one. This brief list is limited to metal and digital foundries and matrix engravers that have issued or preserved original designs that seem to me of lasting value for setting text in Latin, Greek or Cyrillic.

Many of the type designers listed in appendix D (Robert Granjon, William Caslon, Hendrik van den Keere, for instance) also cast and sold their own type. Their foundries are listed again here only if (1) the foundries outlived their founders and developed into independent entities or (2) they are currently active.

The phone numbers, fax numbers and physical locations of foundries are subject to frequent change. Under present conditions, so is their financial health and consequent legal status. Current information is obtainable through the internet and the trade press. Other useful references include the consolidated catalogues of vendors such as Precision Type, in Commack, New York, and FontShop in Berlin, and the websites of on-line retailers such as MyFonts and Identifont.

Adobe Systems, San Jose, Calif. Fundamentally a software company, founded in 1982 by John Warnock and Charles Geschke. Adobe was the original developer of the PostScript computer language – one of the foundation stones of digital typography. It is also, with Microsoft, co-creator of the OpenType font format. In the early 1980s it established a digital foundry and an ambitious type development program directed by Sumner Stone. Adobe has issued digital versions of many historical types as well as original designs by Robert Slimbach, Carol Twombly, Jovica Veljović and many others.

Agfa, Wilmington, Mass. In 1988 Agfa-Gevaert absorbed the Compugraphic Corporation, a manufacturer of photosetting machines and film matrices. A digital foundry known as Agfa-Compugraphic was then formed and passed from hand to hand (e.g., it was for a time part of the Bayer Corporation). In 1997, Agfa acquired the remains of Monotype, and in 1998 a new firm, Agfa Monotype, was formed. Agfa per se issued new designs by Otl Aicher, David Siegel and others.

Amsterdam Foundry, Amsterdam. A metal foundry established in Rotterdam in 1851 by Nicolaas Tetterode with stock from the Broese Foundry in Breda. The firm moved to Amsterdam in 1856 and in 1892 changed its name from Lettergieterij N. Tetterode to Lettergieterij Amsterdam. Typecasting operations waned in the 1970s and ceased altogether in 1988. During the twentieth century it issued new designs by Sjoerd de Roos and Dick Dooijes. The surviving matrices and other materials are now at the library of the University of Amsterdam.

ATF (*American Type Founders*), Elizabeth, New Jersey. This was the largest metal typefoundry in North America, formed in 1892 by amalgamating a number of smaller firms. In its best days, it issued original designs by M.F. Benton, Lucian Bernhard, Frederic Goudy and many others. Though the company began to falter in the 1920s, it clung to life until 1993. Its library is now at Columbia University, New York. Much of the older typographic material is in the Smithsonian Institution, Washington, DC.

Bauer Foundry, Frankfurt. A metal foundry established in 1837 by Johann Christian Bauer. It expanded into an international network toward the end of the nineteenth century. The Bauer Foundry as such ceased to exist in 1972, but one branch of the old empire – the Fundición Tipografica Bauer (FTB) in Barcelona – has survived. (It is separately described in this list.) Bauer issued original faces by its founder and later by Lucian Bernhard, Imre Reiner, Paul Renner, Emil Rudolf Weiss and others. The surviving punches and matrices are now at FTB in Barcelona and at WMD in Leipzig.

Berlingska Stilgjuteriet, Lund, Sweden. A metal typefoundry and printing house important for its castings, during the twentieth century, of original faces by Karl-Erik Forsberg.

H. Berthold, Berlin. Hermann Berthold's metalworks entered the typefounding business in 1893. It acquired the original punches and matrices of J. E. Walbaum and later issued original faces by Günter Gerhard Lange, Herbert Post, Imre Reiner and others. Berthold was involved in the creation of phototype as early as 1935. It ceased casting metal type in 1978 and turned to producing digital fonts in the 1980s. This activity all but ceased in 1993, but the company has resumed selling its own digital fonts. The foundry's collection of punches and matrices is now in the care of the Museum für Verkehr und Technik, Berlin.

Bitstream, Cambridge, Mass. A digital foundry established in 1981 by Matthew Carter and Mike Parker, both of whom later left the company. Bitstream has issued digital revivals of many earlier faces and new designs by Carter, John Downer, Richard Lipton, Gerard Unger, Gudrun Zapf-von Hesse and others.

Carter & Cone, Cambridge, Mass. A digital foundry established in 1992 by Matthew Carter and Cherie Cone. It issues original designs and historical revivals by Carter.

Caslon Foundry, London. A metal typefoundry established by William Caslon about 1723 and maintained as a family business for four generations. It survived as the firm of H.W. [Henry William] Caslon until 1936. Most of the older surviving punches are now in the St Bride Printing Library, London. The newer material passed to Stephenson, Blake. In 1998, Justin Howes acquired rights to the name H.W. Caslon & Co. Under this name, his digital foundry in Northamptonshire issues the series known as Founder's Caslon.

Deberny & Peignot, Paris. Joseph Gaspard Gillé the elder, one of Fournier's apprentices, opened his own foundry in Paris in 1748 and left the business to his son in 1789. In 1827, the novelist Honoré de Balzac acquired this foundry as part of his intended writing, printing and publishing empire. The scheme failed at once, but the foundry was rescued by its manager and bought by Alexandre de Berny.

Gustave Peignot entered separately into the typefounding business in 1865. His own foundry entered its first creative phase under his son and grandson Georges and Charles Peignot, who issued historical revivals of the work of Jean Jannon and created a series of types based on the lettering of the eighteenth-century engraver Nicolas Cochin.

The De Berny and Peignot foundries merged in 1923. Under the guidance of Charles Peignot, the enlarged firm issued new designs by Adolphe Cassandre, Adrian Frutiger and others. When D&P ceased production in 1975, the type drawings and company library went to the Bibliothèque Forney, Paris, and most of the typographic material – including a set of original Baskerville matrices – to the Haas (now Fruttiger) Foundry, Münchenstein. Baskerville's punches, also formerly held by D&P, are now at the University Library, Cambridge.

df Type, Texing, Austria. A digital foundry established in 1999 by the Venetian calligrapher Giovanni DeFaccio and the Austrian printer-typographer Lui Karner. The foundry issues the Rialto family and other text and titling faces, rooted in DeFaccio's calligraphy.

DTL (*Dutch Type Library*), 's-Hertogenbosch, Netherlands. A digital foundry established by Frank Blokland in 1990. It has issued original faces by Blokland, Chris Brand, Gerard Daniëls, Sjoerd de Roos, Gerard Unger and others, and historical revivals of types by Christoffel van Dijck, Jan van Krimpen, J.M. Fleischman and Hendrik van den Keere.

EETS (Εταιρεία Ελληνικών Τυπογραφικών Στοιχείων). Listed here under its English name, GFS: *Greek Font Society*.

Elsner & Flake, Hamburg. A digital foundry established in 1989 by Günther Flake and Veronika Elsner. The firm has produced a large number of digital revivals and made the original digital versions of a number of ITC faces.

Emigre, Sacramento. A digital foundry established in Berkeley in 1985 by Rudy VanderLans and Zuzana Ličko. In 1992, the office moved to Sacramento. The firm issues original faces by Ličko, VanderLans, John Downer and others.

Joh. Enschedé en Zonen (Johann Enschedé & Sons), Haarlem, Netherlands. A printing plant and typefoundry operating from 1743 to 1990. In two and a half centuries of operation, the firm acquired material from many sources, including some of the punches and matrices of J.M. Fleischman and Christoffel van Dijck. During the early twentieth century, it issued in foundry form the types of its chief designer, Jan van Krimpen. In 1990, its stock of matrices and punches was transferred to the Enschedé Museum.

The Enschedé Font Foundry, Hurwenen, Netherlands. A digital foundry established in 1991 under the direction of Peter Matthias Noordzij. It has issued original designs by Bram de Does, Gerrit Noordzij, Christoph Noordzij, and Fred Smeijers.

Esselte Letraset, London. Letraset Ltd. was founded in 1959 as a manufacturer of dry transfer lettering. It was acquired by the Swiss firm Esselte in 1981 and a few years later began to issue its faces in digital form. The digital library now includes both historical revivals and original designs by Michael Gills, Michael Neugebauer and others.

Fann Street Foundry, London. A metal foundry established in 1802 by Robert Thorne. Its creative period came in the 1850s, when it was owned by Robert Besley and issued original designs cut by Benjamin Fox. The surviving material was acquired by Stephenson, Blake in 1905.

Font Bureau, Boston. A digital foundry established in 1989 by David Berlow and Roger Black. It has issued both historical revivals and original designs by John Downer, Tobias Frere-Jones, Richard Lipton, Greg Thompson and others.

FontShop International, Berlin. A digital foundry established in 1989 by Erik Spiekermann. It has issued original designs by Spiekermann, Erik van Blokland, Martin Majoor, Just van Rossum, Fred Smeijers and many others.

Walter Fruttiger, Münchenstein, Switzerland. The Fruttiger Foundry, operating under this name since 1989, traces its roots to an operation founded by Jean Exertier in 1580. For more than two centuries it was known as the Haas Foundry, after Johann Wilhelm Haas, who acquired the company in 1740. It now possesses little material from before the eighteenth century, and in its long life has not been the source of many original faces. In the first half of the twentieth century, however, Haas issued new designs by Walter Diethelm and, in 1951, the first versions of Max Miedinger's Helvetica. It does possess some original Baskerville matrices, acquired by Haas from D&P.

FTB (*Fundición Tipográfica Bauer*), Barcelona. A metal foundry established in 1885. It is the last surviving branch of the old Bauer network and now holds much of the Bauer Foundry's surviving typographic material. From 1922 to 1995 it was known as FTN, the Fundición Tipográfica Neufville – a name still used by the digital arm of the company.

Genzsch & Heyse, Hamburg. A metal foundry established in 1833 and absorbed by Linotype in 1963. It issued both blackletter and whiteletter types designed by Friedrich Bauer, Otto Hupp and others.

Golgonooza Letter Foundry, Ashuelot, New Hampshire. Established in 1980 by Dan Carr and Julia Ferrari, who cast type from Monotype matrices and issue Carr's own faces, some cut by hand in steel and others created in digital form.

Grafotechna, Prague. A metal typefoundry important for its castings of the work of Miloslav Fulín, Oldřich Menhart, Vojtěch Preissig and other Czech designers.

GFS (*Greek Font Society*), Athens. A digital foundry established in 1992. It has issued digital versions of historically important Greek types designed by Ambroise Firmin-Didot, Richard Porson and Victor Scholderer, as well as new Greek designs by Takis Katsoulides and George Matthiopoulos.

Haas Foundry. See *Walter Fruttiger.*

Hoefler & Frere-Jones, New York. Jonathan Hoefler established his own digital foundry in Manhatten in 1989. In 2004 the name was changed to reflect the increased role of his associate Tobias Frere-Jones. The firm has produced important designs by Hoefler and useful digital revivals of the Fell types.

Dr-Ing. Rudolf Hell. See *Linotype.*

Imprimerie Nationale, Paris. A printing house and foundry established by Louis XIII in 1640 as the Imprimerie Royale. With the French Revolution (1789), the Imprimerie Royale became first l'Imprimerie Nationale and then l'Imprimerie de la République. With the coronation of Napoleon I in 1804, it became l'Imprimerie Impériale. After the Restoration of 1815, it was again l'Imprimerie Royale. In 1848, after two more revolutions, it was l'Imprimerie Nationale once more. It has retained this name ever since – except for the hiatus, 1852–1870, under Napoleon III, when it reverted to l'Imprimerie Impériale. It owns the surviving punches and matrices of Jean Jannon (the source of most of the world's 'Garamonds') and a large quantity of historically important material for the typography of Asian languages. Over the years it has sponsored new designs by many hands, including Firmin Didot, Philippe Grandjean, Marcellin Legrand, Louis-René Luce and José Mendoza y Almeida. It is the one surviving institution with punchcutters on salary.

Intertype (International Typesetting Machine Co.), New York. When the basic Mergenthaler Linotype patents expired in 1912, a group of investors had assembled in New York, ready to build a competing, and very similar, machine. Its matrices included new adaptations of foundry faces designed by Dick Dooijes and S.H. de Roos. The firm was involved in phototypesetting as early as 1947. After a merger in the 1950s, it was known as the Harris Intertype Corporation and became a principal manufacturer of photographic matrices.

ITC (*International Typeface Corporation*), New York. Founded by Aaron Burns and Herb Lubalin in 1969 as a typeface licensing and distribution agency. The original domain was limited to phototype. In the 1980s, ITC began to license digital designs as well. Not until 1994 did it start to produce and market its faces directly. For more than a decade, there was a readily identifiable ITC style: a standardized large torso with interchangeable serifs that reduced the alphabet and its history to superficial costume. This Procrustean approach to type design faded in the 1980s. Coincidentally, the company was bought in 1986 by Esselte Letraset. The list includes original designs by Ronald Arnholm, Matthew Carter, Erik Spiekermann, Hermann Zapf and many others.

Klingspor Brothers, Offenbach. A metal foundry established in 1842 and operated under several different names before its acquisition in 1892 by Karl Klingspor. It issued original faces by Peter Behrens, Rudolf Koch and Walter Tiemann. After its closure in 1953, the library and drawings were transferred to the Klingspor Museum, Offenbach, and most of the matrices to the Stempel Foundry, Frankfurt.

Lanston Monotype Machine Co., Philadelphia. The Monotype machine as we know it was devised by John Sellers Bancroft of Philadelphia in 1900. It grew, however, from a series of earlier machines invented by Tolbert Lanston of Washington, DC, beginning in 1887. The American company created to manufacture and sell these devices started slowly and was soon outdistanced by its English counterpart, formed a decade later with the same objective and almost the same name (see below: *The Monotype Corporation*). The American firm nevertheless remained in business, moving to Philadelphia in 1901 and pursuing on a smaller scale its own design agenda. This included cutting mats for historical revivals and original designs by Frederic Goudy, Sol Hess and others. The surviving material was dispersed in 1983.

Lanston Type Co., Mt Stewart, Prince Edward Island. In 1983 Gerald Giampa acquired a collection of patterns and drawings from the Lanston Monotype Company of Philadelphia. With this foundation, he established a digital foundry in Vancouver, moving to PEI in 1994. The library consists almost entirely of digitized versions of American Monotype faces, especially work by Frederic Goudy.

LetterPerfect, Seattle & New York. A digital foundry established in 1986 by Paul Shaw and Garret Boge. It has specialized in titling faces, including many with carefully researched inscriptional pedigrees.

Linotype Library, Bad Homburg. In Brooklyn in 1886, Ottmar Mergenthaler began to sell his newly invented Linotype machine. This led to the founding of the Mergenthaler Linotype Co., Brooklyn, and Mergenthaler Linotype & Machinery Ltd., Manchester, both in 1890. Their German ally, Mergenthaler Setzmaschinen-Fabrik, Berlin, was created in 1896. Many of the early matrices were produced under contract by the Stempel Foundry, Frankfurt, from designs by artists such as Warren Chappell, Georg Trump and Hermann Zapf. Others were produced in England from the designs of George W. Jones, and in the USA from designs by W.A. Dwiggins, Rudolph Růžička and others.

Linotype began producing photosetting equipment in the 1950s, CRT (cathode ray tube) photosetters in the 1960s, and high-resolution laser setters in the 1980s. The German firm, which had relocated to Frankfurt in 1948, merged in 1990 with Dr.-Ing. Rudolf Hell GmbH of Kiel.

In 1997, Linotype's digital foundry was spun off under the name the Linotype Library, which relocated to Bad Homburg, north of Frankfurt, in 1998. It has issued many of the old Linotype faces in digital form, and new designs by Adrian Frutiger, Hermann Zapf and many others. A large collection of early material from the American branch of the company is now at the Rochester Institute of Technology, Rochester, New York, and the University of Kentucky, Lexington.

The Ludlow Typograph Co., Chicago. Washington Ludlow of Chicago began making typecasting machinery in 1906, but the Ludlow caster which his company sold throughout the early twentieth century was a later device, designed and built by William Reade in 1909. The machine casts slugs from handset proprietary matrices and was therefore used for little except display type, but several Ludlow faces have been successfully adapted for digital text composition. The company issued both historical revivals and original designs, chiefly by its director of typography, R.H. Middleton. It ceased operation in North America in 1986. The English arm, founded in the early 1970s, closed in 1990.

Ludwig & Mayer, Frankfurt. A metal foundry established circa 1920 and closed in 1985. The surviving material was transferred to FTB in Barcelona. During its heyday, the firm issued original designs by Jakob Erbar, Helmut Matheis, Ilse Schüle and others.

Mergenthaler. See *Linotype.*

Miller & Richard, Edinburgh. A metal foundry established in 1809 by George Miller, joined by Walter Richard in 1832. The foundry issued original designs by Richard Austin, Alexander Phemister and others. When it ceased operation in 1952, the surviving material went to Stephenson, Blake.

The Monotype Corporation, Redhill, Surrey, England. An entity called the Lanston Monotype *Company* was first formed in the USA in 1887. Another, called the Lanston Monotype *Corporation* (later simply the Monotype Corporation) was formed in England a decade later. For the American firm, see *Lanston Monotype.*

The typographically creative phase of the English firm began in 1922 with the appointment of Stanley Morison as typographic advisor. Over the next few decades, English Monotype cut a number of meticulously researched historical revivals as well as new designs by Eric Gill, Giovanni Mardersteig, José Mendoza y Almeida, Victor Scholderer, Jan van Krimpen, Berthold Wolpe and others. The firm began producing photosetting equipment and photographic matrices in the 1950s, and laser typesetting machines in the 1970s.

In the early 1990s a new and smaller company, Monotype Typography, was spun off to produce and market digital type, including digital reincarnations of the faces originally cut in metal for the Monotype machine. This firm merged with Agfa in 1999, becoming Agfa Monotype. Metal matrices are still made on demand in England by the Monotype Trust.

Nebiolo Foundry, Torino. A metal typefoundry established in 1878 by Giovanni Nebiolo through the amalgamation of several older and smaller firms. It is important for its castings of original designs by Alessandro Butti and Aldo Novarese. Nebiolo ceased operation about 1990.

Neufville Foundry, Barcelona. See FTB.

Norstedt Foundry, Stockholm. A metal foundry, formerly supplied with matrices by Robert Granjon, François Guyot, Ameet Tavernier and others. The surviving material is now in the Nordiska Museet, Stockholm.

Fonderie Olive, Marseilles. A metal foundry which ceased operation in 1978. It issued a number of original designs by Roger Excoffon, François Ganeau and others. The surviving material is now at the Fruttiger Foundry, Münchenstein.

ParaType, Moscow. Successor (as of 1998) to the ParaGraph (or Parallel Graphics) digital foundry, which was founded in 1989. It issues original designs and historical revivals of Cyrillic, Latin, Georgian, Arabic, Hebrew and Greek faces.

Pie Tree Press & Foundry, New Westminster, British Columbia. Jim Rimmer's press and foundry, started in 1960, now produces both metal and digital type by Rimmer and others.

Plantin-Moretus Museum, Antwerp. The printing house and foundry established by Christophe Plantin about 1555 was conserved for nearly three centuries by descendants of Plantin's son-in-law, Jan Moretus. It was converted to a museum in 1877. It includes a rich collection of original material by Claude Garamond, Robert Granjon, Hendrik van den Keere, Ameet Tavernier and other early artists.

Polygraphmash (НПО Полиграфмаш), Moscow. The Institute for Machine Printing. Its drawing office, active from 1938 to 1992, issued type designs by Galina Bannikova, Nikolai Kudryashev, Pavel Kuzanyan, Vadim Lazurski, Anatoli Shchukin and others.

Scangraphic, Hamburg. Formerly Mannesmann Scangraphic, a manufacturer of photosetting equipment. In the 1980s it began to issue digital fonts. These were poorly finished but included one important design by Hermann Zapf.

Schelter & Giesecke, Leipzig. Johann Gottfried Schelter and Christian Friedrich Giesecke established this foundry in 1819. Many of the early faces were designed by Schelter himself. In 1946 the firm was nationalized as Typoart.

D. Stempel, Frankfurt. After its foundation by David Stempel in 1895, this firm absorbed the holdings of many other German foundries. It also issued many original faces by Hermann Zapf, Gudrun Zapf-von Hesse and others, and sold type cast from the original matrices of Miklós Kis. After the foundry closed in 1986, the typographic material was transferred to a museum known as the Haus für Industriekultur in Darmstadt. The tools of Stempel's last master punchcutter, August Rosenberger (who cut the original versions of Zapf's Palatino) are now in the Gutenberg Museum, Mainz.

Stephenson, Blake & Co., Sheffield, England. A metal foundry established in 1819 by John Stephenson, James Blake and William Garnet, using materials acquired chiefly from William Caslon IV. Over time, the firm has added further material from the Fann Street Foundry, the original Caslon Foundry, and other operations. Much of the inherited typographic material is now in the fledgling London Type Museum, though the company still casts and sells some type.

Stone Type Foundry, Palo Alto. A digital foundry established in 1991 by Sumner Stone. It issues Cycles, Silica and other faces designed by its proprietor.

Tetterode. See *Amsterdam Foundry.*

Tiro Typeworks, Vancouver. A digital foundry established in 1994 by John Hudson and William Ross Mills. It is named for Marcus Tullius Tiro, the Roman slave (freed in 53 BC) who served as Cicero's scribe. Tiro has developed extensive expertise in the design and encoding of non-Latin faces, especially those involving many contextual alternates.

Typoart, Dresden & Leipzig. A metal foundry formed in 1946 by nationalizing the existing operations of Schelter & Giesecke and Schriftguss. From 1964 until 1995, when operations ceased, the head of design was Albert Kapr. The surviving typographic material is now at WMD, Leipzig.

URW (*Unternehmensberatung Karow Rubow Weber*), Hamburg. Established as a software firm in 1971, URW was diverted into digital typography by Peter Karow, a physicist excited by typography, who joined it in 1972. It was the original developer of the Ikarus system for digitizing type and of the HZ system for paragraph-based justification. It issued a large number of historical revivals as well as original faces by Hermann Zapf, Gudrun Zapf-von Hesse and others. The firm entered receivership in 1995. Its library has since been distributed by a corporate successor known as 'URW++.'

Johannes Wagner, Ingolstadt. Established at Leipzig in 1902 by Ludwig Wagner and relocated to Ingolstadt in 1949 by his son Johannes. It has acquired matrices from Berthold, Johns, Weber and other foundries, and continues to cast type.

C.E. Weber Foundry, Stuttgart. A metal foundry established in 1827. It issued original faces by Georg Trump and others before it closed in 1971. The surviving material was bought by the Stempel and by Wagner foundries.

WMD (*Werkstätten und Museum für Druckkunst*), Leipzig. A working typographic museum founded in 1994 by Eckehart Schumacher-Gebler. Its large stock of typographic material includes original punches and matrices by Johann Christian Bauer, Lucian Bernhard, Jakob Erbar, Albert Kapr, Paul Renner, Jacques Sabon and many others.

Y&Y, Carlisle, Mass. A digital foundry specializing in fonts and system software for the setting of mathematics and scientific texts. It has issued original designs by Charles Bigelow, Kris Holmes and Hermann Zapf.

FURTHER READING

The items flagged by small caps seem to me essential works of reference or benchmark publications in the field.

1. BOOKS & ARTICLES

Adobe Systems Inc. *PostScript Language Reference Manual.* 3rd ed. Reading, Mass. 1999.

Amert, Kay. "Origins of the French Old Style: The Types of Simon de Colines," *Printing History* 26/27 (1992): 17–40.

Anderson, Donald M. *The Art of Written Forms.* New York. 1969.

Avrin, Leila. *Scribes, Script and Books: The Book Arts from Antiquity to the Renaissance.* Chicago & London. 1991.

Barker, Nicolas. *Aldus Manutius and the Development of Greek Script and Type in the Fifteenth Century.* 2nd ed. New York. 1992.

Benjamin, Walter. "The Work of Art in the Age of Mechanical Reproduction," in Benjamin, *Illuminations.* London. 1970.

Bennett, Paul A., ed. *Books and Printing: A Treasury for Typophiles.* Cleveland. 1951.

Berry, John, ed. *Language Culture Type: International Type Design in the Age of Unicode.* New York. 2002.

BIGELOW, Charles, & Donald DAY. "Digital Typography." *Scientific American* 249.2 (August 1983): 106–119.

Bloomfield, Leonard. *Language.* New York. 1933.

Blumenthal, Joseph. *Art of the Printed Book, 1455–1955.* New York. 1973.

Bringhurst, Robert. "On the Classification of Letterforms" et seq. Parts 1–5. Claremont, Calif.: *Serif* 1–5 (1994–97).

———. *The Solid Form of Language: An Essay on Writing and Meaning.* Kentville, Nova Scotia. 2004.

Burke, Christopher. *Paul Renner.* New York. 1998.

CARTER, Harry. *A View of Early Typography.* Oxford. 1969.

Carter, Sebastian. *Twentieth-Century Type Designers.* London & New York. 1987.

Carter, Thomas F. *The Invention of Printing in China and Its Spread Westward.* 2nd ed, revised by L. Carrington Goodrich. New York. 1955.

Books & Articles

Catalogue of Books Printed in the XVth Century Now in the British Museum. 12 vols. London. 1908–85.

Chappell, Warren, & Robert Bringhurst. *A Short History of the Printed Word.* 2nd ed. Vancouver. 1999.

Chiang Yee. *Chinese Calligraphy: An Introduction to Its Aesthetic and Technique.* 3rd ed. Cambridge, Mass. 1973.

Chicago Manual of Style. 15th ed. Chicago. 2003.

Consuegra, David. *American Type Design and Designers.* New York. 2004.

Coulmas, Florian. *The Writing Systems of the World.* Oxford. 1989.

Dair, Carl. *Design with Type.* 2nd ed. Toronto. 1967.

DANIELS, Peter T., & William BRIGHT, ed. *The World's Writing Systems.* New York. 1996.

Davids, Betsy, & Jim Petrillo. "The Artist as Book Printer." In Joan Lyons, ed., *Artists' Books.* New York. 1985.

Day, Kenneth, ed. *Book Typography 1815–1965.* London. 1966.

DeFrancis, John. *Visible Speech: The Diverse Oneness of Writing Systems.* Honolulu. 1989.

Degering, Hermann. *Lettering.* New York. 1965.

Diringer, David. *The Hand-Produced Book.* London. 1953. Reprinted as *The Book Before Printing,* New York. 1982.

Dowding, Geoffrey. *Finer Points in the Spacing and Arrangement of Type.* 3rd ed. London. 1966.

Dreyfus, John, ed. *Type Specimen Facsimiles.* 2 vols. London. 1963–72.

———. *The Work of Jan van Krimpen.* The Hague. 1952.

Duncan, Harry. *Doors of Perception.* Austin, Texas. 1987.

EISENSTEIN, Elizabeth L. *The Printing Press as an Agent of Change: Communications and Cultural Transformations in Early-Modern Europe.* 2 vols. Cambridge, UK. 1979.

———. *The Printing Revolution in Early Modern Europe.* Cambridge, UK. 1983.

Enschedé, Charles. *Typefoundries in the Netherlands,* translated with revisions and notes by Harry Carter. Haarlem, Netherlands. 1978.

Fairbank, Alfred, & Berthold Wolpe. *Renaissance Handwriting.* London. 1960.

Felici, James. *The Complete Manual of Typography.* Berkeley. 2003.

Fine Print on Type: The Best of Fine Print Magazine on Type and Typography. San Francisco. 1988.

Fournier, Pierre Simon. *Fournier on Typefounding*, translated & edited by Harry Carter. London. 1930.
Friedlaender, Henri. *Typographische ABC: Een beknopt overzicht der grondbeginselen van degelijke typographie.* Den Haag. 1939.
Gaur, Albertine. *A History of Writing.* London. 1984.
Gelb, Ignace J. *A Study of Writing.* 2nd ed. Chicago. 1963.
GILL, Eric. *An Essay on Typography.* 2nd ed. London. 1936.
Goudy, Frederic W. *Goudy's Type Designs.* 2nd ed. New Rochelle, NY. 1978.
———. *Typologia: Studies in Type Design and Type Making.* Berkeley & Los Angeles. 1940.
GRAY, Nicolete. *A History of Lettering.* Oxford. 1986.
———. *Lettering as Drawing.* 2 vols. Oxford. 1970. Reprinted as one vol., 1971.
Grimes, Barbara F., ed. *Ethnologue: Languages of the World.* 14th ed. 2 vols. Dallas. 2000.
[Grinevald, Paul-Marie.] *Les Caractères de l'Imprimerie nationale.* Paris. 1990.
Handbook of the International Phonetic Association. Cambridge, UK. 1999.
[HART, Horace, et al.] *Hart's Rules for Compositors and Readers.* 39th ed. Oxford. 1983.
Hlavsa, Oldřich. *A Book of Type and Design.* New York. 1961.
Huntley, H.E. *The Divine Proportion: A Study in Mathematical Beauty.* New York. 1970.
Huss, Richard E. *The Development of Printers' Mechanical Typesetting Methods 1822–1925.* Charlottesville, Virginia. 1973.
Hutner, Martin, & Jerry Kelly, ed. *A Century for the Century: Fine Printed Books from 1900 to 1999.* New York. 1999.
International Organization for Standardization. *Information Processing: Eight-bit Single-byte Coded Graphic Character Sets.* ISO 8859. Parts 1–9. Geneva. 1987–89.
———. *Information Technology: Universal Multiple Octet Coded Character Set.* ISO 10646. Parts 1–3. [Rev. ed.] Geneva. 2000–2003.
Искусство шрифта: Работы московских художников книги. Москва. 1977.
Itten, Johannes. *The Art of Color*, translated by Ernst von Haagen. New York. 1961.
JASPERT, W. Pincus, et al. *Encyclopedia of Typefaces.* 5th ed. London. 1983.

Jeffery, Lilian H. *The Local Scripts of Archaic Greece.* 2nd ed. Oxford. 1990.

Jensen, Hans. *Sign, Symbol, Script,* translated by George Unwin. London. 1970.

JOHNSON, Alfred F. *Selected Essays on Books and Printing.* Amsterdam. 1970.

———. *Type Designs.* 3rd ed. London. 1966.

Johnston, Edward. *Formal Penmanship and Other Papers,* edited by Heather Child. New York. 1971.

———. *Writing and Illuminating and Lettering.* Rev. ed. London. 1944.

Kapr, Albert. *The Art of Lettering.* Munich/New York. 1983.

———. *Fraktur: Form und Geschichte der gebrochenen Schriften.* Mainz. 1993.

———. *Johann Gutenberg.* Aldershot, Hants. 1996.

Karow, Peter. *Digital Typefaces: Description and Formats.* 2nd ed. Berlin. 1994.

Kenney, Edward J. *The Classical Text: Aspects of Editing in the Age of the Printed Book.* Berkeley. 1974.

Kinross, Robin. *Modern Typography: An Essay in Critical History.* London. 1992.

Knight, Stan. *Historical Scripts.* 2nd ed. New Castle, Delaware. 1998.

KNUTTEL, Gerard. *The Letter as a Work of Art.* Amsterdam. 1951.

Koch, Peter, et al. *Carving the Elements.* Berkeley. 2004.

Lange, Gerald. *Printing Digital Type on the Hand-Operated Flatbed Cylinder Press.* 2nd ed. Marina del Rey, Calif. 2001.

Lawson, Alexander. *Anatomy of a Typeface.* Boston. 1990.

Layton, Evro. *The Sixteenth Century Greek Book in Italy.* Venice. 1994.

Le Bé, Guillaume [le jeune]. *Sixteenth-Century French Typefounders,* edited by Harry Carter. Paris. 1967.

Le Corbusier. *The Modulor.* 2nd ed. Cambridge, Mass. 1954.

Legros, Lucien A., & John C. Grant. *Typographical Printing Surfaces.* London. 1916.

Lommen, Mathieu, & Peter Verheul, ed. *Haagse letters.* [Amsterdam.] 1996.

Lunde, Ken. *CJKV Information Processing.* Sebastopol, California. 1999.

McGrew, Mac. *American Metal Typefaces of the Twentieth Century.* New Castle, Delaware. 1993.

McLean, Ruari. *Jan Tschichold: Typographer.* London. 1975.
———. *Thames and Hudson Manual of Typography.* London. 1980.
Macrakis, Michael S., ed. *Greek Letters: From Tablets to Pixels.* New Castle, Delaware. [1997.]
March, Lionel. *Architectonics of Humanism.* Chichester, West Sussex. 1998.
MARDERSTEIG, Giovanni. *Scritti di Giovanni Mardersteig sulla storia dei caratteri e della tipografia.* Milano. 1988.
Martin, Douglas. *Book Design: A Practical Introduction.* New York. 1989.
Massin, [Robert]. *Letter and Image.* London. 1970.
Meggs, Philip B. *A History of Graphic Design.* New York. 1983.
Middendorp, Jan. *Dutch Type.* Rotterdam. 2004.
Millington, Roy. *Stephenson Blake: The Last of the Old English Typefounders.* London. 2002.
MORISON, Stanley. *First Principles of Typography.* New York. 1936.
———. *Letter Forms: Typographic and Scriptorial.* New York. 1968.
———. *Politics and Script.* Oxford. 1972.
———. *Selected Essays on the History of Letter-forms.* 2 vols. Cambridge, UK. 1981.
Morison, Stanley, & Kenneth Day. *The Typographic Book, 1450–1935.* London. 1963.
Morison, Stanley, et al. *A Tally of Types.* 2nd ed. Cambridge, UK. 1973.
Mumford, Lewis. *Art and Technics.* New York. 1952.
NOORDZIJ, Gerrit. *The Stroke of the Pen.* The Hague. 1982.
———. *De Streek: Theorie van het schrift.* Zaltbommel, Netherlands. 1985.
———. *Letterletter.* Vancouver. 2001.
Pankow, David, ed. *American Proprietary Typefaces.* [Rochester, NY.] 1998.
Panofsky, Erwin. *Perspective as Symbolic Form.* New York. 1991.
Paput, Christian. *La Gravure du poinçon typographique.* Paris. 1990.
Parkes, M.B. *Pause and Effect.* Berkeley. 1993.
Prestianni, John, ed. *Calligraphic Type Design in the Digital Age.* San Francisco. 2001.
Pullum, Geoffrey K., & William A. Ladusaw. *Phonetic Symbol Guide.* 2nd ed. Chicago. 1996.

Pye, David. *The Nature and Art of Workmanship*. Cambridge, UK. 1968.

Re, Margaret, et al. *Typographically Speaking: The Art of Matthew Carter.* Baltimore. 2002.

Ritter, Robert M. *The Oxford Guide to Style.* Oxford. 2002.

ROGERS, Bruce. *Report on the Typography of the Cambridge University Press.* Cambridge, UK. 1950.

Ryder, John. *Flowers and Flourishes.* London. 1976.

Sampson, Geoffrey. *Writing Systems: A Linguistic Introduction.* Stanford, Calif. 1985.

Scholderer, Victor. *Greek Printing Types 1465–1927.* London. 1927.

Senner, Wayne M., ed. *The Origins of Writing.* Lincoln, Nebraska. 1989.

Шицгал, А.Г. *Русский типографский шрифт.* Москва. 1985.

Smeijers, Fred. *Counterpunch.* London. 1996.

Snyder, Gertrude, & Alan Peckolick. *Herb Lubalin.* New York. 1985.

Son Po-Gi. *Han'guk ui ko hwalcha / Kankoku no kokatsuji / Early Korean Typography.* rev. ed. Seoul. 1982.

Spencer, Herbert. *Pioneers of Modern Typography.* Rev. ed., Cambridge, Mass. 1982.

STEINBERG, S.H. *Five Hundred Years of Printing.* 3rd ed., rev. by James Moran. London. 1974. 4th ed., rev. by John Trevitt. New Castle, Delaware. 1996.

STEVENS, Peter S. *Patterns in Nature.* Boston. 1974.

Stevick, Robert D. *The Earliest Irish and English Bookarts.* Philadelphia. 1994.

SUTTON, James, & Alan BARTRAM. *An Atlas of Typeforms.* London. 1968.

Thompson, Bradbury. *The Art of Graphic Design.* New Haven, Connecticut. 1988.

THOMPSON, D'Arcy. *On Growth and Form.* Cambridge, UK. 1917. Rev. ed., 1942; abridged by J.T. Bonner, 1961.

Tracy, Walter. *Letters of Credit.* London. 1986.

Tschichold, Jan. *Asymmetric Typography.* New York. 1967.

———. *The Form of the Book,* edited by Robert Bringhurst. Vancouver. 1991.

TUFTE, Edward R. *Envisioning Information.* Cheshire, Connecticut. 1990.

———. *The Visual Display of Quantitative Information.* 2nd ed. Cheshire, Connecticut. 2001.

———. *Visual Explanations: Images and Quantities, Evidence and Narrative.* Cheshire, Connecticut. 2001.
Twitchett, Denis. *Printing and Publishing in Medieval China.* London. 1983.
Type and Typography: Highlights from Matrix. West New York, NJ. 2003.
UNICODE Consortium. *The Unicode Standard.* Version 4.0.0. Boston. 2003. [Online at www.unicode.org.]
UPDIKE, Daniel Berkeley. *Printing Types: Their History, Forms and Use.* 2nd ed. 2 vols. Cambridge, Mass. 1937.
Vervliet, H.D.L. *Cyrillic and Oriental Typography in Rome at the End of the Sixteenth Century: An Inquiry into the Work of Robert Granjon.* Berkeley. 1981.
———. *Sixteenth-Century Printing Types of the Low Countries,* translated by Harry Carter. Amsterdam. 1968.
———, ed. *The Book through Five Thousand Years.* London. 1972.
Veyrin-Forrer, Jeanne. *La Lettre et la texte.* Paris. 1987.
Warde, Beatrice. *The Crystal Goblet.* London. 1955.
WARDROP, James. *The Script of Humanism.* Oxford. 1963.
WASHBURN, Dorothy K., & Donald W. CROWE. *Symmetries of Culture: Theory and Practice of Plane Pattern Analysis.* Seattle. 1988.
West, Martin L. *Textual Criticism and Editorial Technique Applicable to Greek and Latin Texts.* Stuttgart. 1973.
Wick, Karl. *Rules for Typesetting Mathematics.* Prague. 1965.
Williamson, Hugh. *Methods of Book Design.* London. 1983.
Wilson, Adrian. *The Design of Books.* New York. 1967.
Wittkower, Rudolf. *Architectural Principles in the Age of Humanism.* 3rd ed. London. 1962.
Yardeni, Ada. *The Book of Hebrew Script.* Jerusalem. 1991.
ZAPF, Hermann. *The Fine Art of Letters.* New York. 2000.
———. *Hermann Zapf and His Design Philosophy.* Chicago. 1987.
———. *Manuale Typographicum.* Frankfurt. 1954. Rev. ed., Cambridge, Mass. 1970.
———. *Manuale Typographicum 1968.* Frankfurt & New York. 1968.
———. *Typographic Variations.* New York. 1963. Reissued, New Rochelle, NY. 1978.
Zimmer, Szczepan K. *The Beginning of Cyrillic Printing.* New York. 1983.

2. PERIODICALS

Fine Print. San Francisco. Quarterly. 16 vols, 1975–90. [Complete index published as issue 16.4, 2003. See also *Fine Print on Type* (1988).]

The Fleuron. Cambridge, UK. Annual. 7 vols, 1923–30.

Journal of the Printing Historical Society. London. Annual, 1965– .

Letter Arts Review. Published 1982–93 as *Calligraphy Review.* Norman, Oklahoma. Quarterly, 1982– .

Letterletter. Journal of the Association Typographique Internationale. Münchenstein, Switzerland. Semiannual through 1990, then biennial. 15 issues in all, 1985–96. [See also Gerrit Noordzij, *Letterletter* (2001).]

Matrix. Andoversford, Glos. Irregular, 1981– . [See also *Type and Typography: Highlights from Matrix* (2003).]

Parenthesis. Journal of the Fine Press Book Association. London, San Francisco, etc. Irregular, then semiannual, 1993– .

Printing History. Journal of the American Printing History Association. New York. Semiannual, 1979– .

Serif. Claremont, California. Irregular. 6 issues, 1994–98.

Typografische Monatsblätter. St Gallen, Switzerland. Monthly, then bimonthly, 1881– .

Typographica. London. Irregular, then semiannual. 13 + 16 issues. 1949–59; new series, 1960–67.

Typography Papers. Reading, Berks. Annual, 1996– .

Visible Language. Published 1967–70 as the *Journal of Typographic Research.* Cleveland. Quarterly, 1967– .

3. A SAMPLING OF WEB RESOURCES

Alphabets of Europe: www.evertype.com/alphabets
Ethnologue: www.ethnologue.com/web.asp
International Phonetic Association: www.arts.gla.ac.uk/IPA/ipa.html
Microsoft Digital Foundry List: www.microsoft.com/typography/links/links.asp?type=foundries&part=1
Omniglot: www.omniglot.com/writing/atoz.htm
Type Libraries & Museums: www.tug.org/museums.html
Unicode: www.unicode.org

AFTERWORD TO THE THIRD EDITION

Typography, like language, is more important to me for what it allows to happen than for anything it accomplishes on its own. I hope that in writing a book on the subject I have not given the impression that either typography or design is an end in itself.

A few old friends and typographic mentors are mentioned in the foreword. I owe thanks to many others. These include Christian Axel-Nilsson, Charles Bigelow, Frank Blokland, Fred Brady, Dan Carr, Matthew Carter, Sebastiano Cossia Castiglioni, Bur Davis, James Đỗ Bá Phước, Bram de Does, the late John Dreyfus, Paul Hayden Duensing, Richard Eckersley, Peter Enneson, Christer Hellmark, Richard Hendel, Sjaak Hubregtse, John Hudson, Peter Karow, Peter Koch, John Lane, Ken Lunde, Linnea Lundquist, Jim Lyles, Rod McDonald, the late Michael Macrakis, George Matthiopoulos, William Ross Mills, Thomas Milo, Gerrit Noordzij, Peter Matthias Noordzij, Thomas Phinney, Will Powers, Jim Rimmer, Richard Seibert, Robert Slimbach, Jack Stauffacher, Sumner Stone, Adam Twardoch, Carol Twombly, Gerard Unger, Ken Whistler, Glenda Wilshire, Vladimir Yefimov, Doyald Young and Maxim Zhukov – who have made this a much better book, and its author a less ignorant human being, in a variety of ways.

Translations of the work – especially those into Russian and Greek – have put me increasingly in touch with typographers far more at home than I with Greek, Cyrillic and other non-Latin type. Their careful reading and engagement with the text has taught me many things. In this regard, I'm especially grateful to Vladimir Yefimov and Maxim Zhukov.

Most of the drawings were made by hand for the original edition and recreated for the second in digital form by Glenn Woodsworth.

For those concerned about such things, I might record that the first edition of this book was set in Ventura Publisher software, the second edition in Quark, and the third in InDesign. With each such shift has come a marked increase in technical capability. I have still, in every case, been obliged at times to subvert the software, forcing it to do things its makers didn't foresee, or things they did foresee and expressly excluded.

The book has involved the close testing of many fonts of type, most of them digital, some of them metal. These have come from nearly all the active foundries listed in appendix E, and from some whose operations have now ceased.

It remains the case that I have never yet tested a perfect font, no matter whether it came in the form of foundry metal, a matrix case, a strip of film or digital information. I have tested very beautiful and powerful designs, and extraordinary feats of hardware and software engineering, but no font has crossed my path that could not be improved by sensitive editing. One reason is, the task is never done: no designer can foresee the inner logic of all possible texts and languages, nor all the other uses to which type is rightly put. Another reason is that setting type is a collaborative exercise, like acting from a script or playing from a score. The editing of type, like the editing of music, and the tuning of fonts, like the tuning of instruments, never ends.

There are those who dream of a perfect world in which copyrighted text is translated into copyrighted glyphs through copyrighted rules with no more human intervention than it takes to feed a tape to a machine, while money flows in perpetuity to everyone involved. There are also those who think that putting chairs and air-conditioners in hell will make it just as good as heaven. Actually, working with type is an earthly task, much less like sitting down and turning on TV than like walking on your hands across an ever-varied, never-ending landscape that is otherwise too far away to see.

INDEX

The names of typefaces are italicized in this index, but no distinction is made between generic names, such as *Garamond* or *Bodoni*, and specific ones, such as *Bembo* or *Aldus*.

Sunday

Ben cracked his eyes open through the fog of tequila still lingering in his brain from the night before. Squinting, he could make out the shape of a very attractive naked woman tiptoeing around his apartment collecting her clothes. He closed his eyes and let his head fall back on the pillow with a smile, partly for the memory of the previous night and partly at what a pathetic cliché he had become.

Seeing him awake, she said, "I'm going to run out for some coffee," as she was getting dressed. "Do you want some?"

"Sure," Ben replied, thinking that there was at best a 50 percent chance she would return—at least

those are the odds he would give himself in the same situation.

After she left, Ben hauled himself up and threw on some boardshorts and a T-shirt. He fed his dog and opened the door to his small yard so the dog could go outside and handle his morning business. Reflecting on the coffee/naked woman situation, he decided to hedge his bet with some instant coffee of indeterminate age from his cabinet. He watched the crystals dissolve in the hot water and felt the smell of the coffee start to bring him back to planet Earth. He took a sip and stumbled out the door to check the surf, leaving it unlocked in case Jessica decided to come back. Jessica? Jennifer? He was 98 percent sure that it was Jessica.

He wandered down the park on the bluffs where he could check the waves all the way from the Crystal Pier to PB Point. It was a perfect California day: two- to three-foot waves, slightly offshore winds, sunny with cool water—the perfect hangover cure. Ben trotted back to his house, giddy at what the surf gods had given him and also cursing his drinking, knowing his surf performance would be maybe a 67 percent at best today due entirely to his tequila consumption the night before. (Who drinks tequila at his age anyway?)

He got back to his house—no Jessica, no gourmet coffee. Relieved to a small degree, but also in an equally

small way disappointed, he grabbed his longboard and his wetsuit and jogged down to the Point. It would be less crowded there on a weekend, and the long paddle and the shallow rocks would keep the punters at the beach breaks. Ben surfed the Point for a few hours, getting his share of waves, but he took his time paddling back out after each one to make sure that the bounty was shared. Hunger finally got the better of him, and he took one in, all the way past the stairs to the sand.

Coming out of the water, Ben had the silly grin that he always got after a good surf. Surfing was the only thing that hadn't let him down, avoided him, or outright betrayed him in his adult life. He walked over to his favorite café at the Pier, knowing that the morning crush of tourists with oddball questions such as "What time do the surfers start?" would have died down by now. He dropped his board on the patio, took his wetsuit down to his waist, and got in line. At the cash register, Ben traded pleasantries with Jose, who had worked there for twenty years and was also Ben's neighbor. Ben always envied Jose's simplicity: his simple job and simple life at the beach with his family. Ben's life, until the last few years, had been the opposite—so complicated—and the lingering memories of those complications seemed to continue to make his life feel complicated when, at least from the outside, Ben just pretty much looked like a loser. Ben ordered

his usual, Desayuno Gigante Numero 2. At thirty-six, Ben was still young enough to get away with eating a giant dome of eggs, potatoes, cheese, and bacon for breakfast so long as he kept surfing, but he knew the clock was ticking on his metabolism.

Ben strolled back to his apartment after his late breakfast. Ben lived in a horseshoe of single-story apartments built in the '50s in Pacific Beach, in San Diego, California. He had lived there almost ten years and had no plans to leave. Rent was cheap, and he had a small yard and a garage for his car, his surfboards, and his fishing gear; life was goodish. Pacific Beach was a small community on the water in San Diego, populated chiefly by college students, US Marines from Camp Pendleton partying on leave, and tourists. There was also a small population of old-style beachcombers that Ben fit in with perfectly. These were the types of guys who had originally come back from World War II with very little incentive to fit into regular society after what they had seen and done and had moved to the beach to fish, surf, and drink. They created their own way of life at the edge of the continent and on the fringe of society. These were the guys that Hollywood stereotyped badly with the *Gidget* films. As the urban center pushed toward the water and the rural character of the beach changed with the exit of the last farms, they aged out and were replaced with the Vietnam-era guys, who ended up at the beach for many of the same

reasons as their forebearers and lived much the same life. These crew members were just now phasing themselves out due to a mixture of sun, age, and drugs. Luckily for Ben, the wars of the years 2001–2014 had produced a new crop of misfits for him to hang out with at the beach and get wasted with in between surfs.

On Ben's wall hung four framed documents: two degrees from USC (criminal justice and law), his graduation certificate from the FBI Academy, and his discharge papers from Pelican Bay Correctional Facility. The remaining artwork on the wall consisted of whatever was cheap and had looked decent at a suburban-mall store circa 1999. The rest of his apartment was decorated in the style of late twentieth-century cast-off garbage. You could tell his furniture was at one time nice, but it had been abused and neglected for at least ten years. His beachcomber friends thought he had a "sick pad," which might have been more descriptive than anything else that could be written about it.

Ben's garage, however, was another story. In his garage, he had a rack on the wall for all ten of his surfboards of all lengths, from the rhino chaser to the fish to the longboard, all designed and built for a different purpose, including some designed and built by Ben himself. He had an equally complete rack of wetsuits, trunks, and rashguards all for different water temperatures around the world. On the other side was

another rack of board bags to safely shepherd his boards through the brutish machinations of the modern airline industry. Everything in the garage had a purpose and was overbuilt to it. His surfboard racks were made from diamond plate; his garage floor shined like a ballroom dance floor. He kept both spaces clean—he had learned fastidiousness in prison—but the garage especially so; it was his happy place, brightly lit and filled with purpose as opposed to the apartment itself, which seemed designed to store a living human until it died.

Ben went to his small backyard, watered his potted tomato plant, and then went to the fridge, got a Pacifico, and sat down on his formerly nice couch. He clicked on his TV and took a long draught of beer. He picked up an open copy of *Zen and the Art of Motorcycle Maintenance* from his coffee table (also formerly nice), read a few pages, and set it back down. He grabbed his remote and started scrolling through his Netflix queue, hoping to find something interesting, at least until the beer started to work its magic. He settled on something about the Nazis taking all of Europe's artwork and grabbed another beer. He dozed off as it started to rain. An unknown time later, he slowly became aware of something in the room. He opened his eyes and saw that his front door was standing open; rain was pouring outside. He grabbed a hockey trophy left by a previous tenant from the side table as a means of self-defense and went into the kitchen. Standing

over the sink with a tumbler filled with ice and whiskey was Jessica, soaking wet, with fresh stitches in her head and a blood-stained T-shirt. The dog was with her, looking up at her face and slowly wagging his tail. She looked at Ben and said, quite directly, "You need to help me."

Benjamin Harrison Adams was named after a decidedly mediocre president of the late nineteenth century, one that family lore had as a distant relative. Ben grew up in Evanston, Illinois, a tony suburb of Chicago. His father, Chester, was the grandson of the founding partner of one of the oldest and most well-regarded law firms in Chicago with an entire floor of the Willis (formerly Sears) Tower to themselves. Ben grew up in a typically WASP, East Coast–style environment, filled with country clubs, yacht races, private schools, and various sports befitting the type, such as skiing and tennis.

Unbeknownst to his parents, during his senior year of high school, Ben had only applied to colleges west of the Mississippi. He couldn't articulate it at the time, but the stifling nature of life in the Adams household had started pushing him away. When Ben told his parents that he was headed out west for college, they were beside themselves.

"USC?" they asked incredulously. "What happened to Northwestern like the rest of the family as we discussed?"

They were disappointed to say the least, but they thought perhaps he would come back east for law

school and rejoin the family tradition after he indulged his wildness on the West Coast. He did end up going to law school, but he didn't come back. Staying at USC for law induced yet more gasps from the family. That it was a top-twenty-ranked law school with an exceptional reputation had no bearing; it was so "western" and so "LA" with all the Jews, queers, and unnamed Hollywood types. It was not the path that the family wanted for their son. The final straw came when Ben got accepted for special agent training with the FBI. To the family, public service was by itself so low, but to be carrying a gun and a badge and interacting with the hoi polloi was simply beyond comprehension. The FBI was for Mormons—everybody knew that—Irish Catholics at the very least. It was certainly not for the good WASP stock that Benjamin Harrison Adams came from. It wasn't a complete break, but the family didn't quite embrace him as closely after that. His brothers went into law and banking, spending summers at the yacht club with their kids and otherwise living up to type. The family was humming along nicely with only one piston named Ben misfiring, but at least he hadn't become a jazz musician like his cousin, so he wasn't blackballed entirely. That would come later.

If Ben was honest with himself, the seeds of his exit from polite society had come the first time he took a hydrodynamic piece of fiberglass out into the surf at

Malibu in his second year at USC. Like so many before him, it became less of a sport and more of a disease. At five feet ten inches tall and naturally athletic and lean, he had taken to surfing easily—as easily as one can in an entirely dynamic environment. In addition to his standard university courses, he, like most surfers before him, became an amateur meteorologist, oceanographer, marine zoologist, and geographer. He became all of the things necessary to score good waves in an environment that was completely defined by chaos theory. He checked tide reports, weather forecasts, and underwater-bathymetry charts on the off chance that the millions of surfers that had come before him had missed anything along the coast, and there lay some as-yet-undiscovered surf spot on the California coast. (There wasn't.)

His family certainly would not understand surfing, so he kept it to himself. At holidays, they must have seen the bright tan line across his neck indicating the collar height of a wetsuit, but if they knew what it was, they didn't let on. They probably didn't even notice, as imagination was in short supply in the Adams family. Always athletic (it was expected, after all), from the moment Ben had started surfing, he ceased all his previous athletic pretentions—tennis, football, all of it. Being on the West Coast, his family didn't notice this either—or if they did, they didn't say anything. His obvious continued fitness gave reasonable doubt to any ideas they had

of him as no longer participating in the sports that he had grown up with. He still went skiing with the family over the holidays, but with the lines, the resorts, and the amateur fashion shows, it seemed much less honest to Ben than being alone in the ocean.

He had gotten through the FBI Academy at Quantico, Virginia, easily, scoring expert for marksmanship and getting an award for academics. His surfing skills helped him out in the aquatic portion of training; his only competition in that arena were the former navy SEALs in his class. Because of his overall fitness, he was as good as anyone in defensive tactics, which he liked: it felt good to take out violent aggression in an environment with minimal consequences. He fit in with his class well enough, but his classmates were puzzled that on the weekends, instead of studying in the dorms or partying on M Street in Georgetown, Ben would head to Virginia Beach, Ocean City, Maryland, or the Outer Banks of North Carolina to search for waves. The East Coast can be pretty finicky for surf, but for him, the search was half of the experience; the waves themselves, a bonus. He would return to his dorm room at Quantico on Sunday nights with sandy feet and a bit of a spring in his step as he went back to the serious business of training to be an FBI special agent.

He finished the academy with a high class ranking, which gave him priority in his choice of field office,

getting his third choice, San Diego, after LA, number one, and Honolulu, number two. He was assigned to the money-laundering group in the San Diego field office. In those early post-9/11 days, the job everybody wanted was the Joint Terrorism Task Force, which was a multiagency force run by the FBI and housed in their office. Rookie agents were not usually assigned to JTTF, at least not in that climate, so Ben went to Money Laundering. Ben adapted easily to life as a fed. If you could get past the politics, bureaucracy, and the FBI's almost pathological aversion to risk, the work was interesting and fun. Money Laundering investigations were largely about chasing paper and computer files, but often getting those files required old-fashioned police work, surveillance, search warrants, etc. If he worked hard, kept with the dress code, showed up to the interminable meetings, and didn't rock the boat too badly, he could do his job without too much interference and enjoy doing it.

The end had come about four years into his career at the FBI. Ben had been asked by one of the guys in his unit to help out with a case and sit on a house overnight. It was the early stages of the case, so there wasn't a lot of pressure yet; his only job was to keep the house under surveillance and just note the comings and goings, with appropriate identification of people, vehicles, license plates, etc. It was pretty standard investigations stuff, and since there wasn't to be

any enforcement action, riding solo was fine. There was another agent parked at the end of the block as tactical backup if need be, but more likely he would be called on to clarify whether it was a *2* or a *Z* on a license plate as it went by or whether it was a late-model Buick or Chevy or to give him a heads-up for anybody coming down the street.

The house belonged to an Afghani heroin syndicate that was laundering their money through a string of convenience stores in Southern California. It was a nondescript midcentury-modern house in the middle-class neighborhood of Clairemont. Ben set up around 11:00 p.m. down the street with a good view of the driveway to get any vehicle make, model, or license plates and maybe even a passable description of anybody walking in or out of the house. With a thermos of Jamaican Blue Mountain coffee, decent cheese and crackers, and some kooky talk radio, Ben settled in for the night, rightly thinking that there were much worse ways to earn a living. There was not much action for the first few hours.

Around 1:45 a.m., a silver late-model Ford Taurus, California tag number 7CSY564, with a male driver in his midthirties of medium height and build with dark hair, a medium complexion, and no obvious distinguishing marks pulled up into the driveway, went into the house for about twenty minutes, and then left in

the same car. At around 2:30 a.m. Ben took a drink of his coffee, when he saw a shadow move in his rear-view mirror. Checking again, he saw a male of medium build, height, and complexion in a crouch approaching his car with a gun in his right hand. Ben reacted instantly, his much-vaunted FBI training taking over as designed.

He burst out of the driver's-side door and rotated to face the threat as he pulled his pistol out, raised it up, and fired once. He had been taught to shoot center mass, but he came in a little high and hit his assailant right in the throat, severing the spine and killing him before he fell to the ground. DEA Special Agent Ruben Nunez fired his weapon four times; the first three hit in a tight group right into Ben's chest—his firearms' instructors at the DEA Academy would have been proud. The fourth shot went a little high and to the left, passing through Ben's left trapezius, going wide of the other bullets, likely as a result of Ben's bullet hitting him in the neck. Both Special Agents Nunez and Adams were wearing their ballistic vests; Ben's saved his life, Ruben's did not.

During the aftermath and the following investigation, it was revealed that the FBI case agent hadn't run his operation through the Law Enforcement Deconfliction Center as was protocol. Had he done so, he would have known that the DEA had a takedown

and search warrant planned for the same location that very morning at six. Special Agent Nunez had been there to keep an eye on the house and to make sure that there were no surprises for the entry team in the morning. He saw Ben's unmarked car, confirmed via radio that it wasn't DEA, and went to detain and interview what he believed to be countersurveillance by the bad guys. In retrospect, it was obvious to all that the right thing to do would have been to call for some backup or have a San Diego Police Cruiser come by and pull a traffic stop and field interview on the FBI car, but SA Nunez had a reputation as a bit of a cowboy, so he went to take care of it himself.

The shitstorm that followed included accusations, counter-accusations, denials, insults, and criminal charges. Special Agent Ruben Nunez had a brother who was a San Diego District Attorney and a bit of a cowboy himself. As soon as the funeral was over, he went looking for justice for his brother. The FBI was willing to take the bad press on a bad shoot by one of their agents rather than accept the implication by the newspapers of systemic incompetence of the agency for failing to deconflict. Ultimately Ben was fired and disowned by the FBI and prosecuted by the State of California and District Attorney Nunez for voluntary manslaughter. The proverbial jury of twelve people not smart enough to get out of jury duty convicted him. He was sentenced to six years in Pelican Bay State Prison,

one of California's toughest prisons with the harshest forms of isolation.

Ben was sent there not for the egregiousness of his conduct but for protection: his background in law enforcement would not likely have endeared him to the rest of the general population of California's prison system. That it was for his own protection did little to ease the suffering that was twenty-three-hour lockdown and isolation. Ben treated his imprisonment as if it were law school or the FBI Academy; he knew how to mentally endure unpleasant things. This was obviously on a different scale, but he adapted. He got into yoga and meditation. He could kill hours standing in Warrior One and keeping his mind empty. They kept both his body and mind in reasonably good shape.

Mercifully, the Pelican Bay had a good selection of literature to pass the time as well. He read *The Count of Monte Cristo* no less than ten times and *The Decline and Fall of the Roman Empire* twice—all seven hundred and four pages of it. Prison was mostly about boredom. Ben had read somewhere that the best way to survive captivity was to become "The Gray Man," invisible to everyone else—the type of person not worth antagonizing or even acknowledging. At Pelican Bay, it wasn't as important because he was segregated from the population, but he still had to interact with the guards. So that is what he did; he basically put himself in a trance for

five years. He got the occasional jeer from the guards, but he was mostly treated with civility or otherwise ignored; it seemed that the guards were as bored as he was.

His only real outside contact during that time had been a once-a-week visit with his attorney, a friend from law school named Tyler who was unafraid of suing anybody and everybody if he thought he could squeeze some justice and a nice fee out of it. During these visits, they would discuss Ben's pending case against the FBI for a whole suite of torts related to his gunshot wound, dismissal, and imprisonment. The settlement amount went undisclosed, and no wrongdoing was admitted, but Ben's bank account went into the meaty part of seven figures as a result. Perhaps not surprisingly, virtually none of Ben's family visited. Being a convicted felon, rightly or wrongly, was just too much for them. Ben's brother Asher visited a few times early on but stopped under pressure from his in-laws who had a son running for a highly contested US Senate seat back east.

When Ben got released, the first thing he did was buy an old Jeep, a new quiver of surfboards, and a tent. He proceeded to get lost in Baja California for about five months. He had heard that after release from prison, some people had a hard time adjusting to the freedom and the decision making, preferring

the regimented life of the prison system. Not Ben; he just basked in it, never planning anything longer than forty-five minutes out and bristling at anything resembling an order. He started a bit slow, spending his first week at San Miguel, a mere hour from the border, but eventually he navigated all the way down from Cuatro Casas to Scorpion Bay to Zippers at the end of the peninsula just outside of Cabo San Lucas.

Feeling lonely one night in his tent, he went into Cabo to party, but it had the opposite of the intended effect; the crowds and the noise made him uneasy and defensive, so he slinked away back into the desert and the waves. He hit a few East Cape and Sea of Cortez spots before working his way up the waveless east coast of Baja, surfcasting for his food and reveling in the splendid isolation. Eventually, his beard long enough, his body fit enough, and his clothing dirty enough, Ben returned to Pacific Beach in San Diego, where he rented an apartment month to month a few blocks from the ocean, and where he had remained for seven years.

On the streets in La Paz, he had picked up a medium-sized spotted mongrel dog that he named Geronimo, partly for the scowl that he wore that to Ben looked an awful lot like the scowl that the Apache warrior wore in all of the photographs Ben had seen and partly as an honor to the warrior for his lifelong struggle against the US government that Ben had only

really started to appreciate after his trial and incarceration. Back in San Diego, he would occasionally do some legal work so that to anyone who cared, he could claim to have a job, but mostly he just surfed, read, and drank.

He gave Jessica some new clothes, inspected the work of the emergency-room doctor, and pronounced it fit: seven stitches perfectly lined up across her hairline that wouldn't even be visible in a few months. He reappraised her with a mostly sober perspective: a five-foot-seven-inch brunette in her midtwenties with an athletic but still-feminine body. Ben felt pretty good about his decision-making process for the last twenty-four hours. She sat down on the couch next to Geronimo, who wagged his tail slightly. She closed her eyes, tilted her head back, and took a long drink of whiskey.

"What the fuck happened?" asked Ben.

Jessica exhaled slowly and said, "I'm not really sure..."

"Just start at the beginning."

"OK. This morning I left your place and walked around for a while, looking for a place to get us some coffee. This isn't my neighborhood, so it took me longer than I thought. I found a place on Garnet Avenue, grabbed two coffees and a couple of croissants, and started back here. Because of the convoluted route that I took to find the coffee, it was easier to duck

through the alley behind Fillipi's Pizza Grotto to get back. I only noticed it because I remembered that you wouldn't shut up last night about how great the pizza is there, going on and on about it. I mean c'mon, it's just a fucking pizza..."

Ben had a vague memory flash through his head from the night before of trying to impress her with his cool local- beach knowledge, and he smirked at his own idiocy when it came to trying to get girls.

"Anyway, I ducked down the alley, and two guys fell in right behind me and nailed me on the head with something hard. I fell down to the ground and put my hands up to stop the next blow, and somebody from the end of the alley screamed. I heard a siren chirp, and the guys must have bolted because the next thing I knew, I was staring up at a couple of cops, a bum, and a bunch of other people doing the walk of shame on Sunday morning.

"Did they take your purse?" he asked.

"No, I didn't have one, just thirty-five dollars, my phone, and my ID in my pocket, and they didn't take any of those either."

"They must have been spotted before they could get your cash or worse. So then what?"

"I went to the ER, got my head stitched up, and spent the rest of the day talking with the police, filling out paperwork, and repeating my story no less than fifteen times."

"Strange for a robbery or rape attempt in broad daylight on a Sunday morning, even for PB. What did the police say?"

"They said exactly what you just said, robbery attempt or possible rape attempt."

"Eyewitnesses?"

"Sort of. Several drunk or hungover people said they saw two guys follow me into the alley and nail me on the head with something shiny."

"What about a description? They must have something?"

"I didn't see them. They came up from behind, but the witnesses described them as two guys of unknown race wearing hooded sweatshirts, sunglasses, jeans, and sneakers. Very helpful, I know."

"Wow, that sucks. I guess it could have been worse. I'm glad that you are more or less OK, and I'm actually

very glad you came back. I thought you blew me off, and I was a little bummed."

"Only a little?"

"OK, maybe medium-grade bummed."

"Ha. OK, good enough, but like I said, you need to help me."

"I don't understand, What do you need? How can I help you?"

"Well, last night, when you weren't boring me with tall tales of Filippi's Pizza Grotto, you were telling me what a badass FBI agent you used to be."

Ben cringed as the rest of the evening's memories came back to him in a flood. He had definitely been laying it on thick, trying to keep this girl interested—up to and including dropping the FBI card. It only ever had a fifty-fifty chance of working since half the time they would assume that he was lying since he no longer had the credentials to back up his claim, although it did segue nicely into, "Well, if you don't believe me, I can show you my graduation certificate from the FBI Academy at my apartment." But by the time that desperate line came out of the holster, he was only looking

at a 25 percent chance, at best, of it coming off. It was usually so late in the game at that point that he had nothing to lose, so he would go all in to try to get the girl.

"Jeez, I am sorry about that. I was drinking pretty heavily, and I liked you a lot, so I used all of my best tricks."

"So it's not true?" she asked incredulously.

"Oh, it's completely true, every word of it. I'm just not sure how it was really relevant then or, even more importantly, now."

"I'll tell you how, smart guy. I don't think what happened to me today was random. I think that they were trying to kill me specifically, like in bad movies."

Ben sighed and waited to hear what was sure to be some long-winded and slightly crazy interpretation of what seemed to him to be a random criminal act.

"You don't believe me," she said.

"I have no belief for or against at this point," he said, lying but trying to keep an open mind for the sake of not being a total asshole. "Tell me why you think so."

"Well, right before I got hit on the head, I am pretty sure I heard one of them ask, 'Are you sure this is the girl?' Immediately after this, I heard the other one say, 'Yup,' and then bammo! I got whacked on the head."

"Are you sure that is actually what you heard? You have had a head injury you know."

"No, I'm not sure because I have had a *head injury*, but I think so."

Though dulled by seven years of mild intoxication, the part of Ben's brain that used to be a criminal investigator started swimming upstream toward her story. "OK," he said. "What else have you got?"

"Well, related to today, that is it."

"What do you mean? Have people been trying to kill you on other days? And if so, why didn't you mention this last night, so I could have blown you off and gotten the hell out of there?"

"No, nobody has tried to kill me before, but some strange things have been going on lately."

"OK, let's have it," Ben demanded, motioning with his hand, his flickering brain starting to accept the remote possibility that this might not be total bullshit.

"Do you remember last night when I told you about my master's thesis?"

Ben had a vague recollection of talking about it, but with all the tequila and the noise, all he had really remembered was that it had something to do with water. "Sort of; give it to me again."

"Jesus. How drunk were you? OK, as you may or may not remember, I am working on a master's degree at UCSD in earth sciences, and my thesis relates to the Colorado River Compact of 1922 and how the impending water shortages in the west due to climate change are going to lead to more and more conflict. That is it in a nutshell."

"No wonder they want to kill you; that sounds dumb."

"Fuck you. This is serious stuff. Have you ever heard the expression that whiskey is for drinking, and water is for fighting over?"

"I was just kidding. Please go on."

"Did you even know that in 1934 the governor of Arizona sent the National Guard up the Colorado River to scout an area with which to make war against

California if it didn't guarantee their allotment of Colorado River water south of the Parker Dam?"

"OK, OK; it was only a joke. Tell me how this all relates."

"Fine. I have been researching this project for a year with no issues, just standard academic work with the usual university politics, and as part of my research, I called a professor in Arizona who is one of the leading researchers into the history of water rights of the Colorado River to get some historical context for my thesis, and when I talked to him, he basically told me that he was done working on it and not to call him ever again."

"That doesn't sound that weird."

"Not when I tell it, but the way he spoke it was as if I was a debt collector, not a master's student. He blew me off the way you would if you were at the end of your rope and were freaking out. Also, this is this guy's life's work; to just get out of the field entirely and abruptly doesn't add up to me."

"That seems a bit strange, but it is still a long walk from a university professor in another state having personal problems to somebody trying to kill you. What else have you got?"

"Well, ever since that call, other strange things have been happening to me."

"Like what, for example?"

"Like when I get home to my apartment, I get the feeling that someone has been there. I can't put my finger on why, but it feels like some things have been moved around."

"Anything specific?"

"Nothing that won't make me sound like I am crazy—like I could swear that I had a six-pack of Pacifico in my fridge..."

"Nice."

"Yeah, thanks, but when I came home from class, it was gone."

"Old boyfriend with a key?"

"Nope. I changed the locks as soon as that mutant moved out."

Ben was starting to get interested, not necessarily because he thought that there was any merit to her

story yet, but she was very cute, he liked her attitude, and he really had nothing better to do.

"OK, what else?"

"Lately there have been a couple of guys sitting in a sedan on my street a lot. Every time I leave my apartment, there they are looking right at me and my building, and I wouldn't swear to it, but I think I saw the car again on campus."

"That could be any number of cops, spies, private investigators, or whatever sitting out there for any number of reasons. In San Diego, between SDPD, SDSO, FBI, DEA, HSI, harbor police, secret service, etcetera, there are a million investigations going on all the time all over the city."

"Yeah, but on my street all of the time?"

"Maybe it is a coincidence. Can you describe the guys?"

"No. Dark-tinted windows, but I got a plate number on the car."

"Good girl; what is it?"

"I don't know, it is written down at my apartment. But the car is a dark-blue Ford Crown Victoria."

"Sounds like law enforcement to me, but maybe we can exclude that as a possibility," Ben said, wondering if any of his old friends would bend the rules on running license plates for nonofficial purposes. "OK. Go home and get some rest, and we can take a fresh look at this in the morning."

"Fuck that. I'm staying here. You are going to go to my place, get my stuff, and bring it back here. Please."

Ben bristled a bit at being commanded so, but he was also a little bit excited that she was going to stay and that they were going to have a bit of an adventure together even if it was all for nothing—maybe especially because it was all for nothing.

Ben fired up his jeep and headed out to Mission Valley, the valley home to the San Diego River and the site of the first Spanish settlement in Alta California. Named after the Mission San Diego de Alcala, Mission Valley was now home to car dealers, hotels, shopping malls, and apartments, but with lots of palm trees and opposing hillsides, it wasn't without its charms. He drove past Jessica's apartment complex, a three-story set of buildings around a central courtyard in an architectural style most likely to evoke the word *box*. He had his hat

pulled down low, mostly out of habit rather than any real need for stealth. He spotted the blue Crown Vic with two males parked on the street and cruised past them.

Parking one block over, Ben went into her apartment building through the back door where he wouldn't be seen. He let himself in with the key she had given him. Since the window faced the street where the unknown dudes in the Crown Vic were, he didn't turn on the lights. There was enough light coming in through the window to somewhat find his way around. He could tell even in the dark that the place had been searched. Not the thorough rat-fucking type of a search that law enforcement often does to true dirtbags, but a more professional search by someone actually looking for something specific.

She had told him to grab the messenger bag on the coffee table, which had some of her thesis research and her notes on the guys in the car outside. The bag was there, but it was empty. *Perhaps this adventure was somewhat legit,* Ben thought. He grabbed the bag and went to the bedroom to get some clothes in case she wasn't coming back for a while. Selecting a woman's clothing was way out of his skill set, but he gave it a try. He pulled together enough clothing for a week and a variety of weather and social conditions. He went to the bathroom to get a toothbrush and saw a wetsuit hanging in the shower. He didn't remember her telling

him that she surfed—even hammered, he would have remembered that. He grabbed that as well.

Going back through the apartment, he saw a six-foot-four-inch swallowtail shortboard by Channel Islands behind the kitchen door. He was definitely taking that back to the beach. A quick pass by the refrigerator saw that there were in fact four of an original six Pacificos sitting in their cardboard vehicle. Not caring whether or not these were the missing Pacificos from Jessica's story, he grabbed them and bundled them on top of his now-bulging armload of stuff. He had to make multiple trips to get it all out to his car, but by using the back door to the apartment building and being parked down the block, he was able to get away with it and not be seen by the guys out front.

His booty loaded in the jeep, he crept down the block to get up behind the Crown Vic and jotted down the plate number. The windows in the Crown Vic were cracked, so Ben hid behind the car for a few moments to see if he could catch some incriminating conversation. All he got were their names, Karl and Dennis, a loud fart by Dennis, followed by louder recriminations by Karl, followed by some reference to the stink of Kandahar. It wasn't much to work with but he had to suppress a giggle as he snuck away back to his jeep. He was actually having some fun. That it was becoming

apparent that he was possibly involved in a conspiracy to murder a girl he liked wasn't lost on him. It was just that he hadn't done anything interesting in a long time, and he had a rusty set of investigative skills that wanted to come out and play. This, combined with the persistent state of nihilism he maintained since he had been released from prison, made him feel like he did as a kid, almost like he was playing capture the flag again at summer camp by the lake in the North Woods of Wisconsin. He drove back to the beach smiling, shamelessly drinking one of the Pacificos on the way.

He walked into his apartment with his loot from her place, gently set down the surfboard, and said, "You didn't tell me you surfed!"

"Did you get the stuff?"

"Where do you normally paddle out?"

"What about my research? My notes on the bad guys?"

"Oh, that—sorry. Your apartment has been mildly ransacked, and your stuff was taken from the bag, *but* there were Pacificos in the refrigerator!" he said accusingly as he popped the lid off of one and showed it to her before taking a big drink.

"I bought more, smart guy. What do you mean *ransacked?*"

"Well," he said, wiping his mouth with his sleeve, "it looked like a professional job—nothing destroyed, but everything seemed like it had been gone through, and your messenger bag was empty. I grabbed a bunch of clothes for you and your wetsuit and your six-four Al Merrick, which brings me back around to…"

"I usually paddle out at Scripps before class-happy?"

"I guess. Why didn't you tell me before?"

"You seemed so stoked to be telling me all the ins and outs of getting waves and playing the intrepid, globetrotting surfer; it was kind of cute. I didn't have the heart to stop you."

"Jeez," he said, disappointed.

"So with my stuff gone, we're back to square one?"

"Not exactly. I saw the guys, and I got their plate number. I might be able to twist a few arms and get some idea of who they are."

"Sweet. When do we do that?"

"Start first thing tomorrow."

"You told me last night that you are a lawyer; tomorrow is Monday. Don't you have to go to work?"

Ben gulped at another piece of his act from the previous night coming home to roost. "Not really. I only practice law randomly when certain jobs fall in my lap. For example, a few months ago, I helped an old friend from the Bureau with his divorce, but I don't really work that much."

"So…I don't get it. How do you pay the rent and buy all of those beers? The twenty surfboards?"

"It is kind of a long story, but I'll give you the CliffsNotes version. A few years ago, I sued the FBI for a couple million bucks after they sent me to prison. They settled the case while I was in the can, so once I got out, I didn't really have to worry about money anymore so long as I live pretty simply."

"Prison? Jesus Christ, I haven't the foggiest idea who you are, do I? Why did you go to prison? Although damn, maybe I don't want to know…"

"It isn't quite as bad as you think, or maybe it is, I'll let you decide. Here is what happened…" Ben

proceeded to tell her the whole story without dramatic embellishment for about an hour, after which she seemed slightly relieved—at least of that part of her worry. She still retained her worry about being the target of an assassination attempt. They polished off the remaining Pacificos and fell into bed together in a slightly more sober and slightly less awkward sexual repeat of the night before.

Monday

Ben woke up just as the sky was lightening; he nudged Jessica, whispering, “Let’s go for a surf.”

“Fuck off. Doctor says no ocean for ten days after stitches in cranium. Leave me alone,” she said through her hair covering her face.

Ben got out of bed, changed into his wetsuit, and checked the surf report online. Surfline still showed yesterday’s report, two- to three-foot waves with good shape. He was up earlier than they could check and upload today’s report, so he would have to risk it. He knew that the current swell was fading; he only hoped that there were enough leftovers to remain fun. Geronimo jumped in his jeep while he placed

his six-foot-two-inch Rusty swallowtail in the back. He drove over to Windansea in La Jolla, figuring that at this hour, the famous break would be slightly less crowded with assholes.

As he turned down Bonaire Street, he could see that the waves looked good, and the crowd looked manageable, so he parked and paddled out. Geronimo went on his own shoreline adventure. He was pretty well known among the denizens of that area, and as long as his leashless adventures were confined to the early hours of the morning, he mostly avoided the ire of the well-to-do residents of La Jolla and their friends at the San Diego PD.

Ben surfed for about ninety minutes, getting his share of the peaks that made Windansea famous. He sat furthest out the back, only taking the largest and most infrequent of the set waves, but he still had to bark a few times to keep the sixteen-year-olds who surf there and think they invented the place in check. But he had a good time, with a big drop usually followed by a barrel and then with a big roundhouse cutback—as classic a set of surf moves as there ever was. He got out of the water to see Geronimo covered in sand and violently shaking a big kelp bulb in his mouth from side to side. He gave a whistle, and Geronimo perked his head up, dropped the rotting kelp, and ran over to him.

They both headed back to the jeep parked on Neptune. On his way, he saw Phil standing outside his old beat-up van, a selection of vintage longboards no doubt inside. Phil was the ghost of Christmas future for Ben. The guy lived in PB, had for most of his life, and had worked construction until his thirties when an uncle had died and left him a decent sum of money. Phil quit his job that day and never looked back. He was in his sixties now, having spent the last thirty years hanging around PB, getting stoned, surfing, ranting online with the black-helicopter crowd late at night, and occasionally getting hand jobs from the massage place by the freeway.

"How was it, man?" Phil asked.

"F'ing great, man. You should paddle out right now!"

"Crowd is starting to get ugly out there. I think I'm going to wait another thirty minutes for the tide to come up and go surf the Point."

"Dude, do you ever surf anywhere but the Point?"

"Sometimes," Phil responded and fired up a joint, likely not his first of the day.

"Did you hear about Texas?" Phil asked.

Ben took a small drag of the joint to be polite and said, “No, Phil. What is it this time?”

“It looks like Walmart closed fifteen stores and turned them over to the federal government to be used as internment camps for when they invade Texas and declare martial law.”

“How can they invade Texas, Phil? It is part of the United States. There would be nothing to invade; it would just be a road trip.”

“All of the special-ops units of the navy, marines, and army are staging their invasion under the guise of a training exercise called Jade Helm and are about to declare martial law in Texas. Heck, even the governor has deployed Texas Rangers to keep tabs on it.”

Ben tried to process what exactly he was being told; the circular logic of the truly paranoid failed him. “So let me get this straight—the Texas governor has deployed Texas Rangers to hold back an invasion of navy SEALs, Green Berets, and Delta Force?”

“Yup. That is right.”

“And exactly what chance would you give the Texas Rangers in that scenario?”

"I don't know, man, but trust me, it is happening. You as much as anybody should know what the government is capable of."

"I am not sure which is more offensive Phil, the idea that the governor of Texas is that crazy or that he is willing to pander so badly to his crazy constituents," Ben said and started to walk away. "Take it easy, Phil."

"You too, man. Look out for the FBI!"

Ben flashed a quasi-good-natured middle finger backward at Phil while he and Geronimo walked back to his jeep. They jumped in and headed south to PB.

Back at his apartment, he found Jessica on his computer looking sternly at the screen and drinking his terrible instant coffee. He fed Geronimo and sat down next to her and looked at the screen. On it was a recent article from the *New York Times* about water scarcity in the west with a quote from the professor in Arizona that she had called, which had apparently started this whole situation. She snapped out of her Internet trance and slapped him on the thigh. "Well, big shot, what's the next step?"

"The next step is to change clothes and get some real coffee and breakfast. After that, I will try and run down our only real lead here, which is the license plate of the car outside of your apartment."

"Sounds good to me," she responded, more cheerfully than she should under the circumstances.

They walked down to an old greasy spoon style diner on Garnet Avenue, her cheerful mood turning a bit suspicious as they walked down the streets where she had been attacked the day before. Seated inside at the counter, her mood improved as she could see anybody coming and going into and out of the place. They ordered coffee, and while Jessica perused the menu, Ben took out his cell phone and dialed a number.

"Joe, this is Ben...Pretty good. How are you? Wow, bummer. On that topic, how about we have lunch today?" Ben paused, listening. "No, nothing at all; I just need you to sign something for me for my file related to my fee...I know I didn't charge you a fee, but nobody at the Bar Association would ever believe that a lawyer would work for free, so I need it signed in case I get audited. C'mon, I'll buy...Cool. Point Loma Seafood at 12:30. Bye."

Ben hung up the phone as his huevos rancheros arrived with Jessica's French toast.

"Who was that?" she asked, taking a huge bite of French toast.

"Old friend from the Bureau."

"What was that about signing a bill?"

"Nothing; it was just bait to get him to lunch. I did some legal work for him a few months ago, and now he owes me a favor. I figured I might be able to get him to run that plate for us."

"Why didn't you just ask him that on the phone?"

"Nobody is more paranoid than those who have access to the surveillance capabilities of the US government. If I had asked him to do anything shady on the phone, he likely would have hung up on me and never talked to me again. So I had to lie to him and then drop it on him in a public place where the odds of either of us being under surveillance are low."

"Why would you be under surveillance?"

"I wouldn't, but I am just telling you how these guys and I used to think."

"I don't understand."

"Listen, you don't have to kill somebody to get jammed up working for the government—for example, you could theoretically lose your job just for taking your government-issued car to the dry cleaners on the way home from work. That, according to policy,

would be personal business in a government car. That the government has a dress code and that you would be stopping to get dry cleaning to accommodate that dress code makes no difference. It is just one of the myriad of challenges and hypocrisies that come with being an 1811."

"An eighteen a wha wha?"

"Sorry. An 1811 is the special-agent designation that the government gives to that specific job title. Every job in the government has a classification—all the way from a cook at the White House, to a trail-maintenance guy at the Grand Canyon, to your mail-man. Special agents or criminal investigators are categorized as 1811s, and within that category, there are many different employers, meaning that there are all kinds of 1811s. I worked for the FBI, but there is DEA, secret service, HSI, etc. They're all 1811s."

"God, you make the government sound sexy!" she said with obvious sarcasm.

"Fair point. If you want a really good idea of what working for the government is like, I suggest you read or watch *Catch 22*."

"I have. I love that movie! Is it really like that?"

"Pretty much—if not specifically, at least in spirit."

"Wow. I would not have guessed."

"Of course you would have. Have you ever been to the DMV?"

"Of course—total nightmare."

"The post office?"

"Yes, it's the same nightmare."

"Then you have a very good idea of how most of government operates."

"Yikes, that doesn't make me feel safe at all. If it is so fucked up, then why haven't the terrorists blown us all up into little pieces?"

"Terrorism is a different topic. Terrorism is theater, and statistically there are very few people actually willing to blow people up. It has little to do with law enforcement. Catching terrorists after they act is pretty easy—preventing them from acting is very hard."

"That isn't what the news tells me."

"The news is also theater plus a profit motive. They put on what people want to watch, and that creates advertising dollars, which makes them put on more of what people want to watch, and what people really want to watch are thrilling stories of hordes of brown people spilling over our borders with bombs and guns, bloodthirsty for our heads and our women."

"Have you ever thought about switching to decaffeinated coffee?" she asked Ben as he looked down the counter to the waitress and lifted his cup to signal for more coffee.

"Definitely not."

"Well, you sure are a cynical bastard."

"Well, you seem to like the movies, so I'll quote Richard Burton in John LeCarre's *The Spy Who Came in from the Cold*: 'What the hell do you think spies are? Moral philosophers measuring everything they do against the word of God or Karl Marx? They're not! They're just a bunch of seedy, squalid bastards like me: little men, drunkards, queers, hen-pecked husbands, civil servants playing cowboys and Indians to brighten their rotten little lives. Do you think they sit like monks in a cell, balancing right against wrong?' I love that quote, and I think it applies to Feds as well."

"I haven't heard that before. You must be a blast at parties."

"Sorry, I tend to rant a bit, but it is definitely an ugly world out there. Back to your deal...Besides your dubious Colorado River thesis murder theory, why would someone want to kill you? Are you rich?"

"No, I am not rich. I am a poor grad student, but my family has money."

"Maybe it was a kidnap attempt. How much money are we talking about?"

"Rich by poor-people standards but certainly not rich by rich-people standards."

"You are going to have to explain that to me."

"My overall family is decidedly upper-middle class. My dad is an executive of a big agricultural company in LA. I don't know how much he makes, but my mom never worked, they have two nice cars, live in the suburbs, and they pay my tuition, etc. But it is not like we run out to our estate in the Hamptons every summer and hang out with the Clintons."

"It pays not to underestimate criminal stupidity. Maybe they mistakenly thought that they could get

a good ransom, but the more I think about the professional nature of the search of your apartment, the more that seems unlikely. OK, what else?"

"What do you mean?"

"What is your dad into? Is he a mafia rat? Is he an NSA whistleblower? Cockfighting? What?"

"No! Nothing like that. He is just a guy. He is an executive for a big farming company that farms crops all over California. He makes breakfast and reads the paper on Sunday—totally normal! Every summer, he and my mom take their RV to the national parks. As boring and normal as you can get."

"Has his company angered any labor groups?"

"I don't think so, but who knows?"

"What about environmental groups? Are they hosing children with pesticide?"

"I have no idea, but I hope not. In fact, the company supports all kinds of environmental charities like climate-change research and rainforest preservation."

"What is his job title?"

"He is the regional vice president of operations."

"That sounds terrible, but in a boring way. Seems more like a suicide risk as opposed to kidnapping."

"You are hilarious."

"OK, let's put a pin in that for a while until we sort out who the guys in the car are."

They went back to their breakfast and made deliberate chit chat. She told him what it was like to grow up in the San Fernando Valley and talked about her studies and that her thesis was the culmination of watching the orange groves disappear in the Valley and her dad being in the agriculture business. He talked about growing up in the east and his path of familial departure. Finishing their coffee, they walked around the oceanfront, checking the surf as was habit, and went back to his place to make a plan.

Back at Ben's apartment, Jessica went back online and continued her research. Ben picked up the local paper and thumbed through it. The front page declared that the governor of California had mandated a 25 percent cut in water use to cope with the four-year drought. Farther down on the front page below the fold, Ben read an article titled "Four More

Undocumented Migrants Drown in Canals near Arizona Border." Border-related criminal issues being a hard habit to break, Ben enjoyed the article in that it gave his brain a break from his current situation, and he got a view into a mystery (migrant death) that was easily solved (drowned in canals). Satisfied, he circled back to the headline about the governor and for the first time actively started thinking about metropolitan water use in a place where it never really rained.

Back in Evanston where he grew up, everybody had lawns, everything was green, and it rained all the time. In San Diego, everything was also green, and everybody had lawns, but there was no rain. As soon as you left any sort of developed area, the landscape turned brown as opposed to Illinois, where the landscape didn't really change in that regard—if anything, it grew more verdant. He pondered the folly of building great cities in the desert, and it made him smile. He folded up his paper and got up.

"I have to go meet Joe. Take Geronimo for a walk would you? He gets cranky if I leave him in here too long."

"Sure, but what if somebody tries to kill me again?"

"First, nobody but me knows where you are, which reminds me, turn your cell phone off."

"Law-enforcement paranoia?"

"Exactly, and second, Geronimo will kill anybody who even approaches you. It is one of his best qualities."

Ben walked outside, watered his tomato plant, took off two ripe heirloom tomatoes, and put them on his counter. He looked at Jessica, pointed to the tomatoes, and said, "Don't eat these," as he walked out the door.

"They look pretty good. I wouldn't count on them being here when you get back!" she shouted to his back as he left.

On his way to lunch, he bought two prepaid cell phones and put several hundred minutes on each of them.

He drove down Nimitz Boulevard toward Point Loma. He hooked it right onto Harbor Drive and parked. He slid out of the jeep and walked down the sidewalk, looking at the sailboat masts from the marinas and yacht clubs along the waterfront. He knew that he wasn't unique in this, but be loved the look of sailboats in the harbor. He saw his friend Joe Lanahan sitting outside at a table, and he rose to meet him. Joe had the look of a harried civil servant: bookish, thin, late forties, and slightly stooped. He smiled when they shook hands.

"Ben, how are you? Still looking 10-8 I see," he said, using police radio code for *in service*, presumably meaning that he looked good.

"Good, man. Life is just trucking along. Are things finally sewn up with the ex?" he asked as they walked inside and got in line, eyeballing the transparent cases of fresh fish lined up on ice.

"God no, the divorce is final. And thanks, by the way, but with the kids, it is still a battle every week. She is trying to drive me to eat my gun, and I think it is working." He laughed.

"Classic. Divorce is always tough. I don't think that there is such a thing as an amicable separation."

"You said it, man."

They both walked up to the counter. Ben ordered a lobster roll with an iced tea. Joe ordered the squid sandwich and a bottle of local India Pale Ale called Sculpin. Ben paid while looking askance at him and asked, "Beer at lunch?"

"Fuck it; it's Friday."

"Dude, I am pretty sure that it is Monday."

“Fuck it; it’s Monday,” he said.

Ben traded his iced tea for a Sculpin himself, and they walked to the outside patio and sat down to wait for their lunch.

“So what is it again that you want me to sign?

“Oh, yeah, turns out you didn’t need to. I took care of it. I went through your file again and found it—turns out that you signed it a long time ago.”

“Really? I don’t remember.”

“It was that night where we started going through your finances, and I was telling you about the Community versus Separate Property in the state of California, and we started drinking scotch…”

“Oh, yeah, those were dark times, the scotch helped.”

“Sorry, bud, but it is still good to grab a bite and catch up a bit. Also, I need a favor.”

The waitress came out and brought their food in baskets. She was cute in the way that only seems produced in Southern California.

"Here it comes," Joe said, rolling his eyes and digging into his sandwich.

"What? It is no big deal. I just need you to run a license plate for me."

"Run a license plate? Are you fucking crazy? Did you forget all the ways you can get fucked by misusing government computers?"

"Yeah, I remember. But I also remember you using those same government computers to find out what your wife was up to during your divorce. Besides, you are eligible to retire next year, so who cares?"

"Touché. Fuck it; it's Monday. What is the number?"

Ben handed Joe a slip with the Crown Vic's plate number on it, and they continued to work on their lunch.

"What is it for anyway?"

"This girl I am dating has a Crown Vic parked outside her house all the time, and it has her freaked out. I told her it was probably the good guys but that I would check it out for her. I am trying to impress her

with all my cool government connections. What's the latest with the boat?" Ben asked.

"Same. I am still living on it, slowly making it fully seaworthy bit by bit. I just installed a solar panel last week; the watermaker comes next month. Should be ready to sail the big blue by the time I retire next year. Thanks to your community property lecture, I was able to keep it."

"Sweet. What was it again?"

"Forty-five-foot Beneteau from 2000."

"That's right; that thing is great. Good call hanging onto it."

"My accountant doesn't think so, but thanks. It makes me feel like I am not quite dead yet."

They finished their meals, bussed their baskets, and walked away from the harbor toward the street.

"I'll call you later when I get a hit on this plate."

"Thanks, man. I owe you one."

"No shit."

Back at Ben's apartment, Jessica was printing furiously from the computer. She had a sheaf of papers all related to Colorado River flows. "The guy I called in Arizona was about to come out with some groundbreaking new book or paper that was supposed to change everything we knew about the Colorado River. It had something to do with the amount of water available not being accurate."

"So what?"

"Well, everybody knows that the Colorado River Compact of 1922 is terribly flawed."

"Everybody?"

"OK, at least everybody who studies this stuff. It was flawed in that their data was collected in especially wet years with unreliable estimates and overly optimistic assumptions."

"Which means what, exactly?"

"It means that there isn't enough water to go around. There never was, and that was all before climate change was taken into account."

"OK, what does that have to do with us?"

"Well, from what I can tell online, Professor Gutierrez from the U of A was about to reveal that, based on a decade-long study, even the current estimates were off and that there was even less water than predicted. He was having a hard time figuring out why the current models couldn't account for all of the water, and then all of a sudden, he stopped publishing, fell off the web, and cancelled his classes. I think that between that and my weird phone call with him, he may be our next lead."

"I can't say that I agree 100 percent. Maybe he had a baby, maybe his wife got cancer—people drop things for lots of reasons."

"Well, I think we should go to Tucson and try to track this guy down."

"Really? Doesn't that seem a bit excessive?"

"*No*," she said, pointing to the wound in her head.

"Fair enough. We can leave tomorrow."

Ben's phone beeped with an incoming text message:

> NOT LAW ENFORCEMENT. CAR REGISTERED TO WHITE HOUSE PLUMBERS LLC IN CULVER CITY. DON'T EVER CALL ME AGAIN. JOE

"What is it?"

"A text from Joe. It looks like your minders aren't law enforcement after all."

"Who are they?"

"White House Plumbers."

"Come again?"

"It is an LLC called White House Plumbers, which, strangely, was the name given to Nixon's black-ops guys who did all kinds of illegal shit back in the '70s. The LLC is registered in Culver City."

"Nixon, the dead president?"

"Yup."

"So is that a joke?"

"I have no idea. Maybe it's a cover company, and somebody at the CIA was reading a Watergate book and thought it would be hilarious to name their cover the White House Plumbers? Seems pretty screwed up though, even for the CIA. We can look into it and see who ostensibly owns the company. There will be a trail to follow of public corporate records; it should be easy.

In the meantime, let's go for a surf, get some dinner, and gear up for tomorrow."

"Can't surf, Special Agent Adams," she said, making a dumb face and pointing again at the stitches in her head.

"Right. OK then," he said as he went to the garage and grabbed an old Lis-style fish with two keel fins and his wetsuit. He walked into the alley and toward the water.

Ben wandered down to his usual spot on the bluffs where he could see most of the Pacific Beach surf spots. The fading swell looked like it was hanging on just a bit longer. The Pier looked good, but Ben usually didn't like the salty crowd there. The Pumphouse looked almost as good, and while it was also crowded, it looked to be mostly tourists on squishy foam boards doing their best buoy impressions. Ben figured he would get more waves paddling around the tourists rather than dealing with the crew at the Pier. He paddled out into the shoulder-high surf and made his way to the lineup. He nodded to a guy in his thirties on a longboard.

"What's up, man?" the man asked.

"Same old, same old. The waves look good," Ben responded.

"How is G-Dog? I still have never heard of a dog getting stung by a stingray before."

"I know; it's crazy. Thanks for taking such good care of him, particularly on a Sunday. That kind of stuff just never happens during business hours. That dog loves getting into trouble."

"Just part of the glamorous job of being a vet," he said as he turned on his board, took two quick paddles into a fast chest-high left, and rode it almost all the way to the sand. About midway through the ride, Ben saw him duck down from behind into a possible small-tube ride. He paddled back out, grinning.

"How was that, Bob?" Ben asked.

"Very nice indeed."

They sat for a few moments in silence, waiting for the next set. Bob looked over his shoulder and said, "Don't look now, but here comes our favorite conspiracy theorist," indicating an older guy paddling out.

"Dude, you have to stop selling that guy weed. He's getting more and more paranoid, and his theories are crazier than ever. He told me yesterday that he thinks the United States is going to war with Texas. That

makes no sense on so many different levels. I wouldn't even know where to start."

"Caveat emptor, dude, and it's not my herb that is making him crazy. That is primo stuff with excellent Northern California provenance—none of that blood-soaked stuff from Mexico. That dude was crazy long before I met him," he finished as Phil paddled up on his vintage longboard.

"What's up, guys?" Phil asked. "Did you hear about Texas?"

"See?" Ben said as he turned and paddled outside toward the darkening horizon.

A set of rogue waves was looming, probably 25 percent larger than the typical waves of the day, a good few feet overhead—the last gasp perhaps of the dying swell. Ben had spotted it first and started paddling out for position. The other two dawdled, and as they started scratching for the outside, they got hammered, paying for their tardiness. Ben crested the first one and was in perfect position for the second—he spun and went. The drop was tough on a twin fin of such an archaic design, but he laid into the inside rail of the large swallowtail, the little keel fin hanging on as Ben got completely covered up. He shot out of the tube with a hoot, waved to the guys still paddling in

the soup, and went in to the beach, knowing that he was not going to get another one like that today. He walked back to his apartment where he rinsed off in his outdoor shower, got dressed, grabbed Geronimo and Jessica, and walked down to the Local for dinner. Many beers and nachos later, the three of them passed out back at the small apartment.

Tuesday

The next morning, after the obligatory good coffee, Ben put the bikini top of the jeep on for shade and started packing it for the trip to Arizona.

Jessica came out to the garage and said, "Should we maybe take my Volkswagen Van? It's more comfortable, we can sleep in it, and it will be cheaper?"

"Nah, I guarantee if those dudes really are watching you, they are watching for that van. Nobody knows that we are together yet, so it's better if we go incognito, not to mention, like just about every surfer in California, I used to have a VW Van, and if we are actually planning on making it to Arizona, we had better take my car," he said dryly.

He was starting to get the feeling that this wasn't entirely a lark and that in any scenario that he could imagine, his obsessive-compulsive mechanical disorder related to the fitness of his jeep might prove valuable. Like any good OCD sufferer, he (for obvious historical reasons) had felt somewhat out of control. He knew full well that the idea of control was largely an illusion, but cognitive dissonance being what it was, he soaked in it. He tried to make up for the perceived chaos by controlling every variable that he could, including having gone over every single mechanical, electrical, or other useful bit of his jeep to make sure that mechanical failure was an outside possibility at best.

He could not say the same for Jessica's charming but likely fragile van. She agreed to skip the old bus, and he continued prepping his rig for the trip. After Ben's time in Baja, he always tried to load up for any contingency on a road trip. This included, among other things, a banged-up, tarnished Smith & Wesson .357 magnum with a four-inch barrel familiar to anybody who had watched cop movies in the '80s. Ben wasn't even into guns the way that lots of Americans seemed to be, but as a convicted felon, he was barred from legally owning one, so as an act of rebellion when he got out of prison, he went to the shady neighborhoods east of downtown San Diego and bought one from an equally shady dealer of black-market goods of

all sorts that Ben had been introduced to back when he was a fed and this guy was a paid confidential informant on a case.

The gun rested in a holster in his locked toolbox in the back of the jeep with about a dozen extra rounds. Ben had never actually tried it out. For all he knew, he had paid two hundred and fifty dollars for a gun-shaped paperweight, but either way, it made him feel better. As an agent, he had become used to having a gun at almost all times; as a civilian, even one for whom possession of a firearm was an additional felony, it was a hard habit to break. Perhaps also related to his fear of chaos, he had rationalized its possession by considering it as another tool in his toolbox (literally). He also threw into the jeep a small tent, a camping stove, a tarp, and other assorted things for a trip of unknown destination and duration. They then threw some clothes together, loaded up a cooler with ice, food, and drinks, grabbed a bag of dog food, and hit Interstate 8 eastbound with Geronimo in tow—head sticking out of the side of the jeep in dog bliss.

They blasted over the mountains east of San Diego on Interstate 8 and dropped down to the desert floor of the Imperial Valley. The landscape changed dramatically once they crested the Laguna Mountains that ran the length of the Laguna Salada Fault. The

mountains formed a barrier to any moisture creeping in from the coast, and as you entered the Colorado Desert of southeast California, the bleak moonscape gave them pause as the virtually plantless expanse went on for hundreds of miles ahead.

Jessica used the prepaid phone that Ben had given her to make a room reservation in Tucson as they cruised through the arid plain. Around El Centro, they passed lush fields of industrialized agriculture on either side of the freeway butting up against the lifeless ochre of the sands of the desert with the wide irrigation canals providing the water, siphoned from the Colorado River farther east. It was hard for Ben to process; the juxtaposition between desert and life was just too great, like looking at a photo of Neil Armstrong on the moon with a fishing pole and a tackle box.

As they approached the giant Algodones Dunes west of Yuma, the lush fields disappeared and were replaced by towering sand dunes ten-stories high. It was a Tuesday, and it was hot, so the dunes were peaceful and quiet, but had they gone through on a Saturday, the quiet would have been replaced with hundreds of RVs parked at the base of the dunes as well as hundreds of dune buggies and dirt bikes flying over the sand in a hydrocarbon-fueled orgy that occurred every weekend there. About twenty miles farther on, they crossed from

California to Arizona on the Ocean to Ocean Bridge, which when built in its original form, connected the rest of New Spain to Las Californias over the Colorado River. Even to them looking down, knowing what they knew about drought and reduced water flows, the mighty Colorado appeared so small as to make them wonder whether it was even worth all of the conflict.

They pulled off at Fortuna Avenue to get fuel for the thirsty jeep. There was a taco place attached with a palapa patio perfectly fenced in to let Geronimo nose around for a while as they let some of the heat of the day fade. Ben smiled at the surfboard mounted on the wall two hundred miles from any surfable wave. Jessica ordered four carne asada tacos and two Pacificos in Spanish, and they sat down.

"You speak Spanish?"

"Yup, three semesters in Guadalajara as an undergrad. What about you?"

"I picked up some Spanish on my Baja surf trip, and I might be able to ask where the bathroom is in France, but that's about it."

"That could be useful; we might need that someday."

"Definitely." He said taking a pull on his beer.

"Hey," she said after a few moments, "not to sound ungrateful or to minimize my tremendous abilities in bed, but why exactly are you helping me?"

Ben pondered that for a moment while adding more hot sauce to his taco. "I like you, and there is no swell right now," he replied, taking a bite of carne asada.

"That's it?"

"Maybe perhaps I could dig deeper into my psyche, find some sort of King Arthur complex or some profound yearning for a more human connection, the promise of which you represent; but here, now, under the palapa with the tacos and the beer, I am sticking with that I like you, and there was no swell."

"That's good enough, I suppose," she replied. "And for what it's worth, I like you too, and not just because you're helping me."

Ben raised his bottle to hers with a satisfying *clink*.

Looking around at his immediate surroundings, it was hard for Ben to reconcile the fact that he was in the United States. He had spent so much time in Baja California, he knew it very well, and there was nothing in his field of vision or any auditory clues to tell him that he wasn't actually there. The crowd was

two-thirds Mexican or of Mexican descent, and the dominant language he heard was Spanish. The only real clue might have been that he was looking at a Chevron gas station instead of a government-monopoly Pemex station.

He started to imagine a map of the area, which led to his rudimentary knowledge of the history of the region and the retrospective observation that, although technically part of the United States, he actually lived in part of Alta California and that he lived in the city of San Diego rather than the city of St. Doug or, for that matter, that his former home was properly called El Pueblo de Nuestra Senora la Reina de Los Angeles and not the City of Angels or LA. His mind started down the shared history of the place and the somewhat arbitrary line that separated the two countries that many of the residents tried with some success to pretend didn't exist.

His mind went back to the newspaper article about the drowned migrants who had died trying to prove that very proposition. Geronimo snoozed in the shade while they talked about the United States and Mexico and the shared culture. Jessica, being the film buff, described the scene to Ben from *A Touch of Evil* where the Mexican cop played by Charlton Heston marveled at the 1950s fact that along the US-Mexican border from San Diego to Brownsville, Texas, the border was

nothing but a painted line on the streets of the towns that straddled the border and that there wasn't a single gun along that border—at that time a point of pride between the two friendly countries.

"Boy have times changed," Ben said, thinking of the billions of dollars in guns, trucks, drones, and walls that delineated the twenty-five-hundred-mile border now.

"You said it," she replied, draining her beer and getting up for two more, not asking whether he wanted one.

By the time they got back on the road, the heat had dissipated somewhat. They got more fuel and some hydrating fluids and more beer at Gila Bend, Arizona. Geronimo wandered freely into the desert to handle his business. He dropped a giant turd underneath a metal sculpture of what appeared to be a Tyrannosaurus rex and came proudly trotting back to the jeep. Ben sighed and fished a plastic bag out of the garbage to take care of it, wondering who was really in charge here.

They regained Interstate 8 and eventually merged onto Interstate 10, gaining some elevation as they went through the pass between the mountain ranges surrounding Tucson and seeing the twinkling lights of

what was often called the Old Pueblo in the distance. They pulled into Tucson off of the freeway and onto Miracle Mile, noticing how gritty the place felt. Jessica made the comment that they seemed to be in some sort of film noir as they passed rows of vintage neon advertising the old hotels and prostitutes of similar vintage walking the street.

They made their way downtown and found the Hotel Congress where Jessica had booked them for the night. Ben recognized the old hotel from his studies at Quantico in the FBI Academy. Built in 1919, the hotel had a small claim to fame as being the location of the capture of Public Enemy Number One John Dillinger in 1934. Hiding out in Tucson after a string of robberies, the Dillinger gang had been staying at the hotel when a fire broke out. The guests, including the Dillinger gang, had to escape down the outside of the building on ladders. The original FBI report that Ben had read in the academy as part of his studies had Dillinger tipping the firemen twelve dollars each to go back up and retrieve the gang's luggage. They were recognized on the street and ultimately captured nearby. Dillinger later escaped during a transfer to Indiana and was killed by the FBI six months later in Chicago while coming out of a theater—ironically, after seeing a gangster movie. Ben knew the whole story, having grown up outside of Chicago and having been an FBI agent, and had an interest in crime history, so he was pleased to be staying at the Hotel Congress.

They pulled into the parking lot and Ben pulled out a large, empty duffel bag and dropped it on the ground. Knowing what to do, Geronimo crawled in, and Ben zipped it up and slung him over his shoulder like ordinary luggage. Ben and Jessica checked in with the Geronimo bag and their real luggage and went up to their room. They released the dog and took a shower together—in the interest of water conservation in the era of mega-drought—and then got dressed. Leaving Geronimo to snore loudly in their room, they walked down the grand staircase to the lobby and out onto Congress Street.

The sleek new streetcar glided down its tracks past the old boomtown buildings. It stopped in front of the Hotel Congress as they jumped on toward the University. Ben thought to himself that the train was an unlikely piece of publicly funded infrastructure in such a Republican-dominated state, but considering the last few days, he thought that maybe this wouldn't be the last of his assumptions that would be upended. They got off midway up 4th Avenue at a place called the Hut, which was literally an old Quonset hut. Standing out in a formerly industrial section of Tucson that had gentrified around it, the Hut boasted at the entrance what appeared to be a life-sized or larger replica of a Moai head from Easter Island with glowing red bulbs for eyes towering over the street.

Inside the Hut were a palm-frond bar and lots of Christmas lights, reminding Ben of how the old-time Vietnam vets in Pacific Beach described Da Nang a.k.a. China Beach in 1968. For while the neighborhood outside had gentrified leaving the Hut unaffected, the crowd had also remained ungentrified. It was as if the entire building were protected by the Moai in an antihipster bubble, the patrons being the seedy mix of bar regulars and misfits of desert towns all over the Southwest. Ben and Jessica didn't mind. The drinks were cold, and there was decent live music. They drank and talked and danced until about midnight when they walked back to the Hotel Congress, enjoying the lovely night and unusual adventure.

Ben thought it late enough to forgo the duffel-bag routine and took Geronimo out of the room to water the parched landscaping. They snuck down the stairs after making sure that the night clerk wasn't at the front desk. They wandered around outside for a few minutes, pausing to watch as the Amtrak Southwest Chief rumbled past, making its way from Los Angeles to Chicago. Finished with amateur horticulture, Ben and Geronimo snuck back into the lobby. Startling both of them, the front-desk clerk waved them on and said "nice dog" without even looking up.

Wednesday

In the morning, they went down to the Cup Café in the lobby, again leaving Geronimo to his own devices and kibble breakfast in the room. Ben had a red service-dog vest that he had bought so that he wouldn't get hassled for taking Geronimo places that he didn't belong. He tried to use it sparingly, the marginal ethics of pretending to need a service dog weighed a bit even on Ben's burned-out moral compass. In addition, Ben thought the smells of eggs, bacon, and toast going on at the Cup Café amounted to cruel and unusual punishment, vest or no vest. Jessica produced her sheaf of research as they waited for their large doses of breakfast justice.

"It looks like Professor Jaime Gutierrez's office is number 310 of the Charles P. Sonnet Space Sciences

Building. The streetcar will take us right to the main gate, and hopefully we should be able to find a map on campus," Jessica said.

"OK," Ben said as the waiter brought more coffee and their giant breakfast, found only in America, which probably weighed five pounds each of eggs, French toast, potatoes, and bacon. The plates hit the table with a distinct thud as Ben asked the waiter if he knew of a print shop nearby.

"Sure, right across the street from the main gate to the university. It also has great coffee."

"Thanks, man," Ben said as he dove into his plate. As he was eating, he wrapped up two of his many pieces of bacon to give to Geronimo later.

"Why the print shop?" Jessica asked.

"I'll explain when we get there; it's just a cheap piece of insurance for our adventures."

Ben paid the bill, and they went upstairs for the dog, came out onto the street, and waited for the train.

The train stopped in front of their hotel, and they all three jumped on, Geronimo resplendent in his red

service vest. Everyone on the train complimented him on what a handsome dog he was. A few assumed that Ben was suffering from PTSD from Middle East combat tours and thanked him for his service. He didn't correct them; he just nodded. They rode the few miles through the center of the Old Pueblo. The shops and restaurants they passed were nice but still had that tattered edge of the desert. They filed off at the university's main gate and went into the bookstore/coffee shop/print shop across the street and pressed into the air-conditioned space.

"Do you guys do passport photos?" Ben asked.

"No problem," replied the Rastafarian behind the counter.

"How about a workstation we can use with a scanner, Internet access, and something like Photoshop?"

"No problem," said the Rastafarian again, pointing across the shop.

"Great. Let's start with the photos."

As the guy dug out the digital camera to take their photos, Jessica asked, "What are we doing?"

"Trust me. It will make more sense as we go along."

The Rasta ushered them over to a screen where he snapped off their photos and then returned to the counter to print them. They took the photos and went over to the desk where there was a business workstation set up. Ben quickly went to work, opening up a Microsoft Word document and simultaneously opening the website of the *Cleveland Plain Dealer*. He copied some images from the *Plain Dealer*'s website, pasted them into the Word document, and then scanned in their passport photos and added some text. When he was finished, he printed out what appeared to be two authentic press credentials from the *Cleveland Plain Dealer*, complete with the names Roy Huggins and Annabelle Geoffries.

He showed them to Jessica and said, "In case we are some place we shouldn't be, these might help grease the skids or maybe keep us safe. Hurting journalists is generally bad business."

"Why the *Cleveland Plain Dealer*?"

"I figured it was well known enough to make us seem legit but still obscure enough to be believable and far enough away that hopefully nobody we encounter will actually know somebody who works there."

"Are you just making this all up as you go along?"

"Oh, yeah," he said, looking over to the dreadlocked guy. "Do you guys have a laminating machine?"

"Ya," he said, pointing to the other side of the space.

"It's for an art project," Ben said by way of explanation.

Rastaman just nodded his head.

"Do you see any ethical issue with posing as newspaper journalists?" Jessica asked as they were cutting up their IDs and going through the lamination process.

"Print is dead, Annabelle," he said flatly.

They finished up and checked their work, and to the moderately trained eye, they had two legitimate-looking press passes.

"How about another cup of coffee?" Ben asked.

"What the hell," she replied.

They grabbed a table in the attached café after getting two oversugared and caffeinated coffees.

"OK, so what is our plan? Professor Gutierrez has office hours starting in fifteen minutes, according to the university website."

"Well, I say we go to his office and ask him what all the cloak-and-dagger shit is about."

"That's it? That is the entire plan? I thought that you were some kind of highly trained investigator? Then what is the point of all this *Cleveland Plain Dealer* bullshit?"

"Oh, I was thinking we'd use those to bluff our way into or out of anything sketchy. Interviewing this professor should not even come close to being sketchy. I assume that you and this professor will be on the same page, and the same dudes who bonked you on the head are the same guys that he may, *may* be hiding out from. I still think that he is more likely to have been having a standard midlife crisis, but things definitely seem to be getting weirder in this story. Point is, we shouldn't need these for your professor, but we can use the press passes to bluff people that aren't trying to kill us or otherwise wouldn't want to help us without a little mild coercion, like the ethereal promise of the tangential, fleeting fame of being quoted in the newspaper."

"OK," she said wearily, accepting that there probably wasn't a real explanation that would make any sense in her mind and that maybe Ben was more than just a little bit nutty.

"Let's go. His office building is on the other side of campus."

They finished their five-dollar coffees and walked through the main gate, crossing University Avenue. As they walked through the campus with the manicured lawns, red-brick buildings, and palm trees, it reminded Ben of his time at USC. He smiled at the thought of the bright-eyed university student that he used to be and let out a barely audible *harrumph* at whatever it was he had in fact become. They walked through the crowd of students walking, running, or cycling to class, and Ben's perspective involuntarily changed from that of a former university student to that of a former law-enforcement officer.

He started to think about how a university was a great environment to be in incognito. At any time during the school year, there were any number of homeless dudes, career students, professors, transsexuals, militants, or any other of the myriads of people who cruised around a university campus without being hassled as long as they had a student ID. Sometimes they were even all the same person. A spotted dog

in a service vest, a burned-out ex-federal agent, and a young grad student didn't even register a second glance. Thinking about it, if they needed it, their press cover probably wouldn't even raise an eyebrow here in academia where, intellectually, everything was possible, and everything else was also somewhat believable.

They entered the campus building that housed Professor Gutierrez's office, and since it was during class hours, all of the buildings were open, which Ben thought was another bonus of a college campus for criminals and undercover investigators—both of which they apparently were. They climbed three flights of stairs to his floor and found the office—locked. The office had the hours posted as 10–6 on Wednesdays, and it was 10:15. They decided to wait for a while. Perhaps, as with many academics, punctuality wasn't Jaime's strong suit. They posted up on a bench across the hall, loitering outside a professor's office being another example of something perfectly acceptable on a college campus that would get you hassled and possibly arrested in the outside world. They sat there for about thirty minutes until Geronimo started asking questions.

Ben said, "OK, let's do this."

"Great, do what?"

"Just keep an eye out for me."

"I don't know what that means," she said as Ben approached the locked office door, ignoring her.

In Ben's last year as an FBI agent, the guys in his unit had convinced their supervisor that they needed to go to a weeklong lock-picking school in San Antonio. Nobody really needed that skill, the Money Laundering unit didn't do a lot of black-bag jobs that would require that skill set, but there was money in the training budget, and it was getting close to the end of the fiscal year, so they all went. With his diploma, Ben got a lovely set of picks and the skills to use them. The FBI didn't inventory that stuff, so after he was fired, they stayed with Ben, collecting dust along with a lot of his other tactical gear until this moment.

He pulled out the little leather envelope filled with the picks and went to work. As much art as science, Ben had lost his touch somewhat since he had not been practicing, but he probed and wiggled until he felt the old lock start to give. A meaty *click* and the door swung open. They rushed in, Geronimo right behind, sensing the urgency, and they closed the door behind them. They almost wiped out on the stack of papers and envelopes that had been shoved under the door. Jessica reached for the lights.

"Don't," Ben hissed.

Jess rolled her eyes, thinking that maybe he was taking the James Bond thing a bit too far, but then her head throbbed a bit where she had been hit, and she reconsidered.

Jaime Gutierrez must have been tenured, because his office was ample with a window overlooking the U of A Mall. There was enough light coming in to get an idea of the place. Geronimo quickly jumped up on the leather couch and laid down. A quick survey of the office showed the same professional search Ben had seen at Jessica's apartment. They quietly rummaged through the already pre-rummaged office and turned up nothing of real value: lots of academic papers related to hydrology, mostly from students, some old publications from the professor, including, according to Jessica, his regionally semifamous book from the '80s, *Whiskey Is for Drinking.*

"See," Jessica said, pointing to the title.

Ben rolled his eyes and kept searching. After about thirty more minutes of finding nothing of obvious importance, Jessica sat on the couch next to the dog, and Ben took a seat at the professor's desk. They had created three piles of papers on the desk, one for useless crap, one for possibly useful, and one for maps. Mostly

Ben just liked maps and thought some might make for good art on the wall at his shabby-chic PB bachelor pad.

Ben took out his burner phone and dialed.

"Joe, yeah. It's Ben again. Really? I thought you were kidding. Well, too bad you answered the call; it's your fault. I need another favor...No, actually worse. I need you to track somebody down for me...Yeah, yeah, yeah, but this is related to *real* crime...Listen, if it breaks bad, we can backdate the paperwork and make me a CI. Your boss always liked me; I'm sure that he would sign off on it...Actually, you're right; it would never work. That is a terrible idea, but just help me out anyway, OK? Remember the girl I was telling you about? Well, she reached out to this professor in Arizona, which is where we are now, who was studying the same thing, and he has disappeared from the university, and nobody here has seen him in at least six weeks...Yeah, I interviewed a few people in his department as part of my private investigation..."

Ben continued talking while looking at Jessica and shaking his head *no.*

"Not a deep search. I just need you to find out if he owns property, where those bills go, and if they are current...Yup, his name is Jaime Gutierrez, professor

of hydrology at University of Arizona...DOB? Hold on."

Ben grabbed the copy of *Whiskey Is for Drinking*.

"No, but looking at his picture from 1986, I would guess that he is about sixty-five now, so that should eliminate a bunch. Also, based on his office, I bet he has tenure, so eliminate anything too recent unless it stacks on an older identity...Probably Arizona, but if this guy is hiding out, I wouldn't be surprised to have to go to Montana to dig him up...I know, I know. I promise I'll buy the beers, and I'll help you sail the first leg to Cabo. Fuck it; I'll help you sail the first month of your trip all the way to Panama if G-Dog can come...OK, done. Let me know what you find out. I'll be waiting...Actually it's Wednesday, but I agree—fuck it anyway," he said as he hung up the phone.

"That might help us out a bit," Ben said to Jessica as he moved over to the couch, laid back, and closed his eyes.

"What are you doing?" Jessica asked.

"Waiting; why? What do you want to do?"

"We're going to wait here? In this office?"

"This is our most comfortable option at the moment; it's nice in here, quiet."

"When did he say he was going to search for this guy?"

"He didn't, but Joe was in the office. My guess is that as long as he has already gone to lunch, his supervisor doesn't make him get Starbucks with him, or he doesn't need a car wash for his G Ride, he should get back to us rather quickly—government supercomputers and all that."

Ben got up and went to the desk. He opened the bottom drawer and dug out a bottle of bourbon and fished out two coffee cups out as well. "Some?" he asked.

"Pass," she said, folding her arms and shaking her head. "Geronimo, is he always like this?"

Geronimo sighed and closed his eyes. Ben poured a hefty amount of bourbon in the cup, sat down at the desk, took a drink, and waited. After Ben's second three-finger pour of bourbon, the phone chirped to life.

"Hit me," Ben said in a way that wasn't clear whether he was being playful or was just drunk…OK, spell that please," he said as he scribbled something down.

"That is gold, my friend. Thanks a bunch!" he said and hung up.

"You FBI guys just aren't much for small talk are you?"

"Not really, but I'm sure that he is going to make up for it when he takes me up on that boat-crew offer, and then I will have to hear small talk all the way to Mexico about how his wife fucked him over about five thousand times. Anyway, I've got a good address on Fundicion Street in Ajo, Arizona. It looks like he not only owns the property but also gets cable there, including HBO, and is paying the bill, possibly for some adult movies as well."

"Sweet. Where is Ajo?"

"I haven't the faintest idea, but I bet Senor Gutierrez's computer does," he said as he powered up the computer on the professor's desk and started typing.

The professor had no password protection on his computer, and he even had toner and paper in the printer, so Ben looked up the address, printed out directions, and put them in his bag with a copy of *Whiskey Is for Drinking* and the rest of the documents and maps. On the way out, he also grabbed the stack of papers on the floor.

“Looks like it’s about two hours west of here. You ready to check it out?” Ben asked.

“Let’s go,” Jess replied.

Geronimo had no obvious opinion but seemed up for anything.

They stole out of Professor Gutierrez’s office and locked the door behind them. They walked back to the streetcar and headed downtown. They checked out of the Hotel Congress, loaded up the jeep, fueled up by the university and filled the cooler with ice and supplies, and then headed west on Highway 86 out of town. Arizona’s Highway 86 was a two-lane crumbling strip of asphalt that ran straight west from Tucson through the desert. It passed through a large part of the Tohono O’odham reservation. A part of the country not often visited, this reservation was much like the others in the desert Southwest: hot, dry, and poor.

They motored on through the decrepit consequences of several centuries of Anglo domination and exploitation, turning north toward the town of Ajo, Arizona, at the appropriately named town of Why, Arizona. Ajo looked like a Hollywood set for a film set in a Mexican town of the 1940s. A copper boomtown during the middle part of the last century, since the bust, little had changed. A sun-baked and dust-blanketed town,

Ajo had its own form of charm in that it had been ignored for so long that it was spared any sort of modern development, and the dry desert air preserved the old adobe buildings and whitewashed churches.

Ajo did, however, have current property records and even HBO (and possibly adult movies), so Ben and Jessica were able to track down the address for Professor Gutierrez. Ajo was also small, and it only took them a few minutes to find his house. They turned down Fundicion Street and motored slowly past the address. It was a single-story adobe structure, probably built in the 1930s and kept in good condition. A dirt front yard that presented to the street was hemmed in by a four-foot chain link fence. The blinds were closed, but there was a 1980s vintage Toyota Land Cruiser in the driveway with air in the tires and current registration tags.

They parked on the next block and started walking back. Geronimo didn't need his vest here but probably needed his collar as Ajo looked like the kind of town where stray dogs were shot. Ben scanned the block as they approached the house, and everything appeared normal—or at least normal for a movie set in 1940s Mexico. They walked up to the house and creaked open the waist-high gate. Arriving on the stoop, Jessica knocked on the door. After a few moments, the door cracked open a few inches, and inside

they could barely make out the crusty visage of the University of Arizona professor of hydrology, Jaime Gutierrez.

"Hello? What do you want?" he asked.

Jessica started to answer as Ben shouldered open the door and forced his way in. Dog and Jess behind him, he shut the door quickly and began to peer out of the window shades.

"I'm sorry, Professor, but I think we may have been followed," Ben said before the professor could even respond. Continuing to peer out of the blinds, he glanced sideways to Jessica and barely shook his head to indicate the farce. "It looks like we may have lost them," he finally said, turning to face the professor.

"Who the hell are you two? Who are you running from?"

"Quite probably the same people you are," Ben said. "Maybe Jessica should start at the beginning."

"Let's try that," said the professor, looking like the guy on the book cover but many hard years later: mid-sixties and thin with Einstenian hair and a blazer with PhD-issued elbow patches.

"Professor, I am not sure that you remember me, but my name is Jessica McCoy. I am doing my master's thesis on the impact of climate change on the Colorado River. I am a student at UCSD. I called you a few weeks ago, and you basically cursed me and hung up on me."

"I am not sure that I would characterize my response as a curse, but I do remember you. What are you doing here, and why are you two, plus dog, barging your way into my house?"

"It is something of a long story, but after I spoke with you on the phone, strange things started happening to me as if I was being watched, and I was attacked recently in San Diego. Based on the timing, it may have to do with my research, and it may also have to do with my contacting you. When we spoke, I got the impression that you were scared, possibly for the same reasons that I was attacked. You were my only real lead, so I thought that we needed to talk to you about it."

"Scared? What made you think it was anything other than a bad day when we talked?"

Ben raised his eyebrows and looked at Jess.

"Well, was it?" she responded.

"Actually, no. Maybe I'd better start at the beginning as well. Do you guys want anything to drink?"

"I'll take a Pacifico and some water for the dog if you have it," Ben said.

"Water for me," said Jess.

The professor shuffled off to the kitchen and called back, "No Pacifico, Negra Modelo?"

"Sure," came the response.

The professor came back with two Negra Modelos, a glass of water, and some sort of Tupperware filled with water that he put on the ground for Geronimo, which he lapped up appreciatively.

"OK, so do you guys know that I wrote a book called *Whiskey Is for Drinking*?"

"Yes," they both said somewhat flatly.

"So you read it?" he responded hopefully.

"No," they both said in unison.

"OK," he continued with slightly less enthusiasm. "So I wrote that book in the 1980s when the study of

climate change was in its infancy, and I wanted to write a sequel or perhaps an updated version to account for all that has changed and how much more we know now."

"I can't believe this. You guys are studying the driest, most boring, and narrow topic in the field of science, and this makes you guys a target for murder how?" Ben asked, a bit more stridently than necessary under the circumstances.

"I have no idea," the professor replied. "But, I can tell you this: As soon as I started researching my book in earnest, I started getting threats. It got so bad that I sent my wife to live with her sister in San Miguel de Allende, in Mexico."

"You sent her to Mexico to be safe?" Ben asked, with only a hint of incredulity.

"Yup," he said.

Ben took a drink and let that concept sink in while Jessica got back to the issue at hand.

"What do you think you did that caused these guys to start threatening you?" she asked.

"Again, I'm not sure. I've been thinking about it for weeks, and I really have come up with nothing. But I

can give you a timeline of what I was studying and the questions I started to ask, and maybe you can give me some ideas."

"OK, let's hear that," Jessica said.

"All right, the short version is this: after accounting for bad data from the '20s, revised climate-change estimates, annual precipitation in the Colorado Watershed, and all of the users, there is not enough water."

"It isn't exactly news that there isn't enough water in the Colorado River for all the users," Jessica said.

"That is not what I mean," the professor continued. "What I mean is that there is not enough water coming out of the river to account for all of the water going into the basin."

"I don't follow," Ben said.

Jess had started to understand but said nothing yet.

"Listen, if you have *X* acre feet of water going into the system through precipitation, you need to have *X* amount going out through evaporation, into the soil through infiltration, percolation, and hydraulic

conductivity, etc., minus what is taken by agriculture, and what is left goes into the Sea of Cortez."

"And?" Jessica interjected.

"Going back, water stopped flowing from the Colorado River to the Gulf of California in 1998, and everybody attributed it to the reduced flows related to reduced precipitation, agriculture, climate change, etc. But when I started looking at it closely, the model was missing something. Based on my numbers, water should be flowing all the way through the Colorado River Delta to this day."

"That's it?" Ben asked with mild exasperation.

"Maybe the model is simply wrong; maybe evaporation rates are different throughout the year; perhaps the substrate under the river allows more to percolate than we think?" Jessica proposed with academic coolness.

"I looked at all that. I have spent my entire career studying this stuff, and the model is solid. I was just about to start from scratch and redesign everything when I noticed one very specific piece of data."

"What is that?" Jess asked.

"The model is flawless, accounting for every drop of water going into and out of the system, right up until one specific point on the river, and then the whole thing falls apart, and from that point downriver, there are millions of acre feet per year unaccounted for."

"OK, so did you draw any conclusions?" asked Jess.

"None. It was at this point that my phone started ringing with threats and my pets were poisoned. I sent my wife to Mexico, and I hid out here."

"Why didn't you go to Mexico with her?"

"I don't know. I wanted to maybe keep researching from here, and we weren't getting along that well anyway at that time."

"I knew it! Personal problems!" Ben said, interrupting what had been up until that point a thoughtful discussion between scientists related to their field.

"Can you forget your stupid divorce theory, Ben? I think that we are actually on to something here."

"OK, but I want some validation on personal problems as they impact nutty conspiracy theorists."

"Fine. There may be multiple factors loading on this equation—happy?" said Jess.

"Totally," replied Ben.

"Where on the river does the model fail?" she asked the white-haired man.

"I don't have any maps here, but maybe I could describe it to you," said the professor.

"We actually pulled a bunch of maps from your office, so maybe you could take a look at those?" spouted Ben, trying to add some value.

"Come again?"

"We went to your office looking for you. You weren't there, so we broke in, and by the way, your office had been searched before we got there, likely by the same crew that ransacked Jessica's apartment."

"Don't try to change the subject. What on earth gave you the right to break into my personal and professional space? And I know that she is a master's student, but by the by, who the fuck are you?" asked the professor, getting edgy.

"I'm sorry, Professor. This is my boyfriend Ben. He used to be an FBI agent and he is helping me figure out who tried to kill me."

Ben arched his eyebrows at the *boyfriend* descriptor.

Jessica continued, "A few days ago, somebody attacked me in an alley, and I think that they were trying to kill me, and I think it has to do with my research. My apartment was searched just like your office, and there are two guys camped outside my place watching me. It's all very sinister. So we apologize for ruining your day here, but as a fellow scientist, I think you should help us."

"And to be fair, hiding out in Ajo with the shades drawn watching *The Price is Right* isn't much of a day to ruin," Ben offered, in a poor attempt to smooth out the conversation.

Jess scowled at him and went on, "If we could just show you the maps that we brought here from your office?"

"OK, OK, show me what you have," Jaime capitulated.

Ben unfurled the maps and laid them out.

The professor looked over the maps. "So if you look at this map showing the Colorado River as the

border between Arizona and California, my calculations show the model stops functioning at this point here," he said, putting a stubby finger on the map. "Right in the middle of the Imperial National Wildlife Refuge."

Ben looked at the map as if to discern some detail that would explain the last century's worth of hydrological study of the Colorado River and, not surprisingly, he came up short.

Jessica went over to the professor's cluttered desk and fired up his computer.

"What are you doing?" Gutierrez asked.

"You guys are hogging the map, and perhaps a little twenty-first-century technology might be beneficial here."

With the computer up, she started scrolling through and zooming in and out of satellite images of the area where Arizona, California, and Mexico met. "Professor," she said, "Come take a look at this please."

He went over to the desk and looked over her shoulder. He seemed slightly uncomfortable at the proximity, having been holed up alone for so long.

"This is the point that you say the water stops being accounted for, yes?"

"Yeah, that is it."

"Check it out: If you look due west, more or less along Highway 78, what is this giant agricultural area here south of the Salton Sea?"

"Those are the big agricultural communities around El Centro."

"It is an ocean of green in the desert. How do they get all that water?"

"I haven't studied that area much, but I know that the New River flows north into the Salton Sea, and one of the big draws in that area is the All-American Canal from the Colorado River, which flows that way with much technological and financial help."

"Are those draws by the canal taken into account in your model?"

"Of course."

Jessica thought about it for a minute then asked, "Can that much water account for that much agriculture?"

Ben looked up from his maps, finally gaining some understanding of what she was getting at.

"What do you mean?" asked the professor, trying to get to the fine point.

"Put simply, can the amount of water from the New River, the All-American Canal, plus rainfall grow all of those crops?"

"I have no idea. I don't think anyone has ever looked at that."

"I think we have your new research project," said Ben.

"I don't know, man; there is a reason that I am hiding out here."

"I understand that, but simply put, you have two choices: number one, you can hide out here and watch daytime television for the rest of your likely short life in this place, or number two, we can get to the bottom of this, and maybe you can go back to your cushy university job."

The professor absorbed the truthful implications of that statement. "OK, I'll do some rough calculations and get back to you. How can I reach you guys?"

"Take this phone, and we will call you," Ben said, tossing him one of the burner phones that he had bought back in San Diego.

"Let's head back to SD and keep trying to figure this out," Ben said.

"Why San Diego? Is there some big swell coming or something?" Jess responded.

"Actually, I checked Surfline at Jaime's office—just a medium-sized, long-period south heading in, building today, and peaking over the next few days; it should be fun!"

"You realize that is kind of pathetic, don't you?"

"Maybe, but I am pretty sure that Jaime here doesn't want two new roommates, and we need to post up somewhere and do some more research on the river, the bad guys, etc. And what better place to do that than the beach? Nothing like a good surf session to reset your brain for optimal investigative functioning, I think," Ben expounded.

"Fair enough; I guess we really have nowhere else to go anyway, so the beach it is."

"Great. By the way, Professor, these midterms were stuffed under your door; you really should grade them," Ben said, pulling a bunch of papers from his messenger bag and putting them on his coffee table.

Jaime cocked his head at yet another invasion of his personal and professional privacy. He then closed his eyes, counted to ten, shook his head, and eked out a "Thanks."

They shook hands with the still-marginally antagonized professor and walked out of his house. Ben scanned the area, partly out of habit and partly as a legitimate situational-awareness tool. Geronimo padded along toward the jeep as they followed behind. They piled into the jeep, and Ben pulled out his atlas and started looking at the shortest route back to Interstate 8 and California. Satisfied that he had it, he fired up the jeep and rolled out toward the main road. In his rearview mirror, he saw a familiar, dark-colored Crown Victoria pull onto the street behind them.

"Fek," he said.

"What?" Jess replied, turning around.

"Your friends may have been watching the professor and now are behind us."

"Are you sure?"

"Might be a coincidence. Let's make a couple of turns and see what happens," Ben said, squinting in the mirror.

Geronimo emitted a low growl looking back. At the main highway, they turned southbound toward Mexico instead of north toward Interstate 8. A few blocks down the highway, he watched as the Crown Vic turned to follow. He started accelerating, figuring the risk of a speeding ticket might be worth finding out what those guys were up to. The Crown Vic stayed back but definitely kept them in sight, always far back enough to try and not be too obvious. Their pursuers were good, without Ben's FBI background, they probably wouldn't have noticed being followed. Ben floored the jeep to about seventy-five miles per hour for a few miles and hooked a hard right onto a dirt road. The Crown Vic now sped up to catch them and hooked a hard right as well, abandoning the pretense of being inconspicuous.

Ben bounced down the dirt road, turning left, then right. Out of the corner of his eye, he saw a sign that said Now Entering El Camino del Diablo.

In the back of his mind, there was some flicker of recognition at that name, but it was quickly pushed aside by the car bearing down on them. The jeep was made for this kind of track, the Ford wasn't. As they bounced along, it was clear that the Ford was at its limit. Both going flat out in a comet of dust, they raced along for mile after mile. At about twenty minutes into the chase, which felt like ten hours, they heard a loud *pop* from behind them.

"Holy shit, this just entered another level," Ben said as he reflexively jerked the wheel.

"Did they just shoot at us?" Jess asked incredulously.

"Actually...wait, maybe not," Ben said, looking in the mirror as the Crown Vic faded back into a cloud of dust and flying bits of rubber.

"No gunshots. I think they just blew one of their tires. It looks like we are clear for now," he said, settling his gaze on the road ahead. He let off the throttle and eased into a more leisurely off-road pace, smiling at Karl and Dennis's bad luck.

As they rumbled down the dirt track, Ben slowly started to remember what he knew of El Camino del Diablo. Several months before, he had gotten lost down an Internet rabbit hole late one night after

starting on a jeep bulletin board looking for a fishing-pole mount for the front of his jeep. One of the people on the discussion board had mentioned El Camino del Diablo and what a cool off-road travel objective it was to transect it. From there, he just kept clicking through *Wikipedia* where he had learned the rest.

He had learned that El Camino del Diablo was a trail through northern Mexico and the southwestern United States that had been in use for at least one thousand years. Starting as a footpath that the natives had used to cross the unforgiving Sonoran Desert, the road had been used by conquistadores, missionaries, prospectors, and settlers through the end of the nineteenth century. It was one of the main routes across the desert and was much shorter than sailing around the length of the Baja Peninsula. The route had also been deemed safer as it went through territory nearly absent of hostile native tribes (who presumably had been too smart to be caught dead in such an otherwise naturally hostile area). The route was famous for being littered with cactus and bleached skeletons as well as having scorching temperatures and very little water.

As he read online about El Camino, a light went off and he remembered something. Ben then went into the back of his closet, through his old box of warrants and thumb drives that held all of the nonclassified

stuff that he had kept when he cleaned out his office at the Bureau, including an old PowerPoint briefing from the Border Patrol, leftover from some interagency conference on border issues or something like that. The briefing included a large section on El Camino Del Diablo. According to what Ben had learned from the briefing, the route had been mostly abandoned once the railroad reached Yuma, Arizona, in 1870, but it had experienced a renaissance of sorts over the last thirty years as illegal migrants and drug smugglers from Mexico had been pushed farther into the desert by walls, fences, and enforcement along the urban areas of the border in California and Arizona.

Now El Camino was used almost exclusively by the Border Patrol and the desperadoes heading north. The very same isolation and danger that had made it the so-called safest route for the missionaries made it the safest route for today's breed of fortune seekers. The section that they were on was about one hundred and thirty off-road miles to Yuma. They had plenty of water and food, but looking at the fuel gauge, Ben knew they wouldn't make it on the gas that they had. In the briefing, he had read that there was a border-patrol outpost somewhere along El Camino, and he hoped they could make it there.

Ben explained all of this to Jessica as they cruised through the desert, watching the sun set over the

mountains in the distance. Just after sunset but before the light was gone, the jeep made the coughing sound familiar to anyone who has run out of gas. They coasted to the side of the trail and rolled to a stop.

"Well I guess that is it," said Ben.

"Now what?" Jessica asked as she leaned her head back and closed her eyes.

"Assuming that our one phone doesn't get a signal, we set up camp and hope the Border Patrol finds us before the cartels do."

"Are you serious?"

"Pretty much. I think the real danger from the cartels is getting run over in the middle of the night by a vehicle with no headlights rather than any sort of gun battle, but either way, dead is dead, so we will have to be careful. In case we are here all night, let's set up the tent and get some dinner going," said Ben, cracking open a can of Modelo from the cooler.

"This is a funny coincidence," she said.

"What do you mean?"

"Have you ever heard of Ed Abbey?"

"Maybe—refresh my memory?"

"He was a writer and an enthusiastic and somewhat hypocritical environmentalist. He died in the late '80s."

"Oh, yeah. I think they mentioned him in the academy in our training on eco-terrorists or something like that. Earth First! or something. What about him?"

"Well, two things: one, when he died, his friends took him out to the Cabeza Prieta Wildlife Refuge—which I think we may be in right now—and buried him illegally and had a big party, and two, with your cavalier attitude toward our lives and reckless beer consumption, you actually remind me a bit of him."

"I'll take that as a small compliment," said Ben, polishing off his Modelo and digging around the jeep for the tent and camp chairs. "But for the record, I have every interest in keeping everyone here, including myself, alive."

Jess shrugged and went to the jeep where she found a Jetboil camp stove and some bags of dehydrated camp food. She held two up in the air. "Lasagna or beef teriyaki? I imagine that they both taste more or less the same."

“You call it,” Ben replied.

Jess went to work while Ben finished setting up the tent and chairs. He pulled out two fabric bowls for Geronimo and filled one with water and the other with kibble. He grabbed another beer and sat down in the camp chair. In the distance, some coyotes started yipping over something they had presumably killed. Geronimo perked his head and ears up from his dinner and then went back to it with a barely audible grumble.

“This isn’t so bad,” Ben started. “Kind of like a Baja surf trip with no waves and more danger.”

“Glad that you’re having fun,” she replied.

“Since we have some time to kill, why don’t you tell me more about your backstory. I have the whole environmental grad student and surfer thing, but what about where you grew up, etc.?”

“It’s pretty boring.”

“That’s OK. We have time, and I’d like to know more about you,” he said with a smile.

“All right, I grew up in the San Fernando Valley or just ‘The Valley,’ so I am a valley girl—nothing too

exciting there. My parents are still together, I had a boring childhood, and my dad works for the agricultural company that has one of the last remaining orange groves in the valley. When I was a kid, he told me stories about Mulholland and the LA City Water Company and how they got the water from the Owens Valley to LA for the orange groves, which led me to the movie *Chinatown* and started my enthusiasm for film and for water issues. I started college at UCSD and have been there ever since. That is about it."

"That's interesting," said Ben. His investigative mind was starting to pick up a thin trace of something. "Tell me more about your dad. As we are talking about it, it occurs to me that maybe you were attacked not for what you are into, but for what *he* is into."

"I doubt that. He wears a suit and tie, takes his lunch to work, and has meetings about agriculture and the price of soybeans and alfalfa. It's not really the type of work likely to incite any violence—which reminds me..." she said, changing the subject away from her dad. "Why did you bash in the door on the professor? Seemed a little bit excessive, didn't it?"

"Maybe it was, but it also seemed stupid to argue with him standing on his stoop for half an hour only to have him shut the door in our face, which he most

certainly would have. I thought that if we could get in there quickly and make him think we had a common enemy, he would be more likely to talk to us, and he did."

"Man, you are strange, but he did talk to us, so maybe you are on to something with your weirdness. But you definitely did not make a friend out of him."

"Oh, I don't know. I think he may have warmed up to me at the end a little bit," he said wistfully.

"Not likely, but I have another question. How did they find us?" Jess asked.

"I have been wondering that myself. The professor wasn't too hard to find; maybe they staked him out and spotted us there? Have you contacted anyone since we started this escapade?"

"Not really. I have been texting my parents to let them know that I'm OK, but I have been using the phone you bought."

"They might have your parents' phones bugged, so please stop doing that. Shoot them an e-mail if you have to, but no more phones."

"OK, sorry. I didn't know."

"No worries. I didn't either. That is pretty sophisticated surveillance. I would not have guessed that they were that legit or that we were that important. This is another layer entirely."

Jess started to reply, and Ben held his hand up to silence her. He got up and went to the jeep where he fished out the .357 and tucked it into his waistband.

A hundred yards away, between the teddybear cholla and ocotillo, he heard a rustling. At that moment, out of the desert walked half a dozen lost souls who looked as if they had spent a lifetime in the desert. Ben relaxed a little bit, thinking that in their physical state, they posed no immediate threat. The man leading the pack looked to be about Ben's age with dark mestizo skin.

As he approached, he held up his hand in a peaceful gesture. "*Tienen usted agua?*" he asked Ben, who had just started doing the slow translation in his head when Jess replied, "Of course," and went to the jeep for the five-gallon jerry can that they had of water.

She laid out cups and started filling them. The group, a mix of old and young men, women, and children, guzzled water, which some immediately vomited up, and then they drank some more. They all collapsed on the ground in various states of exhaustion.

Ben had spent enough years working law enforcement in the Southwest that he did not need an explanation from them about their situation. They were obviously a group of migrants crossing from Mexico and hoping to get picked up somewhere in Arizona.

The leader introduced himself as Raul and said, "*Muchas gracias.*"

"*De nada,*" replied Jessica. She followed with, "*De donde eran?*"

"*Hermosillo,*" he replied.

"*Y donde van?*" she asked.

"*Vamos a San Diego,*" he said and switched to near-perfect English. "We live there," he said, indicating one of the women and a ten-year-old boy. We went home for my father's funeral and are now heading back."

"Dude, that is a huge risk to take for a funeral," Ben said.

"I know. I think that this will be our last trip. It used to be much easier. In the old days, we would go home for the *Tres Reyes* or a niece's *quinceañera*, then take a bus, and jump the border at San Ysidro. But after Operation *pinche* Gatekeeper, it became very

hard. If you wanted to get across, you had to pay the cartels and their *estupidos* coyotes. For a while they had tunnels going through the desert near Yuma, and you had to pay, but at least it was *seguro*. But the cartels closed those off a few years ago, and now we still pay and walk. Our *guias* got lost three days ago and disappeared. I know the way, but our normal *tinaja* was empty; there was so little rain this year. We are very glad to have found you and your *agua*. We were so thirsty; we were even hoping to find *la migra*. But now I think we can make Tinajas Altas. There is always water there, but you have to climb," he said forebodingly.

Ben looked down at Raul's feet. He had some cheap tennis shoes that had separated from their soles and then had been taped together. "I am not sure that you can make it to Yuma on those," Ben said as he pulled off his boots and threw them to him.

"*Es la verdad. Muchisimas gracias*," was Raul's reply.

"*Por su puesto*," Ben replied, digging out his flip-flops from the jeep.

Jess started ladling out the dinner that she had made for the two of them to the entire group while Ben grabbed more of the same and started preparing it.

The rest of the group told their stories, which were mostly similar to Raul's. Some had crossed their whole lives. For a few of the younger ones, this was their first crossing. But they all had family in Mexico and the United States, and they regarded the border as a life-threatening inconvenience to be dealt with but not any sort of geopolitical reality. It was just a largely invisible line in the desert bisecting their lives.

Ben and Jessica continued with the food until the entire group had their fill. Raul asked Ben and Jess for a ride out of the desert to Yuma, but when Ben explained the gas and border-patrol situation, some of the migrants crossed themselves in the Catholic way, and some said that they would pray for their deliverance as this desert was a hostile place as if Ben and Jess were the ones in real danger.

Ben was just thinking the same thing about them as they loaded up their gear and wandered off into the night. As they were leaving, Ben handed Raul a compass. Raul thanked him and handed it back, pointing to Polaris in the clear sky and saying that he knew the way. Ben convinced them to take two headlamps, but he didn't think that they would use them so as not to give themselves away, but maybe they could use them to signal for help if they got into real trouble.

They watched them disappear into the night. Ben was left thinking about what they had said about the tunnels. While he had been a fed, Ben would get e-mail updates from the HSI or the DEA after they had found some elaborate drug-smuggling tunnel in San Diego or even in Arizona. Some had included elaborate ventilation systems, lights, and tracks for pull carts. In one memorable case from the 1990s, an entrance had been concealed beneath a pool table. But he couldn't help but think that Raul was mistaken. He had heard nothing about any tunnels near Yuma that had been discovered, and if they hadn't been discovered, why had the cartels stopped using them? Collapse maybe? Something about the tunnels tugged at his mind. Ben, Jess, and Geronimo tucked into the tent for the night with Ben thinking that between the .357 and the dog, they would hopefully be fine. The only sounds they heard as they drifted off to sleep were the nocturnal sounds of Sonoran Desert wildlife.

Thursday

Ben's eyes blinked open to the sound of an approaching engine. He groggily fumbled his way out of the tent to take a look.

"What is happening?" Jessica groaned.

"No idea," was the croaked response.

Geronimo got out of the tent as well and relieved himself on a cactus.

Ben peered into the distance and saw a dust plume from the inbound vehicle heading westward on El Camino del Diablo. When it finally came into view, Ben could make out the rotating red and blue lights on top and the distinct shade of green belonging only

to border-patrol vehicles. “It’s all good. It looks like our salvation is here; just don’t do anything jumpy at first. I am sure this patrol agent usually only encounters bad guys out here.”

Jess climbed out of the tent and went to work getting coffee started.

“That is a great idea,” Ben said. “These guys can’t resist coffee.”

“Who? Oh, yeah, I guess I can share a bit with them,” she replied groggily.

The truck skidded to a stop in a cloud of dust, but the agent did not get out of the truck. The truck just sat there idling menacingly with the lights rotating for a few minutes.

“Probably running my plate,” Ben said to Jessica.

After a few minutes, the door opened and a fit man in his midthirties with mirrored aviator sunglasses got out of the truck. “Is this your vehicle?” he asked.

“That’s right,” Ben replied.

“So are you Ben Adams?”

"Right again."

"The same Ben Adams that did five years at Pelican Bay for manslaughter?"

"Fuck," Ben muttered under his breath. "Yeah, that is me also."

"Dude! It's me, Jimmy O'Connell! Remember?"

"O…Connell?"

"Yeah, man. We met at SAC Lopez's retirement party from the FBI. He started with BP way back in the '80s. I was invited by my A Chief?"

"Whoa, man. Am I glad to see you out here! How have you been?" said Ben, much relieved by their good fortune.

"Great, man. Same old, same old in the desert here. I miss San Diego, but what are you gonna do? Remember that night after we left the party at the Yard House? We went to Cheetah's, and that stripper was all over you? I still can't believe that you chose to go home alone that night. Man that was dumb; she was smoking!"

Ben shrugged sheepishly.

"Then we all ended up on Lanahan's sailboat, and I think you puked your shepherd's pie over the side into the harbor? The fish went crazy for your barf! Ha! That was a great night!" he said, barely keeping it together, laughing at his own story.

"I guess it was pretty good. I forgot about most of it, but yeah, that was a great time."

"What the hell are you doing out here? Who is your friend? And is that coffee?"

"Yes, that is coffee; help yourself. This is my girlfriend Jessica." (Now it was her turn to arch her eyebrows at the characterization.) "And we came out here to try and drive the entire El Camino del Diablo to see if we could do it—kind of a 4x4 adventure tour—and like an idiot, I had too much to drink in Tucson two nights ago, forgot to fill my jerry can with gas, and we ran out right here. We just made camp and figured that you guys would be along sooner or later."

"Well, you are lucky I did find you. El Camino del Diablo got its name for a reason. If the heat or the wildlife doesn't get you, the cartels will. How did you even hear about it?"

"Online on some jeep forum—guys said it was tough and cool to give it a try, so I figured what the hell."

"And you went along with this batshit-crazy idea?" said O'Connell to Jess.

"What am I gonna do? He says it's cool, so I've gotta give it a try."

"Jeez, I wish there were more girls out there like you."

"Thank you very much," she said with a slight bow." She started ladling coffee out while Ben went into the jeep for some food.

Looking back over his shoulder, Ben called out, "Bagel?"

Two affirmative responses.

When Ben came back, he asked, "So is El Camino del Diablo your normal beat? How long have you been out here?"

"I've been working between the Yuma and Tucson sectors since I left SD. Man, I loved San Diego, but do you realize that I bought my house in Tucson with a pool for two hundred thousand? That doesn't even get you a crack house in San Diego. Not to mention working way out here means guaranteed OT, not like you sucker 1811s with your LEAP screw job. I am banking

a ton of dough out here in the desert. Anyway, I was cutting sign on the Vidrios Drag last night, and I got on to a group of about six or seven *pollos*, and then you guys must have tripped an Oscar, so I figured I would come out at first light and see what was up," O'Connell explained.

"*Pollos*? Department of Homeland Security must be behind on their sensitivity training for the Border Patrol."

"Man, you know how it is," O'Connell replied, blushing slightly.

"*Pollos*? Chickens? I don't get it," Jess said.

O'Connell just looked into his coffee.

"The coyotes who smuggle humans call their clients *pollos*. It is not exactly meant affectionately, and apparently BP has taken it up," Ben explained.

Jess gave the border-patrol agent a hard look.

"You are right—my bad. By the way," he said, changing the subject, "I'm sorry about what happened to you, man. I know we haven't spoken since then. But Oscar Nunez is an asshole. I feel bad about his brother, but as I heard it, it was just a bad deal that was the case

agent's fault, not yours—something about not running deconfliction? Anyway, it was a bad break. You didn't deserve it, and I am sorry."

"Don't sweat it, man. It is all in the past," Ben said, brushing it off.

"Do you miss it?" he asked.

"Prison? No."

"Not prison, you asshole, the FBI?" O'Connell asked.

"Not really. I miss the tactical work and some of the friendships and camaraderie, but I don't miss the truckloads of Bureau bullshit that we had to wade through."

"Tell me about it. BP is the same way," he said, draining his coffee.

"So should we throw some gas in your rig and get the fuck out of here before the Sinaloa Cartel cuts our heads off?" he suggested.

"Sounds good to me," Jess replied.

"OK, I only have enough spare fuel to get you to Camp Grip, but we have tons in drums there."

O'Connell pulled a gas can out of his truck and poured it straight into the jeep while Ben and Jess broke down the tent and packed up.

"OK," he said, jumping into his truck. "Follow me."

They piled into the jeep and the two vehicles headed west with the rising sun at their backs, trailing large plumes of dust.

They pulled into Camp Grip, which sat about halfway through El Camino del Diablo as it existed in the United States. Camp Grip was a remote border-patrol outpost used as a staging area for patrols along El Camino, manned by agents from Yuma and Tucson. It had the look and feel (having likely been built by the same contractor at outrageous cost-plus contract rates) of a forward-operating base in Afghanistan, and it functioned largely the same way.

They pulled into the base to a large group of border-patrol agents standing around applauding and jeering the FBI agent for running out of gas in the desert and thereby condemning his former agency as a whole as totally incompetent. It seemed that O'Connell had radioed ahead. It was apparently a pretty slow day at Camp Grip as the jokes about the FBI kept coming. Ben normally thought of himself more as a convicted felon than a former FBI agent, but these guys cared

more about taking the piss out of one of their (and almost everybody else in law enforcement's) favorite targets, the FBI, referring to them as "The Feebs" and "Famous But Incompetent." They could also relate to having been hosed by one's own agency, as it had happened one way or another to almost every one of them, even if just in their minds.

Ben threw a few back at *la migra* for hassling the hardworking tile setters, cooks, and gardeners of the world, but it was all in good-spirited rivalry. In apparent answer, one of their K-9 units even pissed on the tire of the jeep. Geronimo immediately rectified that insult with a tire soaking of his own. It was a small price to pay for fuel and water, and it reminded Ben of his preprison days in the Bureau and the camaraderie associated with such extreme and dangerous work. It felt good. They pulled out of Camp Grip to a chorus of Bronx cheers, and they continued westward.

They continued through El Camino with a new paper map provided by their new friends at Camp Grip. They buzzed along the dusty trail in the postadrenalized bliss of the past two days. As they bounced along, Jess noted that they were approaching the Tinajas Altas Mountains, and they both remembered that Raul had said that his group would find water there. Their mood darkened as they hoped that the group of thirsty migrants had found their way to the water

that they had claimed was high up in the mountains because, as Raul had said, it was very dry this year.

The end of El Camino del Diablo appeared slowly as the dirt track turned into an agricultural dirt road, and the desert turned into fields as they approached the freeway. They had to parallel the freeway for a few miles until they could find the access at the Mohawk rest area (now closed due to DOT budget cuts). Finally escaping El Camino del Diablo and entering Interstate 8, they high fived at having survived the desert and left their jerry can of water at the rest area for anybody who might make it that far on foot. They got back up to freeway speed and into Yuma, Arizona, the town with the unofficial motto "Where is your sense of Yuma?" Likely burned out by the searing sun, Ben reckoned.

They pulled into the downtown area along the banks of the Colorado River near the bridge where they had crossed just days before. As they rolled into Yuma, they pulled into a restaurant called Yuma Landing. They sat among the vintage aviation photos and memorabilia, talking about their options while Geronimo, in full service gear, lounged underneath the table, escaping the heat outside.

"So, it seems pretty clear to me that you are definitely a target at this point. My apologies for not buying

your theory earlier," Ben said, taking a long drink of an Arnold Palmer—for once having a drink without alcohol.

"I told you," she replied in a singsong way, taking a long drink of water herself. "So now what do we do?" she asked.

"I guess I think we should restock with supplies and get out to the river where the professor claims the water disappears. If it is anything like where we have been, it wouldn't surprise me if nobody goes out there. Also, I think that we should call the professor and see if he dug anything up while we were gone."

"You realize that was only yesterday, right?"

"Yeah, but you realize that guy has literally nothing else going on? Did you see his place?"

"Touché," she replied.

The waitress put down their burgers and fries as Ben ordered another Arnold Palmer, and Jess got another water. They might not have recognized it, but they consumed their water and food with an urgency that hadn't been there before their Camino del Diablo experience. Afterward, everything seemed just a little more precious.

"I think that I had better be the one to call him," Jessica said. "He doesn't seem to like you that much."

"OK fine, but I am not the one locked up in Ajo, Arizona, so consider the source when making your judgment."

"Have you taken a good look at your own life lately?" she asked rhetorically, pulling out the second burner phone that they had bought in San Diego. She dialed the number of the first burner phone, which was hopefully charged and still sitting in Ajo with Jaime Gutierrez, and waited.

"Hello, Professor? This is Jess. Are you OK? We were followed leaving your house yesterday. Have you had any problems?" she asked. "Really? Oh that can be a problem. Maybe some locking trash-can lids would keep them out? Have you had any problems with any *people*?" she asked. "Oh, OK, good. We were worried," she said as Ben mouthed *we were?*

She waved Ben off as the professor spoke rapidly on the phone. "Yep…OK. Really? Wow, OK Maybe that is something….OK, what else?" She paused, listening. "I'm not sure how to interpret that, but I'll ask Ben… Yes, he is still with me…I won't…No, he is not a total dick. Thanks a bunch. We will let you know what we

find out. Good-bye." She flipped the phone shut and looked at Ben across the table.

They sat for a beat in silence.

"OK, give it up. What are you holding? Two pair? Full house? What?" Ben asked insistently.

She smiled and said, "The professor said that, subject to a huge margin of error since he had only been at it one day, there is no way that the amount of soybeans, alfalfa, and other industrial agriculture going on around the south side of the Salton Sea could be supported with the water that they are getting. Boom! How about that?"

"OK, now we are getting somewhere."

"There is more. He said that at one point, the Google satellite images had snapped a huge amount of construction equipment staged along Highway 78 between the river and the Salton Sea. I'm not sure what that means, but he seemed to think it was important. He said it seemed like enough gear to build the Hoover Dam."

"That may be nothing, but it sounds interesting. Did he say where?"

"He gave me a mile marker, number ninety-five. He said that there was a dirt road that left the highway and went straight toward the refuge, and about halfway, there were a bunch of trucks where there shouldn't be any."

"What do you say we check it out?"

"I say yes. Looks like you are going to miss your south swell."

"There will probably be another one," Ben said, mostly serious.

They finished their lunch, paid the bill, and jumped back in the jeep. On their way out of town, they stopped, and Ben bought a tablet computer with cellular-data capability that he thought they could use for additional research on the road, and he replaced the boots that he had given to the shoeless Raul with a brand-new pair of Dr. Martens.

They headed west on Interstate 8 through the dunes to the Imperial Valley, where the air became humid, and the landscape turned from brown and lifeless to lush and green fields. They felt the air change from desiccated desert to the hot humidity and bugs associated with lots of water and vegetation. They turned

north on Highway 111 to the intersection with Highway 78 that led east again toward their destination near the Imperial National Wildlife Refuge. The landscape turned back into harsh desert as they left the fields and went east on Highway 78. They passed through a border-patrol checkpoint, but this time there were no friendly ghosts from law-enforcement past. They just gave the obligatory declaration of US citizenship and went through.

Jess asked what the Border Patrol was doing manning armed checkpoints in the interior of the United States, fifty miles from any international border. She said that between the desert and the armed checkpoints, she had to convince herself that they weren't in the Middle East. Ben laboriously explained that the Supreme Court had allowed the border-search authority to extend up to one hundred air miles from the border, creating large swaths of the United States, including the entirety of several East Coast states, where the 4th Amendment didn't fully apply, allowing warrantless searches and seizures with very little regulation or constitutional oversight.

"Are you fucking serious?" she asked when he finished his dissertation.

"I'm afraid so," he replied casually, taking a piece of beef jerky from the center console.

"Well, fuck that. Does New Zealand have the same rules?"

"No idea. Are we moving there?"

"Maybe. This functional equivalent of the border is bullshit."

"Tell it to the judge, sister," he said.

She reached into the cooler and broke out her first beer of the day and slumped in silence in the passenger seat in a funk about border-search authority and the Supreme Court's interpretation.

Watching the mile markers creep up, they got to ninety-five, turned off, and followed a dirt track due east toward the refuge. Not unlike El Camino del Diablo, this unnamed trail cut a serpentine path through the desert, following the undulations of the natural surface. Here and there were large piles of dirt that Ben took to be tailings from failed mining adventures in the area. After about half an hour of dusty driving, they came upon an otherwise nondescript part of the desert, but it was fenced in with ten-foot-high chain link and concertina wire across the top. They estimated it to be a few acres, and in the center appeared to be some sort of concrete platform.

Ben worked his lock-picking magic again on the padlock, secured the gate, and it swung open. They drove in slowly. It appeared as though the entire area had been pounded to dust by large tire tracks that appeared to be quite old and frozen in place in a region of almost no rain. Where other parts of the desert had small shrubs and lichen, inside this chain link was like Mars, nothing lived. It jived with the professor's description of lots of construction equipment moving around. The area had the war-torn look of a nascent land development familiar to anyone who had lived in the modern boom towns of Arizona and had watched nature subsumed in the service of progress. But where those same developments ultimately sprouted strip malls and identical rows of homes after the devastation, this development remained scarred.

They pulled up to the concrete platform and got out. Geronimo went about smelling the entire area and pronounced his opinion with a large dump. Ben left this one where it lay. They jumped up on the three-foot-high platform and looked around. In the center were two large steel doors like the kind you'd find on the streets of New York that lead to the basements of old buildings. They were not secured but were far too heavy for Ben and Jess to lift on their own. Ben backed the jeep up to the platform and secured the brake. He removed two bolts to fold the windshield down, and then he released the long cable from the winch on the

front bumper. Looping it backward over the roll bar, he hooked it on to one of the handles to the big steel door. He fired up the winch, and with a groan, the big door heaved open. When it got just short of vertical, Ben stopped it. They could hear a loud rushing noise emanating from within the concrete, like a jet engine or Niagara Falls.

They slowly approached the concrete platform and climbed up. It was about fifteen feet from the edge of the concrete to the surface of the water below. It was hard to tell the width, but the torrent was at least as wide as the platform, perhaps much wider. What they saw were hundreds of thousands of cubic feet per minute of water rushing past the opening at a speed that would give the Emerald Mile pause. The water was flowing west toward the Salton Sea and the previously described unsustainable agriculture based there.

"Well, that was easy," Ben said.

"Fuck me—this is a big deal," replied Jess. "How could they have built this with nobody knowing?" she asked.

"I don't know, maybe it was just as easy as doing it. Look around, nobody lives here, and not counting the Border Patrol, nobody works here, and those guys are

a pretty recent development on interior roads. Maybe they just fucking did it?"

"OK, then the next question is, who is *they*?" she asked.

Their conversation was interrupted by a short bark by Geronimo and the approach of a white pickup truck labeled Amtrex Security. The truck skidded to a stop outside of the enclosure and two men in their late twenties got out, each in tan battle-dress uniform with the Amtrex logo on the breast and with what appeared to be Glock 19s in chest rigs. They had the swagger of military men who had gone the contractor route: all of the deadly skill with none of the pesky US Department of Defense rules of engagement.

They approached and ordered them off of the platform. Ben and Jess complied.

"What are you two doing out here?" the first one demanded.

Jess started. "We were lost, and we saw this concrete here and thought maybe it was a well where we could get some water for our dog."

Ben looked at her sideways, thinking science was definitely a better career choice for her than acting.

“Do you really expect us to believe that garbage story?” the second asked.

“Listen, fellas, the truth is that we are journalists from the *Cleveland Plain Dealer* and—” Ben said.

“You shut the fuck up, FBI man. We know the truth, but we want to hear what Ms. McCoy has to say about it. Either way, it’s gonna be what it’s gonna be.”

Jess started to speak as Ben quickly drew out his .357 Smith & Wesson and pulled the trigger three times as he raised it to eye level with the barrel right on target. The gun clicked impotently three times in rapid response. The first guard went for his pistol as Ben threw the .357 as hard as he could at the guy’s face, fastball style. The gun found its target where the bullets hadn’t, and the guard’s nose answered in blood.

The guard reflexively brought his hands to his face, and Ben charged him. Ben grabbed the guy’s Glock out of the chest holster as they both tumbled to the ground. By this time, the other guard had his pistol out and was trying to get a clear shot, but Geronimo had the wrist of his gun hand in his teeth and was starting to draw blood.

Jessica jumped behind the jeep, looking for a weapon, and came up with a Spyderco knife from the glove box. She held it upright, unsure what to do. On the

ground, Ben transferred the gun to his left hand and smashed his right hand into the face of the guard on the ground beneath him, raising himself up high enough to line up the sights. Ben snapped off two quick rounds to his left, once again, aiming a little high for how he had been trained, but both bullets caught the standing guard in the head and killed him as his body fell to earth like a sack of potatoes. He then turned the gun to the head of the guard beneath him, still wrestling. He turned his own face away and ended the guard.

Ben dropped the Glock in the dirt and wiped his hands on the dead man's shirt as he staggered to his feet. Geronimo trotted up with his ears down and wagged his tail.

"Good boy, G-Dog," he said, rubbing his head. "Very good boy!"

He walked over to the jeep and grabbed two pieces of beef jerky, bit one, and gave the other one to Geronimo.

Jessica came around from the jeep, still clutching the knife and said, "What the fuck was that?"

"They were about to kill us," Ben matter-of-factly replied.

"How the fuck do you know that?"

"They knew that I was in the FBI, and they called you by name."

"And in your world that means they were going to kill us?" she asked, still incredulous.

"Yes."

"Really? OK, Doc Holliday, walk me through that one."

"OK, first, they had guns—"

"This is Arizona—everybody has a gun!"

"Actually, we are back in California, and, second, he called you by name and knew my background and—"

"Fuck, they did know who we were," she replied in shock.

"Third, he said that it was gonna be what it was gonna be. That sounded pretty fatalistic to me, so I went with the best interpretation under the circumstances."

"You are 100 percent sure of that? What if you were wrong?"

"I'd give it a 5 percent chance that I was wrong, and in that case, we get to live with the guilt of killing two guys, but the thing is that we still get to live."

"Jesus, OK. We should get the fuck out of here."

"Agreed."

"What about those two?" she said, gesturing to the two dead bodies.

"Aqua tunnel for sure," Ben responded with a barely perceptible smile.

"Jesus, OK."

They dragged the bodies over to the concrete slab and hoisted them onto the platform. Ben pulled their ID tags from their shirts and then rolled them into the opening. They fell with an oddly satisfying deep splash and were immediately sucked away by the current. They followed with the guns and other associated detritus of the struggle.

"Shouldn't we have kept at least one of those guns?" she asked.

"Mine didn't work as you saw, and I don't think it is worth the risk of being linked to a homicide with either of their guns—trust me," Ben replied.

"Fair enough. What do we do about the car?" Jessica asked.

Ben jumped into their truck and drove it directly into a ditch, making sure to spin the tires back and forth to make sure that the truck was well and truly stuck. He walked back to the aqua tunnel and tossed the keys in. Ben started lowering down the door with the winch and said, "With any luck, when somebody finds the truck they will think that they got stuck and wandered off and died."

"OK, Mr. Odds. What do think the likelihood of that is?"

"Eleven percent, but at a minimum, it should confuse them for a while, and at the moment, I don't have a better idea. In the meantime, we need a place to hide, regroup, and figure all of this out, and I don't think my place in Pacific Beach is going to work—swell or no swell."

"I know exactly the place. Hand me the map," said Jessica.

Friday

They awoke in their tent, having made camp in the wee hours of the morning after a long night of driving. They were in a broad, shallow canyon in northern New Mexico, filled with the ruins of a grand, ancient city. They were in Chaco Canyon National Park.

"Exactly how is going to a national park laying low?" Ben asked wearily from his sleeping bag.

"Trust me, Ben. Nobody comes here," Jess replied, extricating herself from her bag. "You should make coffee."

"Yeah, OK," Ben said as he also dug himself out of the bag and lumbered out of the tent toward the jeep.

True enough, there was nobody in the campground; it was the national park that time forgot. Being at the end of thirty miles of dirt road in the middle of the New Mexican desert was probably a large factor. Chaco Canyon was the site of an ancient city of thousands linked with the tropical cities of pre-Columbian America through a series of long-distance trade routes. Tropical parrot feathers had been found there with origins thousands of miles away. The site boasted buildings and windows aligned with solar events, the knowledge of which would have taken generations to acquire. Now, there were only the mute masonry ruins of great houses and kivas, the largest collection of Pueblo ruins north of Mexico. The ruins were visible from the campsite as Ben made coffee and got out the stove for some breakfast. Geronimo trotted back from some unknown adventure, his coat filled with various plant life and bird feathers.

Setting up a folding chair, Ben said, "You know, I don't think those piles on the roadside were mining tailings. I bet those were piles of dirt that they had excavated for that tunnel."

"That makes sense. I just can't believe that they could just steal half of the Colorado River underground without anybody noticing."

"Somebody noticed. It was just that that somebody was an unfortunate professor at the U of A—and us!"

"Well that sucks."

"Tell me about it. Turns out that swell is hitting perfectly, according to Surfline. Five to seven feet at Sunset Cliffs," Ben said, looking at his new tablet computer. Setting it down, he asked, "Oatmeal or egg scramble?" as he picked up two bags of yet more freeze-dried camp food.

"Oatmeal, please," she replied.

Ben went to work on the oatmeal while Jess grabbed the computer and started tapping away. "On the satellite maps, it looks like there is one of those concrete-tunnel accesses every mile or so on a straight line from the wildlife refuge all the way to those green fields south of the Salton Sea, but it looks like the one we were at is the only one with a big fence around it. That was probably just where they staged all of the equipment and then just never bothered to take the fence down."

"Hmm, maybe so," she acquiesced uncertainly.

Ben set out breakfast and coffee as well as food and water for Geronimo, and they all ate.

"It says here that at 10:00 a.m. there is a walking tour with one of the rangers around the ruins here at Chaco. You want to check it out?" asked Jessica.

"Sure, let's have a look at this joint," he replied through a mouthful of breakfast.

They met the ranger at 10:00 at the visitor's center, and as anticipated, they were the only ones on the tour.

The ranger seemed excited to have an audience for once and took them around the formerly great city, enthusiastically describing the different buildings and their theoretical usage. He also described how the population of the canyon had peaked around AD 1100 and then declined drastically, likely due to a combination of deforestation and drought, which led to conflict, death, and ultimately abandonment of Chaco Canyon.

"Does this sound familiar?" Jess whispered to Ben. "In a hundred years, Phoenix and Las Vegas could look like this."

Back at the campsite, Ben grabbed the computer and started searching. He searched *Amtrex Security*, the name on the side of the truck back at the tunnel. Using public open-source material, he traced them to a DBA from White House Plumbers LLC out of Culver City,

which was not a huge surprise to Ben at this point. He started searching public records from the tax assessor in the Imperial Valley. The quantity of material was enormous. All of the individual parcels were owned by separate companies, sometimes leased to one another, and always owned by different separate companies, often out of state. This process consumed most of the afternoon, with Ben writing notes, going back to the computer, and then comparing notes. Sitting by a tent next to an abandoned city in the desert meant that there was no way to print anything, so he ended up with a large pile of handwritten notes. After a few hours, he sighed, powered down the computer, and grabbed a beer from the cooler—surprisingly, his first since El Camino del Diablo.

"How did you do?" she asked.

"I don't know. It needs more work. I have most of the parcels linked to a few companies in Delaware, but that is as much as I have. I need to dig deeper to find out who actually controls those properties. One of those companies seems to be the one that owns most of the land that the tunnel goes through. It is something lame like Desert Development LLC. I am going to take a break and get back to it later."

"Do you mind if I take a look?" Jess asked.

"Be my guest. My notes are over there," he said, pointing. "Good luck deciphering them."

"I can handle it," she replied.

Jessica tore into the computer and his notes, switching back and forth from computer to pages and back again. After a few hours of her own, she put down the computer and notes, exasperated. She then went to the cooler for a beer. "It is just a fucking legal maze. LLCs in Delaware leasing land to another LLC in Nevada, who in turn subleases it to a third LLC, and all of the ownership of the LLCs are listed as other LLCs in different states," she said.

"I know. It's brutal. This group is clever and industrious."

"Fuck this," she said, looking around the jeep. She dug out a Frisbee, and Geronimo perked up from inside the tent, barked, and she started throwing it for him.

Ben went back to work on the computer. He started digging deeper on Amtrex again. It turned out that Amtrex shared ownership with one of the big Iraq contractors called BearClaw Logistical Solutions that was famous for a very loose-trigger policy. It appeared that a lot of their personnel was also shared

with Amtrex, working domestically, with BearClaw, working internationally, mostly in the Middle East and Africa. There was a lot of bad press online about BearClaw and very little about Amtrex—no huge surprise there.

He tried to find a client list for Amtrex, but apparently they weren't dumb enough to post that online. He ended up at a charity website and found a photo of the CEO of BearClaw, Erik Kaiser, taken with the CEO of Agricon, Alan Kettner, at some cancer benefit in Santa Monica. In the background, some B-list celebrities were among the crowd. The two were clearly having a good time, their red faces no doubt flushed with high-quality craft cocktails and the giddiness of black-tie philanthropy.

Ben set down the computer and grabbed another beer before entering the Frisbee game with Jess and Geronimo. They played around as the sun went down until it got too dark to see. Back at the campsite, Ben fired up two tiki torches.

"This car isn't that big. Where are you getting all of that stuff?" Jess queried.

"Very smart packing—like a big game of Tetris," Ben replied, starting to feel the warm buzz of the beer. He dug around and came up with some salami and

cheese and started cutting it up to complement the continued beer consumption.

As he worked, Jess sat down and picked up the computer. "What the fuck is this?" she asked as the photo came up from the cancer benefit.

"What?" Ben asked, taking a bite of salami.

"That is my dad!" she said.

"Who is your dad?"

"The guy in the background of this picture who's talking to that guy from that terrible cop movie."

Ben walked over to take a look. In the background among the group was a fit white man in his early sixties wearing an Agricon polo shirt that Jess indicated was her father.

"Hmmm, so your dad works for Agricon, and the CEO of Agricon is obviously chummy with the CEO of BearClaw, who is also on the board of directors at Amtrex—maybe we are on to something? Could just be a coincidence. Here, have another beer and some salami, and we can get into this in the morning," he said, trying to distract her so he could process the implications of the new information.

"Wait a minute, I just found out that the company that my dad works for may be involved in trying to have me killed, and your solution is beer and salami?"

"Definitely. I am not sure that there is a better time for it. The photo of your dad is almost certainly a coincidence," he lied. "This murderous plot of greed and revenge can keep until tomorrow; we are burnt today. If it's true that there is a connection, I promise that we can take a clear-eyed look in the morning."

"Fuck it—do you have any tequila?" she asked, happy to forget about that possibility for a while.

Mission accomplished for the moment, Ben thought. "Actually, as it happens…" he said, walking back to the bottomless jeep.

The current situation temporarily forgotten, they made a fire and drank tequila and beer into the night under the same sky that had silently watched the rise and fall of the Anasazi in Chaco Canyon.

Saturday

They awoke groggily and clambered out of the tent.

"You said something about arising clear eyed this morning, right?" Jess croaked.

"That may have been bullshit. I apologize. Let me set the coffee up as a small token of penitence," he said as he teetered toward the table set up next to the jeep with the stove on it. He got the coffee going, fed G-Dog, and started to get some breakfast together.

Jess came over, and he handed her a cup of coffee. She was just wearing a T-shirt and her underwear, not self-conscious with no one around but the ghosts of

the Puebloan people. “So what now?” she asked, taking a sip of coffee.

“Let me just do some quick searching on these two companies and see what I can come up with online—after we eat, of course,” he said, craning his head back to get a look at her butt.

“Why don’t we just pack up our shit, get to LA, and talk to my dad about this? He is going to want to know, not to mention that he is the one in the best position to do something about it as he is on the *inside*,” she said.

“I guess that makes sense. Give me one hour online, and we can hit the road,” Ben proffered.

“Deal,” she replied, happy to be getting her dad involved. She was sure that he would be able to fix this; he fixed everything.

After breakfast, Jess started tearing down the camp while Ben went online to find out all he could from open sources about Agricon, Amtrex Security, and BearClaw Logistical. He couldn’t get anything too specific, but it was clear from photos and news stories that Agricon was one of Amtrex’s domestic clients. Further research found all sorts of unproven allegations about heavy-handed and possibly illegal activity on the part of

Amtrex, fully in line with the White House Plumbers' moniker and history, plus a full suite of war-crime allegations against BearClaw, with many of the same operators named in both sets of allegations.

The jeep packed up, they headed out of Chaco Canyon and linked up with the former Route 66, now Interstate 40, and headed west for Los Angeles. They made it as far as the mountains of northern Arizona and Flagstaff where they stopped for the night and got a room in the Hotel Monte Vista in downtown Flagstaff. The Monte Vista was a historic but rough hotel with off-track betting in the lobby, it was the type of place where neither their paying cash for a room nor Geronimo's wearing his service vest raised an eyebrow. One got the impression that nobody would care either way what the dog was wearing.

They wandered around downtown Flagstaff as neither of them had been there before. Jess talked about their predicament and how, with her dad involved, it would surely be sorted out. It seemed to be some sort of deep-seated belief that dad would make it all better that Ben thought was clearly misplaced, but he didn't say so. Ben's cynical mind was going the opposite direction, but he was not about to share that with her yet.

Continuing a theme, they grabbed dinner and beers at Diablo Burger and wondered aloud if Raul and

his compatriots had made it through the desert alive and back to their homes in San Diego. Ben thought about calling O'Connell for some intel on the group but figured they had enough of their own problems to contend with at the moment.

Ben looked up from his burger and saw them first, his eyes beating theirs by a half second—based purely on luck—as they came through the door. They were the same shaggy, superfit former special ops type guys that he had known and worked with at the Bureau and he had just killed at the aqua tunnel. They were badly disguised as college students but moved with obvious purpose. Ben grabbed his beer, flipped the table sideways, and pulled Jessica down as the first silenced bullets splintered the wood. The crowd panicked toward the door, ironically in the direction of gunfire.

Ben grabbed Jess by the hand and sprinted low into the kitchen with Geronimo right behind them. They could hear commotion behind them as they burst into the alley. Jess started to run down the alley, but Ben stopped, picked up a garbage-can lid, and stood next to the back door while Jess kept sprinting with Geronimo following her. The first guy burst out through the door, and Ben walloped him in the head with the lid. Bending over him as he hit the ground, Ben yelled, "*Fuck you!*" right in his face.

The second guy came up right behind the first. Ben sprung up and gave the guy a hard uppercut with the lid. It didn't do much damage, but it made his gun go off right in front of his face. The bullet lodged in the plaster above him and caused him to stumble and slip on some grease from the restaurant. He landed in a pile on his partner, stunned and confused.

Ben caught up to Jess sprinting down the alley, and they both turned left onto the street where the now-familiar Ford Crown Victoria was parked. Ben skidded to a stop and asked Jess if she still had the Spyderco knife from the glove box. She fished it out of her pocket and handed it to him. He flicked open the blade and muttered, "And fuck this car," as he forced the blade into the front tire of the Ford. He repeated the same for the back tire into what must have been the spare after their blowout on El Camino del Diablo. The Crown Vic sat hissing as the three of them took off toward the hotel.

Jess packed their gear upstairs while Ben worked countersurveillance in the lobby. They hustled out of there, jumped back into the jeep, and headed out of town. Feeling bitter about the loss of his Diablo Burger, Ben pulled into a drive-through fast-food joint and re-loaded with salt and grease. Jess took a pass since she was too freaked out to eat. They made camp a half

mile off of a dirt road in the Kaibab National Forest west of Flagstaff, parked amid a grove of Ponderosa Pines. After they set up the tent, Ben volunteered for the first watch, promising to wake Jess up at 2:00 a.m. He was so angry at the repeated attempts on their lives that he couldn't sleep, so he decided not to wake Jess and kept watch all night. He kept the coffee going while Geronimo patrolled the area for bad guys and skunks.

Sunday

By morning, his ardor had cooled a bit, and when Jessica woke up, he gave himself a celebratory breakfast beer, having skipped the night before in favor of clearheaded sentry duty.

"I thought that you were going to wake me up at two?" she asked.

"I didn't have the heart. We made a trade although you didn't know it: I stay up all night on watch, and you drive the rest of the way to LA while I sleep. How about it?"

"OK, deal," she said, not sure what the other option was.

She had some coffee while Ben broke down the camp, and they hit the road. Wanting to avoid the freeway as much as possible to keep from meeting their new friends from the past week, Dennis and Karl—formerly of Mosul and Kandahar—who would no doubt be in an extra foul mood, they turned onto one of the remaining sections of Route 66 that hadn't been swallowed up by the interstate-highway system. They swung wide in a large arc toward the Grand Canyon as they went through little towns frozen in time as they had been the day that the freeway had been opened and cut them off from all the traffic bounty that Route 66 used to provide. That they still existed was a testament to the nostalgia of the tourists that still came by occasionally to buy a Route 66 coffee mug or have a slice of pie and pretend that it was still fifty years ago.

Ben missed all of this, of course, because he was sound asleep in the passenger seat while Jess drove and navigated. Geronimo was also of little help, snoring loudly in the back, also tired from the long night. At Kingman, Arizona, they continued due west where the freeway juked south, and they drove into Laughlin, Nevada.

Laughlin was like a miniature second-fiddle Las Vegas on the banks of the Colorado River. The casinos ran free ferry boats across to Bullhead City, Arizona, to

help residents there who didn't have the wherewithal to cross a bridge get their meager cash into the casinos.

They crossed the river and couldn't help but notice that it looked a bit lower. It was probably entirely psychological, knowing what they now knew, but to them it was lower all the same. They stopped for lunch at a casino buffet.

After they were seated, Ben returned to the table, beaming and with a plateful of crab claws and shrimp. "Well, this isn't so bad," he proffered.

"I haven't decided whether or not you are very simple or very complicated," Jess replied.

"I probably used to be complicated, but after five years in solitary confinement, I now tend toward the simple."

"I guess so. That might explain the surf obsession."

"Oh, yeah. I have been meaning to ask you about that. It's like you don't have a problem with surfing at all?"

"You say that like it is alcoholism."

"Oh, it is way worse than alcoholism—or better—depending on how you look at it."

"Well, I just go surfing when I have the time. I enjoy it; that is it. It's only a sport."

"Yeah, right. Surfing is only a sport, like Ebola is only an infection."

"You definitely have problems."

"Maybe so, but they are currently being solved by this all-you-can-eat seafood buffet," he said, arising for another strafing run at the buffet line.

When he came back with a fresh pile of bottom feeders, Jess was finishing up her plate and said, "Listen, I know I have been giving you a hard time, and I think that maybe you like that about me, but I want you to know how much I appreciate what you have done for me, particularly considering that we met drunk at the Tiki less than a week ago."

"Don't mention it. If nothing else, it has been a wild ride."

"But you realize that you have killed two people so far and brutally assaulted two more?"

"Well those first two were probably going to kill us, so they had it coming, and the second two definitely were going to kill us, so I may just kill them

yet. And you forgot the guy I killed that sent me to prison in the first place. I realize that is probably not the normal human experience, particularly for grad students in environmental science or whatever you are studying, but for what it's worth, all of the men I killed and hit with trash-can lids are all in the Club."

"What club?"

"The Killing Club."

"Did you just make that up?"

"Actually, I stole it from a movie, but I liked it, and I am keeping it."

"What the fuck is the Killing Club?"

"It is the club of FBI agents, secret-service agents, soldiers, mercenaries, cartel soldiers, mafiosi, etc. Basically anybody who has trained to take lives and plans for that possibility in their work. Some people call it the *warrior mentality* or some other self-congratulatory bullshit, but I like the *killing club*; it is more honest. It is a changed perspective, and once you accept it, it is somewhat comforting."

"How is that?"

"Once you accept that you can kill and also be killed, there isn't that much to be afraid of anymore, and you are free to just enjoy your plate of crab claws."

"Jesus, I'm not sure what to make of that."

"Well, I saw you go for that knife in the desert. I think at this point that you are at least a probationary member of the Club."

"Fuck that. I want out of the Club."

"Some people don't get to choose, particularly in places like Africa, but in this case, maybe we can wrap this up without you getting a full-fledged membership."

"Let's see if we can't make that happen, shall we?" she asked with a lilt in her voice.

"Indeed," he replied while raising his glass in a partial mock toast, followed by a very real drink.

They piled back into the jeep with a solid haul from the buffet for Geronimo. Heading east around the Dead Mountains Wilderness Area, they turned south on Highway 95 and had no choice but to rejoin the freeway into Los Angeles.

Ben was awake and at the wheel when Jess called home. "Hey, Mom, it's me…I know. No, everything is fine…Yeah, I am coming into LA right now…Is dad home?" She paused, listening. "Oh, OK, I'll go by there first. I have some research questions to ask him…Sure, afterward we will come by for dinner. That sounds good…Yup, all of us. Also I am bringing a friend… Boy? I guess you could say that. You will definitely like him. We'll see you later. We are headed there now."

She clicked off the phone and said, "My dad is at his office in Culver City. I say we go straight there and tell him what we know and see if he can help us. He is going to want to know what is going on with this."

"OK," Ben said warily, not exactly sure that going in the front door of the headquarters of Agricon was the best tactical plan, but lacking a better idea at the moment, he went along with it. "Just direct me in. I don't know Culver City that well," he said.

They cruised past the wind farms of Palm Springs through the San Gorgonio Pass, their thousands of blades chopping through the air in unison. The traffic started building, and they groped their way down Interstate 10 into the LA megalopolis. After what seemed like three hours of city driving, they exited in Culver City. Jess directed them around the surface

streets. They drove past the various midcentury low-rise office buildings until they came upon a white, four-story office complex with a monument sign on the street indicating Agricon Headquarters. Ben rumbled past the building, noticing two surveillance cameras pointed at the front door.

"There was street parking right there," Jess said, pointing.

"Better to park down the block just in case," Ben responded.

"What do you mean?"

"Just in case our friends are still following us," Ben said, only partly lying.

"Ahh, got it—good thinking," she replied.

They parked the car, told Geronimo to stay, and started walking toward the entrance.

"It's Sunday. I assume that they are closed. Are you going to call your dad?"

"No need. I used to intern in the mail room in college, and I still have a key for the back door," Jess said,

holding up a shiny deadbolt key that she had fished from her bag.

"Well played, madam."

They shuffled around the back of the building to the door facing the rear parking lot and let themselves into the building. Ben happily noticed that this entrance wasn't monitored by video. The alarm chirped as they opened the door, but it did not alert as it was not armed at that moment. Somebody had coded it off.

"That was lucky," Jess said. "They didn't have an alarm when I was working here."

Ben's response was only *pfffff*.

They worked their way up the fourth floor and down a long corridor to the executive suites. One of the office doors was slightly ajar; it bore the nameplate of Rory McCoy, VP of Operations. Jess pushed open the door and said, "Daddy, are you in there?"

They both walked in and saw Mr. McCoy sitting at his desk. He had the appearance of a man under an incredible amount of stress. His white hair was tussled, his skin was pallid, and his hands were trembling. "Oh

my gosh, sweetie, it is good to see you!" he said, standing up to hug her.

Ben noticed both the bourbon on the desk and the revolver in the partially open drawer.

"What are you doing here?" he asked, smiling weakly.

"We came because we need your help. We found out some things that you need to know about your company, and maybe we can make it right..."

"Nobody was supposed to get hurt," he mumbled, looking at his lap and collapsing back into his chair, his flimsy façade falling apart.

"What was that?" she asked.

"Nobody was supposed to get hurt. They told me nobody would get hurt, just scared. I'm sorry...It was my job...I had to...I didn't mean it..." he said, trailing off.

"What are you talking about, Dad?" Jess demanded.

Ben started to move to the side of the room to let this play out and to get to within striking distance of that revolver if things went sideways.

"It just got out of control..."

"That's enough, Rory." The voice came from behind, and in walked Alan Kettner, the CEO of Agricon that Ben remembered from the photograph of the cancer benefit. He was followed in by the guys from Diablo Burger, El Camino del Diablo, and Jess's apartment, both of whom were carrying what appeared to be Heckler & Koch MP5s. Their faces were swollen and bandaged as a result of the garbage-can-lid impacts. Ben couldn't suppress a tiny giggle when he saw the damage.

"Fuck you, motherfucker!" the taller one said, pointing at Ben and starting toward him.

"Stand down, Karl," the CEO barked, and the soldier obeyed the order.

"Now, Rory, you need to stop talking now. I am here, and I am now in control of this situation," he said.

Jessica's eyes widened as she processed all of this new information and quickly gained a full understanding of the situation.

"I just have one question Alan: How did you guys dig the tunnel?" Ben asked.

"I'll consider this your last request, Mr. Adams, and I will grant it. I am actually quite proud of that. It was back in the mid-1990s, and we came up with the idea after realizing that the monitoring ability for flows on the Colorado were at best estimates, so we figured we could just take as much as we wanted, and as long as nobody could actually see us doing it, nobody would ever know. And it worked for almost twenty years, by the way!"

"OK, I get the idea. But how did you actually dig the thing without anybody catching on?" Ben asked.

"That was the true stroke of genius in our plan—isn't that right, Rory? I had read a story about a drug tunnel in Arizona that had an entrance hidden under a pool table on one side of the border and behind a bookcase on the other, and it was equipped with climate control, pumps, and lights—very high tech and well engineered. So I reached out to the cartel that had built it and made a deal; it was brilliant," he continued, obviously quite pleased with himself.

"So you just requested that they be your friend on Facebook, they accepted, and it went from there?" Ben asked with a heavy dose of sarcasm.

"It was a bit more complicated than that. I had to track them down in Mexico and convince them that

we weren't DEA and to give up on their own tunnel operations, it wasn't easy. We had some close calls. You remember that guy putting the gun in your mouth, Rory? That was fucking scary! Those were some great times though, eh? Lots of drugs, tequila, and broads. We were like fucking *Scarface*, man! Private jets, yachts—the whole fucking thing!"

Rory said nothing and just quietly wept.

"Anyway, I got off track there a bit. We got their engineers and some of their soldiers to get to work, we formed Amtrex Security to control the sites in the United States, and bada-bing! We got as much water as you please! We then got extremely lucky that the United States invaded Afghanistan and Iraq. We spun off BearClaw with that born-again idiot Kaiser and made even more money!" he continued maniacally. "We did the same tunnel thing with some of their rivers over there too. Nothing as grand as Gaddafi's Great Man-Made River but good stuff, and not to mention, look at how things turned out for him. Am I right?" he said, losing his own plot. "Again, slightly off track there, but after we got BearClaw running, we got these great DOD cost-plus contracts for protection over there. If a US soldier gets killed, it is a political travesty, but for a contractor, we could bill three hundred thousand dollars a year for each one and nobody gave a shit if they got blown up. They paid even our

most outrageous invoices without even blinking. It was fucking unbelievable! A total gold rush."

"And meanwhile, back here, nobody noticed a bunch of cartel guys and special ops digging a giant fucking tunnel in the desert?" Ben asked skeptically.

"Well, nobody that mattered anyway. We had to dump a few wildlife biologists from the wildlife refuge and a few wayward undocumented migrants during construction—maybe more than a few—but they all drowned *accidentally* in the Colorado River; that was it. We also had to bluff the Border Patrol a bit. We even ended up hiring some of their BORTAC and BORSTAR guys to work for us, but outside of that, we looked legit enough that most of those guys working the checkpoints didn't give a shit—we were white with nice trucks, and the cartel guys came in by helicopter. It has been a godsend for our business—I gotta tell ya," he finished, obviously quite pleased with his autobiography.

"Isn't Agricon a big contributor to climate-change research and all that other feel-good environmental shit? I assume that as CEO, all that was at your direction. Don't you think that massive water theft, cartel partnerships, and murder kind of fly in the face of all that?" Ben asked.

"I don't take your meaning?" Alan asked quizzically.

"You don't see some sort of conflict there?"

"Not at all. I care deeply for the environment, and I am very proud of our environmental contributions. Did you know that we preserved fifteen thousand acres of wild land in Arizona for prime pygmy owl habitat? You should see it out there, totally pristine and beautiful, not to mention the owls just love it. I want my kids to live on a nice planet. I drive a Tesla for God's sake. All this other stuff is just business."

"Wow, you guys are fucked up," Ben said.

"I have a legal duty to my partners and shareholders as I am sure you know, not to mention that I have read your file, Mr. Adams, and that is a pretty funny statement coming from you—stones and glass houses and all that."

Ben turned his palms up in a sign of acquiescence to the point.

"Dad? Is any of this true? Speak to me!" Jess shrieked.

Rory just continued to sob softly and stare at his desk. He was definitely 10-7, *out of service.*

"Truth be told," Alan continued, "all this cloak-and-dagger stuff is kind of fun, but the reality is that I definitely

don't enjoy *all* of the murder; it aggravates my ulcer. I am getting too old for these kinds of shenanigans," he said as he casually popped some antacids into his mouth.

"We could have continued indefinitely, in fact, and avoided all of this had the water-monitoring technology not gotten so much better and put Professor Gutierrez on to our aqueduct, followed by you guys. I suspect that even after we kill you guys, I give it an 80 percent chance that within eighteen months someone else will get on to it. So after we get rid of your bodies, we will start looking at other options for our water needs. Maybe we'll just have to actually start paying for it legitimately, or maybe we'll get out of the agriculture business and spin it off as a consulting firm; who knows?" he finished.

"Then why get rid of us at all?" Jessica yelled.

"Quite obviously, the criminal liability is way too large to let any of you leave this room under your own power. In fact, Rory, I know we have been through a lot, but you are obviously no good to anybody anymore," he said as he pulled a small pistol out of his pocket and put one right into Rory's forehead.

Upon impact, Rory's eyes and mouth stuck open in a permanent state of surprise. Jess charged Alan and knocked him over. The two battered special-ops guys

by the door looked on, amused and not reacting, presuming that Jess the grad student did not constitute an actual threat. They watched the tussle with continued amusement as Ben went for the revolver in the desk. Again, reaction still not being as good as action, they were a half second too slow as Ben brought up the gun and took cover behind the still-surprised corpse of Rory McCoy.

As the Amtrex guys brought up their MP5s, Ben shot one straight in the groin and the other in the neck. Not his best work with a pistol, but it bought him a few seconds to move and line up for a better shot. Karl dropped his weapon and put both his hands to his crotch, so Ben focused his efforts on Dennis. With one hand on his neck to stop the bleeding, Dennis weakly raised the submachine gun one handedly and let a burst loose.

Ben hit the ground behind the desk. The burst was wildly inaccurate as it shot out the office window and sent splinters and office bric-a-brac flying off of the desk. Ben now had a good clean shot under the desk at the guy's foot and took it, blowing through his ankle. Ben discovered he was holding a .357 much like the one he had thrown down into the aqua tunnel, but this one in fact worked. The guy screamed and fell to the ground, showing Ben the top of his head. Ben put a pill into his brain with the fourth of his allotted six rounds.

By now, Mr. Groin was fumbling for his gun, and Ben launched like a frog from the ground over to it and sent the gun skidding across the tile. He was looking pale, either from blood loss or the psychological fear of major genital damage. He scooted away and leaned back against the wall, hands still on his balls. Another shot rang out from the combination of Jessica and Alan, and Jessica rolled off with an obvious wound in her right forearm. She cried out in pain and grabbed it tight. Ben trained his gun on Alan and started to squeeze the trigger, thinking that his shot would be perfect this time, his marksmanship pride having been somewhat hurt from his earlier pistol work. As the hammer came back, he stopped when he realized that Alan wasn't moving or at least wasn't moving very much. He still had his gun in his right hand, curled back at an odd angle, and there was a small, smoking hole in his chest that was making a low, whistling noise.

Ben crawled over to Alan and took the gun from his hand. He put his ear down to his chest and listened. He looked over at Jessica and shook his head *no.* Jessica shrugged, showed him her palms as if to say *I don't give a fuck*, and got up and went over to her dad. She sat down on his desk and looked at him. She shed a few silent tears and shook her head. As Alan's chest cavity filled with air, he slowly expired. As he went, he tried to say what appeared to Ben to be *water.* Karl, the special-ops guy from Amtrex, just sat against the wall

wild eyed with both hands on his crotch, clearly afraid to look at the damage. He wasn't spraying blood, so Ben thought that his femoral artery was intact and that he would probably live, but he wasn't going to let Karl know that. Ben got to his feet and felt a sharp pain in his side. He looked down at a 9 mm sized hole in his abdomen. He grabbed a mirror from the desk drawer and looked at his back where a 9 mm exit wound presented itself.

"Fek," he said. "That could be a problem," he continued.

"What about this?" Jessica asked, raising her arm without looking away from her dad.

"Probably not great either," he replied. "But I know a guy…"

"You know a doctor? So do I. He is called St. John's Hospital on 20th street in Santa Monica. We should go over there and see him," she said.

"Do what you want, but there is no way I am going to a hospital with a gunshot wound. Regardless of what page-turning yarn I tell, with my background, they will lock me up and throw away the key."

"You may be right about that."

"Welcome to the club, by the way."

"Fuck that, and fuck you, and also thanks."

"Don't mention it; let's get the hell out of here."

"What about all of this?" she said, turning to face him and spreading her arms to the carnage in front of them.

"Well, if we're lucky, it will look like some sort of interoffice dispute turned deadly, and we were never here."

"And that dude?" she asked, pointing to Karl slumped against the wall, frozen in testicular horror.

"Well, I'm not really up for killing him as he is no longer on the field of battle, so to speak. So my guess is that, assuming that he is not badly injured, he is going to go on the run as the most likely material witness to this clusterfuck of a gun battle, and he probably has the skills to hide very well someplace on the beach in Latin America."

"And if they get him, and he talks?"

"He will have to cop to all manner of high crimes and misdemeanors, so it is probably in his best interest

to make up some shit about these guys sleeping with each other's wives," Ben said loudly to make sure that the guard heard him. He looked over and saw what he believed was a small nod. Maybe he just wanted to believe it, but either way, it was good enough for Ben to hit the road as he was just not in the mood to kill anyone else. As it was, he was way over his bag limit for homicides this week.

"And my mom? What do I tell her?"

"I wouldn't tell her anything yet. Text her that we broke down and are going straight back to San Diego and that you will e-mail your dad the questions that you had. The police are going to be visiting her soon enough. In a few days, come up and tell her the truth. Her life is going to be terrible for a while."

"That really sucks," she replied dryly.

"No argument there. We gotta get something to stop all of this bleeding." Ben shredded his shirt into two makeshift bandages for the two of them, tied them as tight as they could stand, and went to the closet in the office. He took out one of Rory's Brooks Brothers shirts and put it on. "Not bad," he said. Jess just looked away. Ben wiped down the .357 and put it into Rory McCoy's still-shocked hand and rested both in his lap.

They walked out of the building the same way they had come in, being careful not to track any blood down the hallway. Ben noticed with much relief that there weren't any interior surveillance cameras that he could see. They dragged over to the jeep, trying to look as normal as possible, and jumped in. Geronimo whimpered when he saw them. Ben pulled onto the 405 south, grimacing with every bump that the jeep went over as they motored south back to San Diego.

They made only one stop and that was to the Carl's Jr. next to the Trestles parking lot. Ben insisted that he needed some food and a break from driving. Jess didn't believe him for second, knowing where they were and that Ben wanted to check the surf at the famous break, but as he had the more severe bullet wound, she went with it as the three of them walked down to the beach at Trestles and ate the burgers. The sun was going down as the usual crowd at Lowers zipped along the perfect five footers breaking in front of them with the occasional air thrown in.

"The swell did come in after all," Ben said through a mouthful of burger.

"Actually looks pretty nice," Jess conceded.

The sun went down into the Pacific as they finished their beachside dinner and limped back to the jeep,

Geronimo trotting happily along. They pulled off the freeway at La Jolla later that night and headed toward the water.

"OK, so who is your guy?" Jess asked.

"Geronimo's vet—great dude, lives in Bird Rock."

"Your vet is gonna attend to our bullet wounds effectively and be OK with that?"

"Oh, yeah. He sells weed to half of PB on the side; he is no stranger to weirdness."

With that, Ben clicked open his phone and dialed. "Hey, Bob, it's Ben…Yeah, I know it is getting late, and I apologize, but…No, actually, I am good there but could use a little off-the-books medical attention…No, not the clap, you jackass, just a flesh wound…Cool, we'll be by in a little bit."

Jessica could just barely hear the "wait a minute, who is *we*?" coming from the phone as he snapped it shut. They drove down through the Village of La Jolla, past the dealerships of Ferrari, Maserati, and Lamborghini, past Windansea, and down into Bird Rock. They pulled up in front of a small house on Dolphin Place that fronted the ocean on the cliffs above South Bird, one of the better of the La Jolla Reefs.

"Maybe I should have been an animal doctor," Jess said as they walked up.

"The weed bought the house; he just likes animals. I don't think they pay for much around here," Ben responded as he rang the bell on the courtyard gate. They were met by Bob, fit and clean cut in his early thirties, like an actor hired to play an animal doctor on a soap opera. He ushered them in and sat them down, offering a drink of water and greeting Geronimo with a Milk-Bone.

"Beer, please," Ben said.

"Not until we see this flesh wound that we discussed."

"Her first," he said, pointing.

Bob obliged, looking at Jessica's arm. "Not too bad, in and out, no major bleeding—should be OK. Now you."

Ben pulled off his shirt and showed him.

"This one looks quite a bit worse," he said, probing the wound and causing Ben to flinch. "Should be OK. I did a few of these in Afghanistan."

"Afghanistan? What the fuck are you talking about, Bob?" asked Ben, wincing.

"The army sent me to veterinary school; you didn't know that? I was house doctor to a K-9 unit of bomb-detecting dogs based out of Kabul for three years. Soldiers would occasionally come in with gunshot wounds that they would rather not report, and I stitched them up."

"What was that about?"

"Them or me?"

"Both," Ben said.

"Well, I usually didn't ask, but I think it was mostly just being drunk and not handling their weapons properly. But at least once, it was the result of the brother of the mistress of a lieutenant colonel looking to account for family honor. For my part, I just wanted extra money, which reminds me, late-night house call gunshot wounds aren't cheap. You will be getting a bill."

"I had no idea you were such a badass. A vet *and* a vet," Ben said, shutting his eyes and leaning his head back on the couch. He directed Jessica to the kitchen where he had her lay her arm out on the counter next to the sink.

"Yeah, like I've never heard that one before. This is definitely going to hurt," he said as he started cleaning out the wound.

Jessica gritted her teeth as he went to work.

"Don't move," he said to her as he left he room. He came back a few minutes later with a suture kit and a syringe in his teeth. He used the syringe to anesthetize both sides of the wound and proceeded to stitch her up. "OK, you are all set. Stay out of the water for ten days, keep it dry and clean, take these antibiotics as a prophylactic in case that bullet was dirty, and come back, so we can take these out."

"Thanks, Doc," she said.

"OK, your turn, Ben. Jump up on the counter here—same drill but more pain."

Ben did what he was told, complaining about needing booze for medicinal purposes. Doctor Bob relented and poured some single malt down his neck on the table.

"Thanks," he gurgled.

He went through the same procedure, cleaning the wound as best he could, probing around in Ben's abdomen looking for tears, stitching internally where needed, and trying to keep Ben from wiggling around in pain. After about an hour, he had him stitched and upright. "Obviously no guarantees on this work under

the circumstances, but you two should be fine eventually. Now go home, get some rest, and most importantly, get out of here, so I can go to sleep." He sent them out with a half bottle of scotch, two bottles of antibiotics, and a Ziploc bag of Humboldt County's best weed, also for medicinal purposes.

Back at Ben's apartment, Jess drank enough scotch to forget the previous week and blacked out. Ben gave some of the doctor's medicinal weed a try and sat staring at the wall in nihilism as he ultimately fell asleep.

Monday

Ben got up early and wandered out of the apartment with Geronimo toward the beach. He hit the newsstand on Garnet Avenue for a copy of the *Los Angeles Times* and grabbed a cup of coffee at the cart next to the Pier. He sat down and thumbed through the paper. On the front page of the local section below the fold, he saw a piece about the CEO and VP of Agricon found dead in a possible murder-suicide related to a love triangle. The piece didn't mention the other two guys, but it was early yet, and the paper might not have the whole story. He then read down to the official statement of Agricon, which referenced personal problems between the two men and how sad they were to have lost two of the Agricon family in such a tragic way. It was obvious to Ben from the

article that the whole thing was starting to get white-washed over, likely with no further consequences for anybody involved.

As much rage as he felt welling up about that, he also started to feel relief at the prospect that the issue would hopefully remain dead and buried. His sense of justice and accountability belonged to the old Ben; the new Ben would be happy to just be left the fuck alone. He threw away the paper and walked north along the bluffs, checking the surf along the way. The surf was still holding at four to five feet from the south, but he knew better than to rip out his stitches and introduce the ocean into his guts. He would not be surfing for a while.

He continued north to Tourmaline Surfing Park. Entering the parking lot, he saw Phil's van. He walked down to the beach and saw Phil gazing at the surf. He walked up to Phil and nodded, both looking out at the ocean.

"Swell looks good today," Phil said.

Ben nodded again.

"It has been great all week. Where have you been? Baja?" Phil continued.

"No, I have been working, I guess. Arizona," Ben replied.

"That doesn't sound like you."

"No kidding. It wasn't exactly my first choice for things to do this week."

"A girl, I'm guessing? Are you going to paddle out?"

"No, I have some fresh stitches in my side. Looks like I am out of the water for a while."

"Stitches—what happened?"

"Phil, what do your crazy conspiracy friends know about a company called Agricon?" he asked, changing the subject.

"Everything. Why?"

"Just tell me what you've heard."

"Everybody knows this, dude. Those are the guys who, before they changed their name to Agricon, killed Kennedy after he reneged on their deal to produce the fake moon landing. I think they gave it to Haliburton or somebody."

“Got it. Anything else?” he asked, rolling his eyes.

“There are dark Internet rumors that they are in bed with the drug cartels somehow—something about rerouting giant rivers underground—but to be honest, it all sounds a bit farfetched to me; it doesn’t really add up.”

Ben laughed out loud. “Ha!” He slapped Phil on the back.

“What is so funny?” Phil asked.

“Nothing, man. I’m just glad to be back at the beach, and I am glad to see you here. Are you paddling out?”

“Not here. Tourmaline is too crowded. I think I am going to wait for the tide to come up and go hit the Point.”

“Of course you are. Take it easy, man,” Ben said as he started to walk away.

“You too, man. Just watch out for the FBI *and* Agricon!” he yelled.

Ben gave him the customary backward middle finger and kept walking.

APOLOGIES AND ACKNOWLEDGMENTS

Some of the issues presented in this book have some merit, such as the overdraft of the Colorado River; however, this work is entirely fiction. Some of the other facts noted in this book might accidentally be true; however, I believe it best to proceed as if not a single word in this book relates to any actual place or person in the real world. My thanks to all of the southwestern authors and the creators of the subgenre of surf noir for inspiring me to write something down that might otherwise seem very silly.

Made in the USA
Columbia, SC
10 September 2017

This book was designed by Robert Bringhurst.
It was edited and set into type in Canada,
then printed and bound by C&C in Hong Kong.

The text face is Minion Pro, designed by Robert Slimbach.
This is an enlargement and revision of Slimbach's original Minion type
issued by Adobe Systems, Mountain View, California, in 1989.

The captions are set in Scala Sans, part of a family of type
designed in the Netherlands by Martin Majoor. The face was issued
by FontShop International, Berlin, and its affiliates in 1994.

The paper is Glatfelter Laid, made
at the Spring Grove Mill in Pennsylvania.
It is of archival quality and acid-free.

ISBN: 1515355225
ISBN 13: 9781515355229

Camino Del Diablo

Jeremy DeConcini

Kazin further deepens our sense of conflict and diversity. And Alan Wolfe offers an alternative reading of American political culture, especially in our own time, suggesting that Heclo's prophecy of a "coming rupture" may be too dark. Heclo acknowledges the validity of much of what his critics have to say, yet reasserts and reinforces his own main theses.

Readers of these remarkable exchanges will decide for themselves, bringing new insights to the dialogue. That is as it should be, and the broadened engagement will further realize the purpose of Harvard's Alexis de Tocqueville lectures and books—to carry forward in our own time and through our own explorations the questioning about America that the namesake of the series so splendidly practiced when he visited these shores some eighteen decades ago.

THEDA R. SKOCPOL
Director (through June 2006), Center for American Political Studies, Harvard University

Christianity and American Democracy

1

CHRISTIANITY AND DEMOCRACY IN AMERICA

Hugh Heclo

IN THE FIRST TOCQUEVILLE LECTURE IN THIS SERIES, published in 2006, James Ceaser invited attention to what he called "foundational concepts" in American political development. Ceaser defined these concepts as high-level abstractions that serve to ground the explanations and justifications for a polity's other political ideas or general courses of action. The two foundational concepts he invoked were "history" and "nature." The three commentators on the lecture then inquired if "religion" might not also be a foundational concept deserving at least equal time in the discussion.[1] This is the direction in which I intend to turn.

We should begin with an obvious fact: Religion as such has had little significance for American political development. Religion in general can mean anything—from love your enemy's heart to eat your enemy's liver. Asserting the importance of generic "religion" in America is like saying that "economics" was important for Americans while ignoring the fact that the substance of the economic idea was private property; or saying that "geography" was important for American political development but glossing over a physical landscape of frontiers protected by oceans. In America—

and in every other place and time—religion affects political development as this or that *particular* religion, with a substantive content that includes its own distinctive features and variations.

Few people engaged in the myriad of actions that we, in retrospect, call American political development thought of themselves as engaged with some mere analytic category called "religion." If they had done so, they would have been mere social scientists. Rather, Americans filled in the academics' "religion" category with the substance of a richly variegated thing called Christianity. They did so as establishment clerics and radical dissenters, New Light and Old Light Calvinists, fundamentalist Bible thumpers and Unitarian Bible knockers, and on and on. The list of religionists is huge, but it is almost entirely a list, even if nominally, of alleged Christians. Similarly, in the case of those Americans who have not cared much about religion—and throughout our almost 400-year history, many have not—it has been Christianity they have not cared about. And the historically tiny, but increasingly vocal, minority of devout atheists in America has generally consisted of persons turning their backs on Christianity, not rejecters of Muslim, Hindu, or Zoroastrian faiths.

To focus on mere religion in American political development, rather than on Christianity, is to eviscerate any historical understanding. Hence my subject is not religion and American democracy, but Christianity and American democracy. Likewise, the historical presence we need to acknowledge in American political development is Christianity in general as well as Protestant Christianity in particular.[2] Thus the site of our inquiry is America and its political development as an ostensibly democratic, Christian, and predominately Protestant nation. That said, we must not lose sight of the central issue. For the last 500 years, Protestantism has typically defined itself against Roman Catholicism, and that oppositional self-identification is inherently too narrow for our purposes. It is Christianity as such that is the crucial specification of "religion" in all that follows. As we will see, in recent years both Protestant and Catholic versions of traditional Christianity have been coming to define themselves, not against each other, but against another Other, which is in some sense American democracy itself.

In the story line that follows I begin with an essential ambiguity and its historical resolution and go on to discuss a mutual and tensioned embrace between the democratic and Christian faiths. I then identify a growing estrangement and eventual turning point in the 1960s, raising the real possibility of a coming rupture between Christianity and American democracy in the years ahead. This story line is, of course, much too simple to capture everything relevant on this subject. However, I do think it is sufficient to headline the central tendencies of what has happened and is happening, as well as—in the spirit of Tocqueville—to offer a plausible warning about what lies ahead.

For a very long time, the scholarly community has neglected Christianity's role in American political development. I think it is not some accidental oversight that has led academics to resort to the abstract term "religion" rather than the substantive socio-political-doctrinal formation that is Christianity. It is instead a terminological dodge, which serves at least two main purposes. First, social scientists have been comfortable disregarding substantive differences in the content of different religions (and the political implications of any such differences) because to do otherwise risks having to examine their usually unspoken premise that all religions are essentially the same (wish-fulfillments, oppressors' tools, barbaric superstitions, archetypal myths, psychological projections, or just a touching human desire for the approval of supernatural beings). Second, modern social science arose with a determinedly secular outlook which privileged some voices and not others in accounting for the progressive march of democracy. Only the approved secular routes to democracy were highlighted. Those who counted in the pro-democracy movement were the champions of Reason rather than Faith, religious skeptics but not clerics. They were classical humanists inspired by the glories of pagan Greece and Rome rather than Christian humanists inspired by the Bible.[3]

The democracy-as-secularism blinders began to slip when scholars were surprised by the rise of conservative Christian activists in the 1970s. This eruption fit neither the secularization theory of modernity nor the "paranoid" thesis applied to culturally backward fundamentalists. And the scholars of secular academia have been playing catch-up ever since.

Recent events have made it still more academically acceptable to look at religious content. It is now common for western scholars to ponder whether Islam is compatible with democracy. A little reflection should show that to a devout Muslim this is an insulting way of putting the question; the more apt rendition would be to ask if democracy is compatible with Islam. Which way the question is put depends upon whether pre-suppositional faith is put in democracy or the Koran as the legitimate point of departure. Of course, being Americans, we know that the former and not the latter is the right way of putting the question.

But before that typically unthinking thought goes down too smoothly, let us replace the word "Islam" with the word "Christianity." We then would ask, is Christianity compatible with democracy? Or, to reverse the pre-suppositional faith, is democracy compatible with Christianity?

No doubt most Americans today would consider these to be silly questions. In what follows, I hope to show that to dismiss the issue is to take a myopic view of the past, present, and future of American political development. After all, in the larger historical scheme of things, it was not so long ago that Tocqueville identified "the organization and establishment of democracy in Christian lands" as the "great problem of our times."[4] Discerning a solution to that problem was a major reason Tocqueville commended the American experience to his fellow Europeans' attention. We would do well to begin with his insight.

Tocqueville's Insight

Modern readers have difficulty in appreciating how extraordinary the American scene must have appeared to a well-educated young French aristocrat like Tocqueville. Here was a society of vibrant democratic equality and liberty. But it was also a society of no less vibrant Christian institutions and fervor. To sense the surprise and admiration that Tocqueville felt, one needs to understand that at this time any sophisticated European intellectual would know that these two characteristics—democratic liberty and religious authority—did not go together. To think otherwise was to be intellectually naïve and historically ignorant.

The movement known as the Enlightenment, especially in French intellectual circles, had evolved from a complacent deism in the early eighteenth century to a militant, largely atheistic humanism of the *philosophes* by the end of the century.[5] Since "enlightenment" meant liberation of man's reason from tutelage under the guardianship of others, all religious authority could easily be construed as an unenlightened, superstitious fetter on free thinking and free men. Likewise, the religious-political structure known as Christendom, especially in French Catholic circles, had ample historical reason to see claimants for democratic liberty and free thinking as enemies of the one true religion. Thus Tocqueville came from a world of wretched consensus: the contending champions of faith and reason were in ruthless agreement that these were mutually exclusive commitments.

For a time, almost forty-one weeks, Tocqueville had expelled himself from this hothouse atmosphere of French intellectuals, churchmen, and politicians who were forever replaying arguments from the Enlightenment and the French Revolution. He injected himself into a new society, a wholly fresh atmosphere at the margins of an allegedly more "advanced" European civilization. The result for the young man in his late twenties was revelatory.

Tocqueville's observations in the raw new nation convinced

him that it was in Europe, and particularly his own country, where something unnatural had happened. In a "strange confusion" (10), the spirit of freedom and the spirit of religion had been sent spiraling in opposite directions. But in supposedly backward America, where one could observe the "natural quiet growth of society" (26), Tocqueville saw that the forces of religious faith and democratic liberty could exist in harmony and mutual support. Indeed, he saw that the partnership between the two must grow if something more than mere democratic equality was to survive. That "something" worth preserving at all cost was the God-given dignity and grandeur of human beings.

Thanks to the quick and dirty extracts from *Democracy in America* that are commercially produced for classroom use, Tocqueville is frequently misinterpreted as viewing religion mainly as a device for maintaining democracy. This view makes no sense, since Tocqueville clearly considered democracy as an irresistible historical development and inevitable wave of the future. The future of democracy-as-equality is not in doubt for Tocqueville. What is in doubt is democracy as a domain of liberty for preserving man's true dignity. Tocqueville considered the first thing that struck him about America—the religious aspect of the place—as key to preventing the only other more important factor he saw in America—the juggernaut drive of democratic equality—from running amok and degrading humanity.

Here, then, is a very brief sketch of some of the most important things Tocqueville observed about Christianity and American democracy.[6]

Tocqueville saw democratic equality as the God-inspired thrust of all history. This thought was in his first pages of Volume I, published in 1835, and in the concluding pages of Volume II, published five years later (pages 6 and 678–680). Such providential design expressed itself in direct historical movement as well as in the unintended consequences produced by those hostile to this purpose. This overall, apparently irresistible advance of democratic equality suggested to Tocqueville an intention coming from beyond history, and once this pattern is discerned, "effort to halt democracy appears as a fight against God Himself" (6). In the background of such a providential account is the recognition that "Christianity, which has declared all men equal in the sight of God, cannot hesitate to acknowledge all citizens equal before the law" (10). Much later, almost as something too obvious to discuss, Tocqueville describes the contrast with the most profound minds of Greek and Roman culture: "Their minds roamed free in many directions but were blinkered there. Jesus Christ had to come down to earth to make all members of the human race understand that they were naturally similar and equal" (404).

According to one of his biographers, Tocqueville himself was hardly a devout Christian believer.[7] This fact does not diminish the central importance of religion or Christianity in his analytic system. Tocqueville writes as a political sociologist, not a Christian, and generally argues that anything of political and social importance has multiple causes. But for all the importance he assigns to voluntary associations, decentralized administration, *mores* and the laws they produce, religion has the prior importance; it shapes the kind of people who will act in all these venues. "There is hardly any human action, however private it may be, which does not result from some very general conception men have of God, of His relations with the human race, of the nature of their soul, and of their duties to their fellows. Nothing can prevent such ideas from being the common spring from which all else originates" (408). In his last great work, Tocqueville views the inhuman outrages of the French Revolution as stemming from the preceding Enlightenment assault on religion.[8]

Tocqueville believes that for Americans or any other people, the circumstances of their origin are crucial to explaining all subsequent development. Fortunately for this strong claim about path dependency, America offers a unique case in that it allows one to see clearly—that is, undistorted by the travails of Europe's long history—the point of departure of a major nation.

Tocqueville cites several features shared by many early European immigrants coming to America: a common English language and notions of political rights, liberty, and local government; experience with the religious quarrels and intellectual battles shaking Christendom; the middling social status held by most immigrants; the frontier encounter with seemingly limitless supplies of land that undercut any pretensions of a landed aristocracy; and so on. And yet, given the scope and detail of what follows, these are only preliminary observations. Tocqueville clearly lays the main emphasis regarding America's point of departure on the New England colonists. And here is where Tocqueville's insight into our subject begins to emerge most clearly. In his view, it was in the English Puritan colonies of New England "that the two or three main principles now forming the basic social theory of the United States were combined." The New Englanders were distinguished from all other colonists by "the very aim of their enterprise . . . they hoped for the triumph of *an idea.*" Tocqueville proceeds to describe their fervently sought combination of Christian piety, democratic self-government, and republican freedom. This foundation of Puritan principles, he says, spread its influence to enlighten "the whole American world" (29, 30).

Modern readers have little trouble grasping Tocqueville's point that Puritans scored well on the principle of democratic self-government. Neither rich nor poor, the Puritans at America's point of departure were a well-educated, middle-class, homogeneous people who knew how to form themselves into voluntary congregations and into a "civil body politic" of equals (32). Only in Puritan New England had the British Crown supported such organic communities of immigrant families—as opposed to individual adventurers farther south—to form self-governing colonies (33). Well over a hundred years before the Revolution of 1776 or the Constitution of 1787, New England's Puritans had become the founding fathers of American democratic self-government. "Puritanism was not just a religious doctrine; in many respects it shared the most absolute democratic and republican theories" (30). Unlike Europe, America came into political existence from the bottom up, democratic at its historically unencumbered roots.[9]

But these Puritans were also what today we would call religious extremists, and Tocqueville pulls no punches on that score. To the modern mind, he seems determined to undercut his own case by citing in detail the repressive penal codes that resulted from Puritans using the Bible to script their laws. He takes pains to quote laws punishing blasphemy, adultery, and disrespect of parents with death. Sins of idleness, drunkenness, intercourse among the unmarried, tobacco use, and long hair got off only a little more lightly with the Puritan lawmakers. And yet Tocqueville holds up such Puritan legislation as "the key to the social enigma presented to the world by the United States now" (34). How can he claim that these American Puritans set in motion America's "marvelous combination . . . the spirit of religion and the spirit of freedom"? (40)

In fact Tocqueville considered such penal codes shameful invasions of conscience and violations of human spirit. The key point, however, is that "these ridiculous and tyrannical laws were not imposed from outside—they were voted by the free agreement of all the interested parties themselves" (36). Alongside the penal codes was the great host of political laws embodying the republican spirit of freedom. Local independence, broad citizen suffrage with elected officials, free voting of taxes, trial by jury, government responsiveness to social needs—this broad sphere of political freedom was undergirded rather than contradicted by the Puritans' religious convictions. Clearest of all the examples were laws for compulsory public schooling. In good Protestant fashion, enforced taxpayer support for literacy was justified as promoting a knowledge of the Bible in its true sense and original meaning, unclouded by the commentaries and "false glosses of saint-seeming deceivers." Tocqueville answers the anti-religious sneers of France's Enlightenment *philosophes* with American facts: "In America it is religion which leads to enlightenment and the observance of divine laws which leads men to liberty."[10]

Here then was New England's gift of a national template—America's meta-constitution, so to speak—for harmonizing religious ardor and democratic freedom, doing so amid the irresistible historical trend toward democratic equality.

> Religion regards civil liberty as a noble exercise of men's faculties, the world of politics being a sphere intended by the Creator for the free play of intelligence. Religion, being free and powerful within its own sphere and content with the position reserved for it, realizes that its sway is all the better established because it relies only on its own powers and rules men's hearts without external support.
>
> Freedom sees religion as the companion of its struggles and triumphs, the cradle of its infancy, and the divine source of its rights. Religion is considered as the guardian of mores, and mores are regarded as the guarantee of the laws and pledge for the maintenance of freedom itself. (40)

Thus Tocqueville's insight into Christian New England saw that faith and reason, religion and politics, were distinct but, far from being separated in opposition, they could provide each other mutual support. One did not need to decide which blade in a pair of scissors does the cutting or which wing does the lifting.

In three large analytic blocs, Tocqueville subsequently expands his views on this cooperative relationship. The first of these discussions emphasizes Christianity as a main factor in maintaining a democratic republic in America (265–277). The direct influence is one of favoring self-government. This time without mentioning the Puritans, Tocqueville points out that England bequeathed to America a Christian immigrant population that was both democratic and republican: "From the start politics and religion agreed, and they have not since ceased to do so" (265). In the American context, Protestantism gave relatively greater emphasis to republican independence and liberty and Catholicism to democratic equality, but a single democratic and republican worldview prevailed.

Even more important to Tocqueville is the indirect support that Christianity gives to American democracy. Here he spells out the meaning of his earlier generalization that in America, religion takes freedom "by the hand" so as to "sanctify its striving" (10). The problem is that, left undisciplined, liberty loses its value as the means for human flourishing. Especially in a democratic republic, freedom without religious "oughts" and "ought nots" must become disorderly and self-destructive at both the individual and societal levels. "How could society escape destruction if, when political ties are relaxed, moral ties are not tightened? And what can be done with a people master of itself if it is not subject to God?" (271). The two questions are not quite the same.

As for the first question, Tocqueville finds that the needed tightening of moral ties occurs through a single Christian morality which unites the myriad of sectarian differences in America. To be sure, this morality may have trouble in restraining men seized by the many opportunities to enrich themselves in such an open society. But, he says, the balance is righted in domestic life, where marriage ties are strong and women take the moral lead. It is there that Christian morality is translated into the *moeurs* (moral attachments of the heart as well as ideas that shape mental habits) that do so much to maintain America's democratic republic. Men carry over the habits of moral order and restraint learned at home into the public affairs of state (268).

Tocqueville's answer to the second question has been generally underappreciated. The influence of American Christianity covers not only mores but also "reason" (268). With this term Tocqueville harkens back to his idea of politics as a sphere devoted to the free play of intelligence. Here everything is "in turmoil, contested, and uncertain" (40). The scope for political experiment and innovation seems limitless. But then the contempt for old ways and spirit of experiment "reaches the limits of the world of politics . . . in trepidation it renounces the use of its most formidable faculties; it forswears doubt and renounces innovation . . . it bows respectfully before truths which it accepts without discussion" (40). It is the reigning Christianity that checks, retards, and sets the primary assumptions and insurmountable barriers around the otherwise limitless world of politics. Later, in speaking of the American philosophical approach, Tocqueville puts it this way:

> In the United States there are an infinite variety of ceaselessly changing Christian sects. But Christianity itself is an established and irresistible fact which no one seeks to attack or to defend.
>
> Since the Americans have accepted the main dogmas of the Christian religion without examination, they are bound to receive in like manner a great number of moral truths derived therefrom and attached thereto. This puts strict limits on the field of action left open to individual analysis and keeps out of this field many of the most important subjects about which men can have opinions. (396)

No doubt thinking of the contrast with their French counterparts, Tocqueville points out that even American revolutionaries have their dreams circumscribed by the widespread respect for Christian morality and equity. He makes no judgment about Americans' religious sincerity; some profess Christian doctrines because they believe them, and others for fear of looking as though they do not believe them. In either case it is Christianity and respect for its morality that reign over both personal mores and public reason in politics (268–269). Liberty in America is ordered liberty because a people seeing itself as its own political master also sees itself as subject to God. Thus without speaking directly about freedom, religion teaches Americans "the art of being free" and so can be rightly considered the "first" of America's political institutions (267, 269).

What accounts for this powerful hold of Christianity on the American people? Tocqueville asks the question not as a believer, skeptic, or unbeliever, but as a political sociologist. His answer is the separation of church from state, of religion from politics. Again, however, we need to listen carefully to hear what Tocqueville is saying rather than what contemporary slogans in our modern minds are repeating. Tocqueville acknowledges and considers it irrelevant that most of education in America is entrusted to Christian clergy. The separated "politics" which he commends consists in the absence of clergymen from elective or appointive public office, their non-affiliation with particular parties, their disengagement in regard to particular policy opinions (even as they condemn bad faith and selfish ambition on any side of an issue) (272, 517). In other words, "the structure of religious life has remained entirely distinct from the political organization" (396). Eschewing this kind of "political" involvement with the apparatus of government and party competition, religion diminishes what Europeans would regard as its power. But that view, according to Tocqueville, simply reveals the distorted understanding produced by Europe's sad history of religious entanglements with worldly instruments of power. Avoiding those entanglements in America has increased Christianity's enduring strength and public influence, rather than its illusory temporal power.

At this point Tocqueville expands on the nature of religion in general. Religion's sphere comprises the universal and permanent longings embedded in every human heart as it faces the ultimate questions of its own existence (273). Alliance with the fleeting powers-that-be in the world can only diminish this natural claim that religion has on human beings, turning it into something as fragile and changeable as those earthly powers. And in a democratic republic, those political powers are very changeable indeed. Religion with political power is not merely prone to be intolerant, indolent, and unstable; it is prone not really to be religion. In America, organized Christianity assured its enduring influence by disassociating itself from the vicissitudes of political authority and power. The "political" separation of church and state does not safeguard liberty by protecting secular people; rather, it safeguards liberty by protecting religion from being corrupted into something less than itself. Thus religion is necessary to sustain the ordered liberty of democracy, but it must also be separated from the apparatus of political power to offer this necessary assistance (273–274, 410, 517).

Religion provides answers to the primordial questions by which men order their actions in the world. The more that claims of authority are weakened in the political sphere, the more important for human functioning is an authoritative foundation in religion's spiritual sphere. If both religion and politics become a free-form exercise in do-it-yourself living, the strain of this limitless independence will leave men disoriented and willing to seek order even at the price of their liberty.

Thus in looking at the subject in terms of "the interests of this world" (408) and "a purely human point of view" (410), Tocqueville describes the kind of religion that will be needed to sustain the ordered liberty of democracy in the centuries to come. To anchor the thinking of people afloat in a world of equality and freedom, religion must be clear, authoritative, and unchanging in its core doctrines and articles of faith. These doctrines must relate solely to spiritual matters, not human laws, science, or political maxims. In contrast to Islam, here the great merit of the Christian Gospels is that they "deal only with the general relations between man and God, and between man and man" (410). The beliefs that religion professes must accord with the democratic idea of a universal equality of men before the laws of a single God. To retain power in democratic ages, religion must also dispense with external ceremonies that are not essential to its core dogmas. Finally, religion must accept rather than attack the democratic passion for material well-being in this world, even while insisting that the admittedly good things of this life remain secondary to the spiritual kingdom of God (409–414).

Tocqueville clearly believes that Christianity in its natural American condition (that is, unencumbered by European history) does well on all these counts. But he also understands that the spirit of independent opinion pervading democratic populations will be an enduring challenge to any such religious authority. Some people will try picking and choosing among the various doctrines of their religion. But Tocqueville realizes that such efforts to finesse obedience and freedom are unlikely to be sustainable. In the future, the lines of division within democracy will be sharper. Those who take Christian doctrine seriously will move toward the single uniformity of orthodox authority (as he sees it, Catholicism). Others will completely abandon Christianity. Seeking unity in all things, these democratic unbelievers will be drawn to some version of pantheism and will reject Christianity's sharp division between the Creator God and His creation (415–418). As we will see, Tocqueville was not far off the mark.

Tocqueville usually frames his observations about religion and Christianity under the general rubric of their "usefulness." But it is a serious mistake to reduce his view to a narrow, utilitarian conception of religion as simply a means to political ends. The value of religion is not just that it is useful to democracy; it is useful to democratic man because it teaches truths about the human condition. Thus Tocqueville emphasizes that in America the doctrine of "self-interest properly understood" is crucial for countering democracy's tendency toward self-absorbed, short-sighted individualism. This doctrine, however, is ultimately religious rather than political. It appeals to man's reason by challenging him to look beyond his immediate desires and see that his behavior in this world is weighted with ultimate significance for the fate of his immortal soul in the next world.[11] And even with this utilitarian-style argument about Christianity's promise of heavenly rewards for good behavior, Tocqueville immediately goes on to insist that there is something grander than calculations of reward and punishment happening in the Christian mind (500). Faith brings man into thinking God's thoughts about well-ordered living, about doing good to others, and above all, about giving priority to spiritual realities.

Tocqueville has no doubt that the tendency of democracy to unleash passions for physical pleasure, to push individuals toward a short-sighted, brutish materialism, is fully on display in America. His claim is that it is therefore all the more important that religious beliefs counter these democratic tendencies by drawing attention to man's immortal soul and elevating his affections and mere natural reason toward what is majestic, pure, and eternal. Without the active presence of spiritual conceptions in society—the recognition that an integral part of each person is implicated in realities beyond this material world—human beings in the democratic age are in great danger of becoming degraded into something less than fully human (514–517). Becoming self-absorbed in mundane things, they will then be abandoning their true selves.

What can those who govern democratic peoples do to make spiritual conceptions prevail? For reasons already discussed, Tocqueville is firmly opposed to state-established religion or religious leaders officially taking on roles in public affairs. The only answer Tocqueville can see is for politicians to lead by example: "I think that the only effective means which governments can use to make the doctrine of the immortality of the soul respected is daily to act as if they believed it themselves. I think that it is only by conforming scrupulously to religious morality in great affairs that they can flatter themselves that they are teaching the citizens to understand it and to love and respect it in little matters" (517). On that hopeful and somewhat problematic note of incorporating a religious perspective into the high levels of governance, Tocqueville ends this analysis.

The Great Denouement

Spend enough time with Alexis de Tocqueville, and you are likely to come away feeling that anything you have to say is simply a gloss on some chapter, paragraph, or sentence of *Democracy in America*. However, with sufficient diligence, such humility can be overcome. At this point it is helpful to step back from Tocqueville and try to see the larger picture of which he—even with his brilliantly enlarged view—was only a part.

It is telling that when Tocqueville thought about how to make spiritual conceptions endure in society, he could come up only with the suggestion of politicians leading by example. And yet for well over a thousand years Christian church authorities had countenanced the use of any number of other means, fair and foul, to enforce conformity with various spiritual conceptions. They persecuted opponents, and used political power to do so, because they believed it was their sanctified duty to uphold the truth.

Strangely enough, after his discussion of the Puritans, Tocqueville says little about religious liberty in America and even less about the religious freedom clauses in the Constitution's Bill of Rights. He simply notes the common "republican" theme in Americans freely voting their temporal interests in politics and freely pursuing their heavenly interests in religion.[12] Even more striking is that Tocqueville seems oblivious to the vehement political debates swirling around the country as a result of evangelical Christian crusades concerning Cherokee removal, Sunday mail delivery, anti-lottery and temperance legislation, prison and orphanage reform, and a host of other Christian-led, "benevolent society" causes. While opponents of these crusades were complaining about the "Christian party in politics," Tocqueville was blithely assuring readers that Americans had found the key to keeping religion out of politics. Soon the young abolition movement would explode his notion that the underlying Christian consensus had set strict boundaries around political "innovation" and disruptions to society. In short, Tocqueville was touring America amid the political fallout of the Second Great Awakening and hardly seemed to take notice.[13]

My point is not to criticize Tocqueville but to suggest that by the time he visited America in the 1830s, something so important had happened, at such a deep political-cultural level, that it could hardly be noticed.

Coming from post-Enlightenment France, Tocqueville thought the problem was that the friends of democracy were anti-Christian and the Christian authorities were anti-democratic. But that was only one manifestation of the longer-term master problem: How can Christianity and civil government be reconciled with each other? In a thousand ways on a hundred fronts, Christians after the Protestant Reformation muddled their way toward an answer, one that pivoted on the idea of individual liberty of religious conscience. This profound historical achievement, centuries in the making, blended commitments to religious liberty and popular self-government. It produced the "twin tolerations" that we can now see are essential for modern democracy anywhere in the world—the political freedom of elected governments from control by religious authorities, and the religious freedom of individuals and groups from control by the government.[14] The term I have devised to describe this hard-won achievement is the Great Denouement, and it was first won in America.

The history of almost anything is not a pretty picture. (Instances where that is untrue could probably be assembled, but they would make a very small book.) Until we understand why governments could find it quite reasonable to couple religious heresy and political treason, we can never appreciate the monumental historical achievement that had occurred in America by Tocqueville's time. In fact if one simply considers the similarities between religion and government, it can seem quite odd that anyone would imagine the authority of the two should be anything but united. Religious and political regimes are both about governing people. Both lay down rules for doing so. Both regard these rules as expressing moral values, the way things ought and ought not to be. Both insist that these normative rules are authoritatively binding on people. Moreover, any religion is a comprehensive worldview which necessarily includes the political, social, and all the other dimensions of human life. From all this the conclusion would seem to necessarily follow: since God is Lord of all creation and since His truth is one, religious and political authority must be one. If they are not, social peace and godly order are impossible. Looked at strictly in these terms, the Taliban has a point.

But this tidy logic is speaking only of generic "religion." The substance of Christian belief introduces a vast disruption into the whole picture, for two interrelated reasons. First, Christianity from its outset has been a potential threat to any established civil order, whatever the form of government. This is because a Christian life is expected to extend its fundamental allegiance upward to God (loyalty to any worldly kingdom, nation, tribe, or family is always secondary to the Christian's current citizenship in a spiritual kingdom), and to extend its fellowship outward to a universal humanity (where there is "neither Jew nor Greek . . . neither slave nor free . . . neither male nor female"; Galations 3:26). These vertical and horizontal attachments threaten to break the normal boundaries of any political society.

This would be less of a problem but for a second feature: Christianity is committed to the opposite of a spiritual withdrawal from or indifference toward earthly human affairs. Following the model of God's incarnation, believers are taught that the world is to be penetrated, lighted, and salted by their Christian lives. Since their God is so deeply concerned with the affairs of the world, "The notion that we can be related to God and not to the world—that we can practice a spirituality that is not political—is in conflict with the Christian understanding of God." This "prophetic stance" toward government and society can be quite ambiguous, but the call is always to be engaged and critical.[15] Even the ascetic holy men and women of the "desert" in Late Antiquity were not in remote wilds but visible at the edges of towns and villages, where they counseled and bore witness to God's unsettling demands on settled society.[16]

In short, Christianity has some chutzpah: it makes profound moral claims on the powers-that-be while refusing any ultimate allegiance to, or even personal kinship or special friendliness toward, those powers.

After its first 300 years, the outsider Christian religion was brought inside civil power to become the state religion of the Roman Empire (the only way Imperial Rome knew how to think of legitimate religion). However, rather than eliminating the essential problem of Christianity and civil government, this move ultimately intensified it. This is because an "official" Christianity is even more dangerous than an outsider Christianity: it turns out to be dangerous both to itself and to any peaceful political order.

The danger to Christianity from entanglement with official state power is obvious. Worldly power, being worldly, is always ready and willing to use religion to win fights with political opponents. This innate inclination is something wholly inconsistent with the substance of a religion that disavows any dependence on or truck with worldly powers. Following their God's example, Christians are called to the unworldly ideas of loving their enemies and of defending the truth of their religion by suffering and dying, not by ruling and killing.

The second danger—an official Christianity's propensity to upset any peaceful political order—is less obvious to us today but is worth serious attention. For it is from here that we are set more directly on the path toward the Great Denouement.

This danger has its roots in the fact that of all religions, Christianity is inherently and fervently doctrinal in nature. It has been so almost from the beginning (that is, from the days of Paul, Peter, and disputes in the apostles' council at Jerusalem). This enormous doctrinal emphasis is not because Christianity's central core is a checklist of doctrines, but because its centerpiece is a very odd person. In a sense, this person *is* the religion. The essence of the good news, or gospel, is that this man died for believers' sins as foretold by the Jewish scriptures, was buried, rose again, and was seen alive by his disciples.[17] Doctrines have served to translate into human intellectual terms the fact that this person was born, died, and rose again. The fantastic claims and actions surrounding this peculiar person could not help but give rise to fundamental questions demanding answers. The answers were not being sought, in the first instance, by unbelievers but by believers, and not by believers who touched and knew the man Jesus but by the following generations of Christians, who were only going on reports. How are we to understand this person we are believing in? More specifically, how can God have a son? In what sense(s) was

Jesus both God and human? How can it be just for God to kill God to pay for humans' sinfulness? What logic allows God to be one and three? Officially endorsed Church councils tried, but even within the post-Constantine centuries of one empire/one religion, doctrinal divisions among Christians could never be settled. And given that enduring fact over the centuries, the temptation to use political power to settle doctrinal differences was even greater than that of using civil authority to squash mere political opponents.

This recurring temptation reached a climax in the sixteenth-century Reformation. Today we can read about the theological debates, social upheavals, political intrigues, and religious wars but still not fully grasp the shattering quality of what happened. It may help to imagine dropping all the labels that intellectuals later invented and pretend to be just an ordinary person who does not know you are living at the end of the "Medieval Synthesis," amid a "Protestant Reformation" and Catholic "Counter-Reformation," leading up to an "Age of Reason" and "Enlightenment." What you do know in a very general way is that people smarter than you have always said that philosophy (with knowledge from human reason) and theology (with knowledge from biblical revelation) both agree in giving a unified meaning to things, including your life and everything around you. Now into this scene comes crashing one monstrous, incontrovertible fact that people later will call the Protestant Reformation—namely, that all the best thinkers are violently disagreeing. Everything that might be considered traditional authority is at war with itself. How can there be multiple truths in contradiction? Where is there any authority for certifying what is true? The shattering effect of such questions on a once coherent worldview was felt across all aspects of European life.

Various approaches were tried to repair this shattering. The first was obvious: religious-political fights within Europe started, stopped, and restarted in vain efforts to impose the one right Christian and political regime. From this turmoil came legal initiatives for "toleration" (the 1598 Edict of Nantes in France, England's Toleration Act in 1689, and the 1781 Patent of Toleration in the Hapsburg lands). In effect, this second approach gave permission for religious minorities to exist in a nation without persecution or legal oppression.

A third approach sought a return to classic pre-Christian sources. Much of what we now call civic republicanism developed in direct opposition to the ideal of a Christian polity. Following in the footsteps of Machiavelli, who considered Christians too soft and passive for good republican citizenship, Rousseau argued that the two concepts of "Christian" and "republic" were mutually exclusive, particularly because of the former's intolerance.[18] For European thinkers like Rousseau, the problem was not what Christianity had become; the problem was what Christianity is when it is being its most true Gospel self. It unbinds the heart of a believer from the state and society and ties its allegiance to an otherworldly country. By definition, good Christians could not be good citizens.

Washing up from Europe along the Atlantic coastline, all of these approaches were tried in the scattered American colonies during the seventeenth and eighteenth centuries. There was energetic persecution of Baptists and Quakers in Puritan New England, toleration in Catholic Maryland, greater freedom for all sects in Pennsylvania and Rhode Island, mild Church of England establishment in Virginia, and flirtations with Enlightenment deism in various intellectual circles. From this confusing hodgepodge eventually emerged an answer to the conundrum of Christianity and civil authority.

The "doctrine" making for this Great Denouement was produced not by events nor by ideas, but by ideas about events. In the Americans' case, it is important to note that ideas about events were being forged during the late phases of Protestant Reformation and in an isolated setting. Lateness meant that any lessons of experience could be clearer, and that enough time had passed for a certain exhaustion to set in among all the combatants. Isolation meant that the colonists were relatively free to figure things out for themselves, with less interference from "old world" thinking and powerbrokers. The Protestant Reformation did not give the answer to the master problem of Christianity and civil authority; but it did precipitate the answer's emergence, and it did so in America.[19]

For one thing, the Reformation's proliferation of Protestant sects created more Christian heretics than it was generally practical to persecute. Well versed in the European tradition of using state power to settle and enforce doctrinal disputes, the New England Puritans tried persecution but eventually could not keep up. As many observers noted, this religious pluralism was especially prominent in the American colonies as a whole. The result was that Americans tended to be driven toward religious tolerance because there were too many sects to allow them to get away with the intolerance they might have preferred. Moreover, the colonial frontier exhibited a quite fluid sort of pluralism; refusing special privileges for any sect could be the safest course if the benefits for your group might tomorrow be grasped by others. In Massachusetts, for example, the Congregationalists (the original beneficiaries of state support) eventually came to favor disestablishment of religion when Unitarians began sharing the state funds in more localities. Thus James Madison would eventually be led to argue that a bill of rights was unnecessary in America's new Constitution because the true security for religious freedom lay in the religious diversity of the population.[20]

In the second place, the same proliferation created minority religious groups with a self-interest in advocating religious tolerance. Thus even Catholic communities, in contexts where they could not be the dominant church, found good grounds for advocating liberty of religious conscience. Through Catholics the colonists acquired the language of "free exercise" that would 150 years later work its way into the first line of the Constitution's Bill of Rights.[21]

Third, the upheavals of the Reformation spurred Christian

thinkers who witnessed the persecutions and turmoil—thinkers both inside and outside the minority sects—to reconsider the meaning of the Christian gospel in light of these events. The spiritual definition of the Christian church, rather than the worldly identities and props of a visible Church, came into sharper focus.

Finally, as time went on from the seventeenth into the eighteenth century, ordinary Americans in their colonial outposts could continually hear about, without themselves suffering from, the struggles going on in their British homeland—the Puritan revolution against Charles I, the Restoration of Charles II, Monmouth's Rebellion, the Revolution against James II, the Test Act, and so on. One did not need to be a philosopher or even particularly well-educated to learn about the futilities involved in the quest for an official Christianity. In all of this, we see that vital political phenomenon which scholars so often overlook: how thinking generated out of political uncertainties and controversies produced transformations in the meaning of old ideas and the emergence of new ideas.[22]

Since it has been done so well by others, there is no need here to recount the varied steps by which a consensus grew in America on the doctrine of religious liberty.[23] It is enough to highlight the central line of reasoning. The grounding of the argument was theological; that is to say, belief in the doctrine of individual religious liberty came from belief in the content of a particular religious faith called Christianity. The thinking developed mainly through debates in Protestant Christian circles, not between believers and secularists. Like their predecessor John Locke in England, American Christians like Roger Williams, William Penn, Isaac Backus, and many more individuals forgotten to history confronted other Christians. The latter thought that because they were right in their doctrine, they were right in persecuting error. No, came the response from the other believers. A Christian cannot be right in his doctrine if he thinks religious persecution is right.[24] Mostly without realizing it, American Protestants were reviving arguments used by a once-persecuted Christian as he tutored the Emperor Constantine's son. Religion cannot be coerced, but must be voluntary and promoted only by words. "Nothing," Lactantius wrote, "requires freedom of the will as religion."[25]

As the debate went on (and here I will confine myself to Madison's language because it so clearly expresses the emerging consensus on the subject), it became clear that the issue was not simply persecution. At bottom, government involvement with religion was not a political or philosophical mistake. It was a religious error. Authentic Christianity was the response of one's whole being to God's inner call; and that required that man's mind be left free from coercion. To say that government coercion is allowed in matters of a religion is *"a departure from the plan of the holy author of our religion, who being lord both of body and mind, yet chose not to propagate it by coercions on either."*[26] To say that religion should be encouraged by government support is another religious error. True religion could make it on its own, without government's financial support or legal weaponry. This abstention was the Christian thing to do, *"for every page of it [Christianity] disavows a dependence on the powers of the world."*

At this point the argument got to the heart of things. It is each person's duty to God that produces the right to religious liberty. Religion is an obligation produced by the fact of God's creative work *("the duty which we owe to our Creator")*. The right of religious liberty follows from this duty. *("The Religion then of every man must be left to the conviction and conscience of every man; and it is the right of every man to exercise it as these may dictate.")* Thus the right of religious liberty is an individual right, not a group entitlement *("the homage each person determines in conscience to be acceptable to the Creator")*. Authentic Christianity is not a problem of collective allegiances. It is a matter of God speaking to one person at a time, of people responding to God's call one person at a time. Far from logically leading to coercion, belief in the absolute truth of Christianity means understanding that faith is a gift from God and that neither the gift nor its acceptance is a work of man. Logically, the absolute truth of this religion absolutely commands individual religious liberty. From this sort of religious analysis, the political conclusions cascaded:

- The only legitimate authority and support for religion is *"the Governour of the Universe,"* to whose government each person is subject. Religion is *"wholly exempt"* from the *"cognizance"* of civil society or government.
- Any true church is a purely voluntary, spiritual association of individuals following the call of God in their innermost consciences. It can never be rightfully regarded as a creation or instrument of government.
- The right of religious liberty is something more than the obligation of a person to follow his own conscience. That leaves room for human authorities to question whether or not a conscience has been correctly formed in light of religious doctrine. The obligations of conscience are between each person and God, his or her Creator.
- Religious liberty extends beyond mere toleration. Toleration is nothing more than a government permission slip for some groups to practice their religion without official obstruction.[27] However, it is beyond any government's rightful power to permit or not permit religion. The doctrine of religious liberty requires that every government acknowledge its limits in the face of its *"Universal Sovereign."* No one using such words doubted that they were referring to the God of the Bible.
- Protection of religious liberty in society is not an affirmation of man's natural goodness. A free society is God's testing place for separating the wheat from the tares in a world that is corrupted but still in His sovereign control. Man's fallen nature fully and permanently justifies distrust of human power, whether in civil or ecclesiastic robes. Thus religious and political freedoms require the mutual support of each other.[28]

The preceding quotations use Madison's words from a Virginia petition opposing the proposal of popular Governor Patrick

Henry to give public support to teachers of the Christian religion.[29] Scheduled for adoption on Christmas Eve, the plan would have allowed each taxpayer to designate the church of his choice to receive his tax. A second petition, receiving well more than double the number of signatures on Madison's petition, may have been more important in eventually defeating the plan. This petition declared the proposed state support for teaching the Gospels to be against "the Spirit of the Gospels."

Americans in these years were not inventing something new. They were rediscovering something old, in fact something intrinsic to Christianity. But because they were rediscovering this in a context of new historical circumstances, they were also innovating, and they were especially innovative compared to the theological and political dead ends prevailing in Europe. Americans creating the Great Denouement were doing something new because they were believing something old. For centuries—and still today—would-be theocrats said, "Because our religion is true, it must unite with the power of the state." In the Great Denouement, the American Christian impulse in effect said, "Because our religion is true, it must do no such thing." This was more than Protestantism speaking. As the Catholic Church acknowledged two hundred years later, it is the Christian gospel itself that "recognizes and gives support to the principle of religious freedom as befitting the dignity of man and as being in accord with divine revelation."[30]

The cumulative result for Americans was something like an *entente cordiale* between the forces of Christian faith and Enlightenment reason. It was the doctrine of religious liberty that provided the sturdy ship-lap joint in this alliance. To announce that "Almighty God hath created the mind free" could be the preamble to either a Christian tract or an Enlightenment essay.[31] Concepts revealed by the light of reason—inalienable rights of the individual, limited government, social compact theory—were no less evident to the Christian political theology developing out of the Puritan heritage.[32] With two sentences, both making the same essential point, Madison was able to encapsulate the entente between Enlightenment reason and Christian faith: the right to religious liberty is unalienable, first, "because the opinions of men depending only on the evidence contemplated by their own minds cannot follow the dictates of other men: It is unalienable also, because what is here a right towards men, is a duty toward the Creator."[33]

To be sure, such brilliant language could conceal important potential fissures between autonomous reason and divine revelation. To the former, separation of church and state could mean the state's indifference to religion as merely a matter of subjective private opinion and superstition; to the latter, it could mean that man's relation to God is something too important to be contaminated by all-to-human political institutions. For advocates of unimpeded Reason, the inherent rights of natural man could justify every democratic challenge to the divine rights of kings and churches. For believers in biblical revelation, human rights and democratic challenges to the divine rights of kings and churches could only be justified by man's duty to what is absolute and divine rather than finite and human. To champions of human reason, man could be seen as having an inherent right to rule himself; to champions of Christian faith, the divine right of the people could be seen as just another blasphemy. Americans' emerging commitment to religious liberty did not eliminate such tensions between faith and reason, but it did greatly help to diminish them.

The *entente cordiale* between faith and reason was vastly facilitated by the fact that virtually all of the individuals regarded as opinion leaders in America were much more influenced by Scottish common-sense philosophy than by the extreme rationalist claims of the continental Enlightenment. The former was at least loosely Christian, while the latter was aggressively hostile to anything resembling traditional Christianity. Precisely on that account Thomas Paine, despite all of his patriotic good work during the American Revolution, went on to become a *persona non grata* to Americans.[34] As Tocqueville emphasized, it mattered greatly that Americans-in-the-making were not a representative sample of semi-Christianized Europeans ranging from unlettered peasants to insouciant aristocrats. Instead the colonial core in America was a disproportionate sub-sample of Europeans, a marginal rump of common, semi-middle-class people who took their Protestant Christianity quite seriously. With the Great Denouement, such people were also gaining the capacity to mount a new kind of political revolution. The first great Protestant political uprising had been the Peasants' War in Europe (1524–1525), crushed by Protestant leaders using the biblical justification that earthly powers are ordained by God and must be obeyed. A second pulse-beat of Protestant political revolution, far more familiar to the American colonists, was the English Civil War (1625–1649) and the failed Puritan Commonwealth (1649–1660). Here, again invoking biblical justifications, Protestants had attempted to unite executive and legislative power to create an English "Christian nation." Having lived through this, people like John Milton and John Locke helped teach the colonists why this was a religious and political mistake. By 1776, again using biblical justifications, Americans had the capacity not only to fight a perceived oppressor (nothing new in history) but to understand their political revolution in a Christian context of individuals constituting a government to protect their God-given rights, grounded in their duty to God, without preference or penalty of state power in matters of religion. If *that* was what a revolution was about, it had meaning for every human being who would ever live.

In forging an alliance between faith and reason, American leaders demonstrated a hearty disregard for doctrinal differences among Christian sects. One reason was a prudent desire to avoid stirring up trouble while trying to persuade Americans to unite around common political endeavors (fight a revolution, create articles of confederation, empower a truly national government under a new constitution). The evidence is persuasive that the drafters of the 1787 Constitution produced a "godless" document not because of some secular agenda, but mainly because they wanted to avoid inviting sectarian disputes and diversions that might interfere with the ratification business at hand.[35] Gradually, alongside Christianity, Americans were constructing a "public religion," speaking of God in a way that unified rather than divided.[36] It was/is a God that created men in his image, endowed them with rights, took a "providential" interest in human affairs, judged individuals and peoples according to his righteousness and, not least, took a special interest in the American nation.

However, there was a deeper reason for the muting of doctrinal disputes. Alongside religious issues, a parallel debate was going on about the possibilities of republican self-government. The problems here had little to do with church/state tensions and much more to do with doubts about popular sovereignty. Whether a free people could successfully govern themselves for any sustained period of time was a question posed not only by the Founders' knowledge of classical antiquity but by the daily events in the former colonies. If freedom meant the absence of any controls, then the mob rule predicted by classical philosophy and history seemed inevitable. The proper design of republican institutions could help, but even an institutional engineer like Madison had to conclude that the ultimate answer lay in the virtue of the people.[37] A people lacking virtue would not be capable holding on to freedom.

Some were too politic to say it, but if the experiment in self-government was to survive, the nation had to deal not simply with the philosophical problem of virtue, but with a looming virtue deficit in the American people. There were intellectual resources that could be brought to bear from many sides—the intuitions of natural law in Scottish moral philosophy, deistic views of moral reason divorced from spirituality, the civic *virtu* endorsed by classical humanists, and the moral affections inspired by pietism. However, it is fair to say that the main body of American opinion addressed the issue of republican virtue by affirming the central role of religion in moral education. What has been called the "moral calculus" became commonplace in the new nation: republican government requires virtuous citizens, virtue requires morality, and morality requires religion.[38] Freedom, which posed such a problem for democratic government when defined as a lack of controls, was in effect reconceptualized into the idea of autonomy. Autonomy was not a lack of controls but rather self-control, a combination of personal independence and moral responsibility.[39] What was Christian and what was republican could appear to be the same thing. Seneca had urged Rome's elite to rule themselves with unflinching integrity before they ruled others. America's elite was now saying that the same thing had to apply to everybody.

With this move, all sides could be drawn to a "practical" view of Christianity as being more about morality than about particular theological doctrines. Even Jefferson, never one to shun an intellectual debate, was much less interested in attacking the irrationality of his Trinitarian opponents than in strongly affirming their common capacity with Unitarians to uphold social morality and produce upright citizens.[40] Despite the poisonous politics of the day, the moral calculus could help defuse not only doctrinal disputes among Christian denominations but also political hostility between those more and less favorable to popular government. In most cases, those who resisted the democratizing impulse were defeated. In the long run, however, these defeats were made more bearable by the widespread commitment of all sides to the moral calculus and its underlying doctrine of religious liberty. Since Americans had reason to trust each other's commitment to religious liberty, talk of a popular government with Christian-based morality could be seen as a unifying theme rather than the threat of a divisive sectarian agenda.

Thus it came to be accepted that what mattered for a workable republic was a shared morality rather than the details of a shared theology. This moralization of Christianity meant that specific doctrines revealed through Scripture could recede into the public background in favor of the general revelation of right and wrong open to all men. Energized by individual liberty of religious conscience and protected from any politically established church, American civil society could be a "sanctified ground" for citizens to be good and to do good.[41] Teaching the "moral sciences" to awaken citizens' inner moral gyroscopes became established and went on to become a prominent part of educational curricula throughout the country in the nineteenth century.[42]

Without over-generalizations there can be no lectures, not even bad lectures. There is ample evidence to show that the early generations of Americans I have been generalizing about had a complex, highly sophisticated view of the likely conflicts between human reason and divine revelation. Theirs was no naïve view of sweet harmony on this side of Paradise. But I think we do these ancestors no injustice to say that with all the caveats that might be offered, there was a general consensus that reason and revelation overlapped sufficiently—not just for philosophers but for ordinary citizens trying to live decent lives—to make self-government a hopeful, going concern.[43] This consensus assumed that reason in the political realm and revelation in the autonomous religious realm would by and large agree on basic moral standards guiding political action. This mostly unspoken belief was greatly facilitated, and could remain mostly unspoken, because the areas of life subject to national and state governments' policy activity were extremely limited. Of course local government was a much greater presence in people's lives, but then the towns, villages, and counties in agrarian America also constituted more or less cohesive moral communities (even if more socially stratified than pure republican theory or Gospel teachings would endorse).[44]

So in the end—not a final end but an ending of substantial scope—there was a denouement to the puzzle of reconciling Christian religion and civil authority. It was "great" because it found a way out of centuries of argument, mutual recrimination, and suffering. Because it was an end of sorts, the Great Denouement in the young American republic could also be a beginning. Instead of contraries there was a contrapositioning, not something univocal but an equivocal coexistence of reciprocal influences. While the Christian gospel certainly was a key long-term force shaping the democratic vision, organized Christianity and democracy had had an ambiguous relationship throughout their respective histories.[45] In America, for the first time, Christianity and democratic self-government launched themselves together in a kind of double-stranded helix spiraling through time. Christianity and civil government were both now freed from the old dialectic of yes/no, unity or chaos, and became two maybes, moving together, each affecting the other.

A Christian Democracy / A Democratic Christianity

The Great Denouement meant that government (beginning at the national level and eventually extending to state and local governments) would have "no cognizance" of its citizens' religious beliefs. In this context of religious liberty, there was also an open invitation for the nation's overwhelmingly Christian religious groups to enter politics as sanctified defenders of the morality underpinning republican government. Implementing this moral calculus would not violate the Constitution as it was then understood, but failing to implement it would violate Christianity's "prophetic stance" toward the worldly powers-that-be.

In the years after Tocqueville returned to Europe, Christianity helped make a certain kind of democracy and democracy helped make a certain kind of Christianity in America. Space not does permit a complete chronicle of this twisting helix of reciprocal influences; the best I can do is to dip into the stream of events and hold up for examination some specimens of this interaction. Snatched out of a flowing historical context, they unfortunately become rather lifeless, but I think they are three specimens of enduring importance. I will call each of these an "idea" in the philosophical sense of the term, that is, a guiding principle of interpretation that can improve our understanding of the facts we see. These three ideas direct our attention to the meanings given to American life in its historical, individual, and societal dimensions. Using the ideas of history, personhood, and political society, we can consider the mutual influences of American democracy and American Christianity on each other.

AN IDEA OF HISTORY

Christianity helped imbue American democracy with a particular historical outlook that is especially bewildering to foreigners. It is summed up in the unnecessarily exaggerated phrase of William McLoughlin that "American history is thus best understood as a millenarian movement."[46] We can appreciate what this might mean by starting at the level of Christianity's general view of history and then moving to the more specific case of America's millenarian strangeness.

Like its two kindred "historical" world religions (Judaism and Islam), Christianity imparts a linear, content-rich view to time. Time is not mere duration. Other major worldviews from classical antiquity and elsewhere have seen the cosmos and man's existence on earth as either a timeless unchanging order or a cyclical eternal recurrence of birth, growth, maturity, decay, rebirth, growth, and so on.[47] By contrast, in the three Abrahamic religions, history—like Abram—is being called by God to go somewhere. In theological language, they are eschatological religions in that they look forward to the great consummation of a magnificent promise. Impelled by the Word of God, the world is moving toward the fulfillment of God's plan for ending history as we know it. In playing out their part in this plan, the origin and development of each of these religions are denominated in terms of dates and events in a particular temporal order, known through written records.

Over the past two centuries, people in Europe as well as America have translated such a theology of history into secular terms and created this or that philosophy of history.[48] For theology the promise for the fulfillment of all things comes externally, through God's plan for man. For secularized versions, the fulfillment of promise comes through the unfolding of forces within history itself. Examples of such secular philosophies of history are ideologies of progress through science and technology, Marxist class conflict, human enlightenment, and the racial struggle for *Lebensraum*.

Christianity adds something radically historical to this general picture. In fact, this is the radical something that makes it Christianity. The Christian claim is that God invaded historical time by taking on the form and substance of a living human being in a particular place and time. None of the other historical religions even remotely claim such a thing. Given this specifically Christian view, thinking about history now becomes a more ambiguous task. In a sense, the centerpiece of God's plan for history has already occurred in those few years at a marginal province of the Roman Empire. Christianity presents a "realized" eschatology in the coming of the promised Messiah, a man named Jesus, a Jew from an utterly insignificant town called Nazareth in the time of the great Herod dynasty. And yet the Christianity founded on this person also presents an unrealized eschatology, since the end of historical time has obviously not come and is somewhere off in the future. Indeed, this final fulfillment of history awaits the return of Messiah Jesus. The Messiah has come and will come again; the Kingdom of God is already here, and is not yet fully here. A space of special expectancy is opened in history. It is like waiting for the end of a war after the decisive battle assuring victory has already been won. "The time is already fulfilled but not yet consummated."[49]

All this sounds, and is, terribly abstract until we start putting it into the English/American context. The Protestant Reformation taught a return to God and his Scriptural Word, lived out in this world and unmediated by human authorities. Among the most prominent of these newly disputed texts was the Book of Revelation, and especially the lone place in that book where one encounters the insistent prophetic vision of a "thousand year" reign of Christ's kingdom on earth—that is to say, a millennium (Revelation, chapter 20).[50] For an English society thrown into decades of turmoil before, during, and after the Puritan Civil War, interest in the biblical end-time prophecies blossomed. The Puritans coming to America were part of this climate, seeking and defending various interpretations of biblical prophecy about the end-times of history as these applied to all sorts of political events in their world.

It was in this theological-hermeneutic-political context that the early American republic was self-consciously casting aside the traditions of the old world and trying to make sense of itself. Here Tocqueville's focus on the early Puritans as an ideological template for the new democracy misses a crucial development. To put it briefly, the early colonial Puritans were strong providentialists and mild millennialists. However, as they and subsequent generations of Americans tried to make sense of their experiment in self-government, and necessarily did so in a cultural context of Protestant thinking, the struggle to define their political identity pulled Americans' outlook on history in a more thoroughly "progressive" millenarian direction.

The earliest Puritans coming to America were providentialists in that their self-understanding was one of essentially casting themselves and their efforts onto God's sovereign power to make things come right. A highly favored Puritan biblical text finds God's people wandering, heaving up and down on the seas, crying out, comforted, thrown about, oppressed, but in the end brought to "understand the loving-kindness of the LORD" (Psalm 107:4). Likewise, Governor John Winthrop's characterization of the Massachusetts Bay colonists as a "city on a hill"—rhetoric so beloved and so thoroughly misrepresented by later American politicians—was a warning about Providence's judgment. Coming as the concluding application of his main message that the colonists must live together in love, the Governor's biblical metaphor pictured a world watching the call and response between God and these colonists. As Winthrop put it:

> For we must consider that we shall be as a city upon a hill, the eyes of all people are upon us. So that if we shall deal falsely

> with our God in this work we have undertaken, and so cause Him to withdraw His present help from us, we shall be made a story and a by-word through the world.[51]

To understand what Winthrop is saying, we need to realize that this is not an American talking to us, but an Englishman speaking to compatriots out of the depths of the English Christian tradition. Nine hundred years earlier, Baeda (later known as the Venerable Bede) had cast the Saxon military adventurers as a single "English" people united by their Christian religion if by nothing else. Bede's biblical analogues held immense imaginative power, and they became a story of nationhood which no educated Englishman could escape. Like the people of Israel established in their promised land, these island English people were especially held up by God as responsible to God. They were to be blessed for obedience and punished for sin, usually following the Old Testament formula of good and bad times corresponding with good and bad kings.[52] Out of this deep cultural context, Winthrop and the thoroughly English and Puritan colonists of seventeenth-century New England could see themselves as a chosen people but not yet a millennial people. For that, they needed to become more "American."

All millennial views are providential, but not all providential views are millennial. On this subject it is useful to think of a continuum. At the extreme providential end are those who see man as having no role in his God-ordained destiny. This suggests a fatalism and quietism little-favored by Protestants, much less the Puritans. Next would be a view of being used by Providence as something like a test-case or an example for better or worse to others, a model that Winthrop clearly had in mind. From here one might imagine a more positively active role as an exemplar of Providence's work, the city on the hill now "shining" (as it did not for Winthrop) to witness and light the way for others. Closing in on the millennial end, we would come to a still greater engagement in the plans of Providence by securing its possibilities, the rock in the sea and the Promised Land for pilgrim refugees. Finally there is the full-blown millennial view of being the active instrument of Providence's plan for history. Here we come to being not just one of God's chosen instruments but to being *the* chosen instrument to lead the divine scheme of things. The image is nothing less than a first-born redeemer leading the way for others in God's ordained procession into the future. It is straight, 100-proof millennialism.

Obviously these conceptions overlap, and the accompanying images of beacon, rock, promised land, redeemer, and so on have varied throughout American history.[53] However, from early in the republic the dominant tendency that developed in American democracy was to lean into the millennial end of the continuum.[54]

If this millennial vision was not always there, when and how did it appear? According to one author, we must look to the later-generation New England Puritans: "The myth of a divine *telos* for New England did not emerge until the middle years of the seventeenth century, and it did not appear spontaneously. It emerged as the centerpiece of a deliberate effort to reassure and reinvigorate the faithful during a period of doubt and anxiety." On this telling, people who were vexed and troubled by the failure of their own lives to live up to the spiritual hopes of their Pilgrim forefathers (1620–1630) found comfort in identifying themselves with a community that had collectively been sent forth by God and would share its grace as long as the community kept faith with Christ.[55]

Another account finds the time "when destiny became manifest" to be a hundred years later, following the religious upheaval of the Great Awakening and the unexpected terrors of frontier warfare. "It seems that in the 1760's, in the nascent nationalism that followed the French and Indian War, there began to emerge a conception of the colonies as a separate chosen people, destined to complete the Reformation and to inaugurate world regeneration."[56]

A third view emphasizes the millennial move in American political thinking amid the fears of national disunity and a second religious awakening at the end of the eighteenth and beginning of the nineteenth century. These mounting anxieties about the meaning of America were eventually resolved in a new consensus of Christian evangelical patriotism that "included the belief that Americans are a peculiar race, chosen by God to perfect the world. That was clearly the nation's manifest destiny, and it was unique."[57]

Drawing these threads together, it makes sense to conclude that there have been multiple beats in the millennial pulse. These pulsations have found religious awakenings—revitalizing calls for God's kingdom to come into men's hearts—to be simultaneous with Americans' awakening to a national political self-consciousness. America existed in order that political principles of equal rights, self-government, and personal freedom might come into the world. Americans became a people constituted by discovering their faith in those political principles that now seem commonplace. In the ongoing struggles to define their national identity, Americans fitted a political reading of the democratic faith into the millennial framework supplied by certain Protestant versions of the Christian faith. This melding of the sacred and mundane, the religious and political, grew into America's sanctified vision of itself. The sacrality consists in understanding the American experience as something set apart for transcendent purposes in at least three senses.

Turned at one angle, this vision reflected the idea of divine election: God chose America as the agent of his special purposes in history. By superintending the first political revolution that did not simply exchange one set of rulers for another but instead produced a government by the people, Providence intended for America to be something special in the larger scheme of things.

Seen from a second angle, this vision of consecration claims that the nation is not sanctified simply for its own sake. America is charged with a mission in political freedom that has significance for mankind as a whole. There is a story for all people in the heart of America's history, a story that Americans did not put there but are living out. To take only the most recent illustration, one can hear the old theme played at the beginning of George W. Bush's presidency in 2000 and then later given its full-throated declaration in the crisis after 9/11.[58]

It is not just people but time itself that is to be redeemed. Viewed from this third angle, the sanctified vision sees an end to the wreck of history and the beginning of a new time. The claim is that the hold of recurrent time on republics—a political life cycle of birth, maturity, and decay—has been decisively broken in America. A new era has come to renew the world. To take two utter extremes from the religious-political spectrum, the "new light" theologian Jonathan Edwards saw America's spiritual awakening in 1740 and reasoned that "it is not unlikely that this work of God's Spirit . . . is the dawning, or at least a prelude, of that glorious work of God so often foretold in Scripture, which in the progress and issue of it shall renew the world of mankind. . . . And there are many things that make it probable that this work will begin in America." In *Common Sense,* anti-Christian rationalist Thomas Paine urged America's revolutionaries of 1776 to realize that they had it in their power "to begin the world over again. A situation, similar to the present, hath not happened since the days of Noah until now." Although Paine was certainly no believer in revealed religion, much of the public power in his secular-rationalist ideas and rhetoric came from their correspondence with Calvinist and other Protestant ideas in the general cultural atmosphere of the time.[59]

Americans' historical outlook is strange to foreigners because the millennial model of Christian time-reckoning has been brought down to earth in one nation's sense of destiny as a permanent new beginning. The sanctified vision reveals a divinely-purposed nation, on a world-redeeming mission, breaking through historical time with the expectation of a coming kingdom of democracy and freedom across the earth. It would be naïve to think that a great many Americans did not really mean it when they stamped their national seal and, even more significantly, their money with a self-description as the "new order for the ages."

Not only foreigners but many Americans, Christian and secular alike, have criticized the abuses of power that have often accompanied America's sanctified vision. Even in the nineteenth century heyday of evangelical patriotism, critical voices loudly opposed Cherokee removal, war with Mexico, and colonial expansion in the wake of the Spanish-American War.[60] And so it remains today with the Bush doctrine of war on terrorism.[61] But while the exercise of power has always been subject to criticism, it is much rarer to find American voices criticizing the sacral vision itself. Indeed, all the criticisms generally presuppose the vision. Why else imagine that the United States *should* be any different from any other country in ruthlessly exercising its power?

Viewed over the long term, America's sanctified vision has always been Janus-like. One face sees America's hope for the world to lie in the nation's special separateness, a holding back to protect its innocence from contamination in a corrupt world. Over against isolation and non-involvement is the other face, calling for robust leadership to save the world from itself. Each side presumes a final apocalyptic answer to the grayness of things. Each side gives the moral critics of America—criticism that itself presumes the sanctified vision—ample room for maneuver. That space invites alternating critiques between sins of commission and sins of omission. Seen together, these opposing tensions present an idea of history in American political development that is a tortured rather than triumphant millennialism. The image is less a shining city on a granite hill and more a narrow ridge of hard passage, one situated between the pride of withdrawal and the pride of control. Not surprisingly, that walk on the narrow ridge begins to resemble the story of the individual pilgrim Christian journey. It is a very Christian story through which Americans have come to understand their nation as a historical phenomenon.

What then can we say about the other strand of the helix—the reciprocal influence of American democracy on American Christianity's understanding of history? Three points stand out.

First, the religious pluralism embodied in Protestant America meant the loss of control over any authoritative interpretation of Christian Scripture. Unlike the situation for Catholics, diverse views of biblical millennialism could flourish across the Protestant landscape and attach themselves to politics with a wholehearted frontier abandon.

Second, this open-market religious competition, operating in an environment of democratic faith in the common man, pushed Christianity toward popularly appealing versions of millennial doctrine. Pre-millennialism had its appeal—Christ returns to usher in a wonderful earthly kingdom for all true believers regardless of worldly economic, educational, or social distinctions. Even more appealing in the American setting has been the post-millennial view—Christ returns after a millennium that has been prepared for him by a people empowered and made hopeful through the ethos of democracy. The politically pro-activist message for a free people is: get busy! There is much preparation and work to be done in bringing in the kingdom.

Finally, there is the main implication for American Christianity. The thrust of these religious-political developments in America was to supplant, if not obliterate, any orthodox Christian view concerning the meaning of history. After debate in its earliest years, the young Christian church decisively rejected "millennialism," that is to say, the doctrine affirming Christ's 1000-year reign in a coming earthly kingdom. It rejected millennialism as a "Jewish error"—not because early Christians were anti-Semitic (for over a hundred years Christian believers were mostly Jews), but because the idea of an earthly millennium was repeating the Jewish authorities' mistake of expecting the Messiah to re-establish the earthly kingdom of national Israel. For the following 1500 years Catholic teaching and, after the Reformation, all leading Protestant authorities (Luther, Calvin, Knox, and so on) interpreted Scripture to mean something quite different than what came to be accepted as the optimistic American view.[62]

The Christian teaching regarded as authoritative was not premillennial, nor post-millennial. It was "amillennial." With Christ's first coming, the millennium had already arrived.[63] It was understood as a spiritual kingdom populated by those who had been spiritually reborn (the "first resurrection") through faith in Christ. Its thousand years were not calendar years but a poetic expression for the perfect fullness of its duration. Essentially, human history since its culmination with Christ's first coming was not a story or progress, or a regress, or alternations between the two. It was a parenthesis during which two kingdoms, wheat and tares (or in Augustine's metaphor, the City of God and the city of man), existed together awaiting Christ's second coming and last judgment. The fact that the thousand-year reign of Christ with his believers was already here was not a call to quietism (though some took it that way). As noted earlier, the people of the City of God were not meant to be indifferent to matters of righteousness and godly living in the city of man. The remaining period of human history called believers to a watchful, active "waiting" through lives that would bear witness to the world about the true meaning of human existence. In this sense America's Puritan forebears stood four-square with the early Christians. If there was an idea of progress, it was not the positive forward movement seen in the world's affairs. Progress was measured in terms of one's attention paid to the things of God while living in his good, though fallen, world.

With development of the nation's sanctified vision, a quite un-Christian idea of historical progress was gradually imported into American Christianity. It came in sideways, so to speak, not by directly challenging Christian orthodox doctrine but by nudging Christianity's ambiguity about time into a more "optimistic" and can-do attitude that American democracy found appealing. In the older, more "pessimistic," or (let us rightly call it) Christian view of things, any future coming of God's kingdom must necessarily mean the final crisis, judgment, and destruction of what worldly men prize. This historical consummation would mean not only the wheat being gathered but the chaff being burned. The twentieth century's leading scholar of American Protestantism, Richard Niebuhr, looked back on what had become of the once-Christian idea of a coming kingdom and despaired: "It was all fulfillment of promise without judgment. It was thought to be growing out of the present so that no great crisis needed to intervene between the order of grace and order of glory."[64]

In terms of an outlook on history, everything in America became more or less Christian as measured by the cyclical standard of pagan antiquity and at the same time more or less un-Christian as measured from the perspective of orthodox Christianity. From that latter perspective, if America is the redeemer of nations and time, then America is the Christ of history. This notion may be inadvertent, but it is blasphemy all the same.

AN IDEA OF THE PERSON

I have introduced the image of a double helix of mutual influence between American Christianity and American democracy. If we apply this image to understandings of democracy's basic unit of analysis, there may be much that seems commonplace. There is a good reason, however, why certain notions become commonplace: it is because they are regarded as true place-markers worth holding in common.

The basic unit of analysis in democracy is a singularity—the citizen, individual, person, community member, or what have you. But what is the nature of this singularity? Since Christians have historically been a strong presence in America, there has been a general seepage of Christian ideas into understandings of the human material that makes up democracy. The task here is to try to be more specific about how Christianity in general and Protestantism in particular helped shape American understandings of democratic man.

But first a caveat is necessary. It is abundantly clear from the historical record that Christians have violated all of the principles that will be discussed. They have done so actively, especially when their religion has been allied with privileged groups in society.

They have done so passively, by failing to act against evils they verbally condemn. Either way, there is no doubt that Christians at times have helped oppressors preserve and extend their power and privileges. But it is also the eye of religion that identifies such behavior as transgressive "violations" of transcendent norms, and not just unattractive preferences or mistakes in opinion. And it is the voice of religion that demands, not just suggests, the mending of one's wrong ways. Without this religious eye and voice there would be no sense in speaking of the violation or correction of anything. Without the standards, no one would know or care that something being done or left undone was un-Christian.

From its first days, Christianity proclaimed a radical equality before God and, through Jesus, of all men and women everywhere. The God who is "no respecter of persons" acknowledges none of the world's distinctions of rank, station, or anything else. The earliest congregations of Jewish Christians clearly anguished over the obvious implications for Judaism of this radical equality. And they came to a conclusion. The Lord of history had used the nation of Israel for his purposes. But one did not have to become a Jew to be a Christian. There was now a new Israel for all men and women (Acts, chapter 15; Galatians, chapter 3).

Every effort to ally Christianity with human structures of rank and privilege has had to fight against the religion's insistence on a thoroughgoing equality among human beings. On the one hand, there is the formal, or positional, equality before a Creator-God. Placed next to the infinity of their Maker, every finite member of humanity is the equal of every other. On the other hand, Christianity also insists on a conditional equality among humans, and this is understood in two respects. First is the equality grounded through each person being made in the image of God. Dignity is inherent to man because it is derivative from God. Each human being is a God-breathed-in eternal soul that, unlike other earthly creatures, is made capable of knowing and loving its Creator. There is also a second, less flattering version of conditional equality: All are also equal in their fallenness from communion with their Maker. "There is none that understands, there is none that seeks after God . . . For all have sinned and come short of the glory of God" (Romans 3:11, 13). Human beings are not divided between the sinning and the righteous; they are all sinners saved by grace. The aim of these Christian accounts is not to exalt or debase man but to call him to recognize himself and his condition for what it is.

This is an impressive arsenal of egalitarian claims, and American advocates of democratic equality have repeatedly returned to it for sustenance. At least equally impressive is the concept of individuation. Throughout the Bible God calls to humans by their personal names, often bypassing their tribal or other identities. In the New Testament this is radically reaffirmed with the poetic but still extraordinary claim that the hairs on each person's head are "numbered"—known to God not just in their collective sum, but each bar-coded, so to speak. Humans have inherent dignity and worth as individual, personally distinct beings.

The importance of this individuation is overlooked in a common political science claim, generally to the effect that democracy assumes "the essential dignity of man."[65] For whatever portion of American democracy has been influenced by Christianity, this is not true. Pagan philosophers, Enlightenment monarchs, aristocrats, and elites of all sorts have often espoused the essential dignity of man. In America democracy assumes, as Christianity declares, the essential dignity of each person, one at a time.

Amid this equality and individuation of persons, Christianity also seems to make a special point of overturning man's preferred order of nobility and exalting the lowly common person. The second, not the first-born, son is honored. Biblical stories of drama and tragedy are told about common people whose only way into a Greek or Roman play would have been as comic characters to be mocked by the audience. For Jews, the Messiah's earthly line of descent is shown to pass through a sequence of women specifically identified as a liar who sleeps with her father-in-law, a Gentile whore, a servant girl from a foreign nation specially cursed by God, a flagrant adulteress, and an unmarried peasant girl from a widely despised village. The royal purple is laid in an animal feeding trough.[66] For Greek philosophers, from their first encounter with Christianity in the second century, there was no difficulty in pointing out the absurdity and inherent contradiction in this new religion. Philosophical wisdom taught that the divine lies in the eternal realm of perfection of every kind, and true knowledge comes from turning the mind's eye away from the changing sensations of this world. Hence it is patently contrary to divine nature that it should be revealed in a flesh-and-blood historical person.[67]

The Christian affirmations of human equality, individuation, and ordinary life have been critically important grounding influences for thinking about democratic man, but they are not the whole story. Under the pressure of wartime, some Christian thinkers such as Jacques Maritain have wanted to claim that the secular democratic conscience as it developed in the West was wholly and simply the slow absorption of "truths evangelical in origin." With less justification, other Christian writers in recent years have felt a need to credit their religion with every good thing the world might seem to value, from freedom and capitalism to western civilization itself. Besides betraying an unseemly desire to fit into non-believers' idea of progress, such exaggeration hurts a very solid case that can be made for seeing biblical Christian values as one root source in the evolution of the modern democratic self.[68] Such a self could not help bearing the marks of Christianity's radical view of humanity—as equals; as universally exalted, God-breathed-in souls; and as individual persons helplessly fallen into the sin of exalting themselves.

A particular (Catholics would say distorted) view of these concepts followed from the fact that the vast majority of Americans were not just Christians but Protestants. Catholic social thought has traditionally drawn an important distinction between the person and the individual. A person is a spiritual whole endowed with freedom of choice, but also an open whole that demands relationships with others. Not just the heart requires these attachments, but human reason itself "needs to be sustained in all its searching by trusting dialogue and sincere friendship."[69] The self becomes a self in "webs of interlocution" and attachments among family, friends, community associations, and so on. By contrast, the Protestant individual stands as a lone figure on a socially barren landscape of other such figures—the lonely crowd of liberal democracy. If one accepts this distinction, then being Protestant sharpened Americans' understanding of democratic man as an autonomous individual. It was precisely this notion of the autonomy and liberty of individual conscience in the Great Denouement that contrasted so sharply with the Catholic tradition of a guided conscience within the community of the one true Church.[70]

It is often said that "belief in the common man is the core of the democratic creed."[71] This sounds good until one realizes it leaves up in the air what it is that is to be believed about the common man. For centuries, thinking persons claimed that what you could believe about the common person was that he was ignorant, emotion-driven, and capricious. The Protestant Reformation helped to overturn this view and set the democratic faith in fast motion. Through a religious affirmation of the common man's capacities, democracy could be reconceptualized—from the "mass rule" feared by philosophers to the "self government" championed by all right-thinking Christians and republicans. In light of what has followed in our own time regarding the sovereignty of individual choice, we need to be careful here. The Reformation did not assert that what any individual judged to be right doctrine was in fact right doctrine. It did assert the perspicuity of Scripture, through which individuals of every sort (thanks first to God's saving grace) could come to a common and right understanding of the things of God. Hence the massive Protestant emphasis on Bible translations into national vernaculars and literacy for the masses.[72] And hence too the intense, fine-grained emphasis on creedal statements expressing the common understandings in the Reformation era, producing of course different creedal statements that today seem hardly distinguishable. It was not the responsibility of the individual to choose his own version of doctrine; it was his, and her, responsibility to know right doctrine.

To grasp the significance of what Protestantism did, and then redid as it immigrated to America, we might return to the Protestant Reformation while it was still Catholic. In August 1513 a young Catholic professor distributed the readings for his 6:00 A.M. lectures. Twice weekly for over a year, the young Martin Luther taught his students from a specially printed text of the Psalms whose wide margins had eliminated all of the centuries-old commentaries by Church authorities on the texts. Instead, each student was presented with the words of the Bible and the blank space on which to write his own commentaries and observations on each Psalm.[73] This was not heresy but something more radical: it was a different way to think about heresy.

Foreshadowed here was the master idea that exploded into a "reformation" of not only religious but also political thinking. Generations of people would be taught that in searching for truth, a person has to go to the scriptural source for himself, decide for himself, and believe for himself. This was more than just an exalting of the lowly; it was an affirmation of the competence of the common man. There was to be no churchmen's *Regula Pastoralis* for the "care and governing" of parishioners' souls. You care for and govern your own soul. There was to be no more doctrine of "implicit faith," that is, the conception of faith by which individuals in the Church need not fully understand what it is they are to believe. The contrast with the older ways—ways that submerged individual judgment into a community and tradition—could not have been starker. Catholic authorities rightly complained that the Reformers made "individual persons the judges in matters of faith, not only of the Fathers but also of the councils," leaving "almost nothing to the common judgment of the Church."[74]

This religious dispute was also a contest about the presumptions for democracy. The individual's capacity to read and understand Scripture inescapably pointed to the common person's capacity for self-government. If the ordinary person was up to such momentous and eternally important things of the spirit, how could he not be capable of participating in the lesser political things of this world? It is misleading to say that democratic thinking in the West adopted these ideas from Protestant Christianity. Unless one counts the bulky philosophical writings on why democracy is a bad idea, there was no substantial body of democratic thinking preexistent to the Protestant Reformation to do the adopting.

However, we can leave aside the general issue of whether or not Protestantism promotes democracy.[75] The point here is that in the United States, conditions were generally favorable for it to do so. And in doing so, there was a favored understanding of the democratic personality. Protestantism in America carved distinct features into the profile of that individual.

In the first place, the consensus forged in America's Great Denouement established the presumption that all religious sects should be free of government entanglements; to be true to godly worship, everyone should worship God as his or her conscience dictated. In this American setting, the individual was not a philosophical abstraction but a living, breathing human being who could plausibly be recognized as a voluntary figure to himself—not self-sufficient but self-activating and in that sense independent. Likewise, the abstract idea of the church as a voluntary body of believers came to exist as a reality of churches in a religious marketplace, all competing to secure the voluntary attachments of those living, breathing individuals.

Second, while Protestantism emphasized the individuation of religious experience, with each human being standing alone so as to experience divinity authentically and deeply, that individual was a work in progress. Especially in the evangelical version that filled the New England template and spread from there, Protestantism stressed the second, spiritual birth of the individual, the born-again conversion experience. Here religion lined up in America with the reality of a remarkably open society, a place of second and third chances to take up again the opportunities offered by such a "new world."

Third, the American individual as a work in progress could be uniquely unencumbered. Protestant reformers in Europe had taken up the stern Gospel teaching that one must be willing to leave all—to be told that your mother and brothers are standing outside the door seeking you, and respond that only fellow believers are your mother, brothers—and sisters (Mark 3:33; Matthew 12:48). In this sense, the real-life condition in America was very Protestant. It was a setting for continually making and remaking attachments to a changing array of kith and kin. In the vast open spaces, waves of immigrants, and social churning of its cities, America was a solvent that continuously disrupted inherited social status and put into ordinary people's hands the opportunity to challenge authority and make their own way.

Fourth, each of these unencumbered individuals was a roughhewn equal, as good as any other. The practical necessities of surviving in America shredded pretensions of superior and subordinate status in a way that was fully in line with Protestant conceptions of natural, democratic equality. As Tocqueville reported, a European aristocrat could come to America to set himself up as a proprietary landlord; in short time, the facts of the situation would leave him a supplicant for labor—seeking "free hands," as they knew themselves to be. Moreover, every would-be proprietor was likely to find himself and his family lending a democratic hand to cope with the facts of existence in agrarian America. These facts of American life fit well with a Protestant indifference to "religion" as a matter of holy days, holy sites, relics, ritual, or sanctified ornamentation. Worship was expected to be coexistent with everyday life, and this affirmed a dignity in ordinary working people's lives, which as a practical matter also had to be lives of substantial drudgery.

Finally, the Protestant movement did not see the individual as simply standing in contemplation of the divine. Its "beatific vision" was about movement—the pilgrim on a journey through the alien land of this fallen world. That helps explain why *Pilgrim's Progress* had such a massive cultural resonance throughout most of America during at least the first half of the nation's history. Pilgrim's journey is an individual journey, which begins by breaking family ties and on its way encounters only a few temporary companions. All the trials, despair, and waywardness in Pilgrim's trek are not about making his way to salvation. America's Puritans clung to nothing more fiercely than the orthodox Christian view that personal salvation came from unmerited grace through faith and had no part of "works" or making "your own" way to it. Pilgrim's troubles in his progress are *after* his salvation as a believer, as he travels in this world to his heavenly destination. Hope—optimism, if you will—was a firm conviction, not just a wishful fantasy. But the fulfillment of forward-looking hope was a tough, hard slog requiring immense individual effort. The opportunities for upward mobility in America confirmed both the necessity of individual effort to get anywhere and the real possibility of the individual sojourner's dreams coming true.

In short, a Protestant view of forward-leaning, unencumbered, ordinary, and equal individuals was repeatedly reinforced amid the realities of life in America. Whether or not one was a good Protestant and read the Bible and the Puritan Fathers, daily life in America could seem a material version of Pilgrim's progress. Moreover, all of these ideas were revitalized by recurring periods of Protestant revivalism in both rural and urban parts of the nation, and these continued into the twentieth century.

As all of this was going on in America, there obviously continued to be oppressed groups in all the familiar categories of race, class, and gender. The issue here is how people in such oppressive situations were being taught over time to think of themselves in America. I think the historical record shows that when you listen to the voices in any such group at almost any time in American history, you hear talk of disadvantage and exploitation but not of defeat and submission. It is generally true that in America the oppressed were taught to think of themselves as free-standing selves, individuals pushing into the future with legitimate, equal claims to freedom, opportunity, and a better life—pilgrims with a promissory note for the American Dream.

While these Christian and largely Protestant influences were at work on democratic ideas of the person, America was also democratizing the Christian mind. The general effect, as with millennialism, was to push Christian doctrine in a series of popularly appealing directions.

The vast majority of Americans have probably always considered themselves Christians. Today upwards of 85 percent of all adult Americans identify themselves as Christians,[76] and it seems unlikely that earlier historical periods would have had significantly smaller proportions of self-professed adherents. What Americans historically have meant by calling themselves Christians is of course another matter. Here we have to rely mostly on what historians of religion have had to say about any changing understandings of the faith. In this complicated mix of developments, there are some general tendencies that can be sketched regarding ideas of the person in American Christianity.

Despite the plurality of Protestant sects, Christianity seems to have come to America with a core of orthodox doctrines distilled out of the fiery disputes of the Protestant Reformation. As noted earlier, Christianity is centered on faith in a person, not doctrines, but doctrines were important for spelling out what it is that a believer believes about that person and his meaning for the world. Of course, since Protestantism was the point of departure for America, this did favor the Lutheran-Calvinist tradition as against, say, the Thomistic tradition in the Catholic Church. Even so, the differences between Protestants and Catholics, overheated on so many things, were less than might be expected on central points. Nor is this surprising, since both Catholic teachings and

Protestant Reformed theology traced a central line of interpretation on these essentials back to Augustine, and through him to the statements of doctrine in Paul's letters.

One body of such principles dealt with the easily misunderstood view of individuals as "elected" and "predestinated." The very terms summon up images of self-righteous prigs preening themselves in New England churches before going out to look down their noses at their neighbors. In fact, this is exactly the pride of the Pharisee that Puritans believed condemned people to hell and wanted no part of.[77] As doctrine, the election and predestination of individuals had to do with the sovereignty of God in choosing those he would save or not save, and his sovereign power in seeing to it that nothing through all time could prevent that choice from being efficacious.

Another body of fundamental doctrine had to do with original sin and the limitations of free will. Here too the scope for modern misunderstandings is immense. The doctrine of original sin ("the total depravity of man" in Protestant Reformation language) is not a claim that human beings never do anything good. It is that even an individual's best actions are tainted by a prideful rebellion against God's rightful rule in one's life, a fall into the yearning to play God. The bent of every person's willful heart toward this rebellion, known as sin, means that no one in such a spiritual state has the goodness that God's holiness requires for fellowship with him. Individuals do have the capacity in their free will to make choices, but not to love and thus obey God as they should. Thus every human being is born without the ability to be in what should be a natural state of communion with his Creator. During the centuries after 400 A.D., major chunks of Catholic and Protestant Reformed theology were devoted to denouncing as heretical the claim of the Irish monk Pelagius that humans have the capacity to initiate or earn their own salvation. By contrast, the orthodox Christian view has been that unsaved man, being spiritually dead, has no capacity to help God do what only God can do for sinners.

My aim here is not to argue the many intricacies of these doctrines one way or the other. It is to point out that the prevailing tendency was for democratic thinking in America to sweep aside all these views of the individual. The theme is a Christianity that became more aligned with the desires of the people, more democratic or, as we would say today, "market-driven." (This is also to say, less Christian.)

I noted earlier that the Founding Fathers' generation had good political reasons to de-emphasize differences in religious doctrine in favor of a common Christian morality. After 1800 the upsurge of "democratic evangelicalism" gave a much more powerful and sustained push in that same direction.[78] The doctrine of election—some saved and others not—appeared undemocratic in its inegalitarian overtones. Predestination could just as easily be recognized as undemocratic in what it seems to deny about an open future of hope for individuals unencumbered by the past. With little effort, the doctrine of original sin could be perceived as a slam on an American faith in the common man's goodness. The doctrine of limited free will seemed an even worse violation of faith in the common man's capacity to govern himself and work at achieving his full God-given potential. By contrast, traditional Christian doctrine offered hope for, but no faith in, the common man or any other man. Apart from God's grace, each person had all the spiritual potential of a corpse.

Traditional Christian doctrine clearly did grate on what was becoming the American democratic creed. The result was that, over time, such doctrine had its undemocratic rough edges smoothed off, even though substantively speaking these ideas were more the core than the edges of Christian teaching. This smoothing work was done not by secularists and unbelievers but by Christian leaders of the various democratic flocks proliferating in nineteenth-century America. There was no overt design to deny traditional Christian doctrine, but there was an overt incentive and desire to keep the flocks from deserting the shepherds for preaching unpopular, democratically incorrect things. Within the ever-recurring divisions and subdivisions of American Protestantism, the competitive advantage over time—even among American theologians—consistently lay with those preaching more popular views and not with the learned clergy suspicious of a merely emotional religion, sentimentalism, and a Gospel bound to American political values.[79] At any one time one could say that there was simply a question of emphasis, say using Jonathan Edwards' or some other learned distinctions, to offer a more popularly palatable message. Do that long enough and carelessly enough, and one has changed the traditional teaching of the religion—and the theological populists did so.

Usually the first move from the pulpits was to temper public presentations of unpopular aspects of orthodox Christian doctrine, such as God's wrath against sin and the damnation of sinners. The next step, encouraged by and well under way during the Protestant revivals in nineteenth-century America, was to accept outright self-contradiction and embrace popular opportunism. Lyman Beecher, the North's leading revivalist and moral reformer in the first half of the nineteenth century, declared: "I believe that both the doctrines of dependence [man's total dependence on God for salvation] and moral accountability [man's ability and free agency in choosing to be saved] must be admitted. . . . I also believe that greater or less prominence should be given to the one or the other of these doctrines according to the prevailing state of public opinion."[80] The next step was simply to assert the opposite of traditional Christian doctrine as if nothing was happening. By the mid-nineteenth century the nation's revivalist superstar, Charles Grandison Finney, was brushing aside 1500 years of anti-Pelagian doctrine: "The moral government of God everywhere assumes and implies the liberty of the human will, and the natural ability to obey God." By the Civil War era, Lyman's son, Henry Ward Beecher, was achieving an immense public following by concentrating on the pleasures of God's love in popular sentiment and preaching little or nothing about God's judgment.[81]

A careful study of America's leading antebellum theologians

describes how easily they equated America's political morality with Christianity itself. The author, Mark Noll, concludes: "Their tragedy—and the greater the theologian the greater the tragedy—was to rest content with a God defined by the American conventions God's own loyal servants had exploited so well."[82] If this is what was happening in the higher, elite realms of American theology, it is not difficult to imagine what was going on in the free-range, hardscrabble locales of American preaching. Hierarchy and deference to authority or tradition were all but nonexistent in the competitive marketplace of American Protestantism. In this setting, any serious discussion of doctrine would invite only unending debate, confusion, and the threat of driving people to competing churches of a less "highbrow" nature. Thus there was a strong incentive to avoid what ordinary church people considered intellectual speculations (that is, careful efforts to clarify, correct, and responsibly expound doctrine) in favor of the "primitive simplicity" of Gospel truth.[83] And there was this all-important point as well: Appeals to a popular religion of the heart made much more sense than doctrinal expositions because such appeals could be presented to the common man as more authentic. Heartfelt religion seemed truer than a mere intellectual understanding of Christianity, action more useful than contemplation in America's kinetic society.

If theological populism was a constant temptation in the routine weekly sermonizing of American clergy, it was omnipresent amid the excitement of recurring Protestant revivals led by populist preachers across the land. During the nineteenth century, periodic surges of revivalism produced changes in Christian understandings of the individual that made perfect democratic sense. Something seemed to be amiss if Christian faith denied the individual's free will (that is, his or her capacity to choose, to work, and to deserve his salvation), while at the same time America's democratic faith was affirming every person's capacity for self-government in the political realm.

In the early twentieth century, new and much more thoroughly secular forces emerged to push in the same direction. A sense of guilt before God and feelings of shame for sinning were now understood to be unhealthy, psychologically damaging self-conceptions. "The old-time religion" was another name for such conceptions, and in educated circles this was coming to be seen as narrow, illiberal, and judgmental. Despite their importance among intellectuals, however, these new psychoanalytic-therapeutic ideas of the twentieth century were only overlaying influences; they served to reinforce what had already been under way for some decades in the pulpits and revival tents of America's ever more democratic Christianity. In the nineteenth century, Unitarians and other opponents of traditional Christianity had taken special delight in publicizing the doctrinal prevarications of Protestant revivalists as they sought to appeal to mass audiences. By the twentieth century fewer people seemed to notice or care, apart from an outraged subset of Protestant intellectuals who would become known as "fundamentalists." In the main body of American Protestantism, centuries-old articles of faith were becoming an empty shell. As Richard Niebuhr described it, "A God without wrath brought men without sin into a kingdom without judgment through the ministrations of a Christ without a cross."[84] In this more modern, liberal view, to become focused on creedal issues of doctrine was to risk being doctrinaire—an odd worry since there was so little doctrine to be doctrinaire about.

Beyond any particular issues of doctrine, the overall effect was to shove doctrine itself to the sidelines of American Christianity. What prospered instead was an "emotional, legalistic, and superficial folk-theology" that had literally uprooted "large sections of American Christianity . . . from the Church's great tradition." The individual American Christian could be portrayed as a feeling person but not especially a thinking person. By the mid-twentieth century, America's leading religious historian described the modern result as "a kind of 'Christianity of Main Street' . . . and with it an implicit theology—a farrago of sentimentality, moralism, democracy, free enterprise, laicism, 'confident living,' and utilitarian concern for success . . . It has reduced the number of theologically responsive and responsible people, lay and clerical."[85]

Since Sydney Ahlstrom wrote those words almost fifty years ago, the democratizing of the Christian mind has continued to push American Christianity toward a simple fideism with scant regard for doctrinal reasoning. A person is sure of what he believes because he believes it. According to a leading sociologist, since World War II the approach governing religious obligations is modern Americans' strongly held belief in "quiet faith" and "morality writ small":

> People who adhere to such a creed think the best way to fulfill our obligations to others is not by lecturing them about right and wrong, but rather by personal example. They do not believe in absolutes but in balancing what is right with what is practical. They distrust extremes, even those views they consider correct but that are asserted with too much finality. And they feel that one has to do one's best to understand, even when one does not agree with, those who think otherwise.[86]

It appears that in the last half-century many Americans have arrived at a self-understanding that is religious in tone and intent but also nonabsolutist, inclusive, modest and, above all, nonjudgmental of others. Scholars have sought various ways to describe this overall trend. One speaks of a "spirituality of seeking" replacing the "spirituality of dwelling" provided by traditional religion. Another sees competition in America's religious marketplace as being won by self-expression values—"the pursuit of self-realization through personal quests for spiritual insight and fulfillment." A third describes the general trend of "shrinking transcendence." In this process, the "little transcendences" experienced by seekers of spirituality displace the "great transcendences" of salvational religion and its promise to bridge the divide between God and man.[87]

Although none of this represents traditional Christian doctrine, by any normal understanding of the meaning of words this nonjudgmental spiritual quest for self-realization is in fact doctrine. It cannot be anything else, since it is self-evidentially a thoroughgoing claim of what is right and wrong to believe. It is right to believe that all religions teach the same truths; it is wrong to believe that they do not. It is wrong to believe in absolutes without balancing them with what is practical. It is right to seek to understand those with whom you disagree but wrong to seek to tell them why you think they are wrong. It is right to distrust extremes and wrong to trust extremes you think are correct if they have too much finality in being correct.

Nonjudgmentalism, which holds that it is right not to judge others, amounts to a kind of judging without criteria. To assert the non-judgment of others can mean judging others to be worthy of respect, or to be a matter of indifference to you, or to be innocent of anything deserving judgment, or anything else one chooses it to mean. But for those who are not interested in doctrine, it does have the superficial appearance of virtue. The person of nonjudgmental faith in faith appears to be humble and open-minded. But in fact, he is just the opposite. He disdains any need to give reasons to others. He refuses others the respect of engaging in serious disagreement. He holds that to judge is to exclude and to condemn, and so he excludes and condemns anyone who does it.

But in addition to being able to claim the virtue of tolerance, not judging others also opens up a comfort zone for having a relaxed attitude about judging oneself. In this open and tolerant democratic ethos, it is far more desirable to be seen as a seeker than as a true believer (read "fanatic"). In the older Christian tradition, Pilgrim, as a true believer in the revealed Word, is racked in this world by the tribulations of faith, including the doubts and honest questioning that accompany faith on its journey. Today's Seeker is on a more open-ended and wholly self-referential journey to find what satisfies him, the place in a world of unanswerable questions where he can come to psychological rest. The odds are good that Seeker will find the Church of Don't-Be-Too-Hard-on-Yourself. Self-realization does not fit well with the ancient Judeo-Christian precept of self-mortification before God. Thus it is not surprising that among Christians and non-Christians alike, more Americans than ever before are engaged in "new" forms of an eclectic spirituality that has little or nothing to do with the Christian religious tradition.[88] On the contrary, much of this spiritual seeking resembles the pantheism that Tocqueville foresaw in America's future.

The fact is that orthodox Christianity has long rejected fideism. It has been regarded as an error, which mainstream Christianity began attacking in the third century during the days of the first Christian apologists. "It is far better to accept teachings with reason and wisdom than with mere faith," said Origen. According to this ancient view, reaffirmed by Pope John Paul II in 1998, doctrine is the product of reason applied to faith. If believers see only through the eyes of faith and neglect reason, they won't understand what they are seeing. The fideist, who considers religion as an expression of "blind faith," denies the need to give reasons for believing and thereby denies the individual's responsibility for understanding his or her faith. In the third century this opened the door to all sorts of Gnostic cults; in twentieth-century America it opened an even wider door to all sorts of "new spirituality." As John Paul put it, "It is an illusion to think that faith, tied to weak reasoning, might be more penetrating; on the contrary, faith then runs the grave risk of withering into myth or superstition."[89]

In the democratizing process that I have been describing, the exalted individual of Christianity has become exalted indeed. One might say that in the spiritual courtroom for judging righteousness, the individual has been slowly transformed from defendant to prosecutor. In what Ahlstrom called Christianity's "great tradition," God is praiseworthy whether or not He saves any sinner (grace is "amazing" in that any individual in His dock should be let off). The modern democratized Christian appears to offer praise and worship to God for having the good character to save him, with God now implicitly in the dock to explain why He does not save everybody.

Assuming that one is allowed to judge, how should we view this democratized Christianity regarding the idea of the person? Tocqueville, we recall, in considering the characteristics needed if religion was to survive well in the democratic future, put high importance on the issue of doctrine. In his view religion could do well in a democracy only if it gave up external formalities to hold onto its core articles of faith. By that standard, it would not seem that Christianity has survived very well.

There are important reasons for thinking that the demise of doctrine and the rise of nonjudgmental, quiet faith have been a very good thing. By abandoning claims of absolute truth by which the social order and individual behavior can be judged, Christianity has been made safe for democracy. It has helped produce moral citizens who are moderate in asserting any claims to truth and willing to compromise with others to produce practical results. Americans have been able to remain religious in their self-understanding as well as generally tolerant, constructively engaged democrats. Especially in light of the domestic turmoil in other religious societies, these are immense accomplishments.

But to leave the matter there is to be unfaithful to the subject. There is also the claim that religion is not something to be valued simply by the criterion of how well it serves the interests of the state and society. Seeing religion merely as something in service to earthly powers is what Christians in the Great Denouement totally rejected, as did the early Christians in the Roman Empire. This rejection was based on the very religious reason that what is absolute must not be subordinated to what is relative and human. Limiting the power of the state and the organized church over each other was a matter of keeping relative things relative. Over, under, and around all that was the superior matter of man's relation to his sovereign Creator. Christianity did much to shape the idea of the individual in American democracy, mainly it would seem for the better. America drew Christian thinking on that subject in its own democratic direction, mainly for the worse in terms of anything like traditional Christian doctrine.

AN IDEA OF POLITICAL SOCIETY

How did Christianity help build a particular kind of political society in America, and how was the religion shaped in turn by that society? I have already discussed one of the chief influences of Christianity on the idea of political society. The Great Denouement was explicitly about individual religious liberty, but implicitly it presented a more general vision of a political society that could be pluralistic, non-hierarchical, and yet unified, or at least in a very important sense at one with itself. In philosophical terms, evoking such a possible vision was a very Big Deal. From the origins of Greek philosophy, one of the most enduring problems in thinking about political society has been the conundrum of the one and the many. If society is only a many, there can be no unity and chaos must result. If society is unity, there can be no many and the vibrant hues of humanity must be crushed. Christianity entered this intellectual puzzle palace and in effect said, no, unity and plurality can be compatible. Christian theology gave warrant for this seemingly illogical claim: there is one God in three persons. So too did ecclesiology: the Christian community is one body of different, mutually dependent members.

Of course these abstractions could be and were consistent with a medieval hierarchy of such differentiated members, in one great Chain of Being, as it was called. The advent of Protestantism, and the practical experiences of such people in America, flattened pluralism, so to speak, into a horizontal vision of differentiated unity. The one church of Christ, to be the true church of Christ, must exist as a multiple and voluntary body of believers. So said Protestants. Moreover, as noted earlier, America was born religiously pluralistic, and colonial thinking gradually moved to accommodate itself to that inescapable fact on the ground. A singularity could be plural—varied flowers, one bouquet. These were not just poetic metaphors but new conceptualizations introduced into antiquity's debate. As such, they had the capacity to make what was unthinkable into something thinkable. And until a pluralistic society of oneness, an "E Pluribus Unum," became thinkable, there was no intellectually defensible way to work for it. In many ways worth discussing but beyond the scope of this essay, Protestants and Catholics in America brought such intellectual conceptions down to earth as religious associations in civil society that insisted on holding together the seemingly contradictory commitments to human individuality and social solidarity.[90]

Given the actual religious and social conditions in America, this structural puzzle about political society was relatively easy to address (though always difficult in practice to resolve). The problem of stability and change in the new political society was another matter. For classical republican thinking, change meant ultimate decay and collapse, as republics were born, matured, and aged. But the idea of stability could be no less threatening; it seemed to endorse the entrenched powers of every status quo fixed in place against republican liberty. Christianity in America did not really debate this philosophical problem of stability and change. It simply went into action and helped solve it.

At first glance it might seem an absurd idea for religious "pilgrims"—literally, foreigners passing through—to be building anything in their field of transit. In this common view of religion, a truly spiritual person must regard this world as "fly-over" territory that is not worth bothering about. But orthodox Christian dogma has always rejected any idea of believers living a spiritual existence apart from the world. As Christians and particularly as Protestants, many Americans saw themselves called to act in their local world, and their particular ways of acting helped shape distinctive features of American political society.

It might be said that by definition, Protestants are protestors. And there has certainly never been any lack of people in America who are willing to protest. However, it is important to understand that before Protestantism is a "protest," it is an affirmation. Otherwise there would be no basis for protesting. The Protestant political influence in America has not come from people who have primarily thought of themselves as protestors against authority; rather, it has come from people who have seen themselves as affirming the original values that existing authorities have forgotten or corrupted. Authenticity had to trump authority. This has important implications for the kind of "protesting" presence these people have been in American society. As Richard Niebuhr put it:

> The protests of Protestantism—always allowing for the presence in them of rebellious self-assertions—have been secondary, for the most part, to revivals. The movement of protest from generation to generation has followed, not preceded, a movement of reformation, regeneration, awakening, and renewal. And the protest was raised not against the authority of the old, but against its acceptance and establishment of a mediocre form of men's moral and religious existence.[91]

A political society of affirmation and protest not only called people to act in the world; it also continually re-called them to revive from their slacking off. Protestant revival and political renewal fed off each other. In democratic America, the Old Testament's easy way out of blaming bad kings for moral decline was no longer available. One had to dwell on the shortcomings of an entire people, and Protestant democracy could do so in the confident hope of striving for spiritual and moral renewal. Just as the Puritans' godly covenant had the jeremiad as its inevitable accompaniment, so post-revolutionary American political society became accustomed to develop through pulsations of Protestant revivalism. Puritans saw themselves as a chosen people continually on the verge of becoming Babylonians. Revivalists saw America as a Christian nation in repeated grave need of being Christianized.

Thus any simple idea of liberal/conservative, pro- or anti-change, wholly misses the point—which is that "revival" can mean any or all of those things. Protestantism was both a stabilizing and a destabilizing force in American political society. In implementing the moral calculus of republicanism, such religion helped produce stable citizens with at least an expectation (if not always the fact) of responsible moral conduct. Acting under the affirmative impulse to help purify society, these same citizens could be counted on to be destabilizing agents of change. Likewise, their religious energy meant that Protestants were both a dividing force, as they followed a penchant for sticking their noses into other people's business, and a uniting force, as they called all Americans back to widely shared ideals. America has many political stories, but squarely in the center of them is a procession of recurring Protestant revivals, personal awakenings, and religious-political reform movements pressing for institutional change.

These themes began appearing with the first of the noteworthy Protestant revivals to occur in the nation, the Great Awakening in the 1730s and 1740s. For reasons that are not clear, these years witnessed an outbreak of religious fervor across the colonies. Although it varied in different regions, the common experience reported was an awakening to God's call in one's life. Dullness and despair, often superintended by a spiritually dead clergy, were transformed into hope and joy through regenerated hearts.

The spreading revival cut across traditional lines of occupation, region, gender, and race. It overturned churches of unregenerated clergymen and created new congregations and new preachers (including, in the North at least, blacks, Indians, and women) who were "alive to the word of God." The revivals mobilized ordinary people to assemble as they never had before and helped promote a shared identity, the first to actually spread across colonial boundaries. Among the many important implications for political society, perhaps the most significant for our purposes is that the Great Awakening endorsed personal commitments to living in truth even at the price of challenging and rejecting traditional authority. It was the "old lights" of paternal authority who had betrayed the experiential truth of Christianity. Rebellion by the "new lights" was not in the name of new values or the work of a rebellious heart; rather, rebellion was in the name of old, eternally true values, and thus a duty. There is good reason to see the years following the 1740s as an extension of this awakening. Political republicanism and spiritual regeneration were blended to make the independence claimed in 1776 a moral as well as a merely political concept.[92]

Subsequent revivals lacked such revolutionary implications, but they nonetheless had great political importance. For millions of ordinary people, over many time periods, this line of movement from personal regeneration to social regeneration infused American political society with a penchant for moralization, voluntary organization, and popular inclusiveness that would otherwise not have been there. These are precisely the features of American public life that have always evoked knowing smirks from Old World sophisticates amused by Americans' puritanical and innocent approach to public affairs. I will consider each of these three features in turn.

First, revivalism has served to continually re-moralize American politics, a point that is easily caricatured and misunderstood. Europeans have always found it amusing, even touching, to observe Americans' earnest efforts to "clean up politics" and produce "good," rather than merely effective, government. And it is surely true that over the years there have more than enough examples of American reformers' naïveté to keep the snickering going. Abandoning doctrines of original sin in the nineteenth century helped produce a far too rosy view of what could be expected from human beings and their institutions—a foolishness which eighteenth-century Calvinism saw through and to which liberal Protestantism was especially prone.[93]

However, the continual efforts to re-moralize politics did more than just reveal reformers' naïveté. Revivalism imparted a distinctively Protestant tone (now commonly labeled as "puritanical") to American politics. As revivalists viewed the world, a base and unreformed politics interfered with the moral duty to try to cor-rect the failings one saw in society. Such a politics corrupted th benevolent purposes that should guide public action. This way thinking helped teach Americans to view political action in a particular way, as a kind of benevolent problem-solving aimed at purifying and restoring society. Obviously this is not the whole story on political thinking in America, but it needs to be understood as an important and distinctive element of the story that Protestantism contributed.

The Protestants' impulse to moralize politics has deep roots. In this tradition every believer is to be viewed as "his own priest," with no need for churchly human intermediaries between himself and God. And with no confession booth for confiding to a priest, no penance imposed by church authorities, no earthly apparatus of indulgences to get him off the hook with God, every Protestant believer is in a way his own moralist. A proactive stance toward judging what is right and wrong comes with the Protestant territory. At the same time, the individual is not left on his or her own without standards. There is of course the Bible, the Word which each person is to encounter directly. Some efforts to re-moralize politics have found Protestants trying to place the Bible's dos and don'ts more or less directly into legislative enactments. At the same time, there has also been a Protestant moralism that has continuously challenged such "legalism" in the name of a larger Christian calling to benevolence and following the Word that took the form of a person.

The messy historical fact is that both these views of Protestant moralism have been operating during every effort at spiritual and political regeneration. But especially with the nineteenth-century evangelical explosion in America, the dominant emphasis in moral standards was put on "knowing Jesus." This in turn had a very definite meaning for Protestant reformers. While all religions offer their followers enduring rules and positive ideals to be sought, Christianity offers an ideal person. For believers, this person offers (among other things) a perfect model of human exis-nce, a God-man who fully reveals man to himself. By this stan-rd the mark of *agape* love is what it means to be fully human—ther words, to love others selflessly without judging their merits or thinking of one's own needs. Protestant reformers saw such benevolence as wholly consistent with telling those same people that they were doing something wrong and should stop it.

Since evangelical Christianity focused on the individual and his or her moral behavior in society, political reform efforts were often heavily tilted toward public measures against drinking, gambling, prostitution, Sabbath-breaking, and other "vice" issues. The moralization of politics became more confused as industrial development transformed America after the Civil War. Some looked at the joblessness and other urban problems and saw a need to redouble efforts at anti-vice legislation to enforce middle-class propriety and personal responsibility. Others sought new ways of uplifting urban lives with "scientific charity," orphanages, settlement houses, and education. Yet others saw the social evils as something more than the result of individual acts of sinfulness. For them, the need was to apply the "social gospel" to the new large-scale structures of commerce and affirm the moral quality of economic relations with new forms of labor legislation and social insurance.[94] And still others launched the "godly insurgencies" of Populism to try and make the economic and political regime responsive to the interests of the common man.[95] Over the decades, Protestant reformers in conjunction with others pursued all of these causes and many more. If their Christian commitment did not provide all or even most of the answers, it did supply the unmistakable moral energy for social and political reform in America well into the twentieth century.

Protestantism's revivals and reform movements were not about legislating evangelical theology, which as we have seen was in a general state of doctrinal decline. They were mainly about Protestant moralists working out the model of Benevolence, the religious duty of seeking the good of others. To modern eyes they were, of course, committing the ultimate sin of thinking you know what is best for other people. But they did think that, and th busied themselves in the public arena trying to be faithful to t belief. They were rightly dubbed do-gooders, although they p ably would have rather been called "those who hunger and thirst after righteousness." In any case, the issue was not whether a person can be good without God. It was more basic than that. Protestant revivalism helped instill in public life the expectation that in the first place one ought to be good—rather than merely powerful, smart, effective, and all the other attributes the world expects.

The second effect of revivalism on political society is easier to identify and briefly describe. It has to do with learning the politics of voluntary organization in a democracy. Protestant revivals were not identified with particular churches, and they did not aim at strengthening institutional religion. They were mobilizations of ordinary people—a religious populism. Their leaders were entrepreneurs with the common touch rather than representatives of the learned clergy in established church orders. Their expertise was in reaching people, organizing them, and moving everyone forward with a common purpose.[96] Protestantism, which had always been more of a movement than a structure, became in America a way of doing religion and then organizing the same way to do good in politics.

In the early revivals and awakenings, Protestant elders often expressed concern that such occurrences should be spontaneous—the independent workings of the Holy Spirit rather than something "gotten up" by preachers who were skillful in appealing to common people's emotions. In this way, America's religious founders matched the political founders' concern for a virtuous republicanism in which one stood and was drafted rather than "ran" for office by courting the people. And in both cases, the realities of democratic life in the nineteenth century swept aside such views. Soon it was difficult to distinguish the preparations and machinery of mass evangelism from the mass politics of political parties. The conversion of a sinner could be seen as nothing iraculous but rather as the natural result of a properly planned d effectively implemented set of organizational techniques. As of the greatest of the nineteenth-century revivalists put it, ersion "is not a miracle or dependent on a miracle in any sense. . . . It is purely a philosophical result of the right use of constituted means."[97] As the campaigns for moral reform grew more sophisticated, the same pattern repeated itself. Between 1865 and 1920 it was overwhelmingly religious groups who invented and applied the lobbying techniques that later became standard operating procedure for interest groups of all kinds.[98]

In helping Americans learn how to organize politics, Protestant revival and reform contributed something very mundane yet very important to political society: it taught people still experimenting in self-government a practical way to domesticate the question of political power. Political power could be, and was, domesticated by people organizing within a free democratic process to push for needed change. The practical political effect was to house-train an issue drenched in centuries of blood and turn it into something ordinary people could live with—indeed, participate in—amid relative peace.

Finally, the Protestants' revival and reform movements, by their very nature, introduced a pluralist politics of inclusion into the American scene. It was a paradoxical, Protestant kind of inclusiveness in that it was achieved by ever more denominational divisions accommodating differences of race, class, region, and congregational opinion. This conflict within pluralism itself could be portrayed and then celebrated as a series of successes of the American pluralist ideal.[99] In this welter of denominations and moralized politics, it was always difficult for Christian reformers to get around their religion's commitment to human equality. It was this problem—taking form in the early abolition movement's debate over women speakers and "mixed" (that is, male and female) audiences—that almost immediately set in motion the forces that led to the women's movement of the 1840s. If notions of Chri tian equality did not suffice to produce inclusion, then the pr ticalities of movement politics in a democracy did: more pe meant more influence.

In either case, the revivals and reform movements of tant do-gooders opened up new spaces in political soc women and other oppressed groups had never had access to before. Among the earliest and latest beneficiaries were blacks and women. After the abolition and early women's suffrage movements, the coming of industrialization and its attendant social problems gave even more prominence to the "feminization" of Christian social activism. Americans still believed that women's place was in the Christian home, but many American women also believed it was women's place to protect the Christian home. The result was many new mobilizations around measures that would safeguard women and families amid the pressures of urban factory life, as well as against the temptations of bars, gamblers, and low women that were leading men astray. None of these religious-political movements was more formidable than the Women's Christian Temperance Union of Frances Willard and her mass of associates spread throughout the federal political system.[100] From this feminization one could track a corresponding reform movement to reaffirm a "masculine Christianity," especially among disadvantaged young urban males through scouting, the YMCA, and other manly sports associations.[101] And still to come was the much bigger story of the twentieth-century civil rights movement and the pivotal role of black Protestant churches.

For a time moral reform movements succeeded in the legislatures, with laws prohibiting or regulating Sabbath-breaking, alcohol, lotteries, and distribution of immoral literature and birth control through the mail. Ultimately almost all of this anti-vice legislation failed in the first half of the twentieth century, none more spectacularly than Prohibition. By contrast, economic and human rights legislation produced through such efforts—maximum work hours and minimum wage laws, worker safety and nitation, Mothers' Pensions, child protection laws, civil rights iatives—served as the basis for permanent reforms in American institutions. The point here is not to list the successes and s of Protestant reformers in producing new policies, but to the kind of political society they tended to produce. hat score, Protestantism was a powerful civics school. It helped produce a lively, kinetic political society of joiners. It mobilized people who often disagreed with and annoyed others, but also pushed everyone to keep talking. It taught people to pay attention to what is right or wrong in the way American society is behaving itself. In doing that, it taught people to see the social world not as a set of permanent conditions but as a series of problems that need to be "fixed" (itself a uniquely American term). It schooled ordinary people in the confidence that, if there "ought'a be a law" to fix things, then people like you and me have the capacity to make or unmake such a law and set things right. It taught citizens that, whatever you might personally stand to gain, you had better be able to argue that what you want is for the larger good of a moral republic. In short, it taught Americans how to be responsibly democratic.

How then did such a political society affect Christianity? Although the reforming evangelicalism of the nineteenth century taught Americans to equate the Christian gospel with their democratic political society, there were always some Christian voices worried that such political engagements were a distraction from the true purpose of their religion. That purpose, they said, is to fulfill the Great Commission to spread the good news of God's salvation, given through Christ's atonement for human sin. And as these critics pointed out, the early church of believers who knew the flesh-and-blood Jesus left no record of trying to reform the inhumane politics and policies of the Roman Empire.

The ambivalent relationship between Protestant revival and political reform was embodied in Charles Grandison Finney, the leading antebellum evangelist. To old-style Protestant revivalists, Finney was the incarnation of suspicious "new measures" for getting up a revival movement. He mastered the arts of publicity holding all-night prayer sessions and week-long meetings, pray about sinners by name, including women to pray and exho mixed company, attacking unregenerated clergy as spiritual and dead designating the "anxious seat" at the front of a meeting to publicly acknowledge the sinner's repentance. In short, he was a master entrepreneur in mass evangelism. And yet Finney and some Protestant revivalists after him were skeptical about using laws to deal with social evils. Slavery, for example, was a spiritual sin that needed to be confronted by converting slave holders, not by joining the abolition movement. From Finney's antebellum doubts to the mid-twentieth-century opponents of Martin Luther King Jr. in some black churches, the claim has been that Christians do their duty by changing hearts, not laws.

Despite misgivings about marrying Christianity to various worldly projects to do good, there have been few doubts about a larger bond that has grown over the centuries. It is the bond uniting Christianity and the democratic faith in the political society that is America. This general outlook is so pervasive and taken for granted that no single term, such as the old standbys "civil religion" or Americanism, really does it justice.[102] The outlook is philosophical in that it is devoted to democracy as the sole legitimate form of government. It is historical in that it upholds the sanctified vision of the Nation's mission. It is sociological in that it is committed to the American way of life. It is political in that it champions self-government by free individuals. It is all but mystical in invoking "the promise of American life." Theologically, it is possible to imagine a person being a Christian and not believing any of those things, but it is almost unthinkable that one could be an American Christian and not believe those things. To be un-American is to be un-Christian.

None of this is to imply that Americans developed an outlook asserting the converse: that to be un-Christian was to be un-American. The Great Denouement and its long-established results [illegible]noculated Americans against any such theocratic intolerance. The [illegible]estion here is how American political society affected Chris[illegible]ity, and the answer is that it more or less absorbed Christian[illegible] to a political identity.

[illegible]hing for this fusion were all the convergences we have seen [illegible] American democracy and Christianity in the ideas of history, the person, and political society. More than anything else, however, it was war that helped Americans to understand the Christian faith and the democratic faith as virtually indistinguishable. The antecedents for this merging went back to the American Revolutionary War and then, with even greater public force, to the Civil War.[103]

Even so, at the beginning of the twentieth century a significant body of Protestant opinion held itself fairly indifferent to public affairs, and implicitly to America's political fortunes. In the words of the leading revivalist Dwight L. Moody, "I look upon this world as a wrecked vessel. God has given me a lifeboat and said to me, 'Moody, save all you can.'"[104] Beyond that, a growing body of pre-millennialist Protestants found the events surrounding World War I significant only insofar as they might usher in the prophesied second coming of Christ before the millennium. With American entry into the war in 1917, these "fundamentalists" (the term had just been coined) found themselves under devastating attacks from more moderate, mainstream Protestants for being unpatriotic and a threat to national security, possibly with the help of German money.[105] Such incidents gave only a small indication of the larger tendency, under the pressure of events, to merge political and religious identities. Whether one went on to be for or against the League of Nations, the underlying premise took root: America's democratic cause in the world was also the Christian cause.

It was above all the two great wars of the rest of the century—World War II and the Cold War—that seemed to cement the union of democratic faith and Christian faith for America. Writing from the depths of World War II's darkness, Jacques Maritain as a European Catholic expressed the idea that many Americans had already come to understand in their bones: "The democratic im pulse has arisen in human history as a temporal manifestation the inspiration of the Gospel." Maritain went on to quote P dent Roosevelt about the war coalition's aim to establish international order in which the spirit of Christ shall r hearts of men and of nations," as well as Vice President Henry Wallace's claim that "Democracy is the only true political expression of Christianity."[106] If some harbored doubts about America's redeemer role as a Christian nation, fascism helped remove them.

Immediately on the heels of defeating anti-democratic paganism, Americans found themselves turning to lead the worldwide fight against anti-democratic atheism. One did not have to be either a right-wing anti-communist or a Christian to see that once again, America faced a foe devoted to liquidating at the same stroke both Christianity and democracy. As much as anything else, it was their enemies that taught Americans to merge the Christian into the democratic identity. It made perfect sense to see Christian democratic liberty fighting against anti-Christian totalitarian slavery. It was not an illusion to see that freedom's chances might coincide with those of the evangelical message.

Amid these storms, Augustine's image of two cities now became the patriot's assertion of one city. What had been an equivocal relationship was becoming univocal. There was, to say the least, a downside for Christianity in all this. Missing from the view of America as the shining city was Winthrop's understanding that the brightness meant simply exposure; it could be for good or ill in the eyes of both God and the world. And if faithless, it would have been better to stay an unchosen people in history's shadows. That was not just Puritan doctrine and but solid Christian doctrine. However, it was not America's doctrine. By the middle of the twentieth century that doctrine amounted to a generally unqualified assertion of American goodness, especially in light of its enemies, with only the barest sense of judgment looming in the background. America, the carrier of the sanctified cause of freedom and democracy, acquired a purity and ultimacy of meaning hat was all but indistinguishable from worship. Christian Patrio-n could become a way of kneeling before the world while tell-ourself you are not committing idolatry.

the mid-twentieth century the sociologist Will Herberg sur-he American scene and famously concluded that "to be a

Protestant, a Catholic, or a Jew are today the alternative ways of being an American." Generally overlooked is what Herberg saw as the result of this political absorption of religious identity: a religiousness with almost any kind of content or none, a way of sociability or belonging rather than a way of reorienting life to God.[107] Herberg was ahead of his time in catching the drift of things. He just had not yet come up with the terms "spirituality" and "self-realization."

With these results in mind—a generally unchristian view of history, the submergence of recognizably Christian doctrine in favor of a popular religion, the elevation of a political identity at the expense of Christianity's critical and hesitant stance toward even the best of human intentions and claims—what then should we conclude? Tocqueville took as his point of departure the New England Puritans, an admittedly hard act to follow. But if we take that same baseline and look at the span of almost 400 years since then, it is reasonable to conclude that Christianity has probably been better for American democracy than American democracy has been for Christianity.

Coming Apart

Writing from a Birmingham jail in April 1963, Martin Luther King Jr. grieved over the Christian church in America:

> So often it is an arch-defender of the status quo. Far from being disturbed by the presence of the church, the power structure of the average community is consoled by the church's silent and often even vocal sanction of things as they are. . . . If today's church does not recapture the sacrificial spirit of the early church, it will lose its authenticity, forfeit the loyalty of millions, and be dismissed as an irrelevant social club with no meaning for the 20th century.[108]

King's words repeated the time-honored call. Americans must turn revived, more authentic Christian hearts toward political action that will reform society and institutionalize God's call to righteousness and justice. However, his words were also a lament that indicated how, by the middle of the twentieth century, the easy conjoining of American Christianity and American patriotism had produced a fundamental complacency. That self-righteous complacency of a "Christian nation"—long and quietly being eroded by even deeper forces—set the stage for what happened next. That next big thing was, of course, the Sixties. The Sixties were a broad, political-cultural phenomenon that amounted to something much more than just a ten-year span on the century's calendar. With the crucial exception of the early civil rights movement, the reform demands in this period did not come from politically engaged Christians. The push to overturn the prevailing complacency came mainly from secular moralists, for whom the patriotic/Christian worldview was overwhelming evidence for the charge of hypocrisy.

Despite the hoopla of the time, the Sixties were not a sudden breakdown or fork in the road concerning democracy and Christianity in America. To recall the metaphor I invoked earlier, the Sixties were a dramatic confirmation that the two strands in the double helix had been winding away from each other for some time. And if the Sixties were a marker about what had already been happening—a story of America's democratic faith and its Christian faith coming apart—they were also a marker for the future, pointing to the development of two antagonistic stories between those two faiths. That is the subject of this section.

I do not wish to exaggerate the growing antagonism; and here, as usual, Tocqueville offers good advice. Although he was referring to his French peers, Tocqueville might as well have been writing about some of today's Christian activists campaigning to "reclaim America." As he put it, "Imagining unbelief to be something new, they comprise all that is new in one indiscriminate animosity. They are at war with the age and country" (275–276). The coming apart being discussed here does not mean that Christians have been turning their backs on the country. On the contrary, they, like Americans in general, have continued to endorse values of family, piety, and patriotism as a united whole. The current evidence is that conservative Protestants, when compared to Americans of other religious affiliations or no religion, actually have more national pride and feel more strongly that the rest of the world should imitate the United States.[109] But by the beginning of the twenty-first century one could also hear a new separatist theme in respected Christian circles, telling believers not to be unequally yoked to a secularized America. By the same token, coming apart does not mean that actively anti-Christian attitudes have developed among large numbers of Americans, four out of five of whom still identify themselves as Christians. But by the beginning of the twenty-first century, there was a newly articulated view in many quarters that zealous Christians who were politically active posed a threat to the ways of democracy. After several centuries of silence, the old Rousseauian view could now be heard that when Christians are behaving like good Christians, they make poor citizens.

We are speaking of a "Christian problem" for American democracy and a "democracy problem" for American Christians, and it is something much more than a simple, straight-line reaction to the Sixties. In moving through their life cycle, Baby Boomers have produced so many stresses in the nation that they are strongly tempted to think they are always the cause rather than the effect of things. In an important sense, however, the cultural-political-religious outburst known as the Sixties was a fulfillment of tendencies underway for decades. Alongside the convergences in American democracy and Christianity that we have seen (in the ideas of history, personhood, and political society) there were countervailing movements in the twentieth century that at first hardly seemed to be part of any pattern. Yet what was happening in the schools, the courts, and what I will call consumption arts eventually did add up to a new understanding of American public life. It was a development of doctrine that undercut the apparent harmony of American democracy and Christianity. The discord arose slowly and then came out with a crash in the Sixties. What we are likely to notice now is the noise of the crash and not the quieter prelude that occurred throughout the prior decades of the twentieth century.

PRELUDE: THE DEVELOPMENT OF PUBLIC DOCTRINE

The first thing to notice about the development of a new public doctrine is an absence. For roughly three decades leading up to the Sixties, the political voice of conservative Protestantism was barely heard in the mainstream of American public affairs, at least not in comparison with its resounding presence previously in American history. This silence was largely the result of a series of political body blows suffered by Protestant traditionalists during the first third of the twentieth century. Here again we need to gain a deeper perspective on how American political development was intertwined with the turns in American Christianity in general and Protestantism in particular.

At the beginning of the twentieth century, Protestantism in America consisted of a broad and culturally dominant coalition that was trying in various ways to respond to the challenge of "modernism." Natural science challenged any belief in miracles; Darwinian evolution denied man's special creation; and historical criticism threw into doubt the literal accuracy of biblical records. At the same time theological innovators sought to equate religion with morality and to identify the Kingdom of God with the moral progress of civilization. In these and many other ways, modernism—or, as it was also pejoratively termed, "liberalism"—challenged Christians to update their traditional religious ideas to conform to modern culture. In brief, the message was to drop the supernatural baggage.

Protestants, being Protestants, exhibited a variety of responses to this modernist challenge.[110] Some leading and lay Protestants in various denominations were almost embarrassingly eager to adapt to the new outlook. Still, it is fair to say that most of the responses being produced by America's Protestant establishment were more or less conservative—at least in the sense of resisting wholesale conversion to modernism. Within this larger conservative response, some were especially militant in confronting and taking the political offensive against the forces of religious liberalism (both within Protestantism and in the larger society). These more militant champions of traditional views gradually acquired their own identity and, in the 1920s, their own label: "fundamentalists." Lest we fall prey to subsequent caricatures, it is worth recognizing that the fundamentalist faction within conservative Protestantism was not a fringe group of uneducated, backwoods "Bible-thumpers." While remaining close to the dominant evangelical revivalism of the nineteenth century, the fundamentalists of the early twentieth century emphasized a rigorously intellectual dimension of correct doctrine as well as the "heart" dimension of conversion and personal piety. The twelve volumes called *The Fundamentals* that were published from 1910 to 1915 included contributions from over three dozen prominent American and British scholars. These books presented a thoroughgoing critique of modernists' attack on traditional Christianity, along with essays by more popular writers (the series ended with the conversion testimony of a prominent New York lawyer).[111]

By sharpening and insisting on a clear choice between modernism and the truths of Scripture, fundamentalism as a religious-political movement exposed and then widened the fissures existing within America's Protestant establishment in this first third of the twentieth century. The militancy of the fundamentalists meant confrontation.

In the early 1920s, highly publicized fights within mainline Protestant denominations found those now being called "fundamentalists" losing to the more moderate forces who could produce majorities dedicated to keeping peace within a given denomination.[112] As these intra-Protestant battles were being lost, the 1925 Scopes Trial gave national attention to the fundamentalists' crusade in the larger society to legislatively restrict teaching human evolution in the public schools. After dramatic coverage by the national press and the new medium of radio, the humiliation of the fundamentalists in the person of William Jennings Bryan was celebrated by cosmopolitan opinion leaders, who wrote retrospective and largely inaccurate interpretations of what happened.[113] But there was worse to come. In the words of Michael Kazin, "Prohibition was *the* Protestant issue of the day. It had transcendent significance—both because it would cure a social evil that ruined and corrupted millions of lives and because it satisfied, better than any other issue, the urge to purify American culture that had frustrated Christian reformers since the end of the Civil War."[114] The fiasco of trying to enforce the Eighteenth Amendment and then its almost effortless, half-comic repeal in 1933 made the defeat of old-school Protestantism in the public arena seem complete. If anything, the whole Prohibition issue had only enhanced the secularists' cause by portraying Christians as intolerant, self-righteous and, above all, hypocritical. Modernists felt sure they had girdled fundamentalism and left it to die.

The overall effect of these developments was for the defeated conservative Christian forces to retreat into the public and political background. Fundamentalists nurtured their own seminaries, Bible institutes, publications, and radio programs. On the fringes of this subculture in the 1930s and 1940s were populist preachers who railed against "modern ways," liberal conspiracies, and communist plots. Embarrassed by all this, the larger body of thoughtful conservative Protestants tended to simply disappear from publicly visible roles in mainstream universities, journals of opinion, the media, and politics. All in all, in the decades before the 1960s, America's increasingly secular intellectual elites had little trouble relegating Christian traditionalists to the category of anti-intellectual cultural laggards—people who, if not paranoid, were at least suffering status anxiety. And it is probably true to say that by the 1960s, the raucous radio evangelists and others whom the public perceived as Christian fundamentalists did lack the intellectual rigor to match or appreciate their predecessors' volumes of *The Fundamentals.*[115]

Thus it was that the once powerful Protestant conservative forces of earlier times tended to be the dog that did not bark while portentous changes were under way in America's schools, courts, and popular culture. I will briefly sketch each of these contributions to the development of a secular public doctrine.

The Schools. Secularization in public education, as in other spheres, was not some vaguely impersonal, natural process of social evolution. It was the result of an intentional struggle for cultural authority among differing elites, some of whom wished to enhance or maintain Christianity's educational significance while others wanted to reduce or eliminate that influence in favor of purely secular understandings of life.[116] Long before American courts had anything to say on the subject and before Progressive reformers systematized the movement with state-level centralization of school administration and curricula, champions of "modern" ways of thinking were attacking the anti-scientific religious orientation in American public schools. Traditionalists upheld a schoolroom culture of biblical theism as the bedrock of the moral education and social ethics that were to be taught. Modernizers attacked this culture using the new social sciences and advanced educational thinking from German research universities. Elizabeth Cady Stanton summed up the case for secularization in 1897:

> Theology covers the realm of the unknowable . . . The time has come to study religion as a science, an essential element in every human being, differing with climate and civilization . . . The Bible has been the greatest block in the way of [scientific] progress. Why then continue to read it in our public schools? . . . The religion of humanity centers the duties of the church in this life . . . Instead of spending so much time and thought over the souls of the multitude and over delusive promises of the joys to come in another life, we should make for them a

> paradise here . . . If the same laws govern all parts of the universe, and are only improved by the higher development of man himself, we must begin to lay the foundation-stones of the new heaven and the new earth here and now. Equal rights for all . . . will be the triumph of true religion and such [will be] the solution of the problem of just government.[117]

John Dewey and his many fellow reformers went on to establish the crucial linkages between secularization, faith in democracy, and a progressive social and economic policy agenda. While the modernizers' project was not religious in any traditional sense of the term, neither was it thoroughly materialistic (however much biblical creationists attacked the teaching of evolution in the new curriculum). Ordinary Americans would never have countenanced philosophical materialism for their children. Instead, Dewey and allied educational reformers extracted the moral element of Christian theism and naturalized it into an ethics of democracy for this world. The reformers' habitual expropriation of religious language to describe what they were doing simply expressed the fact that democracy, embodied in a new democratic personality, was the religious faith of secular education. Thus in his 1892 essay "Christianity and Democracy," Dewey presented democracy "as the means by which the revelation of truth is carried on. It is in democracy, the community of ideas and interest through community of action, that the incarnation of God (man, that is to say as organ of universal truth) becomes a living, present thing, having its ordinary and natural sense." In the service of this proper social order for social growth, the secularized teacher was sanctified as "the prophet of the true God and the usherer in of the true kingdom of God."[118] Traditional religion could now be seen mainly as an impediment to broader values of tolerance and social inclusion, an inhibition on individual self-expression, and an enemy of free scientific inquiry—all of the things essential for continued human progress.

"Secularization" seems too tame a word for the transformation being implemented by the new professionalized machinery of public education. Traditional religion had claimed to authoritatively teach truth. Now the more authentically human religion of democracy taught an open-ended search for never-final truths. Before, a social ethic that taught all were responsible for all was derived from the higher spiritual responsibility of every human being who must finally stand in judgment before a righteous God. Now the social ethic of equality, freedom, and justice was derived from democratic society itself, with one's religious outlook a purely private appendage. Democracy was a form of government, as Dewey put it, "only because it is a form of moral and spiritual association."

Rightly understood—that is to say, in secular terms—democracy now became another name for experimental, intelligent inquiry by citizens, each equal in his or her human dignity precisely because each was equal in one's freedom to seek out and choose the personal meanings for one's life. Democracy was now taught not just as a way of governing but as a way of living, which is to say religiously. Democracy was a self-directing growth process of secular autonomy for both the society and the individual. Such a democratic society was continually learning to provide the equal conditions necessary for human thriving. Democratic individuals were always pursuing their continuous growth and expression of personality as an end in itself. With "God talk" set out of bounds, the young democrat undergoing such an education was invited to identify with America's secular democratic heroes: Emerson's "endless seeker," Thoreau's individual moving to the beat of a different drummer, Whitman's singer of songs democratic to himself: "Healthy, free, the world before me / The long brown path before me, leading wherever I choose."[119] The all but inescapable implication was that to journey toward self-discovery, one had to leave behind the religion of churches, parents, hand-me-down doctrines, and any idea of natural law.[120] Instead the individual is called to enter a liberated condition of being free to choose among the ideas and practices of any or no religion without being judged or casting judgments. Personal freedom is the ultimate root of moral obligations.

Thus in the modern doctrine of public education, the American seeker for his own truth and the moral advocate for equal rights would be one and the same democratic person. Such a person could be thoroughly skeptical about any absolute truths handed down from traditional religious authority and thoroughly confident in the absolute value of democracy—that is to say, individuals thinking on their own to collectively advance an unquestioned belief in equal rights and human freedom. In this view, traditional religion has been and is a bulwark to the status quo, while spiritually seeking individuals are now the natural allies of social and political progress.[121]

During the first half of the twentieth century, state-level efforts of Progressive reformers to modernize the public school system were reinforced by the thoroughgoing secularization of America's major universities and academic elites. In the vanguard were the new social sciences.[122] Sociologists, often it seems with a deeply anti-religious agenda, helped relativize all religious beliefs. In psychology, there was a particularly good fit with new advanced thinking on the nature of personal freedom; the traditional virtue of suppression of inner drives became the sin of repressing what was most natural and personal, thus violating human freedom. In history, speculations about the meaning or philosophy of history gave way to more scientific methods and middle-range interpretations. Interestingly enough, it was political science that lagged behind public school reformers in giving wholehearted endorsement to the democratic faith. After a good deal of equivocation about the common man's capacity for self-government (especially during the years of economic depression and fascist success), American political scientists chastened by World War II finally signed on to the general democratic faith.[123] In that faith, skepticism about any claims to final truth is the only intelligent position to hold, and only democracy allows free, equal citizens to engage in the open-ended search for personal choices to govern lives, both individually and in common. Social scientists could never quite explain why, but this secular truth of democracy was the one thing in which a person could have absolute faith.

By the mid-twentieth century, at all levels of schooling, the education experienced by any American under public instruction was highly secular. The issue here is not whether this was a good or a bad thing. The point is that this is a thing that happened, something that had important consequences for the development of a public doctrine regarding Christianity and American democracy.

The Courts. It was at this stage that developments in the federal courts legally enshrined and sealed the secularization of public education. This jurisprudence was a second major impulse in the development of public doctrine. As one legal casebook puts it, "Prior to 1940 the Supreme Court of the United States had never upheld a claim of free exercise of religion, had never found any governmental practice to be an establishment of religion, and had never applied the religious clauses of the First Amendment to the states."[124] Starting in that decade, a new and highly complex body of legal judgments developed in an attempt to refine and apply throughout the nation the brief sixteen words of the religious clauses in the First Amendment. The Great Denouement had focused on the individual's right to religious liberty, prohibiting in the process establishment of a national, government-supported church as in the British motherland. Now there gradually developed a stricter judicial call for a total separation of religion and government required by the First Amendment's rule that "Congress shall make no law respecting an establishment of religion." This judicial initiative went on to produce a bewildering array of largely incoherent Supreme Court pronouncements, suggesting to some legal scholars that there are no univocal principles of state neutrality or religious freedom in the relevant clauses, only a jurisdictional prohibition against Congress legislating to create legal privileges or penalties for religion.[125]

Fortunately, we need not try to settle that debate here. The point is that by the mid-twentieth century the Supreme Court had embarked on the creation of a new and immensely elaborate system of rules, the general thrust of which was to favor a thoroughly secular approach to public life, especially but by no means exclusively in public schools. In 1940, the First Amendment's prohibitions on Congress regarding religion were, through interpretation of the Fourteenth Amendment, extended over all state and local levels of government. From there, the Supreme Court in 1947 began splitting the anti-establishment and free exercise clauses of the First Amendment to develop a self-contained "nonestablishment" jurisprudence. This jurisprudence, developed over dozens of cases after the Second World War, applied a strict separationist view, invoking Jefferson's personal metaphor of a "wall of separation" between church and state, and sought to define an absolute principle of state neutrality toward religion.

Probably for most Americans, the developing doctrine of privatized religion was experienced most dramatically in the early Sixties when the Court struck down state-sponsored prayer and devotional Bible-reading in public schools. From this plausible prohibition against government-enforced worship in the schools, subsequent decisions advanced a more thorough ban on government patronage or even acknowledgement of religion. With litigation by offended parties and lower court rulings now an ever-present threat, school administrators and government agencies responded by generally eliminating all provocations that might possibly be construed as an endorsement of religious, much less Christian, views. At the same time, religious traditionalists started to perceive such "neutrality" as the spreading establishment of a single irreligious, secular vision of public life.[126]

Court efforts to moderate the logical conclusions of absolutely strict separation and neutrality only reinforced the doctrine of marginalizing religion's public meaning. Thus even when the Supreme Court would permit public invocations of religion (Sunday closing laws, public Christmas displays, opening prayers at legislative sessions, and so on), it relegated such behavior to "ceremonial deism" and pro forma traditions—a polite way of saying it is all empty ritual.[127] Likewise, when court-enforced public indifference to religion veered into discrimination against religious groups in schools or public settings, the Court responded by requiring equal access for the religiously inclined. The by-product of this equal-seat-at-the-table doctrine has been to confirm religion's place as simply another set of private personal preferences.

The Consumption Arts. Alongside the public schools and federal courts, a third line of twentieth-century development was less "official" but no less doctrinal in uniting a secular understanding of the world and the American democratic faith. Tocqueville had observed that if religion was to continue to counteract democracy's excesses, it would have to moderate, but not try to thwart, democratic man's desire for material well-being. In the 1830s Tocqueville had no idea of how this desire for material well-being would be indulged, molded, and lifted up to form a totalizing way of life in the twentieth century.

Despite booms and busts, America's ongoing industrialization after the Civil War vastly expanded opportunities for mass consumption and opened up new spaces in ordinary life for leisure and entertainment. However, that was merely the necessary prelude. The development I am examining here is the commercial management of desire in filling those opportunities and spaces. No single term—popular culture, mass marketing, consumer society, celebrity culture—seems to do justice to the phenomenon. I will call it the "consumption arts"—an expanding zone of cultural authority created by new technologies for professionally marketing the consumption of material abundance.

Phonograph music, movies, radio, sports, advertising, public relations, market research, department stores, nationally integrated corporations for producing and selling consumer products, the commodification of "entertainment" and institutionalization of "shopping"—these were not just innovations in technology or organization. They were a whole new sphere of social and economic activities ever more professionally crafted, commercially managed, and implemented on a national scale after the beginning of the twentieth century.[128] The aim in all this commercial crafting and managing was not simply to satisfy democratic man's desires for "material well-being." Rather, it was to develop the allure of such well-being, to expand the range of its demands, and to promise the gratification of that desire with never-ending individual consumption choices. And since older, more settled temperaments were less open to such allure, the drive of the consumption arts was always toward the marketing and management of desire for a distinctive youth culture. The assumption being taught was that forward-thinking young people, restless against traditional ways, should set the ever-new standards of what is progressive and thus desirable in music, clothes, language, and relations between the sexes.

The exercise of the new consumption arts was inherently imperialistic, defining an expanding zone of cultural authority quite separate from the traditional forces of family, neighborhood, church, and small-town values. The result was pervasive. From an occasional appearance at the beginning of the twentieth century—a new piece of sheet music for the parlor piano, the annual mail-order catalogue, a half-hour visit to the nickelodeon—the consumption arts by the middle of the twentieth century had grown into an enveloping presence, coextensive with American daily life itself. Children growing up after the Second World War, when Sunday closing laws disappeared almost everywhere, could not have imagined that fifty years earlier major department stores had not only closed but covered their window displays on Sunday. As Americans at mid-century sat enthralled by the new and thoroughly commercialized medium of television, they could not have guessed that a few decades earlier there had been a serious debate as to whether the new medium of radio should be allowed to "invade" the sanctity of our homes with advertising.[129]

It is important to note that this development of the professionalized consumption arts was also irresistibly attractive to democratic politicians.[130] Talk of consumer prosperity as a solvent for public problems allowed one to sidestep difficult questions about redistribution. In a society of consumers, everyone could be a winner. Consumer choice in the competitive economic marketplace was the companion of freedom of choice in the democratic marketplace, both together constituting the American way of life. Not surprisingly, it was not very long before the consumption arts (professional opinion research, marketing and management of the political "sales" campaign) were invading politics itself. By the 1960s, they were becoming the only smart way of doing political business with the public.[131]

Most important, the new cultural form that was developing gave authority to an essentially irreligious view of human existence. With notable exceptions (such as Sinclair Lewis's *Elmer Gantry,* H. L. Mencken's work, or Lawrence and Lee's *Inherit the Wind*), traditional religion was not directly attacked; it was simply undermined relentlessly from one day to the next. Like the preaching of old, the consumption arts gained their power as the pervasive, incessant "articulations" by which people are made aware of what is deemed good and worthwhile. The consistent and unchanging doctrine being taught was simple: in the work, play, and everything else of daily life, the things to pay attention to are those of material existence and its enjoyment. These are the choices that make for satisfaction and self-fulfillment. Other things can be pushed to the margins as matters of easygoing indifference or sporadic attention, or various personal ways of toying with the "big questions." To inject anything seriously religious into this scene would be outré, to say the least. Seemingly indifferent to big, abstract questions, the consumption arts of modern abundance imbued daily life with an implicit philosophy of meaning, namely, that meaning was constructed by individuals making a myriad of wholly self-referential consumer choices. This was the tenacious background theme regarding how the living of one's life was to be understood. It was a radical declaration of freedom (through individual consumption choices) and submission to economic discipline (that is, the work effort required through one's "job" to make ever-growing consumption desires possible). The consumption arts taught a disciplined hedonism. The message was an amalgam of the old-fashioned work ethic in an impersonal economic system and the new-fashioned indulgence in a wholly personalized system of consumption choices—the combination of the two amounting to the democratic creation of one's own meaning for life.

Proponents of the older culture of restraint fought this emerging culture on many fronts. And these proponents of the old understandings lost on all those fronts.[132] What began as cosmopolitan chic among the social, artistic, and commercial elites in the 1920s became increasingly mainstream as the century wore on.[133] By the middle of the twentieth century American Christianity could muster few attempts to moderate, much less thwart, the growing power of the consumption arts.[134] The main religious critics were a few well-known Catholic leaders, like Bishop Fulton J. Sheen, who spoke out forcefully against democratic materialism. As he pointed out in 1948, "What the Western world has subscribed to in isolated and uncorrelated tidbits, communism has integrated into a complete philosophy of life."[135] Such commentary aroused little controversy, presumably because one could still expect a traditional Catholic leader to talk in such old-fashioned ways. By contrast, thirty years later in 1978 the world-renowned Russian dissident Alexander Solzhenitsyn used a Harvard commencement address to say roughly the same thing and was denounced throughout mainstream media and intellectual circles. The great dissident's mistake was to refuse the role of a "liberal" champion of human rights and instead to proclaim an orthodox Christian view that condemned liberal democracy's materialistic preoccupation as something that crushed human beings' religious spirit. This was a message too radically unmodern for late-twentieth-century America. Arthur Schlesinger Jr. observed that Harvard's founding Puritans would have agreed with much of Solzhenitsyn's address, but then quickly added that their more enlightened Cambridge descendants now realized that a workable democratic politics requires a secular view of relative truth rather than a religious view of absolute truth.[136]

Bringing these various threads together, we can see that long before the phenomenon of the Sixties dramatized the fact, and while religious conservatives mostly stood on the sidelines, a distinctive public doctrine was already at work to undermine Christianity's cultural authority for American democracy. Certainly there are variations and qualifications that one might make on each point. However, the following summary seems a fair representation of the developing public doctrine that the schools, courts, and consumption arts, taken together, were advancing. If the contentions in this summary seem obvious, that is only an indication of how deeply the doctrine has taken hold. Again, our earlier categories of history, personhood, and political society are useful in summarizing this developing public doctrine.

History is to be interpreted primarily as a struggle for political, economic, and cultural liberation. After centuries of trying to impose values on others, human beings have become progressively, if painfully, enlightened to see that the chief moral issue is equal respect for the rights of others. Once over that hurdle, the choices freely made by democratic peoples produce an open-ended process of social learning. The liberation of such equal, self-governing individuals is the supreme goal in history because freedom is the essence of man's nature. Thus the march of democracy and the march of secularization have been, are, and will be one and the same.

The *person*, when authentically aware of himself or herself, is an autonomous individual possessing rights freely exercised to express the attributes of personhood. The liberty of each equal person is fully encompassed by the idea of freely making choices.

Choices express one's own unique personality and journey of self-discovery. Liberated from traditional authority, a person's choices are self-justifying because any external judgment is a denial of respect for the inherent dignity of each individual. It is the high calling of each individual to strive to realize his or her own unique potential. The democratic person holds to a "self-reliant piety." Such persons take responsibility for finding their own meaning and fashioning lives worthy of the meaning so created.[137]

A consumer-centric *political society,* seeking to be ever more democratic, has inclusiveness as its central ethos, because inclusion acknowledges and validates each person's journey of self-discovery. A democratic political society is composed of liberated individuals in free association who tolerate all views as equally valid. To lack such tolerance is to be bigoted, discriminatory, and undemocratic. Like the individuals in it, a democratic political society is always open to new truths because no one makes claims to absolute truth, which would render democratic compromise impossible. Since oppression is based on claims to objective truth, it is important for tolerance and human flourishing to affirm that all truth and values amount to matters of personal opinion. Religious commitments, which do make claims to absolute truth, are a personal and private matter that does not belong in the public arena. By contrast, commitment to the democratic faith provides a unifying secular identity that transcends other identities, including religion.

The foregoing account is roughly drawn, and pre-twentieth-century precedents can certainly be found for various particular points. But viewed as an ensemble of ideas, there is a coherent doctrinal quality to what developed. And it developed only in the twentieth century. Understood in this context, the Sixties expressed and gave dramatic impulse to a public doctrine that had been incubating for decades. Traditional Christianity represented a culture of constraint. Democracy required a culture of choice. Quietly but clearly, the battle lines had been drawn. The Baby Boom generation was about to enter the fray.

THE CRASH

By most outward appearances, Christianity and democracy were doing well in the 1950s. Domestic policy had been set on a consensual path. Republicans in the White House and Congress were accepting New Deal social welfare and economic management policies that an earlier generation of Republicans had castigated as un-American socialism. Within that framework, the controversies (mainly civil in tone as the 1960s dawned) concerned whether the federal government should play a role in education, health care, urban planning, and transportation. The war-defined lines of foreign policy consensus also seemed clear enough. Even the excesses of Senator Joseph McCarthy showed that the only real issue was whether one was a hard or a soft anti-communist. Real American communists were so hard to find that politicians occasionally had to invent some. Moreover, Will Herberg and others pointed out that, even though it was religiously shallow, something like an old-fashioned American revival was under way in mid-twentieth-century America. Mainline Protestant as well as Catholic churches were filling up. The young revivalist Billy Graham, the elegant Bishop Fulton J. Sheen, and the positive thinker Norman Vincent Peale were all thriving in the new television media of these times.[138] In the wonderfully clear vision of hindsight, we can see that all this was a facade. Something called "the Sixties" was about to break forth.

With little public notice, a more genuine religious awakening was already occurring in mid-twentieth-century America. The growing civil rights movement in the 1940s and 1950s was centered in many (but by no means all) black Protestant churches, and this ferment seemed to be repeating the time-honored pattern.[139] Driven with a powerful revivalist moral energy, the young postwar movement called on a complacent America to abolish segregation and reform its social and political institutions. Change was not just a political demand. As indicated by the quotation from Martin Luther King at the beginning of this section, the civil rights movement was demanding change as a moral imperative derived from the authentic "sacrificial spirit" of the early Christian church. The movement's mainly Christian leaders combined natural law theory (the duty to disobey unjust laws through the suffering entailed in nonviolence) with an appeal to the sanctified values of both the Judeo-Christian heritage and America's democratic ideals. To be sure, many white Christian groups only passively endorsed the civil rights cause. Yet in doing so, however weakly, the white Christian establishment denied segregationist forces any moral standing comparable to that enjoyed by the leaders of the civil rights movement. Despite the growing turmoil, it seemed that the reciprocating pistons of Americans' democratic faith and Christian faith were powering ahead.

Looking back now, we can see that the mid-twentieth-century civil rights movement embodied the more general transition from an older to a newer version of awakening and reform. The movement originally gained its energy and manpower in the traditional way—a religious revival thrusting itself forward into demands for cultural revitalization and institutional reforms.[140] The African-American religious tradition drew on its deep roots to inspire hope and demand social change. In the early years of the civil rights movement, workshops on nonviolence asked participants to undertake a process of self-purification so that their nonviolent means would be as morally pure as the ends they sought. By the end of the 1960s, however, much of this original religious orientation had been displaced. A vocal and more youthful section of the movement rejected nonviolence and racial integration as capitulations to white supremacy. Especially after the urban riots following passage of the civil rights legislation of 1964 and 1965, assertions of "black power" eclipsed any public awareness of the civil rights movement as an American-Christian cause that all citizens should share. Considering these developments as a whole, it is fair to say that by the 1970s, the religious claims of moral authority in the civil rights movement had been eclipsed by a far more secular, power-based politics. There was a growing sense that "civil rights" was a slogan for one more interest-group coalition, pressing one more set of self-serving demands.[141] At the same time, opposition to the Vietnam War broke the twentieth-century pattern that had merged the American democratic and religious values in fighting foreign enemies. Two months before his assassination in 1968, Martin Luther King Jr. condemned the United States government as "the greatest purveyor of violence in the world today." Revivalism, moral reform, democratic idealism—all the grand old themes seemed to be in play, but nothing was hanging together. Fervor without coherence expressed the liberated view of cultural authority.

Except in one crucial regard, all the political causes of the Sixties modeled themselves on the civil rights movement. The exception was that the moral energy of the new causes and movements was almost wholly secular rather than anything that could be described as traditionally Christian. Despite all the confusion of the times, the Sixties essentially gave expression to the public doctrine that had been in preparation for decades. In other words, the political-cultural phenomenon known as the Sixties was America's first secular Awakening. As such, it represented not an aberration but a radical continuation.

It was a continuation because at their best, Sixties activists affirmed the traditional values of authenticity and democracy, "of faith and deeds, of civic virtue and redemptive sacrifice."[142] It was radical because the old Awakening vision of a redemptive community experiencing individual and collective rebirth was now redenominated into a thoroughly secular cultural framework. The venerable American tradition of moralizing politics was not abandoned, but the moral earnestness was now doctrinally secular rather than religious in its inspiration. The tradition of benevolent problem-solving for the good of others was carried forward, but secular moralists now defined this good as liberating others from oppressive authorities. Faith was not rejected nor, as Tocqueville said, could it be: "Faith is the only permanent state of mankind" (273). But the object of faith changed from transcendent standards that would judge a person's choices and preferences to faith in the individual and collective search for authenticity and self-expression. In earlier times the "prophetic stance" in public life—the critique of misdeeds, call to repentance, and promise of new hope—had been fundamentally Christian. Now the prophetic stance came from within the democratic faith itself. And it was fundamentally secular.

Thus, as in the earlier Protestant awakenings and revivals, the great theme was authenticity and a vigorous rejection of the "phoniness" of pretending to be something other than who you really are, either as a church or as a person. That insistence is what made Puritans Puritans. But unlike everything that had come before, authenticity in the Sixties awakening of secular moralism was entirely self-referential. The revivalists had said that who you really are is a sinner in desperate need of God's grace. Sixties moralists said that who you really are is however you freely choose to express yourself. Similarly, Sixties activists criticized contemporary America not so much for its values as for its hypocrisy. The call was to reform and live out the values of freedom, inclusion, and a never-ending search for social justice. At its best, the Sixties pushed people to face up to unpleasant realities, and it is no accident that the hospice movement had its American beginnings at this time. At its worst, the Sixties mentality became a figure like J. D. Salinger's Holden Caulfield, ridiculously idealistic about his own innocence and sentimentally cynical about everything else in the world.

Like other awakenings, the turmoil of the 1960s soon left in its wake major changes in American public life. Political institutions and public understandings were decisively altered, often in ways that no one deliberately intended. Whether or not the result deserves to be called a "new American political system," the changes were substantial and interlocking in a systematic manner.[143] Before getting to the deeper reverberations, I will mention four immediate changes that are especially important for our present topic. Taken together, they gradually undermined any presumption that there could somehow be a "wall of separation" between what government does and what citizens of any religious or non-religious persuasion think it ought to be doing.

First, previously restricted processes of government decision-making were opened up to public scrutiny and influence. This more participatory format for governing expressed both the democratic faith and the post-Sixties distrust of all authoritative structures of power. Today we take this openness for granted. At the time, it was a sea change in the way of thinking about the policy-making process.

Second, this new access was associated with a permanent mobilization of political activists concerned with issues that now went well beyond the older economic agenda of the New Deal. Instead of "meat and potatoes" material demands for economic security, post-Sixties activists sought to impact social, cultural, "quality of life" issues (as these came to be termed at the time). The new issues did indeed touch all facets of Americans' lives. Not least, these issues directly challenged traditional views of the family, women, sexual morality, and the self-validating quality of personal choice.

Third, the new access and activism revolved around the idea that the one thing of supreme importance in politics is government policy. More than just an expansion of government, it was a new way of thinking about all of political life, a "policy mindedness" that extended from the left to the right of the political spectrum.[144] After the 1960s the authority of the federal government to act became a non-issue; the question was what policy government would pursue, either by its action or by inaction. Influence over policy choices now became the motivation and reward for political activism amid a nonstop flow of contested claims about public problems. To become more democratic was to become committed to a never-ending policy agenda of social problem-solving.

The fourth change—growing reliance on the courts for policy-making—may seem oddly out of place in an era that was demanding public participation in policy-making. The answer lies in the fact that the real aim of political activism was not public participation as such but control over policy decisions. The courts provided a domain well-fitted to give a secular reading to the rights-based claims of individuals and groups. Moreover, the courts' adversarial format and relatively black-and-white decisions could lessen policy activists' dependence on legislators' impure compromises and administrators' unreliable discretion. The only thing needed was legislation and rule changes to expand advocacy groups' access to the courts, and this too is what happened in the wake of the Sixties.

Thus the Sixties brought moral fervor to a secular doctrine that was in substantial tension with traditional Christianity. At the same time, the Sixties produced political-institutional changes that would fully exploit that tension through the now inescapable demand to frame expansive public policies in one way or the other. As this period continued, three distinguished historians of American religion tried to put the turmoil of the times into a larger perspective. Despite their panoramic views, none of the three could escape the notion that a unique dislocation had occurred.

After almost 1100 pages, Sydney Ahlstrom, writing in the mid-1970s, found that the nation had reached a turning point that quite probably ended 400 years of American history. "In summary," he said, "one may safely say that America's moral and religious tradition was tested and found wanting in the sixties."[145] The editors of an even larger multivolume series entitled "Religion in American Life" observed, "At the close of the sixth decade of the twentieth century, commentators on the American scene seem to be of two minds in regard to the status and significance of religion in our culture. . . . sophisticates seem to have given up on God altogether, while the naïve masses simply 'infinitize' their personal and social values and call the nebulous aggregate 'God.'"[146] However, it was the very short book by William McLoughlin that said it best: "Since 1960, we have been in the process of what may well be the most traumatic and drastic transformation of our ideology that has yet occurred." He concluded, "The ferment of the sixties has begun to produce a new shift in our belief-value system, a transformation of our worldview that may be the most drastic in our history as a nation."[147]

REVERBERATIONS

We have seen that Tocqueville celebrated American democratic politics as an arena where everything was contested and open for innovation, but also where a religious-cultural consensus set firm boundaries around that arena. As he put it, in their tumultuous democratic arguments, Americans' contempt for old ways and spirit of experiment "reaches the limits of the world of politics . . . it forswears doubt and renounces innovation . . . it bows respectfully before truths which it accepts without discussion" (40).

The Sixties showed that a different kind of political world had developed. The areas of life subject to public policy choices—understood mainly as government action or inaction in Washington—now had ever-fewer boundaries. And within that expanding political policy terrain, the assumption of traditional Christianity's worldview and supportive "moral calculus" no longer applied. To put the point most generally, the Sixties dramatized a new reality about the American Christian and democratic faiths. Reason in the political realm and revelation in its autonomous religious realm could no longer be counted on to share basic moral standards for guiding political action. More than ever before, cultural authority was a politically contested concept by Americans who no longer seemed to share the same moral universe. By vastly expanding the policy agenda and by making explicit a secular doctrine that was previously developing in hushed tones, the Sixties necessarily provoked important new divisions in religious and political life.

It is fruitless to try to decide whether changes in churches produced changes in political parties, or vice versa. Both were now linked by a double bind: more culturally significant public policy choices had to be made, and among the people active in politics there was a lessened consensus for making these choices. Developments in both America's Christian churches and its political parties testified to this different world that was emerging.

The Churches. It has been said that nothing changed so much in the Sixties as religion.[148] This is a true statement, but we need to be careful in understanding what is true about it. As with the "development of public doctrine" in the democratic faith, in American Christianity the Sixties also produced a fulfillment of tendencies that had been decades in the making. As we saw, conflicts within mainline Protestant denominations found the modernists triumphing over traditionalists in the first third of the twentieth century. The secular awakening of the 1960s revived this conflict and ultimately gave the traditionalist side a new and powerful political impetus. Both Protestant and Catholic versions of American Christianity developed strongly opposed modernist (or liberal) and conservative wings, at times seeming to leave very little room in the middle. However, it was especially among Protestants that the pre- and post-Sixties change in the American religious scene carried the greatest consequences for today's politics.

In 1923 the fundamentalist leader Gresham Machen had declared that "in the intellectual battle of the present day there can be no 'peace without victory'; one side or the other must win."[149] When Machen's side lost, the Protestant establishment did not disappear. Instead, its public face and the orientation of its cultural authority changed. The victors were the mainline denominations and the networks of their leaders embodied in Protestant umbrella organizations (the Federal Council of Churches, 1908–1950, and its successor, the National Council of Churches).[150] Representing roughly 60 percent of American Protestants in the decades leading up to the Sixties, the Protestant establishment's political profile at mid-century went well beyond what such a statistic might suggest. Leaders of the denominations and Councils were the generally accepted spokesmen for American Christianity on public affairs. They claimed to speak not only *for*

Protestants but also *to* Protestants and the larger American public on major public policy issues. At the beginning of the twentieth century, an essentially unified Protestantism had confidently assumed its authority to guide the moral commentary on American public life. By contrast, the post-1920s Protestant mainline leaders were far more self-conscious in institutionally programming their reform messages—itself a sign of eroding cultural authority.

The leaders of the mid-twentieth-century Protestant establishment preferred to think of themselves as moderates rather than liberals, and in fact a broad range of views were represented, from modernist to neo-Orthodox.[151] However, it is also true to say that "moderation" in the Protestant establishment typically meant being generally open to the secular influences of modern culture, and weighted on the liberal side theologically and politically. The denominational leaders and Council officials aimed for an ecumenicalism that emphasized Protestant inclusiveness and unity over concerns with biblical authority and doctrinal clarity, both of which could easily threaten unity. Thus inclusiveness did not include fundamentalists.

Following strongly in the tradition of the social gospel, the leaders of mainline Protestantism sought to apply their inclusive Protestant-Christian vision to the solution of social problems. This typically entailed advocating domestic initiatives to protect labor and promote industrial democracy, to end racial discrimination, and to alleviate poverty through social welfare programs and income redistribution. Many of these proposals and endorsements tracked closely with Roosevelt's New Deal.[152] In foreign policy the Protestant establishment views were humanitarian, internationalist, and at times pacifist. During the Second World War, Protestantism's leaders went so far as to urge creating a postwar "new world order" in which national sovereignties would be relinquished to a world government that could outlaw war, check unbridled capitalism, and protect human rights. After 1945, however, the growing recognition of a Cold War against the expansionist ambitions of atheistic communism quickly brought the Protestant establishment into close alignment with foreign policy leaders in Washington and the Western bloc nations of the new United Nations. Guided by such figures as the Presbyterian lay leader John Foster Dulles and the neo-Orthodox intellectual Reinhold Niebuhr, the social witness of postwar Protestantism became generally congruent with the American status quo and what became known as Cold War liberalism.[153]

The 1960s blew apart any idea of a mainline Protestant establishment.[154] On a variety of fronts, conflicts within the mainline churches found progressive-minded pastors and laity demanding a more authentic social gospel that confronted Americans' complacency and the great issues of the day. Heading the list were racism and civil rights, followed by poverty, hunger, colonialism, and other conditions of social injustice at home and in the Third World. Divisions soon became especially sharp and impassioned when establishment leaders who were aligned with Washington's anti-communist containment policies confronted younger pastors and congregants protesting the immorality of the Vietnam War. Thus mainline Protestantism found itself besieged from both sides. In foreign policy, its identification with hawkish Cold War liberalism antagonized progressives in and outside the churches. In domestic policy, its liberal social activism antagonized the more conservative elements within its denominational coalition.

Upheaval in the Protestant establishment was about much more than topical political causes. Along with the demand for "authenticity" in social action came the requirement for a Christianity that would have "relevance" for the modern generation. Here too the older certainties and coherence of mainline Protestantism crumbled on a range of fronts. Radical Protestant theologians advocated a "non-supernaturalistic" view of God and religion, essentially doubting the meaningfulness of anything like traditional Christianity to contemporary minds. In a book that was immensely influential among many leaders in mainline denominations, Harvey Cox of the Harvard Divinity School applauded the rise of secular urban civilization and its capacity to undercut, relativize, and privatize traditional Christianity. Secularization was now presented as the logical outcome of, and the successor to, biblical religion. In this view the Christian church should focus on social change toward a new, inclusive human community, the church being simply "a sign of the emergent city of man, an outrider for the secular city."[155] The very idea of a professional ministry, specially trained for a salaried career in church administrative structures, fell into widespread disrepute in leading Protestant circles. Meanwhile, on a more personal level, many young Americans reared in mainline church services and Sunday Schools were drawn to what they saw as a more relevant encounter with Christ outside the organized church. After the years of initial fervor in various "Jesus People" movements, many of these people appear to have moved on to conservative congregations.[156]

The Sixties marked a clear turning point. A Protestant establishment that had once taken for granted its privileged place in the wider culture was finally disestablished.[157] While the leaders of mainline Protestantism may have carried the moral high ground in terms of engagement with the humanitarian causes of the time, they lost to the evangelicals in terms of attracting people into their ranks. In the decades leading up to the 1960s, the mainline Protestant denominations had at least maintained their membership in relation to population growth. But even then, the mid-century evangelical/fundamentalist movement was growing faster to become what *Life* magazine in 1958 called a "third force" coming alongside Protestant and Catholic Christianity. By 1960, conservative Christian groups controlled more than 80 percent of the personnel and financial resources of Protestant missions abroad.[158] Worse was to come. From the mid-1960s onwards, the liberal Protestant denominations experienced actual net losses in membership while conservative evangelical churches continued to make mirror-image gains in overall membership and energy. In explaining this shift, social scientists and even analysts friendly to the cause of mainline Protestantism generally reached similar conclusions. The mainline denominations lacked certainty in their core theological beliefs, offered a confused message based on accommodations to secular society, and failed to hold people to a strict, life-changing view of what it meant to be a Christian. With the benefit of hindsight, we can now see that much of the change in conservative and mainline church memberships has been a function, not of people switching churches, but of generations of lower birth rates among women in the more liberal churches compared with those in conservative churches. More babies would seem a natural result of the greater happiness and better sex reported in the marriages of conservative Christians as compared to other couples, but we need not pursue that line of inquiry here.[159]

Whatever the explanation, the fallout from the Sixties was a shift in grassroots numbers and organizational power that would soon have major implications for American democracy and Christianity.

Thus while the mainline Protestant establishment endured its travail, the previously vanquished fundamentalist critics were waiting in the wings and growing in strength. Well before the 1960s, the doctrinally easygoing and politically liberal policy agenda frequently put leaders of the Protestant mainline denominations at odds with more conservative elements of their "united" Protestantism. Indeed, these denominational and Council reformers often doubted that their progressive policy agenda represented more than a minority view in the local congregations.[160] Amid mainline Protestantism's theological uncertainties and political engagements, the fundamentalist cause had passed to a new generation. Its leaders were convinced that traditional Christianity, far from being the relic of a primitive subculture, was the relevant, authentic answer to modern man's anxious condition. Under leaders such as the Chicago theologian Carl Henry and the Boston pastor Harold Ockenga, the National Association of Evangelicals for United Action (NAE) was formed in 1943 to unite conservative, traditionalist Protestants against what they liked to portray as the united forces of Protestant liberalism. The fundamentalist moniker was now self-consciously replaced with the term "evangelical." It was a way for the new generation to reassert the timeless relevance of the Christian "good news" of sinful human beings' redemption through Jesus Christ's atoning death and resurrection—what friends and foes called the old time religion.[161] Evangelical churches called for strict biblical preaching of the gospel of salvation, the sinner's spiritual rebirth, and an emotionally charged new life in Christ. This commitment to a common core of traditional Christianity inadvertently carried with it a potential grassroots advantage of political organization. Unlike its opponents in the Protestant establishment, the NAE grew through a relatively flat, grassroots membership structure that welcomed not only whole denominations but also individuals, congregations, schools, and missions—anyone who might feel they were being misrepresented by the Protestant establishment.

The postwar evangelical movement had been nurtured in the seminaries, Bible schools, missions, and congregations outside the Protestant establishment. At mid-century it was greatly energized by the reappearance of urban mass revivalism. The relevance of the old time Christian gospel was asserted through the immensely popular and professionally orchestrated "crusades" of the young Billy Graham, beginning with his surprising Los Angeles success in 1949. However, it is also true to say that the new fundamentalist/evangelical movement had little interest in heeding any call to become publicly engaged with the rapidly changing culture.[162] To be sure, for evangelicals, as well as for Catholics and other Protestants at mid-century, American power and American Christianity tended to merge into one righteous cause and intensified expression of the American public religion. The point is that for evangelicals, the threats of atheistic communism abroad and godlessness at home served mainly as prompts to call for personal conversion and spiritual revival in the nation, not for direct engagement in politics and public policy. In the growing evangelical churches, mainline Protestantism's gospel of social reform was generally viewed as an un-Christian distraction from the ultimate value of personal salvation in the midst of a degenerating world. An emphasis on social and political activism sidetracked the Gospel.

This position left evangelicals open to a general public perception as social reactionaries, and leaders of the Protestant establishment were not slow to take advantage of this political vulnerability. They charged that making personal conversion the sole answer to life's problems turned Christianity into a socially irresponsible private religion. Evangelism should not be an excuse for the un-Christian acceptance of the corrupt status quo—a backhanded endorsement of racial discrimination, economic injustice, and anti-catholic bigotry. On any fair reading of the events of this time, such criticisms were not far off the mark. At best, the growing fundamentalist/evangelical movement of the postwar years demonstrated an indifference, and often hostility, to the civil rights movement.[163] Evangelicals had little to say about the poverty that coexisted with America's prosperity, and they took the lead in opposing the election of John F. Kennedy on the ground of his Catholicism. For the great causes of the Sixties, white evangelical churches were not missing in action; they never showed up.

No one intended the paradox, but the rapidly growing ranks of white conservative evangelicals were one of the groups most liberated by the Sixties. In several converging ways, they were empowered to eventually become a force in national politics, quite apart from their growing membership rolls.

In the first place, America's first Catholic President became a settled and harmless reality, helping to make evangelicals' anti-Catholicism a moot point.[164] Second, and more important, the passage of civil rights legislation in the 1960s formally neutralized an issue on which evangelicals were immensely vulnerable. Traditionalist Christians were now free to assert their conservative defense of the social order without automatically opening up themselves to charges of racist and anti-Catholic bigotry. Third, it followed that with the end of legal segregation, white conservatives in the South could no longer be counted on to support the

Democratic Party. After a hundred years, openness to Republican politicians' appeals now became a realistic option. Fourth, the Sixties' fulfillment of the heretofore gradually emerging "public doctrine" threw into dramatic, bold relief a clear picture of conservative Christians' foe. The Sixties ethos of cultural openness and nonjudgmentalism, together with the related and expanding policy expectations for the national government, pushed to the fore a new social agenda that directly challenged evangelicals' traditional understandings of family, gender, sexual behavior, and godliness in general. More clearly than ever before, Christian believers in the old time religion thought they could see the true nature of their enemy in this world—soon to be labeled secular humanism.

Finally, and perhaps most remarkable of all, these reverberations from the Sixties created the potential for something that had never before been conceivable among evangelicals—the discovery of common ground with Catholics.[165] In light of the new cultural issues raised by the liberations of the 1960s, it became plausible to think that America needed not a Protestant or Catholic response, but a Christian response to the times. Before the Sixties, the strategic possibilities of a Protestant/Catholic alliance had looked quite different. Catholics' social teaching, along with their longstanding position as outsiders, had often led to sympathetic relations with the liberal and ecumenical reformers in the Protestant establishment on issues of economic justice and racial discrimination. Likewise, with their united Church hierarchy and figures such as Wilmoore Kendall and William F. Buckley Jr., Catholics formed a large and intellectually formidable anticommunist force well-disposed toward Cold War liberalism. However, the Sixties' cultural agenda on issues of family and sexuality struck at what many leaders of the Catholic hierarchy regarded as core moral teachings of the Church. The modernizing reforms regarding Church positions on religious liberty, democracy, the liturgy, and other issues had scarcely been announced by the Second Vatican Council (1962–1965) before a split roughly similar to that among Protestants broke out between more free-wheeling modernists and conservative Catholics. By the end of the 1960s, Catholics at all levels found themselves embroiled in heated internal disputes over issues of "artificial" birth control (that is, contraception), abortion, marriage, and gender roles.[166] The pathway toward previously inconceivable cooperation between American evangelicals and "papists" began to appear.

The turn to political activism among traditionalist Protestants as well as Catholics was not a spontaneous eruption. It was provoked. And it took time for any shared awareness of the provocation to grow. But even though it did not happen suddenly, after the Sixties there was an inexorable quality to the emergence of conservative Christians as a national political presence. With the unfair advantages of hindsight, we can now see that the tipping point for conservative Christians away from civic withdrawal and toward political engagement occurred during the 1970s.

Early in that decade, one of the first Catholic activists to effectively reach out to evangelicals was Phyllis Schlafly. The successful state-level campaigns against ratification of the Equal Rights Amendment to the Constitution began revealing both the new challenge to traditional family/gender values and the power of cooperation among Christian traditionalists. When the Supreme Court's 1973 *Roe v. Wade* decision upheld a woman's right to abortion, Catholic spokesmen at first stood virtually alone in opposition. Disappointed by mainline Protestant leaders who failed to follow through on their avowed support for restrictions on abortion, Catholic activists began cultivating help from evangelical Protestants, many of whom saw the decision as simply another reason to separate themselves from the larger culture. The catalyst for change was what evangelicals came to perceive as Washington's frontal attack on their subculture of Christian schools. The immediate issue involved Internal Revenue Service efforts, again following a federal court ruling, to deny tax-exempt status to Christian schools for practicing de facto racial segregation, even if they were purely privately funded.[167] Contrary to their hopes, this

IRS effort continued after the 1976 election of their fellow evangelical Jimmy Carter to the presidency. Worse, as the Carter administration proceeded, the realization grew that President Carter was quite willing to accommodate core Democratic constituencies and that these were determined to use government policy to advance their broad secular agenda against traditional views of family, sexuality, and religion in public life.

The midwives for delivering this realization were Richard Viguerie and Paul Weyrich, two Catholics and "movement conservatives" in the Republican Party who pioneered the new political technologies of direct mail, computerized information management, and grassroots political mobilization. Billy Graham had already served as the unwitting intermediary when conservative Christians were used and abused by the Nixon administration's electoral strategy for "Middle America." Then, after 1976, conservative Christian leaders felt themselves betrayed by President Carter's series of capitulations to secular and cultural liberals in the Democratic Party. Convinced of the need to stand up politically for their core cultural concerns, a more forceful mobilization of conservative Christians grew behind the presidential candidacy of Ronald Reagan and gained strength in the generally supportive atmosphere of his presidency.[168]

So was the post-Sixties mobilization of conservative Christians mainly a matter of Catholic brains and evangelical foot soldiers? That would be much too crude a view. Far from simply responding to Catholic leadership, Protestant evangelicals produced their own champions to fight against the cultural onslaught of the times. Jerry Falwell's founding of the Moral Majority in 1979 and Pat Robinson's TV ministry are obvious examples. However, there was a grander evangelical call to arms. Even an unsympathetic observer like Gary Wills had to conclude that more than anyone else, Francis Schaeffer galvanized evangelicals to take up the task of cultural criticism and political action.[169] During the 1960s and early 1970s, Schaeffer, a student and admirer of Machen, had electrified young evangelicals by showing that traditional Christianity, especially as inspired by the Reformation, need not be intellectually intimidated. It was fully equipped to critically engage all the art, music, philosophy, and other forms of cultural expression that society had to offer. Academics scoffed at his popularized scholarship, but Schaeffer, in a cascade of lectures and books after 1965, inspired hosts of American evangelicals to engage the ideas and history of western culture with a critically Christian mind.[170] Young Christians in particular felt liberated from the evangelical subculture's narrow-minded dismissal of the larger society's art, philosophy, music, and so on as "worldly." A good Christian should know about Existentialism. He or she could also fight against the plastic, dehumanized society that the Sixties hippies were rejecting. And it was OK to use movie screens instead of hymnals in church.

It would also be crude and obtuse to say that evangelical conservatives were mobilized in the 1970s simply in order to continue practicing racial discrimination in their Christian schools. The IRS tax-exemption issue was merely the dramatic example of a larger narrative being constructed: the courts and federal government were seen as now engaged in a concerted attempt to alter basic Christian patterns of American life. Beginning in 1976, Schaeffer's influential voice turned toward a call for political activism. Driven by the abortion issue as a virtually apocalyptic sign of the decadence and destruction of western culture, Schaeffer's new books, films, and speaking appearances became a pervasive presence in evangelical churches to make the Christian case for political engagement.[171] He pointed out that every previous religious awakening had produced cleansing reforms in our political institutions. The insinuation of secular humanism in our public schools that some had protested locally was now the national agenda in Washington. A "tyranny" hostile to the values of the people—as before the American Revolution—was at work. Continued political quiescence was not an option for Bible-believing Christians.

Thus in the reverberations following the Sixties, the division within both Protestant and Catholic communities has not really been between dogmatic and non-dogmatic Christians. The difference has been which dogma to support—the newer doctrine of individual choice and self-expression, or the traditional doctrines of the Christian past.[172] As Tocqueville rightly observed, "dogma . . . is the essence of religions" (412). At one dogmatic pole of religious activism, modernizers have emphasized personal choice, women's rights, and other aspects of human liberation. At the end of the other dogmatic pole, traditionalists have insisted on submitting any liberation to the authority of established biblical principles and traditional church teachings. In recent years Catholic intellectuals have been especially important in giving this latter conservative movement a coherent, non-denominational, and highly articulate voice.[173] The larger point, however, is that in the aftermath of the Sixties, conservative Protestants and Catholics have both come to see themselves as embattled co-belligerents on public issues of vital significance to their common religious faith, an ecumenical orthodoxy. Their politics has been mostly grievance-based, with a sense that the Christian way of life—their religion's version of "traditional values"—has now come under relentless attack and seems to be losing in modern America.

The Political Parties. These changes on the Christian scene have had their counterpart in the Democratic and Republican parties. The tumultuous Democratic convention of 1972 was an early confirmation of the leftward trend in the Democratic Party set in motion by the events and political causes of the Sixties. With anti–Vietnam War protestors and culturally liberal activists gathered behind the nomination of George McGovern, a distinctly secular segment of the Democratic Party came into unprecedented prominence. Since the 1960s, this vocal segment and its issues have continued to grow in importance within the Democratic Party. Abortion choice, women's rights, alternative life-styles, and criticism of American military power became prominent on the Party's agenda and have remained so. The common underlying theme has been a distrust of traditional authority in the cause of personal freedom. This, more than any spontaneous upsurge in political activities of Christian traditionalists, marked the coming of a new secular/religionist division between activists in the two parties.[174] In the years following 1972, this growth of secular activists' influence in the Democratic Party remained vastly underreported compared to subsequent media alarms about the countervailing and rather belated Republican mobilization among traditionalist Christians.

For the Republican Party, the fallout from the Sixties was a mirror image of this situation; it empowered an already strong conservative insurgency within the Party. This conservative movement was mostly separate from, and a generation earlier than, the appearance of conservative evangelicals on the political scene. The separation now seems counterintuitive, but it should not be surprising. For "movement conservatives," the tie to Christianity ran through Catholic sensibilities by way of intellectual leaders such as Russell Kirk and William F. Buckley Jr.[175] In his 1953 book that launched the movement, Kirk had grounded American conservatism in an outlook premised on western culture's traditional Christian theism. He declared the first "canon" of conservative thought to be

> belief that a divine intent rules society as well as conscience, forging an eternal chain of right and duty which links great and obscure, living and dead. Political problems, at bottom, are religious and moral problems. . . . We do wrong to deny it, when we are told that we do not trust human reason: we do not and we may not. Human reason set up a cross on Calvary. . . . Politics is the art of apprehending and applying the Justice which is above nature.[176]

By 1964, there were enough impassioned conservative activists in the Republican Party to capture the presidential nomination for Barry Goldwater, with his campaign against big government in Washington and military/political timidity in facing communism abroad. However, by the end of that year it was far from clear whether the new conservative forces could ever win a national election. For Republican Party moderates, such as the rising young politician George Bush (defeated as candidate for a Texas Senate seat), Goldwater's crushing loss signaled the need to return to a more moderate, mainstream Republicanism. For movement conservatives like Ronald Reagan, it was a call to spread their "dedication to a philosophy" to an ever-wider popular audience of ordinary working Americans.[177]

The growing turmoil of the Sixties then pushed the conservative cause in exactly that direction. Beginning in 1966 Reagan was rewarded with two terms (1967–1975) in the California governor's office. By the early 1970s, "neo-conservatives"—Democratic Cold War liberals dismayed by the feckless social engineering of Great Society domestic programs and leftist Democratic attacks on their anti-communist policies—began supplying weighty new intellectual talent to the Republican conservative wing. By the end of the decade, the fervent and growing body of conservative Republicans could share the feeling of Billy Graham's fellow religionists that they had been cynically taken advantage of by Richard Nixon and Republican centrists during the 1970s (by now conservative onslaughts had reduced "liberal" Republicans to an inconsequential remnant in the Party). For both of the heretofore separate camps, Ronald Reagan seemed to present a more authentic conservatism, an immensely personable and telegenic blend of Kirk-Schaeffer critiques of the Sixties' political and cultural blunders.[178]

With Jimmy Carter's surprising vault to the presidency, *Newsweek* labeled 1976 the Year of the Evangelical, but at the time it was quite unclear what that might mean politically. By the time of the 1980 presidential contest between Carter and Reagan, the political implications of resurgent evangelical Protestantism were not in doubt. Christians honoring traditional values should be for Reagan. Traditional Christians were, of course, being politically exploited by the Republican conservative movement. The deeper truth is that political professionals and evangelical leaders were now learning to exploit each other.

And what of Ronald Reagan himself in this rapidly boiling political/religious conservative stew? In 1953 Russell Kirk had written that in the "preservation of the ancient moral traditions," conservatism equals talent for re-expressing conviction on those principles to fit the time.[179] On that reckoning, Reagan's conservatism thermometer reading was off the charts. From the beginning of his political career in the 1950s, Reagan had seen and effectively presented himself as a spokesman for the rediscovery of America's traditional values.[180] However, it was primarily what I have called the sanctified vision of America that he reasserted and put on the political/cultural offensive. Rather than a warrior for conservative social causes, Reagan was essentially a sunny denier of any fundamental culture war at home, and a stern affirmer of America's destiny to defeat communism abroad. His enduring assumption was that when the nation's sanctified vision was reinvoked, Americans would respond out of a deeper cultural identity that remained fundamentally fixed and intact. Thus as a rising politician and governor of California, Reagan fought against campus unrest and condemned leftist intellectual influences. However, neither then nor as President did he vigorously use government to promote the culturally conservative policy agenda that the "religious right" was urging on him. In his own way, Reagan was oblivious to the Sixties. To embrace an aggressive cultural conservatism seemed too much like being disillusioned with America, too much like thinking ill of something he loved. Ironically, Reagan's final official warning to the nation was about Americans' loss of memory. He urged the younger generation to recover for themselves the idea of a consecrated nation, in a time when parents were no longer teaching their children about this idealized America.[181]

CULTURAL WARRIORS AND DISGUSTED BYSTANDERS

During and after the Reagan years, the post-1960s religious and political cleavages have manifested themselves in a gradual sorting process between the two parties. Ideologically-oriented liberal and conservative members of the electorate have been more clearly arranging themselves into the Democratic and Republican parties respectively. And the meaning of those ideological terms has increasingly come to emphasize liberal and conservative cultural values rather than simply economic issues. Secular and religious activists continued to be more deeply embedded in the Democratic and Republican parties respectively. But in scoring the capacities for grassroots political mobilization, the advantage has lain with conservative Republicans. The Democrats have had liberal interest group organizations gravitating to Washington policy-making headquarters, especially as the membership and power of labor unions continued to decline. The Republicans, by contrast, in their informal grassroots conservative alliance with tens of thousands of evangelical churches and their millions of congregants, have had people across Main Street America already potentially mobilized. The celebrated young strategist for Richard Nixon's "southern strategy" in the late 1960s would eventually acknowledge that he had thoroughly missed "the depth and importance of religion" in the post-Sixties building of the Republican Party. Forty years later in 2006, he was proclaiming that the Republicans had become "the first religious party in U.S. history."[182]

But can you have a culture war if the people don't come? What was true even in the 1960s and the years immediately following remains true today: distinctly ideological citizens—for or against Sixties thinking, pro- or anti-Christian and secular policy agendas—were and have remained a minority of the total American public. There is good evidence that most ordinary Americans, who tend to be rational and thus only sporadically attentive to politics, see no contradiction in being religious and patriotic on the one hand, and open-minded and liberally tolerant on the other. In terms of their attitudes and preferred policy positions (rather than the choices they are given), most Americans are not polarized, nor have they become more so.[183] In red and blue states alike, the general electorate is largely moderate or ambivalent in its orientation to a host of social issues. Compared to other developed nations, the overall orientation in America is toward "traditional values." But within America, the general public has the quite un-newsworthy quality of being centrist and moderate. An exhaustive study of American data from the World Values Surveys between 1980 and 2000 concludes: "Most Americans are religious centrists, located between the extremes of religious orthodoxy and moral progressivism. Cultural values are not polarized. Most Americans cluster toward the traditional pole of the traditional/secular-rational dimension. There is some evidence of the polarization of moral visions, but this is a tendency, not the basis of two morally opposed camps, because absolutists and relativists still have a lot in common."[184]

In fact, rather than being divided into two warring moral camps, attitudes among the vast majority of Americans on social and cultural issues have been converging rather than polarizing. Since the 1970s public opinion on issues having to do with minorities and the poor, the status of women, crime, homosexuality, personal morality, and so on have become less, not more, polarized. Americans have become more generally tolerant and supportive of equal rights, more committed to individual choice and a live-and-let-live attitude toward what goes on among consenting adults. Even on the politically explosive issue of abortion, Americans appear no more polarized than they were in 1980.[185] When people are asked the more searching question about the actual circumstances when abortion should be legal or not, there does not appear to be a very great difference between churched and un-churched Americans, evangelicals, mainline Protestants, or Catholics. In cases where the polls do show that Americans are closely divided, as on gay marriage, they are not deeply divided in the sense of perceiving the issue to be particularly important.[186] All such information is normally eclipsed, however, because the mass media and political commentators usually consider a good story about polarization more important than an accurate portrayal of good evidence. As one careful study of the subject puts it, "Reports of a culture war are mostly wishful thinking and useful fund-raising strategies on the part of culture war guerrillas, abetted by a media driven by the need to make the dull and everyday appear exciting and unprecedented."[187]

Religious polarization in the electorate is real, but it occurs mostly at the far ends of the spectrum where Americans are either extremely "religious" or extremely "non-religious." Politically speaking, it is the moderate middle that holds power, with stable patterns of religious cleavages in party voting that go back for decades. This is true even when one includes conservative Protestants in the picture. By one estimate, Americans attached to conservative Protestant churches make up 32 percent of the electorate. However, of that percentage, 6 percent are African-Americans in such churches, and they vote overwhelmingly Democratic. White conservative Protestants make up 26 percent of the electorate, but their propensity to vote Republican is only slightly greater (52 percent on average in the 1992–2000 elections) than Republican voting by mainline Protestants (45 percent) and Catholics (41 percent). Even within the smaller subgroup of white evangelical Christians, voting is monolithically Republican only for that subsubgroup of traditionalists who account for slightly under half of such white evangelicals.[188]

It is important not to misinterpret the polarization in party support that has appeared between those who attend church weekly and those who almost never attend. Starting abruptly with the 1992 election, a major gap opened between regular churchgoers and non-churchgoers (a little under 40 percent and about 50 percent of the electorate respectively since the 1970s). Since that time this "churched/un-churched" gap in party voting has declined slightly, but it has persisted on both sides. In other words, the more religious the citizen (defined as faithful church/synagogue attendance), the more likely that person is to vote for and identify as a Republican; and the less religious the citizen, the more likely is his or her allegiance to the Democratic Party. However, the reason for this development does not appear to be that voters' attitudes have themselves become more polarized. Rather, the explanation seems to be that a fairly stable distribution of religious-political attitudes among voters has been forced to choose between more polarized parties and candidates—with a Republican leadership more aggressively asserting conservative moral issues and a religious identity, and a Democratic leadership more sharply secular and non-traditionalist in its moral positions and identity.[189] Presented with the more polarized choices offered by post-Sixties political activists, ordinary Americans naturally make more polarized choices.

It is among the minority of politically active Americans—individuals busying themselves in the work of parties, interest groups, issues, causes, and the public talk of politics generally—that the culture wars have seethed. And this seething polarization has seeped over into the politically attentive, articulate segments of Americans with college and postgraduate professional educations.[190] Among political activists (certainly less than one-fifth of adult Americans), the divisions on social-cultural issues run much deeper than for any ordinary citizens identifying with each party, and those elite divisions have deepened in the past thirty years. Such activists follow a rational strategy for mobilizing money, political attention, activity, and final delivery of the vote. They target the party's base of committed partisans, rather than the broad, moderate, and mostly ambivalent centrist segment of the population. This in turn polarizes the political appeals, nominations, and candidate choices into which the mass of non-polarized voters then have to sort themselves.

Most ordinary Americans would probably agree with the comfortable adage that you cannot legislate morality. By contrast, the activists on both sides of the cultural divide believe you cannot legislate anything else. The question is, whose morality? To put the issue in the negative—as the combatants prefer to do—America's choice is between the repressive, bigoted morality of Christian theocrats, or the debauched, godless morality of secular humanists. It does not make sense to assess the culture wars by surveying people who are uninterested in the subject. The result of developments since the 1960s has been not a polarized American public, but a substantial parting of the ways between the politically active Americans who set the terms of debate for the general public constituted by ordinary Americans. Both sides perceive themselves to be under attack from a determined foe. Both enjoy the self-righteousness that comes with being the aggrieved victims of such aggression. And both find it useful to play the politics of fear against each other.

The Coming Rupture

With the sort of sensible modesty that keeps historians from becoming political scientists, Sydney Ahlstrom once advised his readers that "interpreting the present calls for a seer, not a historian."[191] Here we face no such inhibitions in interpreting the present, as well as the future that it has been setting in motion.

It is a serious mistake to dismiss culture-war talk because it is mainly a combat among a minority of political activists fixated on the religious/secular divide. That it is an elite phenomenon is clear enough. But this is the opposite of saying it is unimportant. Alongside evidence of the "myth" of a culture war among ordinary Americans, there is also good evidence that conflicts among elites are of vastly disproportionate importance for shaping a nation's political future. When modern democracies run into serious trouble, when nations are built, torn down, or acquire a national identity, it has less to do with polarization in the opinion of ordinary citizens and much more to do with the polarization among civic elites.[192]

Thus it is true, but not entirely relevant, that ordinary Americans have a very non-ideological approach to politics. They would like politicians to get on with the practical problems of improving the schools, health care, retirement supports, transportation, the environment, and national security. Nonetheless, there are few things more practical than a person's philosophical-theological outlook. Such "abstract" outlooks become an inescapably practical matter as a self-governing people must now make policy choices that have unprecedented scope and implications. However much the average American would like partisans to just get over culture-war talk, it is not something that is now in anyone's power to get over.

The articulate activists are not wrong in perceiving a fundamental division of outlooks. Their contrasting secular and religious views go beyond just one more opportunity for deliberative democracy to work out a tentative fix for some social problem. Through government policy decisions, Americans are increasingly being asked to consider the most fundamental meanings of human existence, and thanks to accelerating technology, this challenge will only grow with time. The first wave of such existential policy-making has mainly concerned sweeping issues of life and death—abortion, in vitro fertilization, brain death, organ harvesting, embryonic stem cell research, feeding tube removal, assisted suicide, and the like. This leaves aside such relatively "simple" issues as whether government policy should prohibit or, through inaction, passively endorse artificial reproductive technologies for unmarried couples, same-sex couples, or single individuals.

The next wave of policy choices that is already beginning to break concerns the turning of humanity itself into another manmade thing.[193] This takes secularists and religionists, both insisting on their different worldviews of human dignity, into choices regarding the genetic design of enhanced minds and bodies, not only cloning but the creation of embryos from three or more genetic parents, whole brain transplants, organic integration of non-biological and human intelligence, and the merging of man, machine, and animal components into something trans- or post-*Homo sapiens*—in other words, policies, presumably democratically determined, that add up to decisions on what it means to be human. Until our own time, the issue has always been one of using science and technology to repair nature when it fails. Now the issue is whether to do what nature has denied—in effect, to make nature a human artifact. Confrontations with traditional Christianity are inevitable because the choices will be made not as interesting intellectual exercises, but as the decisive, practical exercise of government power over policies. To insist that only secular "public reasons" are acceptable in debating policy choices about the meaning and creation of life, about the management of death, about what it is to be human, is not preserving a public forum of reasoned argument. It is telling religious people to shut up.

Years before academics were spinning theories as to why religious people should have to give public—that is, secular—reasons when debating in the democratic marketplace of ideas, practical political and commercial realities had already begun enforcing that rule.[194] In the early 1960s, it was Christian theologians who initiated a public movement questioning the moral significance of scientists' applications of new technologies regarding things like "test-tube babies." In less than two decades, their voices had been thoroughly marginalized by the demands that on such important issues, the means and ends of public policy had to be discussed in terms held in common by all Americans. Thus what emerged was first, the massive commercialization of a multi-billion dollar conception industry, and second, a new "bioethics" profession. This new profession claims to provide guidance that is neutral toward religion and exclusively secular in arguing moral issues of science and medicine. In this now generally accepted view, all Americans can agree that the goal is to advance a form of human dignity understood solely as autonomy, as well as human beneficence and justice. Being neutral toward religion in this context essentially means eliminating what religion in general and Christianity in particular might have to say about such things. Money, of course, has much to say. In 1978 the first test-tube baby was born; twenty-five years and roughly 3 million babies later, the U.S. fertility industry posted revenues of approximately $3 billion. Using technology that was not available even a decade ago, three-quarters of American in-vitro fertilization clinics now offer pre-implantation genetic diagnosis to weed out undesired embryos before they are transferred to the mother's womb. What began as screening solely for fatal childhood diseases has expanded rapidly to include, at the customer's choice, selection to eliminate embryos with milder childhood diseases, adult disease predispositions (such as colon cancer or arthritis), and poor tissue donation potential. Of the clinics surveyed in 2006, 42 percent were at times eliminating embryos simply for the purpose of selecting boy or girl babies.[195]

The point here is not to offer lamentations or cheers for what happened to the theologians; it is simply to observe that this is what has happened. And it is very likely to continue to happen. This is because there *is* a "Christian Problem" for secular America.

When social scientists survey the general field of religion and politics, they can find good reasons to conclude that the greatest contribution of religion to liberal democracy is in religion's decline, thereby allowing greater individual freedom.[196] Religion is about allegedly absolute truths, and these essential truths of faith are revealed from above, not discovered or invented by humans. It is quite possible to see religion's politics of moral certainty as a recipe for oppression, not democratic compromise. Ever since the French Enlightenment, those of a secular-rationalist faith have argued that there is an inherently irrational, emotional, and arbitrary quality to religious conviction, which leaves only secular reasoning as the appropriate means for intelligent decision-making in the democratic process.[197] The older versions of this argument, standard fare from any village atheist, need not detain us here. As discussed earlier, traditional Christianity is no rejecter of reason, and any secular-rationalist worldview has its own inevitably faith-based premises. In recent decades, however, a more powerful version of the argument has developed out of the democratic faith. For the average citizen, the problem of "public reason in deliberative democracy" sounds like some intellectuals' tempest looking for a teapot in which to happen. But it is a serious issue and deserves more careful attention.

This view of the Christian problem is grounded in understandings of democracy as a discursive process.[198] The philosophical lineaments of this argument go back to the earliest work of John Rawls, extend through legal orthodoxies developed during the 1960s and 1970s abortion debates, and can be heard in the most recent pronouncements of Democratic politicians. That party's rising star, Senator Barack Obama, has put the point succinctly: "Democracy demands that the religiously motivated translate their concerns into universal, rather than religion-specific values. It requires that their proposals be subject to argument and amenable to reason . . . I cannot simply point to the teachings of my church or evoke [*sic*] God's will. I have to explain why abortion violates some principle that is accessible to people of all faiths, including those with no faith at all."[199]

The general argument is as follows. The civil bond among equal citizens is said to be the exercise of reason in the form of arguments seeking to justify collective action through government. Such deliberative democracy (or government by discussion, as it was called earlier) can naturally see religion as a way of dictating the terms of argument or putting an end to discussion altogether. The justifications offered by religion arise from a comprehensive worldview not necessarily shared by other citizens. Its reasons, if solely religious reasons, are inaccessible to other citizens. Thus because they refuse to share the naturalistic, common base of discourse applicable to all citizens, and rely instead on private, revealed knowledge of God, religious voices in public life inhibit and distort the public reasoning essential to democracy.

However, this is more than a philosophical matter of conversational inhibition and distortion. In this view, the Catholic-evangelical-conservative political coalition threatens the secular institutions of our democracy. By rejecting ways of reasoning acceptable to all and seeking to legislate their own sectarian versions of morality, religionists overturn the "liberal bargain" so painfully achieved after Europe's religious wars. According to this bargain, in exchange for state-protected individual rights of religious liberty, religionists would abandon their political ambition to use the state to bring society into conformity with their rigid views of "what God commands." Religionists seeking to impose their moral views on the rest of society threaten to create a volatile politics of impassioned absolutes, where opponents are demonized and the compromises necessary for democracy are made impossible. At the extreme end of this worry, there are imaginings of a conservative Christian theocracy lurking around every corner.[200]

American Christians should not expect to escape this secular criticism and wariness. They *are* in fact called to have a certain kind of undemocratic rigidity. Christians *are* absolutists, in that they believe certain essential truths about human existence have been divinely revealed through the life and work of a unique historical person named Jesus. Christians *are* exclusivist, in that they consider (as do all believers in the law of non-contradiction) that the truths they hold exclude the truthfulness of contrary views denying those truths. Likewise, Christians have to acknowledge that, if true to the articles of faith given in their religion, they are less (or, as they might prefer to say, more) than fully civic. They are required to give ultimate obedience to a "foreign power"—another kingdom which they care for more than they care for America itself. It should be obvious that for someone who truly believes in it, Christianity will and should permeate every aspect of one's life. For such committed believers, Christianity is *the* frame of meaning within which they enact their lives. And it should also be acknowledged that, being human, these Christians will often find it easier to flock together in a holy huddle with fellow believers rather than interact with fellow citizens (though that is not necessarily what their Gospel of love teaches). For reasons such as these, secular Americans can understandably view "pious" Christians as strange and possibly dangerous. They are fellow-believers before they are fellow-citizens. Popular critics now call citizens voting on their cultural values rather than their economic interests "deranged." More than that, moderate Christians, by tolerating their co-religionists who believe in the literal truth of the Bible, are said to be encouraging an irrational and dangerous religious extremism to flourish in America. By the beginning of the twenty-first century a significant minority of the electorate—one-quarter of white voters by one estimate—resembled secular activists in the Democratic Party in their intense dislike of traditionalist Christians.[201]

So there *is* a "Christian problem" in deliberative democracy. But this problem as just described is one of modest dimensions. As I pointed out earlier in discussing the "culture war," this problem cannot reasonably be equated with some generic threat of religious fanaticism or impending American "theocracy." The truly odd (and democratically threatening) thing is to imagine that American democracy would be safer and healthier if religion, which essentially means Christianity in the American context, could somehow be kept out of our contested public life. There are multiple reasons why it makes no sense to think democracy "demands" that serious Christians and other religiously motivated people translate their concerns into universal values and reasoning accessible to citizens of any or no religious faith.[202]

First, the democratic conversation in university faculty clubs may be something that proceeds by exchanging universally accessible reasoning (something I very much doubt), but it is not and never has been true of the democratic real world. American democracy is and always has been full of people trying to get their way on the basis of publicly unreasoned convictions. Why should the religiously motivated be held to standards of universal public reasons that no one else has to meet?

Second, from what we human beings know of one another, it is obvious that reasoned argument is not something that is accessible to all adult citizens. In fact, given that Americans are increasingly besotted by the modern media and permanent political campaigning that seeks, under the best professional guidance, to wholly bypass the recipient's brain, reasoning may be the thing *least* accessible to many fellow citizens. It is ironic that attention to idealized deliberative democracy should coincide in time with the post–World War II triumph of a professionally PR-managed anti-deliberative democracy.[203]

Third, if it is procedurally improper in democratic debate to include unproven religious beliefs seeking to impose moral strictures on others, why is it procedurally proper to allow unproven non-religious beliefs seeking to impose moral views on others? All sides are in the game because they want to win—that is, to do some moral imposing. What sort of pluralism or democracy is it where secularists are entitled to enact policies based on their belief systems but religious people are not?

Fourth, where the most profound issues of justice and humanity are in dispute, it is itself an injustice to tell religious people that convictions of their religious consciences concerning transcendent truths should be considered irrelevant and/or dangerous in the talk of democracy. If religious freedom means "nothing more than that religion should be free so long as it is irrelevant to the state, it does not mean very much."[204]

Fifth, religious passions are politically dangerous, but so are secular passions. Modern history should teach us that we have at least as much to fear from wars of secular ideology as from wars of religious faith. Besides, insofar as they were "religious," the sixteenth- and seventeenth-century European wars were about which religion the state would adopt and enforce. Invoking religious belief and argument on important moral issues of modern public policy is something quite different. Conservative Christians are trying to make their convictions prevail on abortion, same-sex marriage, Intelligent Design, and other issues, just as their opponents are. It would be more dangerous to democracy if they were not trying.

Sixth, there is the inconvenient fact of American history. The evidence it provides shows that on balance, our democratic institutions have survived very well with religiously motivated people invoking their religious convictions to try to make America a more godly place. The liberal bargain was not upset by the loud religious voices of abolitionists, early feminists, Catholic workers' advocates, Populists, Social Gospellers, or the young civil rights movement. There never has been a clear line between "public reason" and the religious beliefs of people trying to change American society for what they regard as the better.

Seventh, just because religious people hold absolutist beliefs and accept religious authority, it does not follow that they must be political authoritarians. That charge is simply the reprise of an old anti-Catholic argument now applied to any committed, Bible-believing Christian. Any reader who has come this far should understand that we live in a country where, on the basis of religious authority, people opposed political authoritarianism and illiberal state power. It was indeed a Great Denouement.

Eighth, if they hope to win majority support, it is certainly politically prudent for religious believers to find secular reasons supporting their preferred positions. That requirement for enlarging, diluting, perhaps even corrupting the purity of one's position is part of the genius of democratic stability. But who are democratic theorists or political pundits to tell religious citizens what forms of political expression are demanded from them? The First Amendment stipulates otherwise.

Finally, to return to the original theme of this essay, the issue is not religion as such but the substantive content of a particular religion called Christianity. Simply to invoke God's will certainly does make further discussion rather pointless. But Christianity, at least the traditional sort extending back through Augustine and Origen, insists that there should be no divorce of faith from reason, that believers are called upon to have an understanding faith rather than a blind faith. Reasoning, including public reasoning, is required because the problem is not God's will but flawed human beings trying to understand God's will. Moreover, Christian believers in the revelation of God are supposed to act on the knowledge that God requires a love of others equal to the love of oneself. Whatever differs from that in thought or deed, to the extent of the difference, is not Christianity.

This is easy to say and impossible to fulfill, but nonetheless it presents an inescapable standard that is supposed to demand Christians' unstinting attention and obedience. A religious belief pointed in that direction would see a better protection against all forms of inhumanity to man than a great many alternatives, including an indifference to whether God even exists. It is true that a politics of moral certainty is a recipe for oppression, not compromise. But this is true for any secular moral certainty as well as for a religious moral certainty. On that score, Christianity does inherently contain an inner corrective. Christianity's "prophetic stance" toward political society is ambiguous, being "humane and engaged but also hesitant and critical."[205] This hesitant and critical view, according to orthodox Christian doctrine, applies first and foremost to the believer's own motives and to the correspondence of his or her own behavior to that of the one person who showed what it means to be really human. This is not the same thing as the democratic faith in deliberative justification, but it would appear compatible with it.

In our nation's last religious awakening, Martin Luther King Jr. tried to teach Americans that Christian power is the power of a suffering love. What secularists have to fear is not Christianity but the abuse of Christianity by people seeking another kind of power. The history of dissent and martyrdom shows that such abuse of the Christian religion has been real and recurrent. History also shows that believing Christians have been willing to throw themselves on the side of dissent and martyrdom to resist the corruption of their religion by the sinful love of earthly power. For those Americans interested in particular political agendas, traditional Christianity has liberal and conservative implications, but it is neither conservative or liberal. It is radically itself.

Much more serious than the Christian problem for democracy is the "democracy problem" for American Christians. The different facets of this problem come into view if we consider the four political options that twenty-first-century Christians face in America, understanding that these are really place-markers along a continuum of engagement and separation.

First, nursing a politics of grievance, some activists on the so-called Religious Right see themselves as besieged by hostile forces and call for a vigorous counterattack. In this view, the loss of Christian values in public life is the direct result of a campaign by ideological secularists. As we have seen, that is partly accurate but it certainly is not the whole truth. The growth of a secular moral discourse is also the result of the mounting pluralism that comes from a nation of seekers who choose their own meanings. With so many multiple perspectives, a pragmatically secular public conversation becomes the one reliable default setting for keeping the conversation going.

The most committed cultural warriors in today's Religious Right dismiss any such subtleties in American democratic development. The most extreme of these essentially seek to subvert the existing order. This view, fortunately rare, can be found among "Christian Identity" and Reconstructionist groups, whose aim is to seize power in churches and eventually legislate a biblically "Christian nation." In essence, the Kingdom of God is to be imposed on earth by worldly power. For reasons already discussed, this is not an option open to orthodox, traditionalist Christians who believe in the fundamentals of their religion.[206] America as a nation of this world can only be the city of man and never the city of God.

That said, there are more numerous proponents of a softer version of this first option. They seek to establish bases of political power in different levels of government and the Republican Party, and from there to "recover" America through legislation expressing Christian values. That is, of course, exactly the vision that worries today's more secular Americans about the whole idea of Christians in politics. They would be surprised to learn that moving the city of man in a more godly direction by amassing political power is something that also worries traditional Christians and evangelical thinkers.[207] This belies a realistic Christian understanding of the problem of worldly power and even the most sincere believer's vulnerability to pride and error. It emphasizes making illegal what Christians consider wrong, at the expense of acting affirmatively on the duties they have to other people.

This is the option represented among the approximately one-sixth of eligible voters who identify with the Religious Right. Since the late 1970s it has produced an ever closer engagement of conservative Christians not just in Republican voting, but in manning the organizational apparatus of the Republican Party, something that is often deliberately hidden from the public.[208] On behalf of their religion, this should worry Christians. Indeed, as Tocqueville teaches us, it should worry any friend of self-government who wants religion to play its vital role in sustaining the ordered liberty of democracy. To do that, religion/Christianity must be itself, not something tied to the apparatus of political power. As usual, Tocqueville put it very well: "When a religion chooses to rely on the interests of this world, it becomes almost as fragile as all earthly powers. Alone, it may hope for immortality; linked to ephemeral powers, it follows their fortunes and often falls together with the passion of a day sustaining them" (274).

The second option for Christians is to accommodate secular democratic discourse and treat one's religious identity just like anything else in the world. This option seems reasonable, but there are also limits, which committed believers will discern. Christians can be committed to the larger democratic goal of talking through things with citizens unlike themselves,[209] and they should be able to demonstrate that their religious opinions are not simply self-referential and beyond reasonable democratic compromises about common goods. This attitude has the advantage of keeping the public conversation going and assuring everyone that democracy is safe from religion. A sense of proportion should tell us that on most issues most of the time, this accommodation works well.

However, a sense of proportion should also tell us that this cannot be true for all issues. For believing Christians, subordinating religion as just another piece of one's worldly identity is exactly what their religion warns against. It is the same accommodation to the culture by modernists in the liberal churches that traditionalist Christians have been opposing for decades. If that is what the democratic conversation requires, then there clearly is a democracy problem. This is especially true as fundamental policy issues on the meaning of human life loom on the horizon. On the one hand, it should be possible to hold a shared understanding between religionists and non-religionists that any comprehensive foundational arguments will occur within basic constitutional rules of fair hearing and basic justice. On the other hand, it is unrealistic to think that full-throated religious talk and political action can be kept at bay on policy issues dealing with essential articles of faith. It is for this reason, 500 years after the disaster of the Reformation, that religiously serious Protestants and Catholics may now be increasingly willing to see themselves as two moments in one Christian movement in history.[210] And America is not necessarily the centerpiece of that history.

With subversion and thoroughgoing accommodation ruled out, the third option—political engagement to find a reasoned public ethic—has been the main course pursued by many thoughtful Christians. By now, sufficient experience has accumulated to define in very stark terms the democracy problem for politically engaged Christian traditionalists.

In the first place, it appears that even thoughtful secular activists and religious activists really do not agree on enough to have a serious argument. Forty years ago, John Courtney Murray could express the hopeful view that "we hold certain truths; therefore we can argue about them." From there he thought the contending sides could go on with the process of reaching tentative conclusions at the "growing end" of the basic consensus.[211] Murray was writing about mid-twentieth-century America. Roughly twenty years later, similar Christian traditionalists—critical of how the fundamentalist Moral Majority was discrediting the public responsibility of religion—launched an effort at political engagement to restore religion's place of public reason to the "naked public square" that had been left by the collapse of the Protestant establishment.[212] The aim of Richard John Neuhaus and others who were ecumenically like-minded was not simply to promote more religious voices in politics. It was to produce a public moral discourse, whose reasoning would draw on transcendent meanings of natural law accessible to all. After another twenty years, by the beginning of the twenty-first century, more experience had accumulated. It seemed to show that given the divergent premises of secularist and Christian worldviews, such a public discussion faced an insuperable barrier.[213]

In the second place, even if there were more shared premises at an intellectual level, it is now clear that engagement in the "public square" must invariably take place on the terms set by America's modern political arena for a so-called democratic discourse. This arena and its rules are not designed to search for truth or to compare rational "deliberative justifications." It is a sophisticated, cynical game designed to manipulate imagery and opinion. In other words, it is a public arena fully invested in the consumption arts. This reality is something far different and more cynical than academics' ideal image of a civic forum or a free marketplace of ideas where, in the competition with error, truth has nothing to fear. It is an arena for the professional marketing of feelings rather than the exercising of reason, and truth has everything to fear. So too do religious activists who decide to engage in the game for public opinion. Those who can be flattered as "God's people" are always easily exploited by politicians inside and outside church walls. Worse than that, Christian political activists are under a constant temptation to invert the true priorities of their faith. According to that faith, flexing political muscle to change America counts as nothing in comparison to the Gospel power to change hearts with the methods of a spiritual kingdom that is not of this world. Christians caught up in politics can easily develop a devotion to power and riches that the first Christian explicitly commanded His followers to reject. Moreover, conservative Christians can be just as willing as liberal ones "to paste Christian labels on essentially secular causes."[214] When conservative Christians present policy opinions as religious doctrine, they risk teaching everyone that doctrine is nothing more than opinion. For reasons such as these, it is not surprising that Carl Henry, who in the 1940s had led the call for evangelical Christians' public engagement, died fifty years later regretting evangelicals' captivity to the market dynamics of American religiosity.[215]

In the third place, the political engagement of traditional Christians has encouraged a majoritarianism—a sort of halfway covenant with mass democracy—which is inconsistent with their faith. Outraged at court decisions over such things as abortion, school prayer, gay marriage, and other issues, Christian activists have mounted vigorous campaigns against a judicial activism that replaces decisions by legislatures of democratically elected representatives. It is a deceptively popular argument to make. With natural-law jurisprudence a relic of the past, politically engaged Christians easily succumb to viewing the essence of law as the will of the political sovereign, namely the people. The problem is that if Christians really do believe what they say, it has to follow that immoral policies on abortion, eugenics, euthanasia, gay marriage, genetic engineering, and so on are just as wrong if passed by fifty state legislatures as they are if decided by handful of Supreme Court justices. Here we are re-encountering an ancient tension between the democratic and Christian faiths. As long ago as the eighth century A.D., *vox populi, vox Dei* was a traditional proverb, and Alcuin, as abbot of Tours and adviser to the great Charlemagne, was compelled as a Christian to warn against it.[216] For an authentic Christian believer, when a government—democratic or otherwise—abrogates the law of God, it loses its legitimacy.

Unfortunately for Christian activists—or as secularists would say, fortunately for American democracy—there is little evidence that more democratic policy-making will produce the majorities for which they hope. In the midst of Christian activists' call for more political engagement by the faithful, this issue is generally overlooked. To date, at least, talk about "reclaiming America for Christ" appears to be mainly good fund-raising talk. It ignores Americans' predominant preference for a "lite Christianity" that marginalizes transcendent claims of faith in favor of cultural claims of self-fulfillment.

While approximately 85 percent of American adults identify themselves as Christians, only 42 percent of Americans say they are absolutely committed to the Christian faith, and a majority of all Americans (60 percent) say they think there is no single religion that has all the answers to life's questions. Between one-fourth and one-third of Americans say that they base their moral decision-making primarily on principles and teachings of religion. For self-professed Catholics this drops to 16 percent, and even among "born-again" Christians, only 40 percent say they rely on biblical or church teachings as their primary source of moral guidance.[217]

In terms of the core doctrinal content that supposedly unites Catholic, Protestant, and Orthodox churches into Christianity as such, recent research makes it clear that the mass of American Christians have very little idea of, or interest in, what it is. As we have seen, the roots of a non-creedal Christianity go far back in American history, and by the twenty-first century it has become fully in tune with a secular culture that endorses individual choice, tolerance of different truths, and distrust of anyone's party line about what morality ought to be. In a transformation of American religion toward tolerance of divergent views, the evidence indicates that Americans are more interested in having religious faith than in the doctrines that define the meaning of their faith.[218] Compared with secular Europe, Americans remain hyperactively religious. But their activity appears less oriented toward seeking a God of theological truth, and very much more toward seeking out a religious community that serves one's personal needs (both utilitarian and aesthetic). This is not surprising, since about half of American Christians say they believe that all religious faiths teach the same basic principles. Reciting the traditional Christian creed at worship, and meaning it, is a countercultural gesture.[219]

It is true that church-going is an outstanding behavioral characteristic of Americans compared with other developed nations. In terms of attending organized religious services, 40 percent of Americans report having attended a worship service in the previous week (that is, excluding weeks containing the major religious holidays). Less often discussed in this measure of religiosity is evidence that such self-reported church-going is apparently—over half the time—a lie. According to independent validation by actual counts, time diaries, and the like, the percentage of Americans actually attending any place of worship in the previous week is probably closer to 20 percent than the widely publicized and self-reported figure of 40 percent.[220] It seems that in America the frequency of going to church is roughly matched by the frequency of lying about going to church.

Beyond bearing false witness to one's pollster, the evidence on behavior outside church is more difficult to gather, but it all points in essentially the same direction. Not only American Christians in general but also born-again evangelicals "are as likely to embrace lifestyles that are every bit as hedonistic, materialistic, self-centered, and secularly immoral as the world in general."[221] As the distinguished preacher and Bible expositor James Montgomery Boice put it in 1996 shortly before his death, "The sad truth is that they [evangelicals] perhaps even more than others have sold out to individualism, relativism, materialism and emotionalism, all of which are the norm for the majority of evangelical church services today. Evangelicals may be the most worldly people in

America." Likewise, the overwhelming majority of Catholics fail to abide by the Church's authoritative teaching on artificial birth control, and apparently very few priests insist on conformity with the Church's natural-law doctrine of contraception.[222] The old hostilities between Protestants and Catholics have indeed diminished in modern America, inasmuch as most people in both Christian congregations now seem to regard individual choice as their *de facto* religious creed and commitment.

In twenty-first-century America, the principle of individual choice appears to be the rock on which must break all hopes of traditionalist Christians appealing to either natural law or democratic majorities. Majorities of Americans consider various things morally wrong, but they are deeply reluctant to make them illegal. This applies to many issues, from abortion and homosexuality to euthanasia and assisted suicide.[223] It will certainly apply to the emerging wave of genetic and other policies for remaking nature. For example, in the largest opinion survey to date, roughly three-quarters of Americans are worried about the future of genetic engineering in designing and treating children like products. However, only 38 percent support any government regulation based on "morality or ethics," while 61 percent support government regulation to ensure the safety and quality of reproductive genetic testing.[224]

Personal choice can easily appear as the sensible middle ground for religious and non-religious Americans alike. It says that where people have such varying opinions, government and law must leave the issue to the choices of individual consciences. Because they are based on one's personal sense of conscience, such choices are self-validating. In this distorted way, Protestantism in a democratic regime of consumer sovereignty has ultimately reaped what it sowed in the Great Denouement. It is a distortion because from the beginning, religious liberty had been grounded not simply on "freedom of conscience," but on the essential God-bestowed dignity of the human person with duties to the God of the Bible. Nonetheless, in modern America the exercise of individual autonomy of conscience is *ipso facto* sanctified, whatever it chooses. Anyone who says otherwise is a judgmental bigot and a potential danger to democracy.

With all moral views reduced to differences of personal opinion, everyone can coexist peacefully so long as no one insists too strongly on any standards for other people. Some Christians will find it possible to accommodate themselves to this public outlook. Other, more orthodox Christians (as well as traditionalist Muslims, Jews, and other religionists) will hear this as a polite way of being told to leave the room. In either case, retailing social morality as the aggregation of individual choices can produce collective results that probably never would have been acceptable as wholesale public policy decisions (policies such as eliminating population groups with certain "defects," or privileging adults' reproductive freedom over the right of children not to be designed by some other human being). It is the same dynamic of choice that has produced the larger popular culture which traditional Christians find salacious, degenerate, and alienating.

Finally, then, for traditional Christians there is the increasingly attractive fourth option of separatism, or what Albert Hirschman called "exit." I expect that many, perhaps most, readers will consider it silly even to be discussing such an option. After all, we live in a time—not unknown in our history—when being super-patriotic and super-Christian is often regarded as the same thing. The overwhelming majority of seemingly traditional Christians (77 percent of conservative white Protestants and 87 percent of self-identified evangelicals) see America as founded on Christian principles, and a clear majority of these people think that Christian morality should be the law of the land. Pollsters find that conservative Protestants have more pride in America than any other religious or non-religious social group. Who would want to exit?[225]

All that, however, is on the surface of things and concerns only current events. In a Tocquevillian spirit, we should try to be attentive to deeper currents. It is here and looking toward the future that we will find devout believers recognizing that Christian political activists who identify their country with their faith are cheapening their religion. In fact, something of an odd-couple agreement is emerging on this option between secular activists (Christians should keep out of public affairs for the good of the country) and those who have been called the new pietists (Christians should keep out for the good of their religious way of life).

The chief worry of such pietists, as with their Pilgrim forefathers who left Leiden, Holland, is likely to be for their children. This view has been fueling the fast-growing home-school and Christian academies movement, although this certainly does not represent full withdrawal into a neo-Amish world.[226] Rather than a sudden exodus, what we may find is a gradual, on-again, off-again disengagement of committed believers in orthodox Christianity from the larger political culture. This may be especially attractive to the coming generation of younger evangelicals, who seem to have a certain empathy for the pre-Constantinian home-church communities of early Christians.[227] The self-critical impulse of their religion may well convince such traditional Christians that the real issue is not to blame or fix the larger culture, of which they have been an active part, but to thoroughly turn their own lives in the right direction. Separatism may well be the course followed by chastened patriots who sense that they have abandoned their first love. The attraction will not lie in separatism but in the yearning to be single-hearted. This is the early Christian vision of an unfeigned singleness of heart, a living-in-truth that makes the whole person available to God and to the united community of fellow believers. The historian John Lukacs once wrote that a person cannot be deeply middle-class and deeply Christian at the same time, and those taking this fourth option will be testifying that one cannot be enculturated by America and deeply Christian at the same time.[228]

In following the path of the Leiden Pilgrims and the early Christian church, believers will be occupying ground where two thoughts have to be held together in a strange union—a vision of reason and revelation, of works in the real world and faith in an unseen world that is even more real. Occasional interventions in the public debate may occur. However, separatists will believe that sustained involvement in America's political culture serves mainly to corrupt. Those taking this fourth option will indeed be trying to return to the vision of a tender, loving Christian community of sanctification, a people commanded to be in the world but not of the world. And from the world's point of view, we can expect that their aspirations for a godly community will be regularly defeated both from without and within the community. But somehow they will see that this does not ultimately matter. In the strangeness of their vision, the most real things in the world are the shadows of an unseen world that knows us by name.

For traditional Christians reluctant to separate, there is simply a sad sense of estrangement. Writing as a new grandmother in the mid-1990s, the distinguished professor of ethics Jean Bethke Elshtain questioned whether there would be a "culture worthy of endorsement and engagement" by the time her granddaughter became an adult.[229] From one day to the next, the elegiac withdrawal can be very quiet and unnoticeable. Such Christians (and no one really knows how many) will be primarily committed to participating in their religion's tradition of Bible study, the Daily Office, and charitable service, taking heart in simply keeping their faith alive amid what they see as the ruins of American culture and Christianity.[230] In any event, it is important to recognize that these intimations of exit are coming not from "backwoods fundamentalists," but from among some of the leading Christian minds in the nation. The democracy problem is becoming a rupture when conscientious Christians doubt if they can any longer give moral assent to the existing regime. Christian discipleship and American citizenship then start forcing very fundamental choices.

And so we come full circle. Although the correspondence is certainly not exact, there is an emerging similarity between twenty-first-century America and the situation that Tocqueville found so tragic and dangerous in his French homeland. It is a condition of devout, serious Christians alienated from the quest for democracy, and of devout, serious democrats hostile to Christianity. I am not saying we are there yet, or that we necessarily must reach that sorry state. But I am saying that this seems to be the general tendency in the movement of things. And in saying this I have tried to bear in mind that "aging scholars, like aging parents and retired athletes, tend to see the present as the past devitalized—all loss, faithlessness, and falling away."[231]

Thus chastised, I remain convinced that it is not this essay but American political development itself that has reopened the hoary issue of the compatibility of democracy and Christianity. In the coming years, the stresses created by this question will vary among the four-fifths or so of Americans who identify themselves to pollsters as Christians.[232] This tension between religious commitment and political allegiance will grow and vary depending on whether the person defines his or her life as a Christian American or an American Christian. Which is the "fundamental" term, and which the mere modifier? Each person's answer will make all the difference in the world and, some believe, beyond it.

2

DEMOCRACY AND CATHOLIC CHRISTIANITY IN AMERICA

Mary Jo Bane

HUGH HECLO IN HIS ESSAY ON DEMOCRACY AND Christianity in America makes the provocative statement that "it is reasonable to conclude that Christianity has probably been better for American democracy than American democracy has been for Christianity."[1] He then goes on to discuss what he sees as a "coming rupture" between the two as American democracy faces a new "Christianity problem" and Christianity faces a new "democracy problem."

In these comments I reflect on the Catholic experience with American democracy, with which Heclo does not deal. I contend that American democracy faced a "Christianity problem" in the nineteenth and twentieth centuries with the arrival of large numbers of relatively intolerant Catholic immigrants, a problem that was solved mainly through politics and through the contributions of Catholics as individuals and communities to American democracy. I then argue that Catholicism faced a "democracy problem," which it solved mainly through doctrinal development, with largely positive practical and theological effects. This history suggests to me that the problems which Heclo argues are facing contemporary democracy and Christianity may be addressed in the same ways, making engagement more possible and separatism less likely.

In making these arguments I use a conception of religion that is not defined solely by doctrine, and one in which doctrinal development is not heresy but an integral aspect of a living religion. I make these arguments from and about the Catholic tradition, although I suspect that they may be applicable to some threads of the Protestant tradition as well. I speak from Catholicism for three reasons: First, it is my own faith tradition and the one about which I am most knowledgeable. Second, because Catholicism takes theology and doctrine seriously, and articulates doctrine in authoritative documents, it is easier to document doctrine and its development in this tradition. Finally, ever since the great waves of immigration of the nineteenth century, Catholicism has been the single largest Christian denomination in America, currently claiming the allegiance of about a quarter of the population.[2]

The Great Denouement

In what ways has Catholic Christianity interacted with American democracy? Let me begin with Heclo's "great denouement," which came about, he argues, because the Christian churches at the time of the Revolution and the drafting of the Constitution developed the doctrine of religious liberty through theological, not simply practical, reasoning. Heclo says: "At bottom, government involvement with religion was not a political or philosophical mistake. It was a religious error. Authentic Christianity was the response of one's whole being to God's inner call; and that required that man's mind be left free from coercion."[3] Heclo suggests that Catholics in the English colonies of North America participated in the project of enshrining this line of reasoning into the structures and practices of the new American republic. Indeed they did. But this was not because religious liberty was a theological principle for Catholics, at least before the great Vatican II

Council of the mid-1960s. At best it was a practical necessity; at worst a great evil.

But luckily for American democracy, its Revolution was fought and its Constitution drafted during a brief period when Catholicism departed in many ways from its history and its future.[4] At the time of the Revolution, Catholics were an extremely small proportion of the population in the English colonies of North America, no more than one percent.[5] Among them were a small group of well-educated, middle- and upper-class Irish immigrants including Charles and John Carroll (a signer of the Declaration of Independence and the bishop of Baltimore, respectively), who are best described as Enlightenment Catholics and their church as republican Catholicism. This small group practiced a humanistic Catholicism that indeed celebrated religious liberty and saw no conflict between Catholicism, the ideas of the Enlightenment, and democracy. As Catholic parishes were being organized in this early period, often without resident priests, boards of lay trustees were formed that owned the properties, and parish governance had democratic features including hiring of pastors by the congregation.

This enlightened, republican Catholicism was tolerated by the Vatican mostly because the Vatican was at a low point in its historical power and influence and had other things on its mind than the tiny church in North America—for example, the destruction of churches and execution of priests in France after their revolution, and the kidnapping of two Popes by Napoleon. Preserving the existence of the Papacy seemed more important than whether a few Catholics in North America were developing their own forms of thinking, worship, and governance.

If the Vatican had forcefully expressed at that time its doctrines denouncing religious liberty as a serious error (as it did both before and after this period), or if the Vatican had been in a position to enforce its doctrines in the American church, or if Catholics had been a larger proportion of the American population at the time of the Revolution and Constitution writing, religious issues in the new republic might have been much more contentious. As it happened, the small Catholic minority within the population joined with Baptists, Methodists, and others in a practical compromise that at least would prevent the establishment of Anglicanism or Congregationalism at the national level. If Catholics had been a larger proportion of the population, and if the views of the Vatican had been better known, it might have been much more difficult to establish tolerance as the norm of the new republic—why should a religion which is not itself tolerant be tolerated by others? But the Vatican was weak and far away, and the Catholic population was small and tolerant. Thus the new republic was able to achieve a "great denouement" in regard to religious liberty. It was very lucky.

The Catholic Immigrants

The relationship of Catholicism to democracy during the period of immigration was very complex.[6] It could easily have gone badly wrong. The waves of immigration that contributed to dramatic population growth and societal change during the nineteenth century began, more or less, with the Irish potato famine of 1845. Between then and around 1865, a million and a half Irish immigrants came to America. As a result of this immigration, by 1860 perhaps 8 percent of the U.S. population was Catholic. The Irish clustered in a few cities and states and were, in those places, a much more real and visible presence than they had been in the colonies. The immigrant presence generated a nativist backlash; the Irish-dominated American church responded in a way that both created a strong American Catholic church and contributed to the cultural and civic underpinnings of American democracy. It was a complicated story.

In addition to sending great waves of immigrants to America, the potato famine in Ireland also contributed to a particular style of Catholicism, described vividly by Charles Morris.[7] Since, according to a prominent cardinal of the time, God had visited the famine on the Irish people as punishment for their sins, they needed to repent, submit to the authority of the church, abstain from (or at least not enjoy) sex, and participate in devotions to the Sacred Heart, the Blessed Virgin, and assorted saints. This style of Catholicism was consistent with theological developments in the larger church at the time, which became known as ultramontanism. (The movement was centered in France but looked "beyond the [Alps] mountains" to the Vatican for direction.)[8] The Vatican aggressively reasserted its authority after the debacles of the French revolution—authority within a strictly hierarchical church, and authority in a sense over the world, which could only be saved by becoming Catholic. This theological development found expression in a number of papal declarations on the primacy of the church, and most starkly in the declaration of papal infallibility in 1870.

The nineteenth-century "infallible" Popes were no defenders of religious freedom. In 1824, Pope Leo XII issued an encyclical condemning a variety of evils of the time, among them religious toleration. An 1832 encyclical repeated the condemnation of "that absurd and erroneous teaching, or rather that folly, that it is necessary to assure and guarantee to whomever it may be the liberty of conscience." Because people "will perish eternally if they do not hold the Catholic faith," if freedom of conscience is allowed, "the pit of the abyss is open."[9] As Noonan summed it up, "What is incontestable is that in absolute terms, without qualification as to context, the pope pronounced freedom of conscience and freedom of religion to be pernicious errors."[10]

The Irish immigrants who poured into America in the mid-nineteenth century were not the elite, educated immigrants of earlier times, but displaced farmers and workers. They brought with them a rigid and devotional style of Catholicism, and were accompanied by a clergy, most (though not all) of whom had been educated in Rome, had absorbed ultramonantist theology, and were fiercely loyal to the Pope. These clergy had been educated to believe, as did the Pope, that error had no rights, that the Catholic church was the only path to salvation, and that both modernism and religious liberty were inventions of the devil.

One can imagine that these attitudes might have posed a problem for American democracy. And indeed there are some fairly horrific stories of anti-Catholic and nativist backlash against Catholics and foreigners. The most famous of these events is probably the burning in 1834 of an Ursuline convent in Charlestown, Massachusetts, after charges circulated (later shown to be baseless) that the convent had kidnapped young girls, kept them prisoners, and forced them to provide sexual services to priests.[11] Two decades of violence against Catholics followed. In the 1880s and 1890s the violence subsided somewhat, but nativism remained strong in the political arena. By 1890 the Know-Nothing Party, the platform of which was anti-foreign and anti-Catholic, had a million members and had captured electoral office in a number of states and cities.

The immigrants responded to (and to some extent fed) nativist anti-Catholicism by coming to perceive themselves and to act as a persecuted, beleaguered minority. The cities in which they settled were developing segregated housing patterns. Within these segregated neighborhoods, Catholic national parishes became the primary form of church organization. The first ones were Irish and therefore English-speaking. But later waves of Catholic immigrants, first from Germany and then from eastern Europe, worshipped in German or Polish or other parishes, according to the customs and in the language of their native countries. These parishes also built schools and developed a network of social activities and benevolent societies, all reflecting the culture and language of their countries of origin.

The sense of being a beleaguered minority was reinforced by a theology which held that there was no salvation outside the Catholic church and that interaction and intermarriage with Protestants were sure routes to hell. This fed the impetus to build Catholic schools, a tendency which was reinforced by the fact that public schools at the time were in fact Protestant schools, often requiring prayer and Bible reading from translations of the Bible that were considered by Catholics to be heretical.

Meanwhile, back at the Vatican, the papacy was asserting its authority over the papal lands as well as over the church. Theological controversies pitted neo-scholastics against historicists. Most important for our story is the theological controversy within the church over the relationship of church and state. Some American bishops and some European theologians were starting to make the argument that the American model of religious freedom and separation of church and state was theologically sound, and that Catholicism was most faithful to its origins when it was freely chosen and separate from the state. This group lost the argument. In 1895, in a letter addressed to the Archbishops and Bishops of the United States, Pope Leo XIII, after first expressing his "esteem and love" for the "young and vigorous American nation," went on to say:

> It would be very erroneous to draw the conclusion that in America is to be sought the type of the most desirable status of the Church, or that it would be universally lawful or expedient for State and Church to be, as in America, dissevered and divorced. . . . [The Church in America] would bring forth more abundant fruits if, in addition to liberty, she enjoyed the favor of the laws and the patronage of the public authority.[12]

Ten years earlier, in an encyclical on "the Christian Constitution of States," the same Pope denounced "that harmful and deplorable passion for innovation which was aroused in the sixteenth century," from which came "all those later tenants of unbridled license" that included the principle "that each is free to think on every subject just as he may choose."[13] Instead, he says, the state

> is clearly bound to act up to the manifold and weighty duties linking it to God, by the public profession of religion. . . .

> Since, then, no one is allowed to be remiss in the service due to God, and since the chief duty of all men is to cling to religion in both its teaching and practice—not such religion as they may have a preference for, but the religion which God enjoins—. . . . it is a public crime to act as though there were no God. So, too, it is a sin for the State not to have care for religion. . . . All who rule, therefore, would hold in honor the holy name of God, and one of their chief duties must be to favor religion, to protect it, to shield it under the credit and sanction of the laws.[14]

Leo makes it clear in the course of developing his argument that "the religion which God enjoins" is the religion of the Catholic church.

So we might conclude that the American Catholic church around the end of the nineteenth century was surely a threat to democracy: a large (now about 16 percent of the population), growing (with higher fertility rates than the rest of the population), inwardly focused subgroup whose doctrine asserted the desirability of an established Catholic religion. The threat, however, did not precipitate a rupture. Instead, three developments occurred.

The first was rivalry between the Irish and the Germans. The Irish were the first large wave of Catholic immigrants to America. They established parishes, attracted priests from both America and Ireland, and came to dominate the Catholic hierarchy of bishops. German Catholic immigrants, who came later, established German parishes, and as time went on they asked for authorization for German-language schools and exclusively German-speaking priests for their parishes. The latter request especially was a threat to the Irish hierarchy. They lobbied vociferously and effectively in Rome against the "special privileges" requested by German American Catholics, and retained their control over the clergy and the hierarchy. Although national parishes remained the norm in Catholic America, the victory of the Irish-American bishops meant that Catholicism was not quite as isolated from American society as it might have been.

The second development was the desire of the Irish American Catholic hierarchy to exercise political power in cities with large Catholic populations. These powerful bishops wanted protections, and indeed privileges, for their Catholic flock; they wanted, for example, fair treatment in public schools and, if they could get it, public financing for Catholic schools. Although they lost most of the specific fights, they did develop into a strong political force. (In the early 1840s Cardinal Hughes in New York endorsed a slate of Catholic candidates for the legislature that agreed with him on the school issues. They won in the city, then won an important victory in the state legislature. Hughes withdrew the Catholic slate he had recruited for the next election, having made his point about Catholic electoral muscle.) And in doing so, they figured out that a platform calling for an established Catholic church might not be the optimum strategy for getting what they wanted. So this message, which was in fact the official Vatican position, was muted, indeed not heard, in America. Catholics, led by their bishops, built in their parishes a strong and rich Catholic religion that was developing, on this important issue, its own implicit doctrine.

The third and most important development was that the strategy of building strong and separate Catholic institutions not only reinforced the power of the hierarchy but also served both the immigrants and American democracy very well. The bishops and their clergy built an authoritarian Catholic church, which asserted and modeled a hierarchical structure and emphasized the importance of obedience. They insisted that Catholics pray only with each other, marry only other Catholics, belong to Catholic fraternal societies, and educate their children as Catholics. They then used their authority and the institutional structure of the church in support of education, strong families, hard work, temperance (not all their efforts were successful), responsibility, and loyalty to the country. Catholics, on average, went to school, worked hard, served in the armed forces, and saved money to buy homes. Their children became professionals and moved to the suburbs.

There were many ironies in this strategy. One was in the pattern of developing and staffing Catholic schools. According to Catholic teaching at the time, there were only two appropriate places for women: the home, where they were to defer to their husbands and raise lots of pious children, and the convent. Given those alternatives, many young Catholic women chose the convent, in which they could be relatively independent, get an education, and practice a profession. They staffed the growing numbers of Catholic schools and managed to provide young Catholics with a pretty good education, at very low cost, in a disciplined and orderly environment. (Another irony was that unmarried Catholic women who were not nuns staffed the public schools of the nation's large cities.) From these schools emerged the Catholic middle class, mostly Irish to be sure, who were in many ways model Americans in their habits, values, and families. And from these strategies grew the American model of mostly peaceful religious pluralism.

Later, at the time of Vatican II, the "success" of the American Catholic church was an important element in bringing about a dramatic shift in Catholic doctrine on religious freedom. That story will come later. Here, I want to make two points. First, Catholicism during the immigrant period posed a potentially serious "Christianity problem" for American democracy. The problem was managed in spite of, rather than because of, important Catholic doctrinal positions. It was managed partly by the chance rivalry of Irish and Germans. It was managed by politics, because the new immigrants settled in concentrated neighborhoods in a few large cities where their leaders, including bishops, were able to build political power and turned out to be pretty good at deploying it. It was managed by Catholic immigrants who developed a successful subculture that was powerfully shaped by religion, even as it muted and later explicitly rejected important doctrinal positions. A significant point here is that religion is more than its doctrine; it is also practice, institutions, habits, and ways of thinking. American democracy allowed the Catholic immigrants to develop a way of life as a subculture within a pluralist society. That subculture was rich in sacraments, symbols, rituals, social structures, and opportunities for community. It provided structure, education, and support; it opened up opportunities in politics and, through politics, in public sector careers; it was very Catholic, very American, and very successful.

My second point is that this period posed a serious "democracy problem" for Catholic Christianity. That problem was eventually solved by a dramatic change in doctrine, first implicitly in the immigrant church and then, at the Second Vatican Council, explicitly. In the case of Catholic Christianity, however, I believe this has proved to be a positive development for the religion, not a negative one. That is because doctrine develops and changes, even in the Catholic church, the most explicitly tradition-bound of all Christian religions.

Religious Liberty as Doctrine

In December 1964 the fourth session of Vatican Council II adopted, by a vote of 1,997 to 224, a draft of a Declaration on Religious Liberty. The key paragraph of that declaration reads as follows:

> The Vatican Council declares that the human person has a right to religious freedom. Freedom of this kind means that everyone should be immune from coercion by individuals, social groups and every human power so that, within due limits, no men or women are forced to act against their convictions nor are any persons to be restrained from acting in accordance with their convictions in religious matters in private or in public, alone or in association with others.[15]

The Council described what it was doing in this declaration as "search[ing] the sacred tradition and teaching of the church from which it draws forth new insights in harmony with the old."[16] The implication of the language in the declaration was that the church was simply restating an old doctrine in a new context.

The declaration on religious freedom may have been so long overdue, so intuitively correct, coming after so many countries in the world had incorporated the right of religious freedom into their constitutions, that most Catholics at the time may have assumed this was indeed the historical teaching of the church. But it was not. Less than a hundred years earlier, as noted above, religious freedom had been denounced by two Popes as a pernicious error. Only a year before, in the third session of the Council, the draft declaration on religious freedom had come close to being rejected on the ground that those in error had no rights; the most the church could condone was tolerance, not rights. Religious liberty, the opponents claimed, could not be justified on theological grounds, though it could perhaps be condoned on practical grounds.[17]

The American theologian John Courtney Murray, who had been instrumental in drafting the declaration, characterized the opposition to it as being not so much against religious liberty as against "the affirmation of progress in doctrine that an affirmation of religious liberty necessarily entails."[18] The bishops hedged their language, but they knew that doctrine was being changed in the Declaration, and they voted overwhelmingly in favor of it. Religious liberty became an official teaching of the Catholic Church.

Religious liberty is not the only example of the development of doctrine in the Catholic Church. The Vatican Council II Constitution on the Church in the Modern World contained a condemnation of slavery,[19] which had been defended by the church for many centuries, and was only officially denounced by this 1965 Constitution. No one at the Council appears to have opposed this change in doctrine, although the record of acceptance of slavery goes back to Saint Paul. The condemnation of usury was gradually abandoned by the Church. In his masterful study of these developments, *A Church That Can and Cannot Change,* John

Noonan suggests that church doctrine on divorce is now in the midst of notable development.[20]

How can this happen? Noonan describes the process as one of the deepening of our understanding of revelation.[21] In the case of the doctrine of religious liberty (or lack thereof), biblical and theological study clearly contributed. The arguments in the Declaration on Religious Liberty are based on newly articulated understandings of the human person, and on a reading of the Gospels that emphasized the freely given and freely accepted invitations to discipleship that Jesus offered.

Two aspects of the historical context were also crucial. First was the fact that the Vatican Council took place in the aftermath of the rise and defeat of Nazism, and in the midst of the Cold War. The power of religious bigotry had become apparent in the rise of Nazi Germany and fascist Italy, and its consequences had been made brutally clear. In the communist Soviet Union and the countries of eastern Europe, the church was struggling to assert the rights of Christians to practice their religion. Some of the strongest statements in the Council debates supporting the Declaration on Religious Liberty came from bishops behind the Iron Curtain.

A second clear influence on the thinking of the Council, and important for our discussion here, was the perceived strength and vibrancy of the American Catholic church. Cardinals Spellman and Cushing (of New York and Boston) came to the Council from an America where Catholics were almost a quarter of the population; where church attendance was high, religious vocations plentiful, and intermarriage low; and where Catholics over the previous decades had financed and built an incredible array of churches, schools, hospitals, and social service institutions. The cardinals argued that the strength of the American church was nurtured, not hindered, by the constitutional framework of religious freedom and non-establishment, and they had the reality of a financially and institutionally strong church to bolster their argument.[22]

In this case, it seems clear that doctrine did develop, that the doctrinal development was positive for the living Catholic faith, and that American democracy contributed to this happy outcome. An indication of the extent of the change in attitude is the positive discussion of American Catholicism and its contribution to Vatican II in a new book by Joseph Ratzinger, now Pope Benedict XVI:

> American Catholics also recognize the positive character of the separation between church and state for both religious reasons and for the religious freedom that it guaranteed them. . . . On the basis of the structure of Christianity in the United States, the American Catholic bishops made a unique contribution to the Second Vatican Council. . . . They brought to the issue and to Catholic tradition the experience of the non-state church (which had proven to be a condition for protecting the public value of fundamental Christian principles) as a Christian form that emerged from the very nature of the Church.[23]

The Aftermath

Ten years after Vatican II, the state of American Catholicism was not so rosy.[24] According to polls conducted and reported by Andrew Greeley, between 1963 and 1974 Sunday Mass attendance by Catholics fell by 20 percentage points, and the proportion of income that Catholics contributed to the church fell by half. In 1974, only 32 percent of surveyed American Catholics believed the Pope was infallible, and only 16 percent believed that contraception was always wrong, down from 52 percent who had expressed belief in this firm teaching of the church in 1963.[25] Greeley suggests that such a dramatic change in Catholic attitudes over this relatively brief period was historically unprecedented.

What happened between 1963 and 1974? The Second Vatican Council, to be sure. Some have argued that the changes made by the Council in Catholic worship and rules for Catholic living (the

English-language Mass and the lifting of the prohibition of eating meat on Fridays, for example), as well as the implication of the Council that the church could change, weakened the church and led to the subsequent declines in belief and practice. But something else happened in the Catholic Church between 1963 and 1974 that may have been more important. In 1968, Pope Paul VI rejected the recommendations of a commission he had appointed to examine the church's teachings on birth control and reaffirmed the church's prohibition on all forms of artificial contraception. The Pope was apparently persuaded that since the church had taught in the past that birth control was wrong, it must be wrong, since the church could not make a mistake on something that affected the lives of the faithful so directly. If he allowed the teaching on birth control to develop and change, he thought, the authority of church and pope would be seriously undermined.

As it turns out—and this is well documented by Greeley's surveys, among others—what weakened the authority of church and pope was their rigidity on this issue. Married Catholics had already rejected the birth control teachings in practice; they knew from the Council-instigated changes in the Sunday liturgy and norms on fasting that church rules could change; and they expected the commission to recommend and the Pope to accept what they saw as eminently sensible changes in the church's teaching on birth control.[26] Large majorities of Catholics simply rejected church teaching on this issue. It seems pretty clear that the problem for Catholicism in the early 1970s was not democracy but its absence—a failure on the part of the hierarchy to learn from the experience of the laity, to respect their conscientious and conscience-driven insights, or even to explain persuasively why the decision was made as it was.

What is perhaps most surprising, however, about American Catholic reaction to the birth control debacle is how many American Catholics stuck with the church through it all. They didn't go to Sunday Mass quite so often, and they dismissed some of the allegedly authoritative teachings of the Vatican, but they mostly stayed. They increased their participation in the Eucharist, and they gave a number of indications that, as Greeley puts it, they liked being Catholic. Their allegiance was dealt another mighty blow in early 2002, with the revelations about clergy abuse of children and the subsequent cover-ups by the church hierarchy. Here too I would argue that the problem was not too much democracy in the church, but not enough transparency, honesty, or remorse. And in this instance as well I would point to the robustness of the church's hold on the loyalty of its members, disillusioned but mostly still Catholic.

Catholics and "the Coming Rupture"

My brief survey of the relationship of Catholic Christianity and American democracy over the centuries suggests that the relationship has been more complicated and also more robust than might be suggested by Heclo's account. American democracy has weathered the potential threats of a powerful religion with official doctrines inconsistent with democracy, and Catholic Christianity has not only weathered but profited from the challenges posed by democracy. The "coming rupture," if one is coming, may also be weathered, by the American and Christian genius for working things out through politics when possible, ignoring unpleasant differences when necessary, and continuing to develop doctrine as theology wrestles with reality.

I look first at the possibilities for political accommodations, again from the perspective of Catholicism. In November 2004, white Catholics constituted 19 percent of the voters, and they gave 53 percent of their votes to George Bush and 47 percent to John Forbes Kerry—a long way from the 68 percent of Catholic votes that went to an earlier Catholic JFK running for President. Catholics who identified themselves as traditionalist voted 72 percent for Bush; as centrist, 55 percent for Bush; and as modernist, 69 percent for Kerry. Sixty-nine percent of Latino Catholic votes went to Kerry.[27]

Before the election, a conservative group called Catholic Answers had distributed millions of copies of a voting guide that advised Catholic voters to attend to five "non-negotiable" issues: abortion, euthanasia, gay marriage, stem cell research, and cloning. The clear implication, which was actually articulated by a few bishops, was that faithful Catholics were morally obligated to vote against their fellow religionist.

Centrist Catholics were clearly an important swing group in the 2004 election: 7 percent of the electorate that gave 55 percent of its vote to George Bush. Judging from the surveys of the attitudes of these voters, it seems unlikely that that they voted on the basis of "non-negotiable issues," since their attitudes on the five issues are conflicted when they are not outright rejecting the hard-line Vatican positions. It seems more likely that these Catholics voted as they did for the same reasons as other Bush voters—that is, they were worried about national security and they didn't much like John Kerry.[28] But at least some of them may have been put off by what they and others perceive as extreme secularism in the Democratic Party. Recent Democratic efforts to talk more about values, to find a position on abortion that is both pro-life and opposed to criminalization, and to express compassion for the poor without advocating big government may or may not succeed with these voters; much will depend, I suspect, on whether these positions are, and are perceived as, sincere. But it is clear that centrist Catholics are an important group of convertible voters, who are likely to be attracted by moderate stands on divisive issues and by policies that effectively address poverty. Perhaps politics, once again, will figure this out, and in doing so, will help to avoid a rupture.

The potential for doctrinal development within the Catholic church as a moderating force on the "coming rupture" is risky to try to assess. This is important, however, because Catholicism is theologically sophisticated at the same time that it is conservative about doctrine. Catholic theologians have done much of the intellectual work for orthodox Christianity over the centuries, and are likely to continue to do so. Certainly contemporary Catholic theologians are exploring issues of moral theology, religious pluralism, and the interaction of church and state, working out a diversity of perspectives grounded in revelation and Catholic tradition. But the most interesting theologian, and the most important, may be the theologian who is now the Pope.

Many liberal and moderate Catholics, myself included, were horrified when Joseph Ratzinger, the enforcer of orthodoxy in his role as head of the Congregation for the Doctrine of the Faith, became Pope Benedict XVI. But might he accomplish the Catholic equivalent of Nixon's going to China? Benedict XVI wrote his first encyclical, *Deus Caritas Est,* on love.[29] The first part of the encyclical is a beautiful and generous portrayal of God as love, and of love, including erotic love, as both a wonderful gift of God and the way in which humans find God. The second part is a meditation on charity as a duty of the church, accompanied by a careful discussion of the state's duty to do justice. The encyclical contains no anathemas, no instructions for voting, no partisan positions. *Deus Caritas Est* will be hard to use as a weapon in the culture wars.

There are some other hints of how Benedict's theology may develop. There is no indication in any of his writings, recent or past, that Benedict is a religious relativist; he clearly does not believe that all religions are equal in either their reflection of truth or their ability to lead humanity to goodness. He forcefully articulates his belief that monotheism, specifically in its Catholic Christian form, is true, that it has universal relevance, and that Christians have an obligation to bear witness to its truth and to invite others to embrace its practice. Benedict clearly accepts, however, the Vatican II formulation of religious liberty and the primacy of conscience, emphasizing that Christianity must persuade by the reasonableness of its doctrine and the attractiveness of Christian lives, not by any form of coercion.[30]

Likewise, there are no indications that Benedict sees room for development in Catholic teachings on abortion, euthanasia, homosexuality, or the importance of the family. His first encyclical did not speak directly to any of these issues (nor did his 2005 Christmas message or his 2006 Lenten message, which discussed poverty, development, and charity); this suggests that they may not be his highest priority as Pope. Nonetheless, in a recently published dialogue with Marcello Pena, Benedict reiterated an uncompromising position on the sanctity of life, the primary importance of the traditional family, and the dangers of moral relativism.[31]

Where there may be room for constructive theological development by Benedict, however, is in the arena of religion and politics. *Deus Caritas Est,* in the context of a discussion of charity and justice, emphasizes the autonomy of both the church as community and the temporal sphere of politics. The church cannot and must not, he says, impose its beliefs and modes of conduct on those who do not share the faith; instead, the role of the church is to "help form consciences" on the basis of reason and natural law and to "reawaken the spiritual energy without which justice . . . cannot prevail and prosper."[32]

In an earlier Doctrinal Note from the Congregation for the Doctrine of the Faith on "The Participation of Catholics in Political Life," Cardinal Ratzinger made the same points about the autonomy of the church and politics. He stressed the obligation of Christians to participate in democratic politics in "the promotion and defense of goods such as public order and peace, freedom and equality, respect for human life and for the environment, justice and solidarity."[33] He also stated that there can be a variety of political and policy approaches that express a correct working out of these principles. He seems to be saying, in short, that Christians have an obligation to take their firmly held beliefs and their challenges to the culture into the political arena, and to work at devising political and policy solutions in the context of democratic politics, through persuasion and the use of reason.

Thus the Pope appears to be developing a theology of what Heclo calls engagement and defining it as an integral aspect of

Christian discipleship. This would seem to leave open the possibility that some of the more contentious issues that politics will face could be addressed with creativity and compromise, rather than, for example, bishops simply announcing that criminal law is the appropriate instrument for delegitimating abortion. If the Pope moves in this direction, it could help to frame a constructive role in politics not just for Catholics but for other orthodox believers.

The Catholic sacramental imagination, as Greeley has described it, sees the world as full of grace, the gift of a good God. It tends to be hopeful, often so when there is not a shred of evidence suggesting reason for hope. I admit to the bias of the Catholic imagination. But I also think there is reason for hope, both in the history and in the present.

3

PLURALISM IS HARD WORK —AND THE WORK IS NEVER DONE

Michael Kazin

AS I THOUGHT ABOUT HOW TO RESPOND TO HUGH Heclo's ambitious and insightful essay, a statement by Richard Hofstadter kept coming to mind. In 1968, at the end of his unappreciated masterpiece, *The Progressive Historians,* Hofstadter sought to transcend the dispute between consensus scholars like Daniel Boorstin and Louis Hartz, and the New Left historians, who were insisting on the central role of conflict, especially over class and race, in American history. Neither group, at the time, was particularly interested in religion.

In 1948 Hofstadter had published *The American Political Tradition,* a classic statement of the consensus position. But twenty years later, he thought that each side was missing the point. Hofstadter predicted: "As more and more historians become aware that conflict and consensus require each other and are bound up in a kind of dialectic of their own, the question whether we should stress one or the other may recede to a marginal place, and give way to other issues." He added, "As practiced by mature minds, history forces us to be aware not only of complexity but of defeat and failure: it tends to deny that high sense of expectation, that hope of ultimate and glorious triumph, that sustains good combat."[1]

In recent years, there has been a renaissance of scholarship about Protestant Christianity in America and its connections both to governance and to social movements. Such historians as William McLoughlin, Nathan Hatch, Mark Noll, Richard Fox, and D. G. Hart have produced compelling analyses of how evangelicalism triumphed not only as a theological position but also as a political style—and how the latter influenced the former.[2]

These works imply a growing consensus: during the nineteenth century, a majority of Americans came to embrace a messianic, anti-hierarchical, Jesus-centered faith. Ironically, at the zenith of the Protestant Century (which only ended sometime after World War I), Americans also began to grow more tolerant of other faiths. As Alan Wolfe writes, "Although premised on one religion's outlook on the world, Protestantism's affinity for individualism, its relatively nonhierarchical organizational style . . ., and—especially in its evangelical form—its commitment to reaching out and spreading the Word helped transform American culture in directions that made it all but impossible for one religion to insist on a privileged status in relationship to others." By the middle of the twentieth century, only atheists and agnostics were denied the pluralist embrace.[3]

Hugh Heclo has written a wonderful synthesis of this scholarship—and has added acute, often witty reflections of his own. In sum, he describes how the long dominion of Protestantism in America established and kept refreshing the individualist cast of American democracy. Better than any previous scholar, he explains how this relationship was shaken during the 1960s but not, I think, destroyed. I also applaud him for emphasizing that the Protestant concern with defining and promoting moral conduct in the public sphere has decisively and continuously influenced American politics and politicians. If we truly have a civil religion, an unwritten pact that both assumes and encourages tolerance toward different faiths within a nationalist framework, then what Heclo calls "the expectation in the first place that one ought to be good" is essential to it.

But what's the point of writing a response if one only dispenses praise? So I want to dissent from one of Heclo's grander assumptions: I believe the consensus he describes was always more fragile and less satisfactory to most Americans than he supposes. He errs in seeing Christianity in the United States as a more or less unified entity that changed little over time, at least until the 1960s. Heclo does not simply rejoice in the marriage of Christianity and democracy in America—he is too good a historian and has too ironic a sensibility for that. But he downplays or ignores some of the most important and long-running cultural and political conflicts within that relationship. If, throughout our history, to be a theist is part of what it has meant to be an American, to battle over the content, meaning, and application of one's beliefs has been just as central to the national narrative.

The result has been an ongoing tension *between* religious Americans—most, but not all of them, Christians—about whether their faith is being practiced in a way that promotes democracy or restricts it to only certain groups in the population. Of course, this tension is sometimes relaxed, and the groups in question both adapt and change their composition and identity over time. But as long as most Americans ground their public moralism in their faith, the tension will probably never be resolved. To take one's religion seriously almost requires a certain amount of conflict with those who seriously disagree.[4]

Heclo neglects the *development* of this charged dialectic, in part, I think, because his focus is more on Christianity than on Christians. If one is analyzing the successful construction of a set of institutions rather than the actions of the people who struggled to define what those institutions should stand for, a sense of popular ambivalence toward those structures can get neglected. Heclo has also chosen to write an episodic style of narrative, which inevitably draws suspicion from a historian. He spends a good deal of time, as one would expect, on the beginnings of the Republic and its early decades, ending during the Second Great Awakening when Tocqueville came for a visit, accompanied by his friend

Gustave de Beaumont. Then, after a few asides about John Dewey, the Scopes Trial, and the Cold War, Heclo leaps into the 1960s for an extended stay.

What occurred during the intervening decades? Among other things, a long series of debates, some of them bloody, about what the relationship should be between democrats and Christians—and sometimes between American democracy and religion itself. It's hardly coincidental that those years included the greatest period of immigration in U.S. history—when, from the 1840s through the 1920s, 37 million people migrated legally across the Atlantic, north from Mexico, and east across the Pacific. Heclo gives barely a nod to how this mass immigration affected the marriage of Christianity and democracy. It is as if all those Catholics, Orthodox Christians, Jews, and Buddhists just leaped happily into a "melting pot" of faiths and races, as Israel Zangwill urged them to do in his 1908 play of that name, which announced that America was "God's Crucible."

But such an assumption neglects the always uneasy, sometimes hostile nature of the interaction between native-born Protestants and the religious newcomers. When Zangwill's drama opened on Broadway, it received the fulsome praise of President Theodore Roosevelt. In his muscular Christianity, TR showed no animus toward Catholics, Jews, or the Eastern Orthodox—as long as they adhered to what he considered to be moral and "true American" standards. Roosevelt also made clear that some coercion would be necessary to speed along the "melting" process and ensure that it would not go into reverse. "We must Americanize them in every way, in speech, in political ideas and principles, and in their way of looking at the relations between Church and State," he wrote in 1894. The immigrant "must not bring in his Old-World religious, race, and national antipathies, but must merge them into love for our common country, and must take pride in the things which we can all take pride in."[5]

That stance is remarkably similar to that which many contemporary native-born Europeans—from the unchurched majority as well as the shrunken precincts of the devout—take toward Muslim immigrants in such nations as the Netherlands, Denmark, and France. Like Theodore Roosevelt, they demand that the Islamic newcomers learn, with state guidance, to conform to national norms of speech, dress, and political behavior. The urgency of such requirements makes clear the natives' dread of the damage an unassimilable horde of foreigners could do to the political and cultural fabric of their nations and of Europe as a whole.

In the United States, the original great fear was that of tyrannical, medieval Catholic hierarchs and the allegedly servile brutes who filled their pews. Puritan settlers brought this dread with them from England, and the American colonists' participation in the Seven Years' War with France strengthened its hold over the dissenting Protestant imagination. On the eve of the Revolution, American evangelicals led protests against the Crown's recognition of the Catholic Church in Canada and accused Anglican bishops of plotting with English politicians to force a popish tyranny on free-worshipping Americans. Paul Revere illustrated the conspiracy theory with one of his most effective engravings, "The Mitred Minuet."[6]

Abolitionists and temperance reformers continued to rail against the Catholic "menace" in the decades just before the Civil War, and the great fear blazed on through the cultural and political skirmishes of Gilded Age America. A powerful 1871 cartoon by Thomas Nast shows frightened and praying schoolchildren on a beach, about to be attacked by a pack of bishops, their mitres shaped like the jaws of alligators—while in the distance sits a public school in ruins and the Capitol building with a cross on top, and the flags of the papacy and of Ireland flapping in the breeze. Nast dramatized conflicts that were taking place over required readings of the King James Version of the Bible in public schools, about how to teach the history of the Reformation and the subsequent wars of religion, and whether tax money could be spent on parochial education.

At the same time, there was often room for compromise. In

New York state, many local school officials kept the sectarian pot from boiling over by allowing Catholics to hold devotional services before the start of classes and inviting Protestants to hold evening prayer services inside the same buildings. But not until the era of World War II did many Catholics shed their suspicions of what their children were learning about their own faith in public school. And Protestant children in small inland towns learned to run quickly past churches where mass was being chanted, lest the whore of Rome seduce them into entering and snatch their souls.[7]

Meanwhile, in state after state, fierce battles over prohibition and immigration restriction, while demographically complex, tended to pit evangelical Protestants against other Christians, particularly immigrants and their children. The struggle over prohibition was particularly long-lived and impervious to compromise. At the head of the "dry army" were two evangelical Protestant organizations—the Women's Christian Temperance Union and the Anti-Saloon League, the latter run by Methodist, Presbyterian, and Congregationalist clergymen. Neither group was shy about pointing out that most brewers and saloon-keepers in industrial cities and factory towns were either Lutherans or Catholics. Not all prohibitionists were evangelicals, but it certainly seemed that all evangelical Protestants were in favor, publicly at least, of what Herbert Hoover would call "the noble experiment." The dry movement succeeded in amending the Constitution, and, throughout the 1920s, the Anti-Saloon League's lobbyists blocked any attempts in Congress to weaken the strict provisions of the Volstead Act. The "experiment" got wrecked by widespread grassroots law-breaking and a well-financed libertarian counter-movement. However, the gradual decline in Protestant nativism that followed the lopsided passage of immigration restriction laws during the same decade also had something to do with it. By the onset of the Great Depression, when more people were leaving the nation than entering it, dry crusaders had a difficult time convincing their fellow evangelicals to keep the old moral standard flying stiffly in the wind.

By then, however, religious animus had left an indelible stamp on American politics. Long before what the historian John Higham called "the tribal twenties," the influx of non-Protestant immigrants had had a large and formative influence on the party system. Hugh Heclo observes, "Tocqueville acknowledges and considers it irrelevant that most of education in America is entrusted to Christian clergy." He affirms Tocqueville's observation that clergy in the early 1830s were not affiliated with political parties. But Tocqueville was writing just before millions of Irish-Catholic migrants and smaller numbers of their co-religionists from Bavaria and the Rhineland began swelling the population of cities across America.

With the presence of all these Catholics, Tocqueville would have had to qualify his remark quite severely. In the North, many evangelical ministers endorsed the Whig Party. The great preacher Lyman Beecher campaigned for William Henry Harrison in 1840, and the messianic humanitarianism of the Whigs owed a great deal to such figures, who included Beecher's enormously influential abolitionist children, Harriet and Henry. Meanwhile, near election time, anyone reading a Catholic newspaper could not have missed the clear preference of its editors and of most local priests for the Democratic Party. This clerical division continued into the Gilded Age, as indicated by a Presbyterian minister's inopportune slur in 1884 that the Democrats were the party of "Rum, Romanism, and Rebellion." In fact, it was big news when anyone in the Catholic hierarchy broke with the Democrats, the party of religious toleration, as did Archbishop John Ireland in 1896 when he backed William McKinley over William Jennings Bryan.[8]

Such religio-cultural skirmishes lasted into the 1920s—when Al Smith and his allies battled the Ku Klux Klan, which recent historians have interpreted as a massive force of men and women dedicated to enforcing the Volstead Act and protecting the unofficial Protestant identity of most public schools. But it wasn't just reactionaries who reviled the Roman Church as a threat to the republic. During the 1908 presidential campaign, some Catholics spoke kindly of William Howard Taft because the Republican nominee, in an earlier stint as governor-general of the Philippines, had negotiated the lucrative sale of huge tracts of land there that were owned by various monastic orders. After Taft's election, his opponent, William Jennings Bryan, received a flood of letters charging that the Vatican had ordered Catholics to vote for the GOP. "How can it be said that our elections are free," asked one correspondent from Cambridge, "when one man in Rome can dictate the choice of . . . voters in this country?" Four years later, Eugene Debs called on his Socialist comrades to "expose" the American Catholic hierarchy "as the rottenest political machine that ever stole the livery of heaven."[9]

American Catholics only shed their image as foes of democracy after the Democrats, their ancestral party, surged into power with Franklin Roosevelt and then led the nation into the Second World War and through the dangerous beginnings of the Cold War. Through the 1950s, both secular liberals and conservative evangelicals accused Catholics of harboring a "dual loyalty" that was not so different from that of Communists who followed the dictates of the USSR. But most Protestants had grudgingly come to accept Catholics as "good Americans"; after all, such pillars of the Church as Bishop Fulton Sheen and Cardinal Francis Spellman played leading roles in the national purging of the Red Menace. In 1960, John F. Kennedy's candidacy and election certainly helped complete the process, although he had to disavow any role for religion in public life in order to assuage lingering fears of papal influence.[10]

Of course, as Hofstadter understood, all these conflicts took place within certain shared assumptions about the limits of political theology and the value of a common, if abstract, civil religion. There was no government-sponsored *kulturkampf* in America, nor did any influential citizens call for re-establishing state churches anywhere, not even in Utah. Meanwhile, Catholics were riven by their own "national question": first German and then

Italian, Polish, Hungarian, and Mexican parishioners demanded priests who spoke their language and were steeped in their traditional rituals of worship and celebration. Some new immigrant churches behaved almost like independent congregations—although the largely Irish hierarchy always managed to pull them back from the brink. But in early-twentieth-century metropolises like Chicago and New York, there was often more cultural pluralism *within* the Catholic Church than between Catholics and Americans of other faiths.

No discussion of pluralism can neglect the role played by American Jews. It was both unsurprising and highly significant that Jewish thinkers were at the forefront of the intellectual movement in the early twentieth century that articulated a cosmopolitan position toward ethnic and religious differences. Fearing both the growth of anti-Semitism and that of nativist bigotry more generally, such writers as Horace Kallen, Franz Boas, Bruno Lasker, and Lillian Wald thought it urgent to parry Christian supremacy—while, at the same, time ridiculing the pernicious nonsense about the supremacy of a "Nordic" race.[11]

Soon after Hitler took power in Germany, opposition to anti-Semitism became the litmus test for American liberals of any faith or none at all—although admitting Jewish refugees from Nazi rule never became a popular cause. But the habitual, if almost always nonviolent, anti-Semitism of most American Christians only came to an end after World War II when they learned about the Holocaust and realized that most Jews wanted to shed their cultural and political exoticism and join the home-owning middle class. Only then was it possible for Will Herberg's trinity of religious identities to gain legitimacy and for most Americans to consider as uncontroversial President Dwight Eisenhower's famous (or infamous) statement, "Our form of government has no sense unless it is founded in a deeply felt religious faith, and I don't care what it is."[12] At the time of Tocqueville's visit, the triumph of pluralism was hardly predictable; it had taken a century of dialectical development to produce the kind of relaxed diversity of faiths that, at least for now, most Americans take more or less for granted.

Despite the erosion of denominational lines in recent decades, there remain important conflicts between major religious groups in America over what ends democracy should serve. Hugh Heclo offers a fine sketch of what "traditionalist" Christians find alarming about contemporary American society. But equally lively alternative traditions on the left, of both ideology and behavior, continue to course through debates about the place of religion and the godly in public life. These minority traditions both derive from and shape the meanings of morality and prophecy for groups which, as Lincoln noted as the Civil War neared its end, "read the same Bible and pray to the same God, and . . . invoke His aid against the other."

The first alternative tradition is that of activist liberal Protestantism itself. Adherents of a Social Gospel are neither as influential nor as self-confident as they were a century ago—or during the 1960s. But many members of such shrunken denominations as the Episcopalians and the United Church of Christ (descendants, ironically, of what were once the established churches in colonial Virginia and New England) are, if anything, more united in their left-leaning interpretation of the Gospels than ever before. For large numbers of people in these denominations, to follow Christ means to welcome gay marriage and preserve abortion rights, to condemn military intervention overseas, and to welcome conflict with conservative authorities—secular or religious. In their view, "charity" has become a synonym for condescension and compromise. As William Sloane Coffin, the late firebrand of the UCC, put it, "Charity in no way affects the status quo, which accounts for its popularity in middle class churches, while justice inevitably leads to political confrontation."[13]

For their part, most Jews, despite their prosperity and high class status, have remained stubbornly liberal on both economic and cultural matters, practicing a species of what one might call "altruistic modernism." This outlook combines the hallmarks of cultural modernism: the freedom to choose one's religion and sexual partners, fluidity of class and ethnic lines, and an openness toward living in a society continually repopulated by immigrants and other cultural strangers. But Jewish modernism is paired with and defined by altruism: Jews tend to feel they have a duty to help the oppressed (or at least to feel guilty about not doing so), to bring about social equality, to practice *tikkun olam* (to repair the world) and the Golden Rule. Activist or not, American Jews are eternally suspicious toward evangelical crusades of any variety—from the right-to-life movement to the invasion of Iraq. The motto of *PM,* a radical daily paper with a largely Jewish staff published in New York City in the 1940s, put it well: "We are against people who push other people around."

The United States provided Jews with an environment in which this ideology could flourish. Even though an informal, folkloric kind of anti-Semitism was once widespread in America (President Harry Truman sneered, after speaking with a delegation of unhappy Zionists, that "even Jesus couldn't satisfy these people"), the hatred of Jews never animated a political party or a major social movement. And Truman, despite his prejudices, still supported the creation of the state of Israel.

For their part, many Catholic thinkers—whether or not they wear a clerical collar or habit—still refuse to share the individualist, anti-statist ethos that animates most Protestants. As two forceful advocates of the Catholic critique recently put it, "We don't think taxes are too high, government is too big, or that the Declaration and Bill of Rights are infallible. We are not against bureaucracy; it does big jobs that can't be done otherwise, and has a certain moral worth that we ought to think about more deeply. . . . We don't believe humans are perfectible, but that bit of wisdom calls for moral realism, not complacency or dropping out." Drawing not just on American texts but on a variety of encyclicals stretching back to *Rerum Novarum* in 1891, such Catholics view solidarity and subsidiarity as guideposts for democratic practice.[14]

The current campaign for a living wage illustrates the strength of this tradition. In support of the policy, Catholic union leaders like John Sweeney of the AFL-CIO, local priests, and student activists at numerous Catholic colleges cite the work of Monsignor John Ryan and the social encyclicals. They either ignore or reject considerations of supply and demand in favor of what Ryan called "distributive justice." At Georgetown University, students who, in the spring of 2005, staged a nine-day hunger strike in support of a living wage cited Catholic social thought more frequently than any secular doctrine. This helped them put pressure on the university president, John DeGioia, who holds a Ph.D. in philosophy and regularly teaches courses about ethics and human rights.

If Hugh Heclo tends to minimize the rivalries and conflicts that have done much to form the history of European-Americans, he says hardly anything about the religious politics of black Americans. Citing the French sage, Heclo claims: "The future of democracy-as-equality is not in doubt for Tocqueville."

In the distant future, perhaps. But in the 1830s, Tocqueville famously warned about the possibility of race war in America. And whatever positive observations he made about blacks were overwhelmed by his affinity for blaming the victim. Recall such statements from *Democracy in America* as "The Negro has no family: woman is merely the temporary companion of his pleasures" and "If he becomes free, independence is often felt by him to be a heavier burden than slavery . . . he is sunk to such a depth of wretchedness that while servitude brutalizes, liberty destroys him."[15]

Gustave de Beaumont, Tocqueville's traveling and research companion, took a quite different and more empathetic view of the matter. In 1835, the same year when the first volume of *Democ-*

racy in America was published, Beaumont came out with *Marie,* a didactic novel written to expose what the author called the deepening "abyss which separates the two races and pursues them in every phase of social and political life." Beaumont was particularly hard on pious whites. The father of Marie, his hero's beloved and a beautiful and refined mulatto, is a rigid sabbatarian. He complains: "They no longer arrest people who travel on Sundays . . . If this disastrous trend is not stopped, all is over, not only with private morality, but with public morality too; there is no morality without religion! No liberty without Christianity!" But this same man refuses to allow his daughter to marry her well-born European suitor because in her veins run some drops of African blood.[16]

Such passages belong to a tradition already begun by black Americans themselves. In contrast to most whites, who believed their religion affirmed and promoted democratic ideals, black Christians tended to see their faith as a prophetic warning, even a scourge of those who quoted the Bible and mouthed the civic religion but betrayed both of them in practice. The writings of David Walker, Frederick Douglass, Henry Turner, Sojourner Truth, W. E. B. Du Bois, and many others are eloquent on this point. As the historian Albert Raboteau writes, "By criticizing white America, blacks assumed a position of moral authority that made them the true exemplars of Christianity in America." That assumption remains alive today. "God cannot be pleased" was the first sentence that Representative Elijah Cummings, chair of the Congressional Black Caucus, uttered at a press conference that Caucus members held to protest the Bush administration's response to hurricane Katrina.[17]

Since the 1960s, white liberal Protestants have echoed this style of jeremiad. They apply it not just to race relations but to military intervention and other examples of what they view as conservative backsliding. Jim Wallis is the best-known example of this tendency, although he grew up in the kind of evangelical, premillennialist church that has become a bastion of the Christian right. In his best-selling *God's Politics*—a series of energetic sermons on a variety of political issues—Wallis calls for a prophetic vision that would begin with the "God question—'How are our kids doing?'" He then moves on to brisk condemnations of terrorism, empire, war, poverty, racism, and corporate greed—all with apt quotes from Scripture.

His point, of course, is that conservative evangelicals are misreading the Bible; the Good Book contains far more references, Wallis points out, about helping the poor than about forbidding homosexuality. Wallis scolds "false Christians," such as General William Boykin, the protégé of Donald Rumsfeld who, in the fall of 2003, claimed that America's "Christian army" was at war with the "idol" of Islam's false god: "Brother Boykin, I believe you are a product of bad theology and church teaching. . . . Why were you never taught in Sunday school about the real meaning of the kingdom of God and the universality of the body of Christ? And why have you never heard that only peacemaking, not warmaking, can be done 'in the name of Jesus'?"[18]

Wallis has lived for a long time in an African-American neighborhood in Washington, D.C., and the "blackening" of such activist Protestants on the left has only increased in the decades since the political and spiritual revival of the 1960s. This is a largely unacknowledged cause of the division that rent the ideological wings of contemporary Protestantism during the heyday of black power and the movement against the Vietnam War, and it shows few signs of closing.

Yet here too, a certain status quo endures. One can view the passions of Wallis and his fellow left Christians as fulfilling the promise of their faith—to guarantee, in Heclo's words, that "there was now a new Israel for all men and women." Or one can point to the continuing, if informal, segregation of the overwhelming majority of churches in America, liberal as much as conservative, as evidence that the turmoil of the 1960s just ended up reproducing older patterns of worship and public piety—even though a certain radical Baptist minister who won the Nobel Peace Prize gets quoted in churches all over the nation.

In other ways as well, what occurred during the 1960s was less of a break in the history of Christianity and democracy in America than Heclo believes. The creation of what Wade Clark Roof has called a "generation of seekers" repeated a pattern seen during the Second Great Awakening and also in the disillusionment with both the Social Gospel and orthodox Protestantism that followed World War I. During each of these periods, large numbers of Christians broke away from their old churches and either joined new ones or followed a more individualist path to spiritual contentment. After World War I, there was as sharp and bitter a split between militant secularists and traditionalist Protestants as after the 1960s; the Scopes trial was merely the best-known skirmish in that particular battle. But by the 1930s, neither Menckenites nor fundamentalists had much influence over the national body politic, and both presidents and pastors were sanding the rough edges off the rhetorical hostilities of the previous decade.[19]

Early in a new century, we may be entering a similar period when strong religious differences matter less in the public sphere than the rhetoric of each side would suggest. Most Americans seem to be transcending the turmoil generated by both the Christian right and its secular and/or liberal enemies during the period from the late 1970s through the immediate aftermath of the attacks on September 11, 2001. The liberal Catholic Peter Steinfels recently labeled the emerging consensus one of "soft secularism"—a respect for religious believers, even the most orthodox ones, as long as they don't press a strong "claim to influence public life." Steinfels is troubled by this development; it rules out any serious dialogue between the devout and the atheist or agnostic, impoverishing talk about the moral basis of politics and leaving each group alone to reinforce the ideas and prejudices of its own adherents. Ironically, Steinfels comments, "soft secularism is the contemporary counterpart to the broad Protestant hegemony that reigned over respectable opinion in nineteenth-century America and still dominates parts of the country."[20] One can regret the cautious, constantly spinning nature of political talk about religion that increasingly marks the current environment. But it is a far cry from the "coming rupture" that Heclo fears.

So Hofstadter's dialectic between conflict and consensus continues to shape how Americans understand both our politics and our religion. It both liberates us and traps us within assumptions of thought and habits of behavior that have become hidebound traditions in our allegedly hypermodernist nation. We may never resolve the question of what role Christianity should play in democratic life because we cannot bear to give up either the ideal of a godly people or the ideal of a self-governing, self-reliant one—although, as Heclo explains, those ideals, if adhered to rigorously, are incompatible. Perhaps, to paraphrase F. Scott Fitzgerald, Americans collectively exemplify the characteristics of a first-class mind: they are able, on a fairly consistent basis, to keep two opposing ideas in their heads at the same time without going crazy.[21]

4

WHOSE CHRISTIANITY? WHOSE DEMOCRACY?

Alan Wolfe

"THERE IS NO SUCH THING AS RELIGION" — OR SO I begin my course on "Religion and Politics" each year. You can imagine, therefore, my pleasure at hearing a similar thought expressed by Hugh Heclo right at the start of his fascinating and provocative Tocqueville Lecture. "Religion as such has had little significance for American political development," he writes. Only social scientists, he continues, believe in something called "religion." For everyone else, there are religions, and for Americans, the most important of those religions is what Heclo calls that "richly variegated thing called Christianity."

And it is precisely with this description that my problems with Heclo's analysis begin. Heclo offers a learned and nuanced *tour d'horizon* of American Christianity, carefully describing how it has changed over time; once a faith which originated in Europe, it successfully met the challenge of flourishing in the United States. In its detail, Heclo's Tocqueville Lecture misses little and comprehends much.

Yet Heclo is also a social scientist interested in making generalizations, and for that purpose, his efforts to establish a link between Christianity on the one hand and democracy on the other do not succeed. The problem, in a nutshell, is this: if religion as such has had little significance for American political development, the same is true of Christianity. There has been no single body of doctrine, no common set of liturgical practices, no agreed-upon list of sins, no account of the specifics of salvation, no conception of grace, no translation of the Bible, no agreement on the relationship between church and state, and no consensus on the way to spread the word of God that is shared by all those Americans who call themselves Christian. Most Americans have not been Christian; they have been Catholic, Baptist, born-again, Lutheran, Pentecostal. Social scientists want to study something called Christianity because it is a unique religion when compared with Judaism or Islam. But within itself, Christianity is so many things that one generalizes about the whole only at one's peril.

The problem this poses for Heclo's analysis should be obvious: the fascinating and illuminating details he offers in the body of his essay about the many ways Christians disagree with each other appear to contradict the claims he wants to make at the beginning and at the end. Generalize to make sweeping conclusions, and one ignores the detail. Pay attention to the detail, and generalization becomes impossible. Heclo is quite aware of this problem: "Without over-generalizations," he writes, as if he had critics like me in mind, "there can be no lectures, not even bad lectures." His is anything but a bad lecture. But the over-generalizations, I believe, lose in precision what they gain in insight. I hope a few brief examples will make the point.

"Of all religions," Heclo writes, "Christianity is inherently and fervently doctrinal in nature." I find this description far too narrow because the exceptions to it are far too great. Some forms of Christianity are indeed doctrinal, but others, including a large number of its evangelical Protestant forms, view doctrine with suspicion, associating it with Catholicism and its presumed distrust of the believer's ability to glean all the doctrine he needs from reading the Bible; I would never describe the Southern Baptist Convention as a denomination that is "fervently doctrinal" in nature even though I would characterize it as one that is fervently

Christian. To be sure, Christians cannot avoid doctrine because, as Heclo notes, their faith in Jesus forces them to ask questions about how a human being could also be divine. And it is also true that Christians should hold fast to doctrine, given the central role that creeds play in so many of their histories. But it does not follow that all Christians lean more toward orthodoxy than orthopraxis; what most distinguishes contemporary fundamentalists is not their doctrine—so long as you accept Jesus into your heart, doctrine matters little—but their insistence on avoiding sinful behavior. Heclo here confuses a part with the whole. He assumes what needs to be known, which is where, along a spectrum of attitudes toward doctrine, a specific form of Christianity locates itself.

At other times, Heclo's use of the term "Christian" suggests the opposite problem; it confuses the whole with the parts. "The Christian claim is that God invaded historical time by taking on the form and substance of a living human being in a particular place and time," he writes. As description, this is true—that is, it effectively differentiates Christianity from other world religions in which God does not send his son to earth. But because identifying the differences between religions takes us to such a broad realm of generality, knowing that Christians believe that Jesus is the son of God tells us very little about the role of that belief in shaping human affairs. It certainly tells us little about what Heclo is trying to explain, which involves a distinctive attitude toward human history that he associates with the United States. "The hold of recurrent time on republics—a political life cycle of birth, maturity, and decay—has been decisively broken in America," he writes, citing both the devout Jonathan Edwards and the doubting Tom Paine. I agree with Heclo that Americans view historical time differently than Europeans do, but I see no relationship between this form of American exceptionalism and Christianity. How could there be? America is exceptional, but Jesus is close to universal. If all western democracies are Christian but only one of them views time millennially, then the explanation of the latter cannot possibly be the former. By attributing to Christianity a determining role in American political development, Heclo rules out ipso facto any form of American exceptionalism; for if America is special, it cannot be because it is Christian, and if America is not special, its Christianity explains everything and therefore explains nothing.

There are at least three major conflicts within the generic thing called "Christianity" that make generalization about it so difficult. The most obvious, and therefore the best place to begin, involves the differences between Catholicism and Protestantism.

Although Heclo is fully aware of these differences, he, as Mary Jo Bane points out in her comments in this volume, spends little time on Catholics; he gives them their due from time to time, but he also devotes most of his essay to Protestants. This makes a certain amount of sense; if most Americans were—and still are—Protestant, then the social scientist who wishes to address religion in America is obligated to deal primarily with the dominant one found here. Yet Catholicism is nonetheless our single largest religious denomination—comprising roughly one-fourth of Americans—and has been that for the past century or so. And so the question poses itself: when we talk about the relationship between Christianity and democracy, are we talking about the hierarchical, priestly, devotional, parish-rooted, Vatican-led, ethnically connected, primarily urban form of Christianity linked with Catholicism, or the congregationally organized, believer-trusting, liturgy-avoiding, plain-spoken, and Southern and Midwestern ones generally associated with Protestantism?

One way to answer this question is to claim, quite plausibly, that in the United States strong differences between religions, including differences between Protestants and Catholics, tend to evaporate. It has been argued, for example, that all American religions take on aspects of the dominant religion, leading Catholics, Jews, and even Muslims to form "congregational" faiths.[1] There may not have been a unified thing called Christianity in sixteenth-century Münster or Flanders, according to this line of reasoning, but there is such a thing in twenty-first-century Scottsdale.

Yet this way of defending Christianity in general does not work to support Heclo's efforts to specify the relationship between democracy and Christianity. For one thing, the "congregational" thesis, if I may call it that, extends beyond Christianity; if Jews and Muslims adopt Protestant styles of worship, then we are back to the even more general thing called religion. Heclo does not choose to go there and neither, at least for the sake of these comments, do I.

In addition, Heclo, as befits the Tocqueville Lecture, is concerned with the period in which American democracy was formed, and in that period, Protestants and Catholics were quite distinct. Both came here from Europe, and in Europe their differences were pronounced: lives were lost, churches were burned, and kings lost their thrones over such questions as whether the Bible should be translated into vernacular language, whether a priesthood was required to interpret its meaning, or whether those priests should or should not be allowed to marry. In importing its citizens, America imported at least some of their religious disputes. In Tocqueville's time, for example, American culture was being strongly shaped by settlers and the descendants of settlers who came from a Scotch-Irish background, and when they left there for Tennessee and back-country Virginia, they brought with them a furiously anti-Catholic form of evangelical Protestant revivalism.[2]

Having brought large numbers of Irish Protestants to our shores in the early nineteenth century, we then turned around and welcomed large numbers of Catholics from the other regions of Ireland later in the century. This looked like a formula for replicating the European wars of religion on this side of the ocean; and that, for a long time, was exactly what happened. There is a debate taking place these days over whether the United States is experiencing a culture war; I find myself on the side of those who believe that, as far as the general American public is concerned, rumors of the culture war are greatly exaggerated.[3] Yet I would never doubt, nor would most historians, that we did experience a real culture war in the nineteenth century, especially in the decades after Tocqueville left our country. This Americanized *kulturkampf* gave us the Know-Nothing Party, battles over the King James version of the Bible, suffrage restrictions (many designed to prevent Catholics from voting), urban political machines (many designed to allow Catholics to vote more than once), Populism, the Spanish American War, and Prohibition—to mention just some of the major developments in American history shaped by distrust between Protestants and Catholics. Heclo knows all these things; indeed, they constitute a substantial portion of his essay. But whenever he makes a generalization, these important differences tend to disappear. Christianity becomes to Heclo what liberalism was to Louis Hartz: both are undeniable realities in American public life, and both frequently imply a consensus that may not always have been there.

Now it is undoubtedly true that many of these once furious debates between Catholics and Protestants have subsided in contemporary America. For the first time in our history, a generic thing called Christianity is emerging, as large numbers of switchers move from one faith to another and as young spiritual seekers respond, not to doctrinal differences between faiths, but to the vibrancy of specific sermons or the charisma of particular clergy.[4] But if there exists a convergence among Christians today, it is difficult to imagine that the Christianity which historically divided them is precisely what is now unifying them. On the contrary, it makes more sense to argue that there is something in contemporary American *culture* that causes all American religions to become similar to each other (just as there is likely something in Nigerian culture that makes all of Nigeria's faiths—Anglican, Catholic, and Muslim—conservative in a worldwide context). Once something resembling a generic Christianity emerges, in other words, it confirms a relationship between democracy and Christianity, but it is not the one discovered by Tocqueville and extended by Heclo: today democracy shapes Christianity more than the other way around.

In addition to differences between Protestants and Catholics, the second major difference among Christians, as I hinted in my comments about the significance of doctrine, divides one kind of Protestant from another. By the time Tocqueville arrived here, American Protestants had already found themselves split into two very different wings, whether they are called "new light" versus "old light," Puritan versus Arminian, or high church versus evangelical. Again, Heclo knows all these things and discusses them with acute understanding of their significance. But he does not, I believe, fully consider the implications for his major thesis that stem from the existence of these differences.

Consider the importance of Lyman Beecher, one of the most important figures in American religious history and a man to whom Heclo rightly devotes attention. In 1832, the year after Tocqueville arrived in America, Beecher moved west, settling in Cincinnati. Beecher, whom the historian Daniel Walker Howe describes as "the Henry Clay of the ecclesiastical realm," was an expansionist among Protestants; with solid evangelical fervor, he wanted to unite as many Protestants as possible, if for no other reason than to head off any emerging threats from Catholicism.[5] A strong believer in progress, Beecher, like so many nineteenth-century evangelicals (and like the leading Whigs of his era), wanted to move beyond a strict form of Calvinism which taught that human beings were pawns in the hands of a capricious God. To do that, Beecher accepted the notion that human beings are blessed with free will, a position far removed from the orthodoxies of Old School Presbyterians (who, by the way, were as likely to be Democrats as New School reformers were to be Whigs). Because no society as dynamically entrepreneurial as this one could have within its religious universe a faith which tells people that they have no control over their destiny, Beecher's view was destined—one is almost tempted to say predestined—to prevail. Jonathan Edwards is our greatest theologian, but we should never forget that his Northampton parishioners kicked him out of his church. Between optimistic and pessimistic forms of Protestantism, the latter invariably lose.

Interestingly enough, Beecher's form of Protestantism, which placed great importance on human moral agency, resonated with the very features of American democratic life which impressed Tocqueville—and, I hasten to add, which impress Heclo as well. As Peter Dobkin Hall suggests, the voluntary association was to society as Beecher's form of evangelical revivalism was to faith: a place in which individuals, through their efforts, could shape the world around them. In Hall's words, "The historical record indicates that the proliferation of voluntary associations in nineteenth-century America involved groups whose theological convictions and religious practices led them to see secular civil society as the most promising arena for exercising moral agency."[6] (One is always tempted to point out, in discussing Lyman Beecher's role in all this, that without such a conception of moral agency, his daughter Harriet would have had a far more difficult time contributing to the abolition of slavery.) If we confine ourselves to the first decade of the nineteenth century, there was, as Heclo rightly suggests, a strong relationship between democracy and Christianity, but—and this is where his tendency to generalize gets him in trouble—the relationship existed primarily between democracy and only one of Christianity's many forms. High church Christianity—the Episcopal Church of the New England Federalists—made little contribution to democracy. The revival churches sprouting up in the Midwest, as Nathan Hatch argues in his book on the Jacksonian period, made a significant one.[7]

It would be one thing if these differences among Protestants concerned what, from the viewpoint of the present, seem like relatively minor matters of doctrine. But they did not; as arguments over free will suggest, Protestants were divided over the most profound theological and philosophical questions in the western tradition. Heclo rightly notes how Pelagian American Protestantism had become by the time of Charles Grandison Finney, but he does not pause long enough to reflect on its meaning: if something is a sin in one era and an accepted truth in another, how unified can the religion be that embraces both points of view? The very Protestant-ness of Protestants makes generalization difficult. If Protestants disagreed with each other over the majestic question of free will, can we expect them to have agreed with each other on the more mundane matter of who should have the suffrage? If they argued furiously over the sacred question of whether Jesus will return to earth before or after the Apocalypse, can we expect them to have been united on the profane matter of a free press? If some of them believed the Bible to be the literal word of God and others did not, would they have had the same position on the tariff? When it comes to differentiating between Christians, in short, it is helpful to point out that some are called Catholics and others are called Protestants. But when it comes to tracing the relationship between democracy and religion, all those who are called Protestants should be broken down into the kinds of Protestants they are.

Once we do that and recognize the bewildering variety of Protestant sects in America, however, we immediately face a third source of division among Christians: each of the many Protestant sects can be as different within itself as all Protestants are among themselves or as all Christians are among themselves. Consider the evangelicals who did so much to influence the course of American democracy in the nineteenth century; as Nathan Hatch points out, many of belonged to the rapidly growing movement called Methodism. Yet if Methodists were evangelicals in the nineteenth century, they are frequently taken as the very definition of a mainline Protestant denomination in the twentieth. So even if we reduce Christian to Protestant and then Protestant to Methodist, we still face the task of specifying whether we mean last century's Methodists or this century's. Nineteenth-century religion is an interesting topic to study and so is twentieth-century religion, but they are different topics. Most religions in theory posit the existence of transcendental truths oblivious to secular trends; most religions in practice adopt themselves to secular trends in order to survive and flourish. There were, when Tocqueville came here, no megachurches, no Promise Keepers, no *Purpose-Driven Life.* Heclo more or less argues that Tocqueville anticipated those events, and on this point I would agree with him. But if he did, their emergence has little to do with anything inside Christianity and a great deal to do not only with democracy—Tocqueville's explanation of just about everything—but with the emergence of exurbs, interstate highways, television, and therapy.

Not only is a contemporary religion such as Methodism different from the Methodism of nineteenth-century revivalism, but the Methodism that produced Hillary Clinton is quite different from the one that produced Laura Bush and, through her, attracted our current President. No other finding of sociologists of religion is more accepted that the one which demonstrates the extent to which mainline churches have lost members, and evangelical ones have gained them, over the course of the past three or four decades. Thanks in part to Mr. Bush's born-again experience, we are now all aware of the fact that while most contemporary Methodists are mainline Protestants, not all of them are. For sociological purposes, we divide Protestantism up into its various denominations. But in American religion, what counts is not the denomination but the congregation. To cite Tip O'Neill, all religion is local. Americans distrust denominations for the same reason they distrust Congress: they identify with the near over the distant, and this, however democratic it may be, makes a mess of the division of Protestants into denominations.

Even when you get inside specific American congregations, however, you are likely to discover what the sociologist R. Stephen Warner found in his exhaustive ethnography of one church in California: congregations are frequently divided, and what divides them is not so much the fine points of theology, but music, gender roles, preaching styles, and dress codes.[8] American religion may be more congregational than it is denominational, but it is also more individualistic than it is congregational. Each American is a church unto himself. (Heclo anticipates this when he writes that "every Protestant believer is in a way his own moralist.") As Heclo is quick to acknowledge, we live now in an era of seekers and switchers, Americans who have a good idea of what they want from religion and, when they do not find it in one particular church, they simply move on to another. It may therefore be true that members of any town's First Methodist Church like their pastor and enjoy the music, but it is not true that they can identify John Wesley or explain why they do not attend a church with the word Baptist in its name. Americans typically do not stay in one church long enough to learn that much about its theology and its history. Intermarriage, job relocation, small groups, soccer leagues—these are among the factors that lead people to join one church or to leave another. This is all very frustrating for the social scientist craving generalizability, as much as it may be exciting to the believer seeking fellowship or authenticity.

To bring this part of my commentary to a close, I would not say of Christianity in particular what Heclo says of religion in general, that it "can mean anything—from love your enemy's heart to eat your enemy's liver." (I know of no single Christian sect that teaches the latter, though someone reading this book may.) But Christianity can mean almost anything, from accepting a Muslim believer as a religious person to insisting that his faith is false, or from believing that God separated the races to believing that he treats members of all of them equally. Something about American religion surely played a major role in shaping American democracy. But whatever that something is, it cannot be a generic form of Christianity whose existence on this earth is difficult, if not impossible, to establish.

Enough on the question of Christianity. Heclo is also concerned with democracy; the whole point of his lecture is to examine the relationship that one has with the other. If it is difficult to define what specifically makes a Christian a Christian, it is not that difficult to define what makes a democrat a democrat. There are, of course, many kinds of democrats, but certain key features of democracy—popular suffrage, representative government, checks on the executive—are relatively uncontested, at least as political concepts go. The United States may not have been democratic in its earlier configurations, but by the time Tocqueville came here, its democratic character had been established. And that character has changed relatively little over time. Indeed, one of the reasons we have the Tocqueville Lectures—or so I assume—is that Tocqueville left us with such a powerful and convincing treatment of this thing called democracy that any discussion of the phenomenon so many years after his death will still have to take him as the starting point. There may not be any Tocquevilles around, but there are Tocquevilles manqués, as we saw recently with the publication of Bernard Henri Lévy's *American Vertigo.*[9]

Heclo offers a profound challenge to anyone who thinks about the state of democracy in America. We usually ask whether religion is compatible with democracy. But shouldn't we ask whether democracy is compatible with religion? For the most devout believers, God comes first and human affairs after. We should not, Heclo warns, dismiss their way of looking at the world; the cost of doing so, he suggests, is "myopia." Democracy is responsive to the people. If the people consider God to be a major factor in their lives, democrats had better pay attention.

Heclo's point here makes considerable sense to me. There is a way of theorizing about democracy—more specifically, about liberal democracy—that all too often treats the views of religious people as incompatible with the requirements of democratic citizenship. John Rawls came close to making an argument along these lines in *A Theory of Justice,* although he went on to modify his views in his later writings. In my book *The Transformation of American Religion,* I cite two other scholars who, I am sure, would raise Heclo's ire.[10] One, the anthropologist Vincent Crapanzano, writes that "one perquisite for democracy is an openness to the position of the other," a capacity he did not find among conservative Protestants; they believe that they "have special access to the truth," an absolutist point of view that renders dialogue impossible.[11] Along similar lines, the political philosopher Stephen Macedo discussed the case of Vicky Frost, a conservative Protestant who did not want her child exposed to ideas she condemned as secular humanist. "Liberal education is bound to have the effect of favoring some ways of life or religious convictions over others," Macedo concluded. "So be it."[12]

Strong faith creates a difficult dilemma for liberal democrats. If they welcome into the public realm individuals who put God first, they will have to share the liberal democratic stage with people who do not assign the same priority to liberal democratic values as themselves. But if they keep them out, they are not acting like liberal democrats, for they find themselves in the business of treating people they believe to be intolerant with intolerance on their part. Certainly a religious believer would bristle about being told that the most fairly arrived at decisions are those arrived at deliberatively, when for that believer the best decisions are those that are revealed.

What Heclo calls the "great denouement" offers a way out of this impasse. If secular liberals in the tradition of Rawls knew more about religion, Heclo implies, they would not be so quick to set reason and revelation against each other. For one thing, religious liberty in America has historically meant not freedom *from* religion, as many secular liberals insist, but freedom *for* religion, as many believers hold. Primarily because of our Protestantism, we developed a religious life quite different from the form found in Europe. There, clericalism confronted anti-clericalism. Here, neither existed. Our believers were not clericalists because they did not bring the power of the state down on behalf of their sects. And our non-believers were not anti-clerical because there was no state church they could attack. Religion was free to play the role of softening the direct confrontation between the individual and the state because it was embodied in civil society rather than in government. Freedom was not license; as Heclo rightly insists, "Autonomy was not a lack of controls but rather self-control, a combination of personal independence and moral responsibility."

This ability of religion to serve as a great denouement, at first glance, is even truer now than it was in the time of Tocqueville. In contrast to Macedo and Crapanzano, I argue in *The Transformation of American Religion* that American culture, including secular culture, has so thoroughly shaped religion that, rather than constituting a danger to democracy, religion, in order to survive, has little choice but to adopt the trappings of modern democratic cultural life. Subject to the dictate of the market in souls, it tempers its message to avoid turning off potential customers. Like politicians, clergy praise the wisdom of their flock rather than emphasize their sins. No one wants to be politically incorrect, or at least not excessively so. Religion is a powerful force that shapes how people act and what they believe. So is culture. When the two conflict in America, religion yields more to culture than the other way around.

This message may not be comfortable for secular humanists who continue to distrust religion, but neither is it a comfort to those, such as the theologian Stanley Hauerwas, who wish to imagine religious believers as "resident aliens," a counter-cultural alternative to the moral thinness of American life.[13] Relying in part on my work, Heclo writes that "Americans have arrived at a self-understanding that is religious . . . but also non-absolutist, inclusive, modest, and, above all, nonjudgmental of others." This is not a description of a nation engaged in a furious battle between reason and revelation. We have our arguments, but we do not have anything like the Spanish Inquisition.

Yet having said all this, I wonder if strong religious believers may still pose a problem for democracy, not because their convictions are so strong and sectarian, but because they are so weak and without content. Our culture is a confessional culture: we admire leaders who are sincere even if we pay less attention to what they are sincere about; we praise those who hold strong convictions even if we fear holding strong convictions of our own; we prefer politicians who appeal to our emotions rather than those who call upon us to increase our knowledge; and we want our leaders to be people of faith so that we need not pay that much attention to the policies they pursue. Watch one of the many preachers on a religious television station and then watch a candidate, even a secular one, running for office. The message may—or, in the age of Bush, may not—differ. The style is the same.

If Christianity has shaped democracy, in other words, it is not in the way it did so in the nineteenth century. Then, as Heclo points out, Christian theologians were anxious to establish the importance of autonomy; like Augustine, they understood that the greater the capacity of human beings to lead lives under their own control, the greater the glory of the God who populated the earth with such special creatures. When Christianity was more intellectual, more demanding, more eloquent, more sin-focused, it produced a certain kind of democratic citizen. Abraham Lincoln may not have been much of a conventionally religious person, but the Christianity of his era was indispensable to the magnificence of his rhetoric. Democracy required virtuous citizens, and, as Heclo notes, Christianity satisfied what politics could not offer. There really was a time when "there was a general consensus that reason and revelation overlapped sufficiently—not just for philosophers but for ordinary citizens trying to live decent lives—to make self-government a hopeful, going concern."

That period exists no longer. Contemporary Christianity could not produce Lincolnesque rhetoric because contemporary Christianity—more specifically, the evangelical form that receives so much attention in politics—resembles Oprah Winfrey more than Jonathan Edwards. (To make the implicit point explicit, I am not generalizing about Christianity as a whole here—if I were, I would be making the same mistake I charge Heclo with making—but talking only about evangelical Protestantism in its more generic forms; as I have argued above, there is a generic form of evangelicalism, strongly influenced by American culture, which crosses denominational lines.)[14] To survive in America's highly emotional, exquisitely individualistic, and depressingly anti-intellectual culture, American evangelical Christianity all too often absorbs, rather than confronts, the culture of narcissism. It gives its followers an important sense of empowerment, a sense of place and meaning, and an avenue for recovery from their dilemmas, but the focus—in evangelical forms, the relentless focus—is on what God can do for you, not what you can do for God. It is the small groups, not the large sermons, that count most in today's megachurch. You come out feeling uplifted. You do not come out feeling intellectually challenged.

This matters because, as Heclo is right to insist, Christianity's location in civil society gives it the special task of teaching the morality that makes democracy work. Unfortunately, however, today's Christian morality, even in its conservative evangelical forms, frequently has little to do with—it is in fact the very opposite of—what the classical thinkers meant by virtue. It does not require us to put aside our self-interest in favor of what is good for the whole. It tells us instead that God hears our prayers and knows what is in our hearts. Citizens shaped by this ethic have difficulty adopting the viewpoint of an impartial spectator or engaging with the Kantian categorical imperative because they all too rarely lift up their eyes to consider the needs of people in worlds very different from their own.

The shape of contemporary American Christianity therefore suggests that there are two ways in which reason and revelation can be at odds with each other. One, the traditional version, suggests that religion's dogmatism and sectarianism stand in sharp contrast to reason's requirements of proof and respect for pluralism. This is the conflict between reason and revelation that Heclo's "great denouement" softens. The denouement between reason and revelation posed in this form posits on the one side liberalism as it exists in practice and conservative religion as it exists in theory. When he discusses the relationship between democracy and Christianity in the latter part of his essay, Heclo assumes the role of prophet more than he adopts the tools of the social scientist. He is concerned with the world as Christians imagine it, a world in which absolute truth is compromised by value relativism and in which time-tested traditions are overthrown for personal convenience. His argument is that genuine Christians, those who really take their faith's doctrines seriously and believe in its conception of authority, will be so uncomfortable with the direction American democracy has taken in the wake of the 1960s that they may well come to consider existing political arrangements illegitimate.

But how many such old-fashioned Christians are there in the United States at this time? True, there are influential Christian intellectuals whose disgust with American culture tempts them into withdrawal, if not, at times, to question democracy itself.[15] But it would be wrong, I believe, to generalize from their examples to the revival of conservative Christianity as a whole. Many ordinary Christians—most evangelical ones—are conservative politically and find themselves more comfortable among Republicans than Democrats. But they are not withdrawing in disgust from the larger culture; if anything, the evangelicals flocking into the megachurches are joining America's emotion-laden and personal testifying culture with enthusiasm. For people such as these—conservative Christians in practice rather than in theory—a second, postmodern conflict between reason and revelation emerges. In this one, religion's refusal to judge, its unwillingness to state firm truth claims, and its tendency to blur all theological and doctrinal disputes confront reason from the side of multiple perspectives and epistemological skepticism. Too narcissistic and inward-looking for comfort, evangelicals have more in common with postmodern literary theorists than they know. Both distrust the authority of science and distrust abstract moral philosophical judgment as well.

There are—there have to be—exceptions to the generalization I have just made, and the most important of these is the movement on behalf of intelligent design. Here is the classic confrontation of reason and revelation, the modern-day Scopes trial. Yet even here, one side—the Christian side—refuses to return to Dayton, Tennessee. We are not defending a theological position, they claim; creationism does that but we are not, or so we say, creationists. No, we believers in intelligent design are followers of Thomas Kuhn; we are challenging the dominant paradigm and merely suggesting that good science look for a more explanatory theory. These claims, as it happens, are not true; intelligent design, it was shown during the Dover, Pennsylvania brouhaha, grows directly out of the creationist movement. Still, it tells us much about the form that today's conflict between reason and revelation takes that defenders of the latter will not adopt the language of the former. They argue for revelation in the guise of liberal ideas of fairness and pluralism of viewpoints—a position that, if taken literally, makes them irreligious or, if not taken literally, makes them hypocrites.

There was a "great denouement" to resolve the older conflict between reason and revelation. There is no great denouement to resolve the new one. Whether the resurgence of contemporary American evangelicalism constitutes a new Great Awakening I leave to others to debate. But even it does, this one has borrowed the enthusiasm of earlier awakenings without the content. Like so much else in contemporary America, it is flashy and exciting, but it does not cut especially deep. Between Joel Osteen, the feel-good preacher at Houston's 25,000-member Lakewood Church, and Jonathan Edwards, I would take Jonathan Edwards any day. I think Heclo would as well. But the prophetic form of Christianity upon which Heclo bases his pessimistic conclusions does not exist in sufficient strength to shatter the softening impact that American culture has had on American religion. One can, if one wishes, long for the return of Jonathan Edwards, but he is not coming back anytime soon.

* * *

And so I come to Heclo's conclusions about what will happen to the United States in the wake of the great denouement's failure to bridge the gap between America's secular and religious components.

Although Heclo notes that this failure originated before the 1960s, that decade plays an enormously important role in his analysis. Traditionally, Americans recognized the existence of a democratic realm "where everything was contested and open for innovation," linked to a religious realm that "set firm boundaries" around democratic innovation. But the 1960s changed all that. On the one hand, policy choices expanded, ranging into such personal matters as sexuality and intimacy. On the other, the ability of religion to guide individual moral conduct atrophied. "Reason and revelation in the autonomous religious realm did not agree on basic moral standards for guiding political action," Heclo concludes. Although Heclo agrees with scholars such as Morris Fiorina and myself that Americans themselves are not that polarized, the emerging gap between reason and revelation is fueling a furious and important culture war among elites. They see the country as divided between "the repressive, bigoted morality of Christian theocrats," as one side holds, and "the debauched, godless morality of secular humanists," as the other insists. Without standards to guide us, secular Americans have a Christian problem and American Christians have a democracy problem.

Heclo is not very optimistic that these problems can be resolved. Christians are absolutists, he points out. They do believe in certain truths that exclude others. They do have an allegiance to a higher power than their nation-state. Secular Americans are correct to view Christians with some suspicion (just as Christians are right to view secular Americans as hostile to them). We face "a condition of devout, serious Christians alienated from the quest for democracy, and of devout, serious democrats hostile to Christianity." Our situation more resembles the France that Tocqueville left than the America that greeted him. We Americans may think we are exceptional, but here we are faced with the conflict between reason and revelation that plagued Europe for centuries.

These are indeed dark conclusions, too dark for my own taste. There are, no doubt, many Christians who are absolutist in their convictions and many secularists who genuinely view faithful people as dogmatic sectarians. But the 1960s united Americans far more than they divided them. We should never forget that the 1960s had a spiritual as well as a secular side; large numbers of Americans came to believe in transcendental truths and otherworldly experiences during that decade, and their attachment to spirituality frequently lived on. And by that I do not mean that they became Wiccans and Buddhists. Some of the most conservative evangelical churches in America—for example, Calvary Chapel in California and its many offshoots—directly appealed to the "Jesus people" who emerged out of the 1960s.[16]

At the same time, many conventionally religious people—the category Heclo and others call "traditionalists"—were in fact touched by the individualism of the 1960s. The experience of being born again owes as much to the 1960s as it does to nineteenth-century revivals. By welcoming Jesus into one's life, the believer makes authenticity of experience more important than adherence to creed. As many scholars have noted, there is a rebelliousness in the act of being born again, a willingness to break with custom and authority, an assertion of individual will, a feeling of personal empowerment.[17] Without the 1960s, American Christianity would not have its rock music, its small groups, its insistence on holism, its testimonials and confessions, its home schooling, even its home churching. Christians may hate the drug culture and left-wing politics which they identify with the 1960s. But they are products of that decade, and their expanding numbers have as much to do with how they absorbed some key aspects of the 1960s as they do with rejecting the messages and personalities brought to us by the political and cultural movements of those years.

America, I conclude in contrast to Heclo, does have a Christian problem and it does have a democracy problem. But they are at root the same. Christianity needs to find a way to retain its commitments to authority and truth as Christians toy with individualism and this-worldly preoccupations. Democracy needs to find a way to preserve its sense of accountability and leadership as Americans focus on their own needs and shy away from grand collective enterprises. Christianity and democracy have both been influenced by American culture, and as a result, they share more in common, even in today's more contentious times, than Heclo acknowledges. There are no large numbers of conservative Christians entering into internal exile in the United States because even though the culture may be repulsive to them in some ways, it is extremely attractive in other ways. We as a country can count on our materialism, our individualism, our populism, and our emotionalism to keep us together, however much any lingering differences of doctrine or faith may divide us.

In conclusion, I want to say a word of praise on behalf of Hugh Heclo. Writing about Christianity is a difficult undertaking because any focus on one religion easily runs the risk of ignoring all the others. Some scholars run this risk more than others. One who illustrates the dangers here is Rodney Stark. His book, *The Victory of Reason,* claims that Christianity, and Christianity alone, made possible the emergence of modern science, democracy, and tolerance.[18] Along the way he deals with the contributions of other faiths—Islam's protection of the classical tradition, the Jewish life of the mind—by simply ignoring them. His excuse is that he is concerned only with Christianity because nearly all modern people are Christian. In his hands, a sociological fact is transformed into religious triumphalism.

Heclo also concentrates on Christianity, and for the same reason that Stark does: most Americans are Christian, hence any study of "religion" in American history most focus on the religion that was actually here. Now I have already made my point that Heclo's idea of Christianity is frequently too broad. But let me quickly add how much I admire Heclo for discussing the Christian contribution to democracy without entering into the triumphalism of a Rodney Stark. In part this is because Heclo discusses Christianity's weaknesses as well as its strengths. It is also a result of the appreciation he shows for how Christianity has changed over time; unlike Stark, he does not believe that once Christians made their presence known in the world, democracy was inevitable. Heclo appreciates contingency and recognizes complexity. His Christianity is more real than Stark's because it is more human. And since democracy is human as well, one comes to understand through Heclo's analysis how the faith of real people contributed to the success of an actual political society.

For this reason, it is not inappropriate to conclude that Hugh Heclo's Tocqueville Lecture follows in the spirit of Tocqueville's book. Like Tocqueville, Heclo admires both American Christianity and American democracy without being an apologist for either. It is an impressive accomplishment, one that, for all the criticisms I have offered in this response, represents a huge step in the much-needed direction of reminding political scientists never again to ignore religion the way we had done for far too many decades.

5

RECONSIDERING CHRISTIANITY AND AMERICAN DEMOCRACY

Hugh Heclo

It is unusual to have a chance to write something, read your critics' comments, and then offer a rejoinder—all in the same book. Of course, I welcome the unfair advantage of having the last turn at bat.

However, it is always the reader who truly has the last word. My overriding hope is that what is said in this book will encourage more serious attention to the vital relationship between Christianity and our American democracy. Since it is a relationship between many Americans' Christianity but everybody's democracy the stakes are high. By the term "serious attention" I mean thinking with care, like grown-ups, and not succumbing to the emotional sloganeering that dominates our public shouting matches on this subject. In the prevailing climate of opinionated extremes—a cocksure mutual deafness being the one thing that unites secular and Christian political activists—such thinking is especially hard work. Nonetheless it is important work, because every attempt to interpret our past is also an implicit effort to understand our present and what may lie ahead. That is a very Tocquevillian thing for us to do, and we should try to do it.

It is no exaggeration to say that today's America exhibits something approaching a mirror image of what Tocqueville perceived in the 1830s. In the democracy he saw, the political world was a place where "everything is in turmoil, contested, and uncertain," but it was strictly limited in scope and undergirded by a "moral world [where] everything is classified, coordinated, foreseen and decided in advance" (40). Today one could arguably reverse his descriptors for those two worlds. What Tocqueville said about the moral world ("obedience is passive, though voluntary") is actually truer of our professionally managed political system, where the political class does politics and the mass of ordinary citizens have politics done to them. What he said about the political world ("there is independence, contempt of experience, and jealousy of all authority") is truer of our moral world, where to judge with fixed standards or decide anything in advance is considered undemocratic bigotry. The result is that it seems harder than ever to get our bearings in such a political society, and more important than ever that we should try to do so.

To that end I have sought, perhaps recklessly, to take the large view of a very big subject. Landscape artists have told me that the choice is not always between using a large brush or a small one. With care, one can paint finely with a broad brush, and that is what I have tried to do.

There are many things that have made us who we are, but the phenomena embraced by the two concepts of democracy and Christianity would surely have to be on any reasonable person's shortlist of those things. My working assumption has been that the interaction between the two should be regarded as dynamic rather than static. In other words, there is development arising from both sides—a tensioned, reciprocating influence between this religion and our democracy. Such a developmental perspective is especially important if we hope to use this large view to gain a better understanding of our present condition and what may lie ahead.

In my lecture I began—and ended—with the outlandish idea that the relationship between democratic self-government and Christianity is problematic. It is not what Americans have been taught to see—some foreordained harmony written into the nature of things. Because of his experience in France, Alexis de Tocqueville had a deep appreciation for this ambiguity. And because of his keen insight, Tocqueville could discern how the American experience produced principles helping to resolve that *problématique.* Christianity, separated from the apparatus of political power, could preserve both its essential nature as a religion and its necessary and rightful influence in democracy. Christianity was teaching Americans not simply how to be democratic, but how to sustain ordered liberty in democratic politics as well as how to uphold the spiritual nobility of human beings against the threats of a materialistic, mass democracy.

Tocqueville's insight then led me to examine a deeper development in America, one that had already shaped what he was able to see in the 1830s. This development was a profound historical achievement. It was a general respect, affirmed in law, for each individual's right to religious liberty. Centuries in the making and never fully completed, this Great Denouement of religious-political claims arose more from the advantages of a particular time and place than from some innate American genius for tolerance. Amid deeply felt religious differences, a Protestant political society gradually convinced itself of the truly Christian reasons for, as well as the enlightened political advantages of, liberty of religious conscience. With this achievement, a new space in public life was opened up—a space for freedom of action in the two distinct, though never wholly separate, spheres of religious belief and civil authority. All we have of this religious freedom, so carelessly enjoyed today, was won for us long ago.

My lecture then tried to describe how, after the eighteenth century and well into the twentieth, this free play of Christian beliefs and democratic politics in America set in motion a tensioned, push-pull interaction between these two powerful impulses (eliciting my image of a double helix). To make this twisting story manageable, I focused on the democracy/Christianity interaction with regard to three subjects: ideas of history, the individual, and political society. By the middle of the twentieth century, something like a mutual embrace between American democracy and Christianity had emerged. I argued that this century and a half of reciprocal influence was largely on the plus side of the ledger for American democracy and on the negative side for Christianity, veering toward un-Christian commitments to worldly progress, autonomous self-realization, and idolatrous patriotism.

The complacency, not to say inauthenticity, of this mutual embrace made it vulnerable to fundamental critique and political challenge. This occurred first with the civil rights movement and then with the broader cultural upheaval that became the Sixties. Amid the turmoil of this time, the best historically-minded observers of religion in American public life sensed that a crucial discontinuity was occurring. How and why was this happening? People like Sydney Ahlstrom, William McLoughlin, and the Niebuhr brothers were not sure. And neither am I. The best I can do, noting the similarity and contrast with America's tradition of religious revivalism and awakenings, is to consider the Sixties as a secular awakening. My lecture sketched the development of public doctrine in our schools, courts, and popular culture that laid the groundwork for this upheaval. By the end of the period, Christianity had lost much and perhaps most of its cultural authority.

Within this larger perspective, I turned to our own times. Despite the rise of the so-called Religious Right in politics and glib talk of an "American theocracy" under Republican presidents,[1] the central tendency of our era is an estrangement. It is a growing, reciprocal alienation between Christianity and American democracy. There is a "Christian problem" for what has come to be understood as deliberative democracy. To an even greater extent, there is a "democracy problem" for American Christians who take their faith seriously. These sets of problems are real, and they are playing themselves out in what we can expect to be a growing struggle between secular and religious political elites. Looming ahead are inescapable public policy decisions on issues weighted with human and religious significance. This threatens to turn estrangement into a coming rupture between serious Christians and our secular democracy.

Such is the story I have tried to tell. In response to my presumptuousness in doing so, three scholars whom I admire have commented in a most kindly and tolerant manner. In what follows I will begin with the common theme that unites the criticisms by Mary Jo Bane, Michael Kazin, and Alan Wolfe, and then consider more particular points brought forward in each of their essays. I will conclude by discussing why any American, non-Christian or Christian, should care about this story I am trying to tell.

Is There Any Such Thing as Christianity?

Taken as a whole, the three comments on my lecture raise an extremely important issue: each of these scholars, in his or her own way, suggests that I have spoken too broadly of Christianity, as if it were one thing. Mary Jo Bane rightfully gives sustained attention to the Catholic presence in America. Michael Kazin just as rightly emphases the many divisions and conflicts among all sorts of Christian groups in our history, so much so that he sees it as an error to view "Christianity in the United States as a more or less unified entity that changed little over time." As a good sociologist, Alan Wolfe pushes the point to its limits by telling us that "Christianity is so many things that one generalizes about the whole only at one's peril. . . . Christianity can mean almost anything."

For two reasons, I am very glad that these scholars' essays are appearing together with my lecture in the same volume. First, the three essays describe important complications that need to be appreciated any time we try to talk about Christianity in America. Topics having to do with Catholicism, anti-Catholicism, denominational conflict within Protestantism, variations in liturgy, doctrine, evangelical mission, moral stances—all this and much more needs to be part of the picture. Working on this lecture was like having to drive too fast through a fascinating and beautiful countryside; it was painful but necessary to neglect one thing after another in order to hew to main themes about the Christian religion itself in the American democratic context. But if my so-called lecture was not going to start resembling Ahlstrom's 1100-page tome, *A Religious History of the American People,* there was simply no alternative to pulling down the shades and keeping the accelerator pressed to the floor. Thanks to these three essays, I can now feel less guilty about short-changing so much of the variegated reality that constitutes Americans' experience with Christianity. My drive-by offenses have, at least to some extent, been redeemed.

Second, the general theme of the Bane/Kazin/Wolfe essays unintentionally offers readers a valuable cautionary tale. The notion that Christianity should not be talked about as if it were one coherent thing reveals a widespread academic blind spot that has persistently trivialized discussions of religion. To be sure, as a matter of behavioral description, it makes perfect sense to point out that Christianity in practice has been far less than a single, unified entity. That observation has its critical force against any claim that Christianity is *only* a single, unified entity. I am saying something different, however—namely that along with all the variations amply demonstrated in the historical record, Christianity *is* something. If it were not some thing, we would not be able to identify variations in the thing that it is. While we rightly want to be attentive to the variations, I do not think we should fall into the opposite error of claiming that Christianity is only the sum of its variations.

This is an important point to consider more closely, especially in our American context where Christian denominations have blossomed in bewildering array and where social science has often pursued a secularist agenda contrived to evade the substantive content of religion.

The underlying theme of the three commentaries is not really that I have done too little, but that I have done too much. They are not saying that I should refrain from talking about the whole of a thing until I have talked about all its parts. They are really saying that there is no one whole thing to talk about as regards Christianity in America.

While the other two comments lend support, the underlying logic of such a view is very well presented by Alan Wolfe. Averting our gaze from "the generic thing called 'Christianity,'" as he puts it, we must begin with the differences between Catholicism and Protestantism. From there, we must attend to the differences among the many Protestant denominations. But our journey into sub-Christianities has only just begun: we must now recognize that the divisions *within* each of the many denominations can be as great as are any differences among all Christians. But wait, there is more. In American Christianity, "what counts is not the denomination but the congregation." And yet there is no resting place here, for congregations are themselves divided—or rather pulverized—into individualized commitments, most of them having little to do with theology. And thus we come to how to think about Christianity: "Each American is a church unto himself." In effect, Christianity has been "sociologized" into a descriptive morass of pointillistic differences.

Obviously this is no genuine invitation to think about Christianity, because we are left with nothing to think about. If this religion that came to America is a free-form exercise defined by whatever particular persons calling themselves Christians happen to believe and do at any particular time and place, then there really is nothing of substance in this (or any other) religion to talk about. This is behavioralism in the social sciences run amok. It is also positivism in philosophy and nihilism in theology run amok. Relentlessly subdividing the subject into its descriptive behavioral particularities, we eventually end up with no subject at all. Christianity as such has no coherent content or meaning—so says such religious minimalism.

That is not true. It is not true because we can look over the centuries and see that there actually is a coherent content, indeed a massively coherent content to this religion. A little over twenty years ago Jaroslav Pelikan finished his monumental five-volume work, *The Christian Tradition: A History of the Development of Doctrine.*[2] I suspect that Alan Wolfe and others of like mind might respond: aha—you see, there is no such thing as Christianity. Its doctrines are so varied and changeable that it takes five volumes even to catalogue them. The answer to this objection is to actually study Christianity and what Pelikan demonstrates about its twenty centuries of life. To be sure, he shows that Christianity is something that can be complex and thus susceptible to development and variation. But it is *something*. That is why you can talk about it in so many ways.

Because Christianity does mean a certain thing—above all a certain person—its doctrine can and has developed. Development of doctrine does not mean a substitution of new for old doctrine, or an evasion of past doctrine, or a successful surrender to some outside source. As G. K. Chesterton put it, "When we say a puppy develops into a dog, we do not mean that his growth is a gradual compromise with a cat. We mean that he become more doggy and not less. Development is the expansion of all the possibilities and implications of a doctrine, as there is time to distinguish them and draw them out."[3] In other words, what Pelikan is showing as development is an advance in understanding the application of what is fundamental; it is a fuller comprehension of what was already there. Professor Pelikan was never one to use words carelessly. His title is not "A Christian Tradition," or "Some Christian Traditions." Or "Bunches of Different Things Christians Have Thought." "The" is a definite article, and it means there is one thing in view. In *Credo,* his later book, Pelikan summed up a lifetime of scholarship devoted to articulations of the Christian faith over the last two thousand years.

> The overwhelming impression that any new reader will carry away from reviewing any of the collections of creedal and confessional texts from various historical periods . . . must surely be their sheer repetitiveness. Above all the creeds from

> the period of the early church, and then once again, though this time at much greater length, the confessions from the age of the Protestant Reformation, do seem to be making the same points over and over and over again. . . . The differences between them, which came out of theological controversy and when sent on to spawn still further theological controversy . . . must at least sometimes seem to any modern reader to be so minute as well as so marginal that only a specialist in historical theology would be able to tell the various confessional positions apart. . . . From this declaration of the Book of Acts that "those who received his word were baptized" we may infer that there was a close connection between the early creeds and the preaching of this "word," the primitive Christian proclamation—or, as it has come to be called also in modern English, the "kerygma" . . . Nor is it a great leap to suppose that this stock outline of the kerygma bore a distinct enough resemblance to the creeds that we now have, in whole or in part, to justify our viewing them as reflecting that outline.[4]

Nor is there any lack today of clear, straightforward explications of what this thing called traditional Christianity is, however rich the forms of its is-ness may be.[5]

To all of this the objection can be raised that doctrine is fine, but there are many American Christians who are far from doctrinal. Quite so. One of the themes throughout my lecture is that American Christians, evangelicals and modern Christians in particular, have been less than doctrinal—especially under the pressures of popular democracy. But so what? That supports the view that "Christianity can mean almost anything" only if we fall into the trap of limiting Christianity to a purely descriptive definition derived from whatever people calling themselves Christians happen to be doing at the time. Such description is important, but it is a grievous error to then conclude that this is all Christianity amounts to. Nothing is more dangerous than an error that is almost true, a half-truth pretending to be the whole truth, and this descriptivist claim is such a half-truth. American Christians might not know a doctrine if it bit them, but that does not mean the religion is non-doctrinal. When the stereotypical backwoods fundamentalist puts up a hand-painted sign on his fencepost saying that "JESUS SAVES," behind that little sign is a world of doctrine. Saved from what? Why does anyone need saving? Why can't they save themselves? How does this Jesus save? And who is this guy to be saving anyone? Like the Molière character who did not know he was speaking prose, our non-doctrinaire believer does not know he is speaking soteriology from the fencepost. But he is.

We might turn the issue around and note that the three commentaries have no comparable objection to my generalized use of the term "democracy." This appears to be because the authors, like many other people, presume there is a greater coherent meaning to democracy than to Christianity as such. Again, Alan Wolfe articulates the general position quite clearly. He points out that there are many kinds of democrats, "but certain key features of democracy—popular suffrage, representative government, checks on the executive—are relatively uncontested, at least as political concepts go."

Really? The fact is that it would be quite easy to start subdividing the alleged common core that Alan Wolfe presents into ever finer variations, and so conclude that democracy "can mean almost anything." Checks on the executive—isn't there a fundamental difference between a parliamentary democracy that scarcely dares impose checks and a presidential, separation-of-powers type of democracy? Representative government—hasn't Robert Dahl taught us how recently this idea has attached itself to the concept of democracy, indeed that the origin of the idea of representation is not even democratic?[6] Popular suffrage—what about those who claim that democracy confined to the political sphere and denied in the economic, market-capitalist spheres of life is no democracy at all? If Christianity has no coherent content and meaning because of the descriptive diversity and conflicts among its adherents, then there surely is no meaning to "democracy" either. It is merely the sum of different ways of being "democratic." Some democracies crush people in the name of the "people's democracy," and others celebrate individualism as if there is no common good. I would contend, in fact, that given the intellectually flabby, sloganeering quality of the democratic faith, the Christian faith's strenuously worked out doctrinal content gives it a far stronger claim to being something real.

In the end, the religious minimalists in social science usually do not really seem to mean what they say. They are drawn to recognize that there really is something there. All three commentators indirectly invoke a general concept of Christianity in delineating differences among its adherents. Mary Jo Bane does so along the Catholic/Protestant axis. Michael Kazin does so in picturing pluralist conflict in American religion. And Alan Wolfe, again being the most explicit, takes the argument all the way over to the other side; in the last third of his comments, it appears there really is such a thing as Christianity. In this vein he wonders if "strong religious believers may still pose a problem for democracy, not because their convictions are so strong and sectarian, but because they are so weak and without content." Religious minimalism now laments that "contemporary Christianity resembles Oprah Winfrey more than Jonathan Edwards." It appears that this Alan Wolfe is attacking the Alan Wolfe who told us earlier that there is scarcely any such thing as Christianity, speaking doctrinally or otherwise. To be fair, he tells us that he is not generalizing about Christianity but speaking only about "evangelical Protestantism in its more generic forms." That is a nice sideways move, but it does not overcome the fact that in the background is a standard to which the author is holding "generic" evangelical Protestants (not evangelical Catholics?). He says something is wrong with a contemporary Christianity that absorbs rather than confronts the culture of narcissism, a Christianity that focuses on what God can do for you and not what you can do for God. Now we are told that there is something deeply flawed in a postmodern Christian evangelicalism that fails to state firm truth claims, that blurs all theological and doctrinal distinctions, and even that refuses to judge! If Christianity can mean almost anything, as the first Alan Wolfe maintains, how can the second Alan Wolfe claim there is anything wrong with a contemporary Christianity, evangelical or otherwise, that does these or any number of other mutually contradictory things outside the Christian tradition? He concludes that we do have a Christian problem in this country. It is that "Christianity needs to find a way to retain its commitments to authority and truth as Christians toy with individualism and this-worldly preoccupations." With the second half of that sentence sucking the meaning out of the first half, both Alan Wolfes apparently want to have it both ways. My conclusion is that the second Alan Wolfe has the better of the argument.

A Closer Look at the Comments

To restate what has sometimes only been implied up to this point, I have been honored by the gracious comments in the three preceding essays. It would be a serious mistake to read my lecture and not to read the three insightful responses of Mary Jo Bane, Michael Kazin, and Alan Wolfe. Each in its own way helps us gain a more rounded view of the subject.

Mary Jo Bane demonstrates how important it is to pay special attention to Catholicism in any consideration of Christianity in America. She points out that in the first place, the small number of Catholics in the early Republic had neither the strength nor the opportunity to pursue the Catholic Church's official opposition to religious liberty of conscience and separation of church and state. This adds support to the more general point presented in my lecture regarding America's historical advantage in dealing with the problem of religion and politics. The colonies' struggle over religious liberty occurred in marked isolation from European power struggles and in the late Reformation era, when a kind of mutual exhaustion, as well as some useful social learning about the advantages of religious toleration, had occurred.

Nonetheless, even in America's earliest years Catholics were making a more positive contribution to the learning of liberty than simply being weak and few in number. Since at least 1636, there has always been a Catholic minority in America. One estimate puts their number at 30,000 out of an American population of 3 million in 1790, a proportion that is roughly double that of Muslims in the United States today. Supplemented by French clerics escaping persecution, the nation's Catholic population before the Irish immigration was mainly English, well-educated, and socially prominent. The patriot and drafter of the seminal 1776 Virginia Declaration of Rights, George Mason, could marry a Catholic without occasioning negative comment. The point is that from the outset, Americans had the benefit of living with a Catholic minority that accepted all the essentials of English-American culture while remaining loyal to their Catholic faith, people who were "truly Catholic and truly American according to the times."[7]

In Bane's account, the contribution of Catholicism to American democracy appears again with the surge of Catholic immigration after the early 1840s. Again, it is a rather negatively formulated contribution. Given the Catholic Church's official hostility to liberal democracy, this large new contingent of religionists was a potential problem. However, as she says, the problem was defused by rivalry between German and Irish Catholics, by the moderation American Catholic leaders had to exercise in achieving political power in their urban strongholds, and by the creation of separate institutions for a Catholic subculture.

All of this makes sense. One can argue, however, that this "problem-solving" strategy of a Catholic subculture had a downside for American democracy. When Catholics boycotted public institutions because "public" meant Protestant, voices with important things to say about the American condition turned inward and were not heard; this was especially true with regard to the social teachings of the church and the moral challenges posed by unfettered capitalism. Likewise, Protestants could dress up their anti-Catholicism with a doctrine of separation of church and state in the public schools. All this opened the way for public schools to drift into a hard-edged secularism. As one scholar of American Catholicism has astutely observed, more constructive leadership from both Protestants and Catholics might have found a way to use federalism (as Germany did) to allow state support for both Catholic and Protestant schools.[8] Our current muddled "neutrality" doctrine of church/state relations might have been the better for it. It is at least worth considering.

Mary Jo Bane next invites us to appreciate how American democracy has been good for Catholic Christianity by encouraging changes in official Church doctrine to favor free exercise of religion and separation of church and state. With two qualifications, I agree this was a positive development.

First, it may be a little misleading to rely on the future Pope Benedict XVI when he commends the American experience of the non-state church "as a Christian form that emerged from the very nature of the Church." My lecture seeks to correct the future Pope (a certain shamelessness is required in my line of work) by taking a larger perspective than that provided by the Church. I try to show that the American contribution was affirming individual religious liberty and a non-state church as "a Christian form" that emerged, not from "the Church," but from the very nature of the religion itself.

Second, I think we would do well to recognize that, even in this positive development of doctrine, there were some downsides for Catholic Christianity. In the wake of Vatican II there was a popular sense that since the Church changed its official teaching on religious liberty and church/state relations, why not do this on other unpopular issues as well? There was continuing pressure to radicalize 1965's *Dignitatis Humanae*. Hence the shock at what Mary Jo Bane calls a failure of Church leaders to learn from and respect the insights of the laity in Vatican pronouncements on birth control. That is only one indicator that many American Catholics are wanting more of the Protestant-style autonomy and less of the traditional guided morality that is supposed to characterize the Catholic community. This is another democracy problem for Catholic Christianity that is not going to go away.

This brings us to the essay's concluding thoughts, which concern what I have called the "coming rupture" between American democracy and orthodox Christianity. Mary Jo Bane is hopeful in seeing two "moderating influences" from the Catholic side regarding this possible danger. But it seems to me that these influences can just as easily be read to support my worries.

As Bane's essay points out, centrist Catholics (7 percent of the electorate) were an important swing vote in the 2004 election, and despite conservative Catholic appeals on non-negotiable human life policy issues, 55 percent of these centrist Catholics voted for Bush on the basis of something other than the non-negotiable moral issues. However, it is also true that more "conservative," observant Catholics *were* apparently influenced by such moral issues and voted even more disproportionately for the Protestant Bush and against their fellow Catholic, JFK II. That larger story of the 2004 election supports the point in my lecture about a possible rupture fueled in part by a split between traditionalist and non-traditionalist wings of Protestant and Catholic denominations alike.

Finally, Bane finds portents of moderating influence in Benedict XVI's first encyclical on the subject of love. With respect, I think that we are misconstruing the message if we think that the commitment to love will mean avoiding what she might consider doctrinal rigidity and what others call the condemnation of error regarding the fundamental teachings of the Catholic Church. As head of the Congregation for the Doctrine of the Faith, Joseph Ratzinger—or as she calls him, "the enforcer of orthodoxy"—was Pope John Paul II's man and not a way of balancing the Vatican ticket with Karol Wojtyla's kinder, gentler papacy. Both men have been fully committed to enforcing Catholic doctrinal orthodoxy against all worldly pressures, whether from the dark side of fascist and communist oppression or from the shiny bright side of liberal, democratic majoritarianism. After the fall of communism, a number of people were shocked to learn that Pope John Paul II was not the evangelizer of democracy, but the evangelizer of Gospel truth to which the will of democracy should be subordinate.[9]

As the 2002 Doctrinal Note from Cardinal Ratzinger's office put it, "The Church recognizes that while democracy is the best expression of the direct participation of citizens in political choices, it succeeds only to the extent that it is based on a correct understanding of the human person. Catholic involvement in political life cannot compromise on this principle."[10] I suspect that John Paul II and Benedict XVI will be found to have a single great theme in their papacies—the inalienable dignity and value of the human person, created in the image of God. Hence such "non-negotiables" in the 2004 election on abortion, euthanasia, cloning, stem cell research. And hence John F. Kerry's problem.

In 2003, even the U.S. Conference of Catholic Bishops (not always a pillar of orthodox rigidity) had this to say about "the faithful citizen":

> Politics should be about fundamental moral choices. . . . It calls Catholics to bring their moral convictions to public life. . . . The faithful citizen is called to test public life by the values of Scripture and the principles of Catholic social teaching. . . . He and she are called to participate in building the culture of life. . . . A consistent ethic of life should be the moral framework from which to address issues in the political arena. . . . Catholics in politics must reflect the moral values of our faith with clear and consistent priority for the life and dignity of the human person, defending human life from conception until natural death and in every condition.
>
> . . . we cannot accept an understanding of pluralism and tolerance that suggests every possible outlook on life is of equal

> value. . . . the legitimate freedom of Catholic citizens [is] to choose among the various political opinions that are compatible with faith and the natural moral law.[11]

It appears to me that for the development of doctrine that Mary Jo Bane hopes to see, there is much disappointment awaiting her. Nonetheless, she is absolutely correct in saying that Catholic theologians have done much of the intellectual work for orthodox Christianity over the centuries. An alliance of co-belligerency between traditionalist Catholics and Protestants has been emerging in our time, and I very much share her hope that Catholic thinkers will develop a "theology of engagement" to help form the conscience of that alliance.

Given Michael Kazin's deep knowledge of populism and American culture, I can certainly understand why he thinks I have spent too much time on "the consensus side of the street." He offers much evidence to show that I have understated the religious conflicts in our history which, together with various points of consensus, have produced a dialectic of development that "both liberates and traps" us.

I would not presume to put myself in the company of the admirable Richard Hofstadter, whom Kazin cites as a model. I would contend, however, that the organizing theme of my whole lecture is exactly the kind of tensioned relationship of consensus and conflict that Hofstadter espoused. It is on these grounds that I picture a double-stranded helix, an image of reciprocal, equivocal contestations of Christianity and democratic politics twisting together through time. Moreover, I describe the development as becoming more conflictual, to the point of being a helix whose two strands are coming apart in the last half of the twentieth century. I think that this amounts to more than my just strolling down the consensus side of the street.

It is true, however, that I spend little time talking about the particular conflicts that Michael Kazin identifies:

- The nineteenth-century conflict between Protestants and immigrant Catholics (though I do highlight the deeper struggle between their contending views of church-state relations, as well as the contrast between Protestant individualism and Catholic social thought).
- The divergent political party alignments of religious groups (but I do point out how, and why, Tocqueville was oblivious to that development).
- The Jewish contribution to America's cultural pluralism (I do cite an exchange between a Jewish supporter and President Washington, because I think it says something important about the cultural pluralism fostered by what I call the Great Denouement concerning religious freedom).
- The racial divide in American religion and politics (although I do discuss the civil rights movement growing out of black churches as the last of our traditional religious revivals, and I use Martin Luther King's words to point out the racial hypocrisy of mid-twentieth-century white churches).

It might well be added that I also do not focus on conflict over gender issues among religious groups, the never-ending fights among Baptists, schisms caused by the charismatic movement, and the like. The reason I don't spend time on these and other conflicts is that they are subjects that have been well worked over. There is a farmer's saying that there's no use plowing a field that has already been harrowed. And academics seem prone to be forever pulverizing the same ground. To keep doing that is the kind of dialectic that really does entrap our thinking.

Especially in light of current religious conflicts in the world, the striking thing about America's religious-political conflicts of the last 200 years is how rarely they centered on religious issues as such. I would contend that by contrast, Americans were more religiously divided in the years prior to 1800 than at any time since. This is not because there were huge numbers of Catholics, or non-Christians, or even a large number of Protestant denominations. It was because the religious differences within colonial Christianity were deeply felt, doctrinally sharp, and politically explosive. Good Puritan congregations could beat and kill Quakers. The young James Madison had his passion for religious liberty stirred by events such as local beatings and the imprisonment of unlicensed Baptist preachers at the hands of Anglican authorities.

By the time of Tocqueville's visit, things had changed. Catholics had always been in America and had come to be generally accepted. The conflicts associated with Irish immigration were less about their Catholicism than about the political, economic, and ethnic challenges these new people presented. The same was true of the Mormons and their persecution from Missouri onwards. Likewise, the "scandal of division" that grew with Protestant denominationalism had less to do with the Christian religion than with forces of race, class, region, and ethnicity.[12] Thanks in large part to the consensus on religious liberty, our nation's "religious" conflicts were only faintly religious. The Great Denouement was a great blessing which we Americans today too often take lightly.

In the same way, one could spend a great deal of time talking about the allegedly "religious" conflicts inflaming today's so-called culture war. However, as I tried to show in my lecture, we should look below the surface of competing publicists' self-serving hyperbole on this subject. When we do, what we mainly find is politicians *using* religion, not religious conflicts driving our politics. Few Americans care about the venerable religious differences over Christology, the means of salvation, infant baptism, and the like. To be sure, religious cleavages in American society and the impact of those cleavages on elections remain important, but they have remained important and largely unchanged for at least the last quarter-century.[13] Christian Americans, and even conservative white Protestant Christian Americans, are a many-splintered thing, but they can be organized as "values voters." That work is done by professional political managers who are adept at such organizing and manipulation. They are not busying themselves in simply upholding the Christian tradition, which by biblical standards would have to give equal time to preaching against divorce, greed, fornication, and indifference to the poor. Both conservative and liberal sides in the culture war have a vested interest in misrepresentation. As Greeley and Hout put it, "If they can puff up the otherness of the opposition, they can rally their base. And by exaggerating how strange the religious right is, demagogues can assure themselves that they will run afoul of very few real people." Typically, what is at issue is not religion but which side is more skilled at the demagoguery.[14]

Instead of replowing all this old ground, I spent a great deal of time in my lecture talking about a conflict that has been underappreciated and that is growing. This conflict strikes at the fundamentals of our culture and political development. It is portentous enough to suggest an emerging rupture between American democracy and Christianity. Given the significance of this conflict, I do not think it leaves me spending too much time dwelling on consensus.

As for being episodic in my treatment (although I would prefer to call them points of inflection rather than episodes), I should plead guilty, at least in part. The alternative to being episodic is to be continuous, and without exceeding my original guidelines by several hundred thousand words, and extending the lecture to several days in length, that was not possible. However, where I think it matters most—over the centuries that produced our crucial doctrine of religious liberty and over the decades in trying to understand the turmoil of the Sixties—I have tried to sketch the ligatures of a long-term, continuous development of forces. On the latter subject in particular, I have tried to show a continuity of forces that came to fruition in what amounted to a secular awakening when the 1960s became the Sixties. I call this continuous line (with apologies to John Henry Cardinal Newman) the development of doctrine regarding democratic and religious faiths. Its description spans more than half of the twelve decades which Michael Kazin suggests I essentially ignored.

For the subject at hand, there is much that deserves to be ignored. By focusing too heavily on conflicts between Catholic Christianity versus Protestant Christianity, or some Protestant Christianities versus others, we risk overlooking the role of mere Christianity itself in American democracy. Likewise, the challenge posed by modern popular sovereignty, especially through policies regarding the fundamental meaning of human life, is not posed to Protestantism or Catholicism but to orthodox Christianity. If we do not see that, we will indeed remain stuck in the tired categories of the past in analyzing American political development. Americans can be Americans without being Christians, but heretofore they have not been able to be Americans without being heavily influenced by their nation's essentially Christian background.

Alan Wolfe's research and books are always teaching me new things, and I very much appreciate his kind comments. But I am afraid I am going to have to begin by trying to escape his embrace. If, as he says, he begins his course by claiming there is no such thing as religion, this is certainly not the thought I was trying to express at the outset of my lecture. What I did say is that religion as such has not been important in American political development, but rather it has been a particular religion called Christianity that has mattered.

Contrary to Wolfe's point of departure, I happen to believe there really is such a thing as religion. The fact that human beings in all times and places have offered different and muddled expressions about this thing suggests to me that we are more likely to be talking about something that is real, even if beyond humankind's poor efforts to grasp it, rather than something that just happens to be made up. This is why I begin my course on "Religion and Politics" with Rudolf Otto's wonderful little book, *The Idea of the Holy.* It does seem that in beautifully diverse ways, human nature is inherently religious. Rather than viewed as a flaw in our rational mind, a reverential religious mentality can be seen as a way to ensure that our public life is authentically human.[15]

Alan Wolfe then goes on to object that I do not follow through on Christianity with what I never said about religion: namely, I fail to realize that there is also hardly any such thing as Christianity. This issue has been discussed above in light of all three essays and need not be repeated here. Wolfe is surely correct that a person generalizes about Christianity only at one's peril, but I am willing to risk that peril, whatever it might be. I feel less imperiled when he goes on to say that what my overgeneralizations "lose in precision they gain in insight." A little less precision for a little more insight? This seems to me to be a very good trade-off.

Wolfe then raises the particular objection that my view of Christianity is too general to explain Americans' exceptional view of history, since Europe was also Christian and did not develop this same millennial view. Here I think he misses the point, because we have to compare the general with the general and the particular with the particular.

In fact, America and Europe did develop the same *general* view of history as linear and progressive, and this is because they did come from the same Judeo-Christian heritage. But they both also developed their own *particular* secularized—I would say bastardized—version of this heritage. In Europe it took the particular form of ideologies of progress such as positivism, socialism, Marxism, and later fascism—all aping the religious idea of a millennial purification of the world. In America this secularized religion of Progress took on a different particularity—partly because it came out of a particular branch of Protestantism and partly because it did so in the very process of forming the nation. The vision became attached to the idea of the nation itself.

The larger point remains that Christianity—the thing itself—has no philosophy of history or historical progress. What it has, and all it can have, is a theology of history. Karl Lowith, a secular

Jew, understood this better than many American Christians ever have. As he put it, "What the Gospels proclaim is never future improvements in our earthly condition but the sudden coming of the Kingdom of God in contradistinction to the existing kingdom of man." Reinhold Niebuhr extended the point by observing that "the New Testament never guarantees the historical success of the 'strategy' of the Cross."[16] With the strategy of vicarious suffering out of love for others comes the promise only of "tribulation in this world." But far from a message of doom and gloom, this is immediately followed by the word of joy: "Be of good cheer. I have overcome the world" (John 16:33). It is difficult to think of anything that is more un-Christian than to expect earthly happiness in some progressive age as a reward for godly living.

History aside, Alan Wolfe and I agree that today our modern democratic culture is shaping Christianity more than the other way around, and that it has been doing so for a long time. As noted earlier, he would like Christians to be more like Christians, that is, committed to authority and truth, even as they continue to "toy with individualism and this-worldly preoccupations"—a comfortable-sounding pilgrim journey. And since the same cultural forces affecting Christianity also affect our democracy, he thinks this democracy "needs to find a way to preserve its sense of accountability and leadership." On the whole, his is a rather contented view. There is nothing to be said about the terrible policy choices Americans will have to make affecting the very meaning of humanity. As a democracy, we "can count on our materialism, our individualism, our populism, and our emotionalism to keep us together." I suppose the question would be, keep us together as what—a collection of materialistic individuals driven by popular appeals to our emotions? Is that a formula for the long-term survival of democratic self-government?

From his concluding remarks, it actually would seem that Wolfe is more worried about American Christianity than American democracy. I am worried about both. What I call the coming rupture concerns a growing possibility that democracy and anything like a genuine Christianity will wholly disengage from each other. Alan Wolfe finds my conclusions "too dark" for his taste. They are also too dark for my taste, but that is irrelevant since any analysis, one hopes, is something more than a matter of personal taste preferences. Despite his preferential taste for the virtues of aristocracy, Tocqueville would certainly have been troubled by the idea of such a rupture, and so should any American, whatever his and her religious affiliation or lack thereof. I will conclude by trying to explain why.

Why Should We Care?

I have argued that, as this new century continues, there is the realistic possibility of a growing disengagement between American democracy and traditional Christianity. Should Christians care? Should non-Christian citizens care? Let us consider each in turn.

At first glance, traditionalist Christians would seem to be the last ones we should think of worrying about. Such people take their faith very seriously and this, as they would have it, means being fully committed to "the faith as received" from the eyewitness apostles in the earliest days of their religion. In any ongoing rupture with America's democratic regime, these Christians will essentially find themselves in a position similar to that of their earliest compatriots in the days of the Roman Empire. They will be one faith among many in a large, sophisticated world empire that is secular but nominally religious, spiritually-seeking in general but well-distanced from the truth claims of Christian revelation in particular. Believers may not turn their homes into virtual monasteries, but as dispersed groups they will form little enclaves trying to hold at bay the influences of public schools, the media, and general culture. Contrary to the hyped fear-mongering of today's televangelists, what they will face is more likely to be pervasive indifference and dismissal as anti-modernists rather than any outright persecution. Insofar as their congregations contain traditionally orthodox Christians, the once hostile forces of Protestantism and Catholicism—each of which a few centuries ago considered the other to be non-Christian—will recognize their kinship in the face of this secular, nominally religious society of seekers.[17] Although such old-fashioned Christians will sense they have little in common with other Americans, the alienation in question will produce a "persecution" that is mostly psychological. Still, I suspect some writer of popular biblical prophecy will discover that these traditionalist remnants within the Protestant and Catholic branches of Christianity are really the Bible's two last witnesses who are foretold to finish their testimony and then be killed by the beast that ascends out of the bottomless pit. Cobelligerency will mean, as prophesied, the two witnesses' dead bodies being left in the street of the great city, "which spiritually is called Sodom and Egypt" (Revelation 11:3–8). A highly profitable book and movie deal will no doubt follow.

The more sober truth is that orthodox Christianity would suffer from such a withdrawal into internal exile in this country. My original essay emphasizes that neither the legal doctrine of church/state separation nor the Christian doctrine of following a king whose reign is not of this world has made religion irrelevant to American politics. From the beginning of our nation, a conditional, non-idolatrous attachment to America has offered Christians committed to their first love an ongoing opportunity to turn their words into deeds. Free to follow the charge of being light and salt in their Master's cause, they have helped make America a source of hope for others. That hope is for justice, freedom, and above all love, things that do not seem to occur naturally in this world. In not pursuing that hope (even while duly noting all that discretion requires concerning attachments to worldly powers), American Christians would be diminished as resident pilgrims in the time and place to which they have been called. Without idolatry toward either, Christians can love their country as they love their neighbor. As one Christian writer has indelicately put it, "Calling ourselves 'a peculiar people' or 'resident aliens' should not become a religiously sanctioned way of giving the finger to our neighbors."[18] Disengagement from American democracy would produce just such a result, and it is something about which Christian believers should certainly worry. Properly discerned, giving an un-civic finger is an un-Christian thing to do.

Fair enough. But why should non-religious or nominally religious citizens care if orthodox Christians have such a serious problem with American democracy that they essentially withdraw? As good democrats engaged in deliberative discourse, aren't we all better off if religious fundamentalists do drop out of public life?

These are valid questions, but they are also too generic for our purposes. They draw us into an unhelpful loop of abstractions about "religion and politics." To return to the opening theme of my lecture, we need to attend to such questions in view of the particular religion that has been integrally related to American political development. Christianity is the religion which some fraction of Americans are likely to be "fundamentalist" about. The issue is whether non-Christians, or the immensely larger number of nominal American Christians, should want citizens who are trying to live their lives fully faithful to the Christian tradition to be an active part of the American democratic future.

Tocqueville's insights start us down the path to see compelling reasons why we should. Those reasons focus on the connection between individual character and the societal prospects for a healthy democracy. American Christians, like all other Christians before them, fail to live up to the ideals of their religion (as expressed in the person of Jesus). But we may all fail even more disastrously if we attempt to live without those ideals in our midst. In at least four crucial ways, traditional Christianity is one important force that can help teach "the art of being free."

First, as Tocqueville pointed out, traditional Christianity comes with an elemental moral code that helps stabilize and order an otherwise chaotic democratic society. It teaches people to be honest rather than lie, to be fair rather than cheat, to keep rather than break promises, to shun selfishness, and all the rest. Of course, there are many citizens who try to behave morally without the Christian God, or any god at all. And certainly there are many immoral Christians. The point is that traditional Christianity makes it its business to ferret out religious hypocrisy. Given the temptations to misuse freedom, it is likely one will be surrounded by a democratic society that simply works better if it has citizens in it who not only try to do the right thing but who know why, because of the teachings of their religion, they are under a personal and higher obligation to actually do it.

Second, the packet of moral imperatives that comes with traditional Christianity includes obligations that regularly lead such citizens to do good works for others. Of course non-religious people often do the same. Again, the point is that Christians are likely to bring a special commitment and energy to such work as a commandment of their creed. To love is a command, not an option. As the British atheist Roy Hattersley has pointed out in reviewing responses to recent natural disasters, if suffering human beings have to wait for atheists and agnostics rather than religious believers for help, they are likely to wait a very long time.[19] Christianity teaches that good works do not get you into heaven. But good works are likely to come from people who believe there is a heaven and that it is their real home. People who have been taught to believe that love is even greater than faith and hope are likely to be people who impart a benevolent, civilized tone to democratic society.

The third factor is the reforming impulse that traditional Christianity carries into society. The religion envisions itself not as a collection of isolated individuals, but as communities of personal attachment sharing a spiritual vision that is meant to be deployed in the world. Here people learn arts of association that, as Tocqueville would say, keep individuals from being atomized and lost in the democratic world of equality. But it goes beyond that. Of the many types of groups making up civil society, the church of Christ is one dedicated—again by the content of its creed—to pursuing a moral vision of the larger society. The inherent tendency is to bring an ethical awareness to every subject, not just abortion and homosexuality but also the environment, scientific research, taxation, and everything in between. The fact that in contemporary America one hears more from Christians on the political "right" rather than the "left" of such issues does not vitiate the general point. The perspective of the Christian mind is inherently reformist and ameliorating, and the positive contributions stemming from this perspective can be spelled out in detail and at great length.[20] Thus Christianity can serve as a democratically valuable force for both stability and ongoing reform.

Finally, once we disabuse ourselves of the heresy of fideism—that is, confining religion to the realm of irrational blind faith—it is clear that Christianity can help preserve the role of reason in democratic discourse about humankind's most fundamental issues. Traditional Christianity holds that faith and reason are not only compatible but essential to each other. In the heat of partisan argument, it is easy for the public to forget that secularist views also start from "unproven premises." Everyone engaged in the great conversation of democracy is arguing for courses of action that are elaborated conclusions built on faith in something or other. If that faith is purely in human reason itself, Christianity asks: is it reasonable to make such a "leap of faith"?

Traditional Christianity insists that we reason about who man is. Like every religion, it claims to have the crucial answers to the big questions of human existence. In the American context, Christianity's contentions help to limit the ultimate arbitrariness of democratic sovereignty by arguing that all is not permitted and man cannot do whatever he wills.[21] And so we return to the worry that lay behind Tocqueville's search for insight into the American experience. Democratic man is pointed in the direction of becoming wholly materialistic, shortsighted, and self-absorbed. Drunk with the sovereignty of his own will, he risks becoming disoriented and psychologically adrift to the point of being willing to give up his very liberty for security. Without transcendent moral reference points for ordering personal and public life, democratic societies will become debauched and alienated from what is most human. This was the worry of Alexis de Tocqueville, and it should worry twenty-first-century Americans as well. Non-believers may not believe the Christians' answers, but a democratic society is surely better off for having to confront the Big Questions rather than pretending they do not exist. Without a strong, publicly engaged Christian presence, America will become a different and not a better place.

But what about the danger for American democracy posed by Christians in the "public square" who claim to be fully convinced, through faith, of God's commandments to do this and to refrain from doing that? I have spoken about that worry in my lecture, but perhaps too abstractly, or maybe too politely. To automatically jam traditionalist, Bible-believing Christians into the category of arrogant, self-righteous, God-is-on-our-side religious prigs in politics is—what shall we say? Arrogant, self-righteous, willfully ignorant secular priggery? In the lecture I spoke of the "prophetic stance" in traditional Christianity, so well discussed by Glenn Tinder.[22] This is far from a call to act with self-righteous certainty in the world's affairs. In putting Babylon on notice, it is also a call that is supposed to put all Christians on a continuous and self-critical watch, demanding to know if they themselves are a prideful and prospering part of the city's wickedness. It lays a finger on the enlivening Christian pulse that has throbbed now for some two millennia, from the sincere worries of today's Christians active in politics, back through the Puritans and the Reformation controversies, through the medieval Catholic reform movements, into the Christian schisms of late antiquity, thence to the Church Councils of Roman Emperor Constantine, and finally back to the original questions of Jesus' Jewish disciples asking their mysterious, risen Jewish teacher when the earthly Jewish kingdom would be restored. His answer, suitably superior to human questioning, was that these truest of first believers were not to know such things. Rather they should get on, when empowered by God's Holy Spirit, with telling other people everywhere in the world what they had seen and experienced. And then, saying no more, this Jesus left them to carry on (Acts 1:6–9).

If it is truly growing out of such a Jewish/Christian tradition, the prophetic stance of today's Christians should have little to do with God-is-on-our-side politics. It should have everything to do with an are-we-on-God's-side politics of self-examination. For traditional Christians, every action that engages the allurements of the world, above all the grand temptation of political power and pride, should by the terms of this religion itself evoke humility, questioning, and doubt—not about God, but about one's own self-righteousness and capacity for self-deception. People with that sensibility, whether citizens or government officials, are a healthy presence in American democracy.

Believing Christians believe they know something—the essential, invaluable, big something—but they are assured by their own sacred texts that they do not know everything, and should act accordingly. While their belief in the truth of their religion may be annoying to others, traditionalist Christians who sincerely try to live out their faith are not people we should want to see retreat from active citizenship. In fact, they make for the kind of companions we should all like to have on board a wandering ship of state as it navigates dark seas. Insofar as they are sincere believers, Christians are likely to be the kind of shipmates who think, like the seventeenth-century Puritan Richard Baxter, "In necessary things, unity; in disputed things, liberty; in all things, charity." One could do much worse by way of fellow passengers.

Notes

Acknowledgments

About the Authors

Index

NOTES

1. Christianity and Democracy in America

1. James W. Ceaser, *Nature and History in American Political Development* (Cambridge, Mass.: Harvard University Press, 2006), 5, 97, 124–126.
2. Reasonable estimates are that, statistically, Protestants moved from near-complete dominance in the colonial and Revolutionary periods to roughly 80 percent of the American population in 1840 and then by 1860 to something around 60 percent, where Protestantism has since remained. William R. Hutchison, "Discovering America," in William R. Hutchison, ed., *Between the Times: The Travail of the Protestant Establishment in America, 1900–1960* (Cambridge, Mass.: Harvard University Press, 1989), 304 and 309, note 3.
3. A discussion of the secularist ideology's approved routes to democratic modernity can be found in David Martin, *On Secularization: Towards a Revised General Theory* (London: Ashgate, 2005).
4. Alexis de Tocqueville, *Democracy in America,* ed. J. P. Mayer and Max Lerner, trans. George Lawrence (New York: Harper and Row, 1966), 286. All subsequent page references and quotations from *Democracy in America* refer to this edition.
5. Peter Gay, *The Enlightenment: An Interpretation* (New York: W. W. Norton, 1995), chap. 7.
6. While Tocqueville frequently uses the generic term "religion," the contexts indicate he is usually thinking of Christianity when he does so. The important exceptions occur when he discusses religion existentially in terms of the universal human yearning for transcendent meaning; he sees all religion as a form of hope natural to the human heart, and its denial as an aberrational distortion of intellect, soul, and human nature itself (409–410). For the most part, however, Tocqueville is explaining his conviction "that at all costs Christianity

must be maintained among the new democracies." *Democracy in America,* 517.

7. André Jardin, *Tocqueville: A Biography* (New York: Farrar, Straus and Giroux, 1988).
8. Alexis de Tocqueville, *The Old Regime and the French Revolution,* trans. Stuart Gilbert (Garden City, N.Y.: Doubleday, 1955), 15.
9. *Democracy in America,* 37. Thus in urging the distinction between elements of Puritan versus English origin, Tocqueville sees the former as accounting for the large sweep of America's democratic landscape, while the elements of English origin consist of relics of aristocratic institutions that can be unexpectedly found in that landscape (41–42).
10. Ibid., 38. Later, Tocqueville becomes more sarcastic toward those "pedants" in Europe who declare the religious spirit Tocqueville admires to be a barrier to Americans' freedom and happiness. "To that I have really no answer to give, except that those who talk like that have never been in America and have never seen either religious peoples or free ones. So I shall wait till they come back from a visit to America" (270).
11. Joshua Mitchell, *The Fragility of Freedom* (Chicago: University of Chicago Press, 1995), 190.
12. "In the United States even the religion of most of the citizens is republican, since it submits the truths of the other world to private judgment, as in politics the care of their temporal interests is abandoned to the good sense of the people. Thus every man is allowed freely to take that road which he thinks will lead him to heaven, just as the law permits every citizen to have the right of choosing his own government" (364).
13. John G. West, Jr., *The Politics of Revelation and Reason* (Lawrence: University Press of Kansas, 1996), 1–3. In his account of "A Fortnight in the Wilds," Tocqueville does offer a brief report of a frontier revival meeting but seems unaware of political implications of such religious enthusiasm in even the most remote parts of America. Appendix V, *Democracy in America,* 745–746. The fictional letter of Tocqueville's younger sister criticizing his failure to report the mixture of religion in American government deserves repeating: "The phenomena I have just reviewed—the commitment in state constitutions to the public worship of God and the enforcement of this obligation by sabbatarian legislation; the use of public funds to endow churches, maintain ministries, commission missionaries, and benefit

religious education; the control of public education by the clergy; the enforcement of a decent respect for the deity and the principal tenets of Christianity by the criminal law; and the submission of the entire sexual life of the Americans to commandments derived from Christian Scripture—point in another, more worldly direction. My brother wrote, just before he ventured upon his analysis of the role of religion in America, 'The principal aim of this book has been to make known the laws of the United States.' It is evident that the bulk of the laws bearing upon religion were omitted from his account." John T. Noonan Jr., *The Lustre of Our Country* (Berkeley: University of California Press, 1998), 110.

14. Alfred Stepan, "Religion, Democracy, and the 'Twin Tolerations,'" *Journal of Democracy,* 11:4 (2000), 37–57.
15. Glenn Tinder, "Can We Be Good Without God?" *The Atlantic Monthly,* 264:6 (1989), 68–82, and *The Political Meaning of Christianity* (Baton Rouge: Louisiana State University Press, 1989), 8.
16. Peter Brown, *The Rise of Western Christendom,* 2nd ed. (Malden, Mass.: Blackwell, 2003), 174–176.
17. This is "the gospel" which Paul says he received and delivered to others. I Corinthians 15:3–8.
18. Jean-Jacques Rousseau, *On the Social Contract,* ed. Roger D. Masters (New York: St. Martin's Press, 1978), 130–131.
19. John T. Noonan, Jr., *Religious Freedom* (New York: Foundation Press, 2001), 117; and Noonan, *The Lustre of Our Country,* 48–49.
20. Speech to the Virginia ratifying convention on the Constitution, June 12, 1788. *The Papers of James Madison,* ed. William T. Hutchinson and William M. E. Rachal (Chicago: University of Chicago Press, 1973), vol. 8, 130.
21. By royal patent, the Catholic convert Lord Baltimore was allowed to found a colony in the Chesapeake area as a haven for English Catholics coming under pressure from the growing Puritan movement. The law of the new colony provided that no Christian should be molested "for or in respect of his or her religion nor in the free exercise thereof." In honor of King Charles's Catholic wife and the Virgin Mary, the colony was named Maryland. Noonan, *The Lustre of Our Country,* 54 and 365.
22. Comments of Jack Rakove in Ceaser, *Nature and History in American Political Development,* 105–108.
23. In addition to Noonan's work, see Thomas E. Buckley, *Church and*

State in Revolutionary Virginia, 1776–1787 (Charlottesville: University Press of Virginia, 1977); William Lee Miller, *The First Liberty: Religion and the American Republic* (New York: Knopf, 1986); Leonard W. Levy, *The Establishment Clause: Religion and the First Amendment* (New York: Macmillan, 1986); Michael McConnell, "The Origins and Historical Understanding of Free Exercise of Religion," *Harvard Law Review,* 103 (1990), 1486–1488.

24. Noonan, *Religious Freedom,* 125.
25. Quoted in Robert Louis Wilken's book review, "In Defense of Constantine," *First Things,* April 2001, 37.
26. This and the following quotations from Madison are taken from Noonan, *The Lustre of Our Country,* 72–75.
27. Gaillard Hunt, "James Madison and Religious Liberty," *Journal of the American Historical Association,* 4:1 (1900), 165–171. As President Washington wrote to a Jewish supporter, "The citizens of the United States of America have a right to applaud themselves for having given to Mankind examples of an enlarged and liberal policy, a policy worthy of imitation. All possess alike liberty of conscience and immunities of citizenship. It is now no more that toleration is spoken of, as if it was by the indulgence of one class of people that another enjoyed the exercise, of their inherent natural rights." President George Washington, "Reply to Moses Seixas, Sexton of Hebrew Congregation of Newport," in Edwin S. Gaustad, *A Documentary History of Religion in America to the Civil War,* 2nd ed. (Grand Rapids, Mich.: Eerdmans, 1993), 278–279.
28. As John Witherspoon, Madison's Calvinist teacher at Princeton, put it, "There is not a single instance in history in which civil liberty was lost, and religious liberty preserved entire." Thomas Miller, ed., *The Selected Writings of John Witherspoon* (Carbondale: Southern Illinois University Press, 1990), 140–141.
29. Noonan has a valuable discussion in *The Lustre of Our Country,* 61–75. Madison's text is worth serious attention: "We remonstrate against the said Bill, 1. Because we hold it for a fundamental and undeniable truth, that Religion or the duty which we owe to our Creator and the manner of discharging it, can be directed only by reason and conviction, not by force or violence. The Religion then of every man must be left to the conviction and conscience of every man; and it is the right of every man to exercise it as these may dictate. This right is in its nature an unalienable right. It is unalienable, because

the opinions of men depending only on the evidence contemplated by their own minds cannot follow the dictates of other men: It is unalienable also, because what is here a right towards men, is a duty toward the Creator. It is the duty of every man to render to the Creator such homage, and such only, as he believes to be acceptable to him. This duty is precedent both in order of time and degree of obligation, to the claims of Civil Society. Before any man can be considered as a member of Civil Society, he must be considered as a subject of the Governor of the Universe: And if a member of Civil Society, who enters into any subordinate Association, must always do it with a reservation of his duty to the general authority; much more must every man who becomes a member of any particular Civil Society, do it with a saving of his allegiance to the Universal Sovereign. We maintain therefore that in matters of Religion, no man's right is abridged by the institution of Civil Society, and that Religion is wholly exempt from its cognizance." James Madison, "A Memorial and Remonstrance," June 1785, in Noonan, *Religious Freedom,* 173–178. See also more generally Merrill D. Peterson and Robert C. Vaughan, eds., *The Virginia Statute for Religious Freedom: Its Evolution and Consequences in American History* (New York: Cambridge University Press, 1988).

30. Vatican Council II, Declaration on Religious Liberty (*Dignitatis Humanae*), 1965, paragraph 12, *www.vatican.va/archive/hist_councils/ii_vatican_council/documents,* accessed 2/13/06.
31. In fact, it was the opening of Jefferson and Madison's "Virginia Statue on Religious Freedom," introduced in 1779, finally passed in 1785, and generally regarded as the first law of its kind.
32. Thomas S. Engeman and Michael P. Zuckert, eds., *Protestantism and the American Founding* (Notre Dame: University of Notre Dame Press, 2004).
33. "Memorial and Remonstrance," in Noonan, *Religious Freedom,* 173.
34. Thus in terms of Henry May's four categories, one is dealing here with the "Moderate Enlightenment," which was "often inextricably mixed with Christian ideas." Henry May, *The Enlightenment in America* (New York: Oxford University Press, 1976), xviii.
35. See Isaac Kramnick and R. Lawrence Moore, *The Godless Constitution: The Case Against Religious Correctness* (New York: W. W. Norton, 1996); Daniel Dreisbach, *Religion and Politics in the Early*

Republic (Frankfort: University Press of Kentucky, 1996); and the debate between the authors of these two books in *Liberty,* May/June 1996, 13–14; November/December 1996, 11–13; March/April 1997, 2.

36. Jon Meacham, *American Gospel: God, the Founding Fathers, and the Making of a Nation* (New York: Random House, 2006), 22–27, 74–75.
37. Speech to Virginia ratifying convention, June 20, 1788, in Robert A. Rutland and Charles F. Hobson, eds., *The Papers of James Madison,* vol. 11 (Charlottesville: University Press of Virginia, 1977), 163.
38. This commonly held view was epitomized in George Washington's Farewell Address: "Of all the dispositions and habits, which lead to political prosperity, Religion and Morality are indispensable supports. In vain would that man claim the tribute of Patriotism, who should labor to subvert these great pillars of human happiness, these firmest props of the duties of Men and Citizens. The mere Politician, equally with the pious man, ought to respect and to cherish them. A volume could not trace all their connexions with private and public felicity. Let it simply be asked, Where is the security for property, for reputation, for life, if the sense of religious obligation desert the oaths, which are the instruments of investigation in Courts of Justice? And let us with caution indulge the supposition, that morality can be maintained without religion. Whatever may be conceded to the influence of refined education on minds of peculiar structure, reason and experience both forbid us to expect, that national morality can prevail in exclusion of religious principle." *www.earlyamerica.com* (accessed 5/10/06).
39. James T. Kloppenberg, "The Virtues of Liberalism: Christianity, Republicanism, and Ethics in Early American Political Discourse," *Journal of American History,* 74:2 (1987), 9–34.
40. West, *The Politics of Revelation and Reason,* 64.
41. James Turner, *Without God, Without Creed: The Origins of Unbelief in America* (Baltimore: Johns Hopkins University Press, 1985), chap. 2; Barbara A. McGraw, *Rediscovering America's Sacred Ground: Public Religion and Pursuit of the Good in a Pluralistic America* (Albany: State University of New York Press, 2003).
42. Ruth Elson, *Guardians of Tradition: Schoolbooks of the Nineteenth Century* (Lincoln: University of Nebraska Press, 1964); Sara Goodman Zimet, "Values and Attitudes in American Primers from Colo-

nial Days to the Present," in Sara Goodman Zimet, ed., *What Children Read in School* (New York: Grune and Stratton, 1972).

43. These and related points are presented in West, *The Politics of Revelation and Reason,* 73–78; Harry V. Jaffa, *The American Founding as the Best Regime* (Claremont, Calif.: Claremont Institute, 1990).
44. Robert H. Wiebe, *Self-Rule: A Cultural History of American Democracy* (Chicago: University of Chicago Press, 1995).
45. See the discussion and related sources cited in John W. De Gruchy, *Christianity and Democracy* (New York: Cambridge University Press, 1995), chapters 2 and 3.
46. William G. McLoughlin, *Revivals, Awakenings, and Reform* (Chicago: University of Chicago Press, paperback edition 1980), xiv.
47. Norman Cohn, *Cosmos, Chaos, and the World to Come* (New Haven: Yale University Press, 1993); Mircea Eliade, *The Myth of the Eternal Return* (Princeton: Princeton University Press, 1954); Christopher Dawson, *The Dynamics of World History* (New York: Sheed and Ward, 1956).
48. Karl Lowith, *Meaning in History* (Chicago: University of Chicago Press, 1949).
49. Ibid., 188.
50. Chapter 20 of St. John's revelation shows the angel of God binding Satan for a thousand years and the souls of martyrs for Christ's sake reigning with Jesus for those thousand years (all of these souls have part in the "first resurrection" with no power of the second death over them, while the rest of the dead remain dead until the thousand years are finished). After the thousand years Satan is loosed, producing a deception of all nations, the gathering of unholy forces against believers, a decisive, quick victory blow from heaven, God's final judgment of all human beings who have ever lived, and the end of historical time.
51. Governor John Winthrop's 1630 sermon aboard the *Arbella,* "Christian Charitee: Modell Hereof," is in Noonan, *Religious Freedom,* 122–123. For much richer accounts of Puritan millennialism than I can discuss here, see James West Davidson, *The Logic of Millennial Thought: Eighteenth-Century New England* (New Haven: Yale University Press, 1977); and Theodore Dwight Bozeman, *To Live Ancient Lives: The Primitivist Dimension in Puritanism* (Chapel Hill: University of North Carolina Press, 1988).
52. Patrick Wormald, Donald Bullough, and Roger Collins, eds., *Ideal*

and Reality in Frankish and Anglo-Saxon Society: Studies Presented to J. M. Wallace-Hadrill (Oxford: Blackwell, 1983).

53. President Ronald Reagan's farewell address to the nation eloquently played on these images: "I've spoken of the shining city all my political life, but I don't know if I ever quite communicated what I saw when I said it. But in my mind it was a tall, proud city built on rocks stronger than oceans, windswept, God-blessed, and teeming with people of all kinds living in harmony and peace; a city with free ports that hummed with commerce and creativity. And if there had to be city walls, the walls had doors and the doors were open to anyone with the will and the heart to get here. That's how I saw it, and see it still.

    "And how stands the city on this winter night? More prosperous, more secure, and happier that it was 8 years ago. But more than that: After 200 years, two centuries, she still stands strong and true on the granite ridge, and her glow has held steady no matter what storm. And she's still a beacon, still a magnet for all who must have freedom, for all the pilgrims from all the lost places who are hurtling through the darkness, toward home." The speech appears in Davis W. Houck and Amos Kiewe, eds., *Actor, Ideologue, Politician: The Public Speeches of Ronald Reagan* (Westport, Conn.: Greenwood Press, 1993), 327.

54. Ernest Lee Tuveson, *Redeemer Nation: The Idea of America's Millennial Role* (Chicago: University of Chicago Press, 1968); Conrad Cherry, *God's New Israel: Religious Interpretations of American Destiny* (Englewood Cliffs, N.J.: Prentice-Hall, 1971); Steven H. Webb, *American Providence: A Nation with a Mission* (New York: Continuum International Publishing, 2004). In an earlier, too often neglected work, Richard Niebuhr presents the developments we are discussing as three overlapping phases in the "notes of faith" of a constructive Protestantism. The first, emphasizing the sovereignty of God, finds believers focusing on their eternal citizenship in heaven, with a relatively static view of society. The second "Kingdom of Christ" phase of revivals and awakenings focuses on the personal experience of Christ's love and reign in the believer, which, it should be noted, is not mere emotionalism but a rule of knowledge in men's minds. The third phase, "the Coming Kingdom," roughly corresponds to what I am discussing as millennialism. H. Richard

Niebuhr, *The Kingdom of God in America* (New York: Harper Torchbook, 1959), first published in 1937.

55. George McKenna, "An Holy and Blessed People: The Puritan Origins of American Patriotism," *Yale Review,* 90:3 (July 2002), 81–98.
56. Tuveson, *Redeemer Nation,* 102.
57. McLoughlin, *Revivals, Awakenings, and Reform,* 105.
58. Thus President Bush before 9/11: "Through much of the last century, America's faith in freedom and democracy was a rock in a raging sea. Now it is a seed upon the wind, taking root in many nations. Our democratic faith is more than the creed of our country, it is the inborn hope of our humanity; an ideal we carry but do not own, a trust we bear and pass along."

    And President Bush after 9/11: "The advance of freedom is the calling of our time; it is the calling of our country. From the Fourteen Points to the Four Freedoms, to the Speech at Westminster, America has put our power at the service of principle. We believe that liberty is the design of nature; we believe that liberty is the direction of history. We believe that human fulfillment and excellence come in the responsible exercise of liberty. And we believe that freedom—the freedom we prize—is not for us alone, it is the right and the capacity of all mankind. . . . And as we meet the terror and violence of the world, we can be certain the Author of freedom is not indifferent to the fate of freedom." President George W. Bush, "Inaugural Address," New York Times, January 21, 2001, 14; and address to the National Endowment for Democracy, November 6, 2003. *www.whitehouse.gov/news/releases/2003* (accessed 1/15/06).
59. Jonathan Edwards, "Some Thoughts Concerning the Present Revival of Religion in New England," *The Works of Jonathan Edwards,* vol. 1, ed. Edward Hickman (Carlisle, Pa.: Banner of Truth Trust, 1974), 381. Thomas Paine, "Common Sense," in *The Writings of Thomas Paine,* ed. Moneurer Daniel Conway (New York: G. P. Putnam's Sons, 1894), 118–119. On Paine in relation to the religious atmosphere, see Stephen Newman and related references in "A Note on *Common Sense* and Christian Eschatology," *Political Theory,* 6:1 (1978), 101–108.
60. Walter A. McDougall, *Promised Land, Crusader State: The American Encounter with the World Since 1776* (New York: Houghton Mifflin, 1998).

61. See, for example, Claes G. Ryn, *America the Virtuous: The Crisis of Democracy and the Quest for Empire* (New Brunswick, N.J.: Transaction, 2004); Michael Northcott, *An Angel Directs the Storm: Apocalyptic Religion and American Empire* (New York: I. B. Tauris, 2004).
62. In saying this, there remains a very significant difference. Catholic teaching presents the Church as the visible society of the Kingdom of God on earth, a claim rejected by Protestant reformers. Reformers retained the idea of the church as the human society through which God's purpose in history is realized, but view this church as composed of all those born again in Christ and not the visible hierarchical Church known to history.
63. St. Augustine, *The City of God,* trans. Marcus Dods (Chicago: Encyclopaedia Britannica, 1952), chap. 20. For a helpful overview, see Arthur W. Wainwright, *Mysterious Apocalypse: Interpreting the Book of Revelation* (Nashville: Abingdon Press, 1993).
64. Niebuhr, *The Kingdom of God in America,* 193.
65. Charles E. Merriam, *The New Democracy and the New Despotism* (New York: Whittlesey House, 1939), 11.
66. Early Christian apologists, not least Paul, took special care in pointing out the glory to God that came from entrusting His good news about the Messiah to socially marginal people whom the world dismisses. Under Jewish law, shepherds, fishermen, tax collectors, and women were not the sort of proper people to give testimony about anything important.
67. Celsus, *On the True Doctrine* (Oxford: Oxford University Press, 1987).
68. See, respectively, Jacques Maritain, *Christianity and Democracy,* trans. Doris C. Anson (New York: Charles Scribner's Sons, 1944), 46; and Charles Taylor, *Sources of the Self* (Cambridge, Mass.: Harvard University Press, 1989). Recent examples of exaggerated claims identifying Christianity with success and progress on the world's terms are Rodney Stark, *The Victory of Reason: How Christianity Led to Freedom, Capitalism, and Western Success* (New York: Random House, 2005); and Thomas E. Woods, Jr., *How the Catholic Church Built Western Civilization* (Washington, D.C.: Regnery, 2005).
69. John Paul II, *Fides et Ratio: Encyclical Letter on the Relationship be-*

tween Faith and Reason (Boston: Pauline Books and Media, 1998), 46.

70. John T. McGreevy, *Catholicism and American Freedom: A History* (New York: W. W. Norton, 2003).
71. Carl J. Friedrich, *The New Belief in the Common Man* (Boston: Little, Brown, 1942), 3.
72. Thus in 1647 the Puritans' General Court of Massachusetts passed a law to create the first publicly supported schools with two declared aims: to foil the efforts of "ye old deluder Satan, to keep men from the knowledge of ye Scriptures," and to ensure that "learning not be buried with ye grave of our fathers." *www.extremeintellect.com* (accessed 5/27/06).
73. Peter Harrison, *The Bible, Protestantism, and the Rise of Natural Science* (Cambridge: Cambridge University Press, 1998), 93.
74. Cardinal Bellarmine, quoted in ibid., 100. In 1546 the Catholic Church's Council of Trent answered the Protestant reformers: ". . . no one, relying on his own skill, shall—in matters of faith, and of morals pertaining to the edification of Christian doctrine—wresting the sacred scripture to his own senses, presume to interpret the said sacred Scripture contrary to that sense which holy mother Church,—whose it is to judge of the true sense and interpretation of the holy Scriptures,—hath held and doth hold." *Decree Concerning the Canonical Scripture, Canons and Decrees of the Council of Trent,* Fourth Session, April 1546, *www.bible-research.com* (accessed 6/11/07).
75. A recent discussion of this more general issue is in Robert D. Woodberry and Timothy S. Shah, "The Pioneering Protestants," *Journal of Democracy,* 15:2 (2004), 47–61.
76. This compares with 89 percent in 1947 when this Gallup poll question was first asked. Gregg Esterbrook, "Religion in America: The New Ecumenicalism," *Brookings Review,* Winter 2002, 46.
77. A usefully brief summary of Puritan beliefs can be found in Nathaniel Philbrick's immensely informative and readable *Mayflower: A Story of Courage, Community, and War* (New York: Viking, 2006), 8–10.
78. See Sydney E. Ahlstsrom, *A Religious History of the American People* (New Haven: Yale University Press, 1972), 385 and Part IV generally.
79. The full story is of course quite complex, and for the period up to the

Civil War it is well laid out in two recent books: Mark A. Noll, *America's God: From Jonathan Edwards to Abraham Lincoln* (Oxford: Oxford University Press, 2002); and E. Brooks Holifield, *Theology in America: Christian Thought from the Age of the Puritans to the Civil War* (New Haven: Yale University Press, 2003). While Holifield lays greater stress on the trained clergy, a central theme in both books is the ultimate ineffectiveness of learned Protestant leaders' resistance to these popularizing trends.

80. Quoted in McLoughlin, *Revivals, Awakenings, and Reform,* 114; see also 121.
81. Debby Applegate, *The Most Famous Man in America: The Biography of Henry Ward Beecher* (New York: Doubleday, 2006).
82. Quotations are from Noll, *America's God,* 441 and 438.
83. Ibid., 442.
84. Niebuhr, *The Kingdom of God in America,* 193.
85. Sydney E. Ahlstrom, "Theology in America: A Historical Survey," in James Ward Smith and A. Leland Jamison, eds., *The Shaping of American Religion,* Volume I in the series *Religion in American Life* (Princeton: Princeton University Press, 1961), 319–320.
86. Alan Wolfe, *One Nation, After All* (New York: Viking, 1998), 56.
87. Robert Wuthnow, *After Heaven: Spirituality in America Since the 1950s* (Berkeley: University of California Press, 1998), chap. 1; Wayne Baker, *America's Crisis of Values* (Princeton: Princeton University Press, 2005), 57; Thomas Luckmann, "Shrinking Transcendence, Expanding Religion," *Sociological Analysis,* 50 (1990), 127.
88. For a survey of the many varieties see Wade Clark Roof, *Spiritual Marketplace: Baby Boomers and the Remaking of American Religion* (Princeton: Princeton University Press, 1999), and Brian D. McLaren, *A New Kind of Christian: A Tale of Two Friends on a Spiritual Journey* (San Francisco: Jossey-Bass, 2001). One author ably summarizes the contrast between the old (i.e., orthodox Christian) and the new spirituality: "The New Synthesis reverses each major tenet of the Revealed Word. The Word's insistence on history as faith's foundation gives way to myth as the universal mode of spiritual expression. Salvation through faith in God's grace yields to the mystical episode as the elemental religious experience. An evolving universe infused with divine consciousness supplants a wholly other God, while human beings evolving toward a divinity of their own are no longer created in the image of such a God." James A. Herrick, *The Making of*

the New Spirituality (Downers Grove, Ill.: InterVarsity Press, 2003), 251.

89. Pope John Paul II repeated the teaching against fideism traditionally upheld by both the Catholic Church and Protestant Reformers such as Luther, Calvin, Knox, and many others. "The truth conferred by revelation is a truth to be understood in the light of reason." John Paul II, *Fides et Ratio,* 48 and 64. Origen is quoted in Robert Louis Willken, *The Spirit of Early Christian Thought* (New Haven: Yale University Press, 2003), 14.
90. For a fuller discussion and related references, see Jean Bethke Elshtain, "In Common Together: Christianity and Democracy in America," in John Witte, Jr., ed., *Christianity and Democracy in Global Context* (Boulder: Westview Press, 2001).
91. H. Richard Niebuhr, "The Protestant Movement and Democracy in the United States," in Smith and Jamison, eds., *The Shaping of American Religion,* Volume I, 31–32.
92. Gordon Wood, *The Creation of the American Republic* (Chapel Hill: University of North Carolina Press, 1969).
93. A fuller discussion of this point would have to acknowledge important differences among not only Protestants but also conservative Protestants on the issue of "engaging the culture." See George M. Marsden, *Fundamentalism and American Culture* (Oxford: Oxford University Press, 1980), chap. 15; and more generally, H. Richard Niebuhr, *Christ and Culture* (New York: Harper and Row, 1950).
94. C. Howard Hopkins, *The Rise of the Social Gospel in American Protestantism, 1865–1915* (New Haven: Yale University Press, 1940).
95. Michael Kazin, *A Godly Hero: The Life of William Jennings Bryan* (New York: Knopf, 2006).
96. Nathan O. Hatch, *The Democratization of American Christianity* (New Haven: Yale University Press, 1989).
97. Charles Grandison Finney, quoted in McLoughlin, *Revivals, Awakenings, and Reform,* 123.
98. Gaines M. Foster, *Moral Reconstruction: Christian Lobbyists and the Federal Legislation of Morality* (Chapel Hill: University of North Carolina Press, 2002).
99. H. Richard Niebuhr, *The Social Sources of Denominationalism* (New York: Henry Holt, 1929), and William R. Hutchison, *Religious Plu-*

ralism in America: The Contentious History of a Founding Ideal (New Haven: Yale University Press, 2003).

100. Theda Skocpol, *Protecting Soldiers and Mothers: The Political Origins of Social Policy in the United States* (Cambridge, Mass.: Harvard University Press, 1992).
101. Clifford Putney, *Muscular Christianity: Manhood and Sports in Protestant America,* 1880–1920 (Cambridge, Mass.: Harvard University Press, 2002); Thomas Winter, *Making Men, Making Class: The YMCA and Working Men, 1877–1920* (Chicago: University of Chicago Press, 2002).
102. Robert Bellah's article still repays attention: "Civil Religion in America," in William G. McLoughlin and Robert N. Bellah, eds., *Religion in America* (Boston: Beacon Press, 1968), 3–23.
103. Harry S. Stout, *Upon the Altar of the Nation: A Moral History of the Civil War* (New York: Viking, 2006).
104. McLoughlin, *Revivals, Awakenings, and Reform,* 144.
105. Marsden, *Fundamentalism and American Culture,* 146–147.
106. Maritain, *Christianity and Democracy,* 58–59.
107. Will Herberg, *Protestant-Catholic-Jew* (Garden City: Doubleday, 1956).
108. Martin Luther King, Jr., "Letter from Birmingham Jail," April 16, 1963, 8. *www.kingpapers.org* (accessed 7/7/07).
109. Andrew Greeley and Michael Hout, *The Truth about Conservative Christians: What They Think and What They Believe* (Chicago: University of Chicago Press, 2006), 83.
110. Variations within the conservative mainstream of the Protestant establishment are described in Marsden, *Fundamentalism and American Culture,* chapter 15, and within Protestantism more generally by William R. Hutchison, *The Modernist Impulse in American Protestantism* (Cambridge, Mass.: Harvard University Press, 1976). Not surprisingly, American Catholics were more self-confident in following Pope Pius X's 1907 condemnation of theological modernism as the "synthesis of all heresies," while accepting limited aspects of the modernist agenda (particularly economic reforms in pursuit of charity and social justice) as consistent with Catholic teaching. See Thomas E. Woods, Jr., *The Church Confronts Modernity: Catholic Intellectuals and the Progressive Era* (New York: Columbia University Press, 2004).
111. The series was reissued in 1917 as a four-volume set, which has been

reprinted by Baker Books, Grand Rapids, Michigan, in 1998. What became popularly known as "the five points of fundamentalism" are the inerrancy of Scripture, the deity and Virgin birth of Jesus Christ, his substitutionary atonement for human sin, his bodily resurrection from the dead, and his premillennial return (or, in Presbyterian circles, the authenticity of biblical miracles). The most cogent intellectual presentation of the fundamentalists' case against modernism is J. Gresham Machen, *Christianity and Liberalism* (Grand Rapids, Mich.: Eerdmans, 1923), reprinted 1981.

112. On the most portentous of these battles, see Bradley J. Longfield, *The Presbyterian Controversy: Fundamentalists, Modernists, and Moderates* (New York: Oxford University Press, 1991), as well as Marsden, *Fundamentalism and American Culture,* chap. 19.
113. Contemporaneous accounts presented the results as indecisive or possibly favorable to the anti-evolution cause, but this did not hinder the subsequent development of the Scopes legend as a decisive defeat for old-time religion. Edward J. Larson, *Summer of the Gods* (New York: Basic Books, 1997), chaps. 8 and 9.
114. Michael Kazin, *The Populist Persuasion: An American History* (New York: Basic Books, 1995), 80.
115. Daniel Bell, ed., *The New American Right* (New York: Criterion Books, 1955); Mark Noll, *The Scandal of the Evangelical Mind* (Grand Rapids, Mich.: Eerdmans, 1994).
116. Christian Smith, ed., *The Secular Revolution* (Berkeley: University of California Press, 2003), especially chaps. 1, 3, and 8.
117. See her debate with Judge Charles R. Grant, "Religious Teaching and the Moral Life," *The Arena,* June 1897, 17:91.
118. John Dewey, "Christianity and Democracy," in *The Early Works of John Dewey,* vol. 4 (Carbondale: Southern Illinois University Press, 1969), 8. The idea of teacher as prophet is discussed in Dewey's *My Pedagogic Creed* (1897) and analyzed in E. Rosenow, "The Teacher as Prophet of the True God: Dewey's Religious Faith and Its Problems," *Journal of Philosophy of Education,* 31:3 (1997), 427–437.
119. Walt Whitman, "Song of the Open Road."
120. Given the well-developed Church teachings on natural law, Catholic leaders were far more aware and articulate than Protestants in criticizing what was happening. As Georgetown University's Stephan McNamee pointed out, "The utter irony of the situation is that the American philosopher [Dewey] who most radically applied the ax to

the principles upon which this democratic government, as we know it in the United States, is erected, is openly hailed as *the* philosopher of democracy!" Quoted in McGreevy, *Catholicism and American Freedom,* 193.

121. Leigh Eric Schmidt, *Restless Souls: The Making of American Spirituality* (San Francisco: Harper, 2005).
122. R. Laurence Moore, "Secularization: Religion and the Social Sciences," in William R. Hutchison, ed., *Between the Times: The Travail of the Protestant Establishment, 1900–1960* (New York: Cambridge University Press, 1989); Christian Smith, "Secularizing American Higher Education," in Smith, ed., *The Secular Revolution.* More generally on this point, see George M. Marsden, *The Soul of the American University* (New York: Oxford University Press, 1994); and Julie Reuben, *The Making of the Modern University: Intellectual Transformation and Marginalization of Morality* (Chicago: University of Chicago Press, 1996).
123. Patrick J. Deneen, *Democratic Faith* (Princeton: Princeton University Press, 2005).
124. Noonan, *Religious Freedom,* xi.
125. Steven D. Smith, *Foreordained Failure: The Quest for a Constitutional Principle of Religious Freedom* (New York: Oxford University Press, 1995). A fuller account of the relevant cases, which supports Smith's point, is John Witte, Jr., *Religion and the American Constitutional Experiment; Essential Rights and Liberties* (Boulder: Westview Press, 2000). That the "separation of church and state" is a twentieth-century innovation in jurisprudence rather than a principle historically founded in the First Amendment is powerfully argued in Philip Hamburger, *Separation of Church and State* (Cambridge, Mass.: Harvard University Press, 2002). The history of our modern conflicts over "legal secularism" is surveyed in Noah Feldman, *Divided by God: America's Church-State Problem, and What We Should Do about It* (Gordonsville, Va.: Farrar Straus Giroux, 2005).
126. Richard John Neuhaus, *The Naked Public Square* (Grand Rapids, Mich.: Eerdmans, 1984). See also Stephen L. Carter, *The Culture of Disbelief* (New York: Basic Books, 1993).
127. *Lynch v. Donnelly,* 465 U.S. 668. Docket Number: 82-1256 (1984).
128. While no single study tells the whole story, one can see the pieces beginning to fit together in Stuart Ewen, *Captains of Consciousness: Advertising and the Social Roots of the Consumer Culture* (New

York: McGraw-Hill, 1976); Warren Susman, *Culture as History* (New York: Pantheon, 1984); Daniel Horowitz, *The Morality of Spending* (Baltimore: Johns Hopkins University Press, 1985); William Leach, *Land of Desire* (New York: Pantheon, 1993); Jackson Lears, *Fables of Abundance* (New York: Basic Books, 1994); Roland Marchand, *Creating the Corporate Soul: The Rise of Public Relations and Corporate Imagery in American Big Business* (Berkeley: University of California Press, 1998). On the cultural messages of marketing to youth, see Juliet B. Schor, *Born to Buy: The Commercialized Child and the New Consumer Culture* (New York: Scribner, 2004).

129. Gary Cross, *An All-Consuming Century: Why Commercialism Won in Modern America* (New York: Columbia University Press, 2000), 132, 127.
130. Alan Brinkley, *The End of Liberalism: New Deal Liberalism in Recession and War* (New York: Knopf, 1995); Robert M. Collins, *More: The Politics of Economic Growth in Postwar America* (Oxford: Oxford University Press, 2000); Elizabeth Fones-Wolf, *Selling Free Enterprise: The Business Assault on Labor and Liberalism, 1945–1960* (Urbana: University of Illinois Press, 1994); Lizabeth Cohen, *A Consumers' Republic: The Politics of Mass Consumption in Postwar America* (New York: Knopf, 2003).
131. Norman Ornstein and Thomas Mann, eds., *The Permanent Campaign and Its Future* (Washington, D.C.: American Enterprise Institute and Brookings Institution, 2000).
132. For a detailed account of this resistance, and its failure, see Cross, *An All-Consuming Century,* 112–143.
133. Nathan Miller, *New World Coming: The 1920s and the Making of Modern America* (New York: Scribner, 2003).
134. A survey of the critics is in Daniel Horowitz, *The Anxieties of Affluence: Critiques of American Consumer Culture, 1939–1979* (Amherst: University of Massachusetts Press, 2004).
135. Quoted in Kazin, *The Populist Persuasion,* 174.
136. Ronald Berman, ed., *Solzhenitsyn at Harvard* (Washington, D.C.: Ethics and Public Policy Center, 1980), 69–71. See also Joseph Pearce, *A Soul in Exile* (Grand Rapids, Mich.: Baker Books, 2001).
137. The Supreme Court famously described this idea in the 1992 case *Planned Parenthood v. Casey:* "At the heart of liberty is the right to define one's own concept of existence, of meaning, of the universe,

and of the mystery of human life." 505 U.S. 833 (1992). Docket Number: 91-744.

138. For a contrary view that such figures were debasing a previous secular purity in the American public arena, see Susan Jacoby, *Freethinkers: A History of American Secularism* (New York: Metropolitan Books, 2004).
139. David L. Chappell, *A Stone of Hope: Prophetic Religion and the Death of Jim Crow* (Chapel Hill: University of North Carolina Press, 2004).
140. In focusing on the movement as such, one is necessarily leaving aside the initiatives begun decades earlier with the Legal Defense Fund and other activities among NAACP elites.
141. An early account along these lines is in John Herber, *The Lost Priority: Whatever Happened to the Civil Rights Movement in America?* (New York: Funk and Wagnall, 1970). This history is carefully reviewed in Taylor Branch, *At Canaan's Edge: America in the King Years, 1965–68* (New York: Simon and Schuster, 2006).
142. Maurice Isserman and Michael Kazin, *America Divided: The Civil War in the 1960s* (New York: Oxford University Press, 2000), 300.
143. Anthony King, ed., *The New American Political System* (Washington, D.C.: American Enterprise Institute, 1978); Richard A. Harris and Sidney M. Milkis, eds., *Remaking American Politics* (Boulder: Westview Press, 1989); Morris P. Fiorina, *Culture War? The Myth of a Polarized America,* 2nd ed. (New York: Pearson Longman, 2006), 187–198.
144. Hugh Heclo, "Sixties Civics," in Sidney M. Milkis and Jerome M. Mileur, *The Great Society and the High Tide of Liberalism* (Boston: University of Massachusetts Press, 2005).
145. Sydney E. Ahlstrom, *A Religious History of the American People* (New Haven: Yale University Press, 1972), 1085. On this theme, see also pp. 2, 1078, 1094.
146. The full quotation is worth repeating: "At the close of the sixth decade of the twentieth century, commentators on the American scene seem to be of two minds in regard to the status and significance of religion in our culture. On the one side there are those of the intellectual avant-garde who insist that 'God is dead,' and that Western culture has entered into a 'post-Christian era.' On the other side are those who call attention to 'the surge of piety in America,' with its accompanying increase in religiosity (if not of authentic religious faith).

. . . In short, sophisticates seem to have given up on God altogether, while the naïve masses simply 'infinitize' their personal and social values and call the nebulous aggregate 'God.'" Smith and Jamison, *The Shaping of American Religion,* 5.

147. McLoughlin, *Revivals, Awakenings, and Reform,* xv and 179.
148. Isserman and Kazin, *America Divided,* 241.
149. Machen, *Christianity and Liberalism,* 6.
150. These "mainline" denominations (following the term for the upscale Philadelphia suburbs connected by the city's mainline commuter train) have customarily included the Presbyterian Church (USA), Episcopalians, Congregationalists (now the United Church of Christ), Methodists, Disciples of Christ, United Lutherans, Reformed Church in America, and American Baptist Churches (but not the Southern Baptist Convention). For a general account of the associated social structures, see E. Digby Baltzell, *The Protestant Establishment: Aristocracy and Caste in America* (New York: Random House, 1964). My discussion of the more political aspects of the Protestant establishment in the period leading up to the Sixties is indebted to the various excellent chapters in Hutchison, *Between the Times.*
151. While accepting historical and scientific critiques of the Bible (and thus rejecting its inerrancy), neo-Orthodox leaders in the Protestant establishment such as Reinhold Niebuhr reasserted traditional Christian doctrines concerning man's inherent sinfulness and God's saving revelation of Himself to man through the Christ of the Bible.
152. Charged with radicalism, President Roosevelt quipped that his program was "as radical as the Federal Council of Churches." Quoted in Robert A. Schneider, "Voice of Many Waters: Church Federation in the Twentieth Century," in Hutchison, *Between the Times,* 110.
153. This did not prevent some more liberal internationalists among Protestant leaders from being investigated as Communist "fellow-travelers" by the House Un-American Activities Committee in the early 1950s. On the whole, it seems fair to say that Cold War liberal elites were mainly impressed and influenced by Niebuhr's political acumen and realism but had little or no interest in his Christianity. Ronald H. Stone, *Reinhold Niebuhr: Prophet to Politicians* (Washington, D.C.: University Press of America, 1981). A useful recent survey of the rise and fall of Cold War liberalism is contained in Peter Beinart's *The Good Fight* (New York: HarperCollins, 2006).
154. Scholars from a wide variety of perspectives offer overlapping ac-

counts of the Sixties as a watershed in the disestablishment of mainline Protestantism. See Robert Wuthnow, *The Restructuring of American Religion: Society and Faith Since World War II* (Princeton: Princeton University Press, 1988); Jackson W. Carroll and Wade Clark Roof, *Beyond Establishment: Protestant Identity in a Post-Protestant Age* (Louisville: Westminster, 1993); Donald E. Miller, *Reinventing American Protestantism* (Berkeley: University of California Press, 1997); and Lyle E. Schaller, *Discontinuity and Hope: Radical Change and the Path to the Future* (Nashville: Abingdon, 1999).

155. Harvey Cox, *The Secular City* (New York: Macmillan, revised edition, 1966), 126. For a sense of this theological and pastoral fervor among self-styled "Christian atheists," see Thomas J. J. Altizer and William Hamilton, *Radical Theology and the Death of God* (New York: Bobbs-Merrill, 1966); and David L. Edwards, ed., *The Honest to God Debate* (Philadelphia: Westminster Press, 1963).

156. On the latter two points, see Marion S. Goldman, "Continuity in Collapse: Departures from Shiloh," *Journal for the Scientific Study of Religion,* 34:3 (1995), 342–353; and Matthew J. Price, "After the Revolution: A Review of Mainline Protestant Clergy Leadership Literature Since the 1960s," *Theology Today,* 59:3 (2002), 428–450.

157. Schematically, this could be seen as the third Protestant disestablishment in American history, the first being the displacement of the learned Protestant clergy by more populist evangelical churches after 1790 and the second being the modernist/fundamentalist fracture after 1920. See Wade Clark Roof, "The Third Disestablishment and Beyond," in Dorothy C. Bass et al., eds., *Mainstream Protestantism in the Twentieth Century: Its Problems and Prospects* (Philadelphia: Presbyterian Church, USA, 1986), 27–37; and more generally Robert T. Handy, *A Christian America: Protestant Hopes and Historical Realities* (New York: Oxford University Press, 1971).

158. Henry P. Van Dusen, "The Third Force's Lesson for Others," *Life,* June 9, 1958, 122–123. On missions, see Grant Wacker, "The Protestant Awakening to World Religions," in Hutchison, *Between the Times,* 267.

159. For an early account sympathetic to the mainline cause, see Dean M. Kelley, *Why Conservative Churches Are Growing: A Study in Sociology of Religion* (New York: Harper and Row, 1972). Largely supportive follow-up studies are by Steve Bruce, *A House Divided: Protestantism, Schism, and Secularization* (London: Routledge, 1990);

Roger Finke and Rodney Stark, *The Churching of America, 1776–1990: Winners and Losers in Our Religious Economy* (New Brunswick, N.J.: Rutgers University Press, 1992); and Donald E. Miller, *Reinventing American Protestantism: Christianity in the New Millennium* (Berkeley: University of California Press, 1997). Regarding birth rates, marital happiness, and family relations, see Greeley and Hout, *The Truth about Conservative Christians,* 105–111, 142, 159–161; and W. Bradford Wilcox, *Soft Patriarchs, New Men: How Christianity Shapes Fathers and Husbands* (Chicago: University of Chicago Press, 2004).

160. William A. King, "The Reform Establishment and the Ambiguities of Influence," in Hutchison, *Between the Times,* 137.

161. Joel A. Carpenter, "From Fundamentalism to the New Evangelical Coalition," in George Marsden, ed., *Evangelicalism and Modern America* (Grand Rapids, Mich.: Eerdmans, 1984). The rapidly growing major evangelical denominations have been Assemblies of God, Church of the Nazarene, Church of God in Christ, and the Southern Baptist Convention. A cogent discussion of doubts as to whether anything was gained after the 1940s in putting a fresh face on fundamentalism by adopting the term "evangelicalism" is in D. G. Hart, *Deconstructing Evangelicalism: Conservative Protestantism in the Age of Billy Graham* (Grand Rapids, Mich.: Baker Academic, 2004). In contrast to the NEA, the American Council of Christian Churches, created by the fire-breathing, super-fundamentalist, and occasionally paranoid anti-communist Carl McIntire, never approached mainstream Protestant status.

162. Carl F. H. Henry, *The Uneasy Conscience of Modern Fundamentalism* (Grand Rapids, Mich.: Eerdmans, 1947). For an early appreciation of Billy Graham in light of the cultural movements of the time, see William G. McLoughlin, *Billy Graham: Revivalist in a Secular Age* (New York: Ronald Press, 1960). A fuller retrospective assessment is William Martin's *A Prophet with Honor: The Billy Graham Story* (New York: William Morrow, 1991).

163. To his credit, Billy Graham insisted on racially integrated audiences. Many of the charges and counter-charges regarding social irresponsibility were conducted through mutual bombardments between the mainline journal *Christian Century* and the evangelicals' *Christianity Today.* For a general account see Mark Silk, *Spiritual Politics: Religion and America Since World War II* (New York: Simon and

Schuster, 1988). A thoughtful analysis of the polite dispute between Graham and Reinhold Niebuhr is offered in Andrew S. Finstuen, "The Prophet and the Evangelist," *Books & Culture,* 12:4 (2006).

164. While Kennedy's candidacy clearly aroused mutual distrust between evangelical Protestants and Roman Catholics, the hostility should not be exaggerated. In contrast to the ferocious anti-Catholicism of the nineteenth century, the conflict in mid-twentieth-century America was more like two butterflies fighting. Neither had the stinger or the venom to do the job.
165. Patrick Allitt, *Catholic Intellectuals and Conservative Politics in America, 1950–1985* (Ithaca: Cornell University Press, 1993).
166. See McGreevy, *Catholicism and American Freedom,* chaps. 8 and 9.
167. In 1971 the federal district court in the District of Columbia ruled in *Green v. Connally* (330 F.Supp. 1150) that, by definition, any organization practicing racial discrimination could not be considered a charitable institution and thus could not qualify for tax-exempt status. An account of the importance of this issue in 1970s political mobilization of evangelicals is contained in Randall Balmer, *Thy Kingdom Come: How the Religious Right Distorts the Faith and Threatens America* (New York: Basic Books, 2006). For a more general discussion of the evangelicals' turn to political action, see Michael Cromartie, ed., *A Public Faith: Evangelicals and Civic Engagement* (Lanham, Md.: Rowman and Littlefield, 2003).
168. Well-balanced historical accounts can be found in William Martin, *With God on Our Side: The Rise of the Religious Right in America* (New York: Broadway Books, 1996), and the second edition of George Marsden's *Fundamentalism and American Culture* (New York: Oxford University Press, 2005).
169. Garry Wills, *Under God: Religion and American Politics* (New York: Simon and Schuster, 1990), 320. Assessments of Schaeffer's career are in Dennis T. Lane, ed., *Francis A. Schaeffer: Portraits of the Man and His Work* (Westchester, Ill.: Crossway, 1986). A critique of his confused theological positions is in Gary North, *Political Polytheism: The Myth of Pluralism* (Tyler, Texas: Institution for Christian Economics, 1989), chap. 4.
170. Among the titles appearing between 1968 and 1975 were *Escape from Reason; The God Who Is There; Pollution and the Death of Man; Genesis in Space and Time; Art and the Bible; Two Contents, Two Realities.* These and other works mentioned in the text can be

found in the five volumes of Francis A. Schaeffer, *The Complete Works of Francis A. Schaeffer* (Westchester, Ill.: Good News/ Crossway, 1985).

171. The most important works in this later period were *How Then Should We Live? The Rise and Decline of Western Thought and Culture* (1976); (with C. Everett Koop), *Whatever Happened to the Human Race?* (1979); and *A Christian Manifesto* (1981). In the last book before his death in 1985, Schaeffer returned to his 1930s separatist roots, warning about believers' accommodation to the world: *The Great Evangelical Disaster* (Westchester, Ill.: Crossway, 1984).
172. Robert Wuthnow, *The Struggle for America's Soul* (Grand Rapids, Mich.: Eerdmans, 1989), chap. 2.
173. See Damon Linker, *The Theocons: Secular America under Siege* (New York: Doubleday, 2006).
174. Geoffrey Layman, *The Great Divide* (New York: Columbia University Press, 2001); Louis Bolce and Gerald De Maio, "Our Secularist Democratic Party," *The Public Interest,* 149 (2002), 3–30.
175. George H. Nash, *The Conservative Intellectual Movement in America Since 1945* (New York: Basic Books, 1976). On Kirk in particular, see W. Wesley McDonald, *Russell Kirk and the Age of Ideology* (Columbia, Mo.: University of Missouri Press, 2004). Russell Kirk's Catholic leanings eventuated in his baptism and reception into the Church at the time of his 1964 marriage. His development as a Christian and a Catholic is traced in Eric Scheske, "The Conservative Convert: The Life and Faith of Russell Kirk," *Touchstone,* June 2003, 41–48. Whittaker Chambers's account of his painful religious journey, from Communism to Quakerism, also had a Catholic "sensibility" that was strikingly influential in the nascent conservative movement of the early 1950s. See Whittaker Chambers, *Witness* (New York: Random House, 1952), 481–485.
176. Russell Kirk, *The Conservative Mind: From Burke to Santayana* (Chicago: Henry Regnery, 1953), 7–8.
177. Pieces by Bush and Reagan reacting to Goldwater's landslide defeat appeared in *The National Review,* December 1, 1964, 1053–1055.
178. The conflict between religious and political conservatism is discussed in D. G. Hart, "Conservatism, the Protestant Right, and the Failure of Religious History," *Journal of the Historical Society,* 4:4 (2004), 447–493; and Andrew Sullivan, *The Conservative Soul: How We Lost It, How to Get It Back* (New York: HarperCollins, 2006).

179. Kirk, *The Conservative Mind,* 7.
180. The question of how conservative, and what kind of conservative, Ronald Reagan was has now become a contested issue of historical inquiry. Assessments from a variety of perspectives are contained in W. Elliot Brownlee and Hugh Davis Graham, eds., *The Reagan Presidency* (Lawrence: University Press of Kansas, 2003).
181. As President Reagan put it in concluding his 1989 Farewell Address from the Oval Office, "Younger parents aren't sure that an unambivalent appreciation of America is the right thing to teach modern children. And for those who create the popular culture, well-grounded patriotism is no longer the style. Our spirit is back, but we haven't reinstitutionalized it. . . . If we forget what we did, we won't know who we are. I'm warning of an eradication of the American memory that could result, ultimately, in an erosion of the American spirit. . . . And children, if your parents haven't been teaching you what it means to be an American, let 'em know and nail 'em on it. That would be a very American thing to do." I discuss the speech and Reagan's political ideas in "Ronald Reagan and the American Public Philosophy," in Brownlee and Graham, eds., *The Reagan Presidency,* 17–39.
182. Kevin Phillips, *American Theocracy: The Peril and Politics of Radical Religion, Oil, and Borrowed Money in the 21st Century* (New York: Viking, 2006), vi, xiii.
183. Fiorina, *Culture War?* 26, 55.
184. Wayne Baker, *America's Crisis of Values* (Princeton: Princeton University Press, 2003), 104. For a general discussion of the different value systems informing liberal and conservative political attitudes, see George Lakoff, *Moral Politics: How Liberals and Conservatives Think* (Chicago: University of Chicago Press, 2002).
185. John Evans, "Have Americans' Attitudes Become More Polarized?—An Update," *Social Science Quarterly,* 84 (2003), 71–90. On abortion, see Ted Mouw and Michael Soel, "Culture Wars and Opinion Polarizations," *American Journal of Sociology,* 106 (2001), 913–943.
186. Fiorina, *Culture Wars?* 83–87 and 118ff.
187. Ibid., 77.
188. These and other reality checks on exaggerated claims about the religious right's impact on election outcomes are contained in Greeley and Hout, *The Truth about Conservative Christians,* chap. 3, and

E. J. Dionne Jr., David Brady, and Pietro Nivola, eds., *Red and Blue Nation: Characteristics and Causes of America's Polarized Politics* (Washington: Brookings, 2007).

189. Ibid., 130–132; 179–181. This considers only whites since African-American citizens, regardless of religious attachments, continue to vote overwhelmingly Democratic.
190. Approximately a quarter of Americans are college graduates. This and related issues are discussed in James Q. Wilson, "How Divided Are We?" *Commentary,* February 2006, 15–22.
191. Sydney Ahlstrom, "Theology in America," in Smith and Jamison, *The Shaping of American Religion,* 317.
192. On those respective points, see Nancy Bermeo, *Ordinary People in Extraordinary Times: The Citizenry and the Breakdown of Democracy* (Princeton: Princeton University Press, 2003); Ernest Gellner, *Nations and Nationalism* (Ithaca: Cornell University Press, 1983); Benedict Anderson, *Imagined Communities* (London: Verso Editions and NLB, 1983).
193. Margaret Somerville, *The Ethical Canary: Science, Society, and the Human Spirit* (New York: Viking, 2000). Informative if rather breathless surveys are contained in Francis Fukuyama, *Our Posthuman Future: Consequences of the Biotechnology Revolution* (Gordonsville, Va.: Farrar, Straus and Giroux, 2002); Gregory Stock, *Redesigning Humans: Our Inevitable Genetic Future* (New York: Houghton Mifflin, 2002); and Joel Garreau, *Radical Evolution* (New York: Doubleday, 2005).
194. John H. Evans, *Playing God? Human Genetic Engineering and the Rationalization of Public Bioethical Debate* (Chicago: University of Chicago Press, 2002).
195. Debora L. Spar, *The Baby Business: How Money, Science, and Politics Drive the Commerce of Conception* (Cambridge, Mass.: Harvard Business School, 2005); Susannah Baruch, David Kaufman, and Kathy L. Hudson, *Genetic Testing of Embryos: Practices and Perspectives of U.S. IVF Clinics* (Washington, D.C.: Genetics and Public Policy Center, 2006), *www.dnapolicy.org* (accessed 10/5/06). Since the survey of 415 clinics produced only a 45 percent response rate (190 clinics), the figures cited for designer babies are probably underestimates.
196. Steve Bruce, *Politics and Religion* (Oxford: Polity Press, 2003).
197. For an insightful discussion of this argument, repeated before and af-

ter the 1960s in many quarters, see Bryan Wilson, *Religion in Secular Society: A Sociological Comment* (London: C. A. Watts, 1966).

198. See the comments of Nancy Rosenblum in Ceaser, *Nature and History*, 130–134.
199. In his first published work, Rawls used the Catholic Inquisition as an example of what, ten years later, he would call the failure to conduct public debate by means of public reason accessible to all. John Rawls, "Outline of a Decision Procedure for Ethics" (1951) and "Constitutional Liberty and the Concept of Justice" (1963), both in Rawls, *Collected Papers*, ed. Samuel Freeman (Cambridge, Mass.: Harvard University Press, 1999). On the legal orthodoxy, see Rawls's Harvard colleague Lawrence H. Tribe, "The Supreme Court 1972 Term," *Harvard Law Review*, 87 (1973). Barack Obama, "The Connection Between Faith and Politics," June 28, 2006. *Www.realclearpolitics.com* (accessed 7/7/06).
200. See Damon Linker, *The Theocons: Secular America under Siege* (New York: Doubleday, 2006); and Phillips, *American Theocracy*. Examples of the recent more hysterical fears can be found in Michelle Goldberg, *Kingdom Coming: The Rise of Christian Nationalism* (New York: W. W. Norton, 2006); Laurenn Sandler, *Righteous: Dispatches from the Evangelical Youth Movement* (New York: Viking, 2006); James Rudin, *The Baptizing of America: The Religious Right's Plans for the Rest of Us* (New York: Thunder's Mouth, 2006).
201. Many references to such derangement are in Thomas Frank's bestseller, *What's the Matter with Kansas? How Conservatives Won the Heart of America* (New York: Henry Holt, 2004). The irrationality of all traditional religions and the threat posed by moderates tolerating Bible-believing Christians is argued in Sam Harris, *The End of Faith: Religion, Terror, and the Future of Reason* (New York: W. W. Norton, 2004), with a reply to his Christian critics in *Letter to a Christian Nation* (New York: Knopf, 2007). The estimate of white voters' dislike of traditionalist Christians is in Bolce and De Maio, "Our Secularist Democratic Party," 13.
202. Fortunately, the "liberal" philosophical and legal orthodoxy on this subject is breaking down. See Christopher J. Eberle, *Religious Conviction in Liberal Politics* (Cambridge: Cambridge University Press, 2002), and the splendid collection of essays in the *Wake Forest Law Review*, 36:2 (2001).

203. Hugh Heclo, "Campaigning and Governing: A Conspectus," in Ornstein and Mann, *The Permanent Campaign,* 1–37; and "The Corruption of Democratic Leadership," in Robert Faulkner et al., eds., *American Democracy: The Great Dangers and What Can Be Done* (Ann Arbor: University of Michigan Press, 2007).
204. Michael McConnell quoted in Jean Bethke Elshtain, "A Response to Chief Justice McLachlin," in Douglas Farow, ed., *Recognizing Religion in a Secular Society* (Montreal: McGill Queen's University Press, 2004), 37.
205. Glenn Tinder, *The Political Meaning of Christianity* (Baton Rouge: Louisiana State University Press, 1989), 8. Thus relying heavily on biblical arguments, former President Jimmy Carter criticizes Christian fundamentalists, not least those leading the Southern Baptist Convention (from which he resigned in protest), for giving political encouragement to foreign policy unilateralism, neglect of human rights, economic inequality, and environmental degradation. Jimmy Carter, *Our Endangered Values: America's Moral Crisis* (New York: Simon and Schuster, 2005).
206. Unfortunately, every use of the term "fundamentalist" now sweeps up into one category all adherents to Christian, Jewish, and Muslim religions who adopt "a militant form of piety." Such militant piety among Christians would presumably include Martin Luther King Jr., John Paul II, Dietrich Bonhoeffer, Dorothy Day, and a host of other inspiring individuals. The option of subversion is more rightly called "post-fundamentalism," for it abandons the compassionate ethic of all world religions in favor of its own apocalyptic vision. Karen Armstrong, *The Battle for God* (New York: Random House, 2001).
207. On the recognition of this danger from two former leaders of the Moral Majority, see Cal Thomas and Ed Dobson, *Blinded by Might: Can the Religious Right Save America?* (Grand Rapids, Mich.: Zondervan, 1999). Along these same lines, Francis Schaeffer's son Franky, who produced his father's films, went on to renounce social activism, abandon Protestantism, and join the Eastern Orthodox Church. Since the mid-1990s, valuable examples of this worry from a more or less traditional Christian perspective are Michael S. Horton, *Beyond Culture Wars* (Chicago: Moody Press, 1994); James Montgomery Boice, *Two Cities, Two Loves: Christian Responsibility in a Crumbling Culture* (Downers Grove, Ill.: InterVarsity Press, 1996); and David Kuo, *Tempting Faith* (New York: Free Press, 2006).

208. John Persinos, "Has the Christian Right Taken Over the Republican Party?" *Campaigns and Elections,* September 1994, 21–24. *www.findarticles.com* (accessed 6/18/06).
209. Jeffrey Stout, *Democracy and Tradition* (Princeton: Princeton University Press, 2003).
210. William M. Shea, *The Lion and the Lamb: Evangelicals and Catholics in America* (Oxford: Oxford University Press, 2004), 283–294.
211. John Courtney Murray, *We Hold These Truths* (New York: Sheed and Ward, 1960), 10.
212. The signature work is Richard John Neuhaus, *The Naked Public Square: Religion and Democracy in America* (Grand Rapids, Mich.: Eerdmans, 1984). Neuhaus begins by observing, "Our quarrel with politicized fundamentalism is not that it has broken the rules of the game by 'going public' with Christian truth claims. Christian truth, if it is true, is public truth. It is accessible to pubic reason. . . . Our quarrel is primarily theological." He later raises the familiar democratic proceduralist objection: "The religious new right . . . *wants to enter the political arena making public claims on the basis of private truths.* The integrity of politics itself requires that such a proposal be resisted. Public decisions must be made by arguments that are public in character. A public argument is transsubjective. It is not derived from sources of revelation or dispositions that are essentially private and arbitrary. . . . Fundamentalist morality, which is derived from beliefs that cannot be submitted to examination by public reason, is essentially a private morality. If enough people who share that morality are mobilized, it can score victories in the public arena. But every such victory is a setback in the search for a public ethic" (19, 36–37; italics in the original).
213. See the symposium discussion on the twentieth anniversary of the publication of Richard John Neuhaus's *The Naked Public Square.* "The Naked Public Square Now," *First Things,* November 2004, 11–26. A more hopeful view of the potential role of natural law in contemporary America is carefully argued in Russell Hittinger, *The First Grace: Rediscovering the Natural Law in a Post-Christian World* (Wilmington, Del.: ISI Books, 2003).
214. Isserman and Kazin, *America Divided,* 241.
215. *First Things,* February 2004, 67.
216. Thomas B. Harbottle, ed., *Dictionary of Quotations (Classical)* (New York: Frederick Ungar, 1958), 308. For a more recent discus-

sion of this theme, see John Howard Yoder, *The Priestly Kingdom: Social Ethics as Gospel* (Notre Dame, Ind.: University of Notre Dame Press, 1984).

217. Trying to get an accurate reading of such points is obviously a murky business that should be approached carefully. The figures in the text are from George Barna, "Practical Outcomes Replace Biblical Principles as the Moral Standard," *Barna Research Online,* September 10, 2001, *www.barna.org* (accessed 6/8/04). The general thematics from Barna's opinion polling can be found in research report titles such as "Americans Are Most Likely to Base Truth on Feelings" (February 12, 2002); "Only Half of Protestant Pastors Have a Biblical Worldview" (January 12, 2004); "Most Americans Feel Accepted by God, But Lack a Biblical Worldview" (August 9, 2005); "The Concept of Holiness Baffles Most Americans" (February 20, 2006).

218. Alan Wolfe, *The Transformation of American Religion: How Americans Live Their Faith* (New York: Free Press, 2003).

219. George Barna and Mark Hatch, *Boiling Point* (Ventura, Calif.: Regal Books, 2001), 190–193; Luke Timothy Johnson, *The Creed: What Christians Believe and Why It Matters* (New York: Doubleday, 2003).

220. A hearty little tussle has developed in the social science literature in the attempt to pin down the extent of "over-reporting" in Americans' self-reported churchliness. Studies have shown a gap between opinion-poll-based and actual-count-based measures of attendance of over 80 percent. The over-reporting appears to be greatest among committed believers and active church members. See Andrew Walsh, "Church, Lies, and Polling Data," *Religion in the New,* 1:2 (1998), 1–8. A particularly careful case study of one well-established suburban evangelical church in the deep South showed a 59 percent rate of attendance over-reporting *by church members.* If one assumed that by "attending church" in the last week respondents meant attending the worship service, the over-reporting/lying rate was 83 percent. The rate of over-reporting for Sunday School attendance was 57 percent. Penny Long Marier and C. Kirk Hadaway, "Testing the Attendance Gap in a Conservative Church," *Sociology of Religion,* 60:2 (1999), 175–187.

221. Michael Horton quoted in a general review of the evidence: Ronald J. Sider, "The Scandal of the Evangelical Conscience," *Books and Culture,* January/February 2005, 8–9 and 39.

222. Donald Critchlow, *Intended Consequences: Birth Control, Abortion, and the Federal Government in Modern America* (New York: Oxford University Press, 1999), 132; Boice, *Two Cities, Two Loves,* 28.
223. Fiorina, *Culture Wars?* 81, 161–164.
224. Genetics and Public Policy Center, *Reproductive Genetic Testing: What America Thinks,* 2005. *www.dnapolicy.org* (accessed 9/22/06).
225. These and similar findings are in Christian Smith, *Christian America? What Evangelicals Really Want* (Berkeley: University of California Press, 2000), and Greeley and Hout, *The Truth about Conservative Christians,* 90.
226. In the 1970s, the government and various home-school groups estimated the home-school population to be between 10,000 and 20,000 students. The latest federal survey puts the number of students being home-schooled as of spring 2003 at approximately 1.1 million, or 2.2 percent of the student population in grades K–12. This represents a 10 percent annual growth rate, given the estimated 850,000 students (1.7 percent of the population) being home-schooled in the spring of 1999. In terms of the most important reason for home-schooling, 31 percent of the students had parents who cited concern about the environment of other schools (such as safety, drugs, or negative peer pressure), and 30 percent had parents who said the most important reason was to provide religious or moral instruction. Another 16 percent of students had parents who said dissatisfaction with the academic instruction available at other schools was their most important reason for home-schooling. National Center for Education Statistics, *Homeschooling in the United States: 2003, Statistical Analysis Report* (Washington, D.C.: NCES, February 2006).
227. See Colleen Carroll, *The New Faithful: Why Young Adults Are Embracing Christian Orthodoxy* (Chicago: Loyola Press, 2002); and Robert E. Webber, *The Younger Evangelicals: Facing the Challenges of the New World* (Grand Rapids, Mich.: Baker Book House, 2002). The substantial divide in religious outlooks of the coming generation can be gauged by comparing two recent books: Naomi Schaefer Riley, *God on the Quad: How Religious Colleges and the Missionary Generation are Changing America* (New York: St. Martin's, 2005); and Christian Smith, *Soul Searching: The Religious and Spiritual Lives of American Teenagers* (New York: Oxford University Press, 2005).
228. Stanley Hauerwas, *A Community of Character: Toward a Construc-*

tive Christian Social Ethic (Notre Dame: University of Notre Dame Press, 1986). A different separatist view emphasizes hierarchy of authority rather than democracy and human rights as a core Christian political teaching. Robert P. Kraynak, *Christian Faith and Modern Democracy* (Notre Dame: University of Notre Dame Press, 2001). On "chastened patriots," see Darrell Cole, *When God Says War Is Right: The Christian's Perspective on When and How to Fight* (Des Plaines, Ill.: WaterBrook Press, 2002). John Lukacs, *Confessions of an Original Sinner* (New York: Ticknor and Fields, 1990).

229. Jean Bethke Elshtain, *Democracy on Trial* (New York: Basic Books, 1995), xv.
230. R. R. Reno, *In the Ruins of the Church: Sustaining Faith in an Age of Diminished Christianity* (New York: Brazos, 2002). The Christian case for getting Christianity out of politics is forcefully presented in Darryl Hart, *A Secular Faith: Why Christianity Favors the Separation of Church and State* (Chicago: Ivan R. Dee, 2006).
231. Clifford Geertz, "A Life of Learning," The Charles Homer Haskins Lecture for 1999, Occasional Paper no. 45, American Council of Learned Societies. *www.acls.com* (accessed 7/7/06).
232. In May 2006 when 820 self-identified Christians were asked whether they thought of themselves first as American or as Christian, 42 percent said Christian first and 48 percent said American first (with 7 percent not responding). For those describing themselves as evangelicals, the proportion of "Christian first" rose to 62 percent. By contrast, 62 and 65 percent of Catholics and mainline Protestants respectively chose "American first." See "Christians First, Americans Second," Pew Research Center, *http:pewresearch.org/datatrends* (accessed 10/19/06).

2. Democracy and Catholic Christianity in America

1. See p. 79 of this volume.
2. My source for most data on religious affiliation is *www.adherents.com.*
3. See p. 27 of this volume.
4. My sources for this discussion of American Catholic history during the colonial and republican period include Jay P. Dolan, *In Search of An American Catholicism* (Oxford: Oxford University Press, 2002), chap. 1, 13–46; James T. Fisher, *Communion of Immigrants: A His-*

tory of Catholics in America (Oxford: Oxford University Press, 2002), chaps. 1 and 2, 1–42; Charles R. Morris, *American Catholic* (New York: Random House, 1997), chaps. 1 and 2, 3–53; and David J. O'Brien, *Public Catholicism* (Maryknoll, N.Y.: Orbis Books, 1996), chap. 2, 9–33.

5. Statistics on numbers of Catholics and percentage of the population that is Catholic, here and later, are from Roger Finke and Rodney Stark, *The Churching of America* (New Brunswick, N.J.: Rutgers University Press, 1992), primarily from chaps. 2 and 4.
6. This section relies on Dolan, *In Search,* chaps. 2 and 3, 47–126; Fisher, *Communion of Immigrants,* chaps. 3 and 4, 41–92; Morris, *American Catholic,* chaps. 3–6, 54–164; O'Brien, *Public Catholicism,* chap. 3, 34–61; and John T. McGreevy, *Catholicism and American Freedom: A History* (New York: W. W. Norton, 2003), Introduction through chap. 4, 7–126.
7. Morris, *American Catholic,* 40–47.
8. Richard McBrien, in his comprehensive survey *Catholicism* (San Francisco: HarperSanFrancisco, 1994), describing the nineteenth-century reaction to the Enlightenment, says: "A rigid traditionalism developed in France (going by the names of Integralism and Fideism), distrustful of all rational reflection in theology and excessively dependent on Papal direction (*Ultramontanism,* literally those who look 'beyond the mountains,' the Alps, to Rome)" (p. 644).
9. This discussion relies to some extent on the sources cited in note 4, but mainly relies on and quotes from a masterful study by John Noonan, *A Church That Can and Cannot Change* (Notre Dame: University of Notre Dame Press, 2005), primarily chaps. 21, 22, and 23, 145–158. The encyclical quoted by Noonan is Leo XII, *Mirari Vos.* (Papal encyclicals take their names from their first few words in the Latin original. The meaning here is "You wonder.")
10. Noonan, *Church That Can and Cannot Change,* 149.
11. Morris, *American Catholic,* 54–60.
12. Leo XIII, *Longinqua,* Encyclical on Catholicism in the United States, 1895, paragraphs 1 (on esteem and love) and 6. Available on the Vatican website: *www.vatican.va/holy_father/leo_xiii/encyclicals/documents/hf_l-xiii_enc_06011895_longinqua_en.html.*
13. Pope Leo XIII, *Immortale Dei,* Encyclical on the Christian Constitution of States, 1885, paragraphs 23 and 24, available on the Vatican

website: *www.vatican.va/holy_father/leo_xiii/encyclicals/documents/hf_l-xiii_enc_01111885_immortale-dei_en.html.*

14. Leo XIII, *Immortale Dei,* paragraph 6.
15. Vatican Council II, Declaration on Religious Liberty (*Dignitatis Humanae),* 1965, paragraph 2. My source for all Vatican Council II documents is Austin Flannery, O.P., ed., *Vatican Council II: The Basic Sixteen Documents* (Northport, N.Y.: Costello, 1996).
16. Vatican Council II, Declaration on Religious Liberty, paragraph 1.
17. This history is thoroughly documented in Noonan, *Church That Can and Cannot Change.*
18. Murray quoted by Xavier Rynne, *Vatican Council II* (Maryknoll, N.Y.: Orbis Books, 1968 and 1996), 460. Xavier Rynne is the pseudonym for the Redemptorist priest Francis X. Murphy, who was present at the Council as an expert adviser and wrote a series of articles for the *New Yorker,* later published as a book, describing in great detail the workings and debates of the Council.
19. Vatican Council II, Pastoral Constitution on the Church in the Modern World *(Gaudium et Spes),* 1965, paragraph 27.
20. Noonan, *Church That Can and Cannot Change,* chaps. 24–27, 161–190.
21. Ibid., 215.
22. A description of the arguments about religious freedom at the Council can be found in Rynne, *Vatican Council II,* 298–303 and 454–456.
23. Joseph Ratzinger, now Pope Benedict XVI, and Marcello Pera, *Without Roots: The West, Relativism, Christianity, Islam* (New York: Basic Books, 2006), 112–113.
24. This discussion relies on Andrew Greeley, *The Catholic Revolution* (Berkeley: University of California Press, 2004). Excellent analyses of the current state of Catholicism in America are provided in Peter Steinfels, *A People Adrift* (New York: Simon and Schuster, 2005), and David Gibson, *The Coming Catholic Church* (San Francisco: HarperSanFrancisco, 2003).
25. Greeley, *Catholic Revolution,* 34–40.
26. Ibid., 41–60.
27. John C. Green, Corwin E. Smith, James L. Guth, and Lyman A. Kellstedt, "The American Religious Landscape and the 2004 Presidential Vote: Increased Polarization," report to the Pew Forum on

Religion and Public Life, 2005, *http://pewforum.org/publications/surveys/postelection.pdf.*

28. Ibid.
29. Pope Benedict XVI, *Deus Caritas Est (*God is Love), 2005, available through the Vatican website: *www.vatican.va/holy_father/benedict_xvi/encyclicals/documents/hf_ben-xvi_enc_20051225_deus-caritas-est_en.html.*
30. The most recent exposition of Benedict's thinking on these issues is Joseph Cardinal Ratzinger, *Truth and Tolerance: Christian Belief and World Religions* (San Francisco: Ignatius Press, 2004).
31. Pope Benedict XVI, *Without Roots.*
32. Pope Benedict XVI, *Deus Caritas Est,* paragraph 28.
33. Congregation for the Doctrine of the Faith, "Doctrinal Note on Some Questions regarding the Participation of Catholics in Political Life," 2002, *www.vatican.va/roman_curia/congregations/cfaith/documents/rc_con_cfaith_doc_20021124_politica_en.html.*

3. Pluralism Is Hard Work

1. Richard Hofstadter, *The Progressive Historians* (New York: Knopf, 1968), 463. For an insightful discussion of his arguments, see David S. Brown, *Richard Hofstadter: An Intellectual Biography* (Chicago: University of Chicago Press, 2006), 188–206.
2. William McLoughlin, *Revivals, Awakenings, and Reform* (Chicago: University of Chicago Press, 1980); Nathan O. Hatch, *The Democratization of American Christianity* (New Haven: Yale University Press, 1989); Mark Noll, *America's God: From Jonathan Edwards to Abraham Lincoln* (New York: Oxford University Press, 2002); Richard Wightman Fox, *Jesus in America* (New York: HarperSanFrancisco, 2004); D. G. Hart, *The Lost Soul of American Protestantism* (Lanham, Md.: Rowman and Littlefield, 2002).
3. Alan Wolfe, "Religious Diversity: The American Experiment That Works," in *Americanism: New Perspectives on the History of an Ideal,* ed. Michael Kazin and Joseph A. McCartin (Chapel Hill: University of North Carolina Press, 2006), 159–160.
4. On the utilitarianism of American religion, see Hart, *Lost Soul.*
5. Quoted in Gary Gerstle, *American Crucible: Race and Nation in the Twentieth Century* (Princeton: Princeton University Press, 2001), 53.

6. Jon Butler, *Awash in a Sea of Faith: Christianizing the American People* (Cambridge, Mass.: Harvard University Press, 1990), 197–199.
7. Benjamin Justice, *The War That Wasn't: Religious Conflict and Compromise in the Common Schools of New York State, 1865–1900* (Albany: State University of New York Press, 2005).
8. John T. McGreevy, *Catholicism and American Freedom: A History* (New York: W. W. Norton, 2003), 123.
9. Leonard J. Moore, "Historical Interpretations of the 1920s Klan: The Traditional View and the Populist Revision," in *The Invisible Empire in the West: Toward a New Historical Appraisal of the Ku Klux Klan of the 1920s,* ed. Shawn Lay (Urbana: University of Illinois Press, 1991), 17–38; Michael Kazin, *A Godly Hero: The Life of William Jennings Bryan* (New York: Knopf, 2006), 166–167; *Letters of Eugene V. Debs,* Vol. 1, 1874–1912, ed. J. Robert Constantine (Urbana: University of Illinois Press, 1990), 560.
10. Many Catholic intellectuals were not happy with JFK's position but held their tongues. See McGreevy, *Catholicism and American Freedom,* 213–214. On anti-Catholicism in the mid-century, see ibid., 166–188.
11. See David Hollinger, *Science, Jews, and Secular Culture: Studies in Mid-Twentieth-Century American Intellectual History* (Princeton: Princeton University Press, 1996), and Diana Selig, "Cultural Gifts: American Liberals, Childhood, and the Origins of Multiculturalism, 1924–1945," Ph.D. diss., University of California, Berkeley, 2001.
12. Contrary to conventional wisdom, Eisenhower was a deeply pious man who considered becoming a minister and told a friend, during the 1952 campaign, "The farther I proceed in political life, the more I believe that I should have striven to be worthy of the pulpit as an avenue of public service instead of the political podium." No president since Wilson shared that sentiment, and Ike's much-derided statement may have helped stir the revival of political religiosity that would become commonplace by the 1970s. See Ira Chernus, "Faith and Fear in the Fifties," *www.spot.colorado.edu.*
13. Coffin, undated quote, cited by Edith Guffey, "Celebrate Micah's Call," Address to New England Women's Gathering of the UCC, March 22, 2006, at *www.news.ucc.org*. Also see Warren Goldstein, *William Sloane Coffin, Jr.: A Holy Impatience* (New Haven: Yale University Press, 2004).

14. Michael Lacey and William M. Shea, "Catholics and the Liberal Tradition: Still Compatible," *Commonweal,* October 11, 2003.
15. Quoted in Garry Wills, "Did Tocqueville 'Get' America?" *New York Review of Books,* April 29, 2004. In much of this piece, Wills, in his debunking zeal, misses the brilliance of *Democracy in America.* But that is not the case with the subject of race.
16. Gustave de Beaumont, *Marie, or Slavery in the United States,* trans. Barbara Chapman (Stanford: Stanford University Press, 1958), 5, 33–34.
17. Albert J. Raboteau, *A Fire in the Bones: Reflections on African-American Religious History* (Boston: Beacon Press, 1995), 63. Some American Indians voiced an analogous critique. In 1916, the Santee missionary Charles Eastman wrote about an elderly Indian on the Great Plains who, after attending Bible study for a week, declared, "I have come to the conclusion that this Jesus was an Indian. He was opposed to material acquirement and to great possessions. He was inclined to peace. He was as unpractical as any Indian and set no price upon his labor of love. These are not the principles upon which the white man has founded his civilization. It is strange that he could not rise to these simple principles which were commonly observed among our people." Quoted in *Talking Back to Civilization: Indian Voices from the Progressive Era,* ed. Frederick E. Hoxie (Boston: Bedford/St. Martins, 2001), 76–77.
18. Jim Wallis, *God's Politics: Why the Right Gets It Wrong and the Left Doesn't Get It* (San Francisco: HarperSanFrancisco, 2005), 155–157.
19. Wade Clark Roof, *A Generation of Seekers: The Spiritual Journeys of the Baby Boom Generation* (San Francisco: HarperSanFrancisco, 1993).
20. Peter Steinfels, "Hard and Soft Secularism," *Religion in the News,* 8 (Winter 2006), Supplement, 6, 11–12. For a counter-argument that mirrors Heclo's, see James Q. Wilson, "How Divided Are We?" *Commentary,* February 2006, 15–21.
21. F. Scott Fitzgerald, *The Crack-Up, with other uncollected pieces, note-books and unpublished letters* (New York: New Directions, 1945).

4. Whose Christianity? Whose Democracy?

1. R. Stephen Warner, "The Place of the Contemporary American Religious Congregation," in James P. Wind and James W. Lewis, eds.,

American Congregations, vol. 2, *New Perspectives in the Study of Congregations* (Chicago: University of Chicago Press, 1994).

2. Anatol Lieven, *America Right or Wrong: An Anatomy of American Nationalism* (New York: Oxford University Press, 2004).
3. For more on this debate see James Davison Hunter and Alan Wolfe, *Is There A Culture War? A Dialogue on Values and American Public Life* (Washington, D.C.: Brookings Institution Press, 2007).
4. For more on this point, see Melinda Bollar Wagner, "Generic Conservative Christianity: The Demise of Denominationalism in Christian Schools," *Journal for the Scientific Study of Religion,* 36 (1997), 13–24.
5. Daniel Walker Howe, *The Political Culture of the American Whigs* (Chicago: University of Chicago Press, 1979), 150.
6. Peter Dobkin Hall, "The Rise of the Civic Engagement Tradition," in Mary Jo Bane, Brent Coffin, and Richard Higgins, eds., *Taking Faith Seriously* (Cambridge, Mass.: Harvard University Press, 2005), 57.
7. Nathan Hatch, *The Democratization of American Christianity* (New Haven: Yale University Press, 1989).
8. R. Stephen Warner, *New Wines in Old Wineskins: Evangelicals and Liberals in a Small-Town Church* (Berkeley: University of California Press, 1988).
9. Bernard Henri Lévy, *American Vertigo: Traveling America in the Footsteps of Tocqueville* (New York: Random House, 2006).
10. Alan Wolfe, *The Transformation of American Religion: How We Actually Live Our Faith* (New York: Free Press, 2003).
11. Vincent Crapanzano, *Serving the Word: Literalism in America from the Pulpit to the Bench* (New York: New Press, 2000), 394–395.
12. Stephen Macedo, "Liberal Civic Education and Religious Fundamentalism: The Case of God v. John Rawls?" *Ethics,* 105 (April 1995), 478.
13. Stanley Hauerwas and William Willimon, *Resident Aliens: A Provocative Christian Assessment of Culture and Ministry for People Who Know That Something Is Wrong* (Nashville: Abingdon Press, 1989).
14. Wagner, "Generic Conservative Christianity."
15. See, for example, *First Things* editors, "Introduction," *First Things,* 67 (November 1996), 21–24.
16. Donald E. Miller, *Reinventing American Protestantism: Christianity in the New Millennium* (Berkeley: University of California Press, 1997).

17. See, for example, Grant Wacker, *Heaven Below: Early Pentecostals and American Culture* (Cambridge, Mass.: Harvard University Press, 2001), 28.
18. Rodney Stark, *The Victory of Reason: How Christianity Led to Freedom, Capitalism, and Western Success* (New York: Random House, 2005).

5. Reconsidering Christianity and American Democracy

1. Kevin Phillips, *American Theocracy* (New York: Viking, 2006).
2. Jaroslav Pelikan, *The Christian Tradition: A History of the Development of Doctrine* (Chicago: University of Chicago Press, 1984).
3. G. K. Chesterton, *St. Thomas Aquinas: "The Dumb Ox"* (New York: Sheed and Ward, 1954), 13.
4. Jaroslav Pelikan, *Credo: Historical and Theological Guide to Creeds and Confessions of Faith in the Christian Tradition* (New Haven: Yale University Press, 2003), 7 and 377–378.
5. See, for example, C. S. Lewis, *Mere Christianity* (New York: HarperCollins, 2001); N. T. Wright, *Simply Christian: Why Christianity Makes Sense* (San Francisco: HarperSanFrancisco, 2006); Joseph Ratzinger (Pope Benedict XVI), *Introduction to Christianity* (Fort Collins, Colo.: Ignatius Press, 2004).
6. Robert A. Dahl, *On Democracy* (New Haven: Yale University Press, 1998), 93–94, 103–106.
7. Thomas T. McAvoy, "The Formation of the Catholic Minority in the United States 1820–1860," *Review of Politics,* 10:1 (1948), 15. The Catholic population estimate is from Sister M. Augustina Ray's *American Opinion of Roman Catholicism in the Eighteenth Century* (New York, Columbia University Press, 1936), which describes the general decline in political opposition to Catholicism in the Revolutionary era.
8. Michael Lacey, personal communication, February 10, 2006. I am deeply grateful to Mike for these and his many other insightful comments on the draft text of my lecture.
9. As the Pope put it, "If there is no ultimate truth to guide and direct political activity, then ideas and convictions can easily be manipulated for reasons of power . . . A democracy without values easily turns into open or thinly-disguised totalitarianism." John

Paul II, *Centesimus Annus,* 46, quoted in George Weigel, "Catholicism and Democracy in the Age of John Paul II," *Logos,* 4:3 (2001), 48.

10. Congregation for the Doctrine of the Faith, "Doctrinal Note on Some Questions Regarding the Participation of Catholics in Political Life," November 24, 2002. *www.vatican.va/roman* (accessed 5/10/06).
11. U.S. Conference of Catholic Bishops, "Faithful Citizenship: A Catholic Call to Political Responsibility," Washington, 2003. *www.nccbuscc.org* (accessed 5/11/06).
12. H. Richard Niebuhr, *The Social Sources of Denominationalism* (New York: Henry Holt, 1929).
13. Recent evidence on this subject is in Andrew Greeley and Michael Hout, *The Truth about Conservative Christians: What They Think and What They Believe* (Chicago: University of Chicago Press, 2006), 43–44.
14. Ibid., 66. For an account of Republican skill on this score, see Thomas B. Edsall, *Building Red America: The New Conservative Coalition and the Drive for Permanent Power* (New York: Basic Books, 2006).
15. Rudolf Otto, *The Idea of the Holy* (New York: Oxford University Press, 1958), first published 1923; Stephen G. Post, *Human Nature and the Freedom of Public Religious Expression* (Notre Dame, Ind.: University of Notre Dame Press, 2003).
16. Karl Lowith, *Meaning in History: The Theological Implications of the Philosophy of History* (Chicago: University of Chicago Press, 1949), 112; Reinhold Niebuhr, *The Nature and Destiny of Man: A Christian Interpretation,* vol. 2 (New York: Charles Scribner's Sons, 1943), 87.
17. Arguments generally favorable to this future possibility are in Mark A. Noll and Carolyn Nystrom, *Is The Reformation Over? An Evangelical Assessment of Contemporary Roman Catholicism* (Grand Rapids, Mich.: Baker Academic, 2005). Pointing in the opposite direction is evidence of lingering anti-Catholicism among white conservative Protestants and an enduring difference between the individualistic versus communitarian ways in which conservative Protestants and conservative Catholics see the world respectively. See Greeley and Hout, *The Truth about Conservative Christians,* 175–177; and Damon Linker, *The Theocons: Secular America under Siege* (New York: Doubleday, 2006).

18. Wilfred M. McClay, "Pilgrims Giving Thanks," *Touchstone,* November 2005, 4.
19. Roy Hattersley, "Faith Does Breed Charity," *The Guardian,* September 12, 2005, 8. Taking a larger view, the philosopher and self-described "methodological atheist" Jürgen Habermas argues that Christianity must remain a fundamental source of nourishment for any European civilization of liberty, human rights, and democracy. See Jürgen Habermas, *Time of Transitions* (Oxford: Blackwell, 2006).
20. John Witte, Jr., and Frank Alexander, eds., *The Teachings of Modern Christianity on Law, Politics, and Human Dignity* (New York: Columbia University Press, 2006). On a popular level, there is a growing chorus of voices calling for a Christian civic engagement from the liberal side of the political spectrum. See Peter Laarman, ed., *Getting on Message: Challenging the Christian Right from the Heart of the Gospel* (Boston: Beacon Press, 2006); Jim Wallis, *God's Politics: Why the Right Gets It Wrong and the Left Doesn't Get It* (New York: HarperCollins, 2005); Jimmy Carter, *Our Endangered Values: America's Moral Crisis* (New York: Simon and Schuster, 2005); Randall Balmer, *Thy Kingdom Come: How the Religious Right Distorts the Faith and Threatens America* (New York: Basic Books, 2006); Michael Lerner, *The Left Hand of God: Taking Back Our Country from the Religious Right* (San Francisco: HarperSanFrancisco, 2006); Bob Edgar, *Middle Church: Reclaiming the Moral Values of the Faithful Majority from the Religious Right* (New York: Simon and Schuster, 2006); Obery M. Hendricks, Jr., *The Politics of Jesus: Rediscovering the True Revolutionary Nature of the Teachings of Jesus and How They Have Been Corrupted* (New York: Doubleday, 2006); and Brian D. McLaren, *The Secret Message of Jesus: Uncovering the Truth That Could Change Everything* (Nashville: W Publishing Group, 2006).
21. Pierre Manent, "Christianity and Democracy: Some Remarks on the Political History of Religion, or, on the Religious History of Modern Politics," in his *Modern Liberty and Its Discontents* (Oxford: Rowman and Littlefield, 1998), 97–115.
22. Glenn Tinder, *The Political Meaning of Christianity* (Baton Rouge: Louisiana State University Press, 1989), 8. Tinder's theme is carried forward in David Dark, *The Gospel According to America: A Meditation on a God-blessed, Christ-haunted Idea* (Louisville, Kentucky:

Westminster John Knox Press, 2005), and in a more secular vein by the PBS journalist Ray Suarez's *The Holy Vote: The Politics of Faith in America* (New York: Rayo/Harper Collins, 2006). For a more personal appeal to Christians in the current regime of deliberately managed divisiveness, see Senator John Danforth, *Faith and Politics: How the Moral Values Debate Divides America and How to Move Forward Together* (New York: Viking, 2006).

ACKNOWLEDGMENTS

I am immensely grateful to Theda Skocpol and Harvard's Center for American Political Studies for giving me the opportunity to present this Tocqueville Lecture and to respond to its thoughtful critics. The result, for better or worse, is something that I probably never would have written otherwise. I also naturally applaud any publication project that allows me the last word by way of rejoinder. Of course, given the length of what is trying to pass itself off as a "lecture," others may just as naturally feel that I have already been allowed far too many words. The three distinguished commentators had originally signed on to respond to a lecture of 12,000 to 15,000 words, but they ended up, without a grumble, being subjected to something well over twice that size. They are indeed noble souls.

While the oral lecture was presented only in outline form at Harvard in March 2006, the full text was made available to the commentators prior to the lecture. The text of the lecture published here has since been elaborated in places and edited for purposes of clarity and accuracy. However, no points of substance have been altered in order to anticipate the three respondents' subsequent comments—a heroic abstention given one's authorial yearning for omniscience. Once engaged in writing my rejoinder, it became clear to me just how indebted I am to Professors Bane, Kazin, and Wolfe for helping me think about this subject. The same debt is due to my friend Mike Lacey and an outside reader for Harvard University Press. Their gracious comments on the entire manuscript saved me from at least some of the worst consequences of my own ignorance. Likewise, the Press's splendid editor, Mary Ellen Geer, helped me appear to be a much more polished writer than I really am. Still farther behind the scenes, deserving but not seeking the honor that should fall to public-spirited people, there are Terry and Betsy Considine. Their support made this book possible.

Finally, I wish to thank my wife, Beverley, for putting up with me during the many times of frustration and ill-temper as I worked on this project. I am sure it seemed like I should be the last person to be writing about Christianity, which is probably true.

Hugh Heclo
White Post, Virginia
October 2006

ABOUT THE AUTHORS

MARY JO BANE is Thornton Bradshaw Professor of Public Policy and Management, Academic Dean, and Chair of the Management and Leadership area at Harvard University's Kennedy School of Government. From 1993 to 1996 she was Assistant Secretary for Children and Families at the U.S. Department of Health and Human Services. From 1992 to 1993 she was Commissioner of the New York State Department of Social Services, where she had previously served as Executive Deputy Commissioner from 1984 to 1986. From 1987 to 1992, at the Kennedy School, she was Malcolm Wiener Professor of Social Policy and Director of the Malcolm Wiener Center for Social Policy. She is the author of a number of books and articles on poverty, welfare, families, and the role of churches in civic life, and the coeditor, most recently, of *Taking Faith Seriously.* She is currently doing research on poverty in the United States and internationally.

HUGH HECLO is Robinson Professor of Public Affairs at George Mason University, a former Professor of Government at Harvard University, and prior to that a Senior Fellow at the Brookings Institution in Washington. Most recently he has been contributing coeditor with Wilfred McClay of *Religion Returns to the Public Square.* He currently serves on the 12-member Scholars' Council advising the Librarian of Congress, and in 2002 was honored by the American Political Science Association with the John Gaus

Award for lifetime achievement in the fields of political science and public administration. For the past twenty-five years, he, his wife, and daughter have operated a Christmas tree farm in the northern Shenandoah Valley.

MICHAEL KAZIN is Professor of History at Georgetown University. He is the author of *Barons of Labor: The San Francisco Building Trades and Union Power in the Progressive Era; The Populist Persuasion: An American History;* and *A Godly Hero: The Life of William Jennings Bryan.* He is also the coauthor, with Maurice Isserman, of *America Divided: The Civil War of the 1960s;* the coeditor, with Joseph A. McCartin, of *Americanism: New Perspectives on the History of an Ideal;* and editor-in-chief of the forthcoming Princeton Encyclopedia of American Political History.

ALAN WOLFE is Professor of Political Science and Director of the Boisi Center for Religion and American Public Life at Boston College. His most recent books include *Does American Democracy Still Work?; Return to Greatness: How America Lost Its Sense of Purpose and What It Needs to Do to Recover It; The Transformation of American Religion: How We Actually Live Our Faith;* and *An Intellectual in Public.* Wolfe currently chairs a task force of the American Political Science Association on "Religion and Democracy in the United States." He serves on the advisory boards of Humanity in Action and the Future of American Democracy Foundation, and on the president's advisory board of the Massachusetts Foundation for the Humanities. In the fall of 2004, Professor Wolfe was the George H. W. Bush Fellow at the American Academy in Berlin.

INDEX